The Tlingit Indians in Russian America, 1741–1867

The Tlingit Indians
in Russian America
1741–1867

~

ANDREI VAL'TEROVICH GRINEV

Translated by

RICHARD L. BLAND

&

KATERINA G. SOLOVJOVA

University of Nebraska Press
Lincoln and London

Library of Congress Cataloging-in-
Publication Data
Grinev, A. V. (Andrei Val'terovich)
[Indeitsy tlinkity v period Russkoi Ameriki,
1741–1867 gg. English]
The Tlingit Indians in Russian Amer-
ica, 1741–1867 / Andrei Val'terovich Grinev;
translated by Richard L. Bland and Ka-
terina G. Solovjova.
p.   cm.
Translation of: Indeitsy tlinkity v period
Russkoi Ameriki, 1741–1867 gg.
Includes bibliographical references and
index.
ISBN-13: 978-0-8032-2214-4 (cloth,
ISBN-13: alk. paper)
ISBN-10: 0-8032-2214-9 (cloth,
ISBN-10: alk. paper)
ISBN-13: 978-0-8032-2071-3 (paper,
ISBN-13: alk. paper)
1. Tlingit Indians—History.
2. Tlingit Indians—Cultural
assimilation.   I. Title.
E99.T6G75   2005
979.8004'9727—dc22
2005012996

CONTENTS

List of Illustrations   vii
List of Tables   vii
Preface   ix
Translators' Introduction   xi
Introduction   1

1. The Tlingit Indians before Contact with Europeans   15
    1. General Characteristics   15
    2. Economic Activities   29
    3. Material Culture   35
    4. Prestige Economy and Potlatch   40
    5. Traditional Social Organization of the Tlingit   50
    6. The Role of War in Tlingit Society   64
    7. Spiritual Culture   69

2. The History of Tlingit Relations with Europeans in Russian America   91
    1. First Contacts (1741–94)   91
    2. Founding Russian Settlements, and Tlingit Contacts with the English and Americans   106
    3. The Indian Revolt of 1802: Reasons and Consequences. Second Founding of a Russian Settlement on Sitka Island. Seizure of Yakutat by the Indians   116
    4. Russian-Tlingit and American-Tlingit Relations (1805–21)   145
    5. Tlingit and Europeans (1821–67)   157

3. The Influence of European Contacts on Tlingit Culture in Russian America   209
    1. Change in the Economic Activities of the Tlingit   209
    2. Changes in the Sphere of Material Culture   225
    3. The Influence of European Colonization on Tlingit Social Organization in Russian America   237
    4. Fighting among the Tlingit in Russian America   252
    5. The Spiritual Culture of the Tlingit in Russian America   253
    6. Linguistic Borrowings   268

Conclusion   275
Documentary Appendix   281
Notes   315
Glossary   329
Bibliography   333
Index   375

ILLUSTRATIONS

Figures

Figure 1. Social-Territorial Structure of Tlingit Society   25
Figure 2. Clan Structure of the Tlingit Tribes   51
Figure 3. The General Structure of Social Organization of
Tlingit Society   55

Maps

Map 1. Settlement of the Primary Linguistic Groups   19
Map 2. Territory of Tlingit and Neighboring Indian Groups   27
Map 3. Russian America: Territorial Administrative Divisions   102
Map 4. Russian, English, and Indian Settlements   134
Map 5. Plan of Novo-Arkhangel'sk in 1836   169

TABLES

Table 1. Ethno-Territorial Division of the Tlingit   26
Table 2. Number of Tlingit from the 19th Century to 1930   29
Table 3. Stratification of Tlingit Society   57
Table 4. Those Serving the RAC at Fort Mikhailovskii, the "Sitka Party,"
and the Party of V. Kochesov in 1802   132
Table 5. Russian Losses in the Clash with the Tlingit in 1804,
by Source   138
Table 6. Prices of Tlingit Furs in Novo-Arkhangel'sk and on RAC Ships
in the Mid-1840s   177
Table 7. Annually Obtained Procurement from the *Koloshi* at the Port of
Novo-Arkhangel'sk, 1842–1860   179
Table 8. Annually Obtained Procurement through Trade with the *Koloshi*
in the Straits, 1842–1860   180
Table 9. Valuation of Furs by the Hudson's Bay Company   197
Table 10. Prices at Which the "Kalosh" Sell Furs on Foreign Ships   201
Table 11. Number of Tlingit Who Accepted Orthodoxy between
1841 and 1860   263
Table 12. Wounded and Dead during the Battle with the Koloshi,
11 March 1855   309

I first became interested in North American Indians when, at the age of 15, I was given a book written by the American ethnographer Oliver la Farge, *Die Welt der Indianer* [The World of the Indians], Berlin, 1974. This beautifully illustrated popular history book truly opened the window on a new and unknown world. It seemed that, in spite of my acquaintance with the novels of James Fenimore Cooper and Mayne Reid, I knew nothing at all about Native Americans, their rich culture, and the interesting and, in many ways, tragic history of relations with the white colonists. From that time I sought to collect all information on North American Indians. However, under the conditions of Soviet Siberia, this was not easily done inasmuch as foreign literature on this theme (especially from the United States) was practically nonexistent in my hometown of Barnaul (near Novosibirsk). Nevertheless, having resolved to seriously occupy myself with the study of history and the ethnography of the Indians, I entered the history department at Altai State University in Barnaul.

Rather quickly I turned to the history and ethnography of the Tlingit in Russian America (that is, when Alaska was under the authority of the Russian Empire): there was almost no information about other Indian tribes in the Barnaul library. Incidentally, I do not regret this. Indeed, the Tlingit created a most rich culture and highly developed art, as well having a very interesting history of relations with the new, white arrivals, principally Russians. It cannot be said that at Altai State University my scholarly beginnings were encouraged, rather they were considered absolutely without prospect, but, fortunately, the university did not hinder me and did not force me to specialize in the history of the Communist Party of the Soviet Union or Siberia. My student diploma work, for which the university committee awarded an "outstanding," had the same title as this book you hold in your hands.

Even before the end of my studies at the university, the well-known specialist in the history of Russian America, Svetlana G. Fedorova, became interested in my research and agreed to become my adviser during my graduate studies at the Institute of Ethnography and Anthropology of the Academy of Sciences of the USSR in Moscow. The thesis I chose for the dissertation remained as before, the "Tlingit Indians of the Russian American Period (1741–1867)." During the course of work on my diploma, and then in my dissertation work, three well-known scholars exerted great influence on my intellectual world view: Svetlana G. Fedorova (already mentioned), the distinguished American ethnographer

Frederica de Laguna, and the leading Soviet (now Russian) Americanist academician Nikolai N. Bolkhovitinov, whose historical school I now follow. Later, the works of the well-known Russian theoretical ethnographer Yuri I. Semenov also influenced my view.

I successfully defended my dissertation in the summer of 1987, and in 1989, having assembled additional archival and literary material, I turned it into a monograph, which in 1991 the academic press Nauka published in Novosibirsk. The book received a positive response in the United States, and in 1996 my good friend, the archaeologist and translator Dr. Richard Bland, began the translation into English. Over the past few years the text of the monograph, including the Documentary Appendix, has been rather significantly expanded and increased, in comparison with the Russian version; additional archival data and information from new Russian and American ethnographic and historical literature has been included. In many ways this is an original work that I hope will be of interest to all readers who are attracted to the traditional ethnographic and historic past of Native Americans, as well as the history of Russian America.

A.V.G.

The author, Dr. Andrei Val'terovich Grinev, holds the position of full professor at the St. Petersburg Humanitarian University of Trade Unions in St. Petersburg, Russia. He has published numerous articles on Russian America and has collaborated with Academician Nikolai N. Bolkhovitinov on a recently published three-volume work entitled *Istoriia Russkoi Ameriki* (The History of Russian America). The present book, which has been substantially updated, was originally published as *Indeitsy Tlinkity v Period Russkoi Ameriki (1741–1867 gg.)* by Nauka in Novosibirsk in 1991.

A number of words from the eighteenth and nineteenth centuries (particularly applying to equipment), as well as words that do not translate into English well, appear in a glossary at the back of the book.

All insertions in curly brackets {} are those of the translators (R.L.B. and K.G.S.); square brackets [ ] are those of the author (A.V.G.). Place names were taken from Donald J. Orth's *Dictionary of Alaska Place Names*, Washington: U.S. Government Printing Office, 1967.

We would like especially to thank Professor Sergei Kan of Dartmouth College, Dr. Ann Simonds of the University of Oregon, Dr. Madonna Moss of the University of Oregon, and David Ramos of Yakutat for reading and commenting on parts of the text. We also owe a debt of gratitude to Dr. Richard Dauenhauer of the University of Alaska for aiding in Tlingit orthography and to Nan Coppock-Bland of the University of Oregon Publications Office for giving editorial advice. We would also like to thank Beth Ina of University of Nebraska Press; Jackie Doyle, our copyeditor; and the anonymous reviewers who contributed substantially to the improvement of the manuscript. None of the above-mentioned persons are responsible for any errors or inconsistencies found in the text. We owe our greatest debt to Dr. Andrei Grinev for permitting us to translate this work.

The Tlingit Indians in Russian America, 1741–1867

Since the early 1980s a number of papers have appeared, both in Russia and elsewhere, dedicated to the Russian period of Alaskan history (1741–1867), including the history of geographic discoveries in this region and the ethnography of the Native population of Russian America. Not surprisingly, great interest has emerged in the history of the interrelation of the Tlingit Indians and the Europeans during the Russian American period and in the influence that Russia had on the Indians' culture and way of life.[1] Collections of documents, monographs, articles, popular books, and works of fiction that directly or indirectly touch upon the question of European contacts with the Native inhabitants of Alaska have been widely published. In this connection, the possibly erroneous idea has developed that this question has been sufficiently studied in Soviet historical research; the adherents of this view refer to general works or to individual articles (Bolkhovitinov 1981:54). However, ethnocultural contacts in Alaska during the Russian period still have not been fully researched, especially considering the broad range of original Russian sources treating this question. The ethnic history of the Koniag, Chugach, and some other Eskimo groups, as well as of several Indian tribes whose lands made up Russian America at the end of the 18th and beginning of the 19th centuries, has been poorly studied, particularly with regard to the Tlingit Indians. The history of relations between the Natives and the Russians is part of the history of Russian America and therefore a part of Russia's past.

The reanimation in recent years of Russian-American dialogue has substantially promoted interest in Alaska's historical past. Materials began to appear in the Russian periodical press that were in one way or another connected with the history and ethnography of Russian America (Belenkin 1988; Larionova 1988; Lopukhin 1989; Shumilov 1989). However, the appraisals, judgments, and facts mentioned in these materials are at times historically inaccurate. Even the authors of such publications often recognize their weakness in this area of study. Thus, A. Shumilov writes, "I recalled the glorious past of Russian America only in order to note with bitterness: Americans know its history significantly better than we" (Shumilov 1989:6). Here Shumilov makes a bold, though accurate, generalization, even if assigning it to the very author who reports in his article that the capital of Russian America—Novo-Arkhangel'sk—was located on Kodiak Island, although it was actually on Baranof Island (Sitka). As for fiction, and sometimes even popular historical literature, the authors' fantasies at times know no limits. Perhaps the most compelling example is in the book by I. Yu. Skarbek *Za trideviat' zemel'* [At the Other End of the World]:

> The Tlingit, which in literal translation means "people in general," lived along the northwest coast of the Gulf of Alaska and on the islands lying along the mainland at the latitude from 52° to 62°, which is approximately from Vancouver Island to Mt. St. Elias. These wild tribes did not look for a permanent place and resettled annually according to convenience. They all had shamans and followed exclusively their fantasies, which resulted in the devil knows what. In any case, their chief personage was, as a rule, the devil himself. The Russians first became acquainted with this people in 1783 (Skarbek 1988:51).

Having consciously kept the "grace" of the author's style, we note that in the quotation given not one sentence corresponds to reality (see chapter 1). Such books, and they appear as a rule in large numbers, give general readers erroneous ideas about the history and ethnography of Russian America.

Annoying errors appear even in contemporary reference literature. Thus, the *Morskoi entsiklopedicheskii spravochnik* [Naval Encyclopedic Reference] notes that the well-known Russian merchant and seafarer Grigorii I. Shelikhov "built shipyards in Novo-Arkhangel'sk" (*Morskoi entsiklopedicheskii spravochnik*, 2:422). This was impossible since Novo-Arkhangel'sk was not founded until 1804, whereas Shelikhov died in 1795. Even *Bol'shaia sovetskaia entsiklopediia* [The Great Soviet Encyclopedia] did not escape such errors. It states that the present-day American city of Sitka (on Baranof Island) was founded by the Russian-American Company in 1799 and was named Novo-Arkhangel'sk in 1804 (vol. 23, p. 480). In fact, the city of Sitka was founded and named Novo-Arkhangel'sk in 1804, whereas in 1799 Mikhailovsk (Novo-Arkhangel'sk) Redoubt was established by the Russians on Baranof Island, and was in 1802 destroyed by the Tlingit (see chapter 2).[2]

In the scholarly literature, there are contradictions and inaccuracies in dates, figures, and the interpretation of individual events, as well as one-sidedness and tendentiousness in evaluating them; this problem is caused in part by researchers who have drawn on an insufficiently broad sphere of sources and literature and by different readings and inaccuracies in the sources themselves. In addition, the ideologized approach to the problem of Russia's colonization of Alaska was characteristic for Soviet historiography. This approach underwent notable changes during the pre– and post–World War II periods. Up to the Second World War, an "accusatory" line predominated in the appraisal of Russia's colonial practices in the New World. An "apologetic" tendency emerges in the works of many Russian authors after the war—connected with attempts to whiten and embellish Russian colonization and to suppress its negative sides (see Grinev 1994a).

Yet any ethnohistorical theme requires that the researcher make a critical analysis and use a multifaceted approach to resolve a problem. Many ethnographic and historic subjects on the history of contacts between the Tlingit and Europeans (primarily Russians), and the consequence of these contacts for the Indians, have not yet been adequately investigated. Regarding the ethnography, for example, there is the question of innovations in Tlingit culture during the Russian American period. As for the historical aspect of Tlingit-European contacts during the period indicated, many disputable and unresolved questions remain. For example, the Indians' seizure of the fort on Baranof Island in 1802 needs to be investigated in greater detail.

Sources for this study include archival documents, travelers' notes, the works of 19th-century historians, and ethnographic works that contain field material, as well as museum collections, geographic atlases, drawings, watercolors, and photographs from the 18th century to the beginning of the 20th century.

Materials from the central archives in Moscow and St. Petersburg and the manuscript divisions of the two largest libraries in Russia, Manuscripts Division of the Lenin State Library and Manuscripts Division of the Saltykov-Shchedrin State Public Library, should be noted first in the rather broad sphere of sources. The most significant collection of documents on the history of Russian America is located in the stacks of the Archives of Foreign Politics of Russia (AVPR). This archive contains especially plentiful materials on the Russian-American Company (RAC), which managed the Russian colonies in Alaska from 1799 to 1867.

Archival data not only significantly enriches any research but helps specify and reverify information in published sources. It also allows reexamination of some of the ideas formed by scholarship on individual subjects in the history and ethnography of Russian America.

Several archival documents on this theme were published while the Russian colonies existed in Alaska. The prominent RAC historian Petr A. Tikhmenev published a variety of valuable materials, including official diplomatic and juridical documents, the correspondence of official persons, and reports by RAC employees, to supplement his work on the company's activities (Tikhmenev 1861:1:Append., 1863:2:Append.). In addition, the Russian-American Company's annual accounts were published (*ORAK 1858 god*, 1859; *ORAK 1859 god*, 1860), as were the *Doklad komiteta ob ustroistve russkikh amerikanskikh kolonii*

[Report of the Committee on the Establishment of the Russian American Colonies] (1863) (*Doklad komiteta*, 1863a, 1863b), and other materials.

Researchers' interest in the history of czarist diplomacy in the Far East and in Russian geographic discoveries in the Pacific Ocean in the 18th and 19th centuries—which increased in the 1930s—prompted the publication of several collections of documents. From the 1940s to the present day, various kinds of archival materials continue to be published (AVPR, Ser. I, vol. III–VII, Ser. II, vol. I–VI; *K istorii Rossiisko-Amerikanskoi*, 1957:58–62). Though these collections contain some data on the history of European-Tlingit relations, as well as on the ethnography of these Indians, the compilers primarily focused on the selection of materials regarding diplomacy, the economics of the Russian American colonies in America, and the history of Russian navigation in the Pacific Ocean. Perhaps most important to us is information found in the *K istorii Rossiisko-Amerikanskoi kompanii* [Toward the History of the Russian-American Company] collection, published in Krasnoyarsk in 1957. Among the materials in the collection that are especially valuable for research is I. A. Kuskov's report, dated July 1(12), 1802, to Aleksandr A. Baranov on the Indians' seizure of the Russian fort on Sitka Island (*K istorii Rossiisko-Amerikanskoi*, 1957:106–123).[3]

In spite of the fact that the archival data would seem to represent the most reliable sources, one must take care when using them, never blindly trusting archival documents that originated with the RAC board of directors, inasmuch as the latter sometimes intentionally and tendentiously distorted the facts. Such distortion was the primary reason for the Indian uprising in 1802. The board of directors sought to blame instigation by foreigners (*K istorii Rossiisko-Amerikanskoi*, 1957:134) for its political miscalculations in colonial Alaska.

Although archival documents are extremely important, it is not possible to create a complete picture of the Russian American past based only on such papers, nor does a survey describe the ethnographic idiosyncracies of Russian America's Native population. A complete picture requires the complex use of different kinds of sources. The notes and memoirs of European (primarily Russian) travelers who visited the Russian colonies in Alaska provide considerable help to those studying Tlingit history and ethnography. First-hand information on the Tlingit appears in the works of such Russian seafarers as A. I. Chirikov, V. M. Golovnin, O. E. Kotzebue, F. P. Litke, and, especially, Yu. F. Lisianskii (1812:6, 7, 14, 18–21, 28–31, 34–43, 63, 68, 73–76). Without diminishing the value of these works, which as a rule contain eyewitness accounts, one notes that they do have a subjective character, most evident in the authors' general appraisal and judgment and their digression into the history of Russian America. For example, Kotzebue, in his book on his voyage around the world between 1823 and 1826, gave an extremely negative characterization of the Tlingit. "It cannot be described," we read, "how disgusting this people seems" (Kotzebue 1987:212). On the other hand, his contemporary I. E. Veniaminov, who observed the Tlingit over the course of several years, held the opposite view: "I was able to see the inhabitants of the Bering Sea, the Unalaska people [the Aleuts of Unalaska Island], the Kodiak people [the Eskimos of Kodiak Island], the Koloshi [Tlingit], and the California Indians of a variety of languages, and knowing as much as possible their capabilities and qualities, it seems to me that the Koloshi of all of them are the best people by their capabilities and activities" (Veniaminov 1840a:112–113).[4]

Data on the Tlingit and their interrelations with Europeans are also contained in the travel descriptions of some foreign observers. Meriting special attention are notes from the voyages of the French commander J. F. G. La Pérouse, the Spanish seafarer A. Malaspina, and the English captain G. Vancouver, and the memoirs of one of the directors of the Hudson's Bay Company, G. Simpson (La Pérouse 1968; Malaspina 1824–27; Vancouver 1830–33; Simpson 1847).

The works of 19th-century historians of Russian America can also be designated as source material. Best known are the works of K. T. Khlebnikov (1835), P. A. Tikhmenev (1861), and the American H. H. Bancroft (1970). It is in the works of these authors that vast factual material on the Russian period of Alaskan history was first summarized and logically conveyed. All these researchers used archival documents, contemporaries' notes on the events described, and eyewitnesses' narratives. Many of the data used by them have been lost; therefore, their works may to a certain degree serve as primary sources (especially the works of Khlebnikov). At the same time, one should never rely completely on information found in their works, as authors of popular literature and fiction often do (see, for example, Markov 1948).

The problem of European influence on Tlingit culture dictates the need to turn to strategies such as ethnographic investigation. The first large and entirely scholarly survey of Tlingit ethnography comes from the prominent Russian missionary and humanist I. E. Veniaminov (1840a), specifically his work *Zapiski ob ostrovakh Unalashkinskogo otdela* [Notes on the Islands of the Unalaska District], which was published in 1840. In it Veniaminov devoted his attention primarily to issues of the Indians' social organization, customs, and, particularly, religious beliefs. It is completely understandable that he should take an interest in the last topic since he, as a priest, could not help but worry about the "errors" of the alien faith.

Almost 50 years after Veniaminov, Archimandrite Anatolii (Kamenskii) occupied himself with missionary activity among the Tlingit. He left behind a small book that was published in Odessa in 1906 and dedicated, like the work of Veniaminov, chiefly to Tlingit spiritual culture (Anatolii 1906). However, in contrast with his predecessor, Archimandrite Anatolii lived in Alaska for 30 years after its sale to the United States; therefore, much of his material treats Tlingit society of the American period and not the Russian American epoch. Also, L. G. Morgan's evolutionist theory, with which he was undoubtedly familiar, influenced the missionary's views.

A professional ethnographer made the earliest ethnographic description of the Tlingit in the first half of the 1880s. During these years the German scholar Aurel Krause conducted his investigations in Alaska. His book summarizes most of the 19th century's study of the Tlingit and is the ethnographic "encyclopedia" of this Indian tribe (Krause 1956).

At the end of the 19th century, the U.S. naval officers lieutenants Albert P. Niblack and George T. Emmons played a large role in the "applied" study of the Tlingit. Stationed in Alaska, both collected many objects of Indian material culture. Emmons himself gathered 11 thousand items, and his collection is the pride of many American museums. Along with acquiring the collections, the naval officers described various aspects of the social and spiritual culture of the northern tribes of the Northwest Coast. And although Niblack succeeded in publishing his large work, furnished with numerous illustrations, as early as 1890, Emmons produced far less: he published only a few articles on the Tlingit (Emmons 1903, 1982), and his numerous notes and memoranda on these Indians, scattered throughout various archives in the United States and Canada, were not published until 1991 after the supreme efforts of F. de Laguna. This researcher labored more than 30 years collecting, deciphering, and logically grouping Emmons's materials into a respectable volume. Some of the sections were written wholly by De Laguna herself or composed of materials selected by her, resulting in a most interesting and valuable ethnographic work that reveals practically every aspect of Tlingit life and culture (see Emmons 1991).

Almost three decades after Krause, field investigations among the Tlingit were conducted by one of America's best-known ethnographers, John R. Swanton. The result of his scholarly research is a large work dedicated chiefly to Tlingit social life, religious views, and language (Swanton 1908).

In addition, Swanton published the first large collection of Indian myths, traditions, songs, and festive speeches, which has served as an important ethnographic source for subsequent generations of American and foreign ethnographers (Swanton 1909).

From 1910 to 1920 the young and talented Indian Louis Shortridge, a descendant of Tlingit Chilkat chiefs, assumed the challenge of studying the Tlingit. He published several articles dedicated primarily to objects of Tlingit traditional culture (preserved in American museums) and the legends and myths connected with them (Shortridge 1919, 1928).

In the 1930s the American ethnographer Kalervo Oberg conducted ethnographic research among the Tlingit of Klukwan. His monograph, *The Social Economy of the Tlingit Indians*, was not published until 1973 (Oberg 1973). Oberg's book elaborates on social aspects of Tlingit society until the arrival of Europeans. Unlike Swanton, Oberg makes significant room for economic issues. Oberg's monograph contains valuable data obtained directly from Indian informants—information concerning, for example, the Tlingit economic cycle, trade activities, and so on, which permits us to include this work in the sources on traditional Tlingit ethnography. In another work, a small but very interesting article entitled "Crime and Punishment in Tlingit Society" (Oberg 1967), this same author examines traditional Tlingit ethics in detail.

In 1947 the American researcher Viola E. Garfield published an article on the Tlingit community Angoon. Garfield, in collaboration with Linn A. Forrest, published a collection of Indian myths that serve as oral illustrations of Tlingit representations on totem poles (Garfield and Forrest 1961).

In the 1950s the American ethnographer Ronald L. Olson performed field work among the Tlingit and was even made an honorary member of the tribe. Like his predecessors, Olson primarily examined Indian society's social aspects. The material that he collected supplemented the information of Swanton and Oberg. The importance of this ethnographic source is defined by a collection of interesting and at times unique legends and facts.

The limitation of subjects in Swanton's, Oberg's, and Olson's works was overcome in significant measure in the works of one of the eminent representatives of American historical scholarship, Frederica de Laguna. Her monograph on the history and culture of the Tlingit of the Gulf of Alaska (De Laguna 1972) is one of the foremost works on the Tlingit. In contrast with the works of her compatriots, which represent ethnographic research, De Laguna's work could more correctly be called an ethnohistory. In the first part of her monograph, De Laguna devotes a rather detailed passage to history and traditional culture and to the innovations and borrowings in it. De Laguna's range of scholarly investigations is significantly broader than that of her predecessors, embracing aspects of material culture, anthroponymics, folklore, shamanism, and so on, which was probably defined by a change in research methodology. De Laguna applied methods from history, ethnography, and archaeology (De Laguna 1960), and employed an unusually broad range of sources, including archaeological data, Indian legends, historical documents, and her own field material. All this makes De Laguna's work a most valuable ethnographic and historic source (Grinev 1994b), especially given the important methodological role of her work in the writing of this monograph.

A student, follower, and good friend of De Laguna, Catherine McClellan, also made a substantial contribution to Tlingit ethnography. As early as the 1950s she published an interesting article on the connection between Tlingit ceremonialism and social structure (McClellan 1954). Later, an equally interesting article dealt with the Tlingit's perception of the first white arrivals, based on information from Indian legends (McClellan 1970a). In the 1960s she began publishing articles on the myths of the interior Tlingit and neighboring Athapaskans—culminating in 1975 with the appearance of a large monograph on these Indian peoples (McClellan 1963, 1970b, 1975).

By the 1980s and 1990s the study of Tlingit spiritual culture and the problem of their Christianization was being fruitfully continued by Sergei A. Kan, a professor at Dartmouth College. In addition to writing several articles (1983, 1985, 1987, 1988, 1991), Kan has written a large, most profound and thorough monograph dedicated to the 19th-century Tlingit potlatch. In addition to ethnographic and historical sources, the author used materials from his own field research and observations between 1979 and 1987: he was adopted by the Tlingit into the Kaagwaantaan clan and participated in a commemorative potlatch. The wealth of factual material presented in the monograph, as well as Kan's theoretical conclusions, make a notable contribution to the ethnography of the Tlingit (see Kan 1989).

Kan undertook 20 years of field work and archival research for his subsequent primary monograph dedicated to the history of Orthodoxy among the Tlingit, *Memory Eternal: Tlingit Culture and Russian Orthodox Christianity through Two Centuries*. For this notable work the author gathered a vast amount of original material that makes his book an invaluable contribution to the study of Tlingit spiritual culture and history. For the theme of our research, the first part of Kan's monograph, which deals with the spread of Orthodoxy among the Tlingit of the Russian American period, is of considerable interest (Kan 1999:25–173).

Other eminent contemporary researchers on the Tlingit include Nora and Richard Dauenhauer (Nora Dauenhauer is Tlingit by birth). They collected, carefully commented on, and published three large volumes of Indian legends, songs, and festive potlatch speeches. The majority of these American scholars' Indian informants were elderly Indians who still remembered the old legends and ceremonies. Because of the Dauenhauers' multivolume work, not only was a significant part of the Indians' oral heritage preserved for the Tlingit themselves but one of the most valuable resources on the spiritual culture and history of these Indians is available to scholars (Dauenhauer and Dauenhauer 1987a, 1987b, 1990a, 1990b, 1994).

The ethnographic works enumerated above, though they are basic sources for studying Tlingit ethnography, do not represent the entire sphere of works on which this research rests. Museum collections and publications about them were also used as specific sources, as were drawings, engravings, and photographs that help represent the distinctive way of life and material culture of the Tlingit. Works dedicated to the Tlingit collections in the Museum of Anthropology and Ethnology (MAE), such as the articles of S. A. Ratner-Shternberg (1927, 1929, 1930), R. S. Razumovskaia (1967), and E. A. Okladnikova (1995), should be mentioned, as should the work of Erna Siebert and Werner Forman (1967). American and European museums' collections of Tlingit material culture and art are described and analyzed in numerous monographs, catalogs, and articles, including works by Bill Holm (Holm 1965, 1984; Holm and Reid 1972), a foremost expert on the Northwest Coast Indians' art, and Aldona Jonaitis (1986), a leading authority on Tlingit art.

Scholarly literature also plays an important role in presenting this book's theme. Two groups of works can be distinguished in the scholarly literature: one is mostly ethnographic, the other historic.

Yuliya P. Averkieva (1941, 1959a, 1959b, 1960, 1961, 1967, 1974, 1981), one of the first Soviet authors to undertake American studies as such, describes various aspects of ethnography. The value of her research lies in the fact that such themes as social organization of Indian society, family relations of the Indians, and potlatch were described in detail and analyzed for the first time in Soviet scholarship.

A profound analysis of the socioeconomic relations that existed among the Tlingit, as among many other peoples of the world, was made by the distinguished Russian ethnographer Yu. I. Semenov (see Semenov 1993). He not only revealed the sources and focal point of the so-called prestige economics that had developed among the Tlingit and other Northwest Coast Indians but also argued convincingly that the Indians' potlatch was first and foremost an economic institution. In general, Semenov's work is of great methodological significance (Grinev 1996b:54). A. M. Khazanov's (1979) earlier large article dedicated to factors and mechanisms of the class formation process should also be noted.

Information on the different aspects of the material and spiritual culture of the Tlingit is found in the works of such contemporary Soviet scholars as G. I. Dzeniskevich (1976, 1985, 1987a, 1987b), A. A. Istomin (1985), R. S. Razumovskaia (1985), E. M. Meletinskii (1979, 1981), and others (Grinev 1986a, 1986b, 1987, 1988a, 1989a; Segal 1972; Fradkin 1985). They raise important questions and introduce new material into scholarly circulation. Nevertheless, the value of these works is somewhat compromised by insufficient sources and a not-always-precise interpretation of factual material (see chapters 1 and 3 of this monograph). In addition, some authors, citing these or other data, do not always indicate the source of the material and occasionally borrow information from other researchers' works without referencing them.

Foreign scholarly literature on Tlingit ethnography is rather diverse. There are both general articles and whole monographs dedicated to describing the Northwest Coast Indian cultures (Adam 1913; Drucker 1955, 1965, 1967; Garfield and Forrest 1961; Goddard 1924; Gunther 1972; Kan 1983; Oswalt 1966; Richards 1984; Rosman and Rubel 1971; Spencer and Jennings 1977; Turner 1979; Wherry 1964). These works help us see parallels and connections between the Tlingit culture and other Indian tribes' cultures and at the same time reveal its specifics. In a series of such works, two monographs by the American scholar Philip Drucker should be noted (Drucker 1955, 1965). In them the author not only analyzes the Northwest Coast Indians' traditional culture but tries to distinguish those borrowings that occurred in the first stage of colonization at the end of the 18th century from those that occurred in the 19th century. In addition, the monographs contain a short summary of the history of Indian-European contacts. Therefore, both of Drucker's works could be termed ethnohistorical.

In general, our subject treats not only ethnographical but historical themes in the Russian American period of the Alaskan past. The distinctive "bridge" between ethnographic and historical works forms the research of ethnohistorians. The contribution of history and ethnography in such works is sometimes uneven. For example, if in Drucker's monographs the ethnographic material predominates over the historical, then in *Contact and Conflict*, a book by the California historian R. Fisher (1977), historical subjects dominate. Fisher analyzes the primary stages of contact between the Northwest Coast Indians and Europeans and comes to several interesting conclusions. He notes in particular two points of view on the consequences of colonization for the Native peoples: some scholars (chiefly historians) see them as quite negative, citing the brutality of the colonial development process, the sharp decline in Indian populations, and so on. Other researchers (primarily ethnographers), by contrast, viewed European colonization—which led, for example, to the flourishing of art and ceremonialism among the Northwest Coast Indians— rather positively. Fisher embraces the "golden mean," pointing out that the character and consequences of colonization for the Native people depended on the period: in the beginning, European colonization on the whole favorably affected the development of Indian society and culture, whereas later, negative effects prevailed. Fisher's book is one of the most fruitful ethnohistorical works because he used unpublished archival documents.

Among foreign researchers' historical works on Alaska, one can cite the large monographs of Clarence L. Andrews (1947), Stuart R. Tompkins (1945), Clarence C. Hulley (1953), and James R. Gibson (1976). In the works of these authors, we are attracted first to the material on Russian American history, and especially descriptions of Tlingit-European contacts during this period. However, American historians base their views of these issues on the rather limited number of published Russian sources; archival materials on Russian America are underutilized. A notable exception is an article by Gibson (1987b) that is dedicated to the Native point of view in the Russian colonization of Alaska; another is an interesting article by Katherine L. Arndt (1988) on the interrelations of the Tlingit, who settled at the mouth of the Stikine River, with the Russians between 1833 and 1867. In both articles, as well as in the recently published articles of J. R. Dean (1994, 1995), Russian archival material is widely used.

It is especially important to mention the monumental biographical dictionary by Richard A. Pierce (1990), an eminent historian of Russian America. This dictionary resulted from the scholar's many years of research in libraries and archives, reference books, and monographs. The biographical dictionary acquaints the reader with Russian America's main historical figures and is a simply irreplaceable research tool. It also contains material on the Tlingit, though, not surprisingly, there is very little mention of them since they were not a major part of Russian colonial society's social structure.

In Soviet historical scholarship, the first research on Russians' activities in Alaska in the 18th and 19th centuries is by S. B. Okun', who in 1939 wrote a monograph on the history of the Russian-American Company. Using extensive factual material and a broad array of archival documents, the author examined the Russians' exploration and settlement of the North American mainland and the role of the Russian-American Company and czarist diplomacy in this process. Okun' not only disclosed the political and economic reasons for the company's establishment and discussed its later functioning but devoted much attention to the interrelations of the RAC with Alaska's Native population. In evaluating these interrelations, the author took a one-sided approach, stressing Russian colonization's negative aspects. At the same time, the researcher accurately saw the Tlingit resistance to colonization as a basic factor undermining Russian supremacy in Alaska.

The theme of Russia's opening up Alaska is discussed in two respectable monographs by N. N. Bolkhovitinov (1966, 1975) and three articles (1981, 1985a, 1985b) in which he elucidates a broad spectrum of problems in Russian-American relations between 1775 and 1815, and 1815 and 1832, respectively. Using considerable factual material (including unpublished archival documents), the author examined in detail the formation and evolution of these relations during the indicated periods. In describing the divisions of Russian American history, Bolkhovitinov discussed both the American-Russian-Tlingit contacts in Alaska and their influences on the diplomatic connection between St. Petersburg and Washington, examining this issue in detail in a scholarly way for the first time. In 1990 Bolkhovitinov's third monumental monograph, *Russko-amerikanskie otnosheniia i prodazha Aliaski, 1834–1867 gg.* [Russian-American Relations and the Sale of Alaska, 1834–1867], was published. The logical conclusion to the two previous works, it is certainly of interest to any researcher of Russian American history.

An early and quite successful historical-ethnographic work in Soviet studies of America was penned by S. G. Fedorova (1971). The author describes the formation and ethnic peculiarities of Alaska's and California's Russian population from the 1700s to 1867 and analyzes Russian colonization trends, their pace, methods, and aftereffects. Fedorova developed a periodization for the history of Russian America that deserves special attention. It is based on the colonization's main directions. The work's structure and the data's course of elucidation are methodologically significant for us.

In addition to the above-mentioned large works on Alaska's Russian period, A. A. Istomin's 1985 article dedicated to Russian-Tlingit relations is of definite interest for our subject. The article is based on a rather broad sphere of sources and gives a profound analysis of Tlingit-Russian relations—this is perhaps the most successful survey so far of contacts between the Tlingit and Russians. It is true that the framework of an article did not permit the author to examine all sides of these contacts and reveal innovations in Tlingit culture during the Russian American period in all their diversity.

In recent years many historical and popular-historical articles on the Tlingit have been published by the historian from Kursk, A. V. Zorin (1994, 1998a,

1998b, 2001a, 2001b), but his works basically detail known historical material and often resemble a compilation, though sometimes he introduces valuable archival material (Zorin 1997).

Thus, the study of this theme in Russian and foreign historical research is still inadequately represented. This monograph attempts to fill this gap to some degree.

§

I consider it my pleasant duty to express my gratitude to all who assisted in the production of this work. Thanks go especially to my former director in scholarship, the eminent researcher of the history and ethnography of Russian America, Svetlana Grigor'evna Fedorova.

I am sincerely grateful for the valuable advice, criticism, and support of Academician N. N. Bolkhovitinov of the Russian Academy of Sciences; doctors of history V. A. Tishkov, L. A. Fainberg, A. V. Vashchenko, and I. N. Gemuev; and doctoral candidates in history R. V. Makarova and S. Ya. Serov.

I am deeply thankful for the attention and help of such employees of the Institute of Ethnography of the Russian Academy of Sciences as L. S. Sheinbaum, N. N. Kulakova, V. G. Stel'makh, Sh. A. Bogina, A. A. Borodatova, P. V. Gribanov, M. T. Kotovskaia, E. G. Aleksandrenkov, I. F. Khoroshaeva, E. L. Nitoburg, L. N. Fursova, I. A. Amir'iants, Z. F. Burnatseva, E. E. Nosenko, N. S. Sobol', L. S. Perepelkin, V. V. Shinkarev, I. I. Krupnik, and others, as well as employees of the Altai Polytechnic Institute, Professor Yu. N. Garber, Docent A. A. Guseva, and chief of RIO V. B. Malakhov.

I would like to express gratitude to my foreign colleagues as well—first to the well-known and meritorious scholar Frederica de Laguna, as well as other researchers of the history and ethnography of Russian America: K. L. Arndt, J. R. Gibson, S. A. Kan, A. A. Znamenski, and R. A. Pierce. I am especially grateful to A. A. Vovnianko and K. Solovjova.

I also extend thanks to the employees of the Central Soviet Archives and especially to those of the Archives of Foreign Affairs of Russia.

Finally, it is impossible not to mention the support of my mother, Nelli Mikhailovna Grineva, whose selfless aid and patience contributed in significant measure to the production of this monograph.

CHAPTER ONE

The Tlingit Indians before Contact with Europeans

~

1. General Characteristics

1.1. Tlingit Territory at Time of Contact

At the end of the 18th century, when regular contacts began with Europeans, the Tlingit Indians occupied a strip of coast in southeastern Alaska from Portland Canal (55° north latitude) in the south to Yakutat Bay (60° north latitude) in the north, including the rocky islands lying offshore—the Alexander Archipelago. The mainland coast and granite shores of the islands are cut up by fjords and bays, and only from the strait at Cross Sound to Yakutat is the coastal belt relatively straight, with just two large bays interrupting it—Lituya Bay and Icy Bay. The Rocky Mountains, with white caps of perpetual snow, separated the "land of the Tlingit" from the interior regions of the continent. On the islands are mountains that, though lower than those on the mainland, are still impressive, with elevations up to 1,500 meters. The highest mountains are located to the north of Tlingit territory, among them rising such giants as Mount Fairweather (*Tsalxaan*, in Tlingit—4,663 meters) and Mount St. Elias (*Uasi-shaa*—5,489 meters). Some of them are dormant volcanoes, for example, Mount Edgecumbe (*Tluk*) on Kruzof Island in the Alexander Archipelago. The hot sulfur springs on Baranof Island are relics of bygone volcanic activity. The curative properties of these springs were known to the Indians from time immemorial. From the mountain peaks slide large glaciers, some of them reaching the ocean, falling into it and creating icebergs. The perpetual snow and glaciers give rise to numerous rivers and creeks, swift and short. Only a few of the small rivers stand out among the others by their dimensions: the Stikine (*Stakin*), Taku, Chilkat, and Alsek (*Altsek*).

The Pacific Ocean, which was the natural western boundary of Tlingit territory, and especially the warm Alaskan current, ameliorates the severe climate of these northern places. The lowest temperature here in January is usually around 0° C, though even 20° C below freezing [−4° F] occurs for short periods. The weather is warmest in August, when the average daily temperature reaches 13° C [55° F] (Krause 1956:54–55). The proximity of the ocean contributes to high humidity. The average annual precipitation reaches 2,000–3,000 millimeters [78–117 inches]. The rainiest month is October and clear weather is characteristic for July. "Continual dreariness, fine rain, and dampness of the air is the usual state of the atmosphere," wrote an old resident of Russian America, K. T. Khlebnikov, "but here, as everywhere, there is no rule without exceptions and good weather occurs. . . . But the prevailing weather is gloomy and rainy, that is, all year is fall" (Khlebnikov 1985:71).

The temperature of the air and the amount of precipitation are greatly determined by the winds, which were noticed by the Tlingit themselves, in whose language were several designations for winds of different directions. A southeasterly wind, bringing rain and dampness, was called *sáanáx*; a southerly wind, usually accompanying clear weather, *dekinaket*; a northwesterly wind, often blowing in fall and winter and changing frequently into strong squalls with hail, rain, and snow, *xóon* ("north").

During the winter, in clear weather, in almost the whole region of Alaska, the northern lights (*gis' óok*) can be seen. The Tlingit believed that these were spirits of the warriors who had died in battle, who light fires in the sky. The appearance of the Northern Lights, according to the notion of the Indians, presaged war and death (McClellan 1975:1:79; Veniaminov 1840a:59–60).

A mild and damp climate and warm sea current promoted abundance and variety in the plant and animal world of southeastern Alaska and the surrounding waters. The coast of the mainland and the islands, even the cliffs and mountains almost to the very peaks, are covered by luxuriant vegetation, mainly coniferous species. Here grow spruce, cedar, larch, hemlock, and pine. Broad-leaf species are represented by alder, willow, and a variety of shrubs. In murky damp forests animals are found in abundance: deer, bears, wolves, mountain sheep, otters, and so on. Birds include ravens, bald eagles, gulls, ducks, geese, and in summer even hummingbirds. The sea along the coast is rich in a variety of fish and sea mammals: seals, sea otters, whales, and others. From March to October numerous schools of valuable fish—herring, candle fish (eulachon), and salmon—go into the coastal waters and rivers of Alaska to spawn.

The rich ecological resources were an important factor in the relatively high degree of development of Tlingit society. Similar natural conditions are characteristic for all of the Northwest Coast, which brought about the formation of the unique Native culture based on fishing for salmon and hunting sea and land animals. The Tlingit lived in the north of this culture area.

1.2. Anthropological Type, Ethnogenesis, Language Association, and Formation of Tlingit Ethnic Territory

Anthropologically the Tlingit belong to the American portion of the large Mongoloid race. Descriptions of the physical appearance of the Tlingit by the various authors generally agree. They are basically a slender, strong, medium-to-tall people (the average height of the Tlingit, according to Boas, is 173 centimeters [five feet seven inches]) with thick black coarse hair, dark eyes, and copper-color skin. The Tlingit's head is rather large, and the face is usually broad and flat. The nose, as a rule, is straight or concave, and lips are of medium thickness (Oberg 1973:6–7). Among the Tlingit is found the pure "Indian" type with relatively long curved (aquiline) nose and distinct profile of the face, and some Indians have rather thick beards and moustaches.

We find the following description of the appearance of a Tlingit in Archimandrite Anatolii, given by him at the end of the 19th century:

> The Alaskan Indian, or Tlingit, is tall, often above six feet, has long, almost round trunk, strongly developed chest and arms, legs somewhat bent at the knees in an outward curve, as among true horsemen of the steppes. However, the curvature of the legs could have been significantly influenced by continual sitting in a narrow boat. The gait is slow and unattractive with a rocking to the sides. . . . The unsightliness of the lower part of the body is compensated by the upper—the head, usually erect and proudly sitting on a thick neck above broad powerful shoulders. The face of the typical Indian man is expressive, strongly outlined, and lively. In the majority of cases the face is round and without beard, but often faces are encountered that are oblong, lean, with aquiline nose. The forehead is not high, but rather broad and almost always reclining back somewhat. The eyes are narrow, but not the same way as among the Chinese or Japanese. Often quite regular eyes are seen. . . . Very beautiful faces are found, especially among the women. . . . But for the color of the skin, which is slightly copper, many a stately Indian man or woman would be difficult to recognize and distinguish from a European (Anatolii 1906:11–13).

In addition, taller stature and proportional build distinguished those Tlingit of the Chilkat community living in the region of Lynn Canal, who much more often had to go on foot over the wooded mountain paths than paddle on the ocean in canoes (Emmons 1991:10).

Data on the ethnogenesis of the Tlingit is scant. They likely began to form as an independent ethnic group about the fourth millennium BC. This can be correlated with the earliest differentiation of the cultures of the coast and the remote regions of the North American continent. During this period the Tlingit language separated from the common trunk of the Na-Dene language family (into which, besides the language of the Tlingit, fall the languages of the Athapaskans and Eyak, the latter having gone out of use literally quite recently) (Krauss 1981:149–151, 154–156; Krauss and Golla 1981:67). Even the first travelers and researchers, who visited among the Tlingit, pointed out the peculiarities of the sound composition of the Tlingit language. The French traveler La Pérouse noted in 1786 that the Tlingit did not speak "b," "f," "p," "v," and sometimes other sounds. On the other hand, the sound "k," as La Pérouse writes, is encountered in almost every word (La Pérouse 1968:410–411). Veniaminov distinguished four phonemic variants of "k" (Veniaminov 1840a:145–146). Therefore, the spelling of some Tlingit words given in this monograph are quite tentative.

The place of origin of the Tlingit, according to Indian traditions, was located to the southeast of their present ethnic territory, in the vicinity of the mouths of the Nass and Skeena rivers, from where resettlement of the Tlingit clans in a northern direction began (Swanton 1908:407, 414; Veniaminov 1840a:28, 82). The legends of some clans, certainly, point to their origin in the depths of the interior or from the Queen Charlotte Islands. The ancestors of these clans, like the local population (most probably Athapaskans and Eyaks), were completely mixed with the Tlingit who settled there.[1]

The Tlingit did not migrate southward since in the south and southeast lived warring tribes of Haida and Tsimshian Indians, who were equal to the Tlingit in their level of socioeconomic development. Both the Haida and Tsimshian, along with the Tlingit, share a culture of settled fishermen of the Northwest Coast of North America. At the end of the 18th century this culture embraced the Native population along the coast of the continent from 45° to 60° north latitude. It was probably the pressure of the Tsimshian from the southeast that led the Tlingit to migrate to the north. The Haida Indians were also expanding outward. A part of the northern Haida moved north from the Queen Charlotte Islands in about 1730 into a region occupied by the Tlingit, and populated the southern half of Prince of Wales Island (Krause 1956:206). This group of Haida that split off was called the Kaigani. Attesting to the fact that the Tlingit lived on this land before the Kaigani are the Tlingit names for the Kaigani villages,

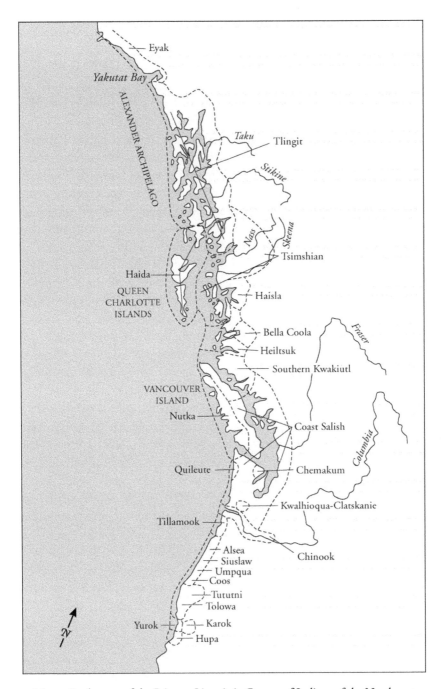

Map 1. Settlement of the Primary Linguistic Groups of Indians of the Northwest Coast of America (end of the 18th century)

including *Kasaan* ("lovely village") and *Sukkwáan* ("grassy village") (Swanton 1908:408). The incursion of the Haida from the south led to the resettlement of several Tlingit clans (particularly, *Teikweidí*) from Prince of Wales Island to the coast of the mainland, as well as to the assimilation and displacement of the autochthonous Athapaskan population. Such a fate, for example, befell the Tsetsaut Athapaskans (autonym—*Wetaltk*, a branch of the Athapaskan Tahltan tribe) who lived in the vicinity of the Behm and Portland canals (Emmons 1911:22–23). The Tsetsaut thus found themselves between the hammer and the anvil: from the west the Tlingit pushed toward them, and from the southeast the *Niska* Tsimshian encroached. In the first part of the 20th century Franz Boas encountered some Tsetsaut Indians who still remembered their language. At this time the pitiable remains of their tribe lived along the upper reaches of Portland Canal as slaves to one of the Tsimshian chiefs (Boas 1924:1).

The Tlingit did not resettle to the east beyond the mountain ranges (at least before the arrival of the Europeans) but rather moved along the coast to the north and northwest. The remote regions of the interior did not attract the Tlingit at this time. The more severe climatic conditions and scant natural resources, as well as the difficulties of adapting their traditional culture to a new ecological environment, limited the expansion of the Tlingit to the east. Their neighbors to the east and north were tribes of Athapaskan hunters—the Tsetsaut, Tahltan, Taku (Taku-Tine), Tagish, and Tutchone.

The Athapaskans, who lived on the coast, were rather quickly assimilated by the Tlingit. Thus, one of the largest Tlingit settlements in the northern part of their ethnic area, Klukwan, was, according to Oberg, still an Athapaskan settlement as recently as 300 years ago (Oberg 1973:56). The Athapaskans from the region of Dry Bay (relatives of the southern Tutchone), and the Ahtna Athapaskans, who were mixed with the Eyak in the region of Yakutat Bay, were assimilated by the Tlingit migrations from the southeast as early as the second half of the 18th century. Pressure from the Tlingit probably led to the resettlement of the Eyaks on the right bank of the Copper River and the expulsion of the Chugach from the region of Controller Bay by the end of the 18th century. At this same time, the Tlingit seized Kayak Island, a territory formerly occupied by the Chugach (De Laguna 1972:1:18, 82, 102–103).

The northward expansion of the Tlingit is likely also corroborated by the data of toponymics. Thus, one of the regions in the northern part of their tribal area is called *xóona*, that is, "northern." Evidently, this region was once the *ultima thule* of the Tlingit tribe, but afterward they settled still farther north, as far as Yakutat Bay (known in Tlingit as *Tlakaik*). De Laguna also points out the Eyak origin of the word *tlakaik* and several other toponyms to the north and south of the bay (De Laguna 1972:1:58–59), indicating that the original inhabitants of this region were Eyaks. The country around Dry Bay is designated by the Tlingit as *Gonako* (*Kunako*). This name was derived from the expression *gunanaa xo* ("among the Athapaskans") (McClellan 1975:1:23–24).

The data of linguistic analysis of the Tlingit language also corroborates that the bearers of this language moved northward, taking the language with them. "Within the boundaries of the area of the Tlingit language the greatest difference between dialects is observed in the southern extremity, which is a consequence of a later spread of the language to the north," writes the eminent Alaskan linguist, Michael Krauss (1981:155–156).

1.3. Ethnic Consciousness and the Ethnonym Kóloshi

The Indians called themselves *tlinkít* (*tlingit, lingit, klinkit*)—"human," "nation," "people"—with the addition of the word *aantkeení*, that is, "people of all settlements" or "people everywhere" (Veniaminov 1840a:28).

The Tlingit distinguished themselves from the Haida (*Deikeenaa*), Tsimshian (*Tsʼootsxán*), Eyaks (Gutéix̱ʼ ḵwáan), Athapaskans (*Gunanaa*), Kwakiutl (*Tʼaawyáat*), and Eskimo (X̱ʼatasʼaak̲). They saw the Haida and Tsimshian as people "equal" to themselves, "of high culture," from whom the Tlingit borrowed many songs, dances, ceremonial equipage, and objects of daily use. Among the Tlingit there was even the expression "work of the Tsimshian" for designating finely made items (De Laguna 1972:1:213–216; Swanton 1908:414). Some Tlingit clans (for example, the *Teeyhittaan* and *Kaasxʼagweidi*) originally sprang from the Tsimshian and Haida, and vice versa; among the Tsimshian was the clan *Kanakada*, which arose from the Tlingit clan G̱aanax̱teidi (Drucker 1955:114; Olson 1967:24, 31, 33–34; Swanton 1908:411). The Tlingit were somewhat condescending toward the Eyaks, seeing them, according to De Laguna, as poor, rather backward relatives (De Laguna 1972:1:213). The collective term *gunanaa* ("strangers" or "strange clan") was used by the Tlingit to designate almost all Athapaskan tribes. They transferred this name in the 19th century to their own relatives, the Tlingit of the interior (McClellan 1975:1:22, 49). The only exception was the Ahtna Athapaskans who lived in the Copper River Valley and procured native copper, for which the Tlingit used the special term *Ikkaa* ḵwáan ("diggers of copper"). The Athapaskans, Krause noted, were treated almost like slaves by the Tlingit, despising their naïveté and poverty (Krause 1956:137). The *tʼaawyáat* ("flat-heads") stood no higher in the eyes of the Tlingit, nicknamed such for the custom of artificially deforming the head. This custom was characteristic for southern Indian tribes, in particular for the Kwakiutl and Salish, who came to the Tlingit usually as slaves bought from the Haida and Tsimshian.

The Tlingit hated and scorned the Chugach Eskimos as their sworn enemies. De Laguna pointed out the fact that in the list of Tlingit words composed by members of the Spanish expedition of A. Malaspina (1791), the word *kutef* (or *kutek*) is translated as "enemy," and in the contemporary Tlingit language of Yakutat Bay this word means "chugach" (De Laguna 1972:1:213). The Tlingit despised the Chugach also for their lack of exogamic clans. According to the ideas of the Indians, the Eskimos entered into matrimonial relations in an unacceptable way, similar to animals. Even the outward appearance of the Eskimos caused aversion among the Tlingit. Their men wore labrets in incisions in the lower lip like Tlingit women.

In Russian sources the Tlingit, as a rule, were designated by the word *Kóloshi* or *Kólyuzhi* (as well as *Kolyushi, Kalyuzhi, Kaloshi*). The ethnonym *Kóloshi* (this form is encountered most often in the sources) evidently originated from the custom of Tlingit women wearing a wood, bone, or stone labret—*kaluzhka*—in their pierced or distended lower lip. The word *kaluzhka* probably originated from the Aleut word *kaluga*, meaning wooden vessel, which was borrowed by the Russians who lived in the Aleutian Islands (Veniaminov 1840a:28). Tlingit labrets are reminiscent in form of wooden saucers or spoons, which probably resulted in the birth of the ethnonym *Kolyuzhi-Koloshi*. However, the German traveler and ethnographer A. Erman, who visited Russian America in the 1830s, was convinced that this term originated from the Russian words *kolot'* ("to pierce") or *kolyu* ("I pierce"), as well as from the derivative adjectives *kolyushchii* and *kolyuchii*. In other words, as an ethnonym, *kolyushi* designates *kolyushchie* ("pierced"), which could be correlated with Tlingit women's custom of piercing the lower lip (Erman 1870:300–301). Nevertheless, the first ("Aleut") variant of the origin of the ethnonym *kolyuzhi/koloshi* is more convincing. The first ethnonym *kolyushi* is encountered in Russian documents in 1783, before direct contact with the Tlingit, when the Russians were conducting negotiations with the Chugach Eskimos and learned from them about this Indian people (Tikhmenev 1863:Append.:5–7). Inasmuch as the negotiations with the Chugach were through an Aleut interpreter and the Russians could not personally see the pierced lip of the Tlingit women, it is logical to assume an "Aleut" origin of the ethnonym *koloshi*. In addition to Tlingit women, the Haida, Tsimshian, and northern Kwakiutl Indians wore these lip ornaments, and judging by the archaeological data, the ornaments were also known among the Bella Coola and Coast Salish (De Laguna 1947:163).

The ethnonym *Koloshi* was used by the Russians in relation not only to the

Tlingit Indians before Contact with Europeans

Tlingit but to other Indians of the Northwest Coast, and occasionally even for designating the Eyak (*Ugalentsi*) and the Athapaskans of the interior mainland ("Tundra *Koloshi*") (Grinev 1986a). Within the bounds of Russian America, the Russians assigned primarily the Tlingit and Kaigani Haida to the Koloshi. Among all the tribes of the Northwest Coast, the longest and most intensive contacts among the Russians were with the Tlingit, and the ethnonym Koloshi is used most often in relation to them. Hence, in the research literature of the 20th century, this term corresponds, as a rule, only to the Tlingit (Efimov and Tokarev 1959:151, 652; Liapunova 1979:225; Hulley 1953:22, 397). The confusion of Koloshi and Tlingit has continually resulted in vexatious misunderstandings. Thus, the notes to the collection of documents on the Russian expeditions in the North Pacific Ocean from 1799 to 1815 indicate that in 1808 the crew of the schooner *St. Nikolai*, which suffered a shipwreck north of the mouth of the Columbia River on Destruction Island, was allegedly pursued by the Tlingit, though in fact these were Quileute Indians (*Rossiisko-Amerikanskaia kompaniia*, 1994:255). For ease of statement, Koloshi from here on will mean only Tlingit. Additional explanation will be reserved for those cases when the use of the term concerns other Indian tribes.

1.4. Intra-tribal Ethnic and Territorial Division

Population Numbers. The Tlingit did not function as a single ethno-social organism, and the tribe lacked centralized institutions of authority. Inherent in Tlingit society were only its own ethnic features: commonality of territory, language (with insignificant dialectical differences), mythology (epic about Raven), ceremonies, and ethnic self-awareness (this was reflected in the general autonym "Tlingit").

From the ethnographic point of view, four main groups could be distinguished in the Tlingit tribe: the southern (coastal) Tlingit belonged to one, the northern (coastal) to the second, the Tlingit of the Gulf of Alaska to the third, and the last group comprised the interior mainland Tlingit (De Laguna 1972:1:15).

The southern Tlingit occupied the coast of the mainland with the attendant islands from Portland Canal in the south to Frederick Sound and Chatham Strait in the north. North from this boundary to Lituya Bay lived the northern Tlingit. In the vicinity of Yakutat and Dry Bay at the end of the 18th century, Gulf of Alaska Tlingit communities were formed, and still later in the 19th century, on the upper reaches of the Taku and Yukon rivers two contemporary communities of interior mainland Tlingit were formed. Only insignificant dialectical differences existed in the language of the northern and southern Tlingit.[2]

Quite recently, a southern relict dialect of the Tlingit language was discovered—Tongass, which has a more archaic system of mutation than the remaining dialects of the Tlingit language (Krauss 1981:167; Swanton 1908:398). The language of the Tlingit of Yakutat Bay was largely different and was distinguished as a special dialect even by early authors (Veniaminov 1846:4, 7). The interior mainland Tlingit spoke the language of their ancestors—Tlingit of the northern branch from the community of Taku (McClellan 1975:1:8, 49)— probably with a small infiltration of Athapaskan words.

Cultural differences sharply contrasted the Tlingit of the first three groups (inhabitants of the coast) from their interior mainland relatives, who were more similar in way of life to their Athapaskan neighbors. Nevertheless, among the coastal Tlingit there existed insignificant cultural differentiation. Thus, the southern groups were more greatly influenced by their neighbors to the south—the Haida and Tsimshian—than were the northern. At the same time, the Tlingit of the Gulf of Alaska still preserved some cultural peculiarities of their Athapaskan- and Eyak-speaking ancestors.

When the Europeans arrived in southeastern Alaska the Tlingit tribe was split into socio-territorial units, or kwáans (Table 1). Scholarly interpretation of these units is fraught with difficulties, and opinions in this regard are contradictory. In the early Russian sources the kwáan was usually defined by the word "settlement." In non-Russian scholarly literature it is variously called "community," "local group," or "tribe." Of course, the majority of researchers point out that the kwáan was not a tribe in the strict sense of the word but only a geographic subdivision of the tribe. De Laguna, in particular, notes that the interpretation of kwáans as independent tribes and their areas as tribal territories reflects neither the actual situation nor the opinions of the Tlingit themselves. In spite of the fact that members of a kwáan were joined by a feeling of local patriotism and family and neighborly connections, they did not form tribes in the sense of a politically organized and autonomous group. For the Indians themselves, belonging to a specific moiety and clan was far more important than belonging to a particular kwáan (De Laguna 1972:1:212).

What in actuality was a kwáan? We will examine this question in more detail since the answer is not clear in the reference literature (*Narody mira*, 1988:443). With the analysis of this concept two aspects can be distinguished: territorial and social. On the one hand, the kwáan was a geographic region with its natural peculiarities and boundaries. On the other hand, it was a certain social group—a joining of the inhabitants of a given region, a territorial form of the

Figure 1. Social-Territorial Structure of Tlingit Society (fragment)

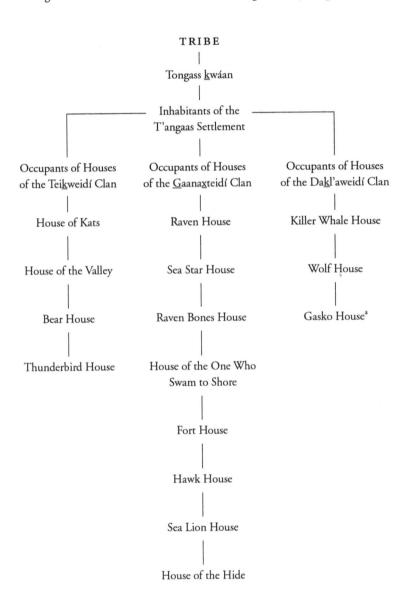

TRIBE

Tongass ḵwáan

Inhabitants of the
T'angaas Settlement

Occupants of Houses | Occupants of Houses | Occupants of Houses
of the Teiḵweidí Clan | of the Gaanaxteidí Clan | of the Daḵl'aweidí Clan

House of Kats | Raven House | Killer Whale House

House of the Valley | Sea Star House | Wolf House

Bear House | Raven Bones House | Gasko House[a]

Thunderbird House | House of the One Who Swam to Shore

Fort House

Hawk House

Sea Lion House

House of the Hide

Source: Figure is based on material from R. L. Olson (1967:10–11).
[a]Gasko: Island off the western shore of Prince of Wales Island.

Table 1. Ethno-Territorial Division of the Tlingit

Subdivision of the Tlingit	Name of the ḵwáan[a]	Note
Tlingit of the Gulf of Alaska	Yakutat (Tlaḵaik) Akoi (village of Akve, Gonakho, Dry Bay) L'tua (Lituya)	Not always indicated—the Lituya region is assigned to the Hoonah ḵwáan, sometimes to the Akoi or Yakutat ḵwáans
Northern Tlingit	Hoonah (village of Kaknau, Icy Strait) [Asanki Harbor] Chilkat (Chil'kat village, Chil'khat [Chilkoot]) Auk (Akut village, Aku, Ak) Kootsnahoo (Kutsnovo village, Khutsinu, Killisnu, Angoon) Taku (Taku village), [Samdam (Saodan)] Sitka (Sitkha village, Shitka)	
Southern Tlingit	Kake (Keku village, Kek, Keku [Kuiu]) Henya (Henu village, Khanego, Tlavak, Klavak) Stikine (Stakhin village, Skatkwan) Tongass (Tongass village, Tankash, Tanta) Sanya (Sanakhan village), Indians of Cape Fox	
Interior mainland Tlingit	Atlin Teslin	Formed in the second half of the 19th century

[a]The names of the ḵwáans are given mainly based on American sources, with regard, however, to their old Russian designations (listed as village). Multiple designations of ḵwáans or their phonetic variants are in parentheses; subdivisions of the ḵwáan, being distinguished sometimes as independent variants, are in brackets.

existence of the society, the result of its areal organization (Figure 1). Veni-aminov wrote, "Above the general name *Tlinkit*, the *Koloshi* have another name according to places, for example: the Sitka *Koloshi* call themselves *Sitkakwáan* or more correctly *Shitkakwáan*, that is, literally, 'those who live there on the sea-

Tlingit Indians before Contact with Europeans

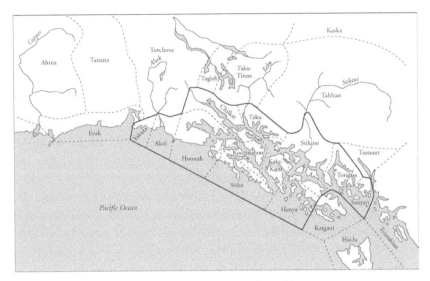

Map 2. Territory of Tlingit and Neighboring
Indian Groups (end of the 18th century)

side of the island bearing the name Shig.' So the others add to the place of
the settlement the word *kwáan*, which properly means *there* or *of there* and is
applied to the names of all the peoples" (Veniaminov 1840a:28–29). De Laguna
gives a similar explanation of the term: "Kwáan is the inhabitants of such and
such place" (De Laguna 1983:71).

The interpretation of the kwáan in Soviet historiography is connected with
the social aspect. This was set forth by Yu. P. Averkieva, who defined kwáan as
"a developing neighborhood community, analogous to a rural community of
agriculturists" (Averkieva 1974:146). However, one can hardly agree with this.
The kwáan itself was not a unitary production and common social group—
some of its settlements were at times several dozen kilometers distant from
each other and in addition did not have a common organ of authority. If the
kwáan is examined from the social point of view, perhaps it can be defined as
a territorial union of communities that was beginning to form.

In the 18th century there were as many as 14 kwáans among the Tlingit. In
one of her works, Averkieva (1960:12) put a table of Tlingit kwáans that was
composed on the basis of the lists of Veniaminov (1840a:29–30), Tikhmenev
(1863:2:341), and Swanton (1908:397). However, Averkieva did not always correctly identify the kwáans noted in these lists. The Tlingit Henya kwáan (the
Henya people) is incorrectly correlated with the Indians of the Hoonah kwáan,

and the Lituya (Akoi) kwáan with the Auk kwáan. The enumeration of the Tlingit kwáans (with synonymous names), composed by the author of this monograph, is placed in Table 1.

The kwáans differed both in territorial dimensions and by the number of inhabitants (from several hundred to several thousand). The most densely populated were evidently the Chilkat, Sitka, and Stikine (Stakin) kwáans.

Family connections among the Tlingit still dominated the territorial ones. Territorial unity was weakly realized by the Indians. Only sometimes, usually when repelling external threat, did unity occur among members of different clans living in settlements of one kwáan.

With regard to number, the Tlingit tribe was one of the largest on the Northwest Coast, and within the realm of Russian America it was the largest Indian tribe. Determining the precise number of Tlingit at the end of the 18th century is not possible. Data from the sources are unclear and contradictory in this regard (Table 2).

The first estimate of the number of Tlingit known to us was given in 1805 by Yu. F. Lisianskii, who determined it to be 10,000 people (Lisianskii 1812:151). However, he did not indicate whether women and children were included in this figure. Almost simultaneously with Lisianskii, N. P. Rezanov, on the basis of information taken by Russian *promyshlenniki* (see glossary) and allied Eskimos, in 1806 produced an approximate calculation of the inhabitants of Tlingit settlements known to the Russians. According to his list, the Tlingit tribe numbered, in fighting men only, more than 10,000. The kwáans of the southern Tlingit—Tongass, Sanya, and Henya—were not included in this (AVPR, f. Gl. arkhiv 1–7, 1802, d. 1, papka no. 35, l. 1500b.–151). This suggests that the total number of the tribe could have been 25,000 to 30,000 people at that time (see documentary appendix 1). One of the best estimates of the Tlingit population between 1740 and 1930 was made by De Laguna (1990b:205).

Contemporary researchers (Hulley 1953:26; Hunt 1976:18; Oswalt 1966:294), as well as some earlier authors (Krause 1956:63), set the total number of Tlingit when the Europeans arrived in Alaska in the 18th century at approximately ten thousand. Averkieva, referring to Veniaminov, mistakenly supposed that at the beginning of the 19th century 6,000 Tlingit lived in Russian America (Averkieva 1974:145). However, in 1839 Veniaminov had written, "The number of *Koloshi* who live within the realm of Russian America, that is, from Kaigan to Yakutat, nowadays does not exceed 6,000; up to 1835, or to the appearance of smallpox, their number was up to 10,000" (Veniaminov 1840b:29). Veniaminov considered in his calculation not only Tlingit but the Kaigani Haida.

Table 2. Number of Tlingit from the 19th Century to 1930

Year	Source	No. people
1805	Lisianskii (1812:151)	Up to 10,000 (only men?)
1806	Rezanov (AVPR, f. GI. arkhiv 1–7, 1802, I. 1, papka no. 35, I. 150ob-151)	More than 10,000 fighting men (not counting the Tongass, Sanya, and Henya kwáans)
1839	Veniaminov (1840a:29–30)	Up to 10,000 Tlingit and Kaigani (only men?) before 1835; 4,500 Tlingit (only men?) or 4,650 (Veniaminov 1840b:57)
1839	Douglas (Petroff 1884:36–37)	5,455 (not counting the Sitka and Yakutat kwáans)
1841	RAC data (*Doklad komiteta ob . . .*, 1863a:132)	Up to 25,000 Tlingit and Kaigani (only men?)
1861	Kostlivtsov (1863:67)	Up to 40,000 Tlingit and Kaigani (only men?)
1861	Golovin (1862:51)	15,000–20,000 Tlingit and Kaigani (only men?)
1861	Verman (Tikhmenev 1863:2:341)	7,839
1870	Scott (Krause 1956:79, 81, 83)	6,500 (not counting the Yakutat, Sitka, and Kuiu kwáans)
1880	Petroff (1884:31–32)	6,431
1890	Chevigny (1944:36)	4,737
1920	Andrews (1947:315)	3,895
1930	Andrews (1947:315)	4,462[a]

[a]The figure entered into the reference book *Narody mira* {Peoples of the World}(1988:433) regarding the contemporary number of Tlingit is astonishing—a total of only 1,000 men, whereas according to American materials at the end of the 1970s there were about 10,000 (see, for example, Krauss 1981:160).

2. Economic Activities

2.1. Primary Occupations

Among the Tlingit, as among the rest of the Indians of the Northwest Coast, the basic economy, fishing, reached a high level of development. Fishing for salmon and preparing it for winter consumption were the chief occupations of the Tlingit during the summer working season. In addition to the many kinds of salmon, the Indians also took herring, halibut, cod, and candlefish. The best herring fishing was off Baranof Island, where Tlingit of various kwáans went to catch fish and prepare roe. Candlefish, whose oil was highly valued by both the coastal and remote interior Indians, were caught around Lynn Canal. But the richest fishing grounds were near the mouth of the Nass River. Not only the Tsimshian but also their neighbors the Haida and southern Tlingit came here to catch candlefish (Olson 1967:88). The Tlingit prepared fish and fish oil annually in large quantities both for winter and for feasts and exchange. The prosperous Indian fishing enterprise insured harvest surpluses and socioeconomic stability, allowing for development of exchange, craftsmanship, accumulation of wealth, development of rank, and the beginning of exploitation of the work of others (Averkieva 1974:137).

Hunting and gathering were important to the Tlingit but they remained second to fishing. The Tlingit men hunted for both forest animals (deer, mountain sheep, and bears) and for marine animals (seals, sea otters, and porpoises). Meanwhile, Tlingit women collected and prepared various berries, roots, tubers, and the bark of coniferous trees. In addition, they collected birds' eggs on the islands, as well as mollusks, crabs, and seaweed along the shore during low tide.

The Tlingit did not occupy themselves with agriculture until the arrival of the Europeans, if one does not consider the growing of a variety of tobacco. The English traveler Vancouver (1833:5:482) was among those who noted the presence of small gardens where this plant grew. But many wild plants were eaten and used for various other purposes. The only domestic animal of the Tlingit was a small type of dog used in hunting bears, deer, and mountain sheep (De Laguna 1960:114).

2.2. The Origin of Craftsmanship

A prosperous fishing industry created a base for the development of craftsmanship. The men made tools, utensils, boats, and weapons; the women wove cloaks; plaited baskets, mats, and hats; and sewed clothing.

Constructing swift canoes, carving totem poles, preparing spoons from antlers, and making wooden battle helmets required special skills. The wood carvers and master boat builders stood out more and more from the general mass of the people (Oberg 1973:84). Fedor P. Litke wrote, "Some crafts among the Koloshi are carried to a substantial degree of perfection. Chief among these is the construction of boats, or, as they are called here [in Russian America], *baty* (a Siberian expression), of which the largest will accommodate from 40 to 60 men" (Litke 1834:162).

Tlingit women achieved great mastery in weaving. Strong and elegant baskets that were impermeable to water and braided from spruce roots, and hats of this same material, often decorated with geometric or totemic designs, were in great demand among neighboring tribes. Especially well known were items made by the women of the Yakutat and Hoonah ḵwáans (Emmons 1903:231–232).

Woven ceremonial cloaks, prepared using a technique the Tlingit borrowed from the Tsimshian, were one of the best examples of the Northwest Coast Indians' art and craftsmanship. The Tlingit wove the cloaks from the down and wool of mountain goats on a bast foundation, usually with a very complex totemic composition. Items from the Chilkat ḵwáan were especially famous, therefore these ceremonial cloaks acquired the name "Chilkat blanket" or simply "Chilkat" in the English-language literature.

The Tlingit knew how to work native copper even before the Europeans appeared in Alaska. They heated copper to a malleable state and, by striking it with stone hammers, gave it the required form. Archaeological excavations in Yakutat show that the Indians used copper for various artifacts: points of arrows, spears, harpoons, knife blades, needles, hooks, and ornaments (De Laguna et al. 1964:85–88). Tlingit master coppersmiths also forged copper plates of a definite form, which were very highly valued among Northwest Coast Indians (Averkieva 1959a:74–77). Oberg's (1973:9) assertion that local copper was used only for making these plates does not withstand criticism in light of archaeological investigations conducted by De Laguna in Yakutat (De Laguna et al. 1964:85–88). However, one cannot agree with De Laguna when she suggests that large plates were made by the Indians only from metal obtained from European traders after their arrival on the Northwest Coast (De Laguna 1972:1:354). This is contradicted by the evidence of Lisianskii, who described a large plate about 90 centimeters high, noting that it was made of native copper, which, in his opinion, gave it its value (Lisianskii 1812:11–12). A similar plate forged from native copper, measuring about 70 centimeters, was seen in 1805 by Rezanov, who wrote that the Indians obtain similar plates from the Copper River and call them *tinnaa* (AVPRI, f. Gl. arkhiv 1–7, 1802 g. d. 1, papka no. 35. l. 470b.).

Even before the arrival of the Europeans, the Tlingit evidently knew and could work iron. In any case, Indian informants reported to De Laguna that iron was known to their ancestors before the arrival of the Russians and that they looked for it in driftwood and pieces of ships along the shore (De Laguna et al. 1964:88–89). The Tlingit could have been taught how to process iron by surviving members of crews of wrecked Japanese junks carried to the Northwest Coast by the current (Gunther 1972:251). However that may be, the first European travelers, who encountered the Tlingit as early as the second half of the 18th century, noted the presence of iron artifacts among them (Shelikov 1971:102).

2.3. Barter

High work productivity, specialization, and the possibility of regularly acquiring surplus products contributed to the development of barter both within the tribe and between the Tlingit and neighboring tribes. Also contributing to this were the ecological differences of some regions of Tlingit territory and the difference between the natural conditions of the coast and those of the interior mainland.

Barter within the tribe, at least up to the arrival of Europeans, was not trade in the complete sense of this word. This was a sort of exchange of gifts between occupants of individual settlements and k̲wáans (especially relatives). True trade exchange existed between the Tlingit and neighboring tribes.

The trade expeditions of the Tlingit went along the sea coast from settlement to settlement or plunged deep into the mainland by specially cleared paths. The Tlingit obtained natural copper from the Ahtna Athapaskans of the Copper River through the mediation of the Eyaks. They resold part of the acquired copper to southern tribes—the Haida and Tsimshian—for slaves, canoes, and carved items, including dentalium shells. The Haida obtained horns of the mountain goat from them, from which they carved handles for buckets and spoons, as well as goat's wool for weaving cloaks (Holmberg 1855:16–17; Rosman and Rubel 1971:36). In exchange the Tlingit obtained from the Haida canoes, which were famous along the whole coast. These canoes, hollowed from huge trunks of red cedar, could accommodate up to a hundred men. The interior mainland Athapaskans supplied furs, elk and caribou hides, fur cloaks, and clothing decorated with porcupine quills to the Tlingit. The Indians of the coast offered the Athapaskans candlefish oil, seaweed, and dried mollusks, handicrafts, shells, and so on. Trade became a significant regular business in Tlingit society, though its goods varied by season. The Indians were usually busy trading in summer until the fishing season began and in late fall after it ended (Averkieva 1974:150–151; Grinev 1986b; Oberg 1973:70; Olson 1936).

2.4. Economic Cycle

Before one characterizes the economic cycle of the Tlingit, one should note the traditional units of time that they used. The year was evidently the largest unit of ecological time known to them. The seasons were reflected in the consciousness of the Indians. They distinguished winter (*táakw*), spring (*táakw eetí*—literally, "the place where winter was"), summer (*kutaan*), and fall (*yeis*) (De Laguna 1972:2:799). In addition, the year was divided into months—*dís*—which designate "moons." The names of most months denote changes

Tlingit Indians before Contact with Europeans

occurring in nature, primarily those related to animal and plant activity (De Laguna 1972:2:800–801). For example, August corresponded to the Tlingit month *kwakaha'dis* ("the month when all the animals prepare their burrows"), and March—*hin tanah kaiyani disi* ("the month when the seaweed grows from under water") (Swanton 1908:426).

The beginning of the Tlingit calendar year, according to Oberg and De Laguna, occurred in July (De Laguna 1972:2:799; Oberg 1973:65), and according to Krause and Swanton, in August (Krause 1956:238; Swanton 1908:426). In August the salmon—the primary food source of the Indians of the Northwest Coast—rush into the rivers of Alaska to spawn. It is not by chance that the indicated period, central to the life of the Tlingit, became the natural chronological boundary. However, as Oberg reports, the economic year proper began among the Indians in March (Oberg 1973:65), and according to materials of various Russian authors—in February (Litke 1834:163–164), when the herring began to spawn. During March and April the Tlingit set off on the spring hunt. The women collected seaweed and shellfish at this time. In May they prepared wild rhubarb, tubers of the Kamchatka lily (sarana), the inner soft bark of hemlock, and so on. That same month they went to the mouths of the large Alaskan rivers for the spawning of shoals of candlefish, from which the Indians extracted large quantities of valuable fish oil (Grinev 1988a:120–121). The peak of Tlingit economic activity occurred from July through September. During these months they fished and stored for future use the salmon arriving in great numbers to spawn in Alaska's rivers. Their regular arrival on the Northwest Coast was the basis of the stability of the Indians' traditional form of life. During the spawning of the salmon, the Tlingit usually moved from their winter settlement to fish camps to harvest the particular fish "crops" (Oberg 1973:70). Having prepared sufficient stocks of fish, the Tlingit set off on the fall hunt. They occupied themselves with hunting all fall and winter. Simultaneously, they devoted great attention to various crafts. They plaited baskets, carved totem poles, and made a variety of implements and tools during this period.

Similar to agricultural peoples after the harvest of the crops, the season of festivals and ceremonies set in. Among the Tlingit the second half of fall and winter was the period of the most active religious-ceremonial life, which peaked in November. During this month the chiefs of the Tlingit households invited their relatives and others to potlatches, which continued into December. The observance of all stages of the economic cycle had a vitally important significance for the Tlingit. Otherwise, hunger and starvation threatened them. Thus, the necessity of timely preparing candlefish oil was one of the chief reasons that the Indians declared a truce with the Russians in 1802 at the mouth of the Alsek River (see chapter 2).

The annual subsistence cycle of the Tlingit was determined by the spawning of the various harvested fish. A similar cycle (with small local differences) was also typical for other tribes of the Northwest Coast (the Haida, Tsimshian, and others).

A smoothly functioning economic mechanism was refined over the course of millennia. The periodicity of the arrival of the exploited fish and the frequent bad weather, which hindered fishing, forced the Indians to procure a larger quantity of fish than was needed for immediate short-term use. It was necessary not only to catch fish but, having processed them, to preserve them for a sufficiently long term, as with the products of hunting and collecting. All this required from the people certain efforts and skills. The natural conditions of the Northwest Coast on the whole, as well as the seasonal changes, promoted an optimal combination of regular and intensive work alternating with rather extensive leisure dedicated to ceremonial life and art, and at times filled with nothing but rest. This is what the Russian naval officer V. P. Romanov wrote concerning this at the beginning of the 1820s: "The Koliuzhi live in their huts like Sybarites: if there is prepared food, they can lie all day between their wives. Becoming bored in the cabin, they throw on their cloak and go down to the shore, sit on a rock or lie on the sand" (Romanov 1825:28). Abundant economic resources and the high specialization of the Indian economy created favorable conditions for the production of the essential surplus of food products. The presence of surplus products caused inequalities in goods, social differences, and the emergence of a simple form of slavery in Tlingit society (Averkieva 1974:137).

The successful relationship of the Tlingit and their environment was thus the fundamental factor in the Tlingit society's rather high degree of development, characterized by an appropriating economy, comparable in level of development to early agricultural peoples (in producing economies). The economic cycle of the Tlingit (as the chronological aspect of interconnection of ecology and economy) was structurally reminiscent of the production cycle of agriculturists of the middle latitudes, for whom the production of vitally important products peaked from May to October, while handicraft activity was most productive from November to March.

3. Material Culture

3.1. Tools and the Means of Transportation

The tools that the Tlingit used to hunt and fish conformed well with the conditions of the catch. Initially these tools were made of wood, bark, roots, bone, stone, and copper.

Fish were procured with the aid of wood or stone dams (locks) or fish traps, as well as hooks, leisters, harpoons, and nets and dipnets. Herring and candlefish, during spawning, were caught by distinctive rakes that consisted of a wooden lath with teeth of bone or copper (Niblack 1890:292). They used a large Y-shaped hook with a carved representation of a man, spirit, animal, or bird to catch halibut. Each hook was named according to this carved image (De Laguna 1972:1:388–389). All the fishing tools were effective and well adapted to local ecological conditions.

The Tlingit hunted on land and sea. The primary tools used in the hunt were bows and arrows, spears, slings, darts, daggers, clubs, and harpoons (for hunting seals and porpoises). They also used all kinds of traps and snares.

The Tlingit used adzes, chisels, knives, scrapers, hammers, and other instruments to make these tools. Their blades were made of stone, bone, shell, or copper and fastened to a handle by animal sinews. They used sandstone and shark skin to polish the tools. The finished artifacts were often painted with various images using a brush made with a grizzly's fur.

The universal means of transportation were canoes, dugout boats of various dimensions. The small canoes were used for fishing and hunting sea mammals, the larger canoes for traveling and trade expeditions. The largest boats were used at war. All these canoes possessed a similar form of body with a raised bow and stern, and the large boats were usually decorated with carvings and ornamentation and even had their own name. In the north, in Yakutat and along the coast of the Gulf of Alaska, the Indians used large skin boats similar to the Eskimos' umiaks, which the Tlingit's Eyak and Athapaskan ancestors of this region probably borrowed from the Chugach. The Indians reported to De Laguna that their ancestors also made one-hatch kayaks and two-hatch baidarkas. Besides skin boats, several other kinds of wooden canoes unlike the common Tlingit type were used (De Laguna 1972:1:330–334). The Tlingit used rafts along the rivers on trade expeditions into the remote mainland (McClellan 1975:1:27). In winter they traveled through deep snow on snowshoes, and for transporting freight they used primitive Indian toboggans.

3.2. Settlements and Dwellings

Tlingit settlements were composed of houses stretched along the shore of a bay or river. Their façades always faced the water. Small settlements had four or five houses and fewer than a hundred people, while large ones had up to 25 houses and about a thousand people (Olson 1967:5) living in these permanent settlements in winter. In summer, during fishing season, the Tlingit made temporary camps of light cabins, huts, sheds, and smokehouses located around bays and along rivers.

Like the other Indians on the Northwest Coast, the Tlingit lived in large rectangular houses with a gabled roof in winter. There were regional differences in the construction of the dwellings of different tribes. The Tlingit, Haida, Tsimshian, and Haisla inhabited the northern type of house (Drucker 1955:54–55).

A house was constructed of thick boards and had four supporting posts within and often four more outside. A small round or oval door hole was covered by a skin or mat, though sometimes the house had a door in the form of a board with a wooden latch. Within the house there was a rectangular pit, and in the center of this was a hearth. In the roof directly above the hearth was a hole for venting the smoke. There were plank beds for sleeping arranged along the walls. The head of the household and members of his family slept behind the partition along the wall opposite the entrance. Storage rooms were located nearby along the sides. The slaves slept at the entrance. The façade and partition within the house were sometimes covered with totemic illustrations, and the corner posts were carved. The totem poles displayed in front of the houses or included in them as elements of construction were probably not as characteristic for the Tlingit as for the Haida and Tsimshian (Krause 1956:86–89). Each large house had its own name (for example, "Large House," "Valley House," "Killer-Whale House," "Frog House," and so on) which could point to the totem of the clan that owned this house, to its location, dimensions, construction, and so forth. In the construction or reconstruction of a house, custom required that several slaves be killed and their bodies thrown into the pits that would be used for the support posts of the house.

In addition to the large "winter" houses, steam baths were built in the Tlingit settlements. In summer fish camps there were huts, wind screens, cabins of poles covered with cedar bark, and small wooden smokehouses (De Laguna 1972:1:302–305).

3.3. Utensils of Everyday Use

Within the Tlingit house, furniture consisted of wooden boxes and chests, mats of grass or cedar bark, blankets of animal skins, and large and small baskets for preserving supplies. The house was illuminated both by the fire and by stone oil lamps. Other implements of the Tlingit household were box-like wooden buckets for water, tongs for pulling out hot stones, wooden plates, dishes and cups, plaited bowls, ladles, scoops, and spoons of wood and horn (De Laguna 1972:1:306–308). At the various ceremonies, they used small bone and wooden spoons to take food from wooden or plaited plates. Many everyday objects were elegantly crafted and decorated with geometric designs or totemic representations inlaid with mother-of-pearl, animals' teeth, and shell. Sometimes the form of the ceremonial cup stylistically reproduced the external view of a totemic animal.

3.4. Dress and Decoration

The dress of the Tlingit is distinguished not only by gender but by season and occasion. Men's everyday summer dress consisted of fur capes or shirts of deer and seal skin, and sometimes included loincloths. The most valuable furs for clothing were sea otter, wolf, beaver, marmot, and especially marten skins; these furs were worn only by rich and aristocratic Indians (De Laguna 1972:1:436). The women wore tuniclike shirt-dresses of tanned deer, caribou, or seal hide, and fur cloaks. On the whole, men's and women's dress differed insignificantly. In summer they usually went barefoot. The head was covered with plaited waterproof hats. In bad weather they also used waterproof bast fiber capes (Oberg 1973:116).

During the cold wintertime, Tlingit clothing included suede combination moccasin-trousers as well as a warm skin and suede jacket. All these items probably originated with the Athapaskans. Soft warm capes and other cold-weather wear, often hooded, were made from bird skins. In addition, in Yakutat they sewed long waterproof shirts, hats, and seal-skin mittens. Hunters wore them for hunting in winter on the shore (De Laguna 1972:1:425–437).

Holiday dress among the Tlingit was somewhat different from everyday dress. It was especially fine among the chiefs and aristocrats, who had Chilkat cloaks, long shirts trimmed with marten or sea otter fur, suede leggings decorated with puffin beaks, as well as wide leather aprons bearing totemic symbols and having long fringes. Aristocratic Indians' headdresses were made from a cylindrical wooden framework with a painted carved wooden plate attached in front that was often inlaid with mother-of-pearl and copper. At the back of the headdress was sewn a mantel of ermine skin, valuable to the Tlingit, and on the upper part of it sea lion whiskers were fastened vertically (Niblack 1890:264). Aldona Jonaitis believes that such head gear was not borrowed by the Tlingit from the Kwakiutl until the mid-19th century (Jonaitis 1986:20–21). In the Museum of Anthropology and Ethnography, several similar pieces of head gear are preserved, including one with an illustration of Raven, which P. P. Doroshin acquired in 1850 (Ratner-Shternberg 1927:96, 101). The chiefs' plaited hats were of very fine workmanship, were painted with totemic representations, and had cylindrical wooden or plaited extensions, the number of which was determined by the number of potlatches the chief had held. The particular type of headdress that chiefs, and especially shamans, wore, was a leather band with mountain goat horns fastened all around it. Sometimes they used wooden imitations instead of real horns. Another kind of headdress, which only the chief had the right to wear on especially solemn occasions, was a wooden hat with an image of the clan totem.

The most popular adornments until the Europeans' arrival were dentalium shells, bone hairpins, and sharks' teeth, which the Tlingit wore as pendants in their ears and nose. The wealthy Indians had ornaments of copper—rings, bracelets, and necklaces. The favorite decorations of a shaman were bears' teeth pendants that often bore a carved symbol.

Occupying a special place among women's decorations was an oval wood, bone, or stone plug, which was inserted into a slit in the lower lip. Its dimensions depended on the age of the woman and could reach eight centimeters among the elderly. This labret indicated a certain social status, and slaves were not permitted to have them (Niblack 1890:257).

Male Tlingit wore their hair to their shoulders, sometimes loose, though often, especially during war campaigns, they bound it in a bun on top. The fundamental difference in appearance between the slaves and free people was that the former wore their hair cut short, while the latter wore it long, especially the women, who sometimes braided it (Kan 1989:62). The shamans never cut their hair (it was believed to have magic powers), wearing several braids instead. To do this, they stuck the hair together with pine resin, which caused the hair to make loud cracking noises when they walked or danced (Anatolii 1906:122).

The Tlingit sprinkled their hair with the down of eagles and other birds during ceremonies. It was customary to paint the face, and sometimes even the body, to protect themselves from sun, cold, and mosquitoes; the paintings were often of totemic figures (Drucker 1955:90). The most common colors were red and black. Tattooing was practiced only among the wealthy Indians.

3.5. Food

The variety of the animal and plant world in Alaska determined the food of the Tlingit up to the arrival of Europeans. It was distinguished by its high caloric value. An almost constant component of Tlingit meals was seal or fish oil. The basic provision was fish, especially dried or jerked salmon, which they dipped in seal oil. Dainty dishes were the roe of herring, salmon, and other fish, dried seaweed, mollusks, and crabs. In addition, the food consisted of the meat of various land animals (deer, mountain goat, mountain sheep, bear, marmots, and so on), as well as sea mammals (seals, sea lions, sea otters, whales, and porpoises). Statements by Georg H. von Langsdorff (1812:2:96) and Veniaminov (1840a:60) that the Tlingit allegedly did not eat whale meat or oil are refuted both by information from travelers and by the Indians themselves (Jacobs and Jacobs 1982:119). Regarding this, Litke wrote: "They drink whale oil from dippers: this is a delicacy, taking the place among them of champagne for our dinner" (Litke 1834:164).

In the food, many kinds of birds and birds' eggs were used as well as various sorts of berries, roots, tubers, and greens. Berries and other plant food were usually preserved using sheep, bear, seal, or fish oil. A substantial part of the Tlingit diet consisted of the inner bark of coniferous trees. They cut the bark off to form a square cake and, after drying it, ate it with fish or seal oil (Niblack 1890:277). It should be noted that significant seasonal variations were observed in the composition of the food.

Food preparation methods among the Tlingit varied. They roasted their food over a fire; stewed it on coals; or, having buried it in the ashes, cooked it in large baskets, throwing hot stones into the water; jerked it in the sun or over a fire, dried it in the wind; covered it with fish or seal oil; and soured it in pits. Among Europeans, some of the Tlingit viands did not tempt the appetite. Archimandrite Anatolii wrote about this at the end of the 1890s: "All dishes are prepared in oil without fail. The most elegant food even up to the present among the Indians is thought to be soured heads of fish and deer . . . The most tasty part is considered the brain, which has turned green. This, of course, takes some getting used to just to be present at the table" (Anatolii 1906:9).

Several food taboos existed among the Tlingit. For example, they never hunted ravens or albatrosses and did not use them for food, probably because of religious prohibitions.

4. Prestige Economy and Potlatch

4.1. Specifics of Economic Relations in Tlingit Society

As already noted above, relatively favorable ecological conditions, rather well-developed tools, and economic specialization permitted the Indians to acquire stable surpluses of goods. Precisely these factors predetermined the formation in traditional Tlingit society of a so-called prestige economy. Its essence was analyzed in depth in a large work by Yu. I. Semenov (1993). We will dwell in more detail on this issue to achieve a better understanding of the development of the economy of a pre-class society, including the traditional economy of the Tlingit.

First we will specify several economic categories without knowing which of the following statements will prompt additional questions. Production is necessary for the normal existence of any society. In the process of production, a relationship emerges among people that is called *production relations* and that includes relationships that are developed in the production process itself and in the distribution, exchange, and use of goods. These relationships depend first on the domination of some *form of property*. In other words, the character of production relations is determined by who controls the primary means of production, including land, hunting and fishing territories, tools, and so on. For example, a capitalist's acquisition results from the fact that the capitalist owns the means of production, that is, the machinery and other technical equipment, and the buildings and structures in which the process of *capitalistic production* occurs.

In deep antiquity property had a common collective character: in indigenous society, some group of early people owned the primary means of production. A man could not survive outside the group without mutual support, sharing the acquired goods with other people and obtaining from them his share. Practically all acquired goods at that time were *necessary, vital*. However, in the course of the evolution of society, with gradual progress and the improvement of tools and production skills, people began to produce more goods than were necessary for physical survival. Thus, along with the necessary goods, *excess* goods appeared. When the developing society became able to regularly produce these excess goods, it became possible to continually expropriate them to other people. In this case, the excess goods are turned into *surplus* goods: created by some people, they are used by others without equivalent compensation, and often in spite of the will or wishes of the producer. In other words, *exploitation*, that is, the appropriation without payment by one part of the society of a share of the communal goods or services created by another part of the society, emerged. Appropriation without payment leads to a *mode of exploitation*: all the goods, or a part of them, are created by the producer not as his property, but as the property of other people who govern the means of production and who frequently govern the producer as well. If the appropriation of goods does not occur in the process of production, but after its completion, then here we are dealing with a *method* and not a mode of exploitation. A method of exploitation is only a form of appropriation and not the creation of the surplus goods. As an example, capitalist or slave-owning exploitation is a mode, while war plunder, tribute, usury, and intermediate trade are related to the methods (Semenov 1993:2:306–307).

However, exploitation emerged only as a consequence of the evolution of tools, forms of property, and production relations. So, in early indigenous society, at an extremely low level of production, the principle of balanced distribution by need or necessity prevailed. With the transition to late indigenous society, when the acquisition of excess goods became a common occurrence, it became necessary to change the principle of distribution, otherwise people simply would not want to create excess goods and become passive objects of "parasitic" kinsmen's exploitation. At this stage of societal development a new principle of distribution arose—distribution based on work. This means, writes Semenov, that the goods a person creates are not for their immediate distribution but for the disposal of these goods to the producer, that is, to his or her individual (but temporary) property. So, along with communal property emerged individual members' property (Semenov 1993:2:324).

But in the society there continued to exist the communal or group property and, accordingly, a person was obliged to share, if only partially, with other people—the co-owners of the communal hunting, fishing, and gathering territories. The society did not permit a person to accumulate material wealth and obliged him to be generous, distributing this wealth to other people. Hence, the group required redistribution, sharing the created goods, but was simultaneously interested in increasing excess goods—which gave it great stability and viability; however, it was impossible to increase the quantity of goods without changing the distribution of work. One person's partial refusal to share with the members of his own community and to transfer excess goods created by him to members of other groups changed the distribution. This transfer gave prestige both to this man and to his group, which he represented. If he held esteem among members of his own community through diligence and generosity, now his authority significantly increased in the eyes of other communities' members. Thus, products and goods began gradually to circulate between two or more communities. So, a system of circulation of excess goods developed at the same time that vital goods continued to be distributed within the community. The formation of this "prestige economy" was in essence a system of prestige gift exchange based on the principle of equivalence in giving and receiving (Khazanov 1979:147–149; Semenov 1993:2:237–239).

The appearance of a prestige economy was a powerful stimulus to work. Indeed, a person could not earn the esteem of others, perform life's most important rites, or atone for crimes if he did not give and return gifts. As a result, production of at least a part of the excess goods became as important as the production of those necessary for survival (Semenov 1979:90, 1993:2:261, 286). Some people, A. M. Khazanov noted, worked more to attain or preserve a higher status and prestige and induced their relatives and followers to do this as well. Those in a position of debt had to work more to compensate for goods accepted (Khazanov 1979:155).

The distribution by work, having emerged, naturally and quickly resulted in property and social differentiation, since individual workers' potential, even within the framework of one community, was unequal. However, the well-to-do person was considered not one who preserved and accumulated property and goods, but one who distributed them to others. Early norms of distribution were preserved (inasmuch as there continued to be group property), but the distribution of at least part of the created goods was already occurring outside the framework of the primary community. In giving goods to a member of another community, a person did not lose them entirely. That is, he lost the goods, but he acquired the right to other goods of equivalent value. Therefore, the more a person gave, the more he could get. In other words, in a peculiar way he became able to accumulate material wealth (Semenov 1993:2:246–247).

If a person initially provided only the products of his own work and that of his family, it was not long before he developed ideas about various ways to use the products of other people's work. Indeed, the recipient of a gift was interested first of all in the quantity and quality of the goods being received from the giver, and not their origin. Therefore, a man's prestige was determined not by his real work contribution but rather by the quantity of property or goods he gave to members of other communities. Those goods could have been created by other people (wives, followers, slaves, and so on). Thus, the development of a prestige economy supposed the exploitation of one person by another and the transition from distribution based on work to distribution based on property. Hence, a man received his share of communal goods only because he was the owner of property (Mauss 1996:140–145; Semenov 1993:2:285, 340).

Returning to the economic relations of Tlingit society, the Tlingit and other

Indian tribes of the Northwest Coast long ago became the textbook example of a people with a "prestige" economy, in light of the basic relations between property and the means of production. These relations differed in great specifics: land, hunting and fishing territories, berry patches, beach areas suitable for coastal collecting, and salmon rivers and creeks were found simultaneously among the properties of both the clan group and its chief. The property was split, divided, incomplete. On the one hand, the clan or its subdivision owned these territories, and this was reflected in the right of each kinsman to use them relatively freely. On the other hand, the heads of the kinship groups were seen as custodians of the group's property (Averkieva 1974:139–140; Semenov 1993:2:335). This was manifested, for example, in the fact that young men of a household, if they hunted individually, were obliged to give large pieces of their game to the chief (Oberg 1973:31). It was the chief who opened hunting season, indicating to his kinsmen where, how, and how many animals each hunter could procure. Finally, only the chief could permit members of other clans to use his clan's territories (De Laguna 1972:1:464). He even received payment for this from outsiders (Garfield 1947:440).

The individualization of the possession of usable territories may have arisen in Tlingit society before Europeans arrived. In any case, R. L. Olson (1967:12) reported that some salmon creeks and small rivers became the property of individual people, usually the household chiefs. V. E. Garfield and L. A. Forrest described the "totem" pole of Tuxekan, which was erected to acknowledge the right of the chief to one of the salmon creeks: on the top of the pole the chief was shown warding off a wolf (the symbol of the Wolf moiety of his kinsmen) from the mouth of the creek (symbolically rendered as a face) and depicted below carved illustrations of salmon "swimming" toward it (Garfield and Forrest 1961:109–111). These data are only from the end of the 19th century, when the process of individualization of ownership rights was occurring under the influence of American capitalistic colonization.

In the traditional economy of the Tlingit, the chief was the proprietor—manager of the primary means of production. But inasmuch as the clan appeared as the owner, the chief was obliged to share the means of production with the clan, supporting and helping poor and infirm kinsmen in particular. However, the latter usually received significantly less game, catch, or products of collecting than the chief received as "custodian" of clan territories from other members of the clan. The chief's income, which substantially exceeded his expenditures, suggests exploitation. As Semenov notes, this form of exploitation was based on the chief's individual use areas. The chief was the owner by virtue of being head of the clan or its subdivision. According to Semenov

(1993:2:335), "The described part of the property was not personal or private, [but] rather official and titular. It was connected not with a person or a group of individuals, [but] rather with a definite office." Khazanov pointed out even earlier that one of the most important functions of the chief was to protect and regulate property rights for the most important vital resources (Khazanov 1979:152).

In traditional Tlingit society land was not owned by the individual but could be parceled out by the leader. This was a special form of exploitation that can be called *redistributive*. A man exploited his kinsmen only while serving as the chief. Once deprived of his office, he ceased receiving surplus goods from his kinsmen. The redistributive method of exploitation, which arose in a natural way within the framework of late indigenous society was, in Semenov's opinion, the first method of exploitation in the history of human society (Semenov 1993:2:307; see also Khazanov 1979:130, 158–163). This *method* of exploitation later changed into a *mode* of exploitation when the chief's property became supreme and the community's property subordinate. In the process of social evolution, the chief's supreme property was transformed into supreme state private property and the chief into a czar, pharaoh, emperor, or the like. In this way the first human antagonistic class formation (a type of society) in history arose, among which the clearest members are the ancient civilizations of Egypt, Assyria, China, and Early Peru. Semenov proposed calling this formation *politarism* (from the Greek word *politiia*—"state"). Underlying politaristic societies was the supreme property of the state, which was based on the fundamental means of production (primarily land) and on the individual as the direct producer. All this was the combined official and private property of the bureaucrats and the communal village property of the peasant societies. The primary mode of exploitation in these societies was state redistribution (in Ancient Rus' [Russia] it bore the name *poliud'e*). It can be noted that politarism was very widely represented in various forms throughout the course of human history (Grinev 1996b).

Besides the redistributive form of exploitation in Tlingit society there existed (though rare) servitude—in which impoverished people and orphans worked for the chief for food (Semenov 1993:2:337). The Tlingit scornfully called these degraded kinsmen, who depended on the mercy of others, "slaves of dried fish." However, wealthy relatives could redeem such a person from his almost slavelike state (De Laguna 1972:1:468–469). In addition, there existed among the Tlingit marriage servitude, the exploitation of wives by husbands without equivalent compensation for their work, as well as slavery, war plunder, and intermediate trade.

On the whole, as has been repeatedly mentioned in Russian historiography, economic relations among the Tlingit were complex and contradictory, typifying societies on the threshold of class formation (Averkieva 1974:154–170; Grinev 1991:62; Mauss 1996:169; Semenov 1993:2:340). Along with the emerging relationship between private property and exploitation, the economic relations of the Indians also had several archaic features that reflected the contradictory, dual character of property. Thus, in Tlingit society there simultaneously existed distribution by need (sharing relations), distribution by work, and distribution by property. This whole complex gamut of economic relations made a profound imprint on all sides of life in Tlingit society.

4.2. Potlatch

The clearest manifestation of the "prestige economy" among the Tlingit, as well as among other Indians of the Northwest Coast, was the "potlatch" (which translates as "to give a gift" in the Nootka language), a well-known ritual that has been studied by several generations of ethnographers. At its core the potlatch was the act of prestige gift exchange, which usually occurred between two or more intermarried clans. This was the mechanism that guaranteed the circulation of excess and surplus goods created in Tlingit society. Besides the potlatch, the Tlingit had other festivals, ceremonies, and feasts. And though they also were a manifestation of a prestige economy, they bore a narrower, individual character. A distinctive feature of the potlatch was the required presence of members of the opposite moiety, who, at the end of the festival, were presented with rich gifts.

This social institution, having great significance in Tlingit life, has repeatedly attracted the attention of scholars. In Soviet ethnographic literature, the potlatch was illuminated and detailed in the works of Yu. P. Averkieva (1960, 1961, 1974).

The Tlingit potlatch was a complex festival lasting no fewer than four days. The most important elements of the potlatch were refreshments, festive speeches, songs, dancing, and the distribution of gifts (foods, furs, crafted artifacts, and slaves). The festivities could be organized both by individual people and by whole lineages. Other festivals and ceremonies existed among the Tlingit too. Members of the opposite moiety were required to attend these festivals, and rich gifts were presented to them at the end of the festival. The potlatch marked a socially significant event, including mourning. Even early Russian authors noted the festivities' special significance for the Tlingit. Thus, Litke, relying on the notes of Khlebnikov, left a rather picturesque description of Tlingit festivals:

Koloshi are the great lovers of feasts—this means immoderate eating and, later, dancing. There was no shortage of pretexts for this: new alliances, new acquaintances, peace and war, any notable event, commemoration of relatives and friends—everything is a reason for these so-called *igrushki*. Igrushki are of two kinds: *domestic*, occurring several times annually between only the closest neighbors, and *public*, in which acquaintances and prominent persons from remote places are invited.

The first are in fall, when food is laid up for winter. The toion, the elder of the clan, entertains his neighbors for several days, during the course of which they eat and dance without stop, alternating between them; finally, the host endows the guests with animal skins, fine leather, blankets, and the like; and together with the whole company moves to another [chief], then a third, and so on, during which they know how to proportion with great delicacy the number and quality of gifts in order that the preponderance was not too great in any individual's favor.

Public igrushki are not given by families, rather by the whole tribe; at them those invited from distant places remain for more than a month. In the settlement, where the igrushka occurs, every dwelling is distinguished by a carved block [wooden model of the totem], which represents some animal, bird, or some other object, and during the whole course of the festival the house is named not by the host, but by a sign board on it. After the craziness is finished under the sign of the eagle, they go under the sign of the raven, bear, sun, moon, and so on. They endow the arriving guests everywhere in proportion to the dignity of each and with the more or less true hope of obtaining from him an equal gift in time (Litke 1834:164–165).

The participants in the potlatch always broke up into three groups. One consisted of the organizers of the festivities, while the others were the invitees, one group being the occupants of the settlement, the second, members of other ḵwáans. If there were no guests from other ḵwáans, then groups were formed from the members of sublineages of the clan or clans of the opposite moiety of their settlement. Thus, for example, at the potlatch of the Sitka Kiks.ádi, the invited Kaagwaantaan were divided into the Basket House group and a group that consisted of the Kaagwaantaan of the Wolf House and Eagle's Nest House (Swanton 1908:434–435). There was a peculiar competition between the two groups of guests, involving the arts of oratory, song, dance, and eating. This

Tlingit Indians before Contact with Europeans

rivalry was sometimes so acute that only the intervention of the host could prevent a bloody clash. Swanton writes that the organizers of the potlatch were always on the alert, and in case of conflict threw themselves between the guests with an image of the totems in their hands, or else uttered the cry of a totem animal of the moiety (Raven, Wolf/Eagle) (Swanton 1908:449).

Veniaminov, who devoted considerable attention to a description of the Tlingit potlatch, distinguished three varieties: funerary, the potlatch proper, and the potlatch in honor of children (Veniaminov 1840a:99).[3] The earliest form of potlatch was the funerary, a festive ceremony. All free Tlingits were obliged to carry out such a potlatch. The Indians reported to De Laguna that even the poorest person in the household was obligated to organize a potlatch in honor of his late relative. Sometimes it took a poor person years to accumulate sufficient property for gifts for the guests. If the relatives did not arrange a potlatch for the deceased, then disgrace fell upon the entire sublineage; other Tlingit began to speak of them as though they were people of a lower rank (De Laguna 1972:2:606). The Indians believed that food and property, which was distributed among guests or thrown into the fire as one called out the name of the deceased, went to the soul of the deceased in the form of "spiritual equivalents." According to the Indians' beliefs, slaves killed at a funerary potlatch had to serve the eminent deceased in the other world. In festive speeches at such potlatches, much was said about the merit of the deceased, his deeds and exploits, and the history of the clan, and the rights of the organizers to this or that territory were substantiated. Speeches were accompanied by songs with the showing of totemic regalia. A period of mourning concluded after the fulfillment of the potlatch.

Especially splendid were a second type of potlatches—those most often held in connection with the construction or reconstruction of a house, or more rarely with the erection of a totem pole or the acquisition of a new totem or totemic object. In this potlatch the usual practice was the sacrifice of no fewer than two slaves (on very rare occasions were the slaves set free). The master of the house was completely ruined by such a potlatch, giving away not only his personal property but sometimes even his wife's fortune (Veniaminov 1840a:103). According to Indian legends, only the great chief of the Naanya.aayí clan, Shakes, could afford to put on eight large potlatches (De Laguna 1990b:220).

The later form of potlatch, as Averkieva noted, was the potlatch in honor of children. At this festival the ears of the children of a wealthy leader were pierced, or their arms or chest tattooed. Each hole in the ears of the child designated a potlatch in his honor. The maximum number of holes was eight (four in each ear). People with pierced ears were considered "elite," "noble,"—"*aanyádi*" among the Tlingit (Veniaminov 1840a:107–108). Slaves were never sacrificed at a potlatch in honor of children. Members not only of the opposite but also of one's own moiety were invited to and acquired gifts at this potlatch; the gifts required no reciprocation. In the ceremonial rites those clear features of the totemic cult, characteristic for the other kinds of potlatches, were absent (Averkieva 1960:64–65).

The potlatch was the center of Tlingit social life. In these ceremonies the wealthy Indian could promote his social status and take a new honorary name. If the initiator of the potlatch was a lineage, then it could acquire the right to new totems or confirm and elevate the prestige of the lineage. Wealth gave the right to a higher status and to privileges, but in order to acquire them it was necessary to publicly give away this wealth. Distributed wealth was not surrendered in vain: the guests were obliged to compensate the potlatch's hosts for their expenditures by arranging their own potlatch at some point.

Prestige derived from public giving at potlatches was spread unequally among the members of the clan who arranged it, being retained primarily by the leaders. It was the chiefs who stood out as the primary distributors at the festive ceremonies, the "conductors" of the potlatch. As members of the clan, they distributed or received most of the most valuable gifts. "If earlier," writes Semenov, "wealth, being distributed at potlatches, secured leadership, then leadership, which emerges from wealth, itself now begins bringing wealth" (Semenov 1993:2:309). Prestige was transformed into social status—a position, and this status in turn brought wealth, the distribution of which again gave prestige.

Using his influence, the head of a lineage decided who of his kinsmen could wear and show more, and who less, of the valuable totemic regalia of the clan; this adornment was visual evidence of status and rank and indicated more or less prestige. This power permitted the chief to regulate social mobility within his clan (Kan 1989:215). The potlatch was therefore used by chiefs as an instrument, and totemic ideas as a distinctive "ideological basis," in the distribution of social roles and statuses.

As S. A. Kan notes, men and women did not play equivalent roles in the execution of the potlatch. Men usually distributed more gifts and wealth than did the women, and bore and demonstrated the most valuable and prestigious totemic objects, prevailed in speeches, and performed the most sacred dances and songs. Correspondingly, the men received the most substantial and valuable gifts (Kan 1989:214–215). The situation was similar concerning payment of blood money for murder: usually the life of a woman was valued at half that of a man. Why was the status of a woman lower? Evidently, it was because she did not participate directly in the affairs of her clan since, after marriage, she moved to her husband's house. Correspondingly, the direct owner of the clan territories were the men, whereas the women were only potential co-owners. Therefore, though women's work could be even more productive than men's, especially in preparing goods for the potlatch, their general status was significantly lower than that of men.

Preparing for the potlatch, members of the clan were obliged to provide the chief with goods and articles as gifts for the guests, "representation," so to speak, for the acquisition of greater prestige for their clan. And this was another channel through which the chiefs might exploit their kinsmen. In every way, the chiefs maintained the potlatch as a socioeconomic institution that gave them power, privileges, and wealth.

In the society of the Tlingit and other Indians of the Northwest Coast, special categories of objects that circulated through prestige gift exchange had been formed. These prestige valuables were often material objects that had no functional significance. First among them were native copper plates that were used exclusively at potlatches, as well as specially dressed deer skins that served as a unit of value (every item could be valued according to how many skins it was worth). In addition, slaves comprised a special category of prestige valuable. Distributing this wealth at the potlatch, the Indian (or lineage as a whole) could raise his social status, pay compensation for insult or murder, receive a new totem, receive an honorary name, and so on.

Though the potlatch was first an economic institution, among the Tlingit it represented a very complex and multifunctional social event. It could never be treated as only a specific kind of exchange, the primary goal of which was confirmation of and an increase in the social position of the distributor—though the potlatch is treated in precisely this way in the contemporary his-torical-ethnographic reference *Narody mira* (1988:592) [Peoples of the World]. In organizing a potlatch, a Tlingit not only increased his prestige but actually strove to bring his inner world into harmonic unity with the universe: joining the world of living people with the world of the ancestors, the past with the present, the real with the beyond. Without consideration for spiritual— psychological events, any description of the potlatch among the Tlingit will be incomplete (Mauss 1996:145). At the potlatch the most important ethnocul-tural information was redistributed and the identification of a person and his status and the place of the clan in the system of clan hierarchy were established. Only after carrying out the potlatch would the soul of the deceased finally join the assembly of ancestral spirits. Thus, the potlatch stood out as the central element of the Tlingit funeral cycle, and according to the ideas of the Indians, the eternal "rotation of the soul," its symbolic immortality, which Kan (1989) discussed so well in his monograph, had to be secured.

5. Traditional Social Organization of the Tlingit

5.1 Clan Structure and the Community

At the base of the Tlingits' social organization lay the matrilineal clan structure. Clan connections and relations comprised the framework, the base on which almost all other social relations (including the day-to-day functioning of Tlingit society) were built or on which they directly or indirectly depended.

The Tlingit tribe is divided into two exogamic moieties—Raven and Wolf (among the northern Tlingit, Eagle). It is true that the Nekadi clan, whose chief totem was the Eagle, was a part of the Sanya kwáan, the members of which could marry members of both moieties. Philip Drucker suggested that the Nekadi are of Tsimshian or Athapaskan origin and were adopted by the Tlingit relatively recently (Drucker 1955:11). Olson simply treated the Nekadi as a people emerging from the Tsimshian (Olson 1967:1).

The chief function of the moieties was regulating marriage relations. The moieties were divided into clans. The Tlingit clan was exogamic and matrilineal and had its own name (for example, L'uknax.ádi, Deisheetaan, Wooshkeetaan, Kiks.ádi, Kaagwaantaan, and so on). Among the other tribes of the Northwest Coast, the Haida, Tsimshian, and Haisla (northern Kwakiutl) also had a matrilineal social organization (Drucker 1955:108).

The Tlingit clan did not have a direct economic function, that is, it was not a production group. It primarily had social functions, including roles in the spiritual culture. According to De Laguna (1972:1:451), certain legends, dances, names, totemic emblems, speeches at potlatches, illustrations applied to the face, battle cries, and even spirits that "visited" shamans, were considered the property of a clan and jealously guarded from strangers. Thus, warriors of the Kiks.ádi, during attacks, hooted like owls, since, according to legend, one of their clanswomen was allegedly changed into an owl (Swanton 1908:417).

Migrations and resettlement resulted in a given clan's members settling in different kwáans and thereby forming localized segments of clans—lineages. Thus, members of the Wooshkeetaan clan lived in the kwáans of Auk, Hoonah, and Kootznahoo, and the Teikweidí were widely settled in many kwáans of the Tlingit ethnic territory, from Sanya in the south to Yakutat in the north (Figure 2). Some (usually small) clans, for example, the Waskinedi (Washinedi)

Figure 2. Clan Structure of the Tlingit Tribes (fragment)

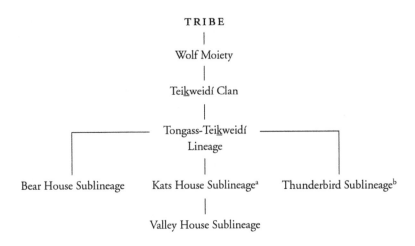

TRIBE

|

Wolf Moiety

|

Teiḵweidí Clan

|

Tongass-Teiḵweidí
Lineage

|

Bear House Sublineage   Kats House Sublineage[a]   Thunderbird Sublineage[b]

|

Valley House Sublineage

Source: Diagram composed of materials from R. L. Olson (1967:11).
[a]Kats: Mythical hero who was married to a she-bear.
[b]According to the material of J. R. Swanton, this house was called *Wanda'it*, that is, "Wanda House."
Wanda: Cloak made of eagle skins, which was used during ceremonial dances (Swanton 1908:400).

in the Kake ḵwáan, had no subdivisions (lineages) in other ḵwáans but were concentrated in only one ḵwáan. In this case the clan and the lineage were one and the same. In some cases these were parts of an earlier clan that had been isolated long ago. For example, the Watanedi clan was in essence a branch of the Kiks.ádi clan (Sitka Kiks.ádi) (Swanton 1908:398–400).

At the local level the lineage performed those same functions as the clan and, in addition, had administrative and military functions and regulated the property rights of the population. It represented in itself a core of the local economic group—the clan community.[4] Though relationship among the Tlingit was calculated along the matrilineal line, the most dominant role in the community was played not by the women but by the men, a dominance caused by avunculocality in marriage (see section 5.4 below); nevertheless, the women were the owners of the primary means of production.[5]

The clan community could be defined as a socioeconomic unit of the "first" or "highest" level, which has united members of different clans. Communities among the Tlingit usually consisted of several households in isolated settlements. The household was the "second," or "lower," level of the community and was the basic economic unit of Tlingit society. The typical Tlingit household was composed of the head (chief) of the house, his brothers, wife, brothers' wives, unmarried daughters, sons under ten years old, nephews, nephews' wives and children, the old people, and the slaves. The household, essentially a fraternal family community, could have has many as 60 members. In each household there were members of different clans and lineages. Though the household was a true working group, the owner of the primary means of production was considered the lineage, and at a lower level, the sublineage, that is, all adult males with full rights who comprised the nucleus of the household. However, in this nucleus of owners, the core stood out—the chiefs, who, along with the group, governed and managed basic means of vital resources. Each sublineage (actually the household as a whole) had a house in the village; had its own territories for hunting, fishing, and collecting; and had its own large canoes, ceremonial objects, and so on.

Though in Tlingit settlements members of different clans and lineages often lived and worked side by side, it is hardly possible to say that they comprised a complex economic group that was above individual clan communities. Economic cooperation within the framework of the settlement was practically lacking. Economic questions were usually decided within the household, and, if necessary, within the clan community. Neighborly connections were limited chiefly by marriage and ceremonial relations and were only occasionally displayed in economic mutual aid and military support. Tlingit society was still a long way from having a proper neighborly community.

Clans, lineages, and sublineages among the Tlingit were not equal in status, since the different communities had different-sized territories, greater or fewer members, and were nearer or farther from trade routes. Therefore, clans and lineages could be of high or low rank. The status of a clan and its segment depended on the amount of property given to members of the opposite moiety's clans in recent potlatches. Wealthy, high-ranking clan lineages possessed the best salmon streams, their houses stood in a prestigious location, such as, for example, the houses of the Gaanaxteidí clan (Chilkat Gaanaxteidí) in the Klukwan settlement (Oberg 1973:57). One cannot agree in this regard with the view of the American structuralist ethnographers A. Rosman and P. G. Rubel (1971:38, 67, 187) that an interclan ranking as such was absent among the Tlingit: this assertion is contradicted by materials collected by a number of authoritative researchers (Oberg 1973:57; Olson 1967:24; Swanton 1908:427).

The Kaagwaantaan of the Eagle moiety in the 18th and 19th centuries acquired such power among the northern Tlingit that any orator of the Eagle moiety might, in a burst of eloquence, call his kinsmen "Kaagwaantaan," even

Tlingit Indians before Contact with Europeans

if they were related to other clans (Olson 1967:13). Thus, acts of social prestige gradually overshadowed the early norms of clan society.

Sublineages of a different settlement, even if they were related to one clan, were also ranked according to the prosperity and number of members of their households. Thus, according to De Laguna, the chiefs of the Kuashḵwáan in Yakutat came from a sublineage of the Raven Bones House. After this sublineage faded out, its high status was inherited by their kinsmen of the Fort House. On the other hand, the people of the Kuashḵwáan of the Moon House were considered of lower rank (De Laguna 1972:1:463).

Examining the evolution of the clans, lineages, and sublineages in historical perspective, it can be noted that their position and rank did not remain unchanged. Some communities that were powerful in the old days became poorer, the number of their members dropped, and the clans that formed them dropped in rank. By contrast, some communities and households, poor in the past, became wealthy and increased in membership so much that their lineages became leaders among the lineages and clans of their settlement or ḵwáan. Notable in this regard is the history of the Deisheetaan clan, reconstructed on the basis of legends recorded by De Laguna (1960:27, 134–135). Originally, the Deisheetaan lived together with the Gaanaxteidí in the Kootznahoo ḵwáan in the position of poor relatives of the latter, and formed their household. The very name Deisheetaan—"occupants of the house at the end of the path (of the beaver)"—attests to the fact that the members of this clan took their origin from separate household members, who comprised the core of the future clan. But after the Gaanaxteidí moved from the ḵwáan and left them their lands, the Deisheetaan increased so much in status that they became the dominant clan in the Kootznahoo ḵwáan. The well-known Kaagwaantaan clan underwent a similar evolution and probably grew from a sublineage.[6] Thus, the development of the clan structure went not only along a descending line, that is, from the clan to the sublineage, but also the other way around. The activity of the local economic groups formed by them—the community and the household—directly influenced the development of these social unities. In the end, it is also precisely from the functioning of the latter that the rank of this or that clan, lineage, or sublineage depended.

Societies with a matrilineal clan structure are generally notable in stability and conservatism (Maretina 1980:98), being inclined to evolve along an extensive path of development owing to the segmentation of the primary clans and their numerical distribution according to population growth and the development of new territories, or owing to expanding—"drawing" neighboring tribes and groups into their clan structure (Grinev 1991:136–137). Being the structure-forming base of the society, clan relations hinder the clan's quality of change. For example, they make much more difficult the appearance of private property and the open exploitation of the ordinary members of the community, as well as complicate the transition from equal distribution to distribution based on work. Tlingit culture's great stability in the face of external influences can be explained by developed clan relations (see chapter 3).[7]

The Tlingit's clan organization has long attracted the attention of researchers. However, much is questionable and contradictory in the organization's interpretation, and some of the stereotypes that scholars developed without proper examination and discussion pass from one work to another. The Tlingit clan has been defined as totemic, yet it is often mixed with other similar but rather autonomous social unities such as community and lineage. Lisianskii (1812:151) and Veniaminov (1840a:32–35), and later the German ethnographers Krause (1956:30) and L. Adam (1913:95–98), distinguished the totemic clan as the basic structural unit of Tlingit society and assumed that moieties of the Tlingit tribe consisted of the Wolf, Bear, Raven, and other clans. The 19th-century American researchers L. G. Morgan (1934:60) and A. P. Niblack (1890:217) and the Soviet historiographers Averkieva (1960:20; 1974:143), S. A. Tokarev (1986:134), G. I. Dzeniskevich (1985:61–62; 1987b:111, 114; 1996:292), and others expressed a similar view. Averkieva, for example, thought that the name of the Tlingit clan derived from its totem (Frog, Bear, Killer Whale, and so on). However, counterarguments point out, first, that the clan was delocalized; second, that it had, as a rule, several totems; and third, that clan names in the overwhelming majority of cases do not reflect the designation of the totems honored in them. Thus, for example, the name of the Teikweidí designates not "Bear clan" (though the chief totem of this clan was the bear) but rather "children of the island of Teko."[8] According to Averkieva's version, the name of the clan ought to sound like xóotsyádi (where xóots is "grizzly bear" and yádi is "children") or xóotsnaa—"Bear clan" (naa is Tlingit for "clan").[9] Analyzing the names of the clans shows, however, that they arose not from totems but from the name of the locality (the G̲aanax̲teidí clan), as well as from the name of the household (Kaagwaantaan). In addition, if we accept Averkieva's point of view, then such clans as Teik̲weidí and Naanya.aayí should be one clan, since they had a common chief totem (the Grizzly Bear). In actuality, these were completely independent clans of different origin and in their names there is not a hint of the clan totem.

In addition, the structural units in Tlingit society were not clearly differentiated in foreign historiography. For example, Rosman and Rubel equate "settlement" and "tribe," defining both as an "independent geographic union"

Figure 3. The General Structure of Social Organization of Tlingit Society

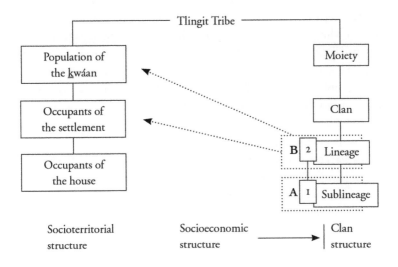

····· Contour of socioeconomic structure, where A is the household, B the clan community
Hierarchical structure
  1: Head of the sublineage and household
  2: Chief of the lineage and clan community

(Rosman and Rubel 1971:36). Thus, in the opinion of the American ethno-historian J. R. Dean (1995:269), clans divided into household groups, each of which consisted of male descendants of the maternal line and their wives. This assertion is incorrect: the households belonged to a socioeconomic structure, whereas the clans were elements of a social organization, and, as exogamic unities, wives and children could not be included in them (since the wife and children belonged to a different clan and moiety). Instead, only men, their unmarried sisters, and nephews were included. The absence of clear termino-logical differentiation is especially manifest to researchers who examine the lower cells of the territorial, economic, and clan structure (Figure 3).

5.2. Social Structure

Long before the arrival of Europeans, Tlingit society had become socially heterogeneous. Investigators usually distinguish three groups: the elite, com-moners, and slaves. But, in fact, Indian society was even more differentiated. On the basis of several works by Russian and foreign researchers, the author attempts to present the socio-hierarchical structure of Tlingit society in the form of a diagram (Table 3). This diagram reflects the stratification of Indian society only in general features, since each of the groups (except the slaves and possibly people of low status) was subdivided into several more ranks.

Rank in Tlingit life was of great significance. High rank gave the right to various privileges, including the right not only to economic valuables (for example, to some fishing grounds) but also to the use of ceremonial and immaterial objects in general (songs, dances, names, and so on). The most significant factor that determined the rank of a person was the wealth that he accumulated and then gave away in the potlatch, but aristocratic origin and conduct were also important (Kan 1989:77–102).

Wealth was concentrated primarily in the hands of the elite—the head of the household, aanyádi and *aankáawu*. They owned the best equipment and slaves and were therefore able to obtain more surplus products than the common people (Averkieva 1960:28). In addition, as already mentioned, each chief was situated in the center of the redistributive system, which enabled him to exploit his kinsmen secretly. The formation of a centralized redistribution system in Tlingit society created an economic and social base for hereditary replacement of chiefs of different ranks. The tendency toward this system can be clearly traced in Tlingit society. Kan pointed out that only the child whose parents belonged to the aristocracy had real chances of climbing the social ladder. Aristocratic parents marked each stage of their child's maturity by generously distributing gifts at potlatches, thereby increasing his "social weight," something common people could not afford to do (Kan 1989:87). Society at this stage of development was itself objectively interested in succession and stability and in the normal functioning of the redistributive system (for the acquisition of regular excess goods); a system of inheriting ruling powers and prerogatives contributed directly to this stability (Khazanov 1979:158). However, it was not always the chief's immediate heir who inherited his status and authority. From our point of view, the hereditary principle in Tlingit society inhibited collective property that might preserve the chief's position: any free Indian could aspire to the status of chief. This event was very rare, but Tlingit society was not a caste system.

In addition to the excess and surplus goods that the commoners and slaves created, trade income was concentrated in the hands of the chiefs. The chiefs, being the ceremonial leaders, were given the richest gifts at the potlatches. The appearance of special terms to designate the wealthy (*landáalx*) and poor (*eshaan*) (Veniaminov 1846:42, 46), as well as to identify servant (not slave) (*kookénaa*) (Olson 1967:31), attests to the stratification by property among the Tlingit. This stratification was very common—property, and the social

Table 3. Stratification of Tlingit Society

Term	Explanation
Chief of a settlement	The Tlingit called a chief of this rank *aankáawu-tlein* (*ankawu-tlen, atlen-ankau*), which is usually translated as "great wealthy person" or "great chief," but literal translation means "great man of the village" (*an:* village; *káau* [*káawu, ka*]: man; *tlein* [*lein*]: great). The *aankáawu-tlein* was the chief of the most influential sublineage, of the most significant lineage (clan) in the village. The word *aan'sáati* (master of the village) also probably served to designate a chief of such rank, as noted by Veniaminov (1840a:60).
Head of a lineage	The Tlingit term was *aankáawu* (*an kawu, amkau*), which is translated usually as "wealthy man" or "chief," but a more precise translation is "man of the village." The *aankáawu* was the head of the leading sublineage of the subdivision of a clan in some villages.
Head of a sublineage	Numerous Tlingit terms exist: *híts'áati* (guardian of the house), *híts'áati* (master of the house), *naa shaade kani* (being at the head of the clan), *Lingit-tlein* (great man).
The elite	People of noble birth and high social position were known as *aanyádi*, which in literal translation means "child of the village." Veniaminov (1840a:108) treats the word *angati* as "noblemen." Not every *an'iadi* was a chief, but every chief was an *an'iadi*. Another word used for the elite was *tl'etakuka*—"pure (white, pure-blooded) human (man)," "crystal personality" (De Laguna 1972:1:463; Kan 1989).
Commoners	*Tlinkit* or *kanash-kide* (the latter term was rarely used) (Oberg 1973:41).
People of low status	The Tlingit term was *nichkakaku*, which possibly translates as "nonentity" or illegitimate child (bastard) (Olson 1967:48). People of low rank were also evidently called *khatak ku'u* (those who lived in the front of the house) (De Laguna 1972:1:462) and *ishan'iadi* (poor children). These people were the illegitimate, paupers, released slaves, and persons whose ancestors were slaves.
Slaves	(*goox*).

elevation that went with it, always accompanied the opposite in society: those who are impoverished by life's vicissitudes (Khazanov 1979:159). And nevertheless, in spite of the noticeable property stratification and the existence of different forms of exploitation in Tlingit society, the society still did not guarantee the existence of the chiefs. As a rule, the latter had to work along with the members of their family. However, the chiefs were wealthy not because of their own work but rather because they exploited the members of their community and their slaves (Semenov 1993:2:342).

Although the Indian society became rather stratified, it should be noted that the authority of the elders and leaders was not great. The heads of the sublineages or households held some of the real authority; the leaders of the lineages (clans) and settlements held nominal titles. F. P. Litke testified: "The government of the Koloshi, as of all societies found in infancy, is patriarchal. The old man in the clan is the leader, whom the Russians call by a word adopted from Siberia: *Toion*. Obedience to him is limited to his family. Whoever has more *kinsmen*, whoever is wealthier, has more slaves, he is more respected; his advice is heard, but he cannot command anything of anyone, and he is served only through good will or money" (Litke 1834:150). The authority, which went beyond the initial clan group's framework, had a tendency to weaken with its rise in the hierarchy. And within the sublineage itself, the elder's authority was weakened in definite measure by the fact that he was related to other members of the sublineage, that is, he was first among equals. Figuratively expressed, he was still not "separate from the people" and did not set himself off from his kinsmen, the more so as his status and rank depended in significant measure on the results of their economic activity. This circumstance permitted De Laguna to state in one of her works that in Tlingit society, a "class" of commoners as such was lacking since full members of the household were younger relatives of the chief and usually had some "profession" (shamans, artist-sculptors, orators, and so on) (De Laguna 1983:74). Kan is of a similar view. He suggests that the arrangement of Tlingit society was not rigid and fixed but rather was mobile and flexible. Here was not a closed-class or closed-caste system; only slaves, who were not viewed as persons of full value, formed a separate group. Any person, sublineage, lineage, or clan could rather easily change its social status by spreading accumulated wealth through the mechanism of the potlatch. In Kan's opinion "common citizens" were simply younger kinsmen of wealthy aristocrats (Kan 1999:8–9, 11). However, one cannot agree with this, since both factually and terminologically (though the terminology was applied only very loosely) in Tlingit society a clan elite (aanyádi) already stood out: the status of the leader was twice (or more) as high as that of commoners, which was clearly manifested by wergild payments for murder (De Laguna 1972:1:462; Oberg 1967:210; Salisbury 1985:41).

Kan notes that the aristocrat in Tlingit society is viewed as a physically and morally pure person, and it is even believed that sorcery does not work on him.

To the Tlingit an aristocrat stood out as the framework, the solid base of the whole society (Kan 1989:91).

The development of the institutional authority in Tlingit society was also controlled by the society's dual-moiety organization, especially with the transition to the territorial level. The chief of the settlement always had a rival in the person of the chief of a leading lineage of the opposite moiety. Among some Indian tribes in which dual organization emerged as a result of competition, social tension was partially removed by means of the institution of two supreme tribal positions: "peace" (civic) and "war" (martial) leaders. Among the Tlingit similar positions at the general tribal level were absent. The development of their authoritative structure was not advanced beyond the rank of leader of the settlement (if there was only one settlement in the ķwáan, then its leader became only the nominal head of the ķwáan).

Special regalia distinguished the leader from his kinsmen: a cloak of marten fur, a long staff, and a ceremonial hat. In addition, a wealthy chief, as a rule, was always escorted by a throng of slaves and nephews—bodyguards. "Without retinue," wrote Archimandrite Anatolii, "the toion did not go anywhere. In order just to sit in his boat or move from one barabara to another, some toions had palanquins and porters. Their dress consisted of expensive furs: sable [marten], beaver, ermine, and so on" (Anatolii 1906:29–30).

In Tlingit society a special place was occupied by shamans, who stood outside the "profane" social structure. In the old days the shaman's dwelling stood in a place of honor in the settlement, and shamanism was profitable (Anatolii 1906:126–127). One of the Tlingit legends speaks of a young woman named June, who was poor, but with the help of her shamanistic art became the wealthiest woman among the Gaanaxteidí of the Tanta ķwáan (Olson 1967:115).

The shaman arranged the *kamlanie*, striving to guarantee success in hunting and fishing, in fighting campaigns, or in treating illness. He "drove away" hostile spirits and predicted the future, obtaining payment in the form of part of a hunter's kill or a fisherman's catch, or some other payment from the relatives of the sick. Since the reason for illness, in the Indians' opinion, almost always consisted of "bewitching," the shaman's chief function was to find the "witch," who was usually then fiercely punished by the relatives of the sick person. It is easy to imagine the influence that the shaman could have over the people of his clan. The leaders purchased the shamans' alliance by offering generous sacrifices, and, supporting one another, the leaders and shamans often had the respect and fear of the whole community (Niblack

1890:25). In sorcery, low-ranking citizens—orphans, women, and slaves—were usually accused rather than influential aristocrats (Kan 1999:19).

The most numerous, though rather amorphous, group in Tlingit society was the commoners. Their personal freedom was unrestricted, and exploitation of commoners was still infrequent. However, this stratum of the population was already not permitted to manage the society's affairs and was gradually distanced from the command of clan territories. The commoner's status was substantially lower than the status of the aanyádi: the life of the latter was "valued" at two to four times that of the life of a person of lower rank (De Laguna 1972:1:462).

Every Indian aspired to elevate his social status. Commoners could attain the position of aanyádi if they were distinguished by outstanding ability in some area. Thus, a carver of wood could grow wealthy by his art, since, as Litke noted, carving a figure on the bow of a large canoe could earn him a slave from the boat's owners (Litke 1834:163). In one of the Tlingit legends that Swanton collected, there is mention of a dancer who used his talent to become rich (Swanton 1909:140).

The poorest commoners formed a separate group with a status similar to that of slaves. It was no accident that they were designated by the term *katak ku'u*, meaning "those who live in the front of the house," which was where the dogs and slaves usually slept. Another contemptuous term used to denote a person of low status was *nichkakwáawu* (*nichkakaku*)—"man of the beach," or *nichkayádi*—"child of the beach or shore." Kan shows that the coast, symbolically, was a marginal area where refuse accumulated and the bodies of dead slaves were thrown. Thus, the term bore a negative semantic load and was directly associated with the social bottom. While the aristocracy was located in the center of the social order, people of low status remained on the periphery (Kan 1989:92–93).

At the very bottom of the social ladder were the slaves. They were entirely deprived of rights in Tlingit society. Slavery was hereditary, which attests to the long development of this institution among the Tlingit. The question of the significance of slavery in the Northwest Coast Indians' society has already been examined in sufficient detail by Averkieva (1941, 1960, 1974). Therefore, only the most salient characteristics will be discussed here.

Slaves among the Tlingit were foreign tribesmen and their descendants captured during raids or purchased from tribes to the south. There were also slaves from the Tlingit tribe, usually coming from distant ḵwáans and taken prisoner during wars. A Tlingit could not keep a person of his own clan as a slave, but he could keep members of other clans of his moiety (Olson 1967:53).

The principal suppliers of slaves to the Tlingit were the Haida. They roved the sea coast in their large red cedar canoes, searching plunder, and even ventured a couple hundred kilometers inland to make surprise attacks on careless villages and bring back slaves (Emmons 1991:40).

Slaves' value was relatively standard, men being valued at one and a half to two times as much as women. As the Indians reported to Emmons, in the old days in the Sitka ḵwáan, a male slave cost 15 tanned elk skins and a female slave 10; in Yakutat they gave 20 pounds of copper or 6 excellent sea otter skins for a male slave, while a female cost only 10 pounds of copper or 5 sea otter skins; and in Kootznahoo a male slave could be bought for 30 fox skins, 10 elk skins, or one Chilkat cape (Emmons 1991:42).

As a rule, slaves belonged to heads of households. Slave labor was used in all difficult household work, fishing, hunting, transportation (they served as oarsmen and porters), and sometimes even in war (Averkieva 1974:151). Nevertheless, slaves were not the main producers in Tlingit society, and they made up less than 10 percent of the population, according to Olson (1967:53).

5.3. The Family and Family-Marriage Relations

Among the Tlingit the so-called Arabian model of relationship prevailed (with a Crow-type generational slant), with the characteristic difference in terms to denote father (*éesh*), father's brother (*sáni*), and mother's brother (*káak*).

The Tlingit were permitted to marry only members of clans of the opposite moiety; violations were punished by death. For the Tlingit, on the whole, monogamy was characteristic. There was no strictly enforced age for marrying. Young men could marry at 17 or 18 years of age; young women entered marriage starting at 15 or 16. The latter, before marrying, had to endure a long seclusion in an isolated hut, which lasted not less than a year and began with the onset of her first menstruation. Violation of this custom could, in the opinion of the Indians, attract the most varied misfortunes (Anatolii 1906:48–50).

The choice of spouse depended significantly on older relatives' recommendations, but neither the bride nor the groom were entirely indifferent to the resolution of this important question, and it happened that weddings were called off because one of the parties objected. Some significance was attached to physical beauty, but this was not the deciding factor in choosing a partner. Social status, however, had great significance. Most preferable, of course, was the union of people of equal rank. Hence, the members of a sublineage of higher rank married members of equal status in sublineages of clans of the opposite moiety. Thus, three of the most influential sublineages of the Gaanaxteidí clan (Raven moiety) in the Chilkat ḵwáan's Klukwan settlement intermarried with

Kaagwaantaan clan (Eagle moiety) sublineages of corresponding rank. On the other hand, lower-ranking sublineages of the Chilkat G̲aanax̱teidí married into equivalent sublineages of the Kaagwaantaan, Shangukeidí, and Dak̲l'aweidí clans (Oberg 1973:40).

Among the Tlingit the tendency was to reduplicate marital connections between the same clans (lineages and sublineages), which, in general, was characteristic of a dual moiety-based society. Therefore, marrying first cousins was not rare.

Before a couple could marry, the suitor had to exchange gifts with the girl's parents (the leaders gave very expensive gifts: furs, slaves, and so on). The girl's family, wanting to know if their future son-in-law was hardworking, often organized "groom shows," during which they paid special attention to the suitor's hands: if they were rough ("like an eagle's talons"), then this indicated that he liked to work, but if they were soft and tender ("like mats"), then the suitor could be rejected as a lazybones (Swanton 1908:429).

Before finally validating the marriage, the young Indian had to work with his future father-in-law for a year, or sometimes even two, to somewhat compensate for the subsequent loss of a female worker. As Archimandrite Anatolii wrote: "For this he moves to the barabara [house] of his fiancée and serves her father and mother. All that he acquires through hunting or other occupation he has to lay at the feet of his fiancée's parents" (Anatolii 1906:47–48). After the suitor "works off" the allotted term, the wedding is arranged and a rather modest party given.

Marriages among the Tlingit, as a rule, were avunculocal; that is, the groom, after the wedding, took his wife to the household of his uncle in the maternal line, whose heir he was. Though the man was also considered the head of the family, the position of the Tlingit woman was also rather high: she was entirely relied upon to run the household and raise the children. Archimandrite Anatolii wrote:

In family affairs the women had rather great authority and freedom. The Indian's wife was not a slave for her husband and not just a work force, as often is the case among savages. She is rather the lady of her husband. In the house, in the family, she has more authority than her husband. While the husband is occupied with public affairs and hunting far from his barabara, his wife runs the house and the family completely and unrestrictedly. Under her management are all the properties and all the supplies of the simple, it is true, Indian economy. At her disposal also comes all that which the head of the family procures (Anatolii 1906:54).

However, the traditional Tlingit family was not a unit in property. There was separate property for husband and wife, since they belonged to different clans. But inasmuch as the wife lived with the husband and used his clan's areas, the goods created by her were received by her husband, and in part by his kinsmen and chief. Usually the husband used the wife's creations at potlatches. Incidentally, the possibility for the emergence of an early form of exploitation, such as marriage servitude, lay here. The need for new workers to produce surplus goods could have been satisfied by a man's marrying a large number of women. Semenov concluded that "the emergence of a prestige economy contributed to the development of polygyny" (Semenov 1993:2:241–242, 317). One must, of course, keep in mind that only some of the wives created excess goods that became surplus commodities in their husbands' hands.

Therefore, polygamy was a rather common occurrence among the Tlingit, especially among the aristocracy. Besides adding to the surplus goods, acquiring new wives granted the aristocratic Indian additional rights and privileges through his in-laws and enlarged the channels of prestige gift exchange. "The wealthy and eminent in a clan of the Koliuzhi," wrote V. P. Romanov, "have up to five wives: they strive through these connections to obtain more dowry and to have more relatives, in order by this to increase their clan and their wealth" (Romanov 1825:21).

Jealousy sometimes caused quarrels and fights among the wives, sometimes ending in death by one woman's dagger (Litke 1834:161). There were no such quarrels when the Indian married sisters—a custom that, in the ethnographic literature, is designated by the term *sororate* (from the Latin *soror*, meaning "sister"). Also among the Tlingit there was the custom of *levirate*, in which the nephew not only inherited his uncle's property after his death but was required to take his widow as a wife, "without respect to how unequal their age," as Khlebnikov testified (1985:81).

A man's infidelity could in the worst case result in his wife's divorcing him. A woman's infidelity was punished more severely: in the best case, she was sent off with the children to her father's household with a demand for the return of "wedding" gifts. In the worst case, the offended husband could kill his wife and her lover. In such a case, the relatives of the latter could not avenge the murder but rather were satisfied by small gifts. If the lover was a close relative of his, the husband could force him to take the seduced wife and properly support her through old age. Some indulgent husbands, usually elderly, permitted the older wife to take a young man into the family as a "semi-official" lover. This role was often filled by a brother, nephew, or other close relative of his, who in early Russian sources was called a *polovinshchik* (Khlebnikov 1985:80–81). According to Kan, a few high-ranking Tlingit women could have several husbands simultaneously (Kan 1999:7). It can be supposed that these were usually brothers. Thus, both polygyny and polyandry directly depended on the spouses' social status and wealth.

In raising children the Tlingit woman is usually helped by her sisters, mother, aunts, and other relatives, as well as by her brother, in whose household nephews up to the age of eight or ten years will live, according to the custom of the avunculate. Children were raised to respect their elders; "children of all ages show their parents obedience and respect especially toward the aged and weak, for whom [they] care with great attention," noted Litke (1834:154).

6. The Role of War in Tlingit Society

6.1. Reasons for the Emergence of Conflict

Armament and Tactics. Fighting encounters occupied an important place in the life of the Tlingit. In Indian legends it is reported that the most frequent cause of interclan conflict was the jealous husband's killing his wife's lover. Similar conflicts often resulted in clan splits and the resettlement of part of the clan in another k̲wáan. Thus, the legends that De Laguna recorded report that after a man killed out of jealousy, which entailed an actual battle between the Kootznahoo Teik̲weidí Valley House and Bear House, the latter were forced to resettle in the Chilkat k̲wáan, where their descendants became known as the Takestina clan (De Laguna 1960:144–146). In addition, the reliable presence of excess goods, which can be forcibly appropriated and redistributed, as well as the possibility of seizing immediate producers (potential slaves), created a basis for numerous inter- and intra-tribal conflicts. The Indians' particular moral-ethics "code," at the base of which lay the custom of blood feud, contributed to the emergence of frequent hostile conflicts as well. "The chief reason for such a warlike character," wrote Archimandrite Anatolii, "is the fact that among the Indians the law of blood feud—'an eye for an eye and a tooth for a tooth'—reigned in full force and was carried out with literal precision" (Anatolii 1906:7–8). It is true that a deviation from ancient norms was emerging in the custom: killing a person did not necessitate killing the killer. Among the Tlingit the practice of paying a particular wergild (expensive furs and shells and other traditional valuables) was formed. If payment were rejected or delayed, the victimized side had the moral right to vengeance. Major crimes were not the only cause for vengeance (and with it possibly hostile conflict). For example, small and unpremeditated offenses or damage to one's property, household, or clan could attract vengeance. Krause adds that the relatives had to demand wergild or take revenge if their kinsman died in a foreign territory or among foreign people, even if he had not been killed (Krause 1956:281).

Frequent wars resulted in the development of improved fighting techniques and equipment. Erecting palisades and other defense equipment around houses, camps, and settlements served as a collective of defense. Such settlements were especially safe if they were arranged on a cliff, from which the defenders could see the approaching enemy from a distance (De Laguna 1972:1:582).

Individual equipment of close combat consisted of three- to four-meter-long spears, heavy carved clubs of wood or whale rib (more rarely stone), and daggers. Some daggers were double-bladed, their handles terminating in another, shorter blade (Goddard 1924:107–108, 158; Ratner-Shternberg 1930:183–186). The dart and bow and arrows were suitable for combating the enemy from a distance. The bow was held horizontally when shot, possibly making it more convenient to aim from a canoe. There was also possibly some Asian influence: Protective equipment included a heavy wooden helmet and visor as well as a cuirass of wooden rods and laths, which was put on over a shirt of thick elk hide. Such armor could successfully withstand arrows and spears and sometimes even bullets from European guns. When fully armed the Tlingit warrior resembled a medieval European knight.

Wars consisted of alternate raids and counter-raids. The Tlingit's fighting expeditions were dispatched in canoe flotillas. "Differing in valor and intrepidness," wrote Archimandrite Anatolii, "they often undertook campaigns by sea in their *yaakw*—large boats—like the Vikings, to great distances, sometimes traveling 150 to 200 miles, that is, about 300 versts, in one day with favorable weather" (Anatolii 1906:4–5). Having quietly sailed to an enemy settlement, the warriors struck by surprise at night or dawn. In a successful attack they either killed the men or took them, along with the women and children, into captivity. A shaman typically accompanied each war party. The shaman's spirits, according to the Indians, protected the war party and predicted the appearance of the enemy, the number killed, and so on (Swanton 1908:450).

Kin and neighbor connections determined the character of intra-tribal clashes. If a quarrel erupted within a settlement, the offended side, after repeated unmet demands for compensation, called for war. In such encounters they tried not to kill, only to wound, and if they got the upper hand, they forced the defeated party to pay the debt. The affair was different if the conflict erupted between members of different settlements or k̲wáans. In this case, vengeance was carefully prepared and kept secret from the women, since they could warn their kinsmen of the impending attack. In war among different settlements or k̲wáans, there was no leniency (Khlebnikov 1985:84).

Hostile conflicts within a tribe occurred, as a rule, only between local subdivisions of different clans. When warriors attacked that part of a settlement where their enemy lived, members of other clans were often only sideline observers or were called out to stop bloodshed and mediate disputes (Oberg 1973:61). Such conflicts probably occurred between local subdivisions of clans of neighboring k̲wáans. When there were raids on other k̲wáans or when they were repelling an attack, the members of different clans of one or even several settlements of a k̲wáan often united. Thus, in one of the legends it is said that all the clans of the Wolf moiety in the settlements of Klukwan and Yendestake of the Chilkat k̲wáan rose up to repel a raid from the south by Tlingit of the Henya k̲wáan. Following that, the Chilkat raided the Henya k̲wáan, sending 60 war canoes. During the surprise attack, about 200 Henya men were killed and about forty women captured (Olson 1967:79).

Clashes with neighboring tribes could be equally bloody. Actual war, which continued for several years between the people of the Stikine (the powerful Naanya.aayí clan) and the Tsimshian, is reported in several Tlingit traditions. Mutual raids were irregularly successful, until finally the chiefs of the Tsimshian decided to completely annihilate the hostile Naanya.aayí clan. Warriors were drafted from four Tsimshian villages and they set out to the mouth of the Stikine in a large flotilla of canoes. At the mouth of the Stikine River one of the largest battles flared. Initially the Naanya.aayí was supported by only the K̲aa X̲'oos Hit Taan clan, but then the remaining clans of the Stikine people entered the battle, bringing to the adversaries a surprise blow from the rear. It was a complete rout for the Tsimshian: the majority of their warriors were killed, the canoes sunk or captured, and the crews taken into captivity and turned into slaves (Corser 1940:23; Olson 1967:80). Only after this was peace concluded, and the Naanya.aayí took as a distinctive "reparation" the honorary Tsimshian name "Sheks" ("Shakes"), which in fact became the name of a whole dynasty of Stikine chiefs; they also took numerous songs, dances, masks, personal names, and the right to use the honorary name "killer whale canoe" (*keet-yaakw*) (Olson 1967:32, 81).

6.2. Education of Warriors and Customs of Fighting

Young men were educated to become strong, tough warriors. With this in mind, boys were made by the age of three to bathe in the sea regardless of the season or weather. After bathing, especially in the winter, they were publicly flogged with rods to teach these future warriors to endure pain (Veniaminov 1840a:97–98). The Tlingit find a basis for such severe procedures in the legend about Duktut (Duktitl), who became a great sea lion hunter as a result (De Laguna 1972:2:890–892; Salisbury 1985:258–260).

In general, the Indians examined the physical condition of newborn boys, especially those of aristocratic origin, and, if they were deformed, often killed the newborn child. A man with physical defects, as Kan notes, simply could not attain high status and rank in Tlingit society (Kan 1989:59–60, 310).

The public highly valued valor on the battlefield, as reflected by their religious views. According to the Tlingit, the spirit of the warrior killed in action became a spirit of the "first category" in the afterworld (Veniaminov 1840a:124). "In battle they were courageous," Litke wrote, "scorned death, not showing however that indifference toward life like the Kamchadal, Aleuts, and inhabitants of Kodiak, who formerly, on any occasion of small importance, or even simply from boredom, were ready to hang or drown themselves" (Litke 1834:155). Veniaminov was more skeptical about the Tlingit's courage, finding that it was rather ostentatious, writing, "And if they are brave, then brave only in safety and with cowards." He opined that this same thing is corroborated in the Tlingit's fighting tactics, which were based on surprise attacks (Veniaminov 1840a:124–125). And yet, in the Russian American period, the Tlingit more than once proved that they were not timid.

The Tlingit's fighting customs were distinctive. Before a war campaign the Indians carried out maneuvers, imitating battle. Four days before the campaign, the war leaders and the shaman began to fast, and, with the other warriors, they observed a long self-deprivation that sometimes lasted a year. Striving to guarantee the success of the fighting expedition, the warriors "killed" and bound, as "captives," wooden effigies. The warriors' wives also had such effigies; immediately before the war canoe was launched, the wives threw these figures to their husbands. The Indians believed that the men who did not catch the figure would be killed. During the raid itself the Tlingit maintained several strict taboos. If a warrior perished in battle, his brothers-in-arms, on the journey home, set up a paddle vertically in his place in the canoe so that the women could see from afar whose husband was not returning from war (Swanton 1908:449–450).

In the case of a successful raid, the Indians approached the clan settlement loudly singing victory songs and displaying the scalps of the slain enemy on the canoe. Scalping was characteristic not only among the Tlingit but also among other Indians of the Northwest Coast. According to Lisianskii, it was the shamans who performed this operation (other sources do not mention this). Lisianskii also reports, "With this hair the barbarians decorate themselves during *igrishche* [festive ceremonies]" (Lisianskii 1812:144–145). If an eminent opponent were killed, the shaman sometimes cut off his whole head. Enemies taken into captivity were often tortured terribly.

Peace between quarreling sides was concluded under solemn conditions and accompanied by the exchange of hostages, who were said to be "deer" (in Tlingit *guwakaan*), a peaceful animal. Khlebnikov clearly described the custom of hostage exchange:

> Both sides go out on a level area with daggers, men and women, and the first [the men], who must seize the *amanat* [hostage] (the preeminent of the opponents and most important through connections of kin and through seniority), show an aggressive look, waving spears and daggers; [they] yell, charge into the midst of the enemy and seize the selected hostage who hides in the crowd of his party. There with a cry of joy, the fulfillment of desires, and the termination of war, they raise him in their hands and carry him to their side. Each side, having exchanged [hostages] in like manner, maintains its hostage in the best way, providing him with all possible services; they do not permit him to walk, rather on every occasion, they carry him in their arms, and so on. The triumph of peace is concluded by dancing from morning to evening and gluttony. Finally, the hostages are taken away to a dwelling of new friends [where they] spend a year or more; then they are returned and once again the endurance of the union [i.e., peace] is acknowledged by dancing (Khlebnikov 1985:84).

On the question of the role of war in Tlingit society, the literature reflects two diametrically opposed views. Thus, Averkieva (1974:152) and A. A. Istomin (1980:57, 1985:146) wrote that war among the Tlingit had the significance of a regular business, that is, wealth could be acquired this way. At the same time, Oberg (1973:78) stressed that war among these Indians was not considered a means of attaining wealth and fame, and was not, consequently, an essential economic and social activity. Oberg also noted that in Tlingit society there was no special stratum of "professional warriors," as was the case, for example, among some of the Indians of the Great Plains.

The truth may lie somewhere between these extremes of opinion. The Tlingit were certainly bellicose—this is noted in all the early sources. The well-developed fighting equipment attested to this as well. However, among the Tlingit, there was no class of people that devoted itself exclusively to fighting. Also, there was no special group of war leaders (the leaders of the warriors were usually the heads of sublineages and their brothers and nephews) distinct from the rest of the Tlingit elite, though the tendency toward the appearance of war leaders is seen in the emergence of special terms for denoting them. Thus, the Indians reported to De Laguna (1972:2:583) that in the olden days a *s' aati* ("captain") commanded flotillas of war canoes, whereas a *x'áan koonáyi* ("general") led the warriors in land battles. These terms, however, do not confirm, as Averkieva (1974:152) thought, that there were war leaders with hereditary names and titles among the Tlingit. There is not a single source giving any data about stable operational war structures, even at the level of the lineage, not to mention about a whole clan's or tribe's fighting organizations.

7. Spiritual Culture

7.1. Tlingit Religious Views and Ideas about the Surrounding World

Tlingit views about the surrounding world were unique. Veniaminov wrote, "One should never lose sight of the fact that among the Koloshi in every phenomenon in nature there are its reasons, its legends and fables" (Veniaminov 1840a:115). They believed the earth flat and the sky solid. The stars, in their beliefs, were fires in the dwellings of the spirits that occupied the heavens, while the sun and moon were living beings that understood human speech.[10]

According to Tlingit myths, the land rested on a gigantic post in the form of a beaver forepaw, which was kept by a subterranean old woman, Agishanuku (Aiishanaku) (Swanton 1908:452). "The Koloshi believe," wrote Veniaminov, "that the earth stands on one large post, which Agishanuku guards and supports; otherwise the earth would long ago have capsized and sunk into the sea" (Veniaminov 1840a:84). The Indians believed that earthquakes occurred because of a struggle between Agishanuku and the Raven, Yel (principal hero of Tlingit myths; see section 7.3). Yel, who became angry at the people for their nonobservance of his decrees, tries to pull the old woman away from the post and upset the land (Swanton 1908:452; Veniaminov 1840a:82). To help Agishanuku defeat Yel, the Indians run out of their houses during earthquakes, sit on the ground, and have a tug-of-war with sticks while singing magical songs (Anatolii 1906:90).

The Tlingit's religious views integrated totemism, animalism, fetishism, magic, animism, and shamanism.

Totemism, the belief in a supernatural connection existing between a group of people and a certain kind of animal, plant, object, or event, held a special place. The belief was closely connected with the social organization of the Tlingit and particularly reflected one of its components—clan structure. Correspondingly, there existed totems of moieties (Raven and Wolf-Eagle), clans, lineages, and sublineages.

To a certain extent it is possible to speak of tribal totemism among the Tlingit if one considers that the world organizer, the principal hero of their myths, was Raven (more precisely, Raven-Man). Among the Tlingit there was apparently also such a type of totemism as individual or personal (the belief that a person can also have his personal totem). This totemism, connected with the cult of personal spirits or protectors, was most common among the shamans.

With an examination of the idea of the "totem" it is necessary to distinguish three of its components: the material prototype of the totem (Raven, Killer Whale, Wolf, and so on); the totem itself—supernatural protector, spiritual symbol of the clan; and the embodiment of the totem in a model (hat, totem pole, or other) or in a flat representation (on cloaks, panels of the house, and such). [11] Various animals were usually depicted as totems, very rarely other natural events or objects. [12] It should be noted that not just any image of the totemic animal was in fact the totem, since: (1) the production of an authentic totem could be entrusted only to a member of the opposite moiety; (2) members of a certain social group had to acknowledge it as a material embodiment of the spiritual essence of their clan; (3) at a potlatch, property had to be given away to members of the opposite moiety in the totem's honor; and (4) the representation of the totem or the right to its representation could be given to people of another clan only in extraordinary cases (Grinev 1989a:38). [13]

The material essences of totems served as a visual symbol of the "reality" of past events that were reflected in clan legends and myths. The most popular and valuable model of the totem was believed to be the ceremonial "clan" hat. The chief appears in this hat, with staff in hand and other regalia, at the potlatch as a member of the clan, its "ancestor," and simultaneously its supernatural totemic patron. According to Oberg the clan's totemic regalia was displayed before those at the potlatch during distribution of gifts to the guests (Oberg 1973:126). The prestige acquired by the potlatch was disseminated to the totem, then through it to the clan and its leader, the clan chief. Therefore,

Tlingit Indians before Contact with Europeans

on the one hand, it is possible to speak of the formation of a special kind of totemic cult among the Tlingit and other Northwest Coast Indians. On the other hand, totemism, and especially a totemic cult, gradually developed into a cult of the leaders and ancestors among the Tlingit.

It is not at all an accident that totems were associated with such events as the *shagóon*. The shagóon can be called the fundamental concept of Tlingit spiritual culture. It is an intricate complex of ideas and associations. Into it come personal and group ancestors, the sacred heritage of the clan—its origin and fate (De Laguna 1972:2:813). Totemic animals, as well as their spirits and images, were included in the shagóon category. In the face of terrible danger, the Tlingit implored the *ax shagóon* (his ancestor-totem-destiny) to help, and most often addressed himself to *kaa shagóon*, that is, "our" collective ancestor-totem-destiny. By the 20th century this term served as a designation for both God and God's law (Kan 1989:69, 313). Some of the visual symbols of the shagóon were the totemic images, in which, according to the ideas of the Indians, the past history, present status, and future of the clan were personified (Jonaitis 1986:67).

The peculiarity of totemism among the Tlingit was that members of one clan could possess several totems; at the same time, common totems existed among several clans. In Indian legends and myths about the origin of totems, people appear as ancestors of the clan, not of the corresponding animals or natural objects. There were also no taboos surrounding the totemic animal (Grinev 1989a:38–39).

Not only were legends and myths connected with totems but so were other components of the Tlingit's spiritual culture. Dances and songs, and speeches at the potlatches, were dedicated to the totems; a warrior dying in battle uttered the cry of the totemic animal; Indians' personal names often came from the totem's name. In addition, members of this or that clan had to be worthy of the totem that belonged to them by their conduct. Thus, it was believed that the Indians of the Teik̲weidí clan were as "brave" as the grizzly bear that their totem invoked, and members of the Kaagwaantaan clan, which honored the wolf, bear, eagle, and killer whale, were "fierce, proud, and intrepid," like the corresponding animals (De Laguna 1972:1:461).

The functions of totems were quite varied. Totems, having as their proto-types concrete natural objects or events, served to connect a group of people with the surrounding world. Like supernatural beings, totems served as "intermediaries" between the real world and the afterworld, and between the world of the spirits and that of man-animals, man-plants, man-cliffs, and so on. On the other hand, the totem figured in the legend of the origin of the clan and, by virtue of this, served to mediate between living people and their ancestors. In addition, retelling the totemic legends and showing the corresponding images at the potlatch strengthened the sense of clan solidarity, and distributing gifts contributed to reinforcing the prestige in the symbol of the clan and its keeper, the clan leader. Finally, representations and models of the totems served as designations of clan property, were used in ceremonies for concluding peace between hostile clans, and were of very great value when paying compensations.

There was a close connection between totemism and the economic, ownership rights of clan use areas, quite popular in Russian ethnographic science. Many ethnographers theorized that the totem served as the symbol of concrete clan use areas (see Averkieva 1960:31, 53, 62–63, 1961:25; Dzeniskevich 1987b:113, 1990:131, 1992:67, 1996:292; Tokarev 1990:71–72). However, this thesis is seriously flawed. The totem or its material image was, in our view, primarily the symbol of the social group and not some territory; if connected it was connected with an area, then it was only through connection with this group, and then indirectly. The clan (or its subdivision) could move to another place, giving up its old territories, but it usually retained its totems. It is true that among the Tlingit there existed so-called geographic totems—various mountains, cliffs, and streams (or, more precisely, their spirits), but they were not numerous, they usually had limited influence, and their natural image was as a rule not an object of economic activity. Thus, Mount Fairweather, one of the highest mountains in Alaska, serves as a totem for the Takdeintaan clan. The spirit of this mountain—properly a totem—was personified as the ceremonial hat *Tsalkantu Shavu Saku* ("Hat [Spirit] of the Woman [Mountain] Tsalkan," that is, Fairweather). This spirit was the vision of one of the shamans of the Dakl'aweidí by the name of Shkik. Another, similar totem, for the Chookaneidí clan, was Glacier in the region of Glacier Bay (Dauenhauer and Dauenhauer 1990b:16–17, 90–91, 392; Olson 1967:117). Kan says, "The term 'totemism' can be applied to their society only very loosely—this was not a classic totemism of Australia, etc." (Kan 1999).

The clan's territorial claims were reflected not in the totem but rather in the clan traditions that were set forth at potlatches, which gave the claims special social significance. At potlatches the history of the clan was related—its origin and migrations, and the acquisition of the totems was reported, and it was explained why the clan had given territories, their origins not otherwise being known to strangers (Olson 1967:12). Thus, a "juridical base" was given to the clan territories, but all clan claims were legitimized only after the potlatch occurred. Evidently it was through this that the role of "copyright," a kind of "intellectual property," became so important among the Tlingit and other Northwest Coast Indians. For example, according to Olson's data, only the Kaagwaantaan had the right to carve the grizzly bear's figure at the top of the totem pole (Olson 1967:40).

If one takes a broader view of this question, then the clan (or lineage) can be identified as a significant social group only after it adopts the totem; that is, it is transformed from a simple group of kinsmen into a collective, now in a position to organize the potlatch in honor of its spiritual essence and occupy, by means of this, a worthy place in the hierarchy of clan groups. The value of the property given away at the potlatch was symbolically "invested" or "applied" to the material images of the totems or the spiritual attributes connected with them. Therefore, valuable donations at the potlatch in honor of a totem, its image, or the formal privileges connected with it (having the right to depict it in a special way, receiving an honorable name "through the totem," singing a song connected with it, and so on) were very important for the Indians. Distributing gifts in honor of the totem established the Tlingit's social world hierarchically and strengthened their prestige and thereby the prestige of the clan group and its chief. A prestige economy, peculiar to traditional Tlingit society, was undoubtedly the reason and prerequisite for prestige totemism to function.

The Tlingit representation of the world was a characteristic, primeval syncretism: a person was an organic part of nature and not set in contrast to the rest of the world. Animals were viewed as rational beings, capable even of understanding human speech. This notion served as a basis for the development among the Tlingit not only of totemism but of animalism. According to Swanton, the grizzly bear, river otter, and wolverine were distinct. The last of them they identified with brave and cunning demeanor, as reflected in the Tlingit saying, "as clever as a wolverine" (Swanton 1908:453, 455–456). The Indians especially respected the grizzly bear. In an encounter with the grizzly, the Tlingit Wolf moiety addressed it with the words, *"Ikoni aiiaka't"*—"I'm on your side" (that is, of your moiety), as well as, *"Ka dutl kanz"*—"Have pity on me" or *"Kat ka tlaketl"*—"Make me lucky" (Olson 1967:117; Swanton 1908:455). It is strange, notes Jonaitis, that in the river otter—a rather inoffensive creature able to bring harm only to the salmon or frog—was concentrated everything wild— all fear and horror of the primitive world and nature (Jonaitis 1986:88, 91–92). The Tlingit steadfastly believed that the river otter (*Kushta-ka*—"River Otter Man") was in reality capable in every way of harming people—charming them, driving them mad, and changing them into werewolves. It was the river otter that carried off the souls of drowned people, and the Tlingit, therefore, most feared dying in water. Not only the drowned but also those who perished in the forest and were not found were changed into Kushta-ka (Emmons 1991:119). Whether one drowned or died in the forest and was not found, the body could not be cremated, and without cremation its soul could not reincarnate in a kinsman; therefore, the soul was believed forever lost: the river otter spirits enslaved it.

Of the small animals known to the Tlingit, they paid most attention to the mouse, whose spirits sorcerers used to help them steal the property of people "corrupted" by wealth (Swanton 1908:471). As strange as it is, we read in De Laguna that a small, harmless frog was, in the eyes of the Tlingit, a dangerous being, and the slime on its skin was believed to be very poisonous (De Laguna 1972:2:831). It was evidently not by chance that shamans' rattles so often bore the frog's image.

Among the sea creatures known to the Tlingit, the killer whale and sea lion, which, according to their ideas, could be powerful helpers of the Indians (especially the shaman), were most respected. Held in no less esteem was the octopus—a clever sea mollusk that has long "arms" and looks like a house of boulders on the sea bottom (Jonaitis 1986:93). With regard to salmon, the Tlingit believe that they form a numerous, powerful tribe of five independent clans (corresponding to the five Pacific salmon species) that live in the ocean far to the west. In spring, during spawning, they paddle to the shore in invisible canoes led by their chiefs. In doing this, the Chum clan, wishing to get to the streams before the others, damages the canoes of the Coho; therefore, the fish of the Coho clan arrive to spawn later (Emmons 1991:104). Of the birds, the raven was most honored. The Indians greatly feared the owl, whose cry allegedly brought misfortune (De Laguna 1972:2:829–830).

The animalistic beliefs of the Tlingit were reflected in their behavior toward animals. Thus, according to De Laguna's materials, the Indians would not kill an animal needlessly nor torture or mock its suffering; that is, they respected all the creatures of the world. To not do so allegedly brought misfortune. Conversely, helping a wounded animal was supposed to bring good luck (De Laguna 1972:2:825).

In addition to totemism and animalism the Tlingit believed in magic, in particular, the supernatural qualities of amulets, which were made chiefly from leaves, flowers, and the roots of various plants (and more rarely of grass, feathers, animal wool, and eagles' claws). Swanton cites a whole list of "magical plants," the names of which speak for themselves, for example: aankáawu k'eikaxwéin—"flower that makes a leader" and tlkewatutl chin naku—"drug that makes everyone obedient." There were other fetishes as well. Swanton reported on a little "magical" box, that Katlian, the leader of the Sitka Kiks.ádi, kept. Carved from wood and tied with ropes and the hair of slaves, it allegedly brought its possessor wealth and fortune after a fast and certain magical rites were performed (Swanton 1908:447–448).

Amulets could be inherited, and friends often exchanged them. Among shamans the speech of the otter was used with special respect, the latter being considered the most powerful fetish (Veniaminov 1840a:63). The braided belt of the shaman symbolized a wood worm that the Indians believed could "penetrate" an enemy village and spy for him (Swanton 1908:464).

Closely connected with fetishism was magic, that is, the belief that certain activities and rituals could supernaturally influence natural events, animals, or humans. The Tlingit believed that sorcerers could harm people with the help of various agents and incantations. Sorcerers, according to the Tlingit, were malevolent, dangerous beings who could fly. The Indians feared and hated sorcerers so much that even the relatives of someone accused of sorcery could kill him. It was usually women who were accused of sorcery (Krause 1956:203; Veniaminov 1840a:76–77). There were also spells to win love, succeed in the hunt, conjure protection, and so on. In order to secure luck in hunting bears, for example, the Tlingit performed certain rituals over the carcass of a dead animal; Veniaminov explained that "from a dead bear after flaying the skin they take off the head and, having decorated it with feathers, similar to a shaman's head, they put it by the fire and sing special songs" (Veniaminov 1840a:89). By singing magical songs, the Tlingit tried to influence the course of the moon so that it would not be obscured, since this was considered a sign of great misfortune (Veniaminov 1840a:85).

The Indians believed that not performing magical rituals before any serious undertaking (battle campaign, hunt, trade expedition, and so on) would have negative consequences, such as bad weather, illness, bad luck on a raid, or hunger.

The Tlingit believed in numerology. As among other North American Indians, the sacred number was "4." Any incantation or magical activity had to be repeated four times or by a multiple of four (usually eight).

The Tlingit believed that the whole world was populated by a multitude of spirits and the souls of people (the basis of the animist beliefs). According to the Tlingit, in the "other world" the spirit of a man occupies the same place he had in life. To provide a wealthy and distinguished man with servants in the other world, during the funeral ceremony the Indians killed one or several slaves, whose spirits were supposed to wait upon the soul of the late chief. A simple Indian's soul was supposed to be accompanied by a dog's soul. In order that the souls be warm in the other world, the body of the deceased was burned on a funeral pyre. His or her remains were rolled up in a skin and put in a box, and this, in turn, was placed in a small wooden house or atop a funerary totem pole away from the settlement. The Tlingit believed that the life of the deceased was in principle no different from the lives of the living, except that the dead did not do any work in their sepulchral world; rather, their continued existence depended entirely on their living kinsmen. Those who died, and in whose honor potlatches were organized, received the spiritual equivalents of goods, which were thrown into the fire or given to the guests. These souls could warm themselves at the central hearths in the houses of the dead in the other world. The souls of those deceased whose names were forgotten had to sit along the wall, far from the fire, and suffer thirst, hunger, and other hardships (Kan 1989:116).

According to the Indians, the soul could return from the afterworld and occupy a newborn of the soul's clan. The Tlingit believed that this reincarnation had occurred when an infant was found to resemble its deceased kinsman. It is possible that the idea of reincarnation was a peculiar reflection of economic relations in Tlingit society, characterized by the regular circulation of excess goods and the strictly cyclical character of the process of economic reproduction.

According to Emmons, the belief in reincarnation resulted in the Tlingit's not fearing death, whether from old age, illness, or war. This complacency manifested itself in the fearlessness of warriors preparing to die to end a blood feud between clans: he calmly went out unarmed to meet his enemies, literally sacrificing himself for peace (Emmons 1991:16). As already mentioned, the Tlingit did fear dying lost in the forest or in water, because their souls could easily be seized by river otters.

According to Veniaminov's data and materials from a Tlingit legend, each person had, in addition to his own soul, a special protective spirit, a "good genius" (Olson 1967:41; Veniaminov 1840a:57). Kan also reported that the Tlingit believed that over the head of each person hovered his patron spirit (*kinaayéigi*). This spirit flew from the person upon death (Kan 1989:309–310). This ethnographer notes that, among the Tlingit, wealth, in and of itself, was not respected or collectively worshipped, nor was there a centralized hierarchy based on riches. Their religion bore a predominantly "individualized" character, with people turning to specific spirits for help (Kan 1999:16). Besides being inhabited by people's souls, the world was occupied by a multitude of animal spirits. Especially honored were the spirits of river otters, like the animal itself. The Tlingit also believed that cliffs, lakes, swamps, glaciers, and so on had spirits. The chief underwater spirit was thought to be Konakadet, who was usually represented as a kind of monster with a large head, legs, and flippers; one glance from it was believed to bring wealth and good fortune (Emmons 1982:82).

Many spirits were associated with certain clans. Thus, for example, the spirits of Chak-ek ("Eagle Spirit") and Kustokan-shawet ("Sun Woman") were the "property" of the L'uknax̱.ádi clan (Oberg 1973:18). The Naanya.aayí clan was of very high rank, and their chief spirit, Tlzhiditin ("Invisible"), was believed to be the supreme leader of all shamanic spirits (Swanton 1908:465).

Most closely connected to animism was shamanism. Among the Tlingit, shamans were more highly esteemed than they were among other Northwest Coast Indians (Swanton 1908:464). Much of the shaman's practice, in De Laguna's opinion, was borrowed from the Tsimshian (De Laguna 1990b:220). The Indians believed that shamans could act as mediators between the world of people and the world of the spirits—*yéik(s)*. Shamans allegedly helped people see the future, find sorcerers or thieves, treat illnesses, protect people from danger, and so on. Though any person, male or female, could be a shaman, female shamans were rare among the Tlingit (Olson 1967:111). A shaman could have several spirit-protectors. The greater their number, the more numerous were the shamanic accessories (masks, rattles, and so on), and the more influential the shamans were thought to be. Each spirit had its name and its songs (Veniaminov 1840a:65). The shamans usually put themselves in a trance by singing, beating on a tambourine, and dancing wildly. Tlingit shamans used hypnosis and autosuggestion to achieve the desired results, especially when treating illnesses and identifying thieves.

The Tlingit's religious views and fantastic ideas combined with knowledge of botany and zoology that they had accumulated and passed from generation to generation. This knowledge helped them in hunting, fishing, and collecting. Their trade activities fostered a rudimentary understanding of applied geography and mathematics. "Though the Indians do not have symbols for numbers and do not know written calculations, they count with sticks, which are tied up in bundles; however, they are great mathematicians and for them to miscalculate is inconceivable," wrote Archimandrite Anatolii (1906:44). In spite of their having certain information about the world surrounding them, the Tlingit's knowledge was still lacking systematization, generalization, and penetration into the essence of objects and events, and naturally could not challenge the age-old foundations of religious faith and superstition. Thus, although the Tlingit knew folk medicine—using curative grasses and roots, the people still sought out shamans and witch doctors.

7.2. Personal Names

A special division of the spiritual culture of any people is anthroponymics, that is, the system of giving names, and the semantics of names. Tlingit anthroponymics was most closely connected with the multifaceted life of Indian society. The Tlingit anthroponymic model was very close to the Arabic classical model, which was formed in the late Middle Ages. This serves as distinctive evidence of the universality of human culture (Grinev 1990:132).

The following factors were important when giving names: sex and age, specific clan and moiety association, parents' social status, peculiarities and personal qualities, social status, and, finally, whether the person being named had children. De Laguna distinguished the following categories of traditional Tlingit personal names: (1) birth or initial real name, (2) childhood nickname or diminutive pet name, (3) adult name or nickname, (4) teknonymic name of several varieties, and (5) honorary or "potlatch" name (De Laguna 1972:2:781–790).[14] It is true that this classification is rather conditional since almost all names and nicknames could change: the teknonymic name could become a birth name, a birth name could be become an honorary one, and so on. With this, the difference between the male and female teknonymic model was insignificant and was manifested in the first instance in teknonyms and, in an indirect way, in honorary names.

The birth name was usually the hereditary name and was passed from generation to generation within the clan. The mother most often called her child by the name of her dead relative whose soul, according to the convictions of the Indians, was "implanted" in the newborn. Dreams, seen by the mother before giving birth, point to this, as does the presence of particular birthmarks. In addition, name selection was influenced by the degree of the mother's affection for the deceased relative, and the social position of the family (De Laguna 1972:2:781–783, 785). Evidently, the names encountered in Tlingit traditions are related to the birth names. The traditional names are not teknonyms and do not correlate with clan totems (where honorary names are more characteristic), for example, Tleḵi (Dancer), Keitl (Dog), Da-Tlein (Large Ermine), and Shaax̱ (Wild Currants) (De Laguna 1972:1:232, 246, 274; 2:789; Swanton 1909:232–233, 399). In addition, a child could immediately be named for several deceased relatives.

Distinct from birth names, children's nicknames and pet names were rarely preserved among adults, much less passed down within the clan. Likewise, the nicknames of adults were not usually preserved, although there were exceptions. For example, a Tlingit chief's wife was nicknamed Shaawát-kege (Stingy

Woman), and this name was inherited by her female relatives (De Laguna 1972:2:788). Slaves who came from other tribes evidently received nicknames because the Tlingit did not know their real names or what they meant. The pet names of slaves from different tribes evidently reflected the physical peculiarities of the slave, or his ethnic origin. For example, in one legend a slave called Xóots-ḵáa (Bear Man) is mentioned; the nickname was bestowed for both his great size and strength. In another tradition a female slave known simply as Young Slave (Shatshkuḵu) is mentioned (Olson 1967:77).

Another variety of nicknames were those given to hostages taken during peace negotiations between clans. Those names were used only during the peace ceremony and were not passed down. The names were usually associated with peace, good fortune, and abundance; among these names were Woman, Salmon Trap, Hummingbird, and so on (Oberg 1967:222). According to De Laguna, the nicknames of peace hostages could also be associated with the totems or valuable property that a clan "seized." Thus, the name Yéil-dleit (White Raven) was received by an Indian of the L'uknax̱.ádi clan from the Kuashḵwáan clan (De Laguna 1972:2:787).

Among Tlingit names, teknonyms formed by adding the words *éesh* ("father") and *tláa* ("mother") to a child's name were often encountered. According to Oberg, teknonymic names were most widespread among women (Oberg 1973:46). If, for example, a child was called Xutsk (Little Bear), then his mother received the name Xutsk-tla, and the father Xutsk-ish. If a person had no children, then he received the name of his favorite dog as a nickname-teknonym (De Laguna 1972:2:784).

Prestige "potlatch" names were a special variety. They were connected with potlatches and emerged as a result of the prestige economy. Honorary names could be received only at a potlatch and in only two ways. In the first case, an adult Indian (usually a chief) organized a potlatch and took a new name. In the second case, a child's parents organized a potlatch in the child's honor (after this the child became an aanyádi, that is, an aristocrat or noble, a status that had to be reflected in his new honorary name). Of course, such names could be borne only by wealthy Indians, primarily the chiefs and their direct descendants and heirs. It is not by chance that potlatch names had the tendency to become distinctive titles. Thus, the traditional name of the head of the Raven House of the Deisheetaan clan was Yel-navu (Dead Raven) (De Laguna 1960:180). However, among the Tlingit, completely changing an honorary name into a "noble" clan title had not yet occurred inasmuch as, on the one hand, the wealthy heir did not always take the honorary name of his predecessor (uncle, grandfather, oldest brother), and on the other, an honorary name could "degrade" and become a common birth name. This metamorphosis occurred when that clan subdivision that received it degenerated and became impoverished, or when the bearer was discredited. As Kan noted, names belonging to a cowardly warrior or a convicted sorcerer could be lost and forgotten (Kan 1989:75, 315, 334).

Nevertheless, in principle, wealth distributed at potlatches permitted "taking" and making any name, nickname, or even insult into an honorary name. The Deisheetaan clan, for example, transformed an insult into an honorary name at a grand potlatch at which they changed the curses that their former kinsmen, the Gaanaxteidí, had cast on them, into honorary names (the offensive expressions were only somewhat changed or shortened). Such was the origin of the Deisheetaan's chiefs' names: Lankushu, Nashukaii, and Kwudaktik (De Laguna 1960:133–135).

However, the cited example more probably belongs to the exceptions. The semantics of honorary names reflected first the spiritual essence of the clan, which is embodied in the totems. It is no wonder therefore that the majority of honorary names was usually associated precisely with totems. Thus, Oberg cited a whole series of similar names belonging to the influential Gaanaxteidí clan, whose chief totem was the Raven: Yéilgok (Beautiful Raven), Andakanel (Flying Raven), Yéilgooxu (Raven's Slave), Danavak (Silver Eyes of Raven), and so on (Oberg 1973:46). These were the names of chiefs, the official organizers of the potlatches. Their wives, though they took an active part in the festive naming ceremony, and especially in preparing the potlatch itself, nevertheless could not expect a totemic name, since they belonged to clans of the opposite moiety (which had its own set of totems). However, as a participant and unofficial sponsor of the potlatch, the wife of the chief could take for herself a new honorary, albeit nontotemic name, "by the potlatch" (Grinev 1990:136–137; see also, Veniaminov 1940a:102–103). It is not an accident, Oberg noted, that the semantics of honorary female names were connected not with totems but with wealth, as, for example, with the name Tonetltitushet (Overflowing [With Wealth] Room) or Tuwetlikaukuke (Giving More than the Value) (Oberg 1973:46–47).

Along with distinctive names and nicknames, the Tlingit often used kinship terms instead of names in daily intercourse. A curious example is cited by the naval officer, V. N. Berkh, who visited Alaska in the early 19th century. When Berkh took a census of a family of a Tlingit chief loyal to the Russians, the chief could not even remember the real name of his wife, since he always simply called her "my woman" (ax shaawát). It was only with the help of a slave that the Russian was able to establish the true name of the chief's mistress (Grinev 1990:139).

On the whole, Tlingit anthroponymics rather fully reflected both the natural and complex social worlds of the Tlingit.

7.3. Morals

Law, as an institution of a class society, was understandably lacking among the Tlingit. Morals took its place (later serving as a basis for common law) and played an important role in regulating Indian society. If one has not examined the traditional morals of the Tlingit, it is impossible to understand many of their behaviors and activities.

A prestige economy led to the emergence of a hierarchical, ranked system that was distinctively reflected in the morals and psychology of the Indians; the formation of their "class" morals in turn influenced their daily conduct. Shame fell on the aanyádi if he was seen performing what the Indians considered "contemptible" slave's work, such as cleaning fish or carrying firewood. It was considered shameful for him to participate in a noisy altercation with a slave or person of low status (Oberg 1967:219). The distinguished aanyádi often ignored a member of the clan who was of low rank and spoke of him not as of a brother but only as of person of such and such a house (Oberg 1973:41).

Slavery as a social institution was reflected in the world view and morals of the Tlingit. Being enslaved shamed not only the slave but his whole clan. A mortal insult for a Tlingit of high rank were the words "Son of a slave!" or "Your ancestors were slaves!" (Olson 1967:17). It was possible to cleanse a person of the shame of slavery only by ransoming him from slavery and rubbing his body with copper plates after he bathed in the sweat lodge. Rubbing with copper plates, according to the Indians, "cleaned away the slavery" (Olson 1967:54).

The aristocratic Tlingit had to control his emotions, behavior, and words at all times. The Indians piously believed in the power of the spoken word to bring good or evil. A person of noble origin had to conduct himself gently, modestly, and with propriety, and to distinguish himself with wisdom, magnanimity, and generosity. He could not brag about his high status, genealogy, or privileges: by observing his behavior and learning his name, clan, and the name of his clan household, anyone could know his rank (Kan 1989:62, 96). In Emmons's opinion, the Tlingit's character was easily determined by noting how they lived in the household, which required great self-control to avert quarrels and other conflicts. He especially noted how taciturn the Indians were during work: traveling with them in a canoe he sometimes heard not a word from them for a whole day (Emmons 1991:18). However, during recreation and potlatches, their speech could flow like a river. In the latter case, as Nora and Richard Dauenhauer note, the skill to craft a ceremonial speech according to form and format and that showed their knowledge of genealogical legends was very highly valued by the Tlingit (Dauenhauer and Dauenhauer 1990b:13–14).

Besides being "symbolic" (that is, evidence of having reached marriageable age), the labrets worn by aristocratic Tlingit may have prevented women from speaking "too much" and "too quickly." And the Indians believed that idle female gossip did not conform to the behavior of an aristocratic person and could easily lead to quarrels, disputes, and even clashes between clans (De Laguna 1972:1:444; Kan 1989:61–62).

Morals in Tlingit society can be characterized as the principle of "moral equivalents." The peculiarities of a prestige economy were distinctly reflected here; a strict accounting of what was given and what was received was common. This accounting was fixed by tradition. The principle of equivalents became a law in blood feuds and governed compensation for any injury, from theft to murder. Veniaminov wrote, "About the Koloshi they say, or at least said, that they are a brutal and blood-thirsty people. But the Koloshi hardly deserve to be called brutal and blood-thirsty, because vengeance for insults is the common law of all savages who have no other law than the internal, innate. The Kolosh does not seek blood, but only demands blood for blood" (Veniaminov 1840a:123).

In the case of murder, the rank of the deceased is also taken into account: for the death of a chief, for example, the life of a chief of the same rank from the murderer's clan must be sacrificed—that is, the murderer himself would live (Oberg 1967:210). "The usual custom is to pay for everything: for the wound, for the insult, for any damage caused even accidentally," wrote Archimandrite Anatolii, adding, "The Indian never gives anything to anyone for nothing. Once something is given to someone, he considers him a debtor his whole life" (Anatolii 1906:42, 51). Even the closest kin had to repay a debt, and payment with interest was considered "good manners," a custom called *k_isch* (Krause 1956:115).

The theft of someone's property was not considered a serious crime among the Tlingit. Veniaminov testified, "Theft is not considered a great vice. A thief either had to return the stolen goods or compensate for the loss but he himself did not suffer (Veniaminov 1840a:110).

In Tlingit society there already existed an unwritten "code of behavior." It was considered indecent to sprawl, display haste, or show curiosity. Deliberate haughtiness, proud bearing, and a sense of dignity were indispensable attributes of high-ranking Tlingit. The Tlingit assumed that an individual's good behavior reflected on the his whole group and, likewise, that bad deeds smudged the character of, that is, disgraced, the entire clan. Aristocrats had to conduct themselves strictly in accordance with elaborate Tlingit social etiquette, that is, to move, eat, speak, and stand with special greatness (Kan 1999:6, 10). Litke observed that the usual facial expression of the Tlingit was "haughty, somber, and even severe." He also wrote, "One distinctive feature of the character of a Kolosh is vanity. To show a Kolosh contempt was to make him your enemy; by contrast, some attention, playing up his vanity a little, is the essence of the most correct means of winning his friendship" (Litke 1834:156, 159).

7.4. Oral Creations

Dances and Games. The Tlingit had a rich folklore, based on a set of myths about the adventures of Raven, Yel. He appeared simultaneously as a cosmic demiurge and a mythological rogue. Thus, according to the stories, Yel, by various means, got the sun, the moon, and stars; procured fresh water from Kanuk (Storm Petrel); obtained fire (scorching his beak); and taught people to build boats, among other feats (Anatolii 1906:65–85; Krause 1956:175–183; Swanton 1909:3–80; Veniaminov 1840a:36–54). In addition, Yel inspired people to be moral. According to the Indians, the stories about his adventures reflect their most ancient history, which began with a mythological flood (De Laguna 1960:129). According to the eminent Russian folklorist E. M. Meletinskii, the Tlingit are the primary bearers of the Raven myths on the American coast and possibly also the primary conduit spreading those myths (Meletinskii 1979:115).

Besides the central epic of Raven there were many other legends and myths among the Tlingit, such as the myth about the gigantic Thunderbird named Ketl, brother of the old woman Agishanuku, who supports the world. Thunder is the noise of Ketl's wings; lightning is the flash of his eyes. He ate whales, snatching them from the ocean and carrying them to the top of high mountains (here the Indians sometimes found animal fossils, which served as evidence of Ketl's existence) (Anatolii 1906:87–89; Veniaminov 1840a:82–83). The legend of Tlinalkkidak ("Offering Wealth") tells of a beautiful woman wandering in the forest carrying a child; an encounter with her brings luck in the hunt (Anatolii 1906:90–95; De Laguna 1972:2:884–885; Garfield and Forrest 1961:117–118; Swanton 1908:412, 460). In the legend about the gigantic cannibal Gutikl, whom the Indians burned, his ashes were transformed into mosquitoes that love human blood no less than did their ancestor (Salisbury 1985:256–257; Wherry 1964:73).

There are popular legends about Kats, a hunter from the Teikweidí clan who married a bear, and about the daughter of a chief who married a bear (Anatolii 1906:104–106; McClellan 1970b; Salisbury 1985:14; Veniaminov 1840a:86–89). Many of these myths, legends, and traditions were widely circulated not only among the Tlingit but among other Northwest Coast Indians (especially among the Haida and Tsimshian), as well as among the interior Athapaskans (see, for example, McClellan 1963, 1970a). The central mythological figure for all these tribes was Raven.

In addition to myths the Tlingit's spiritual heritage included tales about the clans' origins and migrations, and about acquiring totems, honorary names, and so on. For example, the story of Natsitlan, an Indian of the Daktlawedi clan, describes his making from a yellow cedar two killer whales that helped him in his struggle with his wife's brothers. His winning the struggle permitted his clan to lay claim to the Killer Whale totem (Swanton 1909:230–231). In another example from the Deisheetaan clan, legend tells of a supernatural beaver that used a magic bow to kill a chief and used his tail to destroy the chief's clan's settlement (De Laguna 1960:137).

Also related to oral folk creations are potlatch speeches and ceremonial songs. Festive speeches, replete with metaphors, were the prerogative of specially trained, distinguished Indians. The Tlingit highly valued talented orators, and these speakers were often invited to distant kwáans where they received payment of gifts larger than was due their rank (Kan 1983:50, 56). Songs were also often metaphorical. Swanton noted that even the Tlingit could grasp their content only with difficulty. These songs often recalled and explained myths (Swanton 1909:390). Especially valuable at potlatches were the sad memorial songs (Swanton 1908:437). Many songs were the exclusive property of clans and served as a type of currency. The Tlingit often borrowed songs from neighboring tribes, primarily the Tsimshian.

Dances were no less popular among the Tlingit. Lisianskii wrote, "These people dance incessantly; and I have never had occasion to see three Koloshi together that they did not start to dance" (Lisianskii 1812:118–119). Dancing was performed to the accompaniment of the tambourine, rattle, and whistle. Wooden drums in the form of painted boxes with pebbles inside were also used. One of the earliest and quite emotional descriptions of Tlingit war dances is contained in I. I. Banner's *About the Koliuzhi People* (1803):

> The war dance of the Koliuzhskii people, in itself nothing terrible and unpleasant, is produced by the tambourine while the dancers make a semicircle, each taking in hand a death-dealing tool that consists of double-bladed spears [double-bladed daggers], and some use the bow

and arrows, they select in this case a leader who begins the dance, singing about his deeds and the deeds of his ancestors. With every intonation he stamps with his foot and brandishes with his hands, in which all help him and, following him, they precisely keep the time. With this they take on a terrible and frightful appearance, present various distortions and twistings of beastly fury, sticking out the tongue. They roar in a terrible way, make assault on the enemy, produce dreadful battle, menacing encounters, gestures toward killing and arrive through this to a frenzy and might be in such a rage as to wound one another if they did not have the quickness to dodge. In conclusion, it is fairly good fun, joy represents the victory; with admiration they rush and take prisoners, there they exert themselves so completely that they are fiercer than the most predacious animal, preparing the poor sufferers for the most lingering torment and tyranny (*K istorii Rossiisko-Amerikanskoi*, 1957:129).

A similar description of Tlingit dances was left by P. N. Golovin; he, with some irony, observed the Indians who arrived at the Russian fort in January 1861: "In spite of the snow and frost, barefoot dancers carried out their affair superbly—this was purely a dance of the satyrs, something wild, atrocious. The more they danced, the more the excitement built; the dance intoxicates them so that those who yield to it gradually become frenzied and are prepared to dance for several hours running. At such times murders occur among them; changing from dancing to general slaughter is very easy" (Golovin 1863a:6:296).

Dancing was inseparably associated with all festive ceremonies. At potlatches the audience followed the dancer with such rapt attention that even the smallest mistake in his movements was immediately noticed and later discussed at length. The performer was extremely tense and, if after the potlatch he died, the Indians said, "People's looks killed him" (Swanton 1908:435).

The Tlingit also played various games, "sticks" being especially popular. In this game for two, one of the participants shuffled sticks and hid them in bundles under a cedar bark, while the other had to guess in which bundle the "trump" stick, which bore the image of an octopus, lay. Sticks was played along the entire Northwest Coast. O. E. Kotzebue reported that the Indians sometimes lost not only their property but even their wives and children at this game (Kotzebue 1987:217). Tlingit folklore recounts similar cases (Swanton 1909:135–138). Other games included athletic contests, such as running, paddling a canoe, or shooting a bow, in which the Tlingit demonstrated their strength and dexterity.

7.5. Applied Art

Applied art was well developed among the Tlingit, as among other Northwest Coast Indians. As the American researcher N. Feder noted, the art of the Indians of this region was perhaps the most developed and complex in North America, excepting Mexico (Feder 1973:99).

In the representational art of the Tlingit, symbolic direction predominated, the central motif being the stylized representation of the "eye." This element in the form of a circle, oval, or rounded, arced trapezium could not represent merely eyes as such but was used as an articulation—a "hinge" indicating the junction of the body with the arms, the wrist, the legs, the ankles, and the tail or flipper. The "eye" did not always bear the semantic load. Sometimes it was just used to fill (Boas 1955:252). It is precisely through the stylized eye that the art work of the Northwest Coast Indians can be best understood. The prominent American artist B. Holm suggests that this art style originated on the Queen Charlotte Islands and the nearby shores of the mainland, from where it later spread to the north and south (Holm 1965:20). The Russian naval officer Lisianskii attested at the beginning of the 19th century: "The greatest art or craft of the local residents can be considered carving and drawing; judging by the multitude of masks and other carved and drawn things I have seen, I must conclude that each Sitkan [Tlingit of the Sitka ḵwáan] is a master of the mentioned art" (Lisianskii 1812:2:149).

Besides frequently representing "eyes," the art of the Northwest Coast Indians, particularly the Tlingit, typically depicted human skeletons, animals, and fantastic beings. The basis for such illustration was the idea that bones were the chief material component of the body, its inner essence. This belief is reflected in Tlingit art, where various figures appear in "skeletal" form; Indian artists often did not draw or carve all the bones but rather only the most important ones, primarily the vertebrae (Jonaitis 1986:130; Kan 1989:50).

Art also reflected social differentiation in Tlingit society. Jonaitis notes the existence of "elite" art, which the aristocracy owned to emphasize its high status, as well as the existence of the more modest art of the common people. The aristocracy stressed their superiority not only by owning higher quality art objects created by genuine masters of their trade but also by owning a large quantity of art (Jonaitis 1986:98–99).

Stylized representations of animals, birds, fish, people, and supernatural beings, sometimes in very complex compositions, were applied to the surfaces of objects or were carved into them (carvings and drawings were often combined). The subtlety and completeness of this style confirm its lengthy formation in

Northwest Coastal art. This level of development is graphically demonstrated by the drawings and carvings that the Indians made on objects in the collections of the first travelers (Feest 1985:77; Holm 1965:3). In this connection one cannot agree with R. S. Razumovskaia's assertion that the symbolic design allegedly emerged "in the art of the Northwest Indians only toward the middle of the 19th century" (Razumovskaia 1985:90).

The Tlingit's ideas about the organic connection of man and nature, especially man and the animal world and his connection, simultaneously, with the world of myths, were reflected in the symbolism of the images. This symbolism was primarily peculiar to the representation of animals, which were stylized to resemble people: they could have a human face, eyes, trunk, arms, and so on. However, several characteristic features, for example, sharp teeth, protruding ears, or a beak in place of a nose, indicated that it was not a man but a stylized animal. Thus, the figure of a beaver on a totem pole or on a ceremonial dipper's handle had an almost human face and eyes, but the protruding ears, flat nose, projecting incisors, and broad tail spoke for themselves. Other animals and birds were similarly represented; for example, a hawk's head on a battle helmet was reminiscent of a human head, but had a beak-like nose that curved so that its tip entered the mouth (Boas 1955:186–190).

As F. Boas noted, not all representations in the "classic" style of the Northwest Coast "can be deciphered" even by the Indians themselves, especially when one is speaking of the treatment of the multifaceted pattern on ceremonial Chilkat cloaks (see Emmons and J. R. Swanton [Boas 1955:212–221]).

The Indian artist could represent both an animal as a whole and its most characteristic parts (flippers, teeth, and so on). Sometimes the form of the object, which had undergone artistic elaboration, dictated "splitting" the representation into two symmetrical parts. As a result, it became a two-profile representation of the trunk joined by a common head and tail. Carved wooden cups in the form of animals, and illustrations on plaited hats, serve as examples of a similar method. For the "classic" style of the Northwest Coast, a severe symmetry, purity, and clarity of line were generally characteristic. The color scale was rather varied, but the colors black (by which, as a rule, outlines of the basic, primary figure were applied) and red prevailed.

The art of the Tlingit and their neighbors on the coast was also characterized by the poly-iconic artistic method—the combination in one object of several figures or illustrations. To see the second image, one had to move closer to or further from the object. The Soviet researcher E. K. Fradkin was the first to describe this method; he used the technique to decipher the symbolic representations on Tlingit shamans' and chiefs' ceremonial rattles (Fradkin

1985:91–110). However, his interpretation of erotic motifs is questionable: such motifs were never a distinctive part of Tlingit art. By contrast, shamans were strict about fasting and practicing abstinence in preparation for any ritual. According to the Indians, the spirits could punish the shaman, or even kill him, for engaging in sex (Veniaminov 1840a:65).

Many domestic objects, such as weapons, houses, canoes, masks, and so on, were covered with various illustrations and carvings. Especially well-known works of art, executed in the "classic" style of the Northwest Coast, are the widely known totem poles. Such poles were often erected in front of outstanding chiefs' houses or in cemeteries, and in the latter case boxes containing the ashes of the deceased might be located by them (or in them). One to three load-bearing carved posts could be included in the façade of the house. However, on the whole, totem poles were somewhat less common among the Tlingit than among the Haida and Tsimshian.

The term "totem pole" itself is not always correct, since the representations on such poles could be associated with a myth or some important event from the history of the clan and not be reproductions of the totem proper (Segal 1972:321). Proper totem poles were usually erected only at burial huts and represented figures of the corresponding clan's totems (Eagle, Wolf, Killer Whale, Frog, and so on). Thus, Swanton described a pole erected in honor of Dakuket, chief of the Chookaneidí, that consisted of two main elements. One of the elements was the figure of the mythological being Shakanaii ("Mountain Dweller"), a great hunter who was believed to be a Chookaneidí and who served this clan as a totem. The second (upper) element of the pole was an image of an eagle (the moiety-based totem). A box with the ashes of Dakuket was lodged in a hole in the "back" of Shakanaii.

In addition to observing the "classic" style of the Northwest Coast, the Tlingit also used linear geometric design, a pattern the women used to decorate baskets. Such designs were decorative and bore practically no semantic load (see Razumovskaia 1967, 1985:76).

In addition to the Tlingit's symbolic and abstract style in applied art, there was also a realistic style. Such individual works as the battle helmet "Head of the Paralyzed," which is preserved in the Museum of Natural History in New York, is striking for its realistic portrayal.

§

In summary, by the time the Tlingit first encountered Europeans, their society had gone through a rather lengthy evolution. The Indians' fishing economy

Tlingit Indians before Contact with Europeans

guaranteed surplus goods, which stimulated the development of trade, crafts, and the emergence of material and social inequality, including hereditary slavery. The spiritual culture reflected Tlingit society in all its variety. The opening up of Alaska by Europeans, starting in the late 18th century, substantially influenced various aspects of Tlingit life, further accelerating the development of their society.

CHAPTER TWO

The History of Tlingit Relations with Europeans in Russian America

~

1. First Contacts (1741–94)

1.1. Tlingit Contacts before the Second Kamchatka Expedition

The possibility exists that before the arrival of Europeans on the Northwest Coast of America the Tlingit could have had contact with Chinese and Japanese mariners. For example, a Japanese junk that shipwrecked was carried by the current to the Aleutian Islands at the end of the 18th century. Then, in 1815 on the coast of California, the American brig *Forester* came upon a Japanese junk that had lost its mast during a storm. The latter had drifted in the ocean for 17 months, and of its crew of 35 men only 3 survived (Howay 1973:109). Today the possibility of sailing the Pacific Ocean from Asia to America has been proved by the English sailor Brian Platt, who was able to cross the northern part of the Pacific Ocean in 1959 in an Asian junk built in Hong Kong (Voitov 1984:149). However, even if Japanese or Chinese sailors had sometimes arrived among the Tlingit, they left no noticeable trace in the latter's culture and way of life.

It is known that Spanish ships came to the coast of Alaska as early as the 16th century. These were Manila galleons sent from the Philippines to the Mexican port of Acapulco. The Spanish captain Francisco Gali in 1584 approached the Northwest Coast of America at 57° 30' north latitude, though he made no contact with the Natives. Another Spanish captain, Pedro de Unamuno, in 1587 also sailed in northern latitudes along the coast of America (Cook 1973:7; Krause 1956:11–12). It is probable that the Spanish were the first Europeans with whom the Tlingit came into direct contact. In any case, Archimandrite Anatolii referred to Tlingit legends about meeting the Spanish (Anatolii 1906:3).[1]

On the other hand, in the Yakutat Tlingit legends that De Laguna collected, the first Europeans with whom the Indians came into contact were Russians, or more precisely, a Russian woman: she arrived among the Tlingit in a ship that drifted ashore, being the only survivor of its crew. She later married an Indian (De Laguna 1972:1:233, 256).

However, these possible contacts exerted no influence on the fate of the Tlingit, and only the Bering-Chirikov Expedition's "official" discovery of Alaska in 1741 had any lasting effect on them.

1.2. The Second Kamchatka Expedition and Russians in the Aleutian Islands

Bering and Chirikov's Second Kamchatka Expedition was the logical conclusion of that grandiose campaign to "meet the sun" that was started by Ermak. Because of Ermak, Russian adventurers and promyshlenniki (see glossary) rushed into Siberia for *miagkaia rukhliad'* (literally, "soft stuff"), as furs were then called, incidentally "bringing under the high sovereign hand" the local tribes and collecting taxes from them.

At the beginning of the 18th century the western shore of the Pacific Ocean was already well known by the Russians, and the unknown lands farther to the east, about which vague rumors circulated among the local population of Chukotka, beckoned the promyshlenniki (Fedorova 1971:46–52). The czarist government attentively watched the business activity of the promyshlenniki and merchants and for its part took the lead in the research expeditions of M. S. Gvozdev and I. Fedorov (1732) and V. I. Bering and A. I. Chirikov (1728, 1741–42). It was with the Second Kamchatka Expedition that Bering and Chirikov found the coast of Southeast Alaska in June 1741, and thereby began the history of Russian America.[2]

At the same time, the first encounter occurred between the Russians and Tlingit. At 57° 50' north latitude two Tlingit boats approached the packet boat *St. Pavel*, commanded by Chirikov, but contact between the Russians and Indians was purely visual, since the Tlingit did not tie up to the ship, and only by voice and gestures did they invite the Russians to follow them to the shore (several days earlier a boat and a launch with 15 sailors disappeared on this shore without so much as a trace; their fate is unknown to this day) (Lebedev 1951:51–60; Svet and Fedorova 1971). The Dauenhauers suggest that the cries of the Tlingit who were in the boat that approached the packet boat *St. Pavel*—"Agai! Agai!"—was probably the call "Ai k̲aa!" (meaning "Row!") (Dauenhauer and Dauenhauer 1987b:436).

Some authors suggest with more or less assurance that Captain Chirikov's men, who disembarked on the American shore, were ambushed and killed by the Tlingit (Barbeau 1958:18, 76; Gibson 1992:12; Kan 1999:34; Pierce 1990:118).

History of Tlingit Relations in Russian America

Though this hypothesis has every right to be stated, it is doubtful that the Indians could deal with the very well-armed visitors: the Russians had not only rifles, pistols, and sabers but even a small copper cannon and two signal rockets. Modern Tlingit tell a more convincing version of the fate of Chirikov's men. According to them, the Russian sailors who landed on the shore of Kruzof Island seeking fresh water did not return to their ship; their reason was simply that cruelty and oppression prevailed on board. The fugitives were amicably accepted by the local Tlingit and they married Indian women. However, fearing that sooner or later another Russian ship would arrive and they would be hanged or executed as deserters, the Russian sailors loaded canoes and went south with their families. Their descendants headed the most prestigious families in the village of Klawock of the Henya ḵwáan on Prince of Wales Island (Jacobs 1990:3). In fact, the first Spaniards to visit here saw a fragment of a Russian bayonet among the local Indians. At the beginning of the 20th century the schoolteacher O. M. Salisbury stated that the chief of the Klawock village was a certain Robert Peratovich—a Tlingit whose name unquestionably indicated his Russian origins (Salisbury 1962:57).

A short time after Captain Chirikov reached Alaska, the ship *St. Petr*, under Commander Bering, arrived on the American shore at Kayak Island (59° 40' north latitude). The Russian sailors landed on the island, where they found a hut and some of the Natives' everyday objects, but the Russians were unable to make contact with the Natives (*Russkie ekspeditsii*, 1984:263, 271–272). In Averkieva's opinion, the local inhabitants would have to have been Tlingit (Averkieva 1974:141). However, information about the first Russian voyagers who visited this region after Bering, as well as 20th-century archaeological excavations, refute this assertion (Johansen 1963:873–874; Shelikhov 1971:96). The Natives who had come to Kayak Island at the time of the Bering Expedition were probably Chugach Eskimos or Eyak Indians.

Upon their return to the homeland, the crews of the Second Kamchatka Expedition's two packet boats had visited the Kodiak Island region and the Aleutian Islands. From this difficult and dangerous voyage the sailors brought a multitude of skins of fur-bearing animals, including several hundred sea otter skins, the fur being in high demand in China.

The valuable furs and sailors' stories about discovering lands to the east interested the Kamchatka mariners, merchants, and promyshlenniki. "Rumor of this newly discovered land's wealth," wrote the prominent Russian historian V. N. Berkh, "excited the enterprising Siberian merchants, and the stories of Bering's and Chirikov's companions inflamed even more their desire to become rich in sea otter skins" (Berkh 1823:1). As early as 1743 the first ship set out on business for an island that had been named "Bering Island"; others followed, opening up new islands and moving ever farther to the east along the Aleutian chain.

The Russians spent about forty years colonizing the Aleutian Islands. The local Aleuts were conquered and then overwhelmed with taxes. All resistance was suppressed, often with great cruelty (Khlebnikov 1979:86–90, 144). From the free and warlike people the Aleuts were when the Europeans arrived (Liapunova 1987:85–86), they were transformed into a dependent people without rights, about whom P. N. Golovin wrote, "Now the Aleuts are the meekest people, and it can be said, crushed in spirit" (Golovin 1863a:6:292). The Aleuts' complaints to the czarist government about oppression and subjugation by Russian promyshlenniki went unanswered. Their destiny (and that of the inhabitants of Kodiak Island later) was to do the difficult and dangerous work of hunting sea otters on the water, practically as slaves to the Russian colonial authority. Under the influence of colonization the traditional Aleut culture changed. At the same time, the Russians gladly used some elements of it, primarily the skills of baidarka (see glossary) hunting for sea mammals that had been refined for centuries. The subjugated Aleuts were formed into baidarka flotillas—hunting parties under the leadership of Russian promyshlenniki. In 1784 the Ryl'sk merchant Grigorii I. Shelikhov established a colony on Kodiak Island that served as a base for further investigation and the opening up of Southeast Alaska. From here the Russians undertook hunting-trading expeditions in various directions and sooner or later had to encounter the Tlingit.

1.3. The Spanish and the Tlingit (1775–91)

The Russians' success in the northern part of the Pacific Ocean alarmed the Spanish government, which had claimed the entire western coast of America. In 1774 the viceroy of New Spain, Marquis A. M. Bucareli, equipped a naval expedition to the northwestern coast of the North American mainland. However, this expedition's vessels did not reach Southeast Alaska. It was not until the next year that the crew of the schooner *Sonora* succeeded in reaching the Alexander Archipelago, making the first direct contact with the Tlingit.

First, a schooner commanded by a royal military fleet lieutenant, Juan Francisco de la Bodega y Quadra, investigated Bucareli Bay on the western shore of Prince of Wales Island, where the Spanish encountered Kaigani Indians and possibly Tlingit of the Henya k̲wáan. Then the *Sonora* turned to the north and reached Baranof Island. The navigator of the expedition, F. A. Maurelle, noted in his journal such geographic objects as San Jacinto Mountain (Edgecumbe), Cabo del Engaño (Cape Edgecumbe), and Ensenada del Justo (Sitka Bay).

When the Spanish landed on the shore, they noted several Indian (Tlingit) warriors hiding not far from a house fortified by a palisade. Nevertheless, the Spanish, unperturbed, set up a wooden cross—a symbol of Spanish rule—and chiseled another into a cliff. The Indians, who had attentively watched the solemn ceremony but did not understand its meaning, eventually dug up the wooden cross and set it up at their house, having perhaps come to believe that it had some value. The Spanish themselves paid little attention to the local inhabitants: they were not interested in trading with the Indians but rather in "juridically" securing the rights of the Spanish crown to the new territories. Maurelle noted that after several accidental encounters the Tlingit obtained some beads and cloth from the Spanish (La Pérouse 1968:100–102; Maurelle 1781:34–37).

After calling at Baranof Island, the *Sonora* set out still farther to the north (to 58° north latitude) and then turned back, since many of the crew had become ill (La Pérouse 1968:103). It is possible that the crew of the *Sonora* brought smallpox to the Northwest Coast, terribly devastating the Indian population.

The English navigator N. Portlock, having visited the eastern shore of Chichagof Island (Hoonah ḵwáan) in August 1787, noted that the local Native population was very small, probably diminished by smallpox, traces of which he saw on the Indians' faces. Since there were no pock marks on the faces of children younger than 12, Portlock deduced that smallpox had been spread by the Spanish who had visited these places in 1775 (Krause 1956:21). One of the oldest chiefs of the Sitka ḵwáan, Saiginaḵ, told Khlebnikov about the 1770s smallpox outbreak in Sitka: at that time, no more than one or two people in each family had survived (the Tlingit themselves naïvely supposed that Raven had inflicted the illness on them as punishment for frequent civil wars) (Khlebnikov 1985:82).

The smallpox epidemic could also have been brought to the Northwest Coast by a Spanish expedition in 1779, as the American historian W. L. Cook thinks (1973:79). This expedition had the same goal as its predecessor: performing reconnaissance and securing new lands for the Spanish monarchy. Two royal frigates—*La Princessa* (the official name was *Nuestra Señora del Rozario*) and *La Favorita* (*Virgin de los Remedios*)—under the command of Lieutenant Ignacio Arteaga and Bodega y Quadra again visited Bucareli Bay where, according to De Laguna, the Spanish traded with the Henya Tlingit. It is also reported that they bought three boys and two girls (evidently slaves' children) from the latter (De Laguna 1972:1:111). Then the ships, almost without stopping, followed north along the coast to Prince William Sound and then turned south to the shores of California.

After these two Spanish expeditions, the crews of which had had episodic contact with the Tlingit, the Indians were still to encounter members of the Spanish round-the-world expedition of Alessandro Malaspina in 1791 in the corvettes *Descubierta* and *Atrevida*. This time the Spanish sailors visited the Yakutat Tlingit. The Spanish received fresh fish, furs, and crafted artifacts from the Indians in exchange for knickknacks, metal objects, and clothing. At this time, according to Malaspina, the Tlingit were already well acquainted with Europeans, especially English traders. They had not only European axes, pots, and clothing but even three books and a silver spoon, and the young Indians knew several English words (Malaspina 1825:9:168). The Yakutat people exchanged so much clothing with the Spanish sailors that, looking at their costumes one might have thought that the Indians had killed the crew of some Spanish ship and dressed in their uniforms (Malaspina 1825:9:177).

At first the Spanish and Tlingit were friendly; this ended when the Indians stole a sailor's jacket. This incident nearly led to an open clash. Relations were often tense.

Having stayed in Yakutat from May 1 to July 6, 1791, the Spanish corvettes weighed anchor and set off farther north, then returned to Nootka. With this, Spanish-Tlingit contacts were concluded. Though the Spanish were the first Europeans to establish direct contact with the Tlingit, their influence on the Indians' culture and way of life was insignificant. The Spanish goal was not to trade with the Natives of Southeast Alaska or to maintain any other connections with them. As already mentioned, exploring this territory and trying to secure it for the Spanish crown was most important for them. However, Spain, not having sufficient economic, political, and military power to reinforce their claim to the Northwest Coast, was quickly forced out of this region by its old rival, England.[3]

Concerning Tlingit contacts with Europeans, Averkieva erroneously wrote that such Spanish captains as Gabrillo (1542), L. F. de Maldonado (1588), Juan de Fuca (1592), and de Fonte (1640) had visited the region occupied by the Tlingit. Her assertion regarding the Spanish captain Juan Perez (1774) and the English captain James Cook (1778) making contact with the Tlingit is also incorrect (Averkieva 1974:141). It is possible to confirm this, for example, using the American historian W. L. Cook's basic work (1973) on Spanish expeditions to the Northwest Coast, as well as Captain Cook's own notes (1971), which have been examined.

1.4. Tlingit Relations with French, English, and American Fur Traders

The English expansion to the Northwest Coast began with Captain James Cook. In 1778 he sailed the length of the Northwest Coast from Vancouver Island to Kenai Bay (Cook Inlet).[4] On the way home, the renowned captain's companions sold sea otter skins acquired from the Nootka Indians on Vancouver Island for a great return in China. Impressed by Cook's huge profits, English fur traders were drawn to the Northwest Coast starting in 1785. The trade expeditions of Captains Hanna, Meares, Dixon, and Portlock were a prologue to the annual Northwest Coast voyages of English merchants who bought furs from the Indians for resale in China. However, after the Spanish, the first persons to come into direct contact with the Tlingit were not the English but the French.

In July 1786 two French frigates, commanded by the renowned navigator La Pérouse, called at Lituya Bay. According to a Tlingit legend, the Indians mistook La Pérouse's ships for gigantic black birds with snow-white wings and, having decided that Yel had returned to the people, ran into the woods in fear. Eventually an old man dared to canoe to La Pérouse's ship and was met by the friendly French crew. After he had safely returned, the Tlingit began to barter with the French sailors (McClellan 1970a:121–122).

As La Pérouse himself wrote, for the French it was a great surprise that the Indians were well versed in trade, not inferior to Europeans in this respect. The French captain saw that the Indians had a beaded necklace and a small brass knickknack—items that La Pérouse surmised were of Russian origin.

The Tlingit, as La Pérouse reported, were not only experienced traders but excellent thieves. They managed to steal clothing hidden under a pillow in a French officers' tent that was guarded by 12 sentries, as the sailors slept, as well as a musket mounted with silver (La Pérouse 1968:370–372).

La Pérouse himself was convinced that the bay they had discovered would be secured for the French crown and even gave it the name Port des Français. Meanwhile, he acquired a small island in the mouth of the bay from the Indians, for which the latter received several meters of red broadcloth, axes, adzes, bars of iron, and nails (La Pérouse 1968:375). Certainly, France's "new possession" required sacrifices, in the literal sense of the word. On July 13, 1786, in the treacherous whirlpools of Lituya Bay, two launches manned by French sailors sank—6 officers and 15 sailors perished (La Pérouse 1968:388). Shortly before this, and in the same place, several Tlingit canoes owned by the L'uknax̱.ádi clan that were traveling from Kaknau village to Yakutat with a load of furs to trade also sank. The old Tlingit say that the sea currents carried the bales of L'uknax̱.ádi furs across the Pacific Ocean to the shores of Kamchatka, where Russians found them. Having so learned of the wealth of furs in Alaska, the Russians set out across the ocean to America, where they found the Tlingit. As the Dauenhauers note, modern Indian legends use the term "Russians" to identify both the Russians and the French of the La Pérouse expedition, who were the first Europeans to visit treacherous Lituya Bay (Dauenhauer and Dauenhauer 1987b:297–299, 435–436). So, in the Indian legends the actual aims of Russian colonization are interwoven into a single whole with fantastic details and real historical events. The fact is that the Russians did not visit Lituya Bay until 1788, two years after the French.

La Pérouse's sailors traded about six hundred sea otter skins bartered from the Indians during the stop in Lituya Bay, and then the French frigates left for Asia. Modern Tlingit report that the Indian chief who traded with the first white visitors to the shores of Lituya Bay became very wealthy, having obtained iron from the Europeans, the metal most desired by the Tlingit, being one from which they made tools and weapons (Jacobs 1990:2).

Several years after La Pérouse's expedition, another French captain, Etienne Marchand, commanding *La Solide*, traded with the Tlingit. In August 1791 *La Solide* entered Sitka Bay, where the French bought furs from the local Sitka k̲wáan Indians. In all, no more than four French ships visited the Northwest Coast before the end of the 18th century (Howay 1973:12, 16, 18). Thus, the French did not represent any substantial competition for English traders. The French Revolution (1789–94) having begun, the English fleet's blockade of French shores, and a series of Napoleonic wars made French ships' regular visits to the northern waters of the Pacific Ocean impossible. Therefore, French influence on Tlingit culture was insignificant.

The English made direct contact with the Tlingit a year later. In the spring of 1787 the English captain John Meares, on his way from Chugach Bay to Nootka, stopped at Cape Edgecumbe and traded with the Sitka k̲wáan Tlingit (Krause 1956:20). In May and June that same year another English captain, George Dixon, traded with the people of Yakutat and Sitka. Three more English captains—James Colnett, Nathaniel Portlock, and William Douglas—also visited the Tlingit over the years. In exchange for metal items, fabric, clothing, and knickknacks, the English received thousands of sea otter and other furs from the Indians (De Laguna 1972:1:125–132).

After these expeditions the English fur traders' ships began to appear more often around Southeast Alaska, with 35 British ships visiting the Northwest Coast between 1785 and 1794 (Howay 1973:59). Until the mid-1790s British

History of Tlingit Relations in Russian America

merchants were the Tlingit's chief European trading partners, and English wares sold to the Indians significantly outnumbered those of other European governments and the United States.

Striving to classify information about North America's Northwest Coast and to impress its right upon it in hope of good prospects, the British government outfitted George Vancouver's round-the-world expedition in 1791, and between 1793 and 1794 Vancouver visited Southeast Alaska. Exploring the Alexander Archipelago, he noted that the local Indians were already well acquainted with European wares and even had rifles, carbines, and pistols. Members of this expedition also traded with the local inhabitants, but trade was not the expedition's chief goal. The various Tlingit ḵwáans treated the British sailors in different ways. Relations between the English and the Tlingit of the Stikine ḵwáan were friendly; by contrast, the Chilkat ḵwáan once tried to attack the expedition's rowboats (Vancouver 1833:5:468–474). Vancouver especially noted the inhabitants of Southeast Alaska's warlike character and wrote with regret that, having received firearms from European traders, the Indians had become more dangerous (Vancouver 1833:5:510). Vancouver believed that Europeans' dishonest trading methods were at the base of the Indians' animosity (Vancouver 1833:5:237–250).

Guns were supplied to the Tlingit not only by Vancouver's compatriots but also by American traders, the so-called Boston Men, who had appeared on the Northwest Coast in the late 1780s. Only 15 U.S. ships had visited this region before 1795 (Howay 1973:6–24). Some of the American ships undoubtedly also sailed around Southeast Alaska, and their crews had contact with the Tlingit, which was reflected in Indian legends (Olson 1967:87–88).

1.5. Tlingit and Russians (1788–94)

As already mentioned, the first Russian encounter with the Tlingit was during the Second Kamchatka Expedition (1741), which is preserved in the entries in Chirikov's ship's log. The next mention of the Tlingit is in 1783 in the ship's log of Navigator Potap K. Zaikov, who wintered in Chugach Bay (Prince William Sound). The Chugach who visited Zaikov's ship reported about the *"Koloshi,"* who lived to the southeast of Chugach Bay (Tikhmenev 1863:2:Append. 7). The conversation in this case was presumably about the Indians of Yakutat, the northernmost ḵwáan of the Tlingit.

Shelikhov, who settled on Kodiak Island in 1784, having brought the local inhabitants—the Kodiak—under subjection, busily set out to investigate and open the nearby coast of the mainland. By 1786 the Russians had established fortified trading stations on the Kenai Peninsula and were exploring the adjacent mainland (Fedorova 1971:112–117).

In 1788, by order of the Irkutsk governor-general, I. V. Yakobi, who supported all of Shelikhov's efforts to open America, the galliot *Tri Sviatitelia*, under the command of Dmitrii I. Bocharov and Gerasim G. Izmailov, set out from Kodiak Island to the southeast for an inspection of the Northwest Coast. The members of the expedition visited Yakutat and Lituya bays, on the shores of which were Tlingit settlements. Friendly relations developed between the sailors of the galliot and the Natives, and trading began. The Russians then obtained not only a variety of furs from the Indians but two young male slaves (one of them from Kodiak, the other evidently from the Tsimshian Indian tribe). Tlingit chiefs who visited the ship were given Russian copper coats of arms, and to the "head toion" (chief) of Yakutat, Ilkak, a portrait of the heir apparent, Pavel (Shelikhov 1971:99–111). De Laguna suggests that Ilkak (Yelkok) was not chief of the Yakutat kwáan but rather was a chief of very high rank of the Chilkat Gaanaxteidí (he was visiting Yakutat, probably to trade) (De Laguna 1972:1:135). And, in fact, one of the most esteemed names of the Chilkat Gaanaxteidí was Yéilkok, or Yéilgok, the name of the chief of the Whale House of the Chilkat settlement (Emmons 1982:74; Oberg 1973:46). It is possible that Yéilkok was a Chilkat person; however, there is no proof of this.

The Bocharov-Izmailov expedition of 1788 was very significant in the further Russian exploration of Alaska. The coast of the American mainland from Prince William Sound to Lituya Bay had been examined in detail and claimed by the Russians. For the first time, written documentation of direct contact between the Russians and the Tlingit had been produced and an ethnographic description of the latter given.

The members of the expedition and Governor-General Yakobi, as well as Shelikhov himself, assumed that the Tlingit, having accepted the national coats of arms, were now subject to the Russian Empire (Andreev 1948:299, 317; AVPR, f. RAK, op. 888, d. 68, l. 1; Shelikhov 1971:105). As for the Tlingit, they may not have viewed the acceptance of the coats of arms as their voluntary submission. Submission, in the understanding of the Indians, in fact signified slavery, and not one free man, in their estimation, ever voluntarily gave up his independence. In addition, imperfect translation and the fact that there were no Indian terms for such concepts as "empire" and "autocratic rule" inevitably led to the Indians' misunderstanding the Russians.[5] It can be assumed that the Russian copper coat of arms was accepted by the Indians as a clan totem of the Russians or as a valuable adornment (of the rare metal copper). The Tlingit

History of Tlingit Relations in Russian America

may have considered the solemnly given portrait of the heir apparent Pavel as that of a god of the newcomers—Il<u>k</u>ak, in his turn, presented the Russians with an iron amulet in the form of the head of Yel, the Raven; a little bag of magical grass; a representation of the totem; and a drum—objects, from the Indians' point of view, not only valuable but having religio-magical significance. The illusion that the Tlingit had voluntarily become Russian subjects was dispelled four years later.

After Bocharov and Izmailov's 1788 expedition, there was a break in Russian-Tlingit relations during which the Russians took up the initial development of the shores of Kenai Bay and Chugach Bay. In 1792 the director of the Shelikhov-Golikov Company, the enterprising and energetic Baranov carried out an examination of Chugach Bay, at the same time "transfixing" its inhabitants, the Chugach. Baranov was accompanied by 150 two-holed baidarkas (300 Kodiak people), 17 Russian promyshlenniki, and the galliot *St. Simeon* under the command of Izmailov. On June 20 Baranov encamped at Nuchek (Hinchinbrook) Island. That night the Russian camp was surprised by an unprovoked Tlingit attack.[6] The battle lasted several hours. This is how Baranov describes the beginning of this clash:

> In the very depths of night . . . a multitude of armed people surrounded us and from all sides began stabbing and killing the heterodox [Kodiak], and stabbed two of us there who were thrown from sleep, though five men stood guard, but they had crawled so close in the darkness of the night that they saw [them] only at ten paces stabbing our tents, for a long time we fired our weapons without success, since they were dressed in three or four layers of wooden and plaited *kuiak* [armor] and on top of that protected by very thick elk hide cloaks, and on their heads [wore] reinforced helmets with images of various monsters' faces, of which none of our bullets or buckshot pierced, and they genuinely appeared to us in the darkness more frightful than the most hellish devils, and supervising the entire sequence of movements by the voice of the one who commanded, they drew closer to us in an orderly way and as one group ran back and forth, injuring us and the heterodox (Tikhmenev 1863:2:Append. 37).

Baranov himself was nearly killed at the start of the battle. Only the steel mail that he always wore under his clothing saved him. The Indians' charge was checked only by Baranov's discharging the falconet (see glossary). The Kodiak members of the party, seeing that their spears and arrows were powerless against the armor of the enemy, dispersed in panic. Some of them threw themselves

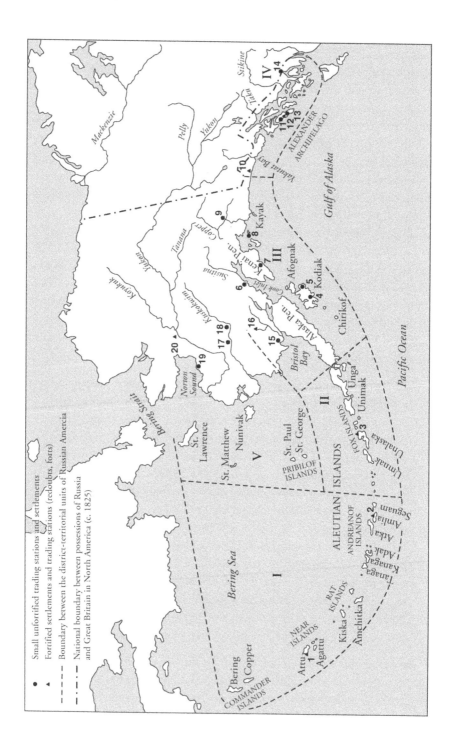

Small unfortified trading stations and settlements

Fortified settlements and trading stations (redoubts, forts)

Boundary between the district-territorial units of Russian America

National boundary between possessions of Russia
and Great Britain in North America (c. 1825)

History of Tlingit Relations in Russian America

into the baidarkas and pushed out to sea; others rushed to Izmailov's galliot, while the rest stumbled around the camp in disarray, impeding Russians' firing handguns and cannons at their adversaries. The battle continued until sunrise. The Tlingit undertook several attacks but finally were forced to flee when Izmailov arrived to help the Russians, having been informed by the Kodiak of the attack. The Indians fell back to their canoes (Baranov attested that there were six) and paddled off in them into the sea.

In this clash with the Tlingit, Baranov lost 2 Russians and 9 Kodiak (12 Kodiak, according to Khlebnikov [1979:25]), and 15 men were wounded. In addition, the Indians took four Chugach, who were being held hostage by the Russians. The Tlingit suffered more tangible losses: 12 dead warriors were found on the battlefield, and they took some of the wounded and dead Indians with them on retreating. The Russians took a mortally wounded warrior prisoner who reported that taking part in the attack were Yakutat Tlingit and their Eyak allies, who had come to take revenge on the Chugach for an attack

---

(*Left*) Map 3. Russian America: Territorial Administrative Divisions. {The modern name has been inserted in curly brackets—*Trans.*}

I—Atkinskii Atka District (center—the settlement of Atkinskoe on Atka Island); II—Unalashka Unalaska District (center—the settlement of Gavanskoe Dutch Harbor-Unalaska on Unalashka Island); III—Kad'iakskii Kodiak District (center—the settlement of Pavlovskii Harbor Kodiak on the island of Kad'iak); IV—Sitkhinskii Sitka District (center—Novo-Arkhangel'sk on Sitka [Baranof] Island); V—Northern District (center—Mikhailovskii Redoubt).

Arabic numbers indicate the most significant Russian settlements in Alaska: 1—the settlement of Port Chichagov; 2—the settlement of Atka (1795, 1826); 3—the settlement of Gavanskoe (Dobroi Soglasie, Illiuliuk) (before 1800); 4—fort, then Trekhsviatitel'skaia Three Saints artel (1784); 5—fortified settlement of Pavlovskaia Kodiak Harbor (1792); 6—Nikolaevskii Redoubt (1786); 7—Voskresenskaia Fort Seward, then changed to an odinochka (1793); 8—Fort Konstantin and Elena (Konstantinovskii Redoubt) (1793); 9—Fort Yakutatskaia Yakutat and the settlement of Slavorossiia (Novorossiisk) (1796); 10—Mednovskaia Copper odinochka (1822); 11—Fort St. Arkhistratig Mikhail (Mikhailovskaia Fort) (1799); 12—Novo-Arkhangel'sk (1804); 13—Ozerskii Redoubt (1810s); 14—Dionisievskii Redoubt (Redoubt Sv. Dionisiia) (1833); 15—Novo-Aleksandrovskii Redoubt (1819); 16—Nushagakskaia odinochka (1830s); 17—Kolmakovskii Redoubt (1841); 18—Khulitnakskaia odinochka (1831); 19—Mikhailovskii Redoubt (1833); 20—Nulato (1839).

The possessions of the Russian-American Company embraced two more districts not indicated on the map: the Rossiiskii Russian District (center—Fort Ross in California) and the Kuril'skii Kurile District (center—on the island of Urup).

the previous year. The Indians risked coming out against the Russians, supposing that if they won they could use the Russians' goods. The wounded Tlingit also reported that his group awaited the arrival of ten more canoes to raid the Kenai people. This compelled Baranov to leave the camp and hurry to Kodiak to take precautionary measures in case of another Indian attack (Tikhmenev 1863:2:Append. 37–38).

This first clash with the Tlingit showed the Russians that they were dealing with a serious opponent. During the course of several hours the Tlingit had withstood not only the fire of handguns but of artillery as well. They had attacked not in a disorderly mob but in ordered rows, clearly under the command of a war leader. Their protective armor turned out to be rather effective for withstanding gunfire. There were only about 150 Yakutat Tlingit and their Eyak allies in this battle (if one canoe held about twenty-five warriors), and though there were at least one and a half times as many Kodiak, experience indicated that the Kodiak were unreliable brothers-in-arms and the Russians would have to fight for themselves.

No legend about this clash with the Russians survived to the middle of the 20th century among the Yakutat Tlingit. In any case, there are no indications of this account in De Laguna's 1972 monograph. But it can be assumed that this unsuccessful storming of the Russians' camp, and the heavy Tlingit losses impeded the Tlingit advance toward Chugach Bay.

The Tlingit attack delayed but did not stop Baranov's (ultimately failed) efforts to bring all the Northwest Coast as far as Vancouver Island under Russian authority. As early as 1793 he had sent a hunting party of 180 baidarkas commanded by E. Purtov south from Chugach Bay. The expedition reached Yakutat Bay, but it was not possible to establish meaningful contact with the Tlingit because of the mutual distrust and suspicion (RGADA, f. 1605, op. 1, d. 352, l. 40b.–5). Most historians, both past and present, do not mention this first hunting party, which visited the Yakutat region in 1793. Descriptions of the hunting parties' journeys to Yakutat and beyond usually begin in 1794.

It was in 1794 that a party of more than five hundred baidarkas set out on a hunt from Kodiak Island, carrying about a thousand Kodiak, Alaskans, and Chugach directed by ten Russians led by Purtov and D. Kulikalov (Tikhmenev 1863:2:Append. 60).[7] The party reached Yakutat Bay, where the Kodiak hunted sea otters and the Russians conducted negotiations with the Tlingit of the Yakutat and Akoi ḵwáans. In the words of an officer of Vancouver's expedition who witnessed the negotiations, the chief of the Yakutat people "used all his eloquence for defining the precise extent of the boundaries of their land and indicating the injustice of the Russians who killed and carried away from there

History of Tlingit Relations in Russian America

the sea otters" (Vancouver 1833:5:438). The Russians, for their part, shamed the Tlingit for the groundless 1792 attack, demanded the return of the four captured Chugach, and asked what had happened to the copper crest left with them in Yakutat in 1788. The Tlingit confessed to the attack, though they reported that the hostages had been sold "farther than the bay of the Chilkats" (evidently to the Auk or Kootznahoo ḵwáan) and there died. The crest, they said, was sold to the Chilkats after the death of Ilḵak and was broken by them (Tikhmenev 1863:2:Append. 64–65).

Though negotiations concluded with assurances of friendship, only a few days later relations between the Russians and the Yakutat became strained. The Indians were irritated by the party's poaching as well as by the fact that the Russians had brought along the Chugach, old enemies of the Yakutat people. In addition, the Indians' resentment might have been evoked by the Russians' almost complete refusal to trade with them (the Russians themselves were experiencing a shortage of European goods). Whatever the case, the Yakutat people seized several Kodiak people, and Purtov, for his part, detained three canoes of Indians, demanding the hostages' return. After lengthy negotiations mediated by the Tlingit of the Akoi ḵwáan, almost all the seized Kodiak were released in exchange for the Indians. On July 3 the party left for Kodiak, taking with it 15 *amanaty* from the Eyak and the Tlingit ḵwáans of Yakutat and Akoi (Tikhmenev 1863:2:Append. 83).[8] Four Kodiak remained hostage among the Yakutat people for the winter.

Purtov's 1794 hunting expedition to Yakutat was a prologue to founding Russian colonies on Tlingit lands. The Russian advance into Southeast Alaska was predetermined by three circumstances: political factors, the extermination of sea mammals in the old hunting grounds, and competition among the trading companies (Fedorova 1971:112–120). Purtov's expedition coincided with Vancouver's expedition, and these summed up the geographic, and to some degree the ethnographic, study of Southeast Alaska beginning with the voyage of Bering and Chirikov.

In 1794 the period of first contact between the Tlingit and Europeans was essentially over. Throughout the previous 19 years the Indians had encountered the Spanish, French, English, Russians, and Americans. With each contact, the Indians became ever more involved in the fur trade that connected the Northwest Coast with a developing world market. European-Tlingit contact primarily consisted of trade exchange. The political struggle among the European powers to rule the northern part of the Pacific Ocean also had an indirect impact on the Tlingit. The isolation of revolutionary France and the ousting of Spain from the Northwest Coast in the mid-1790s left only Russia, England,

and the United States to struggle for primary political opposition domination of this region.

2. Founding Russian Settlements, and Tlingit Contacts with the English and Americans

2.1. The Russians in Yakutat Bay (1796) and the Alexander Archipelago

After his successful expedition to Yakutat in 1794, Baranov, on instructions from Shelikhov (Andreev 1948:338–345), decided to establish a permanent Russian settlement there. According to Shelikhov's plans, this settlement was to become Russian America's granary and potentially its capital. It was proposed that up to 30 Siberian colonists' families settle in the new place to develop agriculture and breed stock.

In the spring of 1795 Baranov sent a hunting party to Yakutat under the command of Purtov and Kondakov and then sent another ship to establish a colony. The hunting party was met with hostility by the Tlingit in Yakutat and so did not stop there. Instead, it continued farther south along the coast. The ship with the colonists, which did not reach Yakutat, returned to Kodiak (Khlebnikov 1835:28). The reason for the Tlingit's hostility, according to Dmitrii Tarkhanov's information, was the *partovshchiki*'s (see glossary) arbitrary use of Indian hunting grounds (OR GPB, Sb. Q. IV. 311, l. 12).

In August 1795 Baranov himself arrived in Yakutat on the one-masted *Ol'ga*. Encountering Tlingit hostility, Baranov "audaciously" (according to Khlebnikov) decided to demonstrate to them the power and accuracy of Russian handguns and cannons, after which, as Baranov himself noted, the Russians "began to live with them in peace" (Khlebnikov 1835:28).

In Yakutat, Baranov negotiated with the primary chief and bought furs from the Indians. Having released the hostages, who had been taken to Yakutat by Purtov in 1794, Baranov now asked the Tlingit chief for his son (or, rather, his nephew) as a hostage. In place of the nephew, Baranov left nine Russians and three Kodiak (under the leadership of a corporal of the Mining Corps, Dmitrii Tarkhanov) and an Aleut female interpreter among the Indians (OR GPB, Sb. Q. IV. 311, l. 5–8; Grinev 1987:91).

From Yakutat, Baranov set off southward into the straits of the Alexander Archipelago. From August to October he visited Cross Sound, Lynn Canal, and Sitka Island, where he encountered and traded with the Tlingit chiefs (Khlebnikov 1835:29; Tikhmenev 1861:1:52–53). Khlebnikov, evidently having read documents of Baranov that are unknown to us, reproduces the characteristics that the latter gave the local inhabitants after making closer acquaintance with them. "This people—populous, powerful, daring, and, having an inclination toward barter and trade—are industrious and diligent. They ably adopt European customs and, with innate cleverness and intelligence, become quickly adapted to firearms" (Khlebnikov 1835:30–31). During the trip the hostile Indians tried to lure the crew of Baranov's small vessel into the straits to seize the ship a couple of times. On the Alexander Archipelago's shores Baranov erected wooden crosses to indicate that this territory belonged to Russia. He wanted to winter on Sitka (Baranov) Island, but severe fall storms did not permit him to approach it. Baranov returned to Kodiak in October with great difficulty (AVPRI, f. RAK, op. 888, d. 121, l. 11–110b.).

While Baranov was in the straits of the Alexander Archipelago, the cutter *Del'fin* was sailing there under the command of Yakov E. (James G.) Shields (Sitnikov 1986:89; Khlebnikov 1861:41). This was the Russians' first thorough investigation of the Alexander Archipelago, the islands of which were discovered as early as 1741 by Captain Chirikov.

In the spring of 1796 a hunting party of 450 baidarkas was again sent to Yakutat, arriving at Lituya Bay. This time there was no friction between the Yakutat and the partovshchiki, since the latter asked the Indians to allow hunting on their hunting grounds and to allow the party to continue south and received their consent (OR GPB, Sb. Q. IV. 311, l. 12). But nevertheless, this year's hunt was not without incident. On the party's return trip to Kodiak the Tlingit took two Kodiak prisoners (Khlebnikov 1979:25).

At the end of June 1796 Baranov arrived in Yakutat on the *Ol'ga,* while the colonists arrived on the *Tri Ierarkha* led by the *prikazchik* (see glossary) I. G. Polomoshnyi (Khlebnikov 1835:34–36; Sitnikov 1986:90). The Russians, left in Yakutat under the command of Tarkhanov, happily wintered there, although they suffered for lack of provisions. Baranov and his people spent two months constructing the fort and settlement at Yakutat Bay.[9] This was the first European colony on Tlingit land.

The Indians, seeing that the Russians were beginning to settle in their territory, decided to establish good neighborly relations with them. The Tlingit were evidently afraid of the numerous and well-armed arrivals. Accompanied by his kinsmen, the "chief toion" of the Yakutat came to Baranov with great ceremony (Tikhmenev 1861:1:54–55). This man was evidently the chief of the Kuashkkwáan, the most powerful kwáan in the Yakutat region (De Laguna 1972:1:223). Judging from the documents, he was called Katkeek or Katkeik, and in Baranov's letters he is mentioned as "the Elder" or "Toion" (*K istorii Rossiisko-Amerikanskoi,* 1957:118; OR GBL, f. 204, k. 32, ed. xr. no. 6, l. 10; RGADA, f. 1605, op. 1, d. 352, l. 120b.).

During the solemn encounter, Baranov, not satisfied with assurances of friendship, asked the old chief to give his relatives as hostages. It is possible that, pressured by Baranov, the old chief handed authority to his nephew, to whom Baranov gave a special paper that confirmed him in this title (Tikhmenev 1861:1:54–55). As we have established, the new chief was the hostage who had been taken to Kodiak the preceding year and had evidently been baptized there. In the documents, he is mentioned as "Toion Fedor," whose godfather was Baranov himself (Khlebnikov 1835:103; OR GBL, f. 204, k. 32, ed. xr. no. 6, l. 30b., 10; OR GPB, Sb. Q. IV. 311, l. 22). It can be supposed that Toion Fedor was one of the first Tlingit to accept Orthodoxy. Baranov surmised that once the head chief of the Yakutat people had accepted the Christian faith and lived among the Russians, he would disseminate Russian Orthodox ideas among the Indians. Judging by the outcome, this theory proved partially true. Toion Fedor was sufficiently loyal to the Russians and, possibly owing to his position, only a few members of the Kuashkkwáan supported the 1805 Tlak̲aik Teik̲weidí revolt against the Russians (OR GBL, f. 204, k. 32, ed. xr. no. 6, l. 30b).

Having stayed in Yakutat for about two months, Baranov took 11 new hostages from among the Tlingit and set out with them to Kodiak (Khlebnikov 1835:36). While he was occupied with building the colony in Yakutat, Shields returned to the straits of the Alexander Archipelago on the *Orel*. On this trip he met with one of the Sitka k̲wáan's head chiefs, who complained to him about the English captain Henry Barber's outrageous conduct. The Indian said that the captain had invited him to his ship and entertained him but then ordered him put into irons; he was not released until the Tlingit paid a ransom of sea otter skins (Khlebnikov 1861:42). This act was evidently the reason that the Indians then captured one of the English sailors, to whose rescue Barber sent an armed launch (Tikhmenev 1861:1:56). Barber's behavior was characteristic of some English and American captains, who, in pursuit of profits, did not limit their means for securing them. Nevertheless, Shields, a Russian, evidently striving to assist his countryman's relations with the Indians, gave Barber the young Tlingit who had been on his own ship and who was loyal to the Russians (AVPRI, f. Snosheniya Rossii s Angliei, op. 35/6, d. 507, l. 16). This act made the Siberian administration suspicious of Shields's loyalty to Russia.

For the Russians who remained in Yakutat (about eighty persons) the winter of 1796–97 was tragic. Thirteen promyshlenniki died of scurvy, as did seven colonists and several women and children (AVPR, f. RAK, op. 888, d. 126, l. 2; Khlebnikov 1985:41). Contention among the leaders increased the new colony's desperate situation. The Yakutat were apparently also drawn into the conflict between the colonists' leader, Polomoshnyi, and the head of the promyshlenniki, Stepan F. Larionov, since, as Baranov himself wrote, "the people with the toion [katkeek] and Fedor there asked me personally to visit and provide better order than is there today" (OR GBL, f. 204, k. 32, ed. xr. no. 3, l. 7). The violence toward and coarse treatment of the Natives by Polomoshnyi and some of the Russian promyshlenniki in Yakutat very negatively affected Russian-Indian relations, which even the official historian of the RAC, Tikhmenev, recognized (Tikhmenev 1861:1:55).

Baranov did not see any prospect in an agricultural colony, since numerous attempts indicated that cereals would not ripen at 60° north latitude. Therefore the Novo-Rossiiskaia colony turned out to be unprofitable, requiring people, goods, materials, and ships needed elsewhere. The only reason to maintain the Yakutat colony was to preserve it as a storage depot for hunting and a place for the partovshchiki to rest en route to the straits of the Alexander Archipelago. In addition, Baranov had few hopes of developing trade here with the various groups of Tlingit, primarily with the Chilkat people. However, there was almost no trade with the Indians since, as a rule, there were not enough European goods in the colonies, especially cloth and clothing. It was necessary, Baranov wrote to the owners of the company, to send no less than two thousand *arshin* of cloth to the colonies "for exchange for furs with the Koliuzh and Chilkat peoples, who hardly look at our *kitaika* {cheap Chinese cotton fabric}, *daby* {another kind of Chinese cotton fabric}, and clothing, and take back the beavers [sea otters]; they trade them to the English who annually visit, and those here [the Kodiak and Chugach] do not look at the *kitaika* with the same eyes as before, and they trade English clothing from the Koliuzhi" (AVPRI, f. RAK, op. 888, d. 121, l. 120b.).

2.2. The Founding of the Russian Fort on Sitka Island (1799)

Yakutat, after the founding there of the fort and settlement, was transformed into a transshipping base associated with the southward movement of the parties into the straits of the Alexander Archipelago. Several dozen guns were distributed to the partovshchiki in Yakutat for protection against possible attack by the Tlingit; the partovshchiki brought their catch from fur hunting here (Davydov 1810:1:122–124). From 1797 the baidarka flotilla began to make regular trips to the Sitka Island region, where sea otters abounded, bringing from there thousands of otter skins. It was Sitka Island that Baranov selected for establishing a new base south of Yakutat in the Alexander Archipelago region. A new colony was also necessary for securing the territories examined earlier for the Russians. Rumors that a special company for trading on the Northwest Coast had been established in England pushed Baranov to hasten the accomplishment of this plan (AVPR, f. Gl. arkhiv 1–7, 1802 g., d. 1, papka no. 1, l. 40b).

Therefore, in the spring of 1799 Baranov sent a large flotilla of 550 baidarkas, the hooker *St. Ekaterina*, and the galliot *Orel* to the Sitka region with the necessary materials and people to found a new Russian colony there. The beginning of the expedition, according to Hubert H. Bancroft, was extremely unfortunate for Baranov. On May 2 the expedition lost 30 baidarkas with 60 Kodiak who drowned at Cape Suckling in a storm on a shoal, and consequently a sudden Indian attack deprived Baranov of 30 more partovshchiki. These losses, according to Bancroft, forced the party to return to Kodiak (Bancroft 1970:386–387).

The above facts, taken from Bancroft's works, appear not to rely on published sources and archival materials. However, Bancroft's information is evidently reliable since he cites a letter by Baranov (authentic, judging by style) describing the Indian attack at Cape Suckling. It is possible that this event is reflected in Chugach oral history recorded by Kaj Birket-Smith and commented on by De Laguna (1972:1:169).[10]

The director himself set off from Kodiak on May 30 in his small *shebek Ol'ga*. En route to Sitka he stopped at Yakutat and found there "great disorder among the affairs and people," the reason for which was a critical conflict between the head of the promyshlenniki, S. G. Larionov, and the steward I. G. Polomoshnyi, who led the colonists. The former, together with the promyshlenniki and the local Indians, presented Baranov with numerous complaints about Polomoshnyi. The director had no recourse except to replace him as head of the Novorossiisk colony, designating the Kursk merchant Nikolai Mukin to replace him (Tikhmenev 1863:2:Append. 139–141).

Baranov left Yakutat on June 30 and reached the west coast of Sitka Island (now Baranof Island) on July 8. Two days before his arrival, almost the entire baidarka party set out for Kodiak. However, on a stopover in the strait between Sitka and Chichagof Islands tragedy befell them: contaminated mollusks that the Native party members ate poisoned a total of 115 Kodiak and Chugach, who died within two hours in terrible pain. The Russian promyshlenniki who were with the party tried to save the Indians, giving them gunpowder, tobacco, ashes, and sal ammoniac with soapy lather as an emetic, but these remedies helped only a few. Khlebnikov, relying on the personal report of the party leader D. F. Eremin, wrote: "The [local] Koloshi, who treated the Aleuts [Kodiak and Chugach] nicely, were dumbfounded by the occurrence and tried to help them by their own methods, but seeing the huge number of dead, became frightened, fearing that the Russians and Aleuts might consider this the activity of their shamanism [more correctly: sorcery], and ran off into the woods" (Khlebnikov 1861:43).

The massive loss of kinsmen so affected the party members who remained that, despite orders and threats from the Russian leaders, they quickly left the strait in panic. Because of the incident, the strait was named Pogibshii "perished" (or Pagubnyi) and is now called Peril Strait. About twenty more Native party members died en route to and while at Yakutat (Khlebnikov 1861:43). And although the "main" party delivered many furs (some 15 hundred adult sea otters were procured) to Kodiak, the loss of at least 135 experienced hunters was almost intolerable and could not help but weaken hunting expeditions in subsequent years.[11] The Natives' distress increased as a result of an epidemic raging on Kodiak and the Kenai Peninsula, and in Yakutat, of which many local residents died (Khlebnikov 1835:47).

Having arrived on Sitka, Baranov found a small artel that was led by Vasilii Medvednikov and brought on the galliot *Orel*. Situating himself on the shore, the RAC director began to acquaint himself with the chiefs of the local Tlingit. He well understood the importance of maintaining friendly relations with the numerous and bellicose Indians. In order to avoid possible friction, he acquired from the Sitka chiefs the parcel of land on which the colony sat, for which "a notable sum" was paid in goods. This purchase was evidently the first time that the Russians established a colony; the promyshlenniki usually did not take into consideration the Native residents' rights to the land and hunting areas.

Negotiations with the Sitkas were successfully concluded, and on July 15, 1799, the Russians laid the foundations for the first fort structures, which they called St. Arkhistratig Mikhail (Mikhailovskii).[12] Toward fall, construction was still not complete, so Baranov and 25 Russians and 55 Koniag from the "main party" wintered there. In addition, 12 women (most of whom were probably Koniag) remained at the new colony where they prepared fish, repaired baidarkas, and processed skins. The women included Anna Grigor'evna—the director's "Native" wife—daughter of the Koniag toion Grigorii Raskashchikov (Tikhmenev 1863:2:Append. 131, 145).

The year of the founding of the colony on Sitka coincided with the time of the final formation, created under the aegis of the government, of the Russian-American Company (RAC), which was supposed to combine trade functions with the functions of colonial administration (Fedorova 1971:120–123, 1981:245). In Alaska the Russian colonies were headed by Baranov, who was officially designated governor of the Russian colonies in America in 1802.

In relations with the Tlingit Baranov was politically cautious. He understood well that to strain relations with the numerous, well-armed, and militant

Indians was dangerous, all the more so since the power of the Russians at Sitka was quite insignificant. Therefore, Baranov tried to win the Tlingit chiefs over with food and gifts. He paid special attention to Skautlelt, whom the Russians called Mikhail, chief of the powerful Sitka Kiks.ádi lineage. At the same time, Baranov strove to make the Indians see him as a legitimate leader. Thus, copper Russian coats of arms were awarded to Skautlelt, who was treated nicely and received many gifts, including an open letter dated March 25, 1800, that spoke of the benevolent concession to the Russians of the place for the colony (Khlebnikov 1835:53–54). As they had in Yakutat, Baranov hoped that the loyally disposed chiefs would help him, if not overriding the will of Indians, then at least neutralizing possible hostile actions.

In spite of the gifts and entertainment, the Sitkans were evidently dissatisfied by the new arrivals' settling on their lands. During the winter of 1799–1800, the Indians visited the fort several times to attend dances, bringing daggers hidden under their cloaks, but the vigilance of Baranov and his people averted possible clashes (Khlebnikov 1861:44; Tikhmenev 1863:2:Append. 147).

Other Tlingit kwáans who had arrived in winter 1799–1800 in Sitka were especially restless, as reported by G. I. Davydov (1812:2:110). Khlebnikov wrote, "In spite of the probably good accord, displeasure arose almost continually among the *Koloshi*. Those who came from distant places reproached the Sitka people, saying that they enslaved themselves to the Russians. They laughed at them, boasted about their freedom, and watched for chances to instigate quarrels and insolently offend the Russians and Aleuts" (Khlebnikov 1835:53–54).

On Easter day in 1800, Baranov sent his female interpreter to the Indian chief with an invitation to join the celebration at the fort, but the interpreter was robbed, beaten, and driven from the Tlingit settlement by visiting Indians. Baranov decided to avoid similar provocations but took care not to strain relations with the Natives. With only 22 Russians and 2 falconets, he went to the Sitka Tlingit settlement, in which there were about 300 well-armed warriors. "We proceeded to march among all to the dwellings of those culprits whom we had been told were prepared to stand in resistance," wrote Baranov, "but, having made only two volleys, found only several old men, while the rest fled." (Tikhmenev 1863:2:Append. 147). The volleys were only to frighten, and no one was injured by them. Baranov assembled the chiefs and compelled the guilty to ask for "pardon." A mutual exchange of gifts and assurance of friendship followed. This act raised Baranov's authority considerably among the Indians.

In April 1800 Baranov set out for Kodiak, having appointed V. G. Medvednikov head of Fort Mikhailovskii. The governor of the Russian colonies in

America continuously adhered to the politics of "peaceful coexistence" with the Tlingit. In the "instructions" to Medvednikov, Baranov required him and his subordinates to observe the greatest care in contacts with the Tlingit and maintain peaceful relations with them:

> Under the circumstances of our present low numbers it is necessary to distance ourselves and be rather circumspect, and to bear patiently insignificant annoyances, which occur from the rudeness and ignorance of the peoples [Tlingit] . . . nor take the least thing from them without bargaining, and without payment, or keep everyone possible from stealing from them and not permitting anyone else, I give additional advice to note the toions . . . with special reception, and when this occurs, to feed them . . . judging that our occupation of their localities requires from our side much gratitude (*K istorii Rossiisko-Amerikanskoi*, 1957:96–98).

Indeed, it was dangerous to strain relations with the numerous Indian people, all the more so because the number of Russians in America was very insignificant, comprising fewer than three hundred men.[13]

With the founding of the fort in Sitka, two parties of baidarkas regularly hunted for sea otters in the region of the Alexander Archipelago. Each spring a large hunting party (250–450 baidarkas), which they called the "chief," "far," or "Koliuzhskii" party, set out for the straits from Kodiak. The other party was formed at Fort Mikhailovskii (90–120 baidarkas) and was called the "Sitka" party.

In 1801 the "far" party, led by Baranov's closest assistant, Ivan A. Kuskov, visited Sitka Island, procuring sea otters, while the "Sitka" party was sent to hunt in Frederick Sound. Everywhere that the "far" party visited, Kuskov "awarded medals and certificates to and befriended" the Tlingit, who, in his words, were very amicably disposed (Khlebnikov 1861:45). Nothing, it seemed, presaged the tragic events of the next year.

2.3. Tlingit and the Fur Trade on the Northwest Coast

While the Russians explored and opened Southeast Alaska, more and more English and American ships began to appear in coastal waters, trading with the Tlingit for the valuable furs. In the second half of the 1790s, American skippers became the chief trading partners of the Tlingit, with the United States seizing the dominant position in the Northwest Coast fur trade, having almost forced their English competitors from it. In 1799, in the region just around Sitka Island, five U.S. ships were trading: the *Hancock, Dispatch, Ulysses, Eliza* (all from Boston), and the *Caroline*, and only one English ship, the *Cheerful* (Andrews 1967:49; Gunther 1972:169). The American traders' dominance can be explained by the fact that the English captains, in order to trade, had to buy licenses from the South Seas Company, which had taken control of British commerce in the Pacific Ocean, and from the East India Company that monopolized English trade in the East. The licenses cost dearly and allowed the sale of furs in China but did not permit the import of Chinese wares to England. Gibson noted that even the powerful Hudson's Bay Company could not remove this double-license blockade (Gibson 1976:155). The American traders, not bounded by any poly-feudal and monopolistic limitations, developed vigorous enterprise along the Northwest Coast. Offering the Indians a wider variety of goods than the English did, and at the same time fiercely competing among themselves, the American fur traders greatly undermined British trade with the Tlingit. The English traders complained to Baranov in 1799 that the Americans had "snatched trade completely from them; on these shores the English had formerly bought two otters for 3 *arshin* {about 71 centimeters of cloth}, and for a gun with a few cartridges from four to six otters, while nowadays as the Boston men began to arrive, their trade was quite undermined and became quite different and unprofitable and from then on they could not rely on who of their countrymen would go from Canton or Bengal [to the Northwest Coast]" (Tikhmenev 1863:2:Append. 145).

It was the American traders who began to bring European wares and products to the Northwest Coast en masse, including broadcloth, clothing, axes, knives, kettles, cooking utensils, and spirituous drinks (Langsdorff 1812:2:75). One of the most popular trade articles continued to be firearms, which American merchants sold to the Tlingit right under the walls of Fort Mikhailovskii on Sitka; this, of course, did not contribute to the safety of the Russian colony. V. M. Golovin wrote: "These savages are so cunning and careful that they tell the Americans they will agree to carry out trade in sea otters only if their ships bring a known quantity of arms and the equipment associated with them, and if not, they will not trade them even one otter" (Golovnin 1864:5:173). Certainly, guns served the Tlingit not only as weapons but also for hunting game and furs, having replaced bows and arrows. The American skippers even sold the Indians light cannons. Among the Sitkans alone, Baranov saw four falconets in 1799 (Tikhmenev 1863:2:Append. 146).

The American traders' enterprise and desire for speculation were truly remarkable. Having noted that the Tlingit valued ermine skin highly, they bought the skins in Russia and soon flooded the Tlingit market with them, so that the value of ermine dropped sharply (Davydov 1810:1:176–177). Another example of American merchants' resourcefulness was the attempt to amass porcelain dentalia, specially made in England. In form, size, color, and luster these artificial shells closely resembled the natural ones, but the Tlingit quickly realized the forgery, and speculation collapsed (Langsdorff 1812:2:113).

Striving to collect the most furs possible, the American traders' ships cruised the straits of the Alexander Archipelago, occasionally wintering over near Tlingit settlements. In trading with the Indians, the sailors exercised the greatest care, since the Tlingit were warlike and had been well armed by the Americans themselves. In 1798 the Chilkats attacked the English sloop *Dragon*, and, when in 1799 the American ship *Caroline* traded in Sitka Bay, the local Tlingit of the Sitka ḵwáan made several attempts to seize it, having cunningly lured the crew ashore (Bancroft 1970:338; Howay 1973:35). Sometimes such acts of animosity were the result of provocation and arbitrariness by previous European and American visitors (see documentary appendix 3). For example, Cow—the well-known chief of the Haida—and two other chiefs of his tribe were seized in 1795 by another British captain, William Wake, of the ship *Prince William Henry*, and were freed only after Wake secured for each Indian 200 sea otter skins from their chiefs. A similar means was applied in 1806 in the Queen Charlotte Islands by the American captain Samuel Hill as well as by several other American captains. In other cases, when the Indians refused to trade, some American captains fired on their canoes and villages with cannons. The Americans did not even shrink from direct slave trade, buying Indian slaves near the mouth of the Columbia River and the Strait of Juan de Fuca for resale to the Tlingit, Haida, and Tsimshian in the north. Sometimes Hawaiians, primarily women, figured as slaves too (Gibson 1992:160–166, 235).

But the Indians themselves were not always friendly toward the white visitors, taking the first opportunity to attack the travelers. Thus, a clash between the English captain Beck and the Tlingit in 1799 ended in a bloody skirmish during which the somewhat aggressively insistent Indians were killed or wounded. The next year, the Tlingit unexpectedly attacked a few sailors from the American ship *Jenny* who had been sent to the shore of a small inlet in Chatham Strait to gather wood. The boatswain and three sailors were killed in the attack, while the first mate, who led the party, barely managed to save himself by swimming away under fire from the Indians. A boat launched from the ship picked him up (Pierce 1990:42, 69).

On the whole, trade between the Indians and the fur traders was peaceful, since both sides wanted to maintain mutually profitable connections. According to Fisher, the European traders and Indians were part of a peculiar economic symbiosis, in which no one benefited from hostility (Fisher 1977:47).

As Kan notes, although the American captains offered the Tlingit a broader assortment of wares at a lower price than the Russians could, they showed less respect for the Indians and their traditions than the Russians did. The Americans were pragmatic and not very diplomatic because they did not want to have permanent settlements on Tlingit land. Rather, they were interested in momentary profits. Their exceptionally businesslike approach explained their unwillingness to honor the local chiefs and aristocrats according to Native traditions, as the Russians did (Kan 1999:58).

As for the Russians, they had almost no trade with the Tlingit during this period since they could not offer the Indians a broad assortment of European wares (from which, in consideration of safety, firearms were excluded). In addition, the goods that the Russians offered to the Tlingit were rather expensive. This was because the Russian colonies chronically lacked European items, a result of the irregularity of shipments, high transport expenses, and officials' abusing their power and neglecting to deliver necessities to the Russian colonies in Alaska. Therefore, the goods that were offered to the Indians were often purchased by the Russians from the English and American ships. Of the few European wares that the Russians bestowed on the Tlingit, a significant number were presented to the chiefs during visits and were not items of trade. Even the Russians themselves were not especially interested in developing trade with the Tlingit, since they preferred to buy furs from dependent Natives at a much lower cost.

On the whole, the period from 1795 to 1801 is characterized by a significant increase in contacts between the Tlingit and the Europeans. The fur trade spread along the Northwest Coast, and the first Russian colonies were founded on Tlingit lands in 1796 and 1799. Between 1795 and 1801 the Tlingit's chief trading partners were businessmen from the United States; the Indians themselves formally became Russian subjects, and their lands became part of the Russian Empire. Found at the extreme eastern boundary of the nation, the Tlingit, until 1867, were the most "eastern" people of Russia.

3. The Indian Revolt of 1802: Reasons and Consequences. Second Founding of a Russian Settlement on Sitka Island. Seizure of Yakutat by the Indians

3.1. The Tlingit Revolt

In 1802 peaceful Russian-Tlingit relations were abruptly interrupted by a revolt of Indians from many kwáans that united to expel the Russians from their

History of Tlingit Relations in Russian America

territories. These dramatic events have repeatedly attracted researchers' attention (Andrews 1967:50–51; Bancroft 1970:401–413; Bolkhovitinov 1966:311–312; De Laguna 1972:1:170–173; Khlebnikov 1861:40–56; Krause 1956:31; Okun' 1939:52; Pasetskii 1970:17; Tikhmenev 1861:1:88–92). However, the reasons for the Indian revolt of 1802, the alignment of the opposing forces, the extent of the parties' losses, and the ultimate consequences of this for the fate of Russian America have, to this day, not been revealed in full measure.

The immediate cause of the revolt was the 1801 murder of the chief of the Kuiu ḵwáan, his wife, and his children by members of the "Sitka" party, as well as the fact that the Russians had kept the chief of the Kootznahoo ḵwáan's nephew in chains for a small offense (*K istorii Rossiisko-Amerikanskoi*, 1957:120; OR GBL, 204, k. 32, ed. khr. no. 6, l. 22). According to Tlingit legends, the cause of the revolt was the Russians' imprisonment of the influential shaman, Stunuku, of the Sitka Kaagwaantaan lineage (Dauenhauer and Dauenhauer 1987b:4).

The first to undergo attack was the "main" party of 450 baidarkas led by I. A. Kuskov, which was setting out from Yakutat to the straits of the Alexander Archipelago to hunt sea otters. This attack occurred on May 23, 1802, at the mouth of the Alsek River, 60 kilometers southeast of Yakutat. The attack was preceded by several days of Tlingit provocations, so that the clash itself did not surprise the Russians. The violent attack was successfully repelled. The Indian warriors feigned flight in an attempt to lure the Russians and partovshchiki within range of the falconets hidden nearby in the woods. Although several hundred Tlingit and about nine hundred partovshchiki fought, there were minimal losses on both sides: ten Indian warriors were killed, while the party was stripped of one Kodiak (the Indians had killed one Chugach the day before), and four more partovshchiki were wounded (one of them died on the return to Yakutat) (*K istorii Rossiisko-Amerikanskoi*, 1957:107–109).

Although the Russians held the battlefield, Kuskov decided to move and set up camp on a small island near the shore of the mainland, since the battlefield was vulnerable to the enemy and the Russians had inadequate ammunition for a prolonged skirmish. While they were crossing to the small island, a panic seized the Native partovshchiki and they took flight in a disgraceful stampede. Their withdrawal was compensated by only a thin line of Russian promyshlenniki, who barely repelled the aggressive Tlingit warriors; but the Russians, facing superior Indian forces, were soon compelled to fall back to their baidarkas. The hasty evacuation to the small island occurred without loss in spite of intense enemy fire. Having entrenched themselves on the island, the Russians and partovshchiki easily endured several shellings from the

Indian warriors who arrived in canoes. The Tlingit, seeing the impossibility of easily routing the party, and fearing the Russians' revenge, decided to forge a peace with them. Encouraging them was the need to get to work storing up candlefish oil, since the candlefish spawning season began in May. Because of the shortage of gunpowder and ammunition, Kuskov agreed to a truce, and soon the sides were exchanging amanaty: the Tlingit gave two sons of chiefs, having received in exchange two Kodiak. In addition, the Indians returned part of the belongings they had seized from the party's abandoned camp (*K istorii Rossiisko-Amerikanskoi*, 1957:109–111).

After this, Kuskov decided to return to Yakutat to replenish his supplies of gunpowder and ammunition; he arrived with his party on May 30. Here he added more men to strengthen the guard at Yakutat, set up cannons, and prohibited the local Russian colonists from leaving the settlement to fish. Having left his sick and wounded and the amanaty at the fort, and having taken three additional Russians, Kuskov and his party set out on June 6 along the seacoast to the southeast. Safely reaching the Alexander Archipelago's northern strait, he learned from the Tlingit that he met that their fellow tribesmen were gathered and ready to attack Fort Mikhailovskii. Alarmed by these reports, on June 17 Kuskov sent a half dozen three-man baidarkas carrying a letter to V. G. Medvednikov, the manager of the fort, warning him of the danger. The envoys returned on June 20 (the Tlingit had seized one of the baidarkas and its crew en route) with the terrible news of Fort Mikhailovskii's seizure and destruction. "It could hardly be told without shuddering," Kuskov reported to Baranov, "how our Novo-Arkhangel'sk fort at Sitka and all buildings were turned into ashes, and the people killed, and the spirit scarcely strong enough to hear this unhappy news" (*K istorii Rossiisko-Amerikanskoi*, 1957:114).

While Kuskov carefully advanced southward from Yakutat to Sitka, the Tlingit, not waiting for his arrival, attacked Fort Mikhailovskii. Judging by eyewitness accounts (Tikhmenev 1863:2:Append. 174–180), the attack was unexpected. A large crowd of armed Tlingit led by Skautlelt attacked the two-story barracks in the middle of the day; Medvednikov defended the fort with half the garrison—the remaining Russians were hunting with the "Sitka" party or doing domestic chores outside the fort.[14] The Indians, having surrounded the barracks, opened up heavy gunfire at the windows and began to break down the door. At Skautlelt's call, a large flotilla of canoes carrying warriors set out from beyond the point to join the Sitkans' attack. The Russians tried to return fire but were unable to withstand the attackers' overwhelming military superiority. Soon the barracks' door was knocked down and, despite direct fire from the cannons inside, the Indians succeeded in entering the barracks,

History of Tlingit Relations in Russian America

setting it afire, and plundering it, having killed all its defenders. According to Indian legend, the roof of the two-story barracks, where the Russians had taken cover, was set afire by two Tlingit women living in the fort; according to other data, it was American sailors who sympathized with the Indians (Dauenhauer and Dauenhauer 1990b:12; Davydov 1812:2:111; Lisianskii 1812:138). The Indians also burned all the remaining structures in the fort as well as the almost completely constructed ship on the shore. The Russians and Kodiak outside the fort were almost all killed, and the women and children were taken into captivity. Tlingit legends report that the nephew and heir of Skautlelt—Katlian—who led the attack on the Russians at the head of the Sitka Kiks.ádi, played the chief role in destroying the fort. He was armed with an unusual weapon—a stone hammer obtained from the Russian smith, and on his head he wore the war helmet of the Raven—the totem of his moiety (Dauenhauer and Dauenhauer 1990b:8).

The day after they seized Fort Mikhailovskii, the Indians annihilated Kochesov's small party as it returned from hunting sea lions. It was probably the rifleman Vasilii Kochesov, identified in Tlingit legends as "Sniper Gidak," who was hunting sea lions as the fort was being attacked. Evidently he was killed only after a great struggle; in the Indian legends Gidak is described with unconcealed hatred. His name itself, write the Dauenhauers, points to an Aleut origin: "Giyak kwáan" denotes "Aleuts" in Tlingit (Dauenhauer and Dauenhauer 1990b:8, 12, 16). Indeed, Vasilii Kochesov was one of the Aleut Russian mestizos or creoles, as they were called in Russian America (his mother was from the Fox Islands).

The "Sitka" party was attacked near Frederick Sound on the night of June 19 and completely destroyed by the Indians (*K istorii Rossiisko-Amerikanskoi*, 1957:114–121; Khlebnikov 1861:45–51; Tikhmenev 1863:2:Append. 174–180). This is how Khlebnikov describes the destruction of the "Sitka party," basing it on accounts of contemporaries of the events:

> The *Koloshi* prepared, pursued the party, and observing its movements, waited at the most favorable place and for the great carelessness of the Aleuts weary from the difficult journey. Scarcely had these latter given themselves over to sweet sleep than the *Koloshi* in a large mass, but without noise, having arrived from the thick forest, and in the darkness of night approaching to a close distance, quickly examined the camp, and then with a cry threw themselves onto the sleeping; they gave none of them time to think of defense, and almost outright destroyed them with bullets and daggers. Very few escaped affliction

by flight, and they hid in the forest; while all the rest were left as sacrifices on their place of rest. . . . Having carried out the killing, the *Koloshi* took from the baidarkas all the otter skins, assembled all the property of the Aleuts and transferred it to boats which had arrived there at a summoning cry from the neighborhood, then cut and broke up all the baidarkas. They did not have any resistance and not one of them lost his life; but enriching themselves with the plunder, they left for their homes with cries of happiness (Khlebnikov 1861:50–51).

According to Khlebnikov, Urbanov's party lost 165 Kodiak in the slaughter (Khlebnikov 1979:25). Some of them were taken captive and killed later during sacrifices at a Tlingit potlatch. Ivan Urbanov, the party's leader, was wounded and seized by the Indians at the very beginning of the attack, but he was able to escape and hide in the forest. Later, some time after the tragedy, he and seven Koniag who had managed to save themselves during the attack were able to repair two baidarkas and reach Sitka in them. Here Urbanov despaired to see the ruins of the fort that the Indians had already destroyed. For him and his companions there was no other course than to try to paddle north to Yakutat. With great difficulty and escaping no few dangers, Urbanov succeeded in reaching Yakutat. Before he arrived, 18 Koniag survivors from the "Sitka" party had managed to reach Yakutat (AGO, razr. 99, op. 1, d. 113, l. 24, 530b.).[15]

Several days after the attack on Fort Mikhailovskii, the brig *Unicorn*, under the English captain Henry Barber, called at Sitka Bay, followed by two American ships: the *Alert*, commanded by Captain John Ebbets, well known to the Russians, having wintered at Fort Mikhailovskii in 1802; and the *Globe*, under Captain William Cunningham. Abrosim Plotnikov, one of the few survivors of the attack, managed to escape to the English brig. Soon the English picked up another Russian and several Kodiak who had hidden on the island's shore. Three days after this, Skautlelt came to trade at the brig with his nephew Katlian. Henry Barber, known for his adventures and thirst for profit, decided to profit personally from the situation that had arisen. He ordered both chiefs seized and demanded that the Indians accompanying them return all the captives and furs taken from the destroyed fort. Should the Indians fail to meet his demands, Barber said he would hang both chiefs on the yardarm. To persuade the Natives to fulfill his demands, the English captain, together with the American skippers, sank some of the Indian canoes with case shot and cannonballs.[16] Many Indians were killed or drowned, and the American captain John Ebbets took some of the survivors captive aboard his ship and exchanged them for captive Kodiak women (Tikhmenev 1863:2:Append. 177–

178). Finally the Tlingit delivered almost all the captives and furs seized in the attack on the fort. The furs were appropriated by Barber, and the former captives were delivered by him to Kodiak, where for their rescue and maintenance he asked 50 thousand rubles. After long arguments with Baranov, the adventurer released the Russians and Kodiak for ten thousand rubles' worth of furs.

These Russian sources are largely in agreement with Captain Barber's ship's log. Thus, Barber wrote that he arrived in the Sitka region on June 28 (by the Gregorian calendar, or June 16, by the Julian calendar), but he encountered neither Russians nor Native party members from the post, which had already been on the island for several years. On June 30 a local Indian chief came to his ship accompanied by three American sailors from the ship *Jenny*, who reported to Barber that three more of the sailors' companions were in the Indian settlement. In addition, the chief and sailors revealed that the Russian fort had been destroyed by the Indians on Saturday, June 26. In the words of the American sailors, the Tlingit forced them to take part in the attack on the Russian post, where up to four thousand sea otter skins were plundered. On July 1 the English captain set off in a well-armed sloop for the Indian settlement in which were more than 30 captive "Russian" women and children. He then visited the ruins of the Russian fort, where he found the mutilated bodies of approximately twenty men. An American deserter who was with Barber reported to him that, in addition to the fort, the Indians had destroyed an almost finished ship of 70 tons displacement that had been in the stocks. At this time, a Koniag spared from the slaughter crept from the woods and asked the Englishman to save him. Captain Barber ordered the unfortunate taken to his ship. Three days later Barber moved the brig to the ruins of the Russian fort where he managed to save two Russian promyshlenniki, one Koniag man, and a woman with a child in her arms, and on the following day, two more Koniag, so that the total number of rescued reached eight persons. On July 6 the chief of the Tlingit again visited Barber's ship accompanied by a wounded Indian and three more American deserters.

The English captain decided to take advantage of the situation, taking the two Indians hostage and demanding that all the Russian colony's captives be freed. The Indians, at musket-point, were forced quickly to release a "Russian" woman who was in a canoe that carried the Indian chief to the *Unicorn* (this woman was being made to bail water from the canoe). [17] On the following day the Indians brought another "Russian" woman and turned her over to the English after laborious negotiations. Then, on July 9, the American ships the *Globe* and the *Alert* arrived in Sitka Bay. Barber arranged with their captains to seize several canoes of Indians to better negotiate the surrender of captives from the destroyed Russian colony. Upon a secret signal, armed boats, along with the three ships, surrounded several canoes that had pulled up alongside the American ships whose crews then tried to capture the Indians who were on board.

The Tlingit desperately defended themselves with knives and tried to fire their muskets, but most of them were wounded and several were killed. The chief's wife and six other men fell captive to the Americans and English, and five medium-size canoes were taken.[18] One of the captured Tlingit was sent to his companions with the demand that they release all the "Russian" captives. Over the course of several days, the Indians surrendered a number of captives, whom Barber later delivered to Kodiak. The total, according to his records, was 8 men (3 of them Russians), 17 women, and 3 children (Shuhmacher 1979:58–60). In his journal Barber "modestly" omits the fact that, besides the captives, he secured a substantial part of the furs pillaged by the Indians from the Russian fort. He also recorded the improvised "trial" of an Indian captive, who, in an attempt to free himself, had wounded two sailors of the *Alert* with a knife; he was hanged for the offense, on the decision of the three ships' officers to teach the other "savages" a lesson (Bancroft 1970:409; Shuhmacher 1979:58, 61; Sturgis 1978:124). In addition, the English captain "forgot" to mention the actual ransom he received from Baranov for the former captives from the Russian fort.[19]

Considering Barber's activities, the RAC board of directors in St. Petersburg suspected that he himself had incited the Indians to "mutiny" (*K istorii Rossiisko-Amerikanskoi*, 1957:134). Later, the official RAC historian, Tikhmenev, also blamed Captain Barber for the Indian revolt, but there was never any real evidence of his participation (other than "hearsay") (Tikhmenev 1861:1:89). Soviet historians maintain their suspicion of Barber (Bolkhovitinov 1966:312; Pasetskii 1970:17), and in the popular literature they often call him a "base and cunning pirate and slave trader" (Paseniuk 1985:94). Although Barber will never be canonized a saint, he was nevertheless not a pirate and did not incite the Indians to revolt. The American captain Cunningham, whose conduct during the Sitka events merits the most severe censure, was in fact a participant in this plot. Cunningham incited the Indians to destroy the Russian hunting party and Fort Mikhailovskii, then, after its destruction, he, Captain Barber, and Captain Ebbets exacted terrible punishment on the Tlingit.

News of the fall of Fort Mikhailovskii reached Kuskov during a hunt at Chichagof Island, forcing Kuskov to hasten his return to Yakutat. He feared that the colony in Yakutat might share the fate of Fort Mikhailovskii. And,

History of Tlingit Relations in Russian America

indeed, on reaching Yakutat he found a multitude of warriors from the Akoi k̲wáan who, as soon as the party arrived, immediately departed to their settlements. According to Khlebnikov, the Tlingit had gathered to attack the fort and settlement the following night, but the party's arrival forced them to abandon the attack (Khlebnikov 1861:53). The destruction of Fort Mikhailovskii panicked the colonists of Yakutat, who almost left for Kodiak. Only Kuskov's persuasion and their lack of sea transport prevented their abrupt departure. Having left two promyshlenniki and about twenty Kodiak in Yakutat to strengthen the local garrison, Kuskov decided to disband the "main" party. At the same time, he sent letters reporting everything he heard to Konstantinovskii and Nikolaevskii redoubts, suggesting that additional precautionary measures be taken against the possible uprising of the local Chugach Eskimos and Ahtna and Tanaina Indians.

What reasons prompted the Indians to take up arms in 1802? The primary reason for the Tlingit revolt lies in the clash between the Indians' and the Russian-American Company's economic interests, which Aleksei A. Istomin (1985:147) has noted. In Tlingit aboriginal territorial waters, the partovshchiki, led by Russians, intensively exploited sea otters, the skins of which were the primary article of Indian trade with the English and American fur traders. This exploitation was the reason for the Indians' discontent, which the Indian chiefs emphasized as being primary during negotiations with Kuskov at the mouth of the Alsek River in 1802 (*K istorii Rossiisko-Amerikanskoi*, 1957:107), when the latter, at the head of the hunting party, set out into the straits of the Alexander Archipelago. It was no accident that the astute Baranov, before the hunting party left in 1802, advised Kuskov to pass by the Tlingit villages with the partovshchiki either early in the morning or in the evening, in order to avoid again provoking the Indians by the sight of others hunting in their waters (OR GBL, f. 204, k. 32, ed. khr. no. 5, l. 60b.).

The Indians were dissatisfied because the Aleut partovshchiki, relying on their greater numbers and the Russian leader's deceit, plundered Indian graves, acts that the Tlingit chiefs discussed with Kuskov during negotiations held on the Alsek River. It is quite probable that the partovshchiki also plundered the stores of dried fish that the Indians had prepared for winter. In any case, in one of his instructions to Kuskov, Baranov demanded that he forbid the partovshchiki from plundering the Indians' food supplies while hunting in the straits (OR GBL, f. 204, k. 32, ed. khr. no. 4, l. 290b.).

Disdainful treatment from some of the Russian promyshlenniki also dissatisfied the Indians. The naval officer Gavriil I. Davydov, who visited Russian America during these years, wrote: "The manners of the Russians in Sitka were not such as to make the Koliuzhi think highly of them, because the hunters began to take the young women from them and commit other offenses against them. Neighboring Koliuzhi blamed the Sitkans for permitting a small number of Russians to dominate them and ultimately turning themselves into slaves. They advised them to kill the hunters and promised to give the necessary aid for this" (Davydov 1812:2:110). In fact, Tlingit legends report that in the early 1800s one Indian from the Sitka Kiks.ádi lineage was mocked during a potlatch in Chilkat. The other Tlingit pointed to the Russians' disgracing his clan. This insult, they say, incited the Kiks.ádi to fight and caused them to attack the Russian fort (Kan 1989:225).

In the opinion of some modern Tlingit, Tlingit enmity toward the Russians arose when the Russians took Indian women as wives without bestowing the traditional gifts on the relatives (Jacobs 1990:4). According to Captain William Sturgis, the Russians at Sitka killed several Indians, whether for real reasons or because they imagined them to be part of a conspiracy, and seized others and sent them to Kodiak, despite the local Indians' own peaceful conduct. It is natural that the captives' and executed persons' friends and relatives thirsted for vengeance against the new arrivals at Sitka (Sturgis 1978:123, 125).

K. T. Khlebnikov wrote that the reason for the "exasperation of the Kolosh" was that the Koniag (not the Russians) had allegedly killed up to ten Tlingit during altercations (Khlebnikov 1861:55). In Kan's (1999:60) opinion, the reason that the Aleuts and Koniag had killed several eminent Tlingit in 1801 was to avenge the loss of their own people who had died of food poisoning from tainted mollusks in 1799, which they ascribed to the sorcery of the Sitka people. Regarding this incident, a scholar referred to the well-known July 1, 1802, letter written by I. A. Kuskov to Baranov, in which the reasons for the Indians' dissatisfaction were enumerated (*K istorii Rossiisko-Amerikanskoi*, 1957:120). In Kuskov's report he actually speaks of the murder of several Indians who were not Sitkas but rather the family of the chief of the Kuiu ḵwáan, who could hardly have had any relation to the Native party members lost in 1799.

Other scholars have made additional attempts to find motives for the Tlingit's actions against the Russians. One theory is that the promyshlenniki's urge to exploit independent Indians as they had earlier done in the Aleutian Islands was a contributing factor (Crass 1992:410; Polevoi and Okladnikova 1994:73). Another, entirely fantastic theory holds that the Tlingit's indignation was provoked by the Russians' delivering copper emblems of the Russian Empire to the Tlingit chiefs, which (according to the Indians' totemic beliefs) allegedly attracted corresponding economic privileges in relations with the Russians (Dzeniskevich 1992:70–71). Whereas the latter theory does not accurately reflect the Tlingit's religious views (see Grinev 1995:120–121), the former theory cannot be corroborated by primary sources. For the most part, the promyshlenniki at Sitka and the RAC simply did not have sufficient power to force the bellicose and well-armed Indians into slavery. The notion that they would do so directly contradicted Baranov's instructions on relating with the Sitka people (*K istorii Rossiisko-Amerikanskoi*, 1957:96).

In enumerating the reasons for the Indian insurrection of 1802, it must not be forgotten that the Indians themselves would not have minded plundering Fort Mikhailovskii and demonstrating their fighting prowess. The desire to loot, for example, was the chief motive for the Tlingit attack on Baranov's camp in Chugach Bay in 1792 (Tikhmenev 1863:2:Append. 35–47).

Another reason for the Indians' animosity was the anti-Russian agitation of several American traders. In his report to Baranov, Kuskov mentioned an American vessel that wintered over from 1801 to 1802 at the Tlingit village of Kootznahoo, the crew of which directly appealed to the Tlingit to destroy Fort Mikhailovskii, extorting the Indians by assuring them that American ships would stop coming to them because the sea otters would soon be exterminated by the Aleut hunting parties and so there would be no furs to trade (*K istorii Rossiisko-Amerikanskoi*, 1957:119). F. I. Shemelin, a manager of the Russian-American Company who took part in the round-the-world voyage of the sloop *Nadezhda* between 1803 and 1806, wrote, "The ship *Globus*, Captain Kiunnen-Zhein, wintered over under the Kootznahoo village" (Shemelin 1818:2:334). The American historian Frederick W. Howay notes the ship *Globe* (*Globus*) from Boston on his list of ships that traded on the Northwest Coast. This ship actually visited the Northwest Coast between 1801 and 1802; its captain, Bernard Magee, was killed in October 1801 by Haida Indians, and the first mate, W. Cunningham, assumed his position (Howay 1973:45).

The official documents of the Russian-American Company and some of its representatives usually identified foreign agitation as the main reason for the Indian uprising of 1802 (*K istorii Rossiisko-Amerikanskoi*, 1957:134; Tikhmenev 1861:1:89). Thus, the former head of the Novo-Arkhangel'sk office of the RAC, K. T. Khlebnikov, wrote:

> The exasperation of these peoples is the product of enlightened envy. The fiend of greed and other base vices was revived among foreigners trading in the straits. They saw that with the occupation by the Russians of Sitka Island they would lose a large number of their advantages because the Aleuts, in comparison with the Koloshi, in essence were the most excellent hunters and the catch of beavers

[sea otters] produced thousands annually; without their participation these thousands would fall into the hands of foreigners. This was the first and most powerful reason to arouse envy in the hearts of the greedy (Khlebnikov 1861:54).

It was advantageous for the company to accuse their trading competitors of instigating the Indian revolt because they could thus secure government aid and privileges. Later, this claim passed from the documents of the RAC and the works of its historians into the works of several prominent contemporary researchers (Bolkhovitinov 1966:311–312; Fedorova 1971:124; Okun' 1939:52; Pasetskii 1970:17). However, one cannot agree with this claim, for even though individual foreign captains agitated against the Russians and sold firearms to the Indians, foreign interference was not the chief reason for the Tlingit revolt. Foreign skippers' appeals could not, by themselves, rally independent Tlingit ḵwáans and induce them to an insurrection against the Russians. Firearms were a more effective means of fighting but by no means the reason for the uprising. Besides, the majority of English and American captains was neutral toward or spoke benevolently of the Russians, which was noted by one of the Russian-American Company's directors, Matvei I. Murav'ev (Narochnitskii 1963–1985:Ser. II, t. V, s. 87–88).

The above reasons for the revolt resulted in unprecedented cooperation among communities and clans previously hostile toward one another. It was not only the Tlingit who took part in the "conspiracy" but also, evidently, the Kaigani Haida and even some Tsimshian Indians. Kuskov managed to learn from the Yakutat Tlingit that in the winter of 1801–02 the chiefs of almost all the Tlingit ḵwáans went to the village of Kootznahoo on Admiralty Island (where the American ship *Globe* wintered over) to plan the attack on Fort Mikhailovskii and the hunting party. Among the so-called conspiracy's participants were, Kuskov reported, the chiefs of "a large island, called Tykinna, near Bobrovyi Beaver Bay toward the Charlotte Islands" (*K istorii Rossiisko-Amerikanskoi*, 1957:119). These were probably the Indian chiefs from Prince of Wales Island. Among the southern Tlingit this island was known as Tan—"Island of the Sea Lion" (Olson 1967:3). It must be assumed that Kuskov's informants—Yakutat people (northern Tlingit)—might not have known this name; they called the island "Dekina" ("Tykinna"), according to the ethnonym of the Kaigani Haida living there. As De Laguna notes, the Yakutat Tlingit could also have used this term ("Dekina") in regard to Tlingit of the Henya ḵwáan—neighbors of the Kaigani Haida (De Laguna 1972:1:216). Kaigani participation in the revolt in 1802 could have been provoked by the murder of a

"Tykinna" toion's sister, the wife of a chief of the Kuiu ḵwáan, by partovshchiki of the "Sitka" party (*K istorii Rossiisko-Amerikanskoi*, 1957:120). Khlebnikov's claim that the Haida from the Queen Charlotte Islands participated in the "conspiracy" against the Russians is doubtful, since the Russians did not hunt around these islands during these years (Khlebnikov 1861:53).

In the winter of 1801–02 "conspiracy," not only did the Tlingit take part— as in all probability did the Kaigani Haida—but those mentioned in Kuskov's report, the "peoples of the special talk, neighbors of the Stikinsk [Stikine people, Tlingit of the Stikine ḵwáan], called Chuchkan" (*K istorii Rossiisko-Amerikanskoi*, 1957:118) also probably participated. De Laguna claims the name of a Tlingit village of the Henya ḵwáan on Kosciusko Island—Shakan—is derived from the word *chuchkan* (De Laguna 1972:1:171). However, such an interpretation is probably incorrect. The word *tsutskan*, as cited by Kuskov, is not a toponym but rather an ethnonym, and we find it in another section of De Laguna's work: tsutskan—so the Tlingit denoted the Tsimshian Indians, who live south along the coast (De Laguna 1972:1:216). Kuskov's claim that the Chuchkan spoke a special language, distinct from Tlingit, corroborates that they were Tsimshian.

Many details of the 1802 events require reevaluation and refinement inasmuch as the sources are frequently incomplete and contradictory. The literature lacks analysis of the documents and sources (an exception is Dauenhauer and Dauenhauer 1987b), and rather uncritical borrowing results in factual errors. [20] In several sources, as well as in some of the scholarly literature, the year of the attack on Fort Mikhailovskii is incorrectly given as 1801 (Davydov 1810:1:109; Drucker 1955:113; 1965:205; Narochnitskii 1963–1985:Ser. I, t. VII, s. 396; Okun' 1939:196) or 1804 (Kotzebue 1987:207; Whymper 1966:73).

Several researchers note that the precise date of the attack on the Russian fort on Sitka Island is still unknown (Andrews 1967:51; Bancroft 1970:402; Hulley 1953:125). In fact the sources disagree as to the exact date. A. Plotnikov, an eyewitness to the events, said that the Indians attacked the fort "about the 24th" (Tikhmenev 1863:2:Append. 174). The attack occurred on June 18 or 19, according to Khlebnikov (1861:45). However, analysis of Kuskov's report shows that Plotnikov and Khlebnikov both gave incorrect dates. According to one of the Kodiak who escaped, he set out with Kochesov's party to shoot sea lions on June 10. After being gone for about a week, that is, until June 17 or 18, Kochesov's party returned to the fort and picked up one of the Kodiak who had remained at the colony and who reported that "yesterday," that is, June 16 (or 17), the Indians destroyed Fort Mikhailovskii. The fort could not have been seized on June 24, as Plotnikov reported, inasmuch as on June 20 baidarkas sent by Kuskov brought news of the attack (*K istorii Rossiisko-Amerikanskoi*, 1957:114, 121).

Only Lisianskii tried to determine the number of Indians who attacked Fort Mikhailovskii, ascertaining that there had been 600 (Lisianskii 1812:138). This number was subsequently used by other authors (Gibson 1979:12; Krause 1956:31; Lazarev 1832:156); however, it is dubious. According to Plotnikov, 62 war canoes came from behind the cape to help the "multitude" of Indians attacking from land (Tikhmenev 1863:2:Append. 174). Putting aside the assumption that there was an average of 15 to 20 men in each canoe (large war canoes held up to 60 men), then no fewer than a thousand warriors took part in the sea-based attack. The total number of Indians who attacked the fort was, in this author's view, closer to 1,500. This is also indirectly corroborated by Khlebnikov, who wrote that the "number of those who attacked can be assumed without exaggeration to be more than a thousand men" (Khlebnikov 1861:47). In light of what has been said, some American researchers' contention that only members of the Sitka Kiks.ádi lineage participated in the attack on the Russian fort is doubtful (Dean 1994:3; Jacobs 1990:3). Though this was one of the most significant lineages, it was scarcely in a position to send more than 15 hundred warriors to battle. Whereas, in her earlier works, F. De Laguna (1960:145–148; 1972:1:172) also assumed that the Sitka Kiks.ádi played the main role in destroying the Russian fort, in later commentaries on G. T. Emmons's work (1991:327) she acknowledges that the Henya, Stikine, Kuiu, Kake, and other Tlingit k̲wáans helped develop the plan of attack.[21]

The Americans supported the Indians, and not just by supplying arms and ammunition. A whole series of early authors mentions the fact that two or three American sailors took part in storming Fort Mikhailovskii (Davydov 1812:2:110; Lazarev 1832:15; Lisianskii 1812:133). This controversial issue has seen practically no research. For example, in the English historian E. Sipes's opinion (1998:42–43) between 7 and 20(!) American sailors, along with a thousand Koloshi, participated in the attack on Sitka. It is known that 13 men deserted the American ship *Hancock* under the command of Captain Crocker during a stop in Sitka Bay in May 1799. In the next several days six of the deserters returned, while seven sailors remained among the Indians (Howay 1973:38–39). Baranov soon took five, and possibly all seven, American sailors into the service of the RAC when, in July 1799, he founded Fort Mikhailovskii on Sitka. Khlebnikov wrote that 11 men had gotten off the American ship; 3 of them came to Baranov, who hired them, while the others remained among the Indians (Khlebnikov 1861:44). However, these data do not agree with the materials of primary sources: no fewer than five American sailors were taken into the service of the RAC. It is true that several more sailors—deserters from Captain Crocker's other ship—the *Jenny*, which visited Sitka in the spring of 1802—could have accepted jobs from the Russians (Howay 1973:50). According to the American captain William Sturgis, the local Indians well understood the difference between their trading friends—the Americans— and the Russian oppressors and so invited the deserters into their village. Some Americans accepted the Tlingit's friendly invitation, while others set off hunting with the Kodiak party. In the Indian village, the Tlingit revealed their intention to attack Fort Mikhailovskii to the American sailors and asked for their help, but the sailors claimed that, naturally, they had refused. In order that the Russians not learn about the intended attack, the Tlingit detained the Americans until the assault had begun, and then released the men to the arriving English and American ships (Sturgis 1978:123–124).

According to Russian sources, the American sailors remaining among the Tlingit were distributed in the following way: one of them (an American originally from Portugal) was sent with the Ivan Urbanov party to Frederick Strait, three others were in the Vasilii Kochesov party hunting sea lions in the vicinity of Fort Mikhailovskii, and another was in the fort itself during the Indians' attack (*K istorii Rossiisko-Amerikanskoi*, 1957:114; Tikhmenev 1863:2:Append. 179). All the men presumably perished during the Indian attacks. But there remain two or more American sailors, evidently from the *Jenny*, who could have joined the Tlingit and taken part in the storming of the Russian fort, but we do not have direct evidence of this. According to the American sailors' own reports, the Tlingit, using force and threats, compelled the sailors to participate in the attack (Pierce 1990:26). According to Russian sources, the sailors volunteered and, before the attack, even instructed the Indians on the weaknesses in the defense of the fort—a likely scenario (Davydov 1812:2:111; RGA VMF, f. 15, op. 1, d. 8, l. 1820b.). Of the seven or more American sailors who stormed the fort, three managed to escape (according to other data, six escaped) (Bancroft 1970:408–409).

The RAC directors were pleased to support the version of events that claimed that American sailors participated in the seizure of Fort Mikhailovskii. Referring to Baranov, they wrote: "The reason for both this misfortune and aid were the Boston ships of the skippers Crocker and Cunningham with their crews, since they not only incited the islanders [Tlingit Indians] to their behavior but traded gunpowder and arms to them, and later, when the Russians were destroyed, they took all the trade from the savages, which consisted of 3700 sea otters and other animals" (Narochnitskii 1963–1985:Ser. I, t. IV, s. 242).

John Crocker himself had visited Sitka for the second time shortly before the *Jenny*'s tragedy (in 1799 Crocker commanded the *Hancock*). Regarding sales of weapons to the Indians, practically all foreign traders who visited Southeast Alaska sold the Natives firearms; to accuse only these two captains would be absurd. The valuable furs plundered by the Indians in Fort Mikhailovskii were taken not by Crocker and Cunningham but by the English adventurer Barber. In general, it should be noted that the RAC board of directors' documents often abound in factual errors and bias.

Also contradictory and imprecise is the evidence regarding the number who perished in and the number rescued from the attack. According to Khlebnikov, the total number of Russians and hunting partovshchiki who perished was more than 200 (Khlebnikov 1861:50–51). The documents support this number. According to this author's calculation, during the insurrection, 24 Russians (including the creole Vasilii Kochesov) and about two hundred partovshchiki perished; of those in Sitka, 23 Russians and 20 to 30 Kodiak were killed (AVPR, f. RAK, op. 888, d. 170, l. 4–40b.; *K istorii Rossiisko-Amerikanskoi*, 1957:106–123; Tikhmenev 1963:2:Append. 174–180) (Table 4). However, many researchers use Tikhmenev's imprecise data in their descriptions of Russian losses at Sitka; Tikhmenev wrote that a total of 20 Russians and 130 partovshchiki perished at Sitka (Alekseev 1975:141; Alekseeva 1998:42; Bolkhovitinov 1966:311; Gibson 1976:14, 1979:12; Krause 1956:31; Pasetskii 1970:17; Roppel 1992:306; Sipes 1998:42–43; Tikhmenev 1861:1:88). Such a number of party members was not at Fort Mikhailovskii on the day of the Tlingit attack—almost all of them were more than a hundred kilometers away, near Frederick Strait, with the "Sitka" party. In the fort itself, there evidently remained several *kaiury* and sick party members. Apparently, Tikhmenev underestimated the total losses among the sick party members. However, several researchers cite clearly exaggerated or simply fantastic data. Some of them write that as a result of the Indian uprising only 45 of 250 Russians escaped (Manning 1953:45). Others report losses of 100 Russians and more than 200 Aleuts (Gibson 1976:14, *Istoriia Russkoi Ameriki*, 1999:2:176). Still others inform us that the Indians killed 408 of 450 defenders at Fort Mikhailovskii and later killed 200 more Aleut hunting party members (Barratt 1981:125; Chevigny 1965:101; Hunt 1976:26). Finally, Dzeniskevich and *Pod flagom Rossii* claim that all the residents of the Russian colony, including women and children, were killed (Dzeniskevich 1992:66; *Pod flagom Rossii*, 1995:184), which is completely untrue.

Data on the number of survivors at Fort Mikhailovskii are fragmentary. According to Rezanov, Barber brought 26 persons whom he had rescued to

Kodiak, 3 of them Russians (AVPRI, f. Gl. arkhiv 1–7, 1802 g., d. 1, papka no. 35, l. 240b.). Barber himself reported that he saved 28 people: 8 men (3 of them Russians), 17 women, and 3 children (Shuhmacher 1979:60). According to Khlebnikov's report, Barber rescued 23 persons. In addition, Khlebnikov wrote that of the "Sitka" party 23 persons were rescued, that is, a total of 46 persons. However, on this same page the author says that 42 persons were rescued (Khlebnikov 1861:50–51). Tikhmenev claims 32 people were saved (3 Russians, 5 Kodiak, and 18 women and 6 children [Tikhmenev 1861:88]). In addition, of the "Sitka" party, its leader, Ivan Urbanov, and 22 Kodiak escaped and eventually managed to reach Yakutat in August. Later, American traders ransomed the creole Afonasii Kochesov, who had been in the "Sitka" party, from Indian slavery and delivered him to the Russians (AGO, razr. 99, op. 1, d. 113, l. 530b.). At the same time, quite a few people (primarily women and children) remained in Tlingit hands. Some of them were not released until 1804, while others, for example, two creole children (mestizos) remained among the Indians—their descendants still live in Alaska (Dauenhauer and Dauenhauer 1990b:14).

Fort Mikhailovskii's seizure by the Indians and the "Sitka" party's destruction dealt a heavy blow to the Russian colonies in America. The richest hunting territories, which provided thousands of sea otter furs in a season, were lost. The great human, material, and financial losses significantly weakened the Russian-American Company and affected the tempo and intensity of the Russians' opening of Alaska. The Tlingit insurrection "moved" the border of the Russian Empire north to Yakutat for two years. Baranov wrote that, because of the loss of Sitka, advancing southward would be impossible, and if a second conquest of the island was not undertaken at once then the whole region of the Alexander Archipelago might slip from Russian control (*K istorii Rossiisko-Amerikanskoi*, 1957:125).

As for the Tlingit, almost all their k̲wáans united to expel the common enemy for the first time. The 1802 insurrection rallied Indians across a territory of about 120 thousand square kilometers with a population of no fewer than ten thousand persons. This was perhaps the largest Native revolt in the history of Russian America. In this connection, one cannot agree with the American ethnographer G. Turner's assertion that the Northwest Coast saw no wars between the Indians and whites (Turner 1979:217).

Table 4. Those Serving the RAC at Fort Mikhailovskii, the "Sitka party," and the Party of V. Kochesov in 1802

"Register of those who died, drowned, and were killed, copied from the last report from Kodiak Island from the chief director master of the collegiate councilor Baranov of the 20th of June 1803" (AVPR, f. RAK, op. 888, d. 170. I. 4–4ob.)	"Stories" of Abrosim Plotnikov (Tikhmenev 1863:174–78)	"Stories" of Katerin Pinnuin (Tikhmenev 1863:2:178–80)	"1802 July 1. Report of I. Kuskov to Baranov in Kodiak . . ." (K istorii Rossiisko-Amerikunskoi 1957:106–123)
1	2	3	4
At Fort Mikhailovskii			
1. Medvednikov, Vasilii Grigor'evich[a]	"	"	"
2. Nakvasin, Prokhor[b]	"	"	"
3. Kuz'michev, Prokopii	"	"	"
4. Zokhtin, Dmitrii	Izokhtin	Izokhtin	
5. Kabakakov, Kharlampii	Kabanov	Kabanov	
6. Rybolov, Egor		"	
7. Pikunyrov, Mikhailo		Pinunyrov	
8. Ovdin, Emel'ian		"	
9. Machul'skii, Kondratii		Machul'skoi	
10. Shanin, Andrei		Shanin	
11. Tiumakaev, Grigorii		Tumakaev	
12. Smirnoi, Nikolai		"	
13. Chiupriianovskii, Andrei		"	
14. Lebedev, Zakhar		"	
15. Martynov, Stepan		"	
16. Chiumliakov, Nikifor		"	
17. Shemelin, Afonasii		"	
18. Malan'in, Ivan (a Kungur peasant)		Kungur	
19. Gerasim, Klokhtin			
20.	Plotnikov[c]	Plotnikov	
21.	Taradanov[c]	"Englishmen"	
In the "Sitka" Party			
1.	Urbanov (Ivan)[c]		Urbanov
2. Karpov, Aleksei	"		"
3.	Kochesov (Afonasii)[c]		"
4.			"Englishmen"
In the Kochesov Party			
1.	Kochesov (Vasilii)		—
2. Kuninovskii, Lev	"		"
3. Evglevskii, Aleksei	"		"
4. Zyrianov, Vasilii	"		"
5.	Baturin (Aleksei)[c]		Three "Englishmen"

[a]Commander of Fort Mikhailovskii.

[b]Deputy to Medvednikov, "head" of the artel of *promyshlenniki*.

[c]People who fled with the Tlingit attack.

3.2. Second Founding of a Colony on Sitka Island (1804)

Baranov did not have the means and people to retake Sitka immediately. In addition, the Yakutat Tlingit were again unstable. So in 1803 Baranov himself went to Yakutat. Here he strengthened the garrison (about a hundred Russians and approximately as many partovshchiki, kaiury, and *kaiurki* stayed with the settlers that winter), laid the keel for two small ships (*Ermak* and *Rostislav*), and departed for Kodiak, having left Kuskov "instructions" concerning the "*akoitsy*."[22] Baranov recommended to Kuskov that, in case the latter undertook hostile activities, he should organize a land warfare expedition against them (employing 70 Russians and 6 light cannons) (Berkh 1823:151; OR GBL, f. 204, k. 32, ed. khr. no. 4, l. 15–21ob.).

Almost two years passed between Fort Mikhailovskii's fall and Baranov's gathering sufficient forces to restore the fort at Sitka. In the campaign against the *Koloshi*, 120 Russians and 900 partovshchiki in 400 baidarkas were mobilized (Lisianskii 1812:15). The party was accompanied by two small ships (two more were sent directly to Sitka), while in Yakutat a large number of handguns were distributed to the partovshchiki, and Baranov's flotilla was sent south.

The unstable union of the Tlingit ḵwáans had apparently already disintegrated. Old interclan and intercommunity enmity defeated the weak coalition in the face of an imminent attack. The first to secede from the union were the Tlingit of the Akoi and Hoonah ḵwáans, which lived closest to Yakutat and could be the first targets of a Russian military expedition. The Indians of these ḵwáans therefore sent their envoys to Baranov to negotiate a truce. Evidently contributing to the success of the negotiations was the fact that the Russians succeeded in taking a son of one of the primary chiefs of the Akoi ḵwáan, Chesnyga, as an amanat[23] (OR GBL, f. 204, k. 32, ed. khr. no. 4, l. 16, 21–21ob., 25).

The Indians of the other ḵwáans were unable to unite when, in June 1804, Baranov's flotilla proceeded into the straits of the Alexander Archipelago. The course of the flotilla did not take it directly to Sitka but rather took it in a large arc past the territory of many ḵwáans (see map). This, it must be assumed, was not an accident: the governor wanted to demonstrate, as much as possible, Russian military might and its power to subdue large numbers of "rebels." Having learned of the Russians' approach, the Indians of individual villages, not strong enough to oppose Baranov's flotilla on their own, left their homes and hid in the woods. The Russians did not linger in the abandoned villages. Only the homes and fortifications of the Kake-Kuiu ḵwáan were

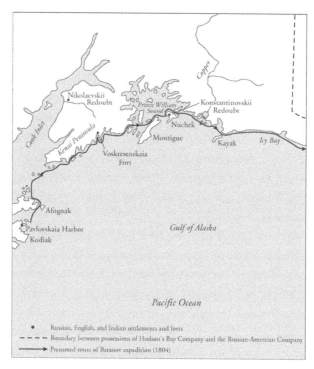

Map 4. Russian, English, and Indian Settlements

burned, this because their warriors had played the chief role in destroying the
"Sitka" party in 1802 (Khlebnikov 1835:81–82; Tikhmenev 1863:2:Append. 183).
Arriving in Sitka, Baranov met the sloop *Neva*, which, under the command of
Yurii F. Lisianskii, was circling the world. The arrival of even a small warship
substantially strengthened Baranov's flotilla.

The Sitka <u>kw</u>áan village on the shore was abandoned, and Baranov occupied
it (September 18), having decided to found a new fort here that later became
the capital of Russian America and was named Novo-Arkhangel'sk. The Sitka
people built a new fort near their old village, fortified it with a palisade, and
equipped it with falconets. The new fort was called Shiksi Noow ("Fort of the
Young Tree," or "Sapling Fort") (Jacobs 1990:4; Kan 1999:63). They evidently
intended to defend this fort with all force and, requiring gunpowder, they
sent a large canoe to Kootznahoo for it. On the return trip the canoe was
intercepted by the *Neva*'s launch and, during a skirmish that occurred along
the way, was blown up when the gunpowder it was carrying ignited (Lisianskii
1812:20). This episode was reflected in a Sitka Kiks.ádi clan mourning song for
the son who perished in the explosion (Olson 1967:45). Most of the Tlingit

History of Tlingit Relations in Russian America

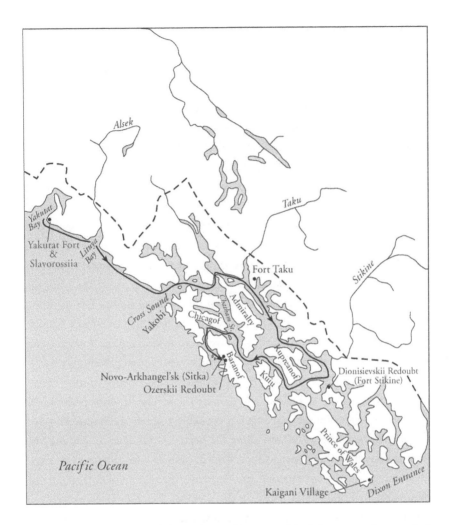

in the canoe drowned, while six (according to archival data, seven) wounded warriors were captured by the Russians (AVPR, f. Gl. arkhiv, 1–13, 1805–1808 gg., d. 12, l. 2; Khlebnikov 1835:83–84; Lisianskii 1812:20). Two of the captured soon died of their wounds, and the remaining were sent to Kodiak on the *Neva*. Khlebnikov wrote that Baranov gave special directions to the Kodiak office of the RAC concerning the Tlingit: "Send them out to distant artels and use them in work just as Aleut workers, and in case of mischief penalize them; however, give them shoes and clothe them" (Khlebnikov 1835:89).

Having been deprived of the gunpowder, the Indians sought peace. However, lengthy negotiations came to a dead end inasmuch as the Sitka people neither freed the captive Kodiak nor gave reliable amanaty, and defied Baranov in refusing to surrender their fort. In addition, on September 24 the Tlingit seized a baidarka and killed two Kodiak partovshchiki. Therefore, Baranov decided to take the fort by storm (its defense was led by Katlian, chief of the Sitka Kiks.ádi).

On October 1, 1804, the Russian ships drew up to the Tlingit fort and began to fire on it. Simultaneously, a party of sailors led by Lieutenant P. Arbuzov disembarked from the *Neva* (with a cannon). At this time Baranov and Lieutenant P. Povalishin led the Russians and partovshchiki, who with the support of four guns approached the fort from the other side. The Tlingit answered fire from the ships and cannons with a strong volley from rifles and falconets. In spite of the hostile fire, the Russians' guns managed to draw up to the fort's gates and storm them. However, when the Indians increased their fire, the Kodiak and some Russians, unable to endure it, retreated. The Tlingit, seeing this, opened the gates and rushed to the attack. Lisianskii ordered increased fire from the ship's artillery to protect Baranov and Arbuzov as they retreated. The storming of the Indian fort thus ended in failure. According to Indian traditions, Katlian again demonstrated his outstanding bravery, overwhelming the Russians and their Native "slaves" in hand-to-hand combat (Jacobs 1990:5; Kan 1999:63).

The next day the Tlingit, encouraged by their success, opened cannon fire on the Russian ships but were unable to damage them. The Russians periodically returned fire. The Indian fort, having probably realized the hopelessness of a long resistance, began negotiations for peace on October 3, sending the Russians amanaty (hostages) and the Kodiak captives over the next few days. However, evidently not trusting the Russians, the Tlingit fled through the mountains to Kootznahoo Strait on the night of October 7, having left the fort to the victors. [24] The next day Partovshchiki pillaged the fort and, on orders from Baranov, burned it (Lisianskii 1812:26–27). Two falconets and up to 20 canoes were seized by the Russians. Only two old women and several dead children, probably of slaves, were found in the fort (Lisianskii 1812:29–30). However, in Kan's opinion, these were not slaves but rather the children of free Indians, who by their cries were able to help the Sitka people secretly leave their fort by making the Russians think that the fort was still occupied. [25] The decision to leave the children behind, Kan points out, had a most negative effect on the reputation of the influential Sitka Kiks.ádi lineage. The murder of children and death of relatives in the clash with the Russians engendered harsh criticism from the Kiks.ádi's in-laws—the Sitka Kaagwaantaan—inasmuch as

History of Tlingit Relations in Russian America

the mothers of the murdered children belonged primarily to that lineage. The Kiks.ádi, according to Tlingit custom, were obliged to compensate the Kaagwaantaan for their losses, but they were not able to do this; therefore, the Kaagwaantaan later acquired the right to claim substantial natural resources from the Kiks.ádi, who were Sitka's initial settlers (Kan 1999:64, 74; see also Sturgis 1978:126).

The source material disagrees on several details about the above events, especially those concerning the date that Baranov and Arbuzov stormed the Indian fort. Lisianskii gives the date as October 1 (possibly Gregorian calendar) (Lisianskii 1812:22), whereas Baranov and Khlebnikov mention September 20 (Khlebnikov 1835:84–85; Tikhmenev 1863:2:Append. 184), and Langsdorff gives August 19 (Langsdorff 1812:2:74). There is also disagreement regarding the number of persons inside the Indian "garrison," or the number of persons each side lost in this clash. In Lisianskii's opinion, there were no fewer than 800 men in the fort (Lisianskii 1812:31). N. I. Korobitsyn, another eyewitness to the storming of the fort, believed that there were no more than 400 people in the fort (but does not indicate whether this was the total population, or only the number of warriors) (Andreev 1944:183). Langsdorff, and later Kotzebue, wrote that the Indian fort was defended by 300 warriors and their families (Kotzebue 1987:207; Langsdorff 1812:2:74). The discrepancy in the data on the Russian and partovshchiki losses during the storming can be seen in Table 5.

No one knows how many Tlingit died during the siege. Lisianskii suggested that their losses were insignificant (Lisianskii 1812:30), whereas archival documents reveal that "the Koliuzhi, who received severe damage and injury to its people, left the fort at night, leaving as well their military supplies" (AVPR, f. Gl. arkhiv 1–13, 1805–1808 gg., d. 12, l. 5). K. T. Khlebnikov reported 30 Indians killed at the walls of the fort, but whether these were Tlingit warriors who died fighting or slaves killed while fleeing is unclear (Khlebnikov 1835:87). According to the Tlingit, they lost many people to hunger and cold when they fled through the forest and mountains. In particular, many old people and children of the Sitka Kiks.ádi perished (Dauenhauer and Dauenhauer 1987b:7).

All these questions need further investigation because the Sitka event of 1804, being a central episode in Russian American history, is of interest to both historians and ethnographers. In a number of serious historical works, the writer relies on only one source to describe these events, and thus relies on inaccurate information.[26]

The Russians' second settling in Sitka was significant for the Russian colonies. Novo-Arkhangel'sk became the most important support point for the

Table 5. Russian Losses in the Clash with the Tlingit in 1804, by Source

Participants in the storming	A. A. Baranov (Tikhmenev 1863:2:Pril. 184)	Lisianskii (1812:24)	N. I. Korobitsyn (Andreev 1944:182)	von Langsdorff (1812:2:74)	Khlebnikov (1835:86)	Tikhmenev (1861:1:107)
Russian *promyshlenniki*		3/?[a]	4/?	3/?	3/9	?/9
Sailors of the *Neva*	8/many	3/several	3.12	3/?	3/2	3/3
Partovshchiki	4/many	Several/?	10/several	Several/?	4/6[a]	?/several

Note: Numerators indicate the dead; denominators, the wounded.

[a] According to Khlebnikov (1979:25), 16 Kodiak perished during the conquest of Sitka.

Russians in Tlingit territory and served as a "springboard" for their further advancement to the south—to California. The exploitation of sea otters continued in the straits of the Alexander Archipelago. The Sitka's defeat forced the Indians to abandon large-scale confrontations with the Russians for a time (Lisianskii 1812:33–34). In October a representative of the Kootznahoo ķwáan, to whose land the Sitkans had gone, came to the Russians with a peace proposal. According to Yu. F. Lisianskii, the envoy, clearly contemptuous of the Sitkans, asked Baranov to allow his relatives to enslave them. Lisianskii quoted the Indians as saying: "In ķutsnov Kootznahoo they have such great disdain for them [the Sitkans] that their name was turned into an invective or a defamation, so that if any child plays a prank, they say to him: 'You're as stupid as a Sitkan'" (Lisianskii 1812:32–33). The arrival of the envoy, and his rhetoric, resulted because he and his relatives seriously feared that the Russians would continue to pursue the Sitkans and, consequently, the Kootznahoo people might become an object of a Russian punitive expedition for sheltering the runaways. However, Baranov diplomatically stated that he was not prepared to interfere in the internal affairs of the Indians: his main concern at the moment was building a new Russian settlement and organizing hunting in the straits of the Alexander Archipelago, for which peace was necessary.

The news of Baranov's second establishment at Sitka quickly spread among the Northwest Coast Indians, and Baranov's authority rapidly grew.[27] By the spring of 1805 the celebrated chief of the Kaigani, Kau, had sent his son to Novo-Arkhangel'sk specifically to meet Baranov and establish friendly relations with him. The Haida from the Queen Charlotte Islands invited Baranov to visit to trade (AVPR, f. Gl. arkhiv 1–7, 1802 g., d. 1, papka no. 35, l. 90b., 49). Fearing the "terrible" (to them) Baranov, and inspired by the effectiveness of the Sitkas' fort, the Tlingit near Sitka undertook to fortify their villages, erecting palisades and falconets purchased from American traders (Tikhmenev 1863:2:Append. 282–283). The Sitka people established themselves on the eastern shore of Sitka Island, where they constructed the sturdy new fort Chatlk-nu ("Fort of Small Halibut") (Dauenhauer and Dauenhauer 1987b:7). After their expulsion from Sitka Bay, they occasionally sent scouts to observe the Russians' construction of Novo-Arkhangel'sk. Neither side took aggressive action; only a careless Kodiak at the ruins of Fort Mikhailovskii was shot by the Indians.

3.3. Indian Seizure of Yakutat (1805)

In July 1805 a peace treaty was finally concluded between the Sitka people and Baranov. Lisianskii, as an eyewitness, clearly described the reception ceremony of a Sitka chief who had arrived at Novo-Arkhangel'sk for the occasion:

We received news of the early arrival of the toion [the Sitka chief] in the morning [July 16, Gregorian calendar], and Mr. Baranov ordered preparations for receiving him. About four o'clock in the afternoon two Sitkan boats appeared along with three of our baidarkas. They all went side by side and those sitting in them approaching the fort began to sing. At this time, our party members began to gather, and the Chugach, assigned to the celebration, to dress in their best clothes and so to speak powder their hair with eagle down [a sign of peaceful intentions]. It must be confessed that looking at this gathering it was impossible to keep from laughing: many of them paced about in only a single quite shabby sleeveless jacket, while others had on under-wear, being otherwise entirely naked, they boasted and delighted in their attire no less than a European dandy in a new stylish kaftan. The Sitkans, having arrived at the shore stopped and, having raised a dreadful howl, began to dance in their boats; the toion himself clowned [made grimaces] more than the others and waved eagle tails. They having scarcely finished this ballet, our Chugach as suddenly began theirs with songs and drumming. This entertainment contin-ued about a quarter of an hour, during which time our dear guests arrived at the wharf and were carried out in boats by the Koniag. I thought that their whole ceremony was finished, however, I was deceived. The Sitkans remained in their boats for several minutes and delighted in the revelry of the Chugach, who with the singing represented ludicrous images. At the end of this the toion was placed on a carpet and carried to the place assigned for him; the rest of the guests were taken by the hands, but without carpets (Lisianskii 1812:115–117).

The arriving Sitkan chief had always been loyal to the Russians and had not taken part in the 1802 attack. After much entertainment and the successful conclusion of peaceful negotiations, Baranov gave the envoy a crimson cotton overcoat adorned with ermine, and his companions received the same in blue. In addition, tin medals were given to all the Indians to recognize their loyalty to the Russians. On parting, Baranov gave the head of the lineage a copper Russian emblem, decorated with eagle feathers and ribbons. At the end of July, Katlian himself arrived in Novo-Arkhangel'sk with a small retinue; Baranov received him with the honor so valued by the Tlingit (Lisianskii 1812:117–121, 128–129). Thus, Kan emphasizes, the chief director understood very well the ceremonial protocol and hierarchical nature of Tlingit society and the role of gifts in maintaining the respect and prestige of the chiefs. The Tlingit legends also report that the Russians received the former territory of the Kiks.ádi, where Novo-Arkhangel'sk was founded, not as a result of conquest but rather for copper coats-of-arms. Thus, neither side "lost face" nor assumed the role of conqueror or conquered (Jacobs 1990:5; Kan 1999:66–67).

After concluding peace with the Sitkans, Baranov sent a hunting party of 301 baidarkas under the command of I. A. Kuskov (Andreev 1944:189) to hunt in the straits of the Alexander Archipelago. The renewed hunting around Sitka Island probably angered the Indians again; this time it was the Kootznahoo who, according to Rezanov, threatened to attack the hunting party (Tikhmenev 1863:2:Append. 201). However, the party returned to Novo-Arkhangel'sk safely, and soon a large part of it, under the leadership of T. S. Demenenkov, set out for Kodiak (sources differ in reporting the number of baidarkas in Demenenkov's party).[28]

On the way to Kodiak, Demenenkov heard from Tlingit that the Yakutat fort and settlement had been seized. After seeing this with his own eyes, and fearing he would be attacked by Indians, he decided to take a large part of his party directly to Fort Konstantinovskii on Nuchek Island in Chugach Bay. The crews of approximately thirty baidarkas, who had grown quite weak from the long passage, decided that, despite everything, they would pull ashore and rest. They managed to avoid an Indian attack and finally reached Nuchek, though a storm sunk the canoes of a large part of Demenenkov's party (Khlebnikov 1985:45).[29]

The source material gives inconsistent dates for the destruction of the Russian fort in Yakutat. Rezanov wrote that Yakutat was seized by "savages" in October (Tikhmenev 1863:2:Append. 278); Tikhmenev relies on him to state, even more vaguely, that this event occurred in the fall of 1805 (Tikhmenev 1863:1:151). These data were later used by researchers (Fedorova 1971:125; Pierce 1990:236; Sipes 1998:43–44), some even indicating that Yakutat was captured in 1806 (Dean 1995:300; Pierce 1990:275, 295, 405). However, judging by the most reliable source (a letter from the manager of Konstantinovskii Redoubt, Ivan A. Repin, to Baranov on September 24, 1805), the fort evidently fell on August 20, 1805 (Tikhmenev 1863:2:Append. 196–197).

The documents also contain evidence of the number of Russians at the Yakutat fort and settlement. The RAC board of directors' report to Emperor Alexander I says that there had been 22 Russians with "faithful islanders," that is, Aleuts, Kodiak, and Chugach, in the Yakutat fort and settlement (AVPRI, f. Gl. arkhiv II-3, 1805–1824 gg., op. 34, d. 7, l. 2). According to Khlebnikov's information, there had been only 12 Russian promyshlenniki led by Larionov in the fort (Khlebnikov 1835:102).[30] The most reliable source, in this author's view, is Rezanov, who used colonial statistics. He reported that in 1805 in Yakutat, under the leadership of Larionov, there were 15 Russian promyshlenniki, 9 settlers with families, a clerk, a blacksmith, and a mechanic. In addition, 20 kaiury and 15 kaiurki lived at the fort (AVPR, f. Gl. arkhiv 1–7, 1802 g., d. 1, papka no. 35, l. 154).

The available Russian sources say almost nothing about the Indians' reasons for attacking Yakutat. The RAC board of directors in St. Petersburg persistently tried to shift the guilt entirely onto the "Boston men" who had sold guns to the Indians (Narochnitskii 1963–1985:Ser. II, t. I, s. 379). In addition, they emphasized the Indians' warlike nature and their "inclination toward fighting and cruelty" (Narochnitskii 1963–1985:Ser. I, t. IV, s. 242). The Natives' "savagery" and the "enlightened" Americans' selling arms to them were the RAC's favorite complaints to the government, and justification for their failure to expand the empire's area to include the whole Northwest Coast. However, contacts between the "Boston men" and the Yakutat people during this period have not been confirmed by the sources. The reasons for the Yakutat uprising likely lay somewhere else. To discover these reasons, Tlingit oral traditions collected by De Laguna (1972:1:233–236, 259–261) are helpful. These legends lead one to conclude that many factors caused the Indian uprising. Chief among them was the fact that the Russians did not permit the Indians to use their traditional fishing grounds. According to legends, the Russians constructed fish dams in Tawal Creek that obstructed the passage of fish into the lake upstream. And, in fact, Russian sources mention two fish dams near the Russian colony in Yakutat (OR GBL, f. 204, k. 32, ed. khr. no. 4, l. 150b.; OR GPB, Sb. Q. IV. 311, l. 17). A shortage of fish evidently led to hunger among the Indians, which was also mentioned in their legends. In addition, when the Indians traveled along the river they had to portage by dragging their heavy canoes, since the Russians opened the dams for free only when the chief passed, whereas they charged a sea otter's skin for ordinary Indians seeking to pass through.

Another central reason for the Indian revolt was that the RAC's employees put the Indians' children in "school" (sending the children amanaty to a school on Kodiak Island that had been organized by Shelikhov) and used them as "slave" labor there to perform light work for the company between classes in Russian and Orthodoxy. From the Natives' point of view, this was slavery.

In Yakutat, as had been the case in Sitka, some Russian promyshlenniki treated the local inhabitants roughly, taking their women and using the Indians for unpaid work. On top of all this, the Russians did not pay the Yakutat people for the land ceded to them for the colony, even though they had promised to do so.

The immediate cause for the Indian uprising, according to one of the legends, was a Russian threat to kill a Native of the Tlaḵaik Teiḵweidí clan because he took nails from a wrecked boat on the shore (De Laguna 1972:1:259–260).

Russian sources do not detail the Indians' destruction of Yakutat. According to Tlingit legends, the fort was seized when almost all the Russians had gone out to catch fish. The few Russians who had remained in the fort were killed by the Indians, having no chance to resist. After this, the Indians fell upon the promyshlenniki returning from fishing and killed all of them as well (De Laguna 1972:1:232–234, 260–261). The legends go on to say that in this uprising the Indians used their classic tactic of suddenly attacking an entirely unsuspecting adversary. Having seized the fort, the Indians plundered and burned it. Five light cannons and five *pudy* of gunpowder fell into their hands, as did some other property belonging to the Russian promyshlenniki and colonists. Some of the items have been preserved among the Yakutat to this day as family relics, including a copper cannon, sheathed sword, and copper kettle that the Indians say belonged to the commandant of the Russian fort (De Laguna 1972:1:261).

It is not clear in the sources who instigated or participated in the Yakutat uprising. I. Repin informed Baranov that Russians in Yakutat had been killed by kaiury and some Yakutat people (Tikhmenev 1863:2:Append. 195). Rezanov wrote that the kaiury committed this act, having possibly been bribed "by the *Koloshi* living at Akoi" (Tikhmenev 1863:2:Append. 278). Baranov also supposed that the fort was seized by kaiury, whom the "Akoi people instructed" (or gbl, f. 204, k. 32, ed. khr. no. 6, l. 30b.). The rac board of directors reported to the emperor that the attack in Yakutat was committed by the "unpeaceful people who lived around this place," that is, the Yakutat people (avpr, f. Gl. arkhiv, II-3, op. 34, d. 7, l. 2).

Comparing the various data, one could conclude that some of the Yakutat people participated in seizing the fort—according to legends, these people were the Tlaḵaik Teiḵweidí (De Laguna 1972:1:233–236, 259–261).[31] It was evidently from this clan that the Russians had recruited the kaiury, since they were afraid to employ people from the powerful Kuashkḵwáan clan for company work. These kaiury may have supported their kinsmen in the uprising against the Russians. Khlebnikov reported that several *Koloshi* of both sexes, seemingly faithful to the company, who "were employed for work and service" lived in the fort (Khlebnikov 1835:102). Legends report that the Tlaḵaik Teiḵweidí were led by a certain Tanuḵ who was supported by only a few of the Kuashkḵwáan clan, since their chief "did not want war with the Russians" (De Laguna 1972:1:260).

More specifically, it was Toion Fedor who did not want war with the Russians, being himself loyal to Baranov.

The number of Russians lost at Yakutat and the number who escaped are unclear. Rezanov wrote that of 40 people at Yakutat in 1805, only 8 men, 2 women, and 3 boys managed to escape (Tikhmenev 1863:2:Append. 278). According to the RAC board of directors, 14 Russians perished "and with them many islanders" (evidently Kodiak and Chugach), while only "four promyshlenniki, four settlers with two women and three children" escaped, being taken captive by the Ugala̲kmiut (Eyak) (AVPR, f. Gl. arkhiv II-3, 1805–1824 gg., op. 34, d. 7, l. 2). They were later evidently released by the Indians or returned for ransom. Among them were the Yakutat settlers Semen Krylatskii, Ivan Shchukin, Stepan Kazantsev, and Fedor Balakin (Grinev 2001:59).

The number of Russians who escaped was possibly larger than the dozen or so cited, since in Baranov's letters a certain "settler Ivanova," a "German," and a settler by the name of Filipov are mentioned; they were captives of the Akoi toion Chesnyga (OR GBL, f. 204, k. 32, ed. khr. no. 6, l. 3–30b., 20).[32] Judging by archival documents, Khlebnikov cites incorrect data in one of his works. According to him, there were a total of 13 Russians in Yakutat and they were all killed by the Indians. Only Larionov's wife and three children succeeded in escaping (Khlebnikov 1835:103). Aurel Krause also cited this erroneous information (Krause 1956:36).

Hence, if there were 28 promyshlenniki and settlers (not counting Russian women and children) in Yakutat in 1805, and 8 men were saved, then there were still 4 Russians among the Indians, of whom at least 1 (Luka Filipov) died as an Indian captive (OR RGB, f. 204, k. 32, ed. khr. no. 6, l. 20). Several Kodiak people escaped as well, also captured by the Indians, and three Chugach, who succeeded in slipping away from Yakutat during the slaughter in a three-hatched baidarka and were the first to report the tragedy to the head of Fort Konstantinovskii (Tikhmenev 1863:Append. Pt. 2:195). By 1809 Baranov had evidently succeeded in rescuing almost all the living captives from Yakutat, which the board of directors reported to the emperor on November 5, 1809 (RGIA, f. 13, op. 1, d. 287, l. 65).

The fall of Yakutat and the destruction of Demenenkov's party was another heavy blow for the Russian colonies. An important economic and strategic base on the American coast was lost. The Russians sustained large material losses. The structures alone in Yakutat were valued (in 1805) at 31,525 rubles—this was, after Novo-Arkhangel'sk, the most expensive Russian colony in Alaska (AVPR, f. Gl. arkhiv I–7, 1802 g., d. 1, papka no. 35, l. 166). The loss of the promyshlenniki at Yakutat, with the chronic shortage of them in Russian America, and in particular the loss of Demenenkov's party, substantially weakened the RAC's position. It was not by chance that Khlebnikov wrote: "This misfortune stopped the progress of industry and in 1806 there were no detachments from Sitka" (Khlebnikov 1985:45).

News of the destruction of the Yakutat colony and fort brought unrest to the Natives in Russian America. The Kenai people (Tanaina Indians), in the words of Rezanov, began to display a "coldness" toward the Russians, while the Chugach and Mednovtsy (Ahtna) openly threatened to attack Fort Konstantinovskii (Tikhmenev 1863:2:Append. 278).

Thus, the armed resistance of the Tlingit and Eyak from 1802 to 1805 suspended Russian colonization for several years in Southeast Alaska. As a result of warlike actions, two Russian forts and a settlement had been destroyed and about 45 Russians and more than 230 Native partovshchiki lost (approximately 250 of Demenenkov's party became indirect victims of the Yakutat conflict), with evidently no less than half a million rubles in direct financial damage. The Indian threat hindered the RAC's powers in the Alexander Archipelago region later as well and did not permit the Russians to establish true sovereignty over the territory.

4. Russian-Tlingit and American-Tlingit Relations (1805–21)

4.1. Tlingit and Russians: A Period of "Cold War"

After the fall of Yakutat, the Russians and Tlingit entered a period of mutual distrust and at times even open hostility. Khlebnikov described the events that followed the destruction of the Russian fort and settlement in detail. He reported that the Yakutat people, encouraged by the victory over the Russians, decided to arrange a raid on Fort Konstantinovskii and the Chugach. However, their campaign ended unsuccessfully. Some of the Tlingit were killed by the Chugach, others drowned during a storm, and the rest were annihilated by the Ugalakmiut. Toion Fedor, who led the expedition, allegedly took his own life (Khlebnikov 1835:103–104).[33] Khlebnikov's information is not confirmed by the archival documents or traditions of the Yakutat people known to this author. In fact, data from the archival sources contradict several of Khlebnikov's claims: the manager of Fort Konstantinovskii was not Uvarov, as Khlebnikov wrote, but Ivan Repin. Toion Fedor did not commit suicide in 1805 but was in good health at least until 1807 when, judging by a letter from Baranov to Kuskov sent through the Ugalakmiut, he invited the governor to come to Yakutat to collect the cannons and captives seized in the Russian fort (OR GBL, f. 204, k.

32, ed. khr. no. 6, l. 50b.).[34] Later Klebnikov's erroneous version was cited in the works of such eminent authors as Hubert H. Bancroft (1970:451–452), Aurel Krause (1956:36), Clarence L. Andrews (1947:81–82), De Laguna (1972:1:175), and R. A. Pierce (1990:515).

Tlingit legends describe the situation that took shape after the Indians' seizure of Yakutat differently (De Laguna 1972:1:261–263, 266–268). The Tlakaik Teikweidí, who destroyed the Russian fort, not only did not organize the raid on the Chugach and Fort Konstantinovskii but, on the contrary, retreated far inland, fearing Baranov's vengeance. Their fears were not in vain. Scarcely having learned of the attack on Yakutat, Baranov ordered a ship equipped for a campaign against the Yakutat people, and only Rezanov's persuasion stopped him (Tikhmenev 1863:2:Append. 240). Of the four three-man baidarkas simultaneously sent to Yakutat to gather information, the Indians seized two, killing six Kodiak (Langsdorff 1812:2:194).

On the Situk River the Tlakaik Teikweidí constructed Chak-nu ("Eagle Fort"). At this time the rumor spread among the Tlingit of Southeast Alaska that the Teikweidí of Yakutat had become very rich, having plundered the Russian fort. Rumors about this wealth prompted the L'uknax.ádi of the Akoi kwáan (with the support of other clans of the Raven moiety) to attack the Tlakaik Teikweidí. In the winter of 1805–06 they organized a raid on Yakutat and attacked Chak-nu but were unsuccessful. After some time (judging by everything, in summer 1806) they nevertheless succeeded in destroying the Tlakaik Teikweidí so thoroughly that they vanished in Yakutat as an independent clan (De Laguna 1972:1:79, 261–263, 266–268).

The Tlingit legends are confirmed by archival sources. Baranov wrote of the Akoi toion Chesnyga who took Russian captives from Toion Fedor, while the Akoi people took possession of things from the pillaged Russian fort after a battle with the Yakutat people (OR GBL, f. 204, k. 32, ed. khr. no. 6, l. 29). Evidently it was the Chesnyga mentioned by Baranov (Jisniya, chief of the L'uknax.ádi, according to De Laguna) who led the march of the Akoi people on Yakutat.

The fall of Yakutat exacerbated the miserable position of the Russian colonies. In the fall of 1805 and winter of 1806 hunger and scurvy reigned in Novo-Arkhangel'sk. Supplies did not arrive, and fishing in the straits was dangerous because of continued skirmishes with the Tlingit. "There is no bread," wrote Rezanov, "and in Sitka they are dying of hunger because with the *Koloshi*, armed with excellent rifles and falconets, there is incessant warfare and fishing must be done under fire" (AVPR, f. RAK, op. 888, d. 173, l. 10b.). To rescue the garrison at Novo-Arkhangel'sk from death by starvation, Rezanov was forced

History of Tlingit Relations in Russian America

to travel to California on the *Yunona Juno*, a ship purchased from the American captain D'Wolf, to seek food.

The shore of Sitka Bay was a traditional meeting place for the Tlingit of different kwáans who came here each spring to fish for herring. The concentration of Indians always introduced the risk of their rallying for a hostile uprising. Therefore, every spring the Russian administration became terribly anxious about Novo-Arkhangel'sk's security.

While Rezanov was in California, the governor of the Russian colonies, Baranov, found himself in a rather unpleasant situation. In the early spring of 1806 more than a thousand Tlingit had gathered in Sitka Bay to catch herring. The garrisons, weakened by hunger and sickness (during the winter, scurvy and hunger had killed 17 Russian promyshlenniki and many Native partovshchiki), found themselves in great danger. Possible attack was prevented only by Baranov's presence in the fort, because the Indians respected and feared him. The possibility of attack was further diminished by the arrival in Novo-Arkhangel'sk of the American ship *O'Cain* commanded by Captain Jonathan Winship, a good friend of the governor. The American unambiguously signaled the Tlingit that, were there an attack, he would be entirely on Baranov's side (Tikhmenev 1863:2:Append. 277). The latter, by means of various tricks, was able to intimate to the Indians that he had supernatural powers, perhaps even those of a sorcerer. Thus, according to the stories of longtime residents, the governor learned of two Indian chiefs' desire to become acquainted with him. Having dressed himself as some kind of monster, and sitting on a high, improvised throne encircled by a fiery wheel of fireworks, he admitted them. They say that the Indians, having scarcely glanced at Baranov, fell unconscious from surprise and fear (Zavalishin 1877:3:10:156). The Tlingit piously believed that Baranov could fly and knew his enemies' plans and intentions. "Thanks to God," wrote Rezanov after returning from California in the summer of 1806, "that at the lowest number of people {Russians} they [the Tlingit] were not brave enough to make a resolute attempt. They genuinely fear Mr. Baranov and his name truly maintains fear throughout the whole region" (Tikhmenev 1863:2:Append. 277–278).

Though the Indians decided not to attack Novo-Arkhangel'sk in the early spring of 1806, a new plan of assault on the Russian fort soon matured among them. In any case, Baranov soon heard that the Indians of the Akoi, Kootznahoo, Chilkat, and Sitka kwáans had joined to seize the Russian fort. He urgently undertook additional precautionary measures: within four days a wooden wall was erected around the colony. The measures Baranov adopted compelled the Indians to abandon the planned attack temporarily. According to Rezanov's words, the "chiefs and leaders of the different peoples fought among themselves from annoyance that they had let slip a favorable time [for the attack] and separated along the straits" (Tikhmenev 1863:2:Append. 277–282).

The Tlingit, however, evidently did not intend to abandon their plans completely. The American captain Brown, having called at Novo-Arkhangel'sk from the straits, informed Rezanov that the chiefs of the Kootznahoo, Chilkat, and Sitka people had gone to the Kaigani to persuade them to join against the Russians. The Tlingit chiefs threatened the Kaigani, saying that if they refused, the Russians would "also settle among the Kaigani" (AVPR, f. Gl. arkhiv 1–7, 1802 g., d. 1, papka no. 35, l. 101ob.). Since Novo-Arkhangel'sk was not attacked, it appears that the Kaigani did not support the Tlingit. Indirect evidence of benevolent relations between the Kaigani and the Russians appears in Rezanov's and Baranov's letters (AVPR, f. Gl. arkhiv 1–7, 1802 g., d. 1, papka no. 35, l. 90ob.; OR GBL, f. 204, k. 32, ed. khr. no. 6, l. 100b.).

In spring 1807 the situation around Novo-Arkhangel'sk again became strained. As Khlebnikov reported, the Tlingit of the Chilkat, Stikine, Kootznahoo, and other kwáans (numbering no fewer than 2,000 persons) gathered in Sitka Bay to fish for herring, and again threatened to attack Novo-Arkhangel'sk. The small Russian garrison Kuskov led (Baranov had gone to Kodiak on business) fell under siege. The Tlingit women who lived among the Russians told Kuskov that the Indians intended to attack the fort. These rumors were confirmed after it became known that the Indians had seized several Aleuts and persuaded them to turn against the Russians, promising them honors and rewards after the fort was taken (Khlebnikov 1835:115–116).

In this critical situation Kuskov decided to separate the Tlingit and thereby weaken them. He invited one of the most influential Chilkat chiefs into the fort and, having arranged a trade meeting with food and gifts, persuaded him to leave the vicinity of the fort with his warriors (Khlebnikov 1835:116). The Chilkat people's refusal to attack evidently demoralized the Tlingit of the other kwáans, and they soon went off into the straits. Rumors of the siege of Novo-Arkhangel'sk, and even of its alleged capture, circulated widely among the Natives and caused unrest among the Chugach, who plotted with several Kodiak and Ahtna Indians who were living in the Russian fort to destroy Konstantinovskii Redoubt. But Russians learned of their plans in time, and the Chugach decided not to attack and instead dispersed (OR RGB, f. 204, k. 32, ed. khr. no. 6, l. 5).

In the summer of 1807 Kuskov attempted to resume hunting sea otters in the straits of the Alexander Archipelago. But the small party of 75 baidarkas he sent under the leadership of Dmitrii Eremin returned with almost nothing since, as Khlebnikov wrote, "it received strong resistance from the *Koloshi*" (Khlebnikov 1985:45).

In March 1808, before Baranov's return to Novo-Arkhangel'sk, Kuskov again sent a party of a hundred baidarkas to the vicinity of Sitka to hunt sea otters; it returned on April 22, having procured 130 skins. Then Kuskov added 95 more baidarkas to this party and sent it under the leadership of Sysoi Slobodchikov to the southern straits of the Alexander Archipelago (Khlebnikov 1985:45). The convoy that was used to protect the baidarka flotilla from Indian attack was the small schooner *St. Nikolai* commanded by the Prussian Khristofor Benzeman, who joined the RAC's service from the American brigantine *Peacock* (Pierce 1990:50). At the same time, the ship *Kad'iak* went into the straits with goods intended for trade with the Tlingit. Both the ships and the baidarka flotilla returned to Novo-Arkhangel'sk on June 20. The party had procured 1,700 sea otters, but the commander of the *Kad'iak*, Navigator Nikolai I. Bulygin, obtained almost nothing from the Indians since they charged too much for their furs and demanded guns and ammunition, which the Russians were afraid to sell them (Khlebnikov 1835:123–124). Thus, the RAC's first attempt to begin more or less widespread trade with the Tlingit in the straits of the Alexander Archipelago was unsuccessful.

And what is more, the RAC's resuming hunting sea otters in the Tlingit ḵwáans' territorial waters in 1809 and 1810 again resulted in Indians' dissatisfaction. The Indians hindered the hunting parties in their attempts to procure sea otters in every area. During skirmishes with the Tlingit in the summer of 1809 several Russian promyshlenniki were wounded and several partovshchiki were killed (Golovnin 1961:336; Khlebnikov 1985:46). In the spring of 1810 Baranov again sent out a hunting party from Novo-Arkhangel'sk under the direction of his assistant Kuskov. The baidarka flotilla was convoyed by two ships: the *Yunona*, under Benzeman's command, and the American ship *O'Cain*, with whose captain, J. Winship, Baranov was well acquainted. The party's voyage along the Alexander Archipelago's southern coasts was not especially successful because of clashes with the Tlingit, particularly in the region of Chatham Strait, during which eight Native partovshchiki where killed. Several Russian promyshlenniki who accompanied the party were wounded (Khlebnikov 1835:134–135). Finally, Kuskov decided to leave the Alexander Archipelago and move south with the party along the American mainland. However, near Dundas Island the baidarka flotilla was nearly attacked by the local Indians (Tlingit or Tsimshian). The American captain, Samuel Hill, who was located near Dundas Island on the brig *Otter*, unequivocally let Kuskov know that he would side with the Indians if there were an open clash with the Russians.[35] The head of the party decided not to tempt fate, and on August 3 returned to Novo-Arkhangel'sk with 1,400 sea otter skins. On the return trip, armed Tlingit lay in wait everywhere for the party, ready to attack at the slightest blunder (Khlebnikov 1985:46).

The Natives' strong resistance compelled Baranov to reject conducting an extensive hunt around the Alexander Archipelago. In a letter to Kuskov on January 20, 1811, he noted that "near and surrounding places turned out to be insecure and dangerous for the hunt, so it is necessary to direct attention farther away, where attempts have already been made, that is the Albion shore, where the people are peaceful" (OR GBL, f. 204, k. 32, ed. khr. no. 12, l. 1–10b.).

The "attempts" that Baranov spoke of occurred as early as 1803, when a hunting party led by T. N. Tarakanov and A. Shvetsov procured sea otters along the shores of New Albion (Upper California) escorted by the American ship *Eclipse* (Khlebnikov 1985:46).[36] This and subsequent successful hunting expeditions to the California shores led to Kuskov's founding Fort Ross there in 1812. Sea otter furs that were procured on California's shores comprised a substantial portion of the furs taken during these years in Russian America. Thus, the hunt in California was able to compensate partially for the loss of the hunts in the straits of the Alexander Archipelago.

The Russians were not able to conduct a hunt immediately to the south of the Alexander Archipelago since all the Northwest Coast (to 40° north latitude) was occupied by warlike "*Koloshi*," to whom American traders had provided arms.[37] This was also the reason that the next Russian colony to the south of Novo-Arkhangel'sk was founded in California, where the local Indians were peaceful, as correctly pointed out by Istomin (1980:57–58). In the scholarly literature climatic conditions favorable to developing agriculture and stock breeding are usually given as the reason for founding the Russian settlement in California.

From 1810 to 1820 the tension in Russian-Tlingit relations, compared with the previous decade, had diminished somewhat, though during these years relations were periodically strained. Thus, in 1813, according to Tikhmenev, Sitka people accumulated arms and arranged a joint attack on Novo-Arkhangel'sk with the Tlingit of neighboring kwáans. However, the "plot" was uncovered in time and Baranov took precautionary measures that forced the Sitka people to give up their plans (Tikhmenev 1861:1:240).[38] The Indians were dismayed that they had not succeeded in killing the Russians who were saved during the sloop *Neva*'s wreck by Sitka Island in January 1813. As naval cadet M. I. Terpigorev, an eyewitness to the events, attested, "the savage inhabitants of this place where the *Neva* wrecked tore their hair with frustration that they did not know of this incident. They said clearly: 'we would have killed all the people and seized the cargo and things cast off so that Baranov would never know' " (AGO, razr. 99, op. 1, d. 7, l. 170b.). However, in the following year the Indians succeeded in killing two riflemen of the RAC near Novo-Arkhangel'sk.

Nevertheless, from time to time the Russians tried to trade with the Tlingit in the straits of the Alexander Archipelago. For this purpose the ship *Otkrytie* was sent out in 1815, commanded by Ya. A. Podushkin, who succeeded in acquiring 486 sea otter skins from the Indians. This was dangerous work and therefore extreme precautions were taken against possible attack by the Natives during the trading. The deck of the ship was enclosed by boarding nets and sail screens; on the forecastle were weapons loaded with case shot; and the whole crew was armed and ready (Litke 1834:1:108). The least inattentiveness and thoughtlessness could have sad consequences: during the voyage among the islands of the Alexander Archipelago the navigator of the ship *Otkrytie* went ashore to gather berries, and not being armed, was taken captive by the Tlingit. The latter took the navigator to the ship and, pressing a dagger to his breast, demanded a ransom from Podushkin—half the ship's cargo, to which, of course, he could not agree. He devised a method of rescuing his subordinate from Indian captivity in the style of the best pirate novels: Podushkin set off south to the Queen Charlotte Islands and lured two chiefs of the local Haida Indians onto his ship, then exchanged them for his careless navigator. Later, reporting the details of this episode to Second Lieutenant Litke, Podushkin coolly continued: "Having gotten back the navigator, I ordered my marksman [Nikolai Zenchin] to shoot the toion who had captured him, who was then sitting on the shore quite near, but, *unfortunately* [emphasis by Litke], the rifle misfired" (RGA VMF, f. 15, op. 1, d. 8, l. 185). It would be interesting to know how many such episodes in Russian America's history remain unknown.

In 1818 the "Baranov era" in the history of Russian America ended. After more than 25 years of service the "Lord of Alaska," as he is called in American literature, left the Russian colonies. The chiefs of many Tlingit ḵwáans gathered to say good-bye to Baranov. To one of them—his old friend, chief of the Auk ḵwáan—the now-former governor gave his chain mail, which he had worn for many years under his clothing and which had repeatedly saved his life (this relic is now located in the National Museum, in Washington, DC) (Miller 1967:156). In the words of one of Kan's contemporary Kaagwaantaan informants, the Tlingit respected Baranov as the Russian *shaade haani*, that is, the chief of high rank, and grieved at his departure from Alaska. Both Russian sources and Indian traditions indicate that members of several ḵwáans gathered at Novo-Arkhangel'sk in 1818 for a special farewell ceremony for this first governor of Russian America (Kan 1999:69–70). Baranov's successors as governors of the Russian-American Company were the officers of the Imperial Naval Fleet, usually captains of the first or second rank, who were appointed in St. Petersburg.

Baranov's first successor, Captain-Lieutenant Leontii A. Hagemeister, soon encountered the Tlingit's warlike nature. In May 1818 two Russian promyshlenniki were killed in the woods not far from Novo-Arkhangel'sk where they were cutting firewood. At first, suspicion as to who had planned the murders fell on Katlian, the well-known chief of the Sitka Kiks.ádi. Hagemeister, learning the location of Katlian's camp, made a surprise appearance there early one morning in three well-armed launches. The Russians' sudden arrival was a complete shock to the sleeping Indians, who initially panicked. Hagemeister hastened to assure the Tlingit through an interpreter that he wanted not revenge but rather negotiations. Finally, the armed Indians, led by Katlian himself, set out in a large war canoe to meet the Russian and approached the governor's cutter. Litke, who had remained in Russian America, vividly describes the subsequent dramatic events in his journal:

> In order to suppress the Tlingit at the boundaries H[agemeister] ordered the other cutter, which had a carronade, to direct its bow toward the *Kolosh* boat and to aim the carronade directly at it; priming fuses were readied; four of the *Koloshi* in their turn leveled their rifles on the people who held the fuses. With these preliminaries, which took the place of an arbitration flag, negotiations began. Katlian asked H[agemeister] why he came. "If you came to kill us," he said, "then it is better you take from me this medal that you hung on me and there my breast (having bared it), kill me." H[agemeister] assured him that he came with no intention of this, but only to find out who killed the Russians, and if his [Katlian's] subordinates, then to give him the guilty ones. Kat[lian] announced that *Koloshi* of another generation [clan] had killed the Russians, that he had learned this from his oldest nephew (RGA VMF, f. 15, op. 1, d. 8, l. 184).

The old chief was right. As it turned out, the Kiks.ádi were not involved in the Russians' killings—the killers belonged to the Kaagwaantaan clan. The latter built a strong fort not far from Novo-Arkhangel'sk and armed it with about ten cannons. Hagemeister decided not to attack the Indian fort, striving to end the affair peaceably. Simultaneously, he ordered the post in Novo-Arkhangel'sk strengthened, and prohibited anyone from going beyond the gates in small numbers and without weapons. The cutter *Konstantin* was sent to the hunting party that was in the straits of the Alexander Archipelago to notify them of the events and issue orders that they be more vigilant since the Indians might try to attack the partovshchiki (RGA VMF, f. 1375, op. 1, d. 26, l. 890b.–900b.).

However, the Kaagwaantaan stopped trying to attack the Russians openly and instead continually sent their scouts to the walls of Novo-Arkhangel'sk. For his part, Hagemeister, while himself seriously ill and having taken the reins of Russian America much against his will, did not want to begin a full-scale war with the Tlingit. Through the mediation of Indian women and members of the Kiks.ádi clan he began to negotiate with the Kaagwaantaan, requiring only the delivery of reliable amanaty and the promise of their never again attacking the Russians. The Kaagwaantaan willingly agreed to the negotiations and the advantageous terms stipulated in them. They, in their turn, of course asked the Russians for hostages. Negotiations with Hagemeister's successor, Lieutenant S. I. Yanovskii, bore fruit, and by the beginning of December 1818 an exchange had been made. The Russians received two nephews of the Kaagwaantaan's head chief, and the Russians handed over two creole boys. Yanovskii hoped that in the course of time the boys would become intelligent interpreters for the RAC (see documentary appendix entries {5} and {6}).

As a result of the events of 1818 the Kaagwaantaan's prestige and glory grew incredibly. They not only had killed two Russians with impunity but had also received hostages, whom they took in order to boast and show them in Kootznahoo. The amanaty taken from the Kaagwaantaan were kept honorably in Novo-Arkhangel'sk like any Russian promyshlenniki. Soon, however, the Indians asked that their hostages be returned, promising to return the creoles taken from the Russians; Yanovskii unwillingly consented, chiefly because the creole boys requested it. The Kaagwaantaan instead gave the Russians two girls who were the nearest relatives of the head chief Tsoutok. The RAC directors, after reading Yanovskii's report of the whole affair, harshly condemned his decision to make unjustified concessions to the Indians and prohibited giving them amanaty from the Russian side in the future (see documentary appendix {7}).

The policy of appeasement that Yanovskii had adopted had certainly succeeded: it became safer for the inhabitants of Novo-Arkhangel'sk to appear outside the city's walls, and trade with the Tlingit increased. However, it was a long road back to genuine good-neighborliness. At the beginning of the 1820s the Indians made several unsuccessful attempts to take Ozerskii Redoubt, which had been erected by the Russians 25 versts about {16 ½ miles south} of Novo-Arkhangel'sk for laying in fish (Lazarev 1950:238; Zavalishin 1877:3:11:219–220).

S. I. Yanovskii, the governor of Russian America between 1818 and 1820, reported to the RAC board of directors in St. Petersburg: "From the time of the colonization of Baranof Island up to the present, if you count the loss of people and other things through the plundering of the *Koloshi* and compare it with the acquisition, how much we have obtained from the occupation of this place, the latter scarcely makes up even a fourth part against the loss." Yanovskii wrote that the purchase of furs from the Tlingit was extremely insignificant compared to the expense of maintaining Sitka (about 50 thousand rubles a year), whereas the sea otters in Sitka's vicinity had already been almost completely exterminated. The only advantage he found was that it was convenient to construct and repair ships at Sitka. Provisions at Sitka did not suffice and the hope of quickly subjugating the local population was unrealized: "The local peoples have more firearms than we, in one Kokoantaiskaia [Kaagwaantaan] fort our amanaty saw more than 10 large cannons" (RGIA, f. 994, op. 2, d. 833, l. 1–10b.). As a result of all this, Yanovskii proposed transferring the capital of Russian America from Novo-Arkhangel'sk to Kodiak. The governor, of course, somewhat exaggerated and dramatized conditions, but his argument made sense. However, after a long discussion the RAC board of directors, interested in expanding southward, changed nothing.

On the other hand, the company did not abandon hope of developing trade with the Tlingit. In 1815 a ship was again equipped to trade in the straits. However, because of a chronic lack of European goods in Russian America, and by virtue of the earlier reasons, RAC trade with the Tlingit could not expand much. "The colonial authorities, limited by prices set by the main office [RAC], were never able in this bargaining to withstand the competition of ships from the United States, and therefore the exchange of furs from the *Koloshi*, always unimportant, became insignificant," wrote F. P. Litke (1834:1:108).

4.2. American Smugglers in the Waters of Russian America

In spite of the fact that Southeast Alaska was formally part of the Russian Empire, foreign fur-buyers continued their illegal trade with the Natives of this region. The dominant position in trading with the Indians during these years (1805–21) was seized by American businessmen. Thus, from 1805 to 1814 forty American ships, and only three English ones, visited the Northwest Coast (Howay 1973:59–105). There was something of a slump in the American sea mammal fur trade with the Indians between 1813 and 1814 because of the Anglo-American War (1812–15). American captains, fearing English cruisers, substantially curtailed their trade operations in the straits of the Alexander Archipelago. But in 1815 they resumed activity on the Northwest Coast with the previous vigor. From 1815 to 1821 about 106 American ships visited the waters of

Russian America (Kushner 1975:26). During this period, the American traders were the chief suppliers of European goods to the Tlingit. Some American ships plied the waters along the coast for years on end, wintering in bays and coves. The commanders of such ships were, as a rule, interested in maintaining friendly relations with the local population. However, contacts between the Tlingit and the Americans were not always peaceful. Thus, on April 2, 1811, the Chilkat people made an unsuccessful attempt to seize Captain Samuel Hill's American brig *Otter*. The captain's second mate and boatswain were lost and six sailors of the brig wounded in the clash. Indian losses were quite substantial, totaling 40 to 50 people (including 13 chiefs). The Tlingit remembered this battle for a long time. Among the Indians killed by Hill was the father of the wife of the well-known Stikine chief, Shakes, who, as the sailors of the American ship *Rob Roy* learned in 1822, intended to seize the first European ship that reached him in retaliation for the death of his father-in-law. Even in 1840 the Chilkat people threatened to destroy the English Fort Taku in retaliation for the bloody clash that had occurred with Hill 30 years before and that had taken several dozen Indians' lives (Gibson 1992:167; Howay 1973:91; Pierce 1990:191).

As S. B. Okun' correctly noted, Americans trading for furs among the Tlingit in fact restricted the RAC's sphere of activity to procuring furs in areas where Natives dependent on the company worked (Okun' 1939:72). The fact that valuable furs from company-controlled territory fell into the hands of competitors undoubtedly irritated the RAC board of directors and the Russian colonies' administration. The sale of guns to the Indians caused special protests from the company. Reports from the RAC board of directors to the imperial government during these years abound in complaints about contraband guns imported by American traders sold at a profit to the Tlingit (AVPR, f. Gl. arkhiv II-3, 1805–1811 gg., op. 34, d. 8, l. 210b.–220b., 98–980b.; Narochnitskii 1963–1965:Ser. I, t. IV, s. 241–243; t. VI, s. 250, 276–279; Ser. II, t. I, s. 529–530). The sale of guns to the Indians had long been an object of diplomatic dispute between St. Petersburg and Washington. However, it never led to anything, since the U.S. government did not intend to limit its citizens' freedom of trade and private initiative, and the czarist government did not wish to aggravate friendly Russian-American relations during these years for the sake of RAC interests (Bolkhovitinov 1966:440–444; *Rossiia i SShA*, 382–387, 394–395, 410, 422–423).

American captains managed to trade for furs among the Tlingit seemingly under the very cannons of Novo-Arkhangel'sk. Thus, in April 1812, the crew of *Atahualpa* acquired 124 beaver skins, 68 sea otter, and 40 river otter, right in Sitka Bay, in only two weeks. And the Indians often obtained firearms from the Americans in exchange for the furs (Gibson 1992:263). This was not a secret to Baranov. Through his informants (a number of Tlingit and Kodiak) he learned about such deeds, though not always in a timely fashion. His patience was exhausted in June 1815 when he received information that gunpowder and guns were being secretly sold to the Indians from American ships standing in the Novo-Arkhangel'sk harbor. Wilson P. Hunt, who was a confidant of the big American fur trader John Jacob Astor, and who had arrived in Sitka on the brig *Pedler*, caused Baranov to be particularly suspicious. Having learned that the English captain William Pigot, who was also in the harbor, had given him a keg of powder, Baranov sent two of his managers to Hunt's brig with the demand that he give them this keg for comparing this powder with some that had recently been found among the Tlingit. Hunt bluntly refused to yield to this seemingly foolish demand, and there was a fight on board the *Pedler* between the RAC employees and the American sailors. At the uproar Baranov himself arrived in a large boat with promyshlenniki and, with another of his boats on the other side of the *Pedler*, boarded the ship by force. The ship was searched, the powder removed, and all the cannons defused (RGA VMF, f. 1152, op. 1, d. 2, l. 40–41ob; VPR:2:1:382–384). Of course, the sides then reconciled and Baranov, to honor the truce, arranged a feast in his residence on the top of the steep rock. Although the governor did not have the authority to take such actions against foreigners, there were many opportunities to do so. Therefore, the foreign skippers sometimes openly laughed at his verbal "commands" about the inadmissibility of trade with the Indians (VPR:2:1:380). Attempts by the RAC's leadership to get the czarist government to impose severe sanctions against foreign smugglers ended unsuccessfully.

The Russians themselves were quite interested in the American traders, since it was only from them that Baranov could obtain the goods and provisions he needed, inasmuch as the supply from Okhotsk was thoroughly insufficient. In addition, Baranov sometimes used American ships for convoying RAC hunting flotillas. However, this practice ended in 1818, after Baranov's retirement from the post of governor of Russian America, when his successor L. A. Hagemeister made a contract on joint hunting with the French lieutenant Marquis Camille de Roquefeuil, who commanded the eight-gun trading ship *Le Bordelais* from Bordeaux. In Kodiak, according to the contract, Roquefeuil was to take 30 two-man baidarkas and 60 Kodiak with several women supervised by two Russian stewards. After this, Roquefeuil set out to hunt sea otters along the Northwest Coast. However, on June 18, when the party of Kodiaks was resting in a temporary camp on the west coast of Prince of Wales Island, it was suddenly attacked by Indians (most researchers say Tlingit, but it is possible that they were Kaigani Haida). Of the 47 people on the shore, 20 were killed on the spot, although they tried to return fire with pistols, while the rest saved themselves by jumping into the water where they were picked up by launches from the ship. Among the survivors were 12 wounded, of whom 3 later died. Roquefeuil himself miraculously escaped by swimming to the ship's launch through the relentless gunfire of the Indians hidden in thickets on the shore. *Le Bordelais* bombarded the shore with cannons for several hours but without visible success. On June 26 Roquefeuil returned to Novo-Arkhangel'sk with the rest of his party (Pierce 1990:425–426). After this tragedy the colonial administration discontinued joint hunting expeditions with foreigners on the Northwest Coast.

5. Tlingit and Europeans (1821–67)

5.1. Tlingit and Russians in the Concluding Period of Russian America

The beginning of the 1820s is the prologue to a new stage in Russian-Tlingit relations and almost coincides with the beginning of a new period in the history of Russian America. According to the chronology detailed by S. G. Fedorova, from 1819 the general direction of colonization in America changed from south to north and northeast. Even the very character of colonization changed (Fedorova 1971:102–136, 1981:244–246). Russian colonization began to become more regulated. The stormy epoch of Baranov's adventures moved into the past. The Russians endeavored to undertake a more general opening of Alaska, focusing on its interior regions. This shift was caused not only by Anglo-American expansion from the south (from 1810 the Americans and English started colonizing the Northwest Coast from the Columbia River to Vancouver Island) but by the exhaustion of the sea otter population in this region, the hunt for which had, up to that point, been the basis of the Russian colonies' economy. The RAC had to make up the resultant deficit of furs by developing trade with the Eskimos and Indians of western and central Alaska.

Changes in the economic base not only reoriented the primary direction of Russian colonization in the north but also affected the socioeconomic sphere. The RAC's quasi-feudal exploitation of Aleuts, Koniag, and Chugach at maritime hunting was pushed aside by nonequivalent trade with the northern Athapaskan and Eskimos. In connection with the general reduction of maritime hunting, the need for the labor of the company's Native slaves—kaiury, who were obliged to supply food and clothing for the RAC baidarka flotillas—dropped significantly. Therefore, between 1815 and 1819, *kaiurstvo* as a social institution finally vanished from the Russian colonies (Grinev 2001:13–15).

The elements of crude noneconomic coercion fell into second place and were replaced by the paternal politics of colonial "guardianship" of the Native population of Russian America. The arrival of enlightened and rather humanely disposed naval officers—representatives of the government, which had decided to more rigorously control its transoceanic possessions—largely contributed to this. Displaying its "paternal care" toward the dependent Natives, the government prohibited the Russian-American Company in 1821 from engaging more than 50 percent of the Koniag and Aleuts in its hunts. In practice, of course, this decree was systematically violated. Nevertheless, the company's managers' despotism and abuse of the Natives were limited by the naval officers' stricter administrative supervision (Grinev 2000:80–84).

The decline in the sea otter catch also adversely affected the socioeconomic position of the common Russian promyshlenniki. The majority of them formerly had the right to part of the value of the furs acquired by the RAC over a four-year period (the half-share system). [39] However, the depletion of the sea otter population between 1815 and 1819 meant that the number of furs falling to the share of the individual promyshlennik quickly declined. The only solution was to instead offer a fixed wage. By 1818, after Baranov was replaced as governor of the Russian colonies and any remaining ideas that the colonies were a viable enterprise had vanished, the ordinary Russian promyshlenniki became salaried, earning 350 rubles; they had to purchase their rations. They were thereby finally transformed from once-voluntary hunters of fur-bearing animals to RAC workers without rights and ensnared by debt. Thus, the elements of early capitalism that early Russian colonization had seen, as well as the quasi-slaveholding relations that took the form of kaiurstvo, were forced out of the Russian colonies at the beginning of the 1820s by colonial politarism. [40] The term "politarism" comes from the Greek word *politeia*— "government" (see chapter 1, section 4.1). Accordingly, politarism is a system based on the primacy of the government's supreme ownership of the basic means of production (especially the land in an agrarian society) and its direct ownership of the producer. In Russian America the government simply temporarily delegated part of its authority to the RAC, having monopolized the company's activity (Grinev 1999:121–122; 2000:84–87). And inasmuch as the company was systematically criticized for its cruel treatment of the Natives, the government decided to introduce order, designating its representatives to the governor's post and simultaneously judicially defining the status and duty of the Native population of Russian America. As a result, these diverse changes between 1815 and 1825 could not help but affect Russian-Tlingit relations.

To regulate the RAC's activity and strengthen its position, the imperial government issued several decrees at the beginning of the 1820s. In 1821 the company's privileges had again been extended for 20 years. Simultaneously, a decree was issued against foreign smugglers operating in Alaskan waters. At the same time, the *Pravila Rossiisko-Amerikanskoi kompanii* [Regulations of the Russian-American Company], which regulated the company's activity, structure, rights, and duties, were promulgated and signed by the czar. The third section of these rules was dedicated to the company's legally establishing relations with independent tribes in Russian America (primarily the Tlingit, of course). In this section employees were ordered to cease trying to subdue the residents of the mainland's coastal zone and "to use every kind of method to preserve their good will, avoiding everything which might stir up suspicion in them about the intention of violating their independence." It was forbidden to require "tribute, taxes, duty or any other kind of gift" from these tribes except the delivery, "according to custom," of amanaty (Tikhmenev 1861:1:57–58). As we see, the Tlingit's resistance forced the imperial government to make definite concessions to them, as reflected in Russian legislation.

Nevertheless, at the beginning of the 1820s Russian-Tlingit relations were seriously tried when Emperor Alexander I ratified the decree of September 4 (16), 1821, in which Russia stated its claims on the American coast to 51° north latitude. Foreign ships were prohibited from approaching Russia's American possessions closer than 100 nautical miles. This point was introduced to suppress all trade (especially of firearms) by foreigners (chiefly, Americans) with "independent Natives" of Russian America. To enforce its claim the czarist government dispatched the naval sloop *Apollon* to Southeast Alaska, and later dispatched the 44-cannon frigate *Kreiser* and the sloop *Ladoga*. The rashness of these decisions was rather evident, since both the Russians in the colonies and the Native population depended in substantial degree on the American ships' supplying goods and provisions. Matvei I. Murav'ev, who had replaced Yanovskii as the governor of Russian America (1820–25), wrote about this in his reports to the RAC board of directors. He particularly feared the discontent of the Tlingit:

> The *Koloshi* clearly see that through us they are deprived of the fur business and trade, because with weapons [which are supplied by the Americans] they can procure beavers, and for beavers they get clothing and many other things they need: blankets, frieze, molasses, and so on and on. From the people whom we have deprived of everything, we can hope for no mercy, no good favor; thus, I will not so much victimize trade with the Americans as think about our own

security and bring the fort into a defensive state. . . . The main office is faced with the sacred duty of providing us for trade with the *Koloshi*, in order not to bring them to despair, and I requested for this in the present requirement a large number of blankets, frieze, and baize, but I would like treble this quantity (Narochnitskii 1963–1985:Ser. II, t. V, s. 88).

Such reports from Murav'ev, on the one hand, and diplomatic pressure from Great Britain and the United States, on the other, forced the czarist government to abolish the decree of September 4 (16), 1821, by the beginning of 1824 and to moderate its territorial "appetite" (Bolkhovitinov 1975:268–292). As a result of concluding the convention with the United States in 1824, and with England in 1825, the Russian American territory was definitively designated, the southern boundary of which was not at 51° north latitude but at 54° 40'. Other concessions by the imperial government were stipulated in the conventions: freedom was granted to foreign ships to navigate and approach the shores of Russian possessions, excepting places of Russian colonies, where for the approach special permission from the local authorities was required. Foreigners were granted full freedom of trade with the local population, excepting only firearms and spirits (Tikhmenev 1861:1:61–66). That Russia accepted the indicated conventions showed the relative weakness of Russian influence in Southeast Alaska.

Despite the not unfounded fears of Governor Murav'ev, during the years the decree was in effect there were no open clashes between the Tlingit and the Russians. First, American traders, despite Russian warships' patrolling the straits of the Alexander Archipelago, did not abandon these places and continued to trade with the Tlingit. The warships did not succeed in seizing a single smuggler. However, the cruisers had other functions. As was noted in the RAC board of directors' documents, "the sojourn of the war ships in the colonies served as reliable protection for them [the colonies] and was a warning to the *Koloshi*" (AVPR, f. Gl. arkhiv II-3, 1805–1824 gg., op. 34, d. 7, l. 390b.). [41]

Second, as Murav'ev noted, old dissension and clan enmity interfered with the Tlingit's rallying for their attack on Novo-Arkhangel'sk (Narochnitskii 1963–1985:Ser. II, t. V, s. 88). It was during these years that a major clash occurred between the Stikine people (primarily the powerful Naanya.aayí clan) and the Kaagwaantaan clan of the Kaknau settlement (more correctly: Kaknuwu—"Fort Partridge") on the north shore of Cross Sound. In this clash the Kaagwaantaan were defeated, and they abandoned the village. Some of them moved to the kwáans of the Chilkat and Akoi, and a majority of them, together with the head chief, resettled at Novo-Arkhangel'sk on Sitka Island (AVPR, f. RAK, op. 888, d. 1006, l. 313).

Third, beginning in 1822 the Russians actually abandoned active hunting around the Alexander Archipelago, both because the sea otter population had become substantially exhausted, and because the Tlingit actively resisted them. Thus, the hunting party of 100 baidarkas that set out in 1821, escorted by two well-armed ships and four launches, procured only 150 skins because the party was tailed by Tlingit who continually shot into the air to frighten the sea otters away, thereby hindering the hunt. According to Murav'ev, the party leader had reported, "They will in no way leave our partovshchiki and though they will not touch our people, they will not permit us to hunt" (AVPR, f. RAK, op. 888, d. 989, l. 2900b.).

In answer to such reports from Murav'ev, the RAC board of directors in St. Petersburg in fact approved stopping active hunting around Sitka. In 1825 the directors of the company wrote to Murav'ev:

> Hunting proper is to be completely forbidden there: by doing this the primary reason for the enmity of the *Koloshi* toward the Russians— competition in hunting fur-bearing animals, with the elimination of which the *Koloshi* will also without doubt willingly sell to the Company the animals they take, as they now sell them to the Americans of the United States. It is known that free exchange with the savages [Indians] can be much greater and more profitable to obtain the animals than by hunting them (RGA VMF, f. 1375, op. 1, d. 4, l. 512).

Surrendering its position in Southeast Alaska, the RAC board of directors even suggested liquidating Novo-Arkhangel'sk, transferring the "capital" of Russian America back to Kodiak. The company did not wish to bear the unwarranted expense of maintaining a large garrison at Sitka. It was suggested that only Ozerskii Redoubt remain and that 50 promyshlenniki with artillery be transferred there and that Novo-Arkhangel'sk itself be burned. As a matter of fact, even Ozerskii Redoubt was almost useless to the RAC—it was suggested it be preserved "for appearances of government," that is, for political reasons connected with retaining Southeast Alaska (RGA VMF, f. 1375, op. 1, d. 4, l. 509–5110b.). However, the plan had to be rejected for several reasons, including the increasingly active penetration of the English of the Hudson's Bay Company (HBC) into territories contiguous with Russian America. It was not until 1832 that the RAC rejected the idea of transferring the colonial center to Kodiak. Simultaneously, the company's main office recommended to Governor Murav'ev and his successor P. E. Chistiakov that they maximally strengthen trade with the Tlingit, and once more emphasized the need to increase Russian influence over them and preserve friendly relations with them even at the cost of completely stopping RAC hunting in Southeast Alaska (RGA VMF, f. 1375, op. 1, d. 5, l. 142–143).

One notes an improvement in Russian-Tlingit relations from the beginning of the 1820s, caused by removing the primary conflict between the Tlingit and the Russians—sea otter hunting in the territories of Southeast Alaska. In the opinion of the American ethnohistorian J. R. Dean (1994:5; 1995:272), by 1820 the Russians had completely stopped hunting in the region of the Alexander Archipelago, and after 1832 in the relatively safe Yakutat and Lituya Straits. This is not correct. The Russians continued to send small parties of Chugach and Koniag to the Yakutat region until the 1860s. For example, in 1852 Governor N. Ya. Rozenberg reported to the RAC's board of directors that during the past year a party consisting primarily of Chugach Eskimos had procured 149 sea otters between Prince William Sound and Yakutat Bay (AVPRI, f. RAK, op. 888, d. 1020, l. 204). It is true that the local Indians were unhappy with the outsiders' incursion into their Native hunting grounds. As early as 1826 Governor P. E. Chistiakov wrote: "Though the inhabitants of these places are indignant about this, because of their small numbers they cannot be a hindrance" (AVPRI, f. RAK, op. 888, d. 992, l. 65). In connection with this there even arose among the RAC board of directors the temptation to reestablish a company village in Yakutat, both to develop trade and to suppress American fur traders' commerce. However, Chistiakov responded negatively to the RAC directors' inquiry about restoring a Russian colony there. In his words, American ships did not go to Yakutat, trade was insignificant there, and the local Indians were hostile and dangerous (AVPRI, f. RAK, op. 888, d. 992, l. 65). The RAC had to abandon active expansion in the Tlingit lands and instead count on their gradual acculturation.

The beginning of rapprochement between the Tlingit and the Russians occurred in 1821, when Governor Murav'ev permitted the Tlingit of the Sitka ḵwáan to settle at the walls of Novo-Arkhangel'sk (Kittlitz 1858:1:218; Lazarev 1832:162). "Governor M. I. Murav'ev," wrote the well-known Russian navigator Fedor P. Litke in 1827, "calculating that, having under his cannons their wives and children and all their belongings, it being much easier to keep them in check and learn all their intentions, permitted them to establish a large settlement by the very side of the fort" (Litke 1834:92). Such proximity could bring only an improvement in relations. The Tlingit gradually became the primary providers of fresh provisions to the Russians in Novo-Arkhangel'sk. The volume of their deliveries increased from year to year. Between 1818 and

1825 the average annual purchase of furs and provisions among the Tlingit was 3,750 rubles, whereas in 1831 the sum of these purchases amounted to 8,000 rubles (Khlebnikov 1985:136). The Russian administration saw trade with the Tlingit as an active means of gradually subjecting and culturally assimilating the independent Natives, as well as a way to maintain peaceful relations with them. Murav'ev significantly raised the price paid for furs purchased from the Tlingit. For sea otter the Russians paid the Tlingit three to five times more (100–150 rubles) than they did the Aleuts or Kodiak. The governor even issued a special directive concerning this, which stated in particular: "Expect of this trade not one of gain for the company, but of one and the same benefit, that the company can acquire friendship and favor from the *Koloshi* toward the Russians" (Khlebnikov 1985:135).

Trade with the Tlingit that was based on new regulations began under P. E. Chistiakov in 1826, and the increase in the purchase price noticeably affected the amount of furs acquired from the Indians, which multiplied by several times at one stroke. Whereas in 1825 the managers of the RAC used goods to buy only 22 sea otters, 22 foxes, and 74 beaver skins from the Tlingit, in 1826 their numbers increased to 95, 169, and 374 skins, respectively. But in 1830 rum became widely traded with independent Indians, both to reduce the cost of the furs and to counteract American and English competitors who supplied spirits to the Tlingit. The RAC had customarily traded wool blankets, a variety of fabrics, cast iron, copper vessels, and Virginia tobacco (Khlebnikov 1985:135–136, 140–141).

Striving to regulate trade with the Tlingit, the Russian administration even proceeded in 1831 to create a special "*Kolosh* market," where managers of the RAC purchased fresh provisions and other goods from the Tlingit.

After the Indian village was founded at the walls of Novo-Arkhangel'sk, the Tlingit chiefs frequently visited the Russian ships. Striving to get close to the Tlingit chiefs, the administration of the Russian colonies distributed documents, certificates, and medals of different kinds. Thus, Murav'ev presented the Sitka chiefs with Russian uniforms that were reminiscent, in the words of D. I. Zavalishin, of the uniform of the Akhtyrskii Regiment of Hussars (Zavalishin 1877:3:10:156). Litke and Ferdinand P. Wrangell confirmed the marked warming in Russian-Tlingit relations between the late 1820s and the early 1830s (Litke 1834:113; Wrangell 1835:116). The incident between the Tlingit and Russians at Ozerskii Redoubt in 1825 was quickly managed by peaceful means (see the documentary appendix entry {8}). The RAC board of directors, advised by Chistiakov about the incident, expressed its complete approval of his and his subordinates' actions and reflected the hope that the occurrence at Ozerskii

Redoubt "will serve the *Koloshi* as a lesson and a warning about daring such impudence in the future. The administration of the company wishes not only to preserve eternal peace and good accord with the *Koloshi*, but to consolidate trade connections with them" (RGA VMF, f. 1375, op. 1, d. 5, l. 193–1930b.).

Such politics were fruitful. As Captain-Lieutenant Litke, who had visited Novo-Arkhangel'sk in 1827, noted, the Tlingit began to show noticeably more loyalty to the Russians than they had in Baranov's time. Shortly before the arrival of his ship in the "capital" of Russian America, a promyshlennik had gone mad and fractured an Indian's skull with a stone; later two Indian slaves had escaped from their master and concealed themselves in the Russian fort. Neither of these incidents had serious consequences, as would have been the case formerly. What is more, the Indian chiefs in the straits of the Alexander Archipelago invited the Russians to establish a trading post among them (in particular, at Kootznahoo). For its part, the administration of the colonies tried to attract the Indian aristocracy to its side. The governor of the colonies and the captains of the ships cruising around the world occasionally organized festivals for the Tlingit that featured solemn speeches about the need to maintain peace, and included desserts of rice porridge and molasses, and glasses of grog, after which the Indians usually sang and danced (Litke 1834:1:156–157, 159).

The RAC board of directors encouraged the development of trade with the Tlingit in every way. In an April 16, 1826, message to the governor of Russian America, the company's directors gave him notice that after the conventions with Great Britain and the United States were concluded, competition with foreign traders could be increased. Therefore, to retain trade with the Indians, the company's directors resolved to pay the Tlingit no less, or even more, for sea otter skins than did American captains. With this goal the RAC leadership was prepared to take such a radical step as to prohibit hunting in the region of the Alexander Archipelago altogether. Their message to the governor stated:

> The governing body of the Company asks you how much it is possible to increase and maintain your trade, not only around Sitka but in all the disputed region to 59 degrees, where foreigners are permitted joint commerce with us. Our own commerce around Sitka became insignificant long ago and, of course, cannot benefit the Company, rather serves in the meantime, as is well known, as the primary reason for the usual hostility of the savages [Indians] against the Russians, and in present circumstances can without doubt damage the success of the suggested trade with them. Therefore, if you see that the cessation of our own commerce around Sitka will have useful influence

for us in trade with the savages and that the Company can be recompensed for loss of business in the trade, in such case the Main office of the Company will accordingly cease business around Sitka, but send parties of Aleuts into other districts [of the colonies] (RGA VMF, f. 1375, op. 1, d. 5, l. 142–143).

Though by the 1830s Russian-Tlingit relations were more stable, genuine neighborly relations would take longer. Regarding the Sitka people who lived at Novo-Arkhangel'sk, Khlebnikov noted,

> The worst of them annually occupy themselves with plans to attack the fort, and as evidence of deftness the daring steal inside the walls on dark and rainy nights, at low water past the old ship *Ametist*, and, having stolen some of the materials in the Admiralty, bring it forth as trophies to their accomplices.
>
> They repeat that we occupied the place where their ancestors lived, deprived them of their gains from hunting animals, and use the best places to catch fish. We, on the other hand, think that we brought them opportunity to sell their products for a profit, provide them with necessary things, and demonstrate cultivation and the use of potatoes and other things (Khlebnikov 1985:185).

The precautionary measures against possible Tlingit attack were worked out in detail even during Baranov's time, and each person in the garrison of Novo-Arkhangel'sk knew his place in case of battle alert. Two to three watches were usually assigned on the ships standing in port, and in the fort itself six posts of 12 guards were continuously on duty. Several dozen cannons (in the batteries of Novo-Arkhangel'sk there were even heavy naval carronades of 24-pound gauge) were loaded with canisters and inspected each week. However, all these measures only checked the aggressiveness of the restless neighbors of the capital of Russian America. To increase defense at Novo-Arkhangel'sk the new governor F. P. Wrangell ordered a new wall erected between 1831 and 1832 to separate the city from the Tlingit Indian village. "In general, this wall," Wrangell wrote to the RAC's directors, "seeming to the *Koloshi* an extraordinary fort, produced in them such an impression that they were made quite meek and careful, not ceasing to be astonished at how it could be erected in such a short time" (AVPRI, f. RAK, op. 888, d. 995, l. 2130b.). With the aid of the new fort wall it was possible to prevent the Tlingit robbing the inhabitants of Novo-Arkhangel'sk. At the same time, Wrangell noted, it became significantly more difficult for the common RAC employee to buy rum from the enterprising

Indian traders who got it from American ships and then resold it to the Russian workers.

The new fort walls, which separated the residents of Novo-Arkhangel'sk from the nearby Tlingit, permitted the colonial administration to try to regulate the purchase of food products from the Indians and to introduce the RAC's monopoly there. Wrangell explained the need for such a step to save the inhabitants of the city from spending too much. The company was prepared to take an intermediary role and buy provisions from the Indians at fixed and low prices and then provide them to the RAC employees in Novo-Arkhangel'sk. In accordance with this decision, the governor issued a special rate for trade with the *Koloshi* at the beginning of 1831 (according to which, for example, a large mountain sheep cost 12 rubles, a halibut 1.5 to 3 rubles, a duck 75 kopecks, and a *vedro* {2.7 gal.} of lingonberries 2 rubles). Henceforth, free trade between the fort's inhabitants and the Tlingit was prohibited, and everything was under the charge of a particular clerk who traded with the Indians every day in the enclosed "*Kolosh* market" where he had his shop (Khlebnikov 1985:140–147).

Though this business of monopolizing trade with the *Koloshi* was profitable for the RAC, the company's common employees suffered, inasmuch as fresh products in short supply began to go almost exclusively to the colonial administration's table, and the workers had to content themselves with salted fish and corned beef. On the other hand, while Wrangell was in charge, the RAC's centralized purchases from the Tlingit notably increased. In the vicinity of Novo-Arkhangel'sk, besides acquiring fresh fish, game, berries, and oil, the company secured wood bark and clay for construction, and sometimes even firewood for heating. In their turn, the Indians began to buy more goods from the RAC, including tobacco, clothing, fabrics, and even bread. The increase in trade contributed substantially to neighborly relations between the Russians and the Tlingit. The inhabitants of Novo-Arkhangel'sk were able to go into the local forest in pairs or small groups, which had been inconceivable a little more than a decade earlier (Wrangell 1839b:13–15).

Interested in consolidating connections with the Tlingit, Wrangell in 1833 sent the brig *Chichagov* into the region of Prince of Wales Island and the Stikine River to negotiate and trade with the local Indians. Gifts that the Russians presented to the Indian chiefs and fair bartering by the RAC's clerks increased the Russians' respectability in the eyes of the southern Tlingit (AVPR, f. RAK, op. 888, d. 351, l. 30–300b.).

However, repairing relations with the hostile Tlingit in the straits of the Alexander Archipelago was not easy. In November 1835 the RAC's directors reported to the Ministry of Finance:

Upon the return of M[r.] Etolin [on the brig *Chichagov* from the mouth of the Stikine], this same mission was entrusted to Lieutenant Zarembo, and, apparently with the notion of these officers, that even with great difficulty, constant patience and substantial cost they scarcely succeeded in executing the orders of the Governor. The *Kolosh* inhabitants of those places, a numerous people, warlike, superstitious and impudent, having become incited by suggestions of envious rivals in trade [foreign competitors] about the rights of Russia to this place and that they would become enslaved by the Russians, were filled with strong suspicion and indignation toward the Russians. Only the continually fair management of the mentioned officers, donation of capital for gifts for the leaders of the savages [Indians], and invariable honesty in trade softened and finally led them to the necessity of requesting that the Governor make a Russian colony among them (RGA VMF, f. 1375, op. 1, d. 10, l. 408ob.–409).

Attempts to expand trade with the Tlingit and Kaigani were not initially fruitful for the Russians, as Wrangell explained:

The *Koloshi* in the straits [of the Alexander Archipelago], trained by traders of the United States, don't sell their furs for prices we pay them in Sitka and which seem extremely high to us: they demand even more in this and it was very difficult to persuade them to make concessions such that as payment in our wares a beaver of large size cost us 15 rubles, medium 10, small 7. . . . Such high prices are less burdensome to us only by the fact that with permission of the main office payment to the *Koloshi* is in part in rum, for 180 percent in rum is applied to the purchase price of the rum, so that payment for a beaver of large size, ⅛ of a *vedro* or by calculation 20 rubles, in fact it costs us about 7 rubles (AVPRI, f. RAK, op. 888, d. 998, l. 1750b.–176).

Nevertheless, the Russian colonial administration, urged by the main office, sometimes went to excessive expense to purchase furs from independent Indians.

A year later, in May 1834, Baron Wrangell sent Kuznetsov, lieutenant of the Corps of Fleet Navigators, on the schooner *Chilkat* to Lynn Canal to the Chilkat people's loyal chief, Annakuts, to find out how furs came from the interior Indians to the coastal Tlingit. In addition, Kuznetsov was supposed to inspect Taku Bay farther to the south, where there was another trade route into the interior (AVPRI, f. RAK, op. 888, d. 988, l. 294–301). Fortified Russian trading posts were planned for this region at the mouths of Southeast Alaska's largest rivers north of Sitka—the Chilkat and Taku. The intention was both to counter English attempts to advance along the rivers' courses deep into the interior, and to obtain furs that were received on the seacoast from the Athapaskans occupying British possessions (Tikhmenev 1861:264–267).

The connections between the Russians and Tlingit were strengthened still further after Dionisievskii Redoubt was founded at the mouth of the Stikine River between 1833 and 1834. Here the Russians annually bought all the Stikine people's furs for 70 thousand rubles (AVPR, f. RAK, op. 888, d. 351, l. 1340b.). The settlement's plot was purchased from one of the Stikine chiefs (see documentary appendix entry {10}), who was awarded a silver medal by Wrangell for assisting the Russians (AVPR, f. RAK, op. 888, d. 998, l. 2800b.–281). A silver medal was also awarded to Shakes, the noted chief of the Naanya.aayí clan, who was considered the Stikine people's main chief. In Russian documents he is usually mentioned as "Shoksha" or "Shekzh." To attract Shakes to the Russian side, a whaleboat was built especially for him in Novo-Arkhangel'sk, and his oldest son (more probably his nephew) was "shown much kindness" and "given presents" by Wrangell (AVPR, f. RAK, op. 888, d. 998, l. 1740b., 201, 306, 428, 4350b.).[42]

The Russian administration thus activated such "Tlingit politics" on its southern borders because of the fear that the English might penetrate this region. The fact is that the Hudson's Bay Company's agents quickly advanced northwestward from the basins of the Columbia and Fraser rivers at this time, establishing one trading post after another along the Pacific coast (see section 5.2). In 1832 HBC ships appeared in the straits of the Alexander Archipelago, while one of its managers, Peter S. Ogden, visited Novo-Arkhangel'sk, where he conducted negotiations with Wrangell (AVPR, f. RAK, op. 888, d. 351, l. 6ob.). News of England's intention of establishing a trading post in the Stikine River region also prompted Wrangell to quickly construct Dionisievskii Redoubt at its mouth (the redoubt St. Dionisii was founded in the fall of 1833, was given for safe keeping to the Stikine chiefs, and was completed in 1834).

The governor's activities were quite timely. By June 18, 1834, an English ship intending to go up the river to establish a trading post appeared at the Russian fort. The schooner was detained at the redoubt. After long negotiations between Lieutenant Dionisii F. Zarembo, who was on the brig *Chichagov*, and Peter Ogden, the chief agent of the Hudson's Bay Company, the English ship was compelled to leave the Russian colonies' territorial waters. This incident prompted the Hudson's Bay Company to demand compensation from the RAC for the losses they incurred. According to archival sources, the English charged

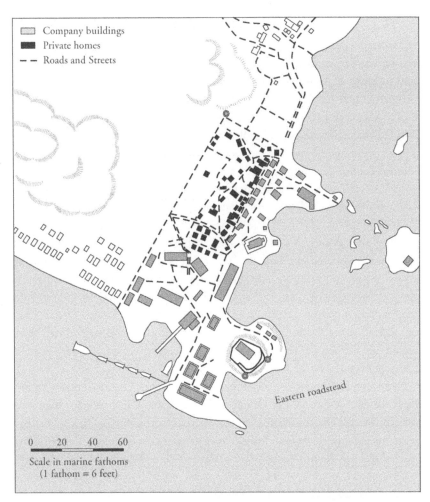

Map 5. Plan of Novo-Arkhangel'sk in 1836 (according to Blashke).
The plan is borrowed from the work of E. E. Blomkvist (1951)

the Russians with not allowing the ship to pass up the river, in violation of the conventions of 1825. The RAC rejected the English charge that its employees had threatened the use of force if the British ship attempted to continue up the Stikine. The Russians asserted that their officer had merely protested the British ship's arriving at the Russian colony without consent from the Russian officer's superior, according to the convention of 1825. The conflicting accounts of this event could have resulted from language difficulties: none of the English knew Russian, and none of the Russians English (AVPR, f. RAK, op. 888, d. 351, l. 1–139).

The RAC also rejected the Hudson's Bay Company's charge regarding the Russians' allegedly inciting the local Indians against the English. On the contrary, according to the RAC, after the incident on the Stikine the English secretly sent interpreters to the Stikine people to give the Tlingit chiefs presents and incite them to revolt against the Russians (AVPR, f. RAK, op. 888, d. 351, l. 60b., 142–142ob.). In fact, considering the Tlingit's economic interests, this anti-Russian agitation could hardly have had much success among them. The Tlingit were apprehensive over their own monopoly in bartering with the interior Indians. Therefore, the Tlingit position in the "Stikine incident" was entirely certain: the Stikine chiefs Shakes and Anakadzho, having been at the negotiations with Ogden, sharply demanded that the English leave the Stikine River (Tompkins 1945:153). The Tlingit well imagined the consequences of the English founding a trading post on Athapaskan lands. "Depriving us of our trade," declared the Indians, "you want to bring us to the position of slaves" (Fisher 1977:32). With this the Tlingit attempted to rely on the Russians' support. Wrangell reported to the RAC board of directors that the Stikine people requested that he not permit the English to pass up the Stikine (AVPR, f. RAK, op. 888, d. 351, l. 250b.). This hostile Tlingit position was one of the chief arguments forcing Ogden to abandon the attempt to open a trading post in the upper reaches of the Stikine (Fisher 1977:32).

By spring 1835 the Stikine people began to show their dissatisfaction with the Russians who had settled in Dionisievskii Redoubt. The reason for their dismay, as the colonial administration managed to ascertain, was Ogden's instigations through the Tsimshian Indians who lived at Fort Simpson. The Russians reacted quickly. Reinforcements were transferred to the redoubt and under D. F. Zarembo's care the impending conflict was settled (Grinev 1996a:72–73, 90; RGIA, f. 994, op. 2, d. 859, l. 10–100b.).

These intrigues of the English were not likely to make the RAC's leadership friendly. Wrangell noted that though these intrigues strained relations with the Indians and complicated company activity, the HBC did not receive equivalent economic gains "since the necessity for personal protection will force our colonial administration to resort in the course of time to such means, from which up to now it had refrained, and to pay agents of the Hudson's Bay Company in kind" (AVPRI, f. RAK, op. 888, d. 351, l. 250b.).

The HBC's illegally selling guns and spirits, in violation of the Convention of 1825, also brought protests from the RAC. This illegal activity, as stated in RAC documents, caused the company not only material but moral damage, since the "natives became exasperated with us, blaming us with oppression, as opposed to the acts of the English who give the savages everything they

History of Tlingit Relations in Russian America

desire" (AVPRI, f. RAK, op. 888, d. 351, l. 141–141ob.). To suppress foreign trade in the southern straits of the Alexander Archipelago, well-armed RAC ships based at Dionisievskii Redoubt or at a temporary post in Tongass Bay at the very southern boundary of Russian America were on watch during every summer navigation. In 1836 the HBC ship *Lama* was evicted from there after the Russians made persistent demands (AVPRI, f. RAK, op. 888, d. 1002, l. 133; d. 1003, l. 245). However, the RAC was itself not always irreproachable on the question of selling spirits and guns to the Tlingit. Yet in his April 1834 report to St. Petersburg, Wrangell, complaining of the high cost of Indian furs, wrote that it was necessary to sell the Natives rum in order to reduce trade expenditures (AVPRI, f. RAK, op. 888, d. 988, l. 1730ob.).

Britain's potentially constructing a trading post on the upper reaches of the Stikine worried the RAC administration. Such a post would threaten the company not only with the loss of furs but with the impoverishment of the Indian middlemen who lived in Russian territory—the Stikine people. Well-armed Tlingit deprived of the proceeds from trade with the interior tribes, the RAC feared, could compensate by robbing and plundering, and this would affect the security of the European colonies in the region (Grinev 1996a:73–74).

The Russians did not compete with the Stikine people in their middleman trade with the interior Athapaskans. In fact, they not only did not hinder the Tlingit in their operations with the Tahltan interior Indians but even encouraged them, giving the Stikine people Russian goods on consignment (AVPR, f. RAK, op. 888, d. 1005, l. 62). For furs, they obtained 25 percent more in goods from the Russians than did their fellow tribesmen in Sitka. Governor Ivan A. Kupreianov wrote to St. Petersburg saying, "Among the Stikines in general the prices are higher as against other places with respect to the rivalry of the English," and he added, "In Sitka the *Koloshi* who trade point to Stikine prices and demand the same" (AVPR, f. RAK, op. 888, d. 1004, l. 76). It was Kupreianov who permitted Ignatii Andreianov, the manager of the Dionisievskii Redoubt, "to make an increase in pay to the *Koloshi*" with molasses, crackers, rum, vests, and caps; and to sell them guns with red butts, shaving kits, and red shirts (the Tlingit valued things of red color above all) for their goods. The Stikine toion Tanakku earned the governor's special favor for promising not to go with his people to the English trading posts but rather to sell all furs only to the Russians (AVPR, f. RAK, op. 888, d. 1004, l. 454–455). The Russians used some loyal Tlingit as secret informants, who during their sea voyages to British possessions in the south were supposed to collect information on the intentions of the English and their politics with regard to the local Indians. Shakes was one such agent.

The 1830s were perhaps the period of greatest Russian activity in the southern part of the Alexander Archipelago. From 1834 to 1839 the RAC's well-armed ships (above all the 14-cannon brig *Chichagov*) regularly patrolled the southern straits, being based usually in Tongass Bay and at Dionisievskii Redoubt. Their task was to turn British and American smugglers out of Russian America's territorial waters. Simultaneously, the Russians strove to expand their trade contacts with the southern Tlingit and Kaigani and to secure the support of their chiefs. In 1836 the silver medal "Soiuznye Rossii" {the Allies of Russia} was given to a Tongass ḵwáan chief, Nekut (Negut, the head chief of the Teiḵweidí Tanta-ḵwáan, in oral histories recorded by Olson [1967:87–88]). In 1837 silver medals were also given to Ankta (Annta, Anta), the chief of the Tanta-Ḵwáan, and to Senaḵet, the chief of the Kaigani. In these same years the Stikine chiefs Kuatḵe, Shekesti, and Ḵuaketli were awarded medals (AVPR, f. RAK, op. 888, d. 1000, l. 32; d. 1001, l. 226). The closest and most friendly relations developed between the Stikine people and the Russians. In 1836 fifteen hundred Stikine people (practically the whole ḵwáan) resettled under the walls of Dionisievskii Redoubt (about twenty Russians were always stationed in it, and a RAC ship annually wintered in the nearest bay). The Indians now built their winter homes near the Russian fort (Arndt 1988:32–33).

Russian ships' frequent visits to the redoubt, negotiations, gifts, and trade greatly promoted rapprochement between the Stikine people and the Russians. In 1837 the distinguished missionary Ivan E. Veniaminov visited the Stikine. Influenced by his preachings, one of the leading Stikine chiefs, Kuatḵa (or Kuaḵte) was the first Tlingit to free two of his slaves instead of sacrificing them, as custom demanded, at a potlatch in honor of the construction of a new home at the redoubt. Since the chief already had a silver medal, the colonial leader asked the government for a special gift—"honorable clothing"—which was approved by the czar (see documentary appendix entry {13}). In fact, Kuatḵa was never given the royal gift since sometime later he compromised himself in the eyes of the Russians by "groundlessly" killing his female slave, and then his brother Ikaaz as well (AVPR, f. RAK, op. 888, d. 1000, l. 32; d. 1005, l. 1690b.; d. 1006, l. 1690b.).

Meanwhile, the "Stikine incident" of 1834 was resolved after long negotiations with an agreement on January 25 (February 6), 1839, between the RAC and the Hudson's Bay Company, according to which the coastal zone of the Russian possessions in America from Cape Spencer in the north to Portland Canal in the south was leased to the English for a period of ten years (AVPR, f. RAK, op. 888, d. 351, l. 215–221).[43] This contract was repeatedly extended until Alaska was sold to the United States in 1867. Thus, almost all the Tlingit who

History of Tlingit Relations in Russian America

lived in the coastal zone of the Russian possessions from 1840 to 1867 formally fell under the control of the Hudson's Bay Company. The lease of the coastal part of the Russian possessions in America must have, according to the idea of the Hudson's Bay Company's director, suppressed the flow of furs from the remote regions of the mainland (up to now a significant part of the furs from this region fell into the hands of the Russians).

The rapprochement between the Tlingit and the Russians in the 1830s also contributed, paradoxically, to the smallpox epidemic that enveloped the entire Northwest Coast and Alaska between 1835 and 1839. In November 1835 smallpox appeared in Novo-Arkhangel'sk and over the course of three months took the lives of 400 Sitka people, that is, almost half the Indians who were living at the walls of the Russian fort (Tikhmenev 1863:2:311; Veniaminov 1840b:31). According to Veniaminov, of the 10,000 Tlingit and Kaigani who lived in Alaska up to the appearance of smallpox, only 6,000 survived (Veniaminov 1840a:29–30). In Indian villages in the straits of the Alexander Archipelago the epidemic did not abate until the summer of 1837. It was, perhaps, the most terrible shock for the Native population of Russian American in the 19th century. The illness, which began in the English possessions in the south, spread like wildfire to the north and quickly reached Alaska, taking with it thousands of Natives' lives.

The smallpox epidemic did not rage everywhere with the same force. Around the Stikine River its disastrous consequences were almost unfelt, whereas in the Kootznahoo ḵwáan entire households died out (Tikhmenev 1863:2:311). This epidemic destroyed the majority of the Tlingit in the Gulf of Alaska region. According to De Laguna's informants, those who died were so numerous that it was impossible to bury all of them right away (De Laguna 1972:1:18, 277–278). This is confirmed by Russian archival documents. By the summer of 1839 I. A. Kupreianov reported to the RAC board of directors that the Yakutat people especially suffered from smallpox (AVPRI, f. RAK, op. 888, d. 1004, l. 406). The epidemic inflicted no fewer losses on the Indians of British possessions. In the opinion of George Simpson, the HBC's director, smallpox took the lives of a third of the Northwest Coast Indians (Simpson 1847:1:207). I. A. Kupreianov, an eyewitness to the epidemic, gives a more modest number, estimating that about a fourth of the Native population of this region died (AVPRI, f. RAK, op. 888, d. 1001, l. 2350b.).

In the opinion of the American researcher D. E. Dumond, smallpox spread to the Tlingit not from the south or east (from British possessions), as is generally accepted in American and Russian historiography, but rather was carried to the Indians from Novo-Arkhangel'sk as a result of unsuccessfully vaccinating the RAC's Native employees (most probably using defective vaccine). [44] The evidence that Dumond cites makes his version quite plausible. The Russian medical men who vaccinated the Natives were undoubtedly moved by the best motives, but the result was quite tragic. Of course, in Russian America it was not a matter of "bacteriological warfare" against independent Natives, such as occurred during the well-known Pontiac uprising against English authority in 1763, when British officers distributed to the Indians blankets taken from people sick with smallpox (Dumond 1996, 2001:78, 82–88).

The large number of Indian deaths weakened their overt and passive resistance to colonization. Moreover, during the epidemic the Russians provided as much help as possible to the Tlingit by giving vaccinations. The Indians confirmed the knowledge and good intentions of the Russians, as well as the inadequacy of their own shamans. As Veniaminov attests, not only the Sitka people but the Indians of other ḵwáans began to arrive in Novo-Arkhangel'sk to get their children vaccinated against smallpox.

The Russian-Tlingit rapprochement that began to take shape in the 1830s was clouded in the spring of 1838. At the end of April 1838 three RAC employees fled Novo-Arkhangel'sk. They intended to make their way south to the English trading posts or to meet up with some American ship in the southern part of the Alexander Archipelago. Two of the deserters, Nikita Karaulov and Nikolai Ivanov, had already once tried to flee to the English, from Dionisievskii Redoubt, but were caught and returned by Tlingit hired by the redoubt's director. The runaways were delivered to Novo-Arkhangel'sk and punished. However, this failure did not stop them. And then in April, having made an agreement with the creole Ippolion Soltanov, they organized a new escape, having this time stolen a canoe from the Sitka people and taken with them two female Tlingit slaves (one of whom served as a guide through the straits). Along the way the runaways occupied themselves with robbing and plundering. First they murdered two Sitka people, then they killed two families of Tlingit of the Kake-Kuiu ḵwáan (killing a total of 11 people). They forcibly took two Tlingit women from these families. Finally, in June the deserters joined in a skirmish with a group of Kake people, during which Karaulov was mortally wounded. The other two runaways were also wounded. On the Indian side of the skirmish, their chief, Ḵukka, was killed and the remaining Indians ran off into the woods (the majority of them having been wounded). After this the deserters were forced to set out for Dionisievskii Redoubt, where they surrendered to the manager, Ignatii Andreianov. The governor, Kupreianov, as well as his aide, Dionisii F. Zarembo, had to take urgent measures to avoid an escalation of conflict. The fact is, a group of armed Kake people soon arrived at Dionisievskii Redoubt intending to kill its manager in revenge for the death of Chief Kukka. They did not do this, but only because the Stikine people who were friendly toward the Russians forced them to abandon this plan. The brig *Chichagov* arrived at the redoubt at this time and began to negotiate payment of compensation to the Kake people for the death of their kinsmen. The RAC paid goods in the sum of 1,237 rubles. Those deserters who remained alive after medical treatment were sent to Okhotsk to appear in court for, as Kupreianov wrote, "their guilt is of great conceit" (AVPR, f. RAK, op. 888, d. 1003, l. 84–85, 201–205; d. 1004, l. 222–228).

The 1840s were the period of the greatest rapprochement between the Russians and Tlingit. The increasing activity of the Hudson's Bay Company in southeastern Alaska forced the Russian administration to pay serious attention to developing multilateral connections with the Tlingit. Contributing significantly to this were the farsighted politics of Adolph K. Etolin, governor of Russian America from 1840 to 1845. From 1840 to 1841, by his order, the first Russian steamship in Alaska, *Nikolai I*, made five trips along the straits to trade with the Tlingit (the Indians themselves having invited the Russians to visit them). In 1841, by Etolin's order, an *igrushka*—a fair with elements of the traditional Indian potlatch—was organized for the Tlingit near the walls of Novo-Arkhangel'sk (this cost the RAC 1,200 rubles) (AVPR, f. RAK, op. 888, d. 1007, l. 267ob.). In 1842 the governor (by request of the Tlingit themselves) immediately hired about 50 Indians to work for the company. Some of them went to work at the Novo-Arkhangel'sk port, and some became sailors on RAC ships. Etolin was entirely satisfied with their service and thought that in the course of time the Tlingit could replace not only the Aleut workers but even the Russians (Mamyshev 1855:246–247) (see documentary appendix entry {18}).

Striving to gradually gain control over "independent Natives," the RAC introduced the title of "head toion of the *Koloshi*" (see documentary appendix 14). The company's selection fell on the baptized Sitka toion Mikhail Kukkan, well known for his loyalty to the Russians (see documentary appendix entries {14} and {19}). On October 10, 1843, Kukkan received czarist gifts that were originally destined for the Stikine chief Kuatke: a brocade kaftan, a brocade girdle with braid and fringe, and a cap with feathers, all valued at an impressive 1,056 rubles 50 kopecks.[45] The chief was also entrusted with a personal seal with the image of a raven sitting on a branch and the inscription "Mikhail Kukkan," as well as a saber. Kukkan was then administered an oath in the Novo-Arkhangel'sk cathedral in the presence of the whole colonial government and a substantial number of baptized Tlingit chiefs and ordinary Indians. In his "promise under oath" to the Russian emperor and the crown prince, Kukkan attested that he would "faithfully and sincerely serve and obey in all without regard to his life to the last drop of blood . . . and in addition, would endeavor to hasten all faithful service and employment by the state in everything possible that concerns His Imperial Highness" (RGIA, f. 18, op. 5, d. 1306, l. 10–11; d. 1312, l. 110b.–130b.).

However, the Russian-American Company's pompously executed action did not lead to the desired results inasmuch as Kukkan's authority among the Sitka people was not great, and most Indians of other kwáans did not recognize his authority. Etolin himself noted that Kukkan could not have had great influence since he was not wealthy. In order to support his protégé, the governor in 1844 ordered that he be given "reciprocal" goods worth 2,327 rubles (AVPR, f. RAK, op. 888, d. 1010, l. 213).[46] With these means supplied to him, Kukkan acquired six slaves (three men and three women), but even after this it was difficult for him to compare to most prosperous Tlingit chiefs. Etolin's direct successor, Mikhail D. Teben'kov, reported to St. Petersburg that Kukkan "by his poverty has almost no influence on the Sitka *Koloshi*, and even less on the *Koloshi* of the straits" (AVPR, f. RAK, op. 888, d. 1013, l. 2790b.).

During these years the Russians strove to preserve friendly relations with the Stikine people. Thus, from time to time they sent a steamship to Dionisievskii Redoubt (Fort Stikine) to find out, the documents report, that "the Natives do not undergo any oppression or insult from the English." The latter, however, were conducting themselves honorably and for the time being not giving the Tlingit cause for dissatisfaction. Dionisii F. Zarembo, who visited there in February 1845, reported to Etolin: "The Stikine toions declared that they [the English] treat them very well and go to extremes of affection" (AVPR, f. RAK, op. 888, d. 1012, l. 28). At the same time, protecting the Tlingit who sided with the colonial administration and making advances to their chiefs had certain political consequences for Russian-English-Tlingit relations (see section 5.2).

Large-scale trade between the Tlingit and the Russians was conducted during Etolin's and Teben'kov's times. A steamship set out along the straits every year to purchase furs and potatoes from the Indians (Tables 6–8). Sometimes the Indians themselves delivered potatoes to Novo-Arkhangel'sk. In 1845 the capital of Russian America saw the arrival of 250 canoes loaded with potatoes (160 of the canoes belonged to the Kaigani and the Haida from the Queen Charlotte Islands). Teben'kov wrote of the Tlingit and Haida: "The industry, enterprise, and activity of this tribe is quite astonishing. In 1844 they delivered to Sitka 300 barrels [of potatoes] and Adolph Karlovich [Etolin], probably not suspecting that they were beginning to increase this exploitation, said: 'no matter how many potatoes you bring, we will buy them all,' and they presently

Table 6. Prices of Tlingit Furs in Novo-Arkhangel'sk and on RAC Ships in the Mid-1840s

Furs	Quantity & name of goods	Rubles
1 sea otter of	7 wool blankets	126
1st quality	5 lbs. gunpowder	5
	10 lbs. of shot or 1 bar of lead	5
	4 packages of cinnabar	3
	1 skein of red wool	0.50
	2 {gun} flints	0.50
	¼ lb. tobacco	
	Total	140
1 {river} otter	1 blanket	18
	or 5 lbs. gunpowder &	10
	1 10 lb. bar of lead	
1 *koshlok*[a]	2 blankets	36
	or 1 rifle	25
1 black bear skin	4 packages of cinnabar	3
	or 1 axe	5

Source: Table is based on materials of Markov (1856:77–78).

[a]*koshlok:* a young sea otter 6 to 7 months old.

[in October 1845] brought 1,060 barrels" (AVPR, f. RAK, op. 888, d. 1012, l. 187–188).

Especially close economic connections developed between the Russians and the Stikine people. The latter were the chief suppliers of fresh provisions for the inhabitants of Novo-Arkhangel'sk. In addition, various handcrafted artifacts and construction materials (bark and logs) were purchased from them. For example, from May 1848 to May 1849 the company obtained 1,360 logs from the Tlingit (Gibson 1976:31). The Indians, for their part, acquired from the Russians a substantial amount of European goods during this same period. In his report to the RAC board of directors, Etolin wrote, "The *Koloshi* have at present drawn so close to the Russians that they consider them their friends and benefactors and, having comprehended the complete advantage to be gained from association with the Russians, cannot remain without relations with them and have become different from those of former times" (AVPR, f. RAK, op. 888, d. 1010, l. 276ob.).

From 1830 to 1840 Novo-Arkhangel'sk was not a "single center of distribution of Russian culture" among the Tlingit, as Istomin and Philip Drucker suggest (Drucker 1965:196; Istomin 1985:152). Dionisievskii Redoubt was under

Russian control for about six years, and trade was rather regular between the Russians and Tlingit on board RAC ships and steamships in the straits of the Alexander Archipelago. In addition, the northern Tlingit regularly traveled to Fort Konstantinovskii on Nuchek Island in Chugach Bay to trade with the Russians (AVPR, f. RAK, op. 888, d. 1006, l. 265–2650b.; d. 1016, l. 252).

In the mid-1840s relations between the Tlingit and the Russians improved so much that the governor, then Teben'kov, reported to St. Petersburg that the "Tlingit problem" had moved into the background among his priorities in Native politics. In fact, Teben'kov did not connect the improvement in relations with mitigating the "temper of the *Koloshi*" or with their special "disposition" toward the Russians but rather with the Tlingit's mystical fear regarding the RAC steamships, which defied wind and current. The largest of the RAC's steamships plying the straits at this time was *Nikolai I*, which had the most powerful armament of all the company's ships: ten cannons, a mount for firing incendiary rockets, boarding nets, and a full set of conventional weapons and firearms.

Another reason for the Tlingit's peacefulness in the 1840s, according to Teben'kov, was the fact that quite a few Indians worked for the Russian-American Company at this time. In a letter to his assistant, Captain of the Second Rank Zarembo, dated May 18, 1846, Teben'kov wrote: "An attack by the *Koloshi* at the present time seems unlikely because the *Koloshi* now serve on almost all our ships as sailors—consequently loyal hostages of our security here" (AVPR, f. RAK, op. 888, d. 1006, l. 265–2650b.; d. 1013, l. 398–3980b.).

Striving even more to draw the Tlingit to them, Teben'kov, following Etolin's example, organized an *igrushka*, for the Indians at the walls of Novo-Arkhan-gel'sk, which occurred on April 12 and 16, 1846 (see documentary appendix entry {22}).

However, a general Russian evil, bureaucracy, negatively affected Russian colonial politics concerning the Tlingit. The governor of Russian America was obliged to contact St. Petersburg with even the least significant questions and at times waited years for the RAC board of directors to give its answer or final decision. The situation in the colonies, of course, could entirely change as they awaited the RAC's decision. In addition, the Russian colonies' administration was entangled in dozens of sections and paragraphs that frequently contradicted real-life requirements. Thus, Teben'kov wrote to the board of directors in May 1847 that he was experiencing substantial difficulty carrying out section 286 of the new Statute of the RAC (of 1844) prohibiting the sale of firearms to the Natives of the Russian colonies. He reported to St. Petersburg: "Cessation of the sale of firearms aroused the general indignation of the *Koloshi*, both the

Table 7. Annually Obtained Procurement from the *Koloshi* at the Port of Novo-Arkhangel'sk, 1842–60

Year	Sea otter	Beaver	River otter	Fox	Bear	Lynx	Sable (marten)	Desman (muskrat)	Mink	Fur seal	Sea otter tails	Wolverine	Wolf
1842	99	215	151	117	103	13	148	65	32	2	84	11	4
1843	136	311	238	93	98		120	16	40		130	8	7
1844	74	253	121		17	3	245				76	11	1
1845	91	187	152	65	29		235				118	13	9
1846	62	93	139	60	1		170		6		64	7	2
1847	158	58	119	29	3		51				141	11	1
1848	44	33	22				7				29	1	
1849	75	444	91	24	4		42		54		96	4	1
1850	139	349	81	68	13	9	200		30	1	135	6	
1851	111	462	65	22	1	7	189		144		114	6	
1852	46	143	15	2			24				58		
1853	1	79			2						7		
1854	1	23					21		30		1		
1855	3	9	2										
1856		15											
1857													
1858													
1859		32			4			4	22		3		
1860		73		1	7		3	5	27				

Source: Golovin (1862:158–159).

Table 8. Annually Obtained Procurement through Trade with the *Koloshi* in the Straits, 1842–60

Year	Sea otter	Beaver	River otter	Fox	Bear	Lynx	Sable (marten)	Desman (muskrat)	Mink	Sea otter tails	Wolverine
1842	32	21	11	12	65	1	34	3	599	24	
1843	62	17	3	8	2					36	1
1844	7	37	19	3	3		5		2		
1845	53	3	12	15	1		27			32	1
1846	80	14	19	18	3		22			61	3
1847											
1848	51	15	22	7	10	6	13			50	1
1849	89	179	45	9		1	23			75	1
1850	121	81	47	37		2				87	3
1851											
1852											
1853											
1854											
1855											
1856											
1857											
1858											
1859					1						
1860	15	15	3	4	4		4	1	12		

Source: Golovin (1862:158–159).

Sitka people and those of the straits. They say that the cessation of the sale to them of rifles and gunpowder takes from them any possibility of obtaining animals, which they can procure only with a gun—and moreover gives them cause to suspect that we intend to subdue them to our power, having deprived them in advance of means of protecting themselves" (AVPR, f. RAK, op. 888, d. 1015, l. 30). In subsequent negotiations with the Tlingit chiefs, Teben'kov never succeeded in convincing the Indians of the necessity of section 286. Wishing to preserve good relations with the Tlingit, and understanding that their claims were just, he ordered that they be given some gunpowder and rifles despite the new RAC statute. Simultaneously, the governor requested further instructions on section 286 from the company's leadership. In his opinion, the sale of ammunition and rifles to the Tlingit was necessary not only for maintaining friendly relations with them but because otherwise the Russians would be living in Novo-Arkhangel'sk without fresh meat, while the Russian-American Company itself was deprived of furs (AVPR, f. RAK, op. 888, d. 1015, l. 290b.–320b.). Not until the end of November 1848 did Teben'kov receive official permission from the RAC board of directors to sell gunpowder and rifles in small quantities to the Tlingit (AVPR, f. RAK, op. 888, d. 1016, l. 429–4290b.).

The generally friendly relations between the Tlingit and Russians in the 1840s were often complicated by small conflicts that never escalated to serious clashes.[47] Aleksandr Markov, the manager of the Russian-American Company, who visited Russian America during these years, wrote:

> I myself was a witness as they pacified the Koliuzhi in the case of some hostile action on their side: if they make noise and gather at the fort, then they the {Russians} sound the alarm, lock up the fort, and begin to try to persuade them verbally to cease the disturbance; when admonition does not work, they fire a cannonball over their heads, which by its whistle scatters the rebellious crowd into the woods and anywhere—and with this all the noise ceases. An unpleasant consequence of these squabbles is the fact that the savages do not come to the market with provisions and do not want to trade. This obstinacy on the side of the savages continues sometimes for a whole week, during the course of which the Russians have no recourse but to remain without fresh provisions (Markov 1856:72–73).

In the early 1850s Russian-Tlingit connections at various levels notably weakened. This was probably caused both by the lack of broad cooperation with the Tlingit by Etolin's successors and by peaceful attempts to acculturate them, as noted by Pavel N. Golovin (1862:49). The frequent change of governors during this period (1850–54) saw three governors: Nikolai Ya. Rozenberg, Aleksandr I. Rudakov, and Stepan V. Voevodskii. Each governor conducted his own politics, which were often quite different from the politics of his predecessors, and thus negatively affected relations with the independent Indians. Especially inconsistent and weak were Rozenberg's "Tlingit politics." In April 1851 he conducted an igrushka, at which about two thousand free Koloshi gathered and which cost the RAC 1,800 rubles (Dean 1995:280). [48] However, cooperation with the Tlingit later declined. From the early 1850s hiring Tlingit to work in Novo-Arkhangel'sk was curtailed. Buying furs from the Indians almost stopped. From 1853 to 1860 in Novo-Arkhangel'sk only five sea otter skins were obtained from the Tlingit (Golovin 1862:101, 158–159) (see also Table 7). After 1851 the steamship that had formerly been sent through the straits to trade with the Indians remained almost entirely in the Novo-Arkhangel'sk port, because the colonial administration feared an attack by the Natives (Golovin 1862:113–114). All these events caused mutual alienation and suspicion. Provocations on the part of the Tlingit became more frequent. In 1850 they caused several quarrels, and even fights, with Russians (at the market and in the forest). Governor Rozenberg, with the mediation of Mikhail Kuḵkan, told the Stikine people that if they did not stop then he would close the market and stop trade with them. In answer to this ultimatum, the Tlingit attempted to seize Novo-Arkhangel'sk the following day. Some of them, armed with rifles, occupied the area behind the buildings and hid in the shrubbery at the walls of the fort. Others, erecting ladders at the wooden tower where the cannons pointed at the Tlingit village, the "*Kolosh* battery," nearly took possession of it. Fortunately for the Russians, the guards were alert and raised the alarm in time. An armed detachment threw down three Indians who were climbing onto the battery and stopped the remainder. Another detachment of Russians was sent to oust the Sitka people who had sequestered themselves near fortified structures. "I myself," reported Rozenberg, "also ran to the battery and with great difficulty talked to them, and succeeded in getting the *Koloshi* to return home and they ceased provoking us to battle" (AVPR, f. RAK, op. 888, d. 1020, l. 318–318ob.).

The following year the Stikine people again began to manifest "insolence." In the spring of 1851 they repeatedly fell upon Russian fishermen and stole the fish from the seines; twice they undermined the fort walls at the laundry and, thus finding themselves in the drying room, carried away many linens; they broke down the fish barn walls and took several *pudy* of salted fish, and in the fall of 1851 they robbed several kitchen gardens around Novo-Arkhangel'sk and, as Rozenberg reported, "had on their part moreover undertaken and performed

History of Tlingit Relations in Russian America

other dirty tricks against Russians as well" (AVPR, f. RAK, op. 888, d. 1020, l. 318ob.–319ob.).

In 1852 the Russians found themselves indirectly drawn into intertribal conflict. At the walls of Novo-Arkhangel'sk a bloody clash occurred between the Sitka people and Indians of the Naanya.aayí of the Stikine ḵwáan who had just arrived. This is known in the English-language literature as the "Sitka massacre." Hostility between the Kaagwaantaan clans of the Sitka and Chilkat ḵwáans, on the one hand, and the Naanya.aayí of the Stikine ḵwáan, on the other, had begun in the 1820s. Legends collected by Olson indicate two possible reasons for this enmity: controversy over the right to use the Killer Whale totem and rivalry over women (Olson 1967:29–30, 77–79). Veniaminov mentions an extremely unfortunate Sitka campaign against the Staḵin (Stikine) people (Veniaminov 1840a:124–125). The Sitka people and their allies, the Kaagwaantaan of the Chilkat ḵwáan, were routed in 1829 and, according to Rozenberg, lost no fewer than 70 warriors (AVPR, f. RAK, op. 888, d. 1020, l. 307ob.–308). According to P. E. Chistiakov, the primary battle between the Naanya.aayí from the Stikine and the warlike groups of Kaagwaantaan of the Chilkat, Sitka, and Kootznahoo ḵwáans occurred a year later, in 1830, and the latter lost from 70 to 110 warriors (Arndt 1988:29). As the Kaagwaantaan themselves declared to Wrangell in 1831, the reason for their defeat was insufficient ammunition (see documentary appendix entry {9}). The skirmish between the hostile clans continued until the 1850s, each Naanya.aayí being "reckoned" at about 40 "unavenged" Kaagwaantaan. Finally, at the beginning of 1851 a truce envoy arrived from the Stikine people and proposed to the Kaagwaantaan that they surrender 12 men and 5 women of the Naanya.aayí clan as slaves as compensation for those murdered, and make up the remaining "blood debt" with furs and European goods. The Kaagwaantaan accepted this proposal and even set off for final negotiations at the mouth of the Stikine. However, the Stikine people did not fulfill their promises and gave the Sitka people only some small gifts. Though peace between the Naanya.aayí and the Kaagwaantaan was formally concluded, the latter were entirely dissatisfied with it. The Stikine people, for their part, feeling its instability, were careful to arrive in Novo-Arkhangel'sk in large parties, and they sent only groups of several people to trade there. Nevertheless, in 1852 there arrived at the Sitka village, as Rozenberg reported, "the Stikine chief Tanaiaka with almost all his clan, with women and children, totaling 50 souls" (AVPR, f. RAK, op. 888, d. 1020, l. 308–310). The Sitka people, long wanting revenge, suddenly fell on the guests during a dance and killed 40 people (25 men, including Chief Tanaiaka, 9 Tlingit noble women, and 6 children). Only three Stikine people were saved (one of them was the son of Chief Tanaiaka). They were able to take shelter in Novo-Arkhangel'sk under Russian protection and then were sent to their Native clan in an Indian canoe. Several women who had come with the Naanya.aayí to Sitka also escaped. According to N. Ya. Rozenberg's report, several women were able to run into the forest during the slaughter, including three Stikine (Naanya.aayí?). Among the fugitives, wrote Rozenberg, were "several Stakine women, who did not belong to this tribe and who were considered related to the Chilkat [that is, to the Chilkat ḵwáan]; these women, who were related to an allied tribe [the Chilkat Gaanaxteidí lineage?], were spared by the Koloshi [Stikine people] and later released to their home territory." Of the women who ran into the woods, some were afterward found dead, evidently from hunger, and the governor had no information about the others (AVPRI, f. RAK, op. 888, d. 1020, l. 312–312ob.). After these events the Stikine, providing themselves with gunpowder and bullets at Fort Simpson for the forthcoming raid on their enemies, reported to the local chief HBC trader William McNeill that the Stikine people had killed four main chiefs and over 50 men, women, and children, having taken two or three women hostage (Dean 1995:287).

In the "Sitka massacre" only one man and one boy died, and several warriors were wounded on the Kaagwaantaan side. The Kaagwaantaan of the Sitka and Akoi ḵwáans were not the only ones involved in the slaughter. Judging by indirect data, the L'uknax.ádi of the Akoi and Yakutat ḵwáans, and even several people from the Sitka Kiks.ádi clan, also took part (AVPR, f. RAK, op. 888, d. 1020, l. 311–315; De Laguna 1972:1:279–284). Based on legend, the Sitka people were led by Yakvan (De Laguna 1960:156), who, according to Swanton (1908:405), was chief of the Star House of the Sitka Kaagwaantaan lineage. He had evidently been baptized, since he is mentioned in the Russian documents as "Kaagwaantaan *Kolosh* Aleksandr Yakvan" (AVPR, f. RAK, op. 888, d. 1025, l. 1020b.).[49]

The colonial administration learned of the intended slaughter almost an hour before it began, but Rozenberg decided to wait, his motivation for nonintervention being paragraph 280 of the Statute of the Russian-American Company, which prohibited company representatives from intervening in the affairs of "independent Natives," excepting cases in which the latter requested it. Rozenberg's position was later repeatedly criticized, including by the RAC board of directors, who usually zealously protected the "honor of the uniform" (*Doklad Komiteta*, 1863a:490–491).

The colonial authority's politics of nonintervention in the conflict between the Stikine and the Sitka peoples in 1852 had serious consequences for the Russians. Rozenberg himself noted in his report to the main office that after this slaughter the "impudence of the *Koloshi*" increased even more. Fearing the revenge of the Stikine people, they began to organize maneuvers in their village at the walls of Novo-Arkhangel'sk, which included firing rifles, and they nearly wounded several Russians. Finally, the governor threatened that if the Indians did not stop the provocation, he would begin exercises on the ships and in the fort, firing cannons through their village. This threat quieted the Tlingit for a while. However, they soon attempted to storm Novo-Arkhangel'sk at night, which did not succeed since the Russians were warned about the intended attack by a Chilkat chief and so took countermeasures. In clarifying the reason for this incident, the Tlingit chiefs told Rozenberg that they had allegedly learned from Tlingit women living with Russians that a massacre of the Indians was coming and had wanted to "forestall" this.

After this incident several more provocations followed, which forced Rozenberg to close the "*Kolosh* market" for a month (the market was opened again only after the urgent entreaties of the Tlingit and promises to "improve").

The Sitka people themselves, wrote Rozenberg, greatly feared the Stikine people's revenge and at night panic often flared in their village at the walls of Novo-Arkhangel'sk, as evidenced by sporadic gunfire. By common effort the Sitka people fortified their village on the forest-facing side with a palisade and, once behind it, fired into the surrounding forest for several hours, suspecting that the Stikine people were concealed there (AVPR, f. RAK, op. 888, d. 1020, l. 320–325).

The Stikine attack that the Sitka people so feared was made not against them but against the Russians. A group of Stikine ḵwáan warriors fell upon a Russian settlement of three houses at Hot Springs (20 versts {about 13 miles} from Novo-Arkhangel'sk). Of the nine RAC employees who were being treated there, one was killed and one wounded; the remainder fled through the mountains to Ozerskii Redoubt (see documentary appendix entry {27}). The Russian settlement was looted and burned. The Stikine people had attacked Hot Springs because they supposed that Sitka people were hiding from them in the settlement (see documentary appendix entry {27}).

Several works describing these events are flawed. For example, Clarence L. Andrews, Clarence C. Hulley, and James R. Gibson erroneously report that in 1852 the Stikine people attacked and destroyed Ozerskii Redoubt (Andrews 1947:117; Gibson 1976:12–13; Hulley 1953:177). In fact, the Stikine attack occurred only on the Russian settlement of three cabins at the Hot Springs. Ozerskii Redoubt, according to the source materials, endured until Alaska was sold in 1867 (Golovnin 1864:5:304).

After destroying the settlement at Hot Springs, the Sitka people, according to Rozenberg, "were in despair," since they feared Russian vengeance for the damage caused. The Indians were calmed only after they gave the governor "three ruffians of the Ku̱kontan clan" as peace hostages. But even before the lapse of the stipulated term, these "three scoundrels," as Rozenberg put it, who were convinced of the Russians' peaceful intentions, asked to go home, and the governor released them from Novo-Arkhangel'sk (AVPR, f. RAK, op. 888, d. 1020, l. 546–547).

After these stormy events came a brief period of calm in Russian-Tlingit relations. "Peace and tranquility were maintained with the surrounding savages," A. I. Rudakov, Captain of the Second Rank who replaced Rozenberg, reported to St. Petersburg on December 2, 1853.

Meanwhile, clouds began to form on the international horizon. The Crimean War approached. A visit to Novo-Arkhangel'sk in August 1853 by the British frigate *Triconmalee* and bellicose articles in the English press alerted the colonial administration and the RAC board of directors in St. Petersburg. The latter proposed to the HBC's directors in January 1854 that they conclude a pact of mutual neutrality of the possessions of both companies in the event of war, especially since the corresponding articles existed in the contracts of the lease of 1839 and 1849. The RAC leadership realized that neither the company's colonial flotilla nor Novo-Arkhangel'sk and the other Russian settlements in Alaska were in a position to withstand a large British war squadron. However, the trading posts and the HBC ships on the Northwest Coast were notably inferior militarily to the Russian colonies' potential, and the main office hoped that the HBC's directors would agree on neutrality. Simpson, for example, considered it mad for the two companies to be involved in war. He feared that the well-armed RAC ships would destroy the HBC steamships and forts on the coast and entirely paralyze British trade in the region. In addition, the warlike Indian tribes (primarily the Tlingit, Haida, and Tsimshian) could be drawn into fighting, which could have unpredictable consequences (Galbraith 1957:163–165; Grinev 1996a:81–82). Therefore, the HBC's directors, with no less enthusiasm than the RAC, supported the neutrality of the two companies' possessions in the approaching war. The Russian and English governments quickly agreed to ratify a neutrality pact inasmuch as it did not affect their strategic interests in the Balkans and Near East. According to the March 1854 agreement, Russian America remained neutral and was formally in the blockade (however, the British fleet in the Pacific Ocean was in no position to form an actual blockade). Of course, RAC ships could be seized on the open sea and the neutrality itself did not extend to the company's trading posts on the

Asiatic coast. Thus, the Indians played an indirect role in protecting Russian America during the Crimean War.

S. V. Voevodskii, occupying the post of governor of the Russian colonies in 1854, adhered to more severe politics with regard to the Tlingit than did his predecessor N. Ya. Rozenberg. In general he did not consider the Indians' use beneficial to the company's work since, profiting from storing firewood and ice (ice was delivered to the Americans in San Francisco), the Tlingit almost ceased supplying Novo-Arkhangel'sk with fresh provisions. In addition, Voevodskii forbade the Tlingit chiefs from freely entering the port to trade, as had been customary before. This prohibition caused a peculiar "strike" by the Indians. They refused to carry out their usual work for the RAC, demonstrating their dissatisfaction. Now only healthy people could be assigned to guard duty, diverting them from their primary work, whereas formerly the sick, weak, and old were usually posted. Though in spring 1854, along with Voevodskii, 22 military sailors arrived in Novo-Arkhangel'sk, they were not able to substantially strengthen its garrison. In fact, somewhat later in the year, about a hundred soldiers and two officers from the Siberian Line Battalion No. 14 were transferred from the port of Ayan to Novo-Arkhangel'sk (Fedorova 1973:162; Golovin 1863b:337). The start of the Crimean War (1853–56) had dictated the need to fortify the Russian colonies in America with regular units, which the military administration of Siberia strove to do in this regard. Nevertheless, the soldiers' presence did not guarantee security for Novo-Arkhangel'sk from Indian action.

On March 10, 1855, several Sitka people fell upon a military sailor who was guarding the company woodshed, and seriously injured him. "The cause for this insolent act," wrote Voevodskii, "was nothing other than that the sentry was seen by them as an obstacle to the theft of company firewood, purchased from them, to be resold a second time to the company, which has quite often happened" (AVPR, f. RAK, op. 888, d. 1022, l. 77). According to Kan's sources, the theft of firewood that belonged to the RAC was, from the Tlingit point of view, a distinct form of revenge and compensation for the various offenses and insults that the Russians had committed earlier, especially those regarding Indian women (Kan 1999:142).

The governor demanded that the Indians guilty of the attack quickly leave the Native settlement at Novo-Arkhangel'sk and never return. In answer, the Sitka people armed themselves with rifles and began to threaten the fort. The Russian garrison was placed on alert. Two blank cannon shots, intended to frighten the Indians, not only did not scare them but in fact infuriated them. Some of them threw themselves at the fort walls and began to chop at the palisade. Others tried to penetrate the port. Another group rushed along the fort walls, intending to pass around it on the woods-facing side by the lake and from there force their way into Novo-Arkhangel'sk. One of the Indians, having shot at point-blank range at the manager F. Kuznetsov, who was on the "*Kolosh* battery," mortally wounded him. This caused the Russians to open fire. The Indians rushed back from the palisade and, having hidden behind stumps and boulders, began to fire upon the fort. Others threw themselves at the "*Kolosh* church," which stood not far from the walls of Novo-Arkhangel'sk, occupied it as a fortified point, and opened fire on the Russian garrison. That part of the Sitka people who intended to rush into Novo-Arkhangel'sk from the woods side had encountered the fire of three field guns from a detachment of Russians sent toward them. Here the Indians, as Golovin noted, had several men killed and wounded, including several women and children who had accidentally found themselves under the bombardment during their flight from the Sitka village into the woods (Golovin 1863b:341). After the skirmish, which continued for about two hours, and during which the Russian fort artillery had been in operation, the Tlingit asked for peace and gave eight people as hostages (AVPR, f. RAK, op. 888, d. 1022, l. 730b.–74).

Discrepancies in the source materials exist both in the general evaluation of this clash and in the losses reported for each side. According to the official reports of the RAC board of directors, Russian losses in the battle numbered 2 killed and 19 wounded (*Kratkoe istoricheskoe obozrenie*, 1861:110; ORAK 1856:35). Tikhmenev and other researchers used this number (Dean 1994:12; Tikhmenev 1863:2:207–208). The RAC inspector, Captain of the Second Rank P. N. Golovin, specifies the Russian casualties as 19 wounded, with 4 later dying from their wounds; thus, 6 people from the Novo-Arkhangel'sk garrison perished (Golovin 1863b:341). Referring to archival materials, the Canadian professor J. R. Gibson writes that as a result of the clash with the Indians in 1855, 7 company employees perished and 16 were wounded (Gibson 1976:12). According to the archival material known to this author (see documentary appendix entry {29}), the official Russian losses included 2 noncommissioned officers and 1 sailor of the naval fleet, 3 RAC employees, and 1 creole; 14 more people were wounded. However, an eyewitness, Dr. Z. S. Govorlivyi, in his medical report indicates a much larger number of Russians wounded. Govorlivyi wrote, "Of 30 wounded in the affair with the Koloshi, 5 died. Such result of the wounds, especially among the young people, depended on the form of the bullets; these were chopped pieces of lead and iron without any form, rather angular for the puncture in the flesh and organs they passed through" (ORAK 1861:106). The divergence of Govorlivyi's information from the official statistical loss (30 and 19, respectively) evidently resulted from the fact that RAC representatives tried to understate the number, and, therefore, in the company reports only those people who had received severe or moderate wounds were included, not the lightly wounded whom the professional Dr. Govorlivyi, for his part, could not ignore.

Tlingit losses during the 1855 clash are not precisely known. Official RAC documents state that the "Koloshi, according to reliable information, lost from 60 to 80 people, killed and wounded" (ORAK 1856:35; Tikhmenev 1863:2:207–208). According to other sources the Indian casualties totaled more than 100 people killed and wounded (*Doklad Komiteta*, 1963b:81; Gibson 1976:12; *Kratkoe istoricheskoe obozrenie*, 1861:110). However, according to Voevodskii's report, it was half the number. "How many among the *Koloshi* were killed," he wrote to St. Petersburg, "I do not know, they wishing to keep up the opinion of themselves conceal this, but it must be suggested that about 50 people were killed and wounded" (AVPR, f. RAK, op. 888, d. 1022, l. 76). The precise number of Russian casualties in this clash are given in the documentary appendix entry {29}.

A diametrically opposite evaluation of the results of the Russian-Tlingit clash of 1855 was given in the official documents of the Russian-American Company and in the reports of the inspectors of its activities. Thus, it was stated in the report of the board of directors: "After a two-hour skirmish, the Koloshi, forced from all places occupied by them, were compelled to ask for quarter and a cease-fire, which was carried out. . . . As a sign of resumption of their submission, they delivered eight amanaty" (ORAK 1856:35). The same opinion is also expressed by the official RAC historian P. A. Tikhmenev, who reported that the events of 1855 ended with the "complete defeat of the savages" (Tikhmenev 1863:2:207–208). On the other hand, the inspector of the RAC from the Naval Ministry, Captain of the Second Rank P. N. Golovin, noted in 1861 that the Tlingit were clearly superior in this battle; in his words, they "well understood that the odds were in their favor and up to this point brag about it" (Golovin 1863b:340). His colleague, the inspector from the Finance Ministry, S. A. Kostlivtsov, shared this point of view (Kostlivtsov 1863:26). Later, the Soviet historian S. B. Okun' also felt that the position of Novo-Arkhangel'sk in 1855 was critical, and only as a result of negotiations with the Indian chiefs was the siege of the city raised (Okun' 1939:196–197). However, analyzing the report of a direct participant of the events—S. V. Voevodskii—it is possible to conclude that during this battle there were neither victors nor losers, although it is possible that the Russians had prevailed to some degree. The Tlingit delivered amanaty and did not demand that the Russians compensate the Indians for their heavier losses.

Several researchers suggest that it was the Crimean War and rumors of it that permitted the Tlingit to attack Novo-Arkhangel'sk in 1855 (Pierce 1990:530–531; Polevoi and Okladnikova 1994:76). However, this is not so. Even the RAC directors, who would not have missed a chance to attribute everything to the intrigues of the English, were forced to note in their reports to the emperor:

> Viewing the reasons for the above-stated encroachments by the savages, the main office is convinced that they have no connection with present political circumstances [that is, war] and that there is no reason to suspect any foreign influence, but these reasons consist of the self-will of the savages which gradually grew from our treatment of them that was too meek and condescending, which they probably understood as our weakness in powers and supposed it possible through this to take advantage of easy pillaging and spoils (RGA VMF, f. 410, op. 2, d. 1082, l. 53–530b.).

The details of the "revolt" were announced to the emperor, who ordered "to declare his good will" to the governor of the colonies "for adopting quick and active measures to stop the emerging disorder." The sailor Mikhail Vasil'ev, severely wounded in the skirmish with the Tlingit, was awarded a cross of the Order of St. George for the "affair with the *Koloshi* of 1855" as a sign of distinction. Two more sailors, a soldier in Siberian Battalion No. 14 and an "employee from the Finnish people," Aleksandr Niuland, were honored with silver medals with the inscription "For Valor" on a Georgievskii ribbon. The wounded officer—Ensign Aleksei Baranov—received the Order of St. Anna, 4th Degree (AVPR, f. RAK, op. 888, d. 1023, l. 920b.).

After the above events, relations between the Tlingit and the Russians gradually normalized and remained stable until Alaska was sold to the United States. "From 1855 no special insolence on their [the Indians'] part was tried," wrote Voevodskii (ORAK 1858 god, 1859:63). An exception perhaps was the attack by Stikine warriors in seven canoes (in September 1855) on four peaceful residents of Novo-Arkhangel'sk who had set out in a Tlingit canoe to Ozerskii Redoubt with two Sitka people. Only one Russian survived this attack. The Stikine people later explained their activities, saying that they assumed the travelers were their enemies, the Sitka people (see documentary appendix entry {30}). These skirmishes with the Indians forced the colonial administration to ask for reinforcements, and in 1857 another hundred soldiers from the ranks of the

Siberian Line Batallions led by officers were transferred from Ayan to Novo-Arkhangel'sk (AVPRI, f. RAK, op. 888, d. 1022, l. 1360b.–137).

Pacifying the Tlingit after 1855 was achieved not only by the transferring of a new military contingent to Novo-Arkhangel'sk but by the epidemic of typhoid fever that struck in 1857. This illness was carried from Ayan to Novo-Arkhangel'sk on the RAC ship *Tsesarevich*, and despite the Russian medical people's efforts it continued until May 1858. The official RAC board of directors' report stated: "This illness was spread also among the neighboring Koloshi. According to their testimony, of those among them who were ill and who remained in their villages no one recovered, whereas of those who resorted to help from our doctors (about a hundred people) very few were sacrificed to the illness. At present the Natives generally understand very well the benefit of medical treatment and quite often come to the doctors in Novo-Arkhangel'sk for advice and even ask to be taken into the hospital" (ORAK 1858:16–17).

I. V. Furuhjelm, who succeeded Voevodskii as governor in 1859, began to conduct the politics of rapprochement with the independent Natives, which Etolin had done with great success. In his official report Furuhjelm wrote:

> I constantly tried to show them trust and not allow quarrels and bloody results between them and gave many of the Kalosh free access to the port where they could become completely familiarized with the conditions of our life. When it was sufficiently prudent I did not let escape an occasion to involve myself in their affairs for the purpose of accustoming them to see in me the leader and mediator who always gives refuge to the innocent among them. Sometimes I paid the Kalosh for injury brought to them by ours [our people], but also required the same of them. In such cases as far as possible I tried to collect personally from the guilty, and not from all, on the basis that if it is addressed to the masses, then the masses become accustomed to act as masses. The result was so satisfactory that the Kalosh did not force me even once to strike the alarm in port and, what is most important, the residents of Sitka [Novo-Arkhangel'sk] were entirely at ease with regard to danger [attack] from the Kalosh (Furuhjelm 1864:21–22).

Purchases of produce from the Tlingit were again expanded. In 1860 the steamship resumed voyages in the straits, visiting various Tlingit villages. When it stopped at the mouth of the Stikine, the local Indians greeted the Russians amicably and even asked them to rebuild their settlement among them. For this they suggested using Dionisievskii Redoubt, which they had preserved after the English abandoned it (AVPR, f. RAK, op. 888, d. 1025, l. 164–1640b.).

During the late 1850s the Russian administration began to more widely engage the Tlingit for work in the port and on ships (Golovin 1862:133). The Tlingit's purchase of goods from the RAC also increased significantly. Whereas they had formerly purchased up to 100 pudy of flour in a year, by the beginning of the 1860s they began to take more than 100 pudy in a month (Golovin 1862:49–50). The improvement in relations between the Tlingit and the Russians is evidenced by the fact that villagers in Nal'tushkan (Kootznahoo kwáan) helped the crew of the steamship *Nikolai I*, which had shipwrecked in Chatham Strait in 1861 (Tikhmenev 1863:2:226–227).

The literature records the mistaken opinion that until Alaska was sold to the United States in 1867, the Russians in Novo-Arkhangel'sk lived under constant threat of Tlingit attack (Gibson 1976:13; Okun' 1939:196). On this the authors usually cite Golovin's and Sergei A. Kostlivtsov's materials, published in the Appendix of the *Doklad Komiteta* 1863b (1863b:339; 1863:69). However, the negative aspects of Russian-Tlingit relations are exaggerated there. The authors, being the official auditors of the RAC's activities, strived to show miscalculations and inadequacies, in particular in relations with the Natives of Russian America. That the Russians by no means lived under siege in Novo-Arkhangel'sk at the beginning of the 1860s is confirmed by Golovin's own statements (1862:47, 110; 1863a:6:291). The Russians were not only not under siege, they actively mixed in the affairs of the independent Natives. In one of his personal letters Golovin described the clash between the Sitka people and the Yakutat people (who came for trade) at the walls of the Novo-Arkhangel'sk fort, a clash that nearly led to great bloodshed. Governor Furuhjelm, having learned of preparations for the intended slaughter, sent a negotiator to the Indians, requiring an immediate truce. When the Indians tried to object to the ultimatum, saying that the Russians did not have the right to intervene in their internal affairs, the governor ordered the guns moved onto the batteries. It was announced to the Tlingit that if they did not cease the "row" and return to their houses, the Russians would open fire on their village. The Natives, knowing that the governor kept his word, hastily dispersed. A truce, mediated by the Russians, was quickly concluded (Golovin 1863a:6:289–295). As we see, the Russians could take rigorous control, at least of the Sitka people who lived at the walls of Novo-Arkhangel'sk. There was not even talk of the Indians' laying siege to the fort. Regarding the Tlingit who lived in the straits, Golovin wrote: "If they are not hostile to us, they are not friendly, rather as they themselves say, 'the Russians are tolerated'" (Golovin 1862:47–48).

The Russians rendered as much aid as they could to the Tlingit. Thus, when a new epidemic of smallpox erupted on the Northwest Coast in 1862,

Furuhjelm persuaded the Sitka people to get vaccinated against smallpox in the Novo-Arkhangel'sk hospital. In addition, he sent a doctor and a medical assistant on the steamship *Aleksandr II* to vaccinate people throughout the straits. Fortunately for the Tlingit, this epidemic turned out to be less virulent than the previous (in the village at Novo-Arkhangel'sk only three people died of smallpox), and therefore the Indians who lived in the straits refused the inoculation (AVPR, f. RAK, op. 888, d. 1026, l. 91–910b., 123).

To strengthen Russian influence among the Stikine people, Furuhjelm paid their head chief a RAC salary of 350 rubles a year and gave him a Russian flag.

The last episode to cloud Russian-Tlingit relations in the 1860s was the murder of the Aleut A. Bashurov who had been out fishing. The Sitkan "*Kolosh* Foma," seized on suspicion of the murder, was exiled to Kodiak by Furuhjelm until all the circumstances of the affair were clarified (AVPR, f. RAK, op. 888, d. 1026, l. 30b., 33–330b.).

After this the Tlingit were not hostile toward the Russians. The last governor of Russian America, Prince Dmitrii P. Maksutov (1863–67) wrote in May 1866: "At the present time we are situated in the most peaceful relations with all *Koloshi*." After a year he reported to St. Petersburg: "In the colonies of the Russian-Amer. Co, according to the final news from the districts, everything is all right, peace and accord having been preserved with the surrounding savages" (AVPR, f. RAK, op. 888, d. 1027, l. 70b.–8, 520b.). In less than six months, on October 18, 1867, the Russian flag would be raised for the last time over Novo-Arkhangel'sk.

Despite the nature of relations between the Russians and the Tlingit, the latter never considered themselves subjects of the Russian Empire and were convinced of the fact that Southeast Alaska belonged to them. They viewed the Russians only as "newcomers" and not as countrymen—and even less as masters of the land (Golovin 1863b:330; Kostlivtsov 1863:238). After learning that the Russians had sold Alaska to the Americans, the Tlingit chiefs gathered to protest this act because, in their opinion, the Russians did not have the right to "sell the country of the Tlingit" (Drucker 1965:207). Later, some Tlingit's attitudes toward Russian rule changed. One of the Chilkat chiefs, Skin-Ya, during an 1899 American-Canadian discussion about the borders of the state of Alaska and the province of British Columbia, recalled the Russians' governing: "I acknowledged the Russians as rulers of this country and always considered myself a Russian subject until the transfer of Alaska to the United States. My fathers and I acknowledged Russian authority over this land for more than fifty years" (O'Grady 1992:337).

The last stage of Russian American history was marked by the greatest rapprochement between the Tlingit and the Russians, peaking in the mid-1840s.

5.2. The Tlingit and the Hudson's Bay Company

After the English-American War (1812–15) the English fur buyers practically ceased their trading expeditions on the Northwest Coast of America. Only at the end of the 1820s do the English again appear in this region, this time under the aegis of the Hudson's Bay Company. In 1825, after finalizing the demarcation of the possessions of Great Britain and Russia in North America and concluding the convention on the freedom of navigators and traders in Southeast Alaska, the Hudson's Bay Company actively began to construct fortified trading posts on the Northwest Coast. In 1827 the English founded Fort Langley at the mouth of the Fraser River, and in 1831 erected Fort Nass at the mouth of the Nass River; the latter was moved to Dundas Island and renamed Fort Simpson in 1834. In 1833 the company built Fort McLoughlin on the Columbia River (Drucker 1965:195; Galbraith 1957:137–138).

The Hudson's Bay Company's plans, wrote the American historian J. S. Galbraith, were primarily calculated to displace the American maritime traders as their chief competitors on the Northwest Coast. For this, agents of the British company worked out a whole system of tariffs on furs, with which they quickly succeeded in almost completely removing American traders from the coast.[50] In 1833 not a single American ship visited the whole Northwest Coast (Galbraith 1957:140). In addition, the Hudson's Bay Company strove to secure the support of the Russians to defeat the Americans. In 1829 Lieutenant Emilius Simpson arrived in Novo-Arkhangel'sk on the ship *Cadboro* with an offer of produce and wares from the HBC for Governor Petr E. Chistiakov and the Russian colonies. Formerly, American skippers had met these needs. The HBC's leadership hoped that, having seized the initiative, it would thus deprive the Americans of one reason to visit the Northwest Coast.

It must be said that Chistiakov on the whole viewed the English proposal rather favorably, and not only for economic reasons. He reported to St. Petersburg that the agreement with the HBC could guarantee the inviolability of Russia's colonies in case of military conflict between Russia and Great Britain. Besides this, he felt that a union between Russian and English companies would give both sides a definite advantage in mutual relations with the independent, warlike Northwest Coast Indians. In Chistiakov's opinion, the new HBC post that the English planned to build at the mouth of the Nass River could "bring . . . less harm than the American ships roaming in those places, because the Hudson's Bay Company, for its personal security, must keep conventions concluded between Russia and England [that is, not sell the Indians guns and spirits]." In addition, the governor indicated in his October 1829 message to the RAC board of directors that the "closeness of the English, it seems to me, provides the Russian colonies not only with political and trade relations against the Kolosh, but also with regard to provisions themselves" (AVPR, f. RAK, op. 888, d. 993, l. 504–508). However, Chistiakov's immediate successors—F. P. Wrangell and I. A. Kupreianov—did not share his point of view.

The quick advance of the English northward to the borders of Russian America and the appearance of Hudson's Bay Company ships in the straits of the Alexander Archipelago greatly alarmed the Russian colonies' administration. Though the British forced American traders from the Northwest Coast almost entirely, the governor of Russian America was only a little pleased, inasmuch as the English continued their predecessors' traditions of equipping the Tlingit with arms and spirits. Besides, the RAC found it difficult to compete with the Hudson's Bay Company because transportation expenses were much higher for goods coming from Russia. The English could pay the Indians three times more for furs than the RAC could (Gibson 1976:200). And finally, establishing a British trading post in the immediate vicinity of Russian possessions threatened to undermine the Russians' position in Southeast Alaska and their trade with the Tlingit. All this also induced Wrangell to establish Dionisievskii Redoubt at the mouth of the Stikine in 1833 to prevent the English from accessing the river's upper reaches. Though the local Tlingit did not oppose the founding of a British post at the mouth of the Stikine, and even invited the English to the village, they were categorically against the English penetrating to the river's upper reaches and, in this, their position agreed with that of the Russians.

Despite their failure at the Stikine in 1834, the English did not desist from their plans to get furs from the Tlingit and Athapaskans of the Rocky Mountains. A Hudson's Bay Company agent, Chief Factor John York, wrote in 1835 that he would give any Tlingit of the Stikine and Tongass kwáans who came to him three gallons of liquor for one beaver skin instead of two gallons (Gibson 1975:114), and in 1837 the manager of Fort Simpson, Dr. J. Kennedy, bought a sea otter skin from the Kaigani for ten blankets, so the fur would not be delivered to the Russians or Americans (Fisher 1977:28–29) (Table 9). These HBC policies were productive. The Russian American governor, Kupreianov, wrote in 1839: "From year to year the *Kolosh* are attracted more and more down from our places to the English border, and in order ultimately not to be too late, support through goods is immediately necessary on our side" (AVPR, f. RAK, op. 888, d. 1004, l. 4030b.).

At the same time, the English continued to try to penetrate the land of the interior Athapaskans, from whom the Stikine people and other Tlingit obtained the bulk of their furs. The English did not advance to the land of the Athapaskans from the coast because the Russians, with the support of the Tlingit, had blocked that path; they approached instead from the Fraser and McKenzie river basins. In 1838 an HBC agent, Robert Campbell, built a post at Dease Lake on Tahltan lands. It existed for only a few months because the local Indians, incited by Tlingit traders, drove the English out of it the same year. The banished English clashed with the Tlingit of the Stikine ķwáan led by Shakes, who was trading Russian goods on the upper reaches of the Stikine. As Campbell himself reported, the Stikine people were in such a hostile mood that his party was, in the end, saved by the friendly female chief of the local Tahltan Athapaskans (Andrews 1947:103; Simpson 1847:1:211).

In 1839, after they signed the treaty to lease part of the mainland coast of Russian America, the Hudson's Bay Company more actively expanded into the lands of the Tlingit and the Tlingit's trading partners. On June 1, 1840, the English, per their agreement with the Russian-American Company, occupied Dionisievskii Redoubt, having renamed it Fort Stikine (sometimes calling it Fort Highfield). [51] This same year, they built Fort Taku (officially, Fort Durham), which had been well fortified with bastions, on the shore of Taku Bay (north of Fort Stikine). However, by 1843 the Hudson's Bay Company had to evacuate this post after several clashes with the local Tlingit of the Taku ķwáan (Hulley 1953:162; Simpson 1847:1:215). The HBC considered it more advantageous to use ships to trade with the Indians here. Instead of outposts in the distant "Russian" north, the English established Fort Victoria on the southern end of Vancouver Island in 1843; in 1846 they transferred HBC headquarters there. Victoria was quickly turned into one of the most lively trading centers in British Columbia.

Meanwhile, Fort Stikine's position became less secure over the years. As A. Markov (1856:88), a RAC manager, recalled, when the Russians left Dionisievskii Redoubt, the Stikine people expressed regret and met the English with open hostility. Having visited Russian America in the 1840s, Markov wrote:

> Several times the Stikine Koliuzhi attempted to burn the whole fort in which the English had settled; but careful and strict guards did not allow the savages to perfect this disastrous plan. The English were at this time in such a position in relation to the savages as the Russians had been during Baranov's time. However, the requirement in goods, which became almost necessary in the domestic life of the

Table 9. Valuation of Furs by the Hudson's Bay Company

Quantity and type of ware	Furs
400 medium *tsukli* (dentalia shell)	1 large beaver[a]
120 *tsukli* of the 1st grade	1 beaver
1 blanket of black frieze, 2 mugs of rum with water, and 4 packages of tobacco	1 beaver
2(?) white blankets, 2 mugs of rum with water, and 4 packages of tobacco	"
25 *arshin* of gray narrow calico	"
25 *arshin* of white calico	"
10 lbs. of powder and 25 lbs. of shot	"
1 barrel of powder of 2 *pudy* 25 lbs.	10 beavers
1 steeltrap	1 large beaver
5–10 *arshin* calico	1 {river} otter

When American traders appeared along the coast
the value changed somewhat:

2 blankets (one of them expensive)	1 beaver
1 barrel of powder of 28 lbs.	2 beavers
1 barrel of powder of 2 *pudy* 25 lbs.	5–6 beavers

Note: The table is created from I. A. Kupreianov's report of the 25th of May 1840 to the RAC board of directors: "On secretly learning how much and in what kind of goods the English pay the *Kolosh* in our region for various furs . . ." (AVPR, f. RAK, op. 888, d. 1005, l. 317–318).

[a]If an Indian sold the HBC 20 large beavers, he received an encouragement gift: a frock coat with cloth trousers, cotton shirt, four mugs of rum with water, one tin bucket, a red belt ("which is used among the *Kolosh* for decoration of the ears"), several flints, four packages of tobacco, and a knife. If the Indian exchanged ten beavers he received as a gift a shirt, four mugs of rum with water, four packages of tobacco, and a red belt. If the Indian traded five beavers he received only four mugs of rum, four packages of tobacco, and a few flints.

savages, compelled the latter to gradually draw nearer to the English and initiate with them the trading of furs (Markov 1856:90).

Despite established trade relations, the Stikine were occasionally hostile toward the new arrivals. Chief Shakes initiated most of their "plots" against the English; in the words of the HBC governor Simpson, Shakes has been "spoiled by the indulgence of the Russians." Fortunately for the English, Shakes had little influence on the "tribe," though he was considered the head chief of the Stikine people. Simpson noted that "Kuatkau," the second "chief of the tribe," by contrast, remained loyal to the English. The mutual hostility of Shakes and Kuatkau was some guarantee of preserving the fort (Simpson 1847:1:211–212). Simpson's reference to Kuatkau, chief of the Stikine people, is undoubtedly a reference to Kuat_ka (Kuat_ke), whom the Russian colonies' administration intended to reward with royal gifts (brocaded kaftan, belt, and hat) because he was the first Tlingit chief to reject human sacrifice at the potlatch. They intended to make Kuat_ka a RAC agent to the Stikine people. However, the colonial administration's faith in Kuat_ka proved unjustified, and they instead turned to Shakes; in the end, the czar's gifts were bestowed on the Sitka toion Mikhail Kuk_kan. Kuat_ka, evidently dissatisfied with the Russians' change of policies, sided with the English.

The Tlingit's dissatisfaction with the English increased after the latter occupied Fort Stikine, because the English cut the price they would pay the Stikine people for furs, setting a tariff equal to the price they had paid the Tsimshian at Fort Simpson. As Shakes told the English, if they introduced a higher price for furs than Fort Simpson instead of following the Russian example in trade, all would be well (Gibson 1992:118; Klein 1987:109). In 1842 the Tlingit of several _kwáans besieged Fort Stikine, trying to exploit conflicts among the Hudson's Bay Company's employees.[52] It was the timely arrival of an English steamship and an armed Russian ship that saved Fort Stikine from complete destruction (Simpson 1847:2:181). After this incident the English and Tlingit peacefully traded with each other for several years. However, in June 1846 Fort Stikine's manager appealed to the Russians for aid to Novo-Arkhangel'sk because the Stikine people had once again laid siege to the post. The arrival of the Russian steamship and the mediation of RAC officials helped reconcile the Indians and the English.

M. D. Teben'kov, who was then governor of the Russian-American Company, was busy clarifying the reasons for this conflict, which the head of Fort Stikine had accused the Russians of causing. In the Englishman's opinion, the reason for the Indians' hostility could be found in the "Russian potlatch" that Teben'kov had established for the Tlingit in April 1846. The Stikine people now required that the English agree to a similar arrangement. In addition, the head of Fort Stikine protested to the Russian colonies' administration about their selling rum, which violated the agreement between the RAC and the HBC. Teben'kov, in his report to the RAC board of directors (and copied in part to the HBC administration), cited some different arguments on this question: "First, this igrushka emerges from the common course of things. This is the epoch of the modern chronology of the Tlingit, their Olympiad; in it I establish five years of tranquility—in relations with them. . . . Second, this was entertainment—it {rum} should be drunk here, and the rum not distributed. There was no trade there, rather a celebration." Teben'kov attested that in the "Russian potlatch" 15 3/8 *vedra* {about 40 gallons of rum} were

History of Tlingit Relations in Russian America

"used in *podchivanie*," that is, to entertain, 1,600 people. In other words, each Indian got a cup of rum. The real reason for the "discord" between the Stikine people and the English, Teben'kov wrote, was that the latter did not take one of the influential Stikine chiefs, who wanted to travel to Fort Simpson, on their steamship. The refusal offended the Indian, and he forbade his fellow tribesmen to trade with the English or to furnish them with provisions. Besides this, Fort Stikine's garrison was small (16 men, including 9 sick Hawaiians), and this gave the Tlingit high hopes for easily seizing and plundering the post (AVPR, f. RAK, op. 888, d. 1014, l. 80b.–100b.). In 1846 conflict between the Stikine and the English nearly led to the evacuation of Fort Stikine's garrison, which its manager wished to do.

In 1847 Fort Stikine was again besieged and the English once more appealed for Russian aid. D. F. Zarembo, who had arrived on the steamship in October, again succeeded in reconciling the two sides (AVPR, f. RAK, op. 888, d. 1016, l. 2650b.–266; Mamyshev 1855:249). As L. F. Klein notes, the Indian threat caused panic among the HBC employees, but in reality there is no mention of killings or other serious incidents between the English and the Stikine people in the company's reports (Klein 1987:111). Nevertheless, the HBC management decided to leave Fort Stikine in 1849 and chartered the brig *Konstantin* from the RAC to transport its employees and goods to its southern posts. While the HBC was evacuating the fort, about two thousand Indians gathered, shocked that the British had dismantled part of the post's structure. They shouted at the HBC employees that they had no right to do so because this was Russian property. The situation became terribly strained and it fell to Leontii Garder, the commander of the Russian brig, to intervene and calm the Natives. He commissioned the Stikine chiefs to protect the remains of the structure while he took the English to their destination (Arndt 1988:35–36).

The Chilkat people also displayed hostility toward the English after Robert Campbell in 1848 established a trading post at Fort Selkirk in the territory of their trading partners, the Athapaskan Tutchone. In 1852 the Chilkat people sent a war expedition 300 miles inland to seize and destroy this English trading post. The British traders who fell captive were set free after being warned not to return to the Tlingit's trading territory (Drucker 1955:22). In this campaign to Fort Selkirk warriors of all the Chilkat clans participated, led by Shotridge (Chartrich or Klo-Kuta), an influential Kaagwaantaan chief (Emmons 1991:39). James Douglas, the British governor of Vancouver Island, wanted to punish the Chilkat people and requested aid from the Russians. However, the Russian American administration were indifferent to the governor's request but promised not to hinder the English as they sought and punished the guilty, who were formally considered Russian subjects (AVPR, f. RAK, op. 888, d. 1021, l. 1890b.).

Of course, the relations between the Tlingit and the English were not limited only to clashes and hostility. Their relationship was based on mutually beneficial trade, the Tlingit trading with the agents of the HBC not only at Fort Stikine and on HBC ships that visited the straits of the Alexander Archipelago but themselves carrying out long trading voyages in British Columbia to the south. On such journeys they usually set out in flotillas consisting of 10 to 12 canoes. There was always the danger of being attacked by Indians of other tribes along the way. As Olson recounts from Tlingit tradition, the "contemptible Kwakiutl" repeatedly attacked such flotillas to capture Tlingit for slavery, but, as a rule, they did not succeed (Olson 1967:92).

Fort Simpson became a trading center in Dixon Entrance soon after it was founded. Here, the Tsimshian, Haida, Kaigani, and southern Tlingit met and bartered (Niblack 1890:337; Simpson 1847:1:206). However, by the 1850s its dominance in trade shifted to Victoria. Even the northernmost Tlingit, the Yakutat people, went there to trade their furs for English goods (De Laguna 1972:1:351).[53] And the Kaigani, as Furuhjelm noted, generally stopped calling at Novo-Arkhangel'sk from 1857 onward, preferring to sell their furs and wares in Victoria (AVPR, f. RAK, op. 888, d. 1025, l. 810b.).

In the early 1860s "gold fever" erupted on the Stikine. In British Columbia the rumor spread that rich alluvial gold deposits had been found on the river's upper reaches. By March 1862 an English schooner had arrived at the mouth of the Stikine with the first party of prospectors. Having purchased several canoes from the Tlingit, they set out up the river. In May of the same year about twenty schooners gathered at the mouth of the river delivering new parties of prospectors. Quarrels often flared between the new arrivals and the local Indians. The Stikine people even killed some of the gold seekers, appropriating their possessions. They tried to shift blame for the deaths from themselves to the Russians, claiming that they had killed the prospectors under orders by the governor of Russian America. In turn, the Russian colonies' administration sent an armed steamship to the mouth of the Stikine for "stopping possible disorder." A party of Russian prospectors led by the engineer technologist Petr A. Andreev had simultaneously headed up the river. It was quickly ascertained that the alluvial gold deposits on the upper reaches of the Stikine were very poor, and interest waned (AVPR, f. RAK, op. 888, d. 1026, l. 79–790b., 880b.–89, 90–91, 92–93).

In the 1860s new competition in the form of small traders from British Columbia arrived to challenge the Hudson's Bay Company and the Russian-

Table 10. Prices at Which the "Kalosh" Sell Furs on Foreign Ships

	Rubles/ kopecks
For a sea otter or female sea otter:	
9 blankets for the amount	140
1 box of gun powder of 4 lbs	6
1 box of shot of 5 lbs	3
5 packages of Virginia tobacco	2
1 cook's knife	1
1 horn comb	0.50
1 file	1.50
2 small tin bowls	4
5 packages of dye [cinnabar]	3.75
10 pieces of {gun} flint and vodka of 2 to 5 bottles as a present	0.20
Total	161.95
For 2 beavers:	
1 blanket or calico of 25 arsh[in]	20
1 fox, dark brown: 1 blanket	20
1 fox, sivodushka [a variety of red fox]	20
1 fox, red	20
1 river otter, large	20
1 river otter, medium	20
1 bear, large: 15 ar[shin] cotton print at 1 ruble per	15
For 5 pieces of lynx on a cape:	
1 blanket 20 rubles and 1 cotton print shirt 6 rubles	26
1 wolf, large: 1 blanket, medium	18
1 wolverine: 1 blanket	20
fur seal: 1 blanket, medium	18
10 pieces of tarbaganov [marmots] on a cape: 1 blanket, medium	18
12 sable [marten], fine: 1 blanket	20

Source: Appendix to the Doklad Komiteta . . . (1863b, Table XII).

Note: "Moreover, before the trading and exactly the same at the conclusion of the trade, they give vodka, especially to those who have procured the most furs."

American Company in the southern part of the Alexander Archipelago. Whereas the RAC and HBC had, in 1842, by mutual agreement, abstained from openly selling liquor and firearms to the Indians, these independent traders began to deliver large quantities of rum to Southeast Alaska (Table 10). In Furuhjelm's official report, he wrote:

The acquisition of furs in the Kolosh straits, besides their significant increase in value, in the majority of cases was made impossible other than with spirituous drinks. It is quite natural that under such conditions company trade in this locality must be entirely broken off in spite of all effort to maintain it. Speaking in general, the situation of this part of our colonies was entirely changed with the appearance of gold in British Columbia. Everywhere that even some small profit is present the company meets rivalry with small tradesmen who have preference in trade with the trusting savages by the great advantage of not being limited by any rules, even the ones that are illegal. However, here it should be added that the Kaloshi from the Stakin, from Keku, and even from Kootznahoo—while being attracted to Victoria in part by novelty, in part by high wages and the possibility of selling their women—nowadays much less than formerly, occupy themselves with hunting animals (Furuhjelm 1864:28–29).

One of the small British traders, a certain Vincent Baranovich (apparently a Croat, being considered a subject of the Austrian Empire), appeared in Novo-Arkhangel'sk in 1863 and requested that Furuhjelm permit him to trade with the Stikine Tlingit and the Kaigani of Prince of Wales Island, as well as to take up residence among the "Kaigani," for which he agreed to become a Russian subject. Furuhjelm emphatically refused the adventurer, whom he characterized in his report as a "smuggler" and "scoundrel," and ordered him to leave Russian American territory (AVPR, f. RAK, op. 888, d. 1026, l. 87ob.–88). Baranovich and his "brothers in profession" were not quite ready to abandon a profitable business. They settled among the Kaigani and southern Tlingit and continued to import spirits and other goods from the British possessions. This enterprise was, of course, not without danger. Thus, in August 1865 the Tlingit of the Kake ḵwáan killed the captain and three sailors of the small English schooner *Royal Charlie*, which was smuggling in the waters of Russian America (the Indians themselves lost four or five warriors in the skirmish).[54] After this encounter the schooner was towed to the Tlingit village and looted.

The smugglers were not the only ones to suffer from the Tlingit's hostility. In May 1865 Tlingit of the Taku ḵwáan returning from Victoria boarded and plundered a small English schooner in revenge for the hanging of two of their clansmen in Victoria (AVPR, f. RAK, op. 888, d. 1027, l. 60ob.–70ob., 109).

Prince Maksutov, then governor of Russian America, conducted a special investigation of the above incidents and concluded that the Kake Tlingit were innocent since the captain of the *Royal Charlie* had first gotten the Indians drunk on rum and then killed one of them with his revolver. The Tlingit of the Taku ḵwáan were actually guilty, but Maksutov had neither the desire nor the ability to punish them, despite the HBC's insisting it be done. The fact is, the relations between the Russians and the Tlingit during this period were good, and breaching them for Britain's interests was not part of the governor's plans. Should the Russians oppress or attack the Tlingit, all the southern Tlingit ḵwáans could unite against the administration, and then the Russian colonies themselves would have to turn to the Russian Pacific squadron for aid (AVPR, f. RAK, op. 888, d. 1027, l. 70b.–8).

Meanwhile the HBC's leadership sent Novo-Arkhangel'sk endless complaints and requests to suppress the British smugglers who had settled in the Russian possessions and had substantially undermined the HBC's trade with the Tlingit. However, the Russian colonial leadership was simply not in a position to effectively blockade the straits of the Alexander Archipelago, which were populated by independent and well-armed Natives. In Maksutov's opinion, even sending a battle cruiser to the colonies would not slow illegal trade. Maksutov assessed the situation with the British smugglers, writing: "There is no possibility of tracking down these dealers and catching them since they all, having taken *Kolosh* women, sort of enter into a kin relationship with *Koloshi*. The *Koloshi*, considering them their relatives, take their side, lay up their wares for them, and deliver them to other villages, so that even if in the straits there are no Europeans or Americans in person, their trade nevertheless continues and at the present time takes on ever broader dimensions" (AVPR, f. RAK, op. 888, d. 1027, l. 1080b.–109). British smugglers did not leave Southeastern Alaska even after Russian America was sold to the United States.

Between the 1830s and 1867 Tlingit contacts with the English bore a complex, at times even contradictory, character. Mutually beneficial trade was interspersed with conflicts and clashes. And though the English (along with the Russians) were the primary suppliers of European wares during these years, the Indians recognized that the English had even less right to control them than did the Russians. (It is not by chance that during a clash with the English, the Russians were often the mediators, since the Tlingit respected the Russians' authority.)

5.3. Tlingit and Americans between 1821 and 1867

The czarist government's decree of 1821 prohibiting foreign ships from approaching Russian American possessions to within 100 nautical miles elicited a strong negative response in American and English diplomatic circles, and engendered the extreme dissatisfaction of American traders. In answer, the

American captains began not only to sell firearms to the Indians, as earlier, but to provoke the Tlingit to attack the Russians. Thus, Governor Murav'ev reported that a captain of one American brig had sold powder and rifles in Kootznahoo for almost nothing, assuring the Indians that the rifles would soon prove useful against the Russians (Narochnitskii 1963–1985, Ser. II, t. V, s. 87). However, no serious Tlingit uprisings against the Russians occurred while the September 4 (16), 1821, decree was in effect (see section 5.1 of this chapter).

Numerous American trading ships plied the straits of the Alexander Archipelago for years, and their crews purchased valuable furs from the Natives. They usually wintered in the Hawaiian Islands or at some Indian village on the Northwest Coast. A favorite place for the American ships to stop was Tongass Bay (Port Tongass). Thus, in August 1822 there were five American ships there: the *Frederick, Lescar, Hamilton, Owhyhee,* and *Rob Roy* (Howay 1973:148–149, 154, 157).

After the 1824 conventions between Russia and the United States on the establishment of a border and the regulation of trade and navigation in Alaska were signed, the Americans continued to trade with the Tlingit, now legally. It is true that the Americans continually broke the agreement by selling the Indians guns and spirits, sometimes right in the roadstead or in the Novo-Arkhangel'sk port. At times this led to an open clash of interests among the Tlingit, Americans, and Russians. Thus, in 1827 there was an incident with the brig *Active*, commanded by W. Cotting. When the brig departed from Novo-Arkhangel'sk port, four canoes of Sitka people joined it, and the American captain began to trade guns and rum with them in exchange for furs. An influential chief, Nawushkeitl, was on board the American ship at this time. Suddenly, the wind increased and the canoes fell behind the brig, which then disappeared over the horizon. Consequently, the Tlingit, thinking that their chief had been taken away forever, began to openly express their dissatisfaction with the Russians. It was because the Russian administration prohibited them from trading with the Americans in the port that they were forced to follow the American ships into the open sea. The Sitka people decided that, from then on, they would not permit the Tlingit of other kwáans to trade with the Russians in Novo-Arkhangel'sk. Fortunately, the brig soon returned, with Nawushkeitl aboard, and the Sitka people settled down (AVPR, f. RAK, op. 888, d. 992, l. 254–256ob.; RGIA, f. 18, op. 5, d. 1282, l. 3–5ob.).

However, despite the advantageous convention, American ships appeared less frequently in the straits of the Alexander Archipelago from the mid-1820s onward, and by the 1830s American fur traders only occasionally visited this region. By this time the sea otter was almost completely extinct on the North-

History of Tlingit Relations in Russian America

west Coast, and competition from the Hudson's Bay Company had increased. But Tlingit-American contact did not cease. The American fur traders were replaced by whalers who worked the northern part of the Pacific Ocean.

By 1791 the first American whalers—*Beaver* from Nantucket and *Rebecca* from New Bedford—had appeared in the Pacific Ocean (Barbeau 1958:112). Later their number increased significantly, and they began to call in the northern part of the Pacific Ocean more often. In 1841 American whalers appeared in the waters of Russian America, and some of them entered the straits of the Alexander Archipelago to rest the crew and trade with the Indians, trading guns and rum for food and furs (Golovin 1862:113).

In August 1843 the whaler *Hamilton* arrived in the port of Novo-Arkhangel'sk. Its captain, John Cole, began to buy furs from the Sitka people despite prior warnings made from A. K. Etolin (AVPR, f. RAK, op. 888, d. 1009, l. 479–479ob.). The Russian colonies' administration, limited by strict regulations, could not cope with such "insolent guests."

The following facts attest to the scope of the whaling industry. In the summer of 1850 alone, a fleet of 144 whalers plied the waters near the Bering Strait; the next year there were 145. Certainly, the number of ships lost in 1851 was unprecedented: more than seven whalers suffered shipwreck or were crushed by the ice in Russia's arctic waters (AVPR, f. Gl. arkhiv 1–9, 1852, d. 15, l. 5–50ob.). The Russian-American Company's 1844 attempt to limit sailing in their waters, intended to dissuade "willful" foreign whalers, was unsuccessful inasmuch as the brig *Chichagov*, which had been designated expressly to patrol the region, was in no position to guard such a gigantic area of the northern part of the Pacific Ocean on its own (RGIA, f. 18, op. 5, d. 1321, l. 10b.–44ob.).

American-Tlingit relations during this period were not limited to trade between the Indians and the whalers in the straits of the Alexander Archipelago. In the middle of the 19th century, the southern Tlingit, with the Kaigani and Haida, participated in expeditions to Puget Sound (U.S. territory) farther to the south. During the 1856 war between Oregon's Indians and the American settlers, the latter feared that the "northern Indians" would join the local Natives, characterized by the American historian G. W. Fuller as those "pirates of the great interior seas." Therefore, when a large group of Haida and Tlingit encamped at Port Gamble, the captain of the American steamship *Massachusetts* demanded that they leave U.S. territory. The Indians refused, after which the American ship bombarded it. The Indians sustained heavy losses, their canoes and provisions were destroyed, and they were finally forced to surrender. After this the Indians were deported to Victoria, and from there they returned home. In revenge for the shelling at Port Gamble, the Indians later seized two American schooners and killed the crews. In the 1856 clash an influential Tlingit chief from the Kake ḵwáan perished. In 1857 the Tlingit sent a special fighting expedition to Oregon to avenge the chief's death, and the fighters killed the American colonel A. N. Eby, taking his head to Alaska as a trophy (Duff 1964:237).

Alaska's sale to the Americans was no happy occasion for the Tlingit because, in Krause's words, they were well acquainted with the American whalers' "dispositions" (Krause 1956:46). It was with interest that the Indians observed the Russian flag being lowered and the American one being raised on the parade ground at Novo-Arkhangel'sk on the historic day of October 18, 1867. Because the Indians were not allowed in the city, they watched the ceremony from their canoes in Sitka Bay. The Tlingit later realized the significance of the change of flags, and it occurred to them to evict Alaska's new owners. The Indians held several war councils, but a Chilkat chief, probably the Kaagwaantaan chief Chartrich (Shotridge), calmed his fellow tribesmen, pointing out that the Americans had too many cannons (Krause 1956:46, 266).

On the whole, 1821 to 1867 was characterized by relatively limited American-Tlingit relations, compared to the preceding period's relations or to Tlingit-Russian or Tlingit-English relations.

§

Summarizing the history of Tlingit-European contact, it should be noted that affairs under the Russian American administration had a certain dynamic: peaceful relations and trade alternated with confrontation and clashes.

The Tlingit were among the first Northwest Coast Indians whom European travelers encountered (the Bering-Chirikov expedition in 1741). Exploration of Southeast Alaska and the development of the fur trade there during the last quarter of the 18th century led representatives of Spain, France, England, Russia, and the United States to make contact with the Tlingit. These Indians' relations with the Russians played a special role in their own fate, inasmuch as from the late 1700s to 1867 their land was nominally part of the Russian Empire. The Russian-American Company's direct and indirect encroachments on the Natives' economic or political independence elicited stubborn resistance from the latter. None of Alaska's Native tribes was so resistant to Russian colonization as the Tlingit, who had free access to firearms, great experience in warfare, and a territory whose geography favored guerilla warfare—when the battle was going poorly, the Indians could easily hide in the forests or fjords, or among the islands. The Tlingit succeeded in preserving their independence

History of Tlingit Relations in Russian America

under Russian American rule because there were few Russian settlers in Alaska. This fact prefigured the RAC's failure to subdue the numerous and well-armed Tlingit unassisted.

The Tlingit reacted similarly to English attempts to secure Natives' land and the lands of the Natives' trading partners. Tlingit resistance forced the English to temporarily abandon the colonization of several regions of northwestern Canada and the territories leased from the RAC in 1839.

However, relations between the Tlingit and the Europeans were not based on conflicts but rather on mutually beneficial trade, which became an important part of the life of these Indians during the period of Russian America.

CHAPTER THREE

The Influence of European Contacts on Tlingit Culture in Russian America

~

1. Change in the Economic Activities of the Tlingit

1.1. Fishing, Hunting, and Collecting

Europeans' arrival on the Northwest Coast led to several changes in many but not all spheres of Tlingit economic activity (the term *economic activity* is used here in the broadest sense of the word). Fishing, hunting, and gathering dominated the Indian economy.

Fishing, central to Tlingit society, was influenced least. Being well suited to local ecological conditions, it had developed successfully and achieved stability over the course of hundreds or thousands of years. An Alaskan researcher of the 19th century, Ivan I. Petroff (1884:67–69), wrote that the Tlingit's fishing equipment was more effective than that of the Europeans. More than that, the Europeans, particularly Russians, are known to have borrowed Tlingit methods of processing and storing fish. In 1800, Aleksandr Baranov wrote in his "admonitions" to the manager of Fort Mikhailovskii, V. G. Medvednikov: "But I would like for the fish to be prepared by smoking in the same manner as among the local people [Tlingit], by cleaning and cutting and hanging under a shed and outdoors, if not a half then a third thus prepared for a test, because by Kodiak preparation more than half of the fish's body is thrown away" (*K istorii Rossiisko-Amerikanskoi*, 1957:104).

The only innovation that indirectly influenced fishing among the Tlingit was perhaps the wider use of metal in fishing gear (iron hooks, fish-spear points, steel butcher knives, and so on), which greatly aided their procuring and preparing fish. The stability of the fishing industry conservatively influenced the rest of Tlingit culture, as did the Indians' political independence throughout the entire period of Russian America.

Changes in hunting methods were more notable. Hunting increased, and with it productivity, because more effective hunting tools (spears and arrows with iron points, firearms, and steel traps) were introduced. According to the naturalist and traveler Georg H. von Langsdorff, by the beginning of the 19th century all hunting by the Tlingit was done with guns; the bow and arrow were used only to hunt sea otters. As the American captain John D'Wolf reported to him, the Americans at this time brought so many guns to the Northwest Coast that it was possible to acquire them cheaper there than in England (Langsdorff 1812:2:113). Later, guns began to be used even to hunt sea otters, having finally forced out the bow and arrow, which afterward served only as toys for boys and hunting weapons for teenagers.

Influenced by market demands (the Europeans were primarily interested in valuable furs), the Tlingit began to hunt with an eye to trade. Meat hunting, which had dominated in the past, was displaced by fur hunting; hunting for sea otters, the procurement of which had been practically absent among the Tlingit in the past, became common. This shift in the hunting industry was reflected in Tlingit spiritual culture. In preparing to hunt sea otters, the Tlingit would hire a shaman and observe taboos and rituals no less complex than those kept in preparing for a fighting expedition (Tikhmenev 1863:2:347–349).

During the Russian American period several innovations were introduced in the Tlingit methods of hunting sea otters. They borrowed the circular hunt method from the Aleuts and Kodiak, who were more experienced in sea mammal hunting (De Laguna 1960:112). "Just like the Aleuts, the *Koloshi* surround a herd of beavers {sea otters} and shoot them, but not with arrows, rather with guns," wrote Tikhmenev (1863:2:347).

The Sitka people's position as neighbors of Novo-Arkhangel'sk predetermined some peculiarities of their economic activity: they became the primary suppliers of fresh meat to the Russians, and hunting for market game therefore began to occupy a prominent place in their affairs. For example, I. G. Voznesenskii, who visited the "Kolosh market" on November 22, 1844, noted that the Tlingit brought more than ten mountain sheep, a multitude of partridges, grouse, and ducks, as well as huge round blocks of rendered sheep fat for sale that day (LO AAN, f. 53, op. 1, ed. khr. 2/2–1, l. 29).

Along with fishing and hunting, collecting continued to be an important part of the Indian economy. During this time, traditional collecting was supplemented by primitive agriculture. The Tlingit had borrowed the practice of cultivating potatoes from the Russians in the early 1820s. Agricultural skills had existed even earlier among the Tlingit—they grew one variety of tobacco. The Indians succeeded to such an extent in cultivating potatoes that before long they were able to sell them to the Russians. The Kootznahoo people

Influence of European Contacts on Tlingit Culture

were especially good potato farmers (Markov 1856:79); in recognition, the Tlingit now call the crop the "Angoon potato" (after a Kootznahoo ḵwáan village) (Jacobs and Jacobs 1982:128). The Russians also taught the Tlingit to grow turnips. In the early 1840s RAC *prikazchiki* managers acquired dozens, or perhaps hundreds, of barrels of potatoes and turnips from the Tlingit as the Russian steamships moved through the straits (AVPR, f. RAK, op. 888, d. 1009, l. 426; d. 1010, l. 506; d. 1025, l. 110).

The Tlingit did not adopt the Russian tradition of raising livestock, although there were opportunities: in Novo-Arkhangel'sk most families kept cattle, hogs, chickens, and even horses. However, the number of livestock was insignificant. The English and American traders who visited the waters of Southeast Alaska occasionally had domestic animals aboard, which is reflected in the Indians' stories (Olson 1967:88). Nevertheless, the Tlingit showed no inclination for animal husbandry, having neither the necessary skills nor the economic interest; besides, the Northwest Coast's climate and geography hindered raising livestock on a large scale. Therefore, one cannot agree that in the 1820s the Tlingit raised large numbers of hogs, as Gibson has argued (1976:98), especially since we find nothing about Tlingit animal husbandry in any Russian sources.

1.2. Handicrafts

The Europeans' arrival on the Northwest Coast significantly stimulated handicraft production among the Tlingit. New kinds of raw materials and instruments and market expansion contributed to this. The Tlingit were able to get scrap iron, copper sheets, fine leather, paints, and other raw materials for making varied handcrafted items from the Europeans. Using metal instruments enabled the Tlingit to sharply increase the number of wood, horn, and bone items. In addition, the quality and the artistry of the items improved, and the work of preparing raw materials for plaited crafts was made somewhat easier.

The form and assignment of items did not change substantially. Traditional Tlingit artifacts continued to be widely demanded in the intertribal market, especially among the interior Athapaskans, who bought the Tlingit's plaited baskets, painted carved boxes and platters of wood, iron daggers, Chilkat cloaks, and so on (Grinev 1986b:117). Crafts made by Tlingit masters were in high demand among the inhabitants of Novo-Arkhangel'sk, chiefly the Aleuts and Eskimos, as well. Especially popular were the watertight baskets, mats, rattles, masks, copper and horn bracelets, and wood and black slate pipes, as well as the traditional Tlingit conical hats (Litke 1834:109; Markov 1856:84). The Tlingit sold plaited European-style hats to Russian and American sailors (the Indians themselves did not wear such hats) (*Novoarkhangel'sk i Koloshi*, 1862:31). The

RAC also bought these hats from the Tlingit, evidently for resale in California (Litke 1834:109). Plaited from spruce root, the hats were apparently copies of European top hats. Several such plaited top hats are preserved in Leningrad's Museum of Anthropology and Ethnography (Razumovskaia 1967:101).

The Europeans' arrival also saw the production of new kinds of handicrafts. These included cloaks made of European fabric and decorated with broadcloth and mother-of-pearl buttons. [1] The Russian-American Company purchased them from the Tlingit for subsequent resale to the northern Athapaskans. Thus, L. A. Zagoskin, traveling in the lower Yukon, had several very expensive "Kolosh cloaks" among his goods to trade with the local Indians. Only one of the Athapaskans he encountered could afford to buy such a cloak, giving 15 beavers for it (Zagoskin 1956:280).

The Tlingit's pre-contact blacksmith and metalworking skills underwent further development when the necessary raw materials (primarily iron, but also copper, tin, silver, and lead) could be purchased from the Europeans. Traditional metalworking methods were preserved as well. The Indians worked iron the same way that they had earlier worked copper. The metal was heated on a fire, forged, then ground and polished. The Tlingit began to make awls, knife blades, adzes, and points for arrows, spears, and harpoons from iron (De Laguna 1972:1:412). However, iron daggers are the most well-known artifacts of the Tlingit smiths. These knives usually had an artistically executed, carved or engraved handle, and sometimes a second short blade. "Their double-bladed daggers, decorated with sparkling shells, are surprising in neatness of finish," wrote Litke (1834:109). Several such daggers are in the MAE's collections (Ratner-Shternberg 1930:183–186).

Despite the widespread introduction of iron, the Tlingit continued the traditional working of copper, making masks, daggers, bracelets, rattles, and copper plates. They also acquired "half-finished" copper plates from the Russians; what these latter plates were is not known. The Hudson's Bay Company also sold copper plates to the Tlingit. According to Yu. F. Lisianskii, the plates obtained from the Russians cost 20 to 30 times less than those forged of Native copper, the latter being valued at 20 to 30 sea otter skins (Lisianskii 1812:11–12). The standard copper plate, according to K. Oberg, was about 60 centimeters long, 46 centimeters wide, and 12 to 16 kilograms in weight. Such a plate cost no less than five or six slaves (Oberg 1973:117). However, it is possible that the plates underwent fabrication after the Tlingit bought them; their form was changed and they were engraved on the back and (often) painted according to the master's taste. E. Curtis suggested that the Indians had engraved the copper plates to resemble the icons they had seen among the Russians (Curtis

1970:145). Copper plates were sometimes presented to loyal Tlingit chiefs as a valuable gift (see documentary appendix entry {31}). Thus, the "chief toion of the Stikine people," Mikhail Kukkan, was rewarded with such a plate in 1860 (AVPR, f. RAK, op. 888, d. 1025, l. 1090b.).

The jeweler's business arose through European influence when the Europeans started manufacturing silver bracelets with Northwest Coast–style engravings. The Russians brought the craft of silver engraving to the Tlingit in about 1800, in the opinion of Christian Feest (1985:71). Feest's assertion, however, is doubtful because the Russians did not supply the Tlingit either with silver or silver goods at this time. Certainly, in 1790 the Russians sold (or gave) the Tlingit copper bracelets, the engraving on which could have influenced the Indians to create similar items. But, in my view, the development of this branch of handicrafts occurred later—around the mid-19th century, when the Indians had amassed sufficient silver (silver coins, ornaments) from European traders.

According to Emmons, after meeting the European traders, the value of copper as a metal for making decorations dropped significantly among the Indians, and it was soon displaced by silver. The Tlingit have suggested that Mexican dollars were initially used as a source for silver. The Tlingit evidently obtained Mexican dollars from Russians who traded in California, where by 1812 Fort Ross had been established. It is possible, although doubtful, that the medals that the governor of Russian America awarded to loyal Indians were also a source of silver. Finally, after Americans appeared on the Pacific coast in the 1840s, the American silver dollar was used for its silver (Emmons 1991:189).

Another branch of handicrafts that began to form among the Tlingit under European influence was metalsmithing. Khlebnikov (1985:87) noted that by the mid-1820s some Tlingit were occupied in the repair of guns.

Although Indian handicrafts developed under Russian American rule, they nevertheless did not form an entirely independent branch of the economy. Rather, handicrafts existed chiefly to satisfy basic requirements, serving personal needs. Only a relatively small quantity of handicrafts was traded, and no separate stratum of craftsmen formed in Indian society.

1.3. Inter- and Intratribal Trade and Trade with the Europeans

Of all spheres of Tlingit economic activity, none was more significantly influenced by European colonization than bartering. Indeed, most contacts between the Indians and Europeans occurred for bartering or in the presence of bartering. Trade was the basic channel through which European culture penetrated Indian society.

The Europeans' arrival on the Northwest Coast stimulated further trade development. Growth in the production of traditional items of exchange (with the introduction of more modern tools), a significant increase in the assortment of goods exchanged, and the market's broadening because of the fur trade all stimulated trade. Exchange within the tribe, which had earlier taken the form of gift exchange, now began to resemble true trade. At the basis of this change lay economic gain and not the maintenance of kin relations (Oberg 1973:107). "Thus," wrote Veniaminov in the 1830s, "one of the toion's children, who began trade with several beaver skins, had in the course of three or four years obtained for himself eight slaves, an excellent boat, a wife, several guns, and a multitude of items and, in a word, became a wealthy man (Veniaminov 1840a:117–118).

The Tlingit substantially expanded their contacts with tribes to the south (Tsimshian, Haida, and others), as well as with the Eyak and Chugach to the northwest. The Eyak's assimilation by their southern neighbors (the Tlingit) increased after the Tlakaik Teikweidí were destroyed in 1806. Trade, strengthened by intermarriage, contributed to this. "Many Ugalentsi Eyak have Kolosh girls while the Koloshi, the reverse, have Ugalentsi wives and by means of this kinship have close relations. The Yakutat toion Klemuk settled among the Ugalentsi in 1826," Khlebnikov wrote (1979:52). The Russian missionary Nikolai Militov, who visited the Eyak in June 1859, wrote in his journal: "Now it is necessary to sail farther to the south to the Ugalentsi. The Ugalentsi belong to a clan of ferocious Kolosh: language, morals, customs, dress, way of life—everything is the same as among the Kolosh" (Yakimov 2001:214). By the time Russian America had been sold to the United States (1867), the Eyak, who lived along the coast from Yakutat Bay to the mouth of the Copper River, were in fact already no different from the Tlingit; during the first American census of Alaska's population (1880) they were counted among the Tlingit (Petroff 1884:28–29). In the opinion of the well-known Alaska linguist M. E. Krauss, between 1785 and 1825, the Eyak, pressured by the Tlingit, relocated northwestward into Chugach territory near the mouth of the Copper River and lost their Native lands to the southeast, which were occupied by the Tlingit who then assimilated the local Eyak (Krauss 1982:12).

The Tlingit also influenced the culture of the Chugach Eskimos. This influence is graphically demonstrated by Chugach household items found in the American museums and the MAE. Plaited Chugach crafts, primarily baskets and hats, clearly show Tlingit influence, having been decorated in the style of the Northwest Coast. The form of the wooden platters and the zoomorphic representations on them, as well as mountain goat horn spoons with totemic engravings on the handles attest to these influences (Birket-Smith 1953:59–67; Razumovskaia 1967:102–104).

For the Tlingit, even more significant than contacts with the Eyak and Chugach were trade connections with the interior Athapaskans. The depletion of fur resources in Tlingit territory in the 1830s and the relative saturation of their internal market by European goods led to the coastal Indians' actively expanding trade into the interior. Tlingit trading parties, sometimes numbering up to 100 people, traveled 100 kilometers from their Native villages, reaching, in the North, the middle course of the Yukon, and, in the East, the upper reaches of the Stikine. Some Tlingit traders remained among the Athapaskans for two or three years in order to amass more furs (Olson 1936:211–214).

While the interior Indians generally could offer the Tlingit only furs and various animal hides, the Tlingit, because of the intermediary trade of the Europeans, had an immense selection of wares. Therefore, besides their traditional products, such as fish oil or dried mollusks, and handicrafts like the "Chilkat" cape and plaited baskets, Tlingit traders furnished the Athapaskans with metal kettles, axes, knives, guns, mirrors, beads, cinnabar, flour, and so on. Sometimes the Tlingit sold slaves to the interior Indians. These were expensive: the Chilkat people could trade a captive to a prosperous Tutchone for a bale of furs as high as his head (McClellan 1975:2:504–505). The Stikine people to the south also sold slaves to the Tahltan Athapaskans. A male slave cost 100 beaver skins, a female 50 (Emmons 1911:29). The coastal traders became rich in the intermediary trade. The Chilkat people reported to Oberg that their ancestors had obtained a flintlock rifle from the white people for a bale of furs equal to the height of the gun, and then sold the gun to the Athapaskans for a pile of furs as high as two rifles (Oberg 1973:110). According to Krause, the Tlingit unscrupulously cheated the Athapaskans in the exchange for furs and treated them almost as slaves (Krause 1956:137).

Over the course of several decades the Tlingit were among the few intermediaries between the European fur traders and the interior Athapaskans. "Their passion to be mercenary is innate and they are the chief middlemen in trade among the remaining Natives," wrote the Russian naval officer P. N. Golovin about the Tlingit (1862:45–46).

There were especially close relations between the Tlingit and the Tahltan, Tagish, and Southern Tutchone, whose cultures the coastal Indians significantly influenced (Grinev 1986b:120–122; McClellan 1975:2:501–518). Sometimes the Athapaskans came down from the mountains to the seashore, which was reported in the 1820s in Russian sources: the naval officer V. P. Romanov wrote:

The Koloshi say that there is a people living to the north, in the mountains, whom they call Konnak [that is, *gunanaa*—"foreign clan"] . . . they say that these people sometimes come to the Chilkat for trade: these people are different from the Koliuzh both in way of life and in language; formerly they had as weapons bows and arrows with stone *kopeitsi* [points], but now they get guns and gunpowder from the Chilkat Koliuzh, and in exchange for this they bring them fox and sable [marten] skins and native copper (Romanov 1825:26).

However, the Tlingit themselves strove in every way to bar the Athapaskans from access to the sea, where they could directly contact European traders. The chief of the Tahltan, who wanted to see a European ship at the mouth of the Stikine, had to give 500 beaver skins to the Stikine chief for protection during the "excursion" (Emmons 1991:7).

Over the course of the 19th century, active trade influenced the Athapaskans to borrow many elements of material and spiritual culture from the Tlingit. It was the latter who taught the Tutchone to make wooden traps for fish, and the Tahltan to cure salmon (MacLachlan 1981:459; McClellan 1981b:497). Evidently, the Tlingit legend of the Wealthy Woman and the Frogs circulated among their interior neighbors (McClellan 1963:124). Similar borrowings undoubtedly promoted the Tlingit language as the language of trade. The culture of the seaside Tlingit, by contrast, was not significantly influenced by the Athapaskans. The influence that there was was found primarily in the sphere of material culture. The Tlingit evidently began to use Athapaskan buckskin moccasins and trouser-moccasins more; the Athapaskans brought these to Novo-Arkhangel'sk to sell to the Russians, according to H. J. Holmberg (1855:19). Especially popular among the Tlingit were the interior Indians' marten and marmot fur capes.

The Ahtna, Northern Tutchone, Han, and even the Kaska and Sekani also had periodic contact with the Tlingit in the mid-19th century. During this time the Tlingit not only traded with the Athapaskans but tried to secure a position on their lands. In the first half of the 19th century the Chilkat people of Klukwáan village built the trading community of Nukva'ik on the upper reaches of the Alsek. However, life in the more severe interior climate seemed difficult to them, and after the smallpox epidemic of 1835–39 they returned to the coast (McClellan 1981b:496). The Stikine people had several small settlements in the Stikine River Valley up to where it met the Iskut River, but the Tahltan Athapaskans checked their advance into the interior (Teit 1906:338, 347). The Tlingit of the Taku and Auk kwáans were the most successful in expanding into the Athapaskans' lands. By 1840 the Athapaskan-speaking Taku Indians (Taku-Tinne) who lived on the upper reaches of the Taku and Yukon rivers had assimilated or dispersed, and the Tlingit formed the two modern communities of interior Tlingit—Atlin and Teslin—in the occupied region (McClellan 1981a:469). On the whole, trade between the coastal Indians and the interior Athapaskans contributed to significant change in the Athapaskans' culture. In addition, trade with inland Indians extended the Tlingit's trade routes to the upper and middle Yukon in the North and to Puget Sound in the South, thereby increasing their ethnic territory.

Tlingit-European trade has already been discussed (see chapter 2). We will not review the assortment of items traded but will instead focus on the Indians' evolving needs for various European goods over the course of Russian American history. From first contact with Europeans, the Tlingit were chiefly interested in metal items (primarily sheet iron). Firearms soon became the most popular ware; later it was fabrics and European clothing; and afterward, food products and spirits (Berkh 1808:7). By the mid-19th century the most demanded goods—the demand for which never diminished—were wool blankets, tobacco, ammunition, and rum. The practical Tlingit, being wealthier than, for example, the Athapaskans, never showed great interest in beads and trifles. This was noted as early as 1788 by G. G. Izmailov and D. I. Bocharov: "They greedily trade for a variety of clothing, iron, kettles, and boilers; other things like beads they do not take so willingly" (Shelikhov 1971:102).

Trying to obtain as many furs as possible, some English and American fur traders offered Indians traditional exchange goods, such as tanned elk hides traded from the Indians of the Columbia Basin, dentalia obtained from the Nutka Indians, and even slaves purchased from the Kwakiutl, in addition to European wares (Drucker 1965:194). The first mention of the Americans' selling slaves to the Tlingit was documented by the Russians in 1802 (*K istorii Rossiisko-Amerikanskoi*, 1957:119). According to F. I. Shemelin, the "Boston men" sold Polynesians—Natives of the Hawaiian Islands—to the Northwest Coast Indians for sacrifices (Shemelin 1816:1:158). Later O. E. Kotzebue wrote that American slave traders traded Oregon Indians to the Tlingit, Haida, and Tsimshian (Kotzebue 1822:2:70–71).

The Russians, especially when they first made contact with the Tlingit, sometimes also acted as middlemen in intertribal trade, supplying the Tlingit tanned elk hides, sea lion whiskers, marmot cloaks and parkas, ermine skins, and walrus bone obtained from Natives employed by the company, in exchange for sea otter skins (OR GBL, f. 204, k. 32, ed. khr. no. 4, l. 10b.). They undertook mediating primarily because they lacked European goods. Later,

HBC agents also sometimes acted as intertribal mediators, supplying the Tlingit with dentalium and abalone shells and sharks' teeth in exchange for traditional adornments (De Laguna 1990b:209).

To strengthen the "effect" of their trade, the Russians followed several elements of traditional Native etiquette. Trading was never begun directly by exchange. It was always preceded by a more or less solemn ceremony, during which they treated the Tlingit and gave them small gifts, and they in return performed their songs and dances. This is what the RAC prikazchik Aleksandr Markov writes about this:

> How ceremonially the savages gather on the ship on this day, which is appointed for their entertainment! From different sides of the bay quietly come large boats, in each of which sit 20 painted savages, with feathers, dressed in their best attire. With drums and songs they paddle to the ship, arranging all the boats in a row not far from it, and show their friendly disposition by dancing, which consists of various twistings, during the continuation of which they incessantly sprinkle themselves with eagle down; then in a sedate way they climb onto the deck, where they are entertained by rice porridge with molasses. . . .
> At the end of the feast, when the savages begin to leave, it is necessary to give each a leaf of tobacco for the journey; and some of them, incidentally, even steal some; in doing this they are very artless (Markov 1856:75–76).

Only on the second day, after such ceremony, does the actual trading begin—a long procedure that requires no little patience on the Russians' part. The Indians, wishing to sell their furs more profitably, bargain for a very long time, and at the end of the transaction they still require at least a small supplement (a so-called *istak*).

Ideas of the "value" of goods between the Tlingit and Russians did not always coincide. Markov recalled, "For example, for a large otter they give them 1 blanket at 18 rubles, or, instead of that, 5 pounds of gunpowder and one 10-pound lead slab, which amounts to 10 rubles; for a yearling sea otter 2 blankets, 36 rubles, or one gun that costs 25 rubles" (Markov 1856:77).

In trading operations the Tlingit conducted themselves like experienced and deft businessmen. They often engaged in various stratagems and skillfully used competition between the European traders themselves (see documentary appendix entry {8}). At times they withheld furs, waiting for a profitable market. Thus, in 1835 the HBC agent J. York noted that the Stikine people, though they had furs, did not hurry to sell them to the British, hoping that the

Influence of European Contacts on Tlingit Culture

American traders they were waiting for would give them a better price (Gibson 1975:114). In February 1837 Stikine people who had arrived in two canoes to trade furs told the English in Fort Simpson that on their way they had seen a "large ship" to the south in Tongass Bay. This rumor was pure invention and was started by the Tlingit to raise the value of their furs (Gibson 1992:124).

The intensification of trade in Tlingit society during the Russian American period led to the appearance of goods that functioned as money. Initially, slaves, dentalia shells, furs, and tanned deer hides were the units of value and wealth (Khlebnikov 1985:86). "Instead of currency," wrote Litke, "they use *rovdugi* {deer hides}; for a slave 15 to 20 *rovdugi* are paid, for a beaver {sea otter} 5 or 6, for a good boat 10 to 15" (Litke 1834:110).

By the mid-1830s the European wool blanket had become the common and sole trade equivalent for all the Northwest Coast Indians. Any item or service could be valued at a definite number of blankets. In addition, the Sitka people, and possibly Tlingit of other ḵwáans, accepted the "colonial currency" of Russian America—leather "marks" from the RAC and Russian banknotes—which, as the sources mention, the Indians used in accounts with the Russians, as well as among themselves, evidently (Golovin 1863a:5:180–181; 6:284; Zelenoi 1865:80:9:58). I. V. Furuhjelm, striving to limit uncontrolled exchange between the Sitka people and the inhabitants of Novo-Arkhangel'sk, in 1860 categorically prohibited trading with the Tlingit outside the "Kolosh market" or using marks or money to pay the Indians for their goods (AVPR, f. RAK, op. 888, d. 1025, l. 800b.). But the decree was systematically violated. Thus, commodity-monetary relations began to penetrate the Tlingit economy in the Russian American period.

1.4. Potlatch

Contact with the Europeans even caused several changes in the ancient Indian custom of the potlatch. The development of the fur trade and the enrichment of a broader circle of people (in addition to the chief, other members of the household became wealthy) possibly led some Tlingit to seek higher status within Tlingit society by conducting personal potlatches (Averkieva 1974:163). Potlatches were soon arranged more often, and the wealth given away more liberally. After European colonization began, another variety of potlatch appeared—the potlatch of rivalry (Drucker 1965:197). This type was characterized by sharp competition between chiefs or whole lineages (which often belonged to the same moiety) and their rivals in a struggle to attain a higher rank than the rival. The property in such a potlatch was not so much given away as destroyed, manifesting a contempt for wealth. Furs and blankets were cut up into strips and shreds, copper plates were broken or dropped into the sea, and so on. Respect for deceased kinsmen also served as a formal cause for destroying accumulated wealth, as in the traditional potlatch. This is apparently the reason that in 1847 the L'uknax̱.ádi arranged an enormous potlatch at the walls of Novo-Arkhangel'sk—striving to attain a rank comparable to that of the Sitka Kiks.ádi, the recognized leaders of the Raven moiety in the Sitka k̲wáan (see documentary appendix entry {24}).

During the potlatch a child's helix was pierced, ushering him or her into the status of *aanyádi*, this custom was gradually eliminated. "In Sitka almost every Kolosh has the ears pierced, but they are almost all pretenders," wrote Veniaminov (1840a:108).

Contacts with Europeans led to such negative innovations as drinking alcohol at potlatches. At such ceremonies not only were guests from the opposite moiety now invited but also members of the host's moiety. Drinking spirits frequently transformed the potlatch into a drunken orgy that often concluded in bloody clashes (Oberg 1973:118).

There were also some changes in the types of property distributed at the potlatch. Whereas, formerly, slaves and copper plates were considered basic gifts, after contact with the Europeans, blankets were added to the list and, later, money. With the diminishing number of slaves, the Tlingit most often substituted piles of blankets of equivalent value as potlatch offerings. Sermons by the Orthodox missionaries and measures by the colonial administration sought to eradicate the tradition of ritually killing slaves during the potlatch. In a report to the RAC central board, I. A. Kupreianov wrote that he himself had repeatedly told the Tlingit chiefs who gathered in his home that human sacrifice at the potlatch was intolerable, and he recommended instead selling the slaves and using the income to organize a commemoration for the dead (AVPR, f. RAK, op. 888, d. 1002, l. 295ob.). In 1847 Teben'kov prohibited ritual slave killings at Sitka (Mamyshev 1855:248–249).It appears that the Sitka people observed this prohibition, at least partly. An Indian informant reported that in 1850 four slaves doomed to die were freed after the chief of the Sitka Kaagwaantaan touched them with his staff at the potlatch. These slaves immediately went into the fort to live among the Russians, since they were not permitted to live among the Tlingit (Anatolii 1906:23). The emancipated slaves, expelled from Indian society, were, in effect, "dead."

The Indians evidently viewed the festive receptions that the Russians organized for "delegations" of Tlingit chiefs as curious potlatches. Such gatherings had some features of potlatches: guests (in this case, the Tlingit) singing and dancing, entertainment, and often gifts from the "hosts." It is not surprising

Influence of European Contacts on Tlingit Culture

therefore that the Tlingit donned ceremonial attire used exclusively at pot-latches to attend these festivities (Veniaminov 1840a:104). Litke recorded a similar account in his diary, having visited Novo-Arkhangel'sk on the sloop *Kamchatka* commanded by the well-known Russian navigator V. M. Golovnin:

> 11th of August [1818]. A full-dress visit by Katlian, elder of the Sitka toions with a great retinue, in which were eight of his nephews, several of whom had wives. The ceremonies were being observed as with the first visit [to the *Kamchatka* by the Tlingit of Chief Kukkan], only with much more splendor. First, on the elevated middle part of the boat stood his oldest nephew, who directed the whole cere-mony. When all the necessary songs had been sung, Katlian, having until then sat among the others, got up from his place, took off his customary flat-topped hat, in place of which the nephew gave him a pointed one (very similar to a Chinese one) and made a speech, which our interpreter was not able to properly explain, but its meaning was that Katlian repeated his assurance that he wanted very much to live at peace with the Russians and that with the arrival of the new leader [V. M. Golovnin] a new sun began to shine. V[asilii] M[ikhailovich Golovnin] showed his gratitude and asked him to come aboard the ship; then he [Katlian's nephew] gave him still another hat (it is dif-ficult to describe it: the illustration by M[ister] Tikhanov represents it better), the top of which was covered with down; the chorus began to sing a new song and beat time on the boat with the oars; in its continuation Katlian shook a rattle similar to the above-described and continually shook his head, causing the down from his hat to fly everywhere. At the end of the concert our guests came on board and were entertained as well, like the first [visitors—Chief Kukkan with his kinsmen, whom the Russians fed crackers with molasses and a glass of grog] (RGA VMF, f. 15. op. 1, d. 8, l. 1810b.–182).

In the 1840s the Russians themselves tried to use the potlatch for rapproche-ment with independent Natives. In 1841 A. K. Etolin organized something like a fair for the Indians, with elements of the traditional potlatch. According to V. N. Mamyshev, up to 500 "honorable Koloshi" were gathered at this "Russian potlatch." News of this celebration spread among other Indians throughout the straits of the Alexander Archipelago, and at a subsequent similar fair 1,500 free Indians, not counting slaves, gathered in Novo-Arkhangel'sk (Mamyshev 1855:246–247).

On the whole, during the Russian American period the Tlingit potlatch was in its prime and continued for a rather long time—until the early 20th century, playing an essential role in Indian social life.

1.5. Hired Work

The arrival of Europeans on the Northwest Coast led to the appearance in Tlingit society of such socioeconomic phenomena as hiring-for-work. From the start of contact with the Russians, the Tlingit entered into temporary service as interpreters and translators. F. A. Kashevarov recalled that by 1796 at least two female Tlingit translators had lived among the Russians: Sitka Aniushka and Yakutat Aniushka (Sitnikov 1986:97). Baranov mentioned another interpreter—Olena of the Auk ƙwáan—in an 1801 letter to Kuskov (OR GBL, f. 204, k. 32, ed. khr. no. 4, l. 2). Niktopolion Gedeonov ("Interpreter Gedeon") served more than 30 years (until his death in 1855) as "chief Kolosh interpreter" for the RAC. His rather exotic name came from his godfather, Hieromonk Gedeon, who in 1806 baptized the young Akoi *amanat* Tygike in Kodiak (RGIA, f. 796, op. 90, d. 273, l. 630b.). Another Gedeonov, Kalistrat, served as an interpreter for the Russians, but he died in 1832, having served fewer years than Niktopolion. In his "Notes," Hieromonk Gedeon mentioned Nikostrat (Kalistrat?) Ľkaina, who had been baptized by him in 1806 along with other amanaty "of the Kolosh people" (RGIA, f. 796, op. 90, d. 273, l. 630b.). Kalistrat Gedeonov received 350 rubles a year for his work with the company; in 1831 F. P. Wrangell added 100 rubles to his salary "for zealous service" (AVPR, f. RAK, op. 888, d. 995, l. 35, 47). Nikostrat Gedeonov died on August 26, 1832, at the age of 44 from tuberculosis, according to R. A. Pierce (1990:162). As "young interpreters"—assistants of Niktopolion Gedeonov—"*Koloshenka* Mar'ia," the widow of the Russian "servant" Matvei Kabachakov; "Kolosh Pavel Kuchkeke"; and Gavrila Kategan, a nephew of Mikhail Kuƙkan, are also mentioned in the documents. Kuƙkan had been sent to the port of Ayan to study Russian (AVPR, f. RAK, op. 888, d. 1020, l. 346; d. 1024, l. 1300b.).

But it was not only as translators that the Tlingit worked among the Russians. In a letter to Kuskov dated May 24, 1808, Baranov mentions a certain "Kolosh" Zabiyakin who, being in the service of the company, plaited hats in Kodiak, then went as a sailor on a RAC ship to Kamchatka (OR GBL, f. 204, k. 32, d. 6, l. 240b.). After the Sitka people settled at Novo-Arkhangel'sk, the Russian settlers began to hire them to work in the gardens, deliver firewood, and perform other services (Khlebnikov 1985:205). However, until the 1840s hiring Tlingit—whether by the company or by private individuals—was episodic. This was because there was relatively limited contact between

Russians and Tlingit at that time. Besides, performing monotonous regular work did not come easy to the Tlingit: "They [the Tlingit] could be skilled sailors, but there is no possibility of drawing them from their natural habits. For example, the young ones serve several years, acquiring a good position and the usual salary, then tire and leave," wrote Khlebnikov (1985:185). Later, in 1864, Governor I. V. Furuhjelm noted in his report: "I continually hired the Kalosh for work in the port and on ships, several decent carpenters were formed of them, but in general it must be noted that not being associated with work from infancy or at least to constant occupation, they are found generally lazy and capricious in work, and therefore I would consider as a quite useful measure taking Kalosh youths in training of various skills" (Furuhjelm 1864:23). In Kan's opinion, the Tlingit did not usually work for long among the Russians but rather left the service after some time to stress their independent status, distinguishing themselves from the permanent Native RAC workers at Novo-Arkhangel'sk—the Koniag and Aleuts—whom they viewed as "Russian slaves" (Kan 1999:76).

The first large group of Indians was hired by the RAC in 1842. Some of them remained in Novo-Arkhangel'sk to perform general labor at the port, while others became sailors on company ships (Mamyshev 1855:247). Both sailors and port workers were paid a standard monthly wage of 30 rubles in goods; in addition, the Indians were issued work clothing when they were hired (AVPR, f. RAK, op. 888, d. 1008, l. 3460b.–347). On the crew of the brig *Velikii Kniaz' Konstantin*, the first of the European ships to enter the mouth of the Amur in 1846, there were three Tlingit sailors: Ignatii Kal'tin, Kastuk, and Sergei Muskkin (AVPR, f. Gl. arkhiv II-5, 1844–1860 gg., op. 38, d. 3, l. 47–470b.).[2] Ivan, the son of Niktopolion Gedeonov, served as first mate on the brig *Shelikhov* in 1855 (AVPR, f. RAK, op. 888, d. 1022, l. 151, 170).

Of course, from the mid-1840s through the 1850s hiring Tlingit for RAC work was curtailed and wages were somewhat lowered. In 1847 Governor M. D. Teben'kov gave special instructions to the Novo-Arkhangel'sk office to establish the following tariffs: a monthly wage to a Tlingit worker need not exceed 24 rubles in banknotes, and a daily wage only 1 ruble in banknotes. This resulted, first, from excess supply in the workforce, and second, from the fact that the Tlingit, finding a new source of earnings as company employees, significantly reduced the supply of fresh provisions in Novo-Arkhangel'sk. As Teben'kov wrote, "Now, if 10 Koloshi are necessary for work, 100 appear, and the denial of a job has an influence. It is a pity only that this willingness produces detriment to provisions. The Koloshi, employed in summer to work in the port, on ships, and for laying in firewood, having made a supply of this for themselves, in fall and winter are devoted to laziness and by this deprive us of fresh provisions in the market" (AVPR, f. RAK, op. 888, d. 1014, l. 350). In instructions to the Novo-Arkhangel'sk office, Teben'kov also stated: "Limit the hiring of Koloshi at the present time to 20 persons, and this precisely for one purpose—their great nearness to us" (AVPR, f. RAK, op. 888, d. 1015, l. 97).

Some Tlingit who entered the service of the Russian-American Company were sent to work in Kodiak and even Mikhailovskii Redoubt on the shore of Norton Sound in the lower Yukon. In 1843 two Tlingit women—Achkuka and Katerina Sakikan—were sent as "workers" to Kodiak. They were given an annual salary of 60 rubles in banknotes. In 1852 an "employee of the Company from the Koloshi," Vasilii Nikolaev, went to Kodiak on the schooner *Tungus* (AVPR, f. RAK, op. 888, d. 1009, l. 468–469ob.; d. 1020, l. 88–89ob.). When the "gold rush" began in California, six Tlingit were among the prospectors that the Russian-American Company sent there (Mamyshev 1855:280). The party of prospectors comprised four Russians and six Tlingit led by Lieutenant of the Corps of Mining Engineers P. P. Doroshin. From February 26 to April 16, 1849, the prospectors extracted 1 *pud*, 7 pounds, 44 *zolotniki*, and 12 *doli* about {43 pounds} of pure gold, and 6 pounds, 50 zolotniki, and 70 doli of silver {more than 6 pounds} (AVPR, f. RAK, op. 888, d. 1020, l. 113; Mamyshev 1855:280). Tlingit participation in the California gold rush is underreported in the scholarly literature, as indicated by the statement of S. B. Okun' that the discovery of gold in California was "nothing but a loss" for the RAC (Okun' 1939:143–144). However, this loss cannot be accepted inasmuch as the company made about 20 thousand rubles net profit (by colonial value) from trade in California in 1849, not counting income from the sale of the gold extracted by Doroshin's party (more than 19 kilograms) (AVPR, f. RAK, op. 888, d. 1018, l. 133–134; Mamyshev 1855:280–281).

In 1850 Teben'kov sent the schooner *Tungus*, carrying another party of prospectors (including four Tlingit), from Novo-Arkhangel'sk to the mouth of the Kaknu River (Kenai Peninsula), where in 1848 P. P. Doroshin discovered evidence of gold. However, this expedition was unsuccessful, since the gold deposits turned out to be very poor (AVPR, f. RAK, op. 888, d. 1018, l. 93–93ob.).

According to Golovin's and S. A. Kostlivtsov's testimony, in the early 1860s the Tlingit worked as sailors and stevedores in the port, delivered firewood in Novo-Arkhangel'sk, and procured ice, which the RAC sold at a profit in California (Golovin 1863a:6:278; Kostlivtsov 1863:115). Usually a Tlingit worker's wage during these years amounted to 10 to 15 rubles in banknotes per month plus rations from the company.

Hired Tlingit workers were used not only by the Russians but also by

Influence of European Contacts on Tlingit Culture

the Americans and English. For example, 20 Tongass ḵwáan Indians served as sailors on the American brig *Bolivar Liberator* in 1834 (Ogden 1941:178). American skippers may also have engaged Tlingit as sea otter hunters, as is related in an Indian legend (Olson 1967:41). It is interesting that the Tlingit also served as translators, guides, paddlers, and so on for the HBC (Corser 1940:25; Simpson 1847:1:213).

However, hired work during the Russian American period affected very few Tlingit. The formation of an "Indian proletariat" had barely begun.

2. Changes in the Sphere of Material Culture

2.1. Dwelling and Settlement

Tlingit material culture was practically unaffected by European influence. It was under Russian influence that the Tlingit replaced the mobile wooden shields used for smoke ventilation on their roofs with fixed wooden covers (De Laguna 1990b:208). In addition, the Tlingit door opening was made rectangular and a wooden door was hung, at least at Sitka, as depicted in I. G. Voznesenskii's illustrations in the mid-1840s (Blomkvist 1951).

When relations with the Russians were strained, the Tlingit reinforced their fortified structures. Settlements began to be fenced in with thick timber palisades. Houses within the fort were frequently connected by subterranean passages, and the forts themselves were built on cliffs, making them hard to reach. G. H. von Langsdorff, who in 1805 visited the Sitka fort, which they had built on the shore of Chatham Strait after Baranov defeated them in 1804, described it as a strong fortification on a high cliff. The fort consisted of a palisade of thick timbers that surrounded the Indians' houses. A high, natural earthen rampart provided additional protection from artillery fire. The natural approach to the fort was protected by an abatis of large tree trunks (Langsdorff 1812:2:110). One such fortification is depicted in a Stikine plan sketched by Lisianskii in 1804 (Khlebnikov 1985:43). The Indians' fortifications were so strong that the light artillery of the Europeans was frequently powerless against their wooden walls (Lisianskii 1812:30). N. P. Rezanov urgently asked the RAC's central board to send mortars—special heavy artillery used in the siege of forts. "One shell thrown at them," wrote Rezanov, "would reduce the pride of this people who, building forts from mast poles in three rows and having better rifles and falconets, consider themselves invincible" (Tikhmenev 1863:2:Append. 282–283).

2.2. Household Items

By the time of early contact with Europeans, foreign household objects had already begun to reach the Tlingit. In 1791 the Spanish navigator Malaspina saw among the Yakutat people several pots and a silver spoon, which, he presumed, had been obtained by the Indians from the English Captain Dixon in 1787 (Malaspina 1825:9:168). The Tlingit gladly acquired from the European fur traders household items, specifically, cast iron, iron, and copper kettles and pots; tin buckets and mugs; and pewter spoons that surpassed their traditional implements in several ways. The Yakutat people, for example, borrowed cups and the word for designating them from the Russians (De Laguna 1972:1:410). By 1805 Lisianskii wrote that the Stikine people were preparing their food in "European kettles," and prosperous Indians had "many European dishes" (Lisianskii 1812:146). Greatly popular among the Tlingit were thick blue and white porcelain platters and bowls, which the Hudson's Bay Company furnished. Sometimes the American captains even delivered items of China porcelain to the Indians (De Laguna 1972:1:393). The Tlingit also bartered with American traders for Cantonese camphor wood trunks. Wealthy Indians usually kept their treasures in these trunks; another chief of the Sitka Kiks.ádi, Nawushkeitl (Naushket or Navushkekl), had several such trunks (Erman 1870:2:316). According to Veniaminov's testimony, these trunks were quite expensive: in Novo-Arkhangel'sk the Russians gave no less that 70 rubles for one Cantonese trunk; the Indians paid six or seven sea otter skins (Veniaminov 1840a:121–122).

In the collections of the MAE is a small table on short legs that probably had a ceremonial function. I. G. Voznesenskii acquired it from the Tlingit in the mid-1840s (Ratner-Shternberg 1929:297, 301). It must be assumed that the appearance of such tables among the Tlingit resulted from Russian influence.

The Tlingit chiefly borrowed items useful in their everyday life. However, despite the widespread use of European items, the latter could not entirely replace traditional Tlingit implements during the Russian American period.

2.3. Tools of Labor and Means of Transportation

Trade with the Europeans and intensified intertribal connections meant that many innovations affected Tlingit material culture during the Russian American period. Convinced of the superior properties of iron and steel, and acquiring this raw material from the Europeans in large quantities, the Tlingit quickly almost entirely replaced traditional tools of stone, bone, copper (blades), and wood (clubs) with nearly identical iron implements. This replacement likely

Influence of European Contacts on Tlingit Culture

occurred by the mid-1790s, as evidenced by the already high demand for scrap iron and iron items (from which points, blades, and so on were made).

In addition, the Tlingit also borrowed European instruments and tools such as axes, hatchets, saws, steel knives, files, awls, needles, and scissors. Traditional hunting implements like the bow and spear were gradually replaced by the more effective gun, which was used to hunt both forest and sea animals.

European contact influenced the Tlingit to equip their large canoes with masts and sails, beginning in the 19th century. A canoe could have three masts, each of which usually bore a rectangular sail. Initially, sails of bast-fiber mats (Markov 1856:84) or elk hides (De Laguna 1972:1:341) were used; later, canvas was employed. Unlike the ships of the Polynesians and other peoples of Oceania, Drucker noted, the Northwest Coast Indians' sailing canoe could not maneuver against a lateral or head wind because it lacked a keel. Therefore, the sail on the Indian canoes was raised only in a fair wind. Nevertheless, the advantages of using a sail (to increase the canoe's speed and preserve the paddlers' strength) were evident to the Indians (Drucker 1965:194–195). Equipping canoes with sails enabled the Tlingit to make long voyages to the south in the second half of the 19th century. According to De Laguna, the southern Tlingit preferred the large 20-meter red cedar canoes of the Haida because they could carry two masts with square sails and transport from six to eight tons of cargo. The Tlingit (as far north as Yakutat) acquired Nutka Indian canoes from far to the south (De Laguna 1990b:208).

The Russians also used Tlingit canoes in Novo-Arkhangel'sk. According to H. J. Holmberg, a large Tlingit canoe cost about eight hundred rubles in banknotes in Novo-Arkhangel'sk in the 1850s (Holmberg 1855:27). For example, in 1842 the RAC purchased three canoes from the Indians for a party of Aleuts who were then sent off to hunt near the shores of Kamchatka, and in 1853, the RAC purchased several more canoes for Unga Island (AVPR, f. RAK, op. 888, d. 1008, l. 90; d. 1009, l. 63; d. 1021, l. 360b.). Wooden Tlingit canoes permitted the Aleuts to hunt unhampered in icy conditions, whereas sharp pieces of ice often damaged their own skin baidarkas.

The strengthening of intertribal contacts during this period led to the spread of some of the other tribes' tools and means of transportation to the Tlingit. Trading saw a large number of the better-quality Eskimo bows, which surpassed the simple bows of the Northwest Coast Indians, come to the Tlingit. The Yakutat people had especially many of them. Sometimes the Tlingit also bought flat bows from the interior Athapaskans (Niblack 1890:286, pl. 26, fig. 115). In the Tlingit collection of the American museums one encounters the atlatl, which the Tlingit evidently bought from the Eskimos or Aleuts in the

19th century (Holm 1972:62–63; Niblack 1890:pl. 27, fig. 127). Such atlatls were often engraved, sometimes encrusted with mother-of-pearl, and probably used not as hunting implements but rather as expensive toys or as attributes of the shamanic cult. In any case, no known sources reveal how the Tlingit used them in hunting. Only De Laguna's informants—the Yakutat people, neighbors of the Chugach Eskimos—reported that their ancestors sometimes used the atlatl to hunt deer (De Laguna 1972:1:369).

Some groups of northern Tlingit were using skin baidarkas and baidars, evidently traded from the Eskimos, when the first RAC hunting parties appeared in the northern part of the Alexander Archipelago. A three-hatched baidarka and baidars, in which Indians of the Akoi and Hoonah ḵwáans approached the ship of the American Captain Kimball, are mentioned in one of Baranov's letters (OR GBL, f. 204, k. 32, ed. khr. no. 6, l. 2).

2.4. Food

From their first contact with Europeans the Tlingit encountered food that was new to them. Several legends recount their initial perceptions of European products. For example, in a Teiḵweidí clan legend about one of the first encounters with American traders, it says that the Indians obtained rice, crackers, and molasses, which they accordingly took for fly larva, tree fungus, and "water from the village of the river otters" (that is, werewolves) from the newcomers.[3] Considering how strange and dangerous they thought this food was, they threw it away. What is more, the young pig given to the chief of the Teiḵweidí was "adopted" by the chief and taken into Indian society "with the rights of an aristocratic child" (Olson 1967:87–88).

However, the Indians became accustomed to the new food rather quickly and even grew fond of it. The Stikine Indians who visited Captain Vancouver in 1793 made it clear to the Englishmen that the best gift for their (the Indians') chief was sugary molasses and bread (Vancouver 1830:4:287). From the 1820s the potato and to some degree the turnip became widespread among the Tlingit. The potato was so readily adopted and integrated into the Indians' cuisine that the present-day Tlingit consider it their own Native food (Jacobs and Jacobs 1982:128).

In exchange for furs the Indians received rice, flour, grits, hardtack, molasses, and sugar from the Europeans. During the period of maritime fur trade an especially large amount of rice (from China and India) was delivered to the Northwest Coast. According to Rezanov, in 1805 the English captain Barber had up to 2,000 pudy {72,000 pounds} of rice on his ship to sell to the Indians. As Barber affirmed, the latter were so partial to rice that they were prepared to

Influence of European Contacts on Tlingit Culture

give an otter skin for one pud {36 pounds} (AVPR, f. Gl. arkhiv 1–7, 1802 g., d. 1, papka no. 33, l. 1460b.).

The popularity of European products among the Tlingit is confirmed by many facts. For example, the Indians entertained the American captain D'Wolf and the naturalist Langsdorff, who visited the Sitka fort in 1805, not only with fish but also with millet and molasses (AVPR, f. Gl. arkhiv 1–7, 1802 g., d. 1, papka no. 35, l. 26). Rice porridge with syrup or molasses was a favorite delicacy of the Tlingit, and the Russians regaled them with this dish during ceremonial receptions in Novo-Arkhangel'sk or on the ships that arrived from Russia (Kotzebue 1987:217). Litke, describing a reception on the sloop *Kamchatka* in 1818, noted that the Tlingit chief Kukkan and his retinue were treated with sugar, molasses, and a glass of grog on the upper deck after dances. [4] The visitors ate "with great appetite and poured the remaining molasses into their hats and took it with them," according to Litke (RGA VMF, f. 15, op. 1, d. 8, l. 1780b.). The Tlingit sometimes obtained bread from the Russians, which, Litke reported, "quite pleased" them (1834:114). In the 1860s the Tlingit purchased more than 100 pudy of flour a month from the RAC (Golovin 1862:50). The Indians adopted the Russian custom of drinking tea, which they themselves reported to De Laguna (De Laguna 1972:1:410).

The arrival of the Europeans acquainted the Indians with alcoholic drinks. The Americans, who mostly brought West Indian rum, prospered considerably trading spirits. Initially, however, rum and vodka were not popular among the Tlingit (Berkh 1808:8; Langsdorff 1812:2:96). Only over time did spirits become commonly traded between the Europeans and the Tlingit. The Tlingit were also often given a gift of rum at the conclusion of trade or as a bonus for work. By the 1830s the Indians had so much vodka and rum, chiefly from the Americans and English, that they started selling it to the residents of Novo-Arkhangel'sk. Wrangell noted that as a result of this some Russian promyshlenniki gave the "shirt off their back" and even became indebted to enterprising Tlingit traders. Drunkards often "forgot" to pay their debt, which usually caused quarrels and animosity between the Indians and Russians (AVPR, f. RAK, op. 888, d. 995, l. 214).

The abundance of spirits led to alcoholism in the Native population. Drunkenness often ended in tragedy: an accidental death or a murder. Such cases are described in Tlingit legends (Olson 1967:92). Drunken quarrels also led to clashes among the Indians, as occurred in 1841 between the two clans of the Sitka kwáan after an intoxicated chief killed another Indian. Only the intervention of the Russian administration averted a subsequent clash (Simpson 1847:2:204–205).

The Russians also provided the Tlingit with rum. Officially, selling spirits to the Indians was permitted in the Russian colonies only from 1832 to 1842, but it had occurred earlier (Khlebnikov 1985:140). [5] Later, however, the colonial authorities, pursuing the RAC legislation and an agreement with the Hudson's Bay Company to prohibit the sale of spirits to the Indians, completely suppressed this practice (*Doklad komiteta*, 1863a:166). Although the residents of Novo-Arkhangel'sk continued to illegally sell spirits to the Tlingit until Alaska was sold, the scope of sales was quite small, with the total quantity of spirits that the Russians sold the Indians being substantially less than what the English and Americans had supplied. Therefore, one cannot agree with Drucker that Russian-Tlingit trade was distinguished by "a large amount of alcoholic beverages" (Drucker 1965:205).

Tobacco, which they obtained from European and American traders, became very popular among the Tlingit. According to Khlebnikov, the Tlingit purchased only Virginia tobacco and would not buy Russian Cherkassian tobacco (Khlebnikov 1985:205). Tobacco was chewed (mostly by the women) and smoked (mostly by the men). One cannot agree with Dzeniskevich's assertion that among the Northwest Coast Indians the ritual of smoking tobacco was a widespread old tradition (Dzeniskevich 1985:68). In fact the Tlingit, Haida, and other Indians of this region knew only one variety of tobacco before the Europeans' arrival; however, they did not smoke this "Native tobacco" but rather chewed it after mixing it with shredded and burned shell or wood bark (De Laguna 1972:1:411; Krause 1956:208). Tobacco smoking became widespread only after the arrival of the whites (De Laguna 1990b:212; Kan 1989:322), and smoking known only in the very south of the Northwest Coast, to the Yurok (Gibson 1992:224).

2.5. Dress and Decoration

In the Tlingit's material culture, the Europeans most influenced dress and adornment. Traditional dress (made from buckskin and animal hides) was difficult to manufacture, because both procuring the raw material and preparing it were laborious processes. European fabric and clothes could be obtained for a fur, which was easier for the Athapaskans to procure than deer or skins. In addition, the comparatively moderate climate and the Indians' physical tempering permitted them to make do with European dress or fabric even in winter, explaining its great popularity among the Tlingit.

The Tlingit borrowed European dress, fabrics, and decorations during the period of early contact, and the Indians' demands for these items did not decrease. [6] Europeans influenced Tlingit dress in two ways: first, in supply-

Influence of European Contacts on Tlingit Culture

ing European fabric to the Indians to make traditional dress, and second, in selling them ready-made European clothing. The fur traders took European and Chinese fabrics to the Northwest Coast: frieze, baize, broadcloth, linen, sailcloth, cotton, and flannel. In the 1820s gray American calico was especially in demand among the Sitka people. In those years the Russians often used it to trade with the Indians (Khlebnikov 1985:203). The Tlingit prepared the simplest kind of clothing—cloaks (earlier they were sewn only from skins)—from European fabrics. Also, cloaks of blue broadcloth were highly valued in the 19th century (AVPR, f. Gl. arkhiv 1–7, 1802 g., d. 1, papka no. 35, l. 35; Lisianskii 1812:119, 129). By the mid-19th century the everyday dress of the Indians along the whole Northwest Coast included wool and baize blankets, having almost completely replaced other fabric cloaks. English blankets were preferred over the American ones (Anatolii 1906:43), and for one red blanket the Tlingit gave two blankets of other colors (Markov 1856:78).

The ceremonial Chilkat blankets gradually yielded to showy blue or black blankets, which the Indian women bordered with red broadcloth and several rows of mother-of-pearl buttons or silver badges. Such blankets were popular among the Northwest Coast Indian aristocracy in the mid-19th century.

European dress came to the Tlingit in no little quantity. American traders took overcoats and outer clothing of wool and flannel into Southeast Alaska; the Tlingit especially desired sailors' clothing (Langsdorff 1812:2:97). From English, American, and Russian traders the Tlingit obtained shirts, frock coats, jackets, trousers, and stockings. European dress and blankets gradually became the index of wealth for Indians. The prosperous Tlingit amassed such a quantity of European dress and blankets as to substantially surpass sensible use. In addition, they rarely wore this clothing except during ceremonial receptions in Novo-Arkhangel'sk or on Russian ships (Khlebnikov 1985:83; Litke 1834:158; Veniaminov 1840a:127). Not knowing how various components of the European costume should be worn, some Indian dandies wore their European attire such that Russian travelers smirked to see them (Markov 1856:47).

Striving to secure the Tlingit chiefs' support, the Russian colonies' administration presented them with various gifts, including dress (usually paramilitary-style uniforms). The Tlingit chiefs were first "presented" with uniforms by Governor M. I. Murav'ev during the first half of the 1820s, and this practice was preserved. Litke wrote, "A hundred rifles could not bring such happiness to them [the Tlingit] as the Russian uniforms given to the toions. In them they put on airs of the most comical form." In a footnote Litke adds that after the sloop *Seniavin* had arrived in Novo-Arkhangel'sk, the Indians, having seen single-breasted uniforms on the sloop's officers, demanded that all those uniforms previously given be altered to single-breasted, "in order that in them they did not lag behind us [Russians] in anything" (Litke 1834:156). The most expensive clothing was bestowed on the "chief toion of the Sitka people," Mikhail Ku_kkan, as a royal gift. P. N. Golovin in 1860 described Mikhail Ku_kkan as being dressed "in a brocade gown with silver fringe and tassels; a crimson silk belt with gold fringe drew in his stomach; above the belt, on a black strap, hung a navy saber; in his hands he held a three-cornered hat, the form of hat of Frederick the Great, but with a high plume of white, blue, pink, yellow, and black feathers" (Golovin 1863a:5:179).

The chiefs and amanaty donned the Russian uniforms for ceremonial receptions arranged by the colonial administration. Recalling the attire of the Sitka chiefs who came to the ceremony to mark the RAC inspectors Golovin and Kostlivtsov's arriving in Novo-Arkhangel'sk, Golovin wrote: "At this time the Koloshi were in their festive costumes, that is, the Russian toion Mikhail in a frock coat of a fleet skipper and three amanaty of the Koloshi in blue dress coats and pantaloons with red stripes; the remaining toions threw on over their shirts showy blue blankets bordered all around by red broadcloth and small silver badges" (Golovin 1863a:6:282). Russian uniforms were essentially changed into distinctive honorable dress for a small group in the Tlingit aristocracy. The HBC agents at Fort Stikine also tried to use military uniforms as gifts to the Stikine chiefs in the 1840s, striving to secure the Indians' friendship for the English (Klein 1987:106).

Toward the mid-1830s a stereotype of Tlingit dress was formed that persisted until the end of the 19th century. The usual dress for both women and men remained a long shirt of European fabric and a cotton or wool blanket. Of the traditional dress there were only the fur cloaks, which were worn in especially cold weather, and trouser-moccasins borrowed from the Athapaskans.

European footwear of the Russian American period was not popular among the Tlingit. The overwhelming majority of Indians went barefoot, as before, or in harsh weather wore moccasins. Only the wealthy chiefs had boots and shoes, wearing them on especially solemn occasions (Golovin 1863a:6:282). During the period of maritime fur trade, American skippers sometimes brought high-top boots to the Northwest Coast (Morison 1922:56), but, judging by everything, they were not popular among the Indians.[7]

European head wear was likewise not adopted by the Indians. This can probably be explained by the fact that their own waterproof plaited hats were far better adapted to the peculiarities of the Northwest Coast's damp climate. Cotton scarves brought by the Europeans evidently pleased the Tlingit women

Influence of European Contacts on Tlingit Culture

since, according to Bishop Nikolai, they happily wore them tied on their heads in the manner of Russian women (Nikolai 1893:86).

In addition, at potlatches some of the Yakutat people at the end of the 19th century wore caps very reminiscent of those worn by Russian soldiers in the Crimean War. The Tlingit themselves pointed out that they borrowed the style from the Russians (De Laguna 1972:1:440). The Indian element of this head gear was a sparse fringe. It is possible that the caps that the Russians had given to the Indian chiefs had served as models (AVPR, f. RAK, op. 888, d. 1011, l. 322).

Trade with the Europeans also brought diversity to the assortment of Tlingit decorations. European contact brought with it beads: of especially high value were light-blue beads, which, in the words of the Indians, could be worn only by a "master of slaves" (De Laguna 1972:1:445). The evidence suggests that this was a Venetian bead that the Indians bought from the Russians (OR GBL, f. 204, k. 32, ed. khr. no. 5, l. 20b., 50b.). However, beads were not significant in Tlingit decoration. Silver, copper, and iron rings, bracelets, and earrings became far more widespread and popular among them.[8] During the period of maritime fur trade, the Indians used small bells, sewing thimbles, and mother-of-pearl buttons widely as decoration for clothing, and preferred brass buttons and American, European, and Chinese coins as earrings and pendants (Andrews 1967:48; Niblack 1890:266). In addition, the Tlingit bought cinnabar from the Russians to paint their faces and bodies and purchased red wool used particularly by the aanyádi to indicate their high social status. Long threads of red wool were strung through holes in the helix. The number of holes (and consequently threads) corresponded to the number of potlatches that had been arranged in honor of this person.

During the Russian American period the custom among Tlingit women of wearing labrets in their lower lips as decoration gradually waned as contact with Europeans increased. The labrets became noticeably smaller and were often replaced by silver pins. Some of the Indian women rejected this ancient custom altogether (Litke 1834:160). On the other hand, influenced by the coastal Tlingit (because of expanded trade in the 19th century), the women of the Southern Tutchone, Tagish, and interior Tlingit began to wear labrets in their lower lips, which was noted by American travelers as late as the 1890s (McClellan 1975:1:319).

Silver medals became a distinctive decoration among loyal Tlingit chiefs during the Russian American period. The Indians first obtained them from the English of Vancouver's expedition in 1793 (Vancouver 1830:4:131).[9] In 1805 Rezanov brought 250 medals (25 gold, 24 large silver, and 201 small silver) with ribbons of the St. Andrew and St. Vladimir orders to the Russian colonies

(AVPR, f. Gl. arkhiv 1–7, 1802 g., d. 1, papka no. 1, l. 2, 6–9). During this same year Rezanov personally gave a silver medal to one of the main chiefs of the L'uknax̱.ádi clan of the Akoi Chesnyge k̲wáan (OR GBL, f. 204, k. 32, ed. khr. no. 4, l. 33). Up until Alaska was sold to the United States, the Russian colonial administration honored many Tlingit chiefs of different k̲wáans with this high reward. We will treat this question in somewhat more detail because it was incompletely examined in the article by Dean (1995). Thus, in 1803 the imperial government granted Chamberlain N. P. Rezanov, the head of the first Russian round-the-world expedition, 325 medals (25 gold, 25 large silver, and 275 small silver with blue ribbons of the orders of St. Andrew and St. Vladimir). Before arriving in Russian America, Rezanov awarded these medals to several dozen people, including some crew of the naval sloop *Nadezhda* and employees of the RAC (AVPRI, f. Gl. arkhiv 1–7, 1802 g., op. 6, d. 1, papka no. 1, l. 2–9; Chepurnov 1993b:78). He brought another 250 medals (25 gold, 24 large silver, and 201 small silver) to Alaska in 1805. Rezanov personally awarded some of them in Unalaska, Kodiak, and Novo-Arkhangel'sk specifically to RAC stewards, promyshlenniki, and Native elders who had distinguished themselves. Thus, in 1805 Rezanov bestowed a silver medal on Chesnyga, one of the main chiefs of the L'uknax̱.ádi clan of the Akoi k̲wáan, who the previous year had helped Baranov in his punitive expedition against the Sitka (OR GBL, f. 204, k. 32, ed. khr. no. 4, l. 33). On one side of the medal he received was the profile of the young Emperor Aleksandr I and an inscription around the edge that said B[OZH'EI] M[ILOST'YU] ALEKSANDR I. IMPERATOR I SAMODERZHETS VSEROSS[IISKII] [Divine Gracious Aleksandr I. Emperor and Absolute Ruler of All Russia]; on the back was an image of a column topped by the imperial crown and the inscription "ZAKON" (the emblem of the justice of the Russian Empire). On the back, along the upper edge, ran the inscription: "ZALOG BLAZHENSTVA VSEKH I KAZHDOGO" (Guarantee of Bliss of Each and Every One), and beneath: "KORONOVAN V MOSKVE = SENT[IABRIA] 15 D[NIA] 1801" (Crowned in Moscow—September 15, 1801) (Chepurnov 1993b:78).

Before his departure from the colonies in 1806, Rezanov gave his remaining medals to Baranov, who until then had given the Natives "badly worked" homemade tin and copper medals (Lisianskii 1812:119; RGIA, f. 994, op. 2, d. 829, l. 100b.). This same year, in St. Petersburg, another kind of silver medal was created to be awarded to Native elders in the Russian-American Company's possessions. On the front of the new medals was the state emblem of the Russian Empire with the monogram of Czar Aleksandr I, and on the back was inscribed "SOYUZNYE ROSSII" (Chepurnov 1993b:98).[10] Distinct from those Rezanov had brought earlier, these were not called medals in the Russian colonies but rather *serebryanye znaki* [silver badges]. In 1808, four hundred silver badges were delivered to the colonies in one shipment: it is no wonder that this is the medal most often found in museums and private collections. These badges were usually worn on a ribbon of the order of St. Vladimir and were given exclusively to the Natives. In 1840 A. K. Etolin gave special instructions not to give them to the Aleuts and Koniag as dependent "non-Russian" subjects but to award silver badges to the Kolosh and other "independent savages" (AVPRI, f. RAK, op. 888, d. 1006, l. 258). Throughout the entire Russian American period a variety of silver medals was received by a few dozen Tlingit. For example, in 1818 L. A. Hagemeister awarded a medal to the well-known chief of the Sitka Kiks.ádi, Katlian, who had led the Indian warriors during the clash with the Russians from 1802 to 1804. Nawushkeitl had a large silver medal bearing the emperor's image, as did chief Koadchini of the Hoonah ḵwáan (AVPRI, f. RAK, op. 888, d. 998, l. 201; d. 1006, l. 81ob.– 82). When awarded a medal the Indian always received a certificate ("documentation") of the award signed by the governor of the Russian colonies (see documentary appendix entries {13, 15, 17}). Dean assembled a special table of all possible awards (medals, certificates, and others) that especially loyal Tlingit and Haida Kaigani (predominantly chiefs) had received from the Russians between 1824 and 1862 (Dean 1995:274).[11] His attempt to connect the time of the award and the territorial residence of those being given awards is very interesting; he concludes that the "chronology" and "geography" of the awards were clearly connected with the dynamics of Russian colonial politics, since the primary goal of the awards was "commercial orientation" to strengthen connections with the Indians in the face of the threat of Anglo-American trade competition (Dean 1995:295).[12] Nevertheless, Dean concludes that, on the whole, the practice of distributing medals and certificates was ineffective. Thus, despite the fact that in 1830 Russian medals were awarded to several Stikine chiefs, the Stikine preferred to trade with the British (Dean 1995:276–279). This was not strange when one considers the higher quality, greater assortment, and lower cost of English wares. In addition, Dean's analysis, indicating that the various awards in the middle of the stormy 1850s speak of the fact that the Sitka Kaagwaantaan were on the Russians' side during this period, while the responsibility for the attack on Novo-Arkhangel'sk in 1855 fell on one of the clans or lineages of the Raven moiety. The Russians' recognition of the leading role of the Kaagwaantaan in the Sitka ḵwáan confirms this (Dean 1995:291, 293).

Russian silver medals did not become an obligatory part of the Indian chiefs' festive attire, since not all of them had medals. Moreover, after someone who had been awarded a medal died, the medal was returned to the Novo-Arkhangel'sk RAC office, which then usually sent it to St. Petersburg, since it was considered the property of the czarist government.[13] Thus, the number of medals in Russian America gradually decreased. By the 1840s the colonial authority was wondering how best to reward the loyal Kolosh; A. K. Etolin's 1840 prohibition against giving scarce medals to Aleut and Koniag elders was particularly relevant to this. In February 1845 the RAC board of directors solicited the Department of Mining and Minerals to produce 100 medals patterned after the silver badges of 1806 but bearing the monogram of the reigning Nikolai I. However, in March the department notified the RAC that a new stamp had to be carved to mint the new medals because the emperor's monogram and details of the image of the two-headed eagle had to be changed (RGIA, f. 37, op. 19, d. 71, l. 1–30b.). The RAC administration evidently decided to abandon this expensive undertaking, especially since the company had begun to experience substantial financial difficulties by 1843 (Bolkhovitinov 1999:3:77). Therefore, in the 1850s the Russian American colonial authority began awarding loyal Tlingit money, copper plates (traditional Tlingit gifts), and certificates without medals.

Dentalia shells, sharks'-teeth pendants, and bone pins were among the traditional decorations that continued to be used. Old cultural forms (in both decoration and dress) persisted because European traders themselves, especially the Russians, supplied the Indians with raw materials to produce them. For example, the RAC supplied the Tlingit with the ermine furs and sea lion whiskers necessary for making a chief's head gear. On the other hand, the Russian traders purchased dentalia from the Indians for resale to the northern Athapaskans (at 30 rubles per 100 shells), which maintained their value in the eyes of the Tlingit (Litke 1834:110).

On the whole, by the mid-19th century the Tlingit had begun to wear clothing predominantly of European fabrics and also to amass large quantities of European clothing. There was especially much of it among the southern Tlingit, who traded at the Hudson's Bay Company posts, and among the Sitka people.[14] One must therefore disagree with Drucker's assertion that dress made of cloth was rare among the Sitka people until Alaska was sold to the United States (Drucker 1965:197). A large number of sources provide data to refute this (Golovin 1862:48; Holmberg 1855:18; Khlebnikov 1985:80; Kittlitz 1858:1:221).

Influence of European Contacts on Tlingit Culture

3. The Influence of European Colonization on Tlingit Social Organization in Russian America

3.1. The Dynamics of Integrative Processes within the Tribe

The fact that the Tlingit were ethnically different from the Russians created a complex and sometimes contradictory situation during the Russian American period. The Russians' arrival in Southeast Alaska, founding settlements on Tlingit lands, and hunting sea otters in Tlingit waters engendered the Indians' active resistance. The Russian threat to Tlingit economic interests, as well as to their independence, led different communities and clans to rally a common tribal coalition. However, the coalition did not last long. By 1804 the union had disintegrated, and although the Tlingit chiefs more than once attempted to revive it between 1806 and 1809, they failed. The reasons why these efforts failed were long-standing intercommunity and interclan alienation and, as events indicate, the lack of a direct Russian threat to Tlingit independence. After confronting the Russians, the tribes resumed their intertribal relations as before: periodic clashes between clans alternated and coexisted with trade activities and contact at different levels. However, the relationship of these fighting-trading tendencies changed. While fighting between Tlingit clans in the Russian American period occurred no more often than before the Europeans arrived in Alaska, as Khlebnikov observed, internecine war around Sitka became rarer (Khlebnikov 1985:85). The Russians themselves strived in every way to reconcile the Tlingit clans to strengthen their own influence on the independent Indians and, above all, promote the expansion and security of trade. In orders given on March 23, 1838, to D. F. Zarembo, the commander of the brig *Chichagov*, Kupreianov pointed to the need to forge a peace between the Chilkat and Stikine Tlingit, for which "all possible means" should be used (AVPR, f. RAK, op. 888, d. 1002, l. 166). The Russian administration in the person of some of the governors (for example, A. K. Etolin and I. V. Furuhjelm) contributed in some degree to preventing intratribal conflicts. In 1861 S. A. Kostlivtsov wrote of I. V. Furuhjelm's politics: "Though some of the former Governors also find in this enmity an advantage for the Russian colonies, the present Governor and I find in this disagreement an important inconvenience for the Company. All the tribes of the Kaloshi before quarreled between themselves, who, not daring to leave their dwellings for hunting and gathering, only from fear of each other, they deprived the Company on the one hand of items of produce and on the other of goods in fur" (Kostlivtsov 1863:88).

In spite of individual conflicts during the Russian American period (the most serious was the 40-year conflict between the Naanya.aayí and Kaagwaan-taan clans), trade and communications undoubtedly increased. This objectively promoted integration within the tribe. In addition, the intensification of intratribal contacts and interethnic connections contributed to the further formation of the Tlingit's ethnic consciousness. Another process common along the whole Northwest Coast was the resettlement of Indian populations to European trading posts and forts. Starting in the 1820s, not only the Native Sitka people but also members of other ḵwáans, in particular the Kaagwaan-taan and the Ĺuknax̱.ádi from the ḵwáans of Akoi and Hoonah, began to take up residence at Novo-Arkhangel'sk. In 1837 the Stikine people established a new settlement near Dionisievskii Redoubt. In 1852 N. Ya. Rozenberg wrote of the composition of the Tlingit who lived at the walls of Novo-Arkhangel'sk: "In the Kolosh settlement the Sitka Koloshi proper are no more than ⅓ of the population, the remaining ⅔ of the Kolosh consists of every riffraff from all the Kolosh Straits attracted here by the desire to profit from the various jobs being carried out at the Company Port" (AVPR, f. RAK, op. 888, d. 1020, l. 325ob.).

3.2. The Evolution of the Social Organization

During the period under examination, the fundamental basis of Tlingit society—the clan structure—did not undergo qualitative changes, although it continued to evolve successfully by means of simple quantitative segmentation as the Tlingit expanded into new territory. The Eyak and neighboring Atha-paskan groups were "drawn into" Tlingit clan structure, which undoubtedly contributed to their rapid assimilation. They even borrowed from the coastal Indians the names of their clans and corresponding totems, for example, the Killer Whale totem, a living prototype of which had never existed deep in the interior. Among the Tahltan Athapaskans on the upper reaches of the Stikine such matrilineal clans were noted as *Karch-otti* and *Tukk-kla-vei-ti*, the names of which repeated the designation of Tlingit clans of the Kachadi and Daktlauedi (Emmons 1911:13–18, 27; Grinev 1986b:120–121).

Strong clan connections in Tlingit society were one of the essential factors that prevented the disruption of the Indians in the face of European colonization; however, the integrating function of clan relations alternated with destructive ones during interclan conflicts.[15] This and other factors compelled the Russian colonial administration to abstain from wide-scale punitive actions against the Tlingit. D. P. Maksutov noted that the Russians were in a position to destroy Indian villages and seize and punish chiefs, but the consequences

Influence of European Contacts on Tlingit Culture

of these measures could be quite serious: "The Koloshi, and even the Kaigani, who live in the straits from the Stikine to Icy Strait comprise as it were one family: the Taku Koloshi are related to and friends with the Stikine, Keku, and others. The Stikine Koloshi are related to the Keku, Kootznahoo, and others—thus, in affecting some, you will certainly stir them all up" (AVPR, f. RAK, op. 888, d. 1026, l. 70b.).

During the Russian American period clan connections among the Tlingit were still so strong that they repelled the colonial administration's attempts to alienate the Indians by creating a class of loyal Natives, principally among the chiefs. Of course, a small number of informants from among all the Tlingit regularly supplied information about their fellow tribesmen's plans and activities. The commandant of Fort Mikhailovskii, Medvednikov, was repeatedly warned about Indian plans to attack the fort. For example, in 1805 T. S. Demenenkov, the head of the hunting party, learned "from faithful Koloshi" that the Yakutat fort had been captured. According to Langsdorff, one of the Sitka chiefs was ostracized for revealing that he supported the Russians after Baranov expelled the Sitka people from their fort in 1804 (Langsdorff 1812:2:106). But such examples were not characteristic of the Tlingit. And, of course, this small number of collaborators was not in a position to prevent Tlingit protests and plots from 1802 to 1809 and from 1850 to 1855.

Whereas clan relations during the period were in fact unchanged, the social institution of slavery nevertheless underwent a quite notable evolution. Expanded production of traditional goods meant that Indian society needed additional labor. Because the Indians profited in trading fur with the Europeans, the former were able to obtain a greater number of slaves than before. Whereas the number of slaves in Tlingit society had not been great before the Europeans' arrival (Olson 1967:53), after colonization of the Northwest Coast began, the number of slaves grew noticeably. Prosperous Indians in the 1820s could own 30 to 40 slaves, according to Khlebnikov (1985:86). Tlingit stories reveal that the wealthiest chief of the Naanya.aayí, Shakes, at one time had 200 slaves, some of whom themselves also possessed slaves (Olson 1967:54). According to Simpson, who visited the Northwest Coast in the early 1840s, slaves comprised about a third of the Native population of this region (Simpson 1847:1:211).

Owning slaves remained the chief marker of wealth and high social status. As noted in 1840 by the HBC agent James Douglas, Shakes was considered the most influential chief, not because he had a large following but rather because he had 24 slaves to paddle his canoe, catch his fish, hunt for him, and perform other duties. Most slaves were women and children—men usually perished during battle and, even if they became slaves, they were better able to run away from their masters. Therefore, they were often resold to other tribes to discourage thoughts of escape or insubordination (Gibson 1992:233–234).

Whereas the primary source of slaves in pre-contact times was from fighting expeditions, post-contact they were obtained chiefly through exchange. The Northwest Coast's largest slave traders during this period were the Tsimshian Indians, who traded with the Tlingit. However, by the mid-19th century the number of slaves in Tlingit society had gradually declined. Averkieva erroneously, in this author's view, connected this trend with the czarist government's prohibition of slavery (Averkieva 1974:153). In fact, the Russian American colonies' administration (but not the czarist government) prohibited only the sacrificial offering of slaves at potlatches, not slavery as such. In addition, the prohibition concerned only Sitka people, and the Tlingit of other ḵwáans generally ignored it (*Doklad Komiteta*, 1863b:250–251). In 1840 Etolin wrote,

> It is sad to see that all the pains and persuasion on our part toward the restraint of cruelty and atrocious customs of the Koloshi remain almost in vain—if our advice and good example have an effect on some of them, this is quite small and only on those who, so to speak, live under our eyes, of which there was an example on the 13th of July of this year when two of the Sitka Kolosh toions, Naushketl' Nawushkeitl and Sḵagataelch', desiring to honor the memory of their dead relative, Toion L'taniḵ, each wanted to kill a slave in commemoration, but by my urgent persuasion agreed, instead of killing these unfortunate victims, to exchange them to distant Koloshi for furs, and to sell us these latter (AVPR, f. RAK, op. 888, d. 1006, l. 169ob.–170).

Sometimes the Russians ransomed slaves (especially if they were young or if they adopted Orthodoxy) (see the documentary appendix entries {24, 34}).

Dean notes that Russian politics regarding slavery among the Tlingit was sometimes contradictory. On the one hand, the Russians stimulated the purchase of slaves by their protégé—the "chief Sitka toion" Mikhail Kuḵkan, having given him significant means with which to acquire them. On the other hand, the Russians required that nonvoluntary workers be freed, although this requirement only pertained to those sentenced to death at a potlatch. In addition, the Russians encouraged the ransom or resale of slaves, which in certain measure could stimulate the slave trade. The Tlingit could scarcely draw "lessons of civilization" from such instruction, notes the American researcher (Dean 1995:291).

Such contradiction in the Russian stance toward slavery, writes Kan, logically resulted from the state of Russian society itself, wherein the repressed were found in bondage (semi-slavery) to the government or landlords. In addition, as already stated in chapter 2, before the 1820s the Russian-American Company itself enslaved part of the colonies' Native population, calling them "kaiury" (Grinev 2000). Even the humanely disposed missionary I. E. Veniaminov proposed buying up to 50 male slaves in 1844, to maintain the conservatory and seminary in Novo-Arkhangel'sk. From the missionary's point of view, using such church servants was preferable to hiring workers dependent on the RAC. In another case Veniaminov proposed obtaining slaves from the Tlingit to train in the seminary so that they could later be used as interpreters and church lay-brothers (Kan 1999:121–122, 169).

The Tlingit chiefs often gave slaves that were intended for sacrificial offering at a potlatch to the RAC, or else set them free. For example, 3 male slaves and 16 female slaves, who earlier in a similar situation would certainly have been killed, were released by the Sitka chiefs in Novo-Arkhangel'sk in 1861 (AVPR, f. RAK, op. 888, d. 1025, l. 1200b.). Some slaves ran away from their cruel masters and found refuge in the Russian fort (AVPR, f. RAK, op. 888, d. 989, l. 1790b.). The gradual disappearance of slavery among the Tlingit, beginning in the mid-19th century, was evidently not the result of administrative decrees from the Russian (and then American) authorities but rather the consequences of European colonization on the whole.[16] The reduction of slavery in the Native population of the Northwest Coast resulted from epidemics and alcoholism, the United States's and Great Britain's suppressing raids, and missionary activity among the Indians, among other reasons.

The development of the Northwest Coast fur trade generally buoyed the Tlingit economy and promoted prosperity among the Native population during the Russian period of Alaskan history. The class that grew rich by trading with the Europeans and by acting as middlemen to other Indians grew. This trend meant that "nouveaux riches" appeared among the once-simple commoners, who began to lay claim to the rights and privileges of the old clan aristocracy (Averkieva 1960:28). Epidemics, which at times caused the complete disappearance of aristocratic families and their replacement with people of previously low rank, also contributed to increased social mobility. Consequently, the authority of the chief, already becoming insignificant, was further weakened. The colonial administration strove to counteract the process of weakening authority in Tlingit society by supporting individual members of the Tlingit aristocracy, giving them medals, honorary certificates, and gifts of clothing, goods, rum, and the like. Some received a special salary from the RAC (see documentary appendix entries {31, 32}). The company paid 360 rubles annually to "Chief Toion" Mikhail Kukkan (Aleut elders received 250 rubles).

From the beginning of the 1860s subsidies of 240 rubles were given to Sergei Sergeev, a baptized chief of the Sitka Kaagwaantaan (Kostlivtsov 1863:89). However, the Russian administration's artificially reinforcing individual chiefs' authority so that they could rely on them politically were not successful. Tlingit society's firm clan structure, the Indians' political independence, and the objective tendency for the chief's authority to weaken, as well as the Tlingit's subjective resistance to establishing investitures among them, hindered Russian attempts to secure the chiefs' loyalty.

3.3. Interethnic Contacts

Interethnic contacts in this region grew significantly starting with the maritime fur trade and the colonization of the Northwest Coast. Besides the Russians, English, and Americans, the Tlingit encountered representatives of many other nations and peoples. For example, there were often many Hawaiian, Indian, Chinese, Filipino, and other sailors on English and American ships. The ethnic composition of Novo-Arkhangel'sk was also quite varied, including not only Russians but also Swedes, Finns, Yakuts, Germans, Poles, Ukrainians, and not a few Russian Aleut and Russian Eskimo mestizos (creoles). In the 1840s creoles comprised about half the population of the Russian American capital. Along with the English and Scottish, there were French Canadians, mestizos, Iroquois, and others working for the Hudson's Bay Company (Galbraith 1957:21). Not a few of the new arrivals, especially on American ships that traded on the Northwest Coast, were Polynesians, primarily Hawaiians (they sometimes comprised half the ship's crew). Hawaiians were skilled sailors whose salaries were far lower than those of European or American sailors. The English of the Hudson's Bay Company also hired Hawaiians. Thus, in 1834, of the 59 men at the Fort Simpson garrison, 14 were Hawaiians (Gibson 1992:212).

For many years fugitive American sailors lived among the Tlingit, and, in the late 1850s, British smugglers and gold prospectors lived among them as well. As early as 1793 Vancouver encountered among some Stikine people who visited him a young man in a blue camisole and trousers "who smoked cigars like the Spanish—through the nose—and who loved tobacco very much," and supposed that this was a Mexican who had deserted a Spanish ship (Vancouver 1830:4:306–307).

From the early 19th century, the Tlingit themselves ventured on long sea and land expeditions, acquainting themselves with the Athapaskans of the middle course of the Yukon (calling them "Aiyan") to the north, and with the Indians of Vancouver Island and Puget Sound to the south. Several Tlingit were hired onto European ships and sailed throughout the entire Pacific Ocean

Influence of European Contacts on Tlingit Culture

region; some of them even completed round-the-world and halfway-round-the-world voyages. The Tlingit chief Klukar traveled to Canton and back on an American ship, during which time he learned to speak English well. In 1810 he sent his son on a trip to Boston with Captain Lemuel Porter's ship *Hamilton* (Gibson 1992:126). Governor M. I. Murav'ev reported to St. Petersburg that "many Koloshi have been to Boston, and some are also educated there" (VPR 1982:2:5:87). In 1841 G. Simpson wrote about one such Indian, named Henya Joy (that is, "Joy from the Henya ḵwáan"), who, as a boy, had been taken on an American ship from Alaska to the United States. He later returned to his kinsmen, and HBC agents occasionally used him as a navigator and translator (Simpson 1847:1:213).

The Tlingit also visited Russia. Thus, in 1817 the RAC directors wrote to Baranov from St. Petersburg: "The Kolosh Sergei Kolobov, whom you sent on the *Suvorov*, having been a healthy, smart, and modest man beyond expectation, because he was not vaccinated against it there or on the way, became a victim of smallpox" (AVPR, f. RAK, op. 888, d. 988, l. 52ob.). Other Tlingit whom Baranov sent to study in St. Petersburg evidently suffered a similar fate. Among them was the brother of the Sitka chief Nawushkeitl. "They all unfortunately did not return to inspire their fellow countrymen with reliable information on European enlightenment and the might of Russia," wrote Khlebnikov (1835:200). Later, several children and young Tlingit (including girls) whom the Russians sought to educate accompanied their foster parents to Russia (see documentary appendix entry {35}). For example, Lieutenant Ivan I. Bartram's family raised two Tlingit girls, one of whom completed school in Novo-Arkhangel'sk and afterward worked as a teacher in Alaska. Enokh Furuhjelm, the youngest brother of I. V. Furuhjelm, governor of Russian America, took with him to his Native Finland a young Indian girl, formerly a slave, whom he had bought from a Sitka chief in 1859 for wares valued at 650 rubles. She was baptized into the Lutheran faith and attended a school for girls in Helsinki, where she successfully studied arithmetic, Swedish, drawing, writing, and sewing. However, she died of typhus in 1868, at the age of 13 (Pierce 1990:152, 361) (see also documentary appendix entry {35}).

On one occasion, a Tlingit's visit to St. Petersburg served science. The Tlingit christened Andrei Tenḵentin (Tiḵontin) was taken at his own request aboard *Imperator Nikolai I*, which, in 1860, was setting off on a round-the-world voyage. The Indian wanted to see the capital of the Russian Empire. In 1861 he arrived in St. Petersburg, and here the well-known members of the Russian Academy of Sciences, Vladimir Middendorf and Leopol'd Padlov, took an interest in him, with Tenḵentin's help gathering information on the Tlingit language (Pierce 1990:419, 504). As it turned out, the Stikine Tenḵentin knew Tsimshian in addition to his Native language. After Tenḵentin's lessons with the scholars the governor of the RAC intended to send the Indian home on his ship that was going around the world in the fall of 1862 (ORAK 1862:45).

Nonetheless, the Russian colonial administration not only often failed to promote direct contacts between the Russians and the Tlingit but strove to restrict and regulate contact in every way possible, fearing they would otherwise lose control over the situation. For example, in 1838 Kupreianov instructed the captain of the RAC ship *Nikolai*, Evgeni A. Berens, that the crew of the ship be "not allowed" to visit the Tlingit settlement at Novo-Arkhangel'sk, entertain the Natives, or sell them rum without his permission (AVPR, f. RAK, op. 888, d. 1002, l. 208–2080b.).

The Tlingit attitude toward the Russians was quite contradictory. On the one hand, the prosperity and power of the newcomers, as evidenced by their dress, wealth of goods, weapons, large ships, and so on, delighted them. On the other hand, the Europeans conjured feelings of alienation in the Indians, inasmuch as European behavior did not always meet Tlingit moral standards. For example, the Europeans did not understand the concept of clans and moieties and, consequently, did not know how to behave within this structure. The Tlingit conceived of the European hierarchy as consisting of masters and slaves. I. I. Banner, the director of the Kodiak office of the RAC, in 1803 stated that "in their disposition it is noticed that they cannot endure the yoke of the law; complete independence and revenge are their most primary passions, because of which they do not fit in social life, and seeing us subordinated to some order of management and obedience, despise us" (*K istorii Rossiisko-Amerikanskoi*, 1957:130). A Sitka chief expressed this even more eloquently in a conversation with Governor Chistiakov: "We . . . though in comparison with you are very poor and helpless, at the same time do not serve anyone, and you, with all your power and knowledge, are yet servants of your emperor" (Kittlitz 1858:1:219).

It is interesting to note that representatives of different Tlingit ḵwáans appraised the Russians in different ways. For example, according to De Laguna, the Yakutat people had extremely negative assessments of the Russians (De Laguna 1972:1:217), whereas the Stikine considered the Russians their friends and continued to describe them as such until the mid-20th century (at the same time, they had negative recollections of the English of the Hudson's Bay Company) (Corser 1940:24).

The Tlingit were extremely hostile toward the Aleuts, Kodiak, and Chugach, who, under Russian leadership, hunted in Tlingit territorial waters (Kittlitz

Influence of European Contacts on Tlingit Culture

1858:1:238). The enmity was mutual. "It is remarkable," wrote Litke in 1818, "that the greatest enemies of the Koloshi are the Aleuts, and conversely, the Koloshi hate the Aleuts much more than the Russians. If the Aleuts catch some of the Koloshi, they will certainly kill them, and the Koloshi never show the Aleuts mercy" (RGA VMF, f. 15, op. 1, d. 8, l. 1850b.). The Tlingit's hostility toward the Chugach (and later toward the Aleut and Kodiak) derived from their contempt for the fact that the Chugach acknowledged their dependence on the Russians. This is what representatives of the RAC central board wrote in 1863: "The enmity between them was constant, through various personal conflicts, but this was hatred of equal to equal; from the time of the recognition by the Aleuts and other tribes of the Russian's authority over them, the Koloshi not only hate them, but finally despise them, calling them the disgraceful name '*Kalgi*,' that is, slaves" (*Doklad Komiteta*, 1863a:529).

It was mostly men who came to Russian America from the mother country, and it was they who largely comprised the hunts' workforce. This fact, as well as the Russian-American Company's encouraging mixed marriages (for political and economic reasons), resulted in the growth of the colonies' mestizo population (Fedorova 1971:186–187). The children of Russians and Aleuts, Eskimos, and Indians were called "creoles" in Russian America. Until the 1820s the number of Russian Tlingit creoles was insignificant, and Russians' partnering with Indian women was relatively rare and seen as "illicit" inasmuch as such unions were not sanctioned by the Church. A certain number of mestizos evidently lived in Yakutat—the Tlingit region first settled by the Russians. Indian legends mention a young Russian Tlingit mestizo from the Yakutat Teiḵweidí (Tlaḵaik Teiḵweidí?), named Jivak, who was enslaved for a long time in the Hoonah ḵwáan before he escaped to Novo-Arkhangel'sk to live among the Russians (Olson 1967:55, 116).

After Fort Mikhailovskii was founded on Sitka Island (1799), several Tlingit women lived there continuously with the Russians. One of them—the daughter of the Sitka chief Dlḵetin—returned to the Russians after they reestablished their fort on the island in 1804 (Langsdorff 1812:2:100). To prevent a repeat of the events of 1802, Baranov and Rezanov strove to mitigate tension between the Russians and Tlingit by establishing kin relations between the two. Dr. G. H. von Langsdorff passed on to the Sitka people Baranov's request that "wenches" be sent to the fort. But Langsdorff was unsuccessful. Evidently the Indians' defeat by the Russians during the second occupation of Sitka Island was still fresh in their memory (AVPR, f. Gl. arkhiv 1–7, 1802 g., d. 1, papka no. 33, l. 250b.).

Beginning in the 1820s Tlingit-Russian contact became more frequent and began to bear a more ordered and regular character, especially after the Sitka people settled at Novo-Arkhangel'sk. The chronic shortage of women in the Russian settlement was compensated for to some degree by relationships of the promyshlenniki and sailors with Tlingit women. These were usually casual and illicit encounters, ultimately fostering prostitution among the Indian women (Khlebnikov 1985:139). "Kolosh concubines, no less than European dancers, know how to bankrupt their worshippers and examples are many that the earnings of promyshlenniki are entirely squandered on the toiletry of their beauty, without regard to any of the efforts of the Director to stop this disorder," wrote Litke (1834:109). Illicit relations were common until Alaska was sold to the United States. "Some of the workers and soldiers [in Novo-Arkhangel'sk] buy women slaves [bond servants] from the toions and keep them at their own expense," noted Golovin (1862:87). However, not all the men would permit themselves to have "temporary wives," inasmuch as this was both rather expensive (25 to 30 rubles per month) and condemned by the Russian clergy (Golovin 1863b:379).

However, Russian men's relationships with Tlingit women significantly helped maintain peaceful relations with the Indians. The Russians learned from the Indian women of "conspiracies" that the Tlingit formulated, and not a few Russians were saved thanks to Indian women's help. The women participated in negotiations during conflicts, contributing in every possible way to their peaceful settlement (Litke 1834:92, 113). On the other hand, uncontrolled relationships with Tlingit women could have serious consequences for the Russians. The latter often lured or abducted Indians' wives and daughters; such insults were, of course, not forgotten. F. P. Wrangell warned Dionisievskii Redoubt's personnel about this in 1834. In the instructions to S. Moskvitinov, the first manager of this redoubt, he wrote, "by no means admit Kolosh women into the Redoubt to live, since from them a multitude of displeasures and harmful consequences can happen for the Company: they retell everything they hear to their countrymen and lie in addition, which can often destroy good accord" (AVPR, f. RAK, op. 888, d. 998, l. 309, 314). However, the exigencies of real life overpowered the governor's instructions, and by the time Kupreianov had succeeded Wrangell in 1838, several baptized Tlingit women were living in Dionisievskii Redoubt. The governor was forced to resign himself to the inevitable, though he tried to regulate marriage between the Russian promyshlenniki and Indian women. Kupreianov wrote a letter to I. Andreianov, the new manager of Dionisievskii Redoubt, saying:

Influence of European Contacts on Tlingit Culture

In the authorization being obtained by you: In dealing with Kolosh wenches baptized into our faith and living with Employees of the Company, I direct you in this regard to precisely observe the same rules as are followed in Novo-Arkhangel'sk, that is, that baptized Kolosh women, though united with Russians in illicit marriage, be held as if separated already from other Koloshi, their relatives, who by no means should have any right or influence over them while they live with the Russians, it being the same also that the children begat by Russians and Baptized Kolosh women be baptized and considered now entirely separated from the Koloshi—all this they and the rest of their relatives should know in advance (AVPR, f. RAK, op. 888, d. 1002, l. 161–161ob.).

In addition to illicit unions, there were also lawful marriages between Russian men and Tlingit women. A. P. Lazarev reports that several Tlingit women were married to Russian promyshlenniki in the early 1820s (Lazarev 1832:166–167) (see documentary appendix entry {16}). But the church evidently recognized few of these Russian-Tlingit families officially. Picking them out of the population of Novo-Arkhangel'sk is difficult, inasmuch as the Tlingit women who married Russians were most probably registered as "dependent Natives," Aleuts and Kodiak. Thus, in his treatise on the Russian colonies, F. P. Wrangell noted that among the Natives who lived in Novo-Arkhangel'sk there were Kolosh women and their children, but he did not categorize them separate from the population as a whole (Wrangell 1835:111–112). Tlingit women who married Russians were, on the whole, faithful wives and decent women (unlike the Aleut and Eskimo women) and maintained their families well, according to Veniaminov (1840a:119). Tlingit women occasionally married creoles, Aleuts, and Yakuts who lived in Novo-Arkhangel'sk. For example, documents for 1834 mention the Yakut Vasilii Pavlov, who requested the colonial administration's "permission to enter into lawful matrimony with the baptized Kolosh woman Aleksandra." And in 1845 the Aleut Semion Kashkak begged for similar "permission" regarding "the betrothal by him of a bride, the Kolosh girl Anna Kakot" (AVPR, f. RAK, op. 888, d. 998, l. 2ob.; d. 1011, l. 16–16ob.).

Besides Russians and creoles, sailors from American and English ships married Tlingit women, as did employees of the Hudson's Bay Company. Some American sailors (usually deserters) lived among the Indians. Governor Murav'ev reported to the RAC central board that there were several "Boston men" among the Koloshi (Narochnitskii 1963–1985:Ser. II, t. V, s. 87). The British lieutenant E. Simpson, who visited the southern Tlingit between 1827 and

1828, corroborated this information, noting the evident growth of the mestizo population as a result of contact with American sailors. These connections forged a notably friendly relationship between the Indians and the Americans. Soon after Dionisievskii Redoubt was transferred to Hudson's Bay Company control, more than half of the post's employees asked Simpson, a company director, for permission to marry a local Native woman; he consented (Simpson 1847:1:231). It is well known that from 1850 to 1860 British smugglers in the southern part of the Alexander Archipelago married Tlingit women, striving thereby to strengthen their position and connections with the Indians and so expand their trade.

Both lawful and illicit connections between European (primarily Russian) men and Tlingit women increased the mestizo population. "Many of the Russians," reported Chistiakov as early as 1828, "were married to Kolosh women or were supporting one, who had begat children" (AVPR, f. RAK, op. 888, d. 993, l. 62). By the mid-1840s mestizos comprised a sizable part of the Sitka people, according to Markov (1856:87). The American ethnographer K. Oberg pointed out that in Sitka, Russian Indian mestizos were very numerous (Oberg 1973:7). "Creoles from Kolosh women are incomparably prettier than creoles from Aleut women; among the first the features of the face are rather regular, large eyes; among the second the type of face is purely Mongoloid: flattened nose, squinting eyes—just as among the Kalmyks," Golovin noted (1863a:6:277). Some mestizos had light skin and even red hair (Gibson 1992:239). Veniaminov emphasized the industriousness, diligence, and decency of Russian Tlingit mestizos in contrast to other mestizos (Veniaminov 1840a:120–121). Nevertheless, the Russian clergy succeeded in finding among the Russian Tlingit creoles some worthy candidates for the lowest Church offices. Such a one was Emel'ian Molchanov, who was born in the early 1820s in Novo-Arkhangel'sk to a Russian promyshlennik and a Tlingit woman (evidently of the Kaagwaantaan clan). After finishing the Native school, he was appointed a sexton in St. Michael's Cathedral in 1837, spending some time also as a clerk in the RAC's Novo-Arkhangel'sk office. Molchanov knew how to read and write in Russian, knew the catechism, and was fluent in his mother's Native language. Nevertheless, after several years he was sent to serve at the Orthodox mission on the Nushagak River. After returning to Novo-Arkhangel'sk in the mid-1840s, Molchanov was assigned second deacon of the local cathedral in 1847. However, his Church career was soon aborted by his bad behavior: he assaulted a young Russian woman and became a drunk, alcohol being the downfall of many creoles (Kan 1999:130–131).

An even more notable figure was the creole Ivan Zhukov, who was born in about 1825 in the Novo-Arkhangel'sk redoubt on the Nushagak River to a Russian father and Tlingit mother. As a youth in the early 1840s Zhukov served as an apprentice on RAC ships, and then from 1844 served as a Tlingit interpreter in Novo-Arkhangel'sk. He sometimes attended the local seminary and could eventually have become a priest for the Tlingit. However, like Molchanov, he discredited himself, was expelled from the seminary, and was sent as a kind of exile to Ozersk Redoubt. Nevertheless, Hieromonk Mikhail tried to bring Zhukov to teach Russian to the Tlingit children and instruct seminary students in Tlingit. The RAC administration compromised, permitting Zhukov to return to Novo-Arkhangel'sk, having appointed him official interpreter at 500 rubles a year plus 5 rubles a month to teach Tlingit. Zhukov turned out to be a capable interpreter and teacher, and, according to the petition of Bishop Veniaminov, by 1845 he had been rewarded 85 rubles for successfully translating the Gospels into Tlingit. Between 1849 and 1850 Zhukov was awarded another monetary prize for translating several chapters of the New Testament and a few other religious texts. However, shameful behavior (evidently debauchery and drunkenness) again discredited him in the eyes of the colonial leadership, and in 1850 he was sent to Kodiak, although he was later returned by the RAC to Novo-Arkhangel'sk (Kan 1999:131–132).

Some Russian Tlingit mestizos could even go to St. Petersburg to get an education. Thus, Zakhar Petrovich Chichenev, a creole whose father was an Irkutsk petty bourgeois and whose mother was a Tlingit, was sent to the capital to study medicine in 1819. Several years after returning to the colonies, he was hired by the RAC and worked for many years as a clerk in various district offices—from the Pribilof Islands to Fort Ross in California, earning the rather substantial salary of 500 rubles. In 1847 Governor M. D. Teben'kov found Chichenev a lazy, marginally capable, and irresponsible worker who entirely neglected the accounts, and intended to send him to Kodiak or leave him in Novo-Arkhangel'sk with a salary of 350 rubles (Pierce 1990:87–88).

RAC employees preferred officially marrying Russian Tlingit creoles, and not pure-blood Indians. Thus, for example, all three daughters—Irina, Natalia, and Matrena—of the "company employee" Matvei Kabachakov and the baptized "Kolosh woman Maria" were married to Ivan Prokof'ev (1836), Karl Dal'strem (1838), and Prokopii Larionov (1939), respectively (AVPR, f. RAK, op. 888, d. 1000, l. 3540b.–355; d. 1003, l. 48–480b.; d. 1004, l. 3120b.–313). It is curious to note that some creole women left their lawful Russian husbands and went to live among the Tlingit, as in the 1843 case of Matrena Kabachakov (Larionov). Later two governors of Russian America, Teben'kov and Rozenberg, reported to St. Petersburg on the unfortunate fate of an "employee of the company," Semion Pavlov, whose wife, the creole woman Avdotia, ran away from him to the Koloshi and, finding protection among them, left Sitka. The deceived husband was thus evidently unable to secure her return (AVPR, f. RAK, op. 888, d. 1018, l. 1450b.) (see also documentary appendix entry {26}).

Because relationships were matrilineal, mestizos (born of Tlingit women) were naturally included in Tlingit society and not discriminated against by the pure-blooded Tlingit (unless, of course, their mothers were slaves) (see documentary appendix entries {20, 21}). Their having "Russian blood" could be a source of pride for an Indian, according to R. L. Olson (1967:116). Kan reports that a good acquaintance—a Tlingit woman of high birth named Charlotte Young (whose Indian name was Tlaktoowu), who had an important role in the Indian Orthodox community in Sitka—was proud of her Russian ancestors (Kan 1999:xii–xiii).

In addition to their being more European-Tlingit marriages, there were also more Tlingit-Athapaskan and Tlingit-Eyak marriages, which undoubtedly contributed significantly to the Eyaks' and Athapaskans' assimilation. Even among the Athapaskan Ahtna, who lived in the Copper River Valley, there is a clan whose members consider the Tlingit their ancestors (De Laguna and McClellan 1981:645).

Interethnic connections and marriages between Tlingit and other peoples during the Russian American period caused conflicts and multidirectional trends. Intermarriage contributed to peace as much as to instability (for example, one reason for the Tlingit revolt in 1802 was the Russian promyshlen-niki's taking the Indians' wives). During a casual skirmish with the Tsimshian, the Tanta Teik̲weidí chief Kakklen (Kak-tlen) was lost and his son Skautli-etl (Skautliel), who belonged to the Tanta G̲aanax̲teidí (a sublineage of the K̲as'ittan—the Elk–Cow Hide house), was severely wounded or killed. The Tlingit decided to take revenge on the Tsimshian for the death of their eminent kinsman. At this time the G̲aanax̲teidí had six guns and arranged an ambush on the shore where the Kitkatla usually returned in their canoes. According to legend, they first fired on the chief, who was standing in the bow of a canoe. After he fell into the water and the canoe capsized, the Tlingit avenged themselves on the crew. According to clearly exaggerated legends, this was how the G̲aanax̲teidí succeeded in destroying more than 20 Tsimshian canoes. Then they plundered the Kitkatla camp and returned in triumph to their Native clan. After this, a new chief of the Tanta Tekuedi, called Kudena—nephew and heir of the murdered Kakklen—did not want peace, and the chief of the Kitkatla Tsimshian, Visheksh, would not be killed in revenge for the death of his un-cle.[17] At this time the Tlingit, fearing their enemies would launch a retaliatory raid, built Fort Kasatki (Kit-nu) on the shore of one of the islands and then set off on a new raid on the Tsimshian, which Kudena led. Kudena commanded a huge flotilla of 40 war canoes: all the clans of the Tanta kwáan equipped their warriors in the south against the common enemy. Four shamans (one from each clan) accompanied the expedition.[18] During a surprise attack on the Tsimshian fort, the Tlingit managed to take about twenty women and children captive (including Visheksh's nephew), because the warriors were away. After this success the Tlingit of the Tanta kwáan, led by Kudena, moved to Ketchikan where they built a new fort, which they were able to defend during the siege of the Tsimshian who sailed there in 70 canoes led by Visheksh. After this, the Tlingit returned to old Fort Kit-nu, where, according to legend, they began to suffer from insufficient provisions. This was evidently a direct consequence of the fighting because the Tlingit, fearing a second attack from the Tsimshian, did not leave the fort to hunt or fish. Finally, even Kudena agreed to make peace with Visheksh. He set off with four canoes to the Tsimshian near Old Metlakatla, where there was a trading schooner. Kudena had a letter that the American captain John Ebbets had given to his uncle Negut. The letter enabled him to board the ship along with his people and be delivered straight to Old Metlakatla, where peace was quickly concluded with Visheksh, and Kudena himself was taken as a hostage (Olson 1967:88–89).

This legend records two factors that traditional legends had not. The first is that the Gaanaxteidí Tlingit used highly effective firearms to kill their powerful enemies, and second, white traders served as mediators. Evidently firearms use amounted to little once there was widespread hand-to-hand fighting among the heavily armed warriors, and they significantly increased the defensive potential of the Indian forts, the direct storming of which could have led to extraordinary losses among the attackers. All this made ambush tactics preferable. This is directly attested to by Veniaminov, who described the defeat of a Sitka Kaagwaantaan war party by warriors from a Stikine kwáan. In this battle in the bloodiest 19th-century Tlingit interclan war, the Stikine people killed many enemy fighters with guns, having set an ambush atop a cliff above the Stikine camp on the shore of an islet. Veniaminov recounted: "If the Stakin [Stikine] people were in fact brave, all who remained might have been taken captive. But, on the contrary, three or four [Stikine] were successfully taken (including the son of their toion Katmian, whom, however, they released out of kindness, as the Stakin say); nevertheless, the remaining [of the Stikine] left home not having been pursued by anyone, in spite of the fact that they were small in number" (Veniaminov 1840a:124–125). Intertribal enmity and the Tlingit's interclan wars ended only after the transition of Russian America to the jurisdiction of the United States and the establishment of tighter control over the Indians' lives by the American military and missionaries.

4. Fighting among the Tlingit in Russian America

Contact with Europeans did not alter the tactics of conducting fighting activities by the Tlingit: as before, there were unexpected attacks, night strikes, and war raids in flotillas of canoes. European-Tlingit contact essentially influenced the materials used in war. Within a rather short period, the bow, club, and spear, the Indians' basic tools for distant and close combat, were almost completely replaced by firearms. By 1794 the Vancouver Expedition participants saw rifles, carbines, pistols, and muskets among the Tlingit (Vancouver 1830:4:295, 299–301; 1833:5:472). In the late 1850s revolvers also appeared among the Indians (Golovin 1863a:5:181; 6:289). The Tlingit, convinced of the substantial advantages of firearms, began to demand primarily rifles, powder, and bullets in their trade with the Europeans. Initially, only wealthy chiefs owned rifles. For a period the rifle was one of a clan's most valued possessions, along with houses, boats, totems, and so on. At this time rifles were even given names (De Laguna 1972:1:263). However, after a while American and English traders had brought so many rifles to the Northwest Coast that the Natives started cutting the rifle barrels into rings, according to V. N. Berkh (1808:7). In the mid-1820s O. E. Kotzebue wrote that the ordinary Tlingit had no fewer than two rifles (Kotzebue 1987:213).

American traders even sold the Indians light cannons. In 1799 Baranov personally saw four one-pound-caliber falconets among the Sitka people (Tikhmenev 1863:2:Append. 146). In 1819 S. I. Yankovskii, the governor of Russian America, reported to St. Petersburg that there were more rifles among the Tlingit than among the Russians, and the Kaagwaantaan clan had more than ten large cannons in their fort (RGIA, f. 994, op. 2, d. 833, l. 1).

The Indians not only held a large number of firearms but also quickly learned to master their use. Kostlivtsov, who observed the "maneuvers" of the Sitka people at Novo-Arkhangel'sk, noted with surprise that they "produced the same rapid fire as marksmen of the regular infantry" (Kostlivtsov 1863:158).

The cold European weapons (saber, cutlass, and lance) were not especially popular among the Tlingit in hand-to-hand combat; they preferred the traditional dagger, which, during the Russian American period, was of course made of iron and steel.

The Tlingit's protective armor certainly evolved. The wooden armor, helmets, and visors gradually lost their significance (as firearms were used more).

Although they were still sometimes used until the 1860s (Golovin 1863a:6:289), they were usually replaced by lighter and more comfortable armor of tanned elk hide. In addition, at the beginning of the 19th century, American traders brought the Tlingit short vest-jackets of elk hide with iron bands sewn across the chest "so that a bullet could not penetrate," as Yu. F. Lisianskii wrote (1812:143).

New to Tlingit methods of collective defense was the equipping of some forts with cannons. In 1804 the Sitka people used cannons to defend their fortified settlement during its siege by Baranov's detachments (Lisianskii 1812:30). The use of artillery by Natives who were the socioeconomic equals of the Tlingit was rare in the colonies.

As already stated, during the Russian American period intratribal conflict appeared to become a rarer occurrence. At the same time, the use of firearms made for bloodier clashes. "The low population of this region {Southeast Alaska} can be explained by the large number of intertribal wars, which are carried out with fury and bitterness rare even for savage peoples," wrote O. E. Kotzebue (1987:214).

During the Russian American period, as trade developed, contacts between the Tlingit and members of other Indian tribes became more frequent, and these contacts were not always peaceful. In the early 19th century, the southern Tlingit, together with the Kaigani and Haida, undertook a devastating raid on southern tribes with the aim of taking slaves, sowing terror and panic among the Kwakiutl and the Indians of Puget Sound (Drucker 1965:75). From the 1830s to the 1850s Tlingit of the Taku and Sanya ḵwáans made several war raids on the Athapaskans of the Taku Tinne and Tsetsaut (Boas 1924:1; Teit 1906:347). From time to time, conflicts flared between the southern Tlingit and the Tsimshian, Kaigani, and Haida. One clash between the Tanta ḵwáan Tlingit and the Kitkatla clan of the Tsimshian is related in oral traditions that Olson recorded (1967:88).

5. The Spiritual Culture of the Tlingit in Russian America

5.1. Religious Views

Tlingit spiritual culture during the Russian American period was significantly less influenced by the Europeans than was material culture. Unable to explain some phenomena, the Tlingit were inclined to attribute them to supernatural forces. For example, I. E. Veniaminov wrote that a mill in Novo-Arkhangel'sk that had burned down after being struck by lightning in 1827 was, according to the Indians, burned down by Ketl—the giant thunderbird (Veniaminov 1840a:83). The Tlingit had a similar explanation of the loss of the promyshlennik Matvei Kabachakov, who drowned while herring fishing; V. P. Romanov reported: "They think that the herring asked the evil spirits to give them the company employee Kabachakov because he had previously allowed them no peace, and the spirits told the shamans this" (Romanov 1825:18).

Baranov used Tlingit superstition deftly, tricking the Tlingit and winning their praise as a great shaman. F. P. Litke wrote: "Baranov, by his behavior, inspired in them such respect for himself that many considered him a sorcerer to the point that when one time (in 1810) on the shore a rocket was launched, the Koloshi who were then on the sloop *Diane* said that this was Baranov flying" (RGA VMF, f. 15, op. 1, d. 8, l. 182). In 1806 Rezanov wrote: "They [the Tlingit] greatly fear Mr. Baranov and truly his name alone holds the whole region in fear" (Tikhmenev 1863:2:Append. 277–278). Possibly only Baranov's presence in Novo-Arkhangel'sk in the winter of 1805–06 kept the Tlingit from attacking the garrison of the fort, which was weak from hunger and illness. As Markov reported, Baranov (wearing chain mail under his clothing) gave captive Tlingit a bow and arrows and commanded them to shoot him directly in the heart, thereby convincing them of his supernatural power. The arrows always bounced off the unharmed Baranov, eliciting the Indians' respectful fear (Markov 1856: 51–52).

Though totemism, as a sphere of Tlingit religious views, was not much changed in the Russian American period, there were some innovations. According to Tlingit legend, a chief of the Tanta kwáan named Tleki made his totem a sailing ship (Olson 1967:87). According to H. P. Corser, a totem of the chief of the Stikine people, Shakes, was the Russian double-headed eagle (Corser 1940:17, 24). However, these new emblems were not, of course, totems in the true sense of the word, inasmuch as they were clearly different from them in both their origin and their association and function. Therefore, one cannot agree with some eminent American researchers of the Tlingit, in whose opinion several exotic objects, not peculiar to the Indians' traditional culture, were transformed into totems (for example, a pig, a white man) (Kan 1989:74–75, 345; Oberg 1973:44; Olson 1967:38). In fact, such figures can more properly be called "totemlike objects." Usually such images served as illustrations of concrete events in the clan's history or of a remarkable fact in the biography of this or that chief who erected a ceremonial pole. These objects were not connected with supernatural powers, that is, they did not have a religious basis, and in addition, they were not worshiped by subsequent generations of Indians (Grinev 1995:119–120, 123). A single possible exception is the Cow totem among the Ḵas'ittan clan of Sitka (a branch of the Koskedi-Kuskedi clan who lived in the Sitka, Hoonah, and Akoi ḵwáans). De Laguna suggests that in fact this is not a cow but rather a forest bison that the ancestors of the Indians had seen deep in the mainland; according to other researchers, however, the Ḵas'ittan obtained a cow hide from the Russians (De Laguna 1972:71, 82; compare Oberg 1973:43–44; Olson 1967:44; illustration: Emmons 1991:32). In this author's view, this totem's history refers to events in 1802, when the Tlingit seized and plundered the Russian fort at Sitka and killed not only almost all its defenders but also the cows that were kept at the settlement. The Ḵas'ittan, who participated in the battle, adopted the form of this animal that was exotic to them as a totemic "trophy." Such a fate possibly awaited the Russian Empire's two-headed eagle as well, the copper image of which the first Russian voyagers handed over to the Indians. The Tlingit viewed it as a valuable totemic symbol of the new arrivals (Grinev 1995:123).

As a consequence of Tlingit-European contact, written certificates, diplomas, documents, and medals fell into Indian hands and were carefully preserved, passed on by inheritance, and at times even shown at potlatches along with clan totems (Anatolii 1906:27; Oberg 1973:110–111; Olson 1967:89). From this fact Yu. P. Averkieva erroneously concluded that these European relics "functionally replaced totemic symbols as evidence of certain rights and privileges" (Averkieva 1960:38). One cannot agree with A. A. Istomin's statement that these objects functioned within the limits of clan traditions, even though "they had a source and symbolized not the clan origin but certain authority beyond the clan" (Istomin 1985:151). Nevertheless, it should be stressed that it was not so much a matter of the totems' coming from different sources as of the fact that new relics did not functionally replace traditional totems as symbols of prestige but rather coexisted with them. In addition, if totems personified an entire social group's prestige, written certificates elevated the authority of only the person physically possessing it. And finally, in honor of clan totems, sacrifices were made to raise their "value," whereas, judging by the available data, offerings were not made for paper certificates. According to P. A. Tikhmenev, the first evidence confirming a chief's rank was issued in 1796 by A. A. Baranov when the Indians themselves requested this for their chief in Yakutat (Tikhmenev 1861:1:54–55). This "bureaucratic" practice was preserved (see documentary appendix entry {19}). In addition, documents were issued to the Indians by the Russians for their loyalty or services. The colonial administration completely supported these documents' prestige among the Indians: Tlingit who had such papers sometimes received special rewards and gifts (Golovin 1863a:6:284).

English and American traders also sometimes gave the Indians letters, notes, and certificates of a very different kind. For example, some letters contained warnings about the cunning and trickery that the possessor of the papers had attempted during trading; subsequent visitors viewing the papers would know what to expect from the Indians. Not knowing how to read, the Tlingit kept such letters among their greatest valuables (Oberg 1973:111–112).

During the HBC agents' stay at Fort Stikine the local Tlingit, who traded with the Tahltan living far inland, requested that the English give them assurance certificates, similar to those that the Russians gave, evidently in order to impress their trading partners. In 1841 even the eminent Naanya.aayí chief Shakes requested this of the head of the fort (Dean 1995:298).

European influence somewhat weakened the Tlingit's faith in the spirits' power. River otters, which the Tlingit had greatly respected (and whose spirit they had especially feared), lost their dominant status after the Europeans arrived. "Up to the arrival of the Russians none of the Koloshi would in general even dare to touch any otter, but at present they kill them for trade, not fearing and not seeing any evil in this," wrote Veniaminov (1840a:64).

In the Russian American period Tlingit faith in shamans was shattered because the shamans proved powerless to avert the smallpox epidemics. Tlingit confidence in European medicine grew. Golovin wrote that after their clash with the Yakutat people in 1861 at the walls of Novo-Arkhangel'sk, the Sitka people turned not to their shamans but to the Russian doctor to help the severely wounded (Golovin 1863a:6:290). Certainly contributing to the elimination of shamanism was Orthodox missionaries' activities among the Tlingit, which began in the 1830s, as well as some Russian administration actions. The colonial leadership sometimes managed to save the lives of people accused by shamans of sorcery, which discredited the shamans' authority. For example, in 1861 two Indian women of the Sitka kwáan were saved from torture and death only because the Russians intervened (Kostlivtsov 1863:71).

5.2. Tlingit Art and Games

The appearance of metal instruments and new kinds of raw materials led to the flowering of Tlingit applied art, primarily to artistic carving. During the Russian American period this art, almost unaffected by outside influence, experienced its "golden age." "Here you do not see one toy, even the simplest, not one tool, nor any vessel, on which there would not be a multitude of different images, and especially on boxes and chests, the lids of which are faced moreover with shells resembling teeth," wrote Yu. F. Lisianskii in 1805 (1812:149). During this time the Tlingit masters created such complex compositions as the carved panel in the Whale House at the Chilkat ḵwáan's Klukwan settlement (Feder 1973:109).

The form and purpose of the artistically executed artifacts were almost unchanged. Only occasionally did an object whose form copied things entirely foreign to traditional culture leave a Tlingit carver's hand: one master carved a ceremonial rattle in the form of a double-headed eagle that imitated the old Russian emblem (Niblack 1890:pl. 8, fig. 307); another creation was a smoking pipe in the form of a ship's cannon (De Laguna 1972:3:104).

The Tlingit themselves not only made artistic artifacts in large quantity but at times ordered some that they especially liked from the Europeans. In 1841 Etolin requested that the RAC's central board send about fifty masks to the colonies to trade with the Indians. He wrote that the masks

> should not be such as we usually use in a masquerade, rather the most misshapen disguises, by special order, with long noses, thick lips and teeth, with beards, and if possible with hair, and that they be somewhat larger than the usual masks. . . . It doesn't matter if they are heavy, only that they be strong and as ugly as possible. The Koloshi urgently request such masks and I hope that in comparison with the price in Russia it will be possible to sell them here to the Koloshi rather profitably for the company (AVPR, f. RAK, op. 888, d. 1007, l. 260–2600b.).

In 1843 the masks Etolin ordered were delivered to the colonies but failed to entirely justify his hopes, inasmuch as he noted: "They, though pleasing to the Koloshi, seem to them flimsy and therefore do not move well in the course of trade" (AVPR, f. RAK, op. 888, d. 1009, l. 342).

The expansion of interethnic connections during this period resulted in the Tlingit's borrowing other tribes' dances. Tsimshian dances, and particularly those of the interior Athapaskans, became especially widespread (Olson 1967:67). According to De Laguna, the Yakutat people loved to imitate the Chugach Eskimos' dances (De Laguna 1972:1:213). They sometimes also borrowed legends and songs. It was probably in the 19th century that the custom of "singing competitions" arose. It was considered a great honor to win such competitions because it allegedly attested to the victor's spiritual superiority. It was seemingly not by accident that the Yakutat people, striving to beat their old rivals, the Sitka, sent people to the Copper River in 1860 to borrow songs from the local Athapaskan Ahtna. However, this did not help the Yakutat people. The Sitka people knew more songs because, before the competition, they had learned the songs of the Kodiak people who lived in Novo-Arkhangel'sk. The

Yakutat people were so ashamed to lose that they threw themselves, armed, on the victors, and only luck and Russian intervention averted a bloody clash (Golovin 1863a:6:289).

During the Russian American period the Russians taught the Tlingit to play checkers (De Laguna 1972:2:577). Competitions such as target shooting also date back to this time. Similar contests were organized between the Indians and the Russian promyshlenniki and sailors and held at the walls of Novo-Arkhangel'sk. In the bay by the fort there were competitions between regattas of paddled boats: Russian launches and jolly boats, Aleut baidarkas, and Tlingit canoes (Zavalishin 1877:3:11:219).

5.3. The First Literate Tlingit

During the Russian American period the Europeans made their first attempts to give a primary education to some Tlingit, these being amanaty. There they learned to speak Russian and, as the indirect evidence attests, to write it. In a letter to I. A. Kuskov, Baranov mentions a chief of the Akoi ḵwáan, Chesnyga, to whom Kuskov should give a note if needed (or GBL, f. 204, k. 32, ed. khr. no. 4, l. 250b.). From this one can conclude that Chesnyga knew how not only to speak the Russian language but also to read and write it.

In 1806 in Kodiak several Tlingit amanaty (including Niktopolion Gedeonov) were trained at the technical school that Hieromonk Gedeon founded. Two grades taught courses in reading, writing, grammar, short catechism, arithmetic, history, and geography (RGIA, f. 796, op. 90, d. 273, l. 63–640b.). Unfortunately, we have no information about whether these young Tlingit passed the whole course and how their studies influenced their later fortunes.

Indeed, the Tlingit Prokopii Mal'tsov (we only know his Christian name), who learned to read in St. Petersburg, met with a tragic fate. He found himself in Russia's capital at an early age and was tutored by the RAC director M. M. Buldakov. A good learner, the young Indian successfully finished his technical school course in naval architecture and set off for the colonies in 1812 on the sloop *Neva* to become a shipbuilder in Novo-Arkhangel'sk. However, this man, probably the first Tlingit educated in Europe, perished in 1813 in the terrible shipwreck on Sitka's shores (Pierce 1990:341).

In a school later founded in Novo-Arkhangel'sk, several Tlingit were trained at different times to read Russian and possibly study some other subjects. Veniaminov reported: "Though up to the present there are yet no attempts on a large scale to teach the Koloshi reading, writing, and so on. But judging by three people . . . it can be said that the abilities of the Koloshi in this regard are not only not inferior to the abilities of the Aleuts and creoles [mestizos] but even much superior" (Veniaminov 1840a:115) (see also documentary appendix entry {13}). Simpson noted that Shakes's son knew how to read and write in Russian, which he had learned in Novo-Arkhangel'sk (Simpson 1847:1:212). In 1841 a Hoonah kwáan chief sent his son to the Novo-Arkhangel'sk school to learn Russian in order to become an interpreter for the RAC. During the second half of the 1840s, Mikhail Kukkan's nephew, Gavrila Kategan, studied at the port of Ayan, and in 1858 another young relative of Kukkan, Saklia, was also sent there (see documentary appendix 28). In the spring of 1860 two more young Tlingit, Kachaty and Tsukane, were sent to train in Ayan (AVPR, f. RAK, op. 888, d. 1007, l. 318; d. 1024, l. 1240b., 1260b., 1300b.; d. 1025, l. 48). In 1861 Golovin wrote that there was one young Kolosh, a former slave who had been given to the Russians by his master, among the pupils of the Novo-Arkhangel'sk school (Golovin 1863a:6:286). The Russians themselves tried to learn and teach the Tlingit language. Thus, among the various subjects that were taught in the Novo-Arkhangel'sk ecclesiastical seminary was the local Indians' language (Markov 1856:85).

Along with the secular authority's attempts to educate some Tlingit, the Orthodox missionaries actively joined this effort toward the end of Russian America's existence. Thus, in fall 1864 the priest Ivan Petelin began to instruct Tlingit children (primarily boys) in a special "Kolosh school" financed by Prince Maksutov, the colonial governor. By December the students were acquainted with the Russian alphabet and could read a few words. However, attendance in the school dropped after Petelin's departure from Novo-Arkhangel'sk in the first half of 1865 (Kan 1999:157–158).

Throughout the history of Russian America, it seems that no more than 20 Tlingit received primary education, whereas among the Aleuts, literate people numbered in the hundreds at that time. The reasons for widespread illiteracy among the Tlingit probably lay in the Natives' complete independence and the relative weakness of Russian-Tlingit connections. In addition, the Russian-American Company, because of the restricted means available to it, could not provide large-scale instruction in reading and writing to the Natives inasmuch as there was no guarantee that the Tlingit "would work off" the cost of their instruction after finishing grammar school or technical school.

5.4. The Russian Orthodox Church and the Tlingit (1795–1867)

The Russian Orthodox Church's influence on the Tlingit has been examined from all sides in the primary monograph of Sergei Kan—one of the greatest specialists in Tlingit ethnography—and therefore I will dwell on only the essential aspects of this theme.

The Russian promyshlenniki began to implant Christianity in Russian America as they explored the Aleutian Islands. Some Natives' acceptance of Orthodoxy promoted the formation of a stratum of "islanders" loyal to the Russians, which undermined the Natives' unity and facilitated exploitation. The company tried to create a similar stratum of loyal Natives among the Tlingit. But, as the Russian researcher S. G. Fedorova correctly notes, "Christianity in Russian America carried in itself two opposing tendencies: on the one hand, the striving to attract the aboriginal peoples into the bosom of the church (and consequently, also into submission to the Russian-American Company); and on the other, the undoubted enlightened role of some ministers of worship, such as I. E. Veniaminov (Fedorova 1971:238). However, the ultimate goal of the Orthodox missionary was Tlingit subordination to the Russian state. Kan turns his attention to this aspect, emphasizing the close connection between the Orthodox Church and the state, which is reflected in Church documents and instructions (Kan 1999:92).

One of the first baptized Tlingit was the head chief of the Yakutat people's nephew, known in Russian sources as "Toion Fedor," whose godfather was A. A. Baranov himself (OR GBL, f. 204, k. 32, ed. khr. no. 6, l. 10; Khlebnikov 1835:103). Toion Fedor accepted Orthodoxy in the winter of 1795–96 when he lived at Kodiak as an amanat. Other amanaty—sons and nephews of Tlingit chiefs—were later baptized there as well, and the colonial administration was very interested in attracting them to its side. For example, documents mention the son of the chief of the Akoi k̲wáan, formerly an amanat. He was evidently baptized, since he was known to the Russians as Pavel or Pavel Rodionov (*K istorii Rossiisko-Amerikanskoi*, 1957:109–111; OR GBL, f. 204, k. 32, ed. khr. no. 6, l. 2). It can be supposed that his godfather was Ensign F. Ya. Rodionov, who was stationed in Alaska at the end of the 1790s. It is also known that in 1806 five young Tlingit became Orthodox; they were trained at the Kodiak school (RGIA, f. 796, op. 90, d. 273, l. 64). Following the amanaty, ordinary Tlingit began to become involved in Christianity. At first these were Indian women who were wives of Russian promyshlenniki and lived with them in Novo-Arkhangel'sk; then some chiefs, primarily of the Sitka, joined: for example, Naushket (Nawushkeitl), who accepted Orthodoxy in 1823 (Lazarev 1832:166–167; Litke 1834:114–115). However, Russian success in spreading Christianity among the Tlingit was insignificant until the late 1830s. Among the Sitka people who lived at Novo-Arkhangel'sk, where Russian influence was especially strong, there were only 20 baptized Indians at that time (Tikhmenev 1861:1:298). "With all the intensified and concerned care, they succeeded in baptizing only some Indian women and marrying them off to promyshlen-

Influence of European Contacts on Tlingit Culture

niki," wrote A. P. Lazarev in the early 1820s (1832:166–167). [19] Only after a smallpox epidemic (1835–39) did the number of Christian Tlingit begin to grow noticeably. The shamans' decreasing influence fed this trend, as did the colonial administration's flexible politics and the start of Orthodox missionary activity among the Tlingit in the early 1840s. Thus, in 1834 the distinguished Alaskan missionary I. E. Veniaminov, who later became Archbishop Innocent and then Metropolitan of Moscow and Kolomensk, was transferred from the Unalaska District to Novo-Arkhangel'sk. Kan's analysis of the missionary's journal shows that his efforts to enlighten the Kolosh had very modest results initially. Between August 1834 and October 1836 Veniaminov was able to baptize only nine Tlingit men and women, the majority of whom lived at Sitka. This low number resulted from the fact that the missionary insisted on baptizing the Indians only at their own request and not after coercion by a priest. In addition, he was against the RAC practice of distributing gifts to newly baptized Natives (Kan 1999:93–94). In 1838 Veniaminov departed the colonies for St. Petersburg, where he was designated Bishop of Kamchatka, the Kuriles, and the Aleutians in 1840 by resolution of the emperor and the Holy Synod. He returned to the colonies in 1841; however, by this time he was not devoting much attention to Christianizing the Kolosh (Pierce 1990:523–524).

Nevertheless, in the early 1840s more Tlingit began to convert to Orthodoxy. Hieromonk Mikhail, who arrived in Novo-Arkhangel'sk in 1841, played a large role in this process as he influenced dozens of Sitkans to become Christians. By Easter 1843 there were already 102 Christians among the Tlingit, including 2 shamans (Tikhmenev 1861:1:269). In 1844 the number of Kolosh baptized was especially high—65 men and 30 women. This was the "richest" year for newly baptized Tlingit during the Russian America period. However, serious illness forced Hieromonk Mikhail to leave his Native flock and return to Russia in 1845. By this year the Orthodox parish membership numbered 172 Indian men and 38 Indian women. Mikhail's departure had a very negative effect on Tlingit conversion to Orthodoxy, and in 1845 a mere four Indian men and five Indian women were baptized (Kan 1999:127; see also Table 11). [20]

Having replaced Mikhail in Novo-Arkhangel'sk in 1847, Priest Petr Litvintsov tried, with varying success, to continue his predecessor's work of Christianizing independent Indians. By 1855 the number of Tlingit baptized was fluctuating between 9 and 65 a year (Golovin 1862:147–150). By this time about 25 to 30 percent of the Sitka population had been converted to Orthodoxy. According to Litvintsov, in the early 1850s ever more Indian men and women began visiting the church, and a few were having their children baptized. In spite of certain Orthodox successes, most Tlingit were skeptical about Christianity. Veniaminov recalled that when Indians were asked why they turned away from the Church, they said: We don't want to become like the Russians—lying, brawling, and immoral people." It was difficult for the missionaries to dispute this judgment inasmuch as a large number of Russian promyshlenniki and creoles living in Novo-Arkhangel'sk led a far from godly life (Kan 1999:136–137).[21]

The Tlingit-Russian clash in 1855 had clearly negative consequences for conversions: in the four years from 1855 to 1858 only eight Indians were baptized. Not until 1859, when the new governor I. V. Furuhjelm instituted his policies of rapprochement with the Kolosh, did the number of baptized Tlingit grow, with 40 people converting to Orthodoxy in 1861 (Golovin 1862:147–150). In 1860 the priest Ivan Petelin was assigned to preach to the Tlingit. He tried to attract the toion Sergei Katliak, the influential chief of the local Kaagwaantaan, to attend church activities but was largely unsuccessful. The Christian doctrines' weak influence on the Indians' religious perception speaks to the fact that some families of baptized Tlingit, who initially agreed to bury their relatives in the ground as part of a Christian ceremony, then dug up their remains and burned them, following the traditional notion that souls "froze" in the cold ground. Thus, for example, in 1864 Petelin learned that Toion Maksim (whose Indian name was Taasu) had cremated the bodies of two relatives. Kan notes that Maksim explained that, without traditional burial ceremonies and a memorial potlatch, the Indian could not achieve the status of his deceased uncle and thereby secure his deserved place in the clan hierarchy (Kan 1999:154–156).

In mid-November 1864 Petelin made a mission voyage through the straits of the Alexander Archipelago on the RAC's steamship. On board he conducted several services for the Tlingit of the Kake and Kootznahoo ḵwáans and baptized some of them, including children. The head of Angoon Village, Yelnawu (Dead Raven), who belonged to the dominant Deisheetaan clan, even expressed the desire to be baptized in Novo-Arkhangel'sk the following year (1865). In Kan's opinion, the aristocracy showed its interest in Christianity to ease trade contacts with the Russians (Kan 1999:158–159).

In November 1865 Hieromonk Feoktist Obraztsov made a similar mission trip on the steamer *Velikii knyaz' Konstantin*. He visited the ḵwáans of Kootznahoo, Hoonah, Taku, and Kake, where he gave the sermons from the Holy Scripture and was able to baptize several Indians. In this same year the senior monk Nikolai Militov was transferred to Novo-Arkhangel'sk from the Kenai Peninsula's mission to serve in the "Kolosh church" that had been constructed especially for the Tlingit. He tried to read the prayers in Tlingit, but his bad pronunciation provoked laughter among the Indians. Many of them, formally

Influence of European Contacts on Tlingit Culture

Table 11. Number of Tlingit Who Accepted Orthodoxy between 1841 and 1860

Year	Men	Women	Year	Men	Women
1841	4	—	1852	2	17
1842	38	4	1853	22	19
1843	66	4	1854	14	14
1844	65	30	1855	1	1
1845	4	5	1856	—	—
1846	9	—	1857	1	2
1847	8	19	1858	—	3
1848	12	23	1859	15	8
1849	5	6	1860	8	11
1850	3	32			
1851	30	31			
Total				221	206
Grand total					427

Source: Appendix to the *Doklad Komiteta ob ustroistve russkikh amerikanskikh kolonii* (*Doklad Komiteta*, 1863b, Table IV).

Christian, preferred to occupy themselves with domestic affairs or to bathe in the sea, even on holy days. When Militov asked the converts to bring more of their fellow tribesmen to church, the "head toion of the Sitka," Mikhail Kukkan, answered: "The Kolosh are bad people; they want to be baptized only if they can have an honorable godfather who can provide them with something." Having failed to Christianize the Tlingit, senior monk Nikolai returned to his mission on the Kenai Peninsula in March 1866, saying he had never seen such rude and mendacious "savages" as the Kolosh (Kan 1999:159–163).

The priest Nikolai Kovrigin was the last Russian missionary to try to steer the Tlingit toward Christianity before Russian America was sold to the United States. Like almost all his predecessors, Kovrigin understood practically nothing of the Indians' traditional, social, and religious life or their language, and his activities therefore had little success. It is true that he succeeded in baptizing two chiefs—Toion Nikolai Kakuk and the Sitka chief Iushkenat, as well as several Indians of the Kake, Chilkat, Yakutat, and Kootznahoo kwáans who came to Novo-Arkhangel'sk between 1866 and 1867 (Kan 1999:163–168).

All told, about 560 Tlingit were converted to Christianity during the Russian American period, according to Kan (1999:151, 168). The overwhelming majority were Sitka people who lived at Novo-Arkhangel'sk. The colonial administration supported the baptized Indians in every way possible, seeing in them potential bearers of their politics and the Russian culture. It was from among them that the "chief Kolosh toion," Mikhail Ku<u>k</u>kan, was chosen. And in 1838 Shakes's son was baptized in Novo-Arkhangel'sk and named "Nikolai" (AVPR, f. RAK, op. 888, d. 1003, l. 123–1230b.). The English captain Edward Belcher noted that the Russians clearly preferred to employ Tlingit who professed Christianity over those who did not, although he believed they were no different from pagans by any virtues (*Materialy dlia istorii*, 1861, vyp. 1, s. 205).

Tlingit were never allowed free entrance into Novo-Arkhangel'sk, and the Indian parishioners could visit the Novo-Arkhangel'sk cathedral only for large church festivals. Therefore, the Orthodox church called In the Name of the Holy Trinity was constructed beside the Kolosh settlement at the walls of the Russian fort between 1846 and 1848 especially for the Tlingit (Donskoi 1893:23:859; Mamyshev 1855:258). However, the new "Kolosh church" was not popular among the Indians. The Tlingit, especially the aristocrats, preferred to go to the service at St. Mikhail's Cathedral in Novo-Arkhangel'sk where all the colonial administration was gathered; they felt that attending services in the poor Native temple would compromise their prestige. Senior monk Militov, who served in the "Kolosh church" between 1865 and 1866, sadly concluded: "The high-ranking Kolosh never come to this church; they probably suppose their dignity is lower to pray together with their servants and subordinates," and the baptized chief of the Sitka Kaagwaantaan, Sergei Kaliak, told Father Nikolai Kovrigin that the "Kolosh church" was not for him but rather for the slaves; on festive days he himself dressed in his uniform and attended the church service in St. Mikhail's Cathedral along with the Russian officers (Kan 1999:129, 137, 143, 152, 163, 166).

In order to make sure that the prayers and sermons reached the Natives, they were read in Tlingit. The first attempts to translate the religious texts into Tlingit are from Baranov's time, during which the Lord's Prayer was translated into the Sitka people's language (OR GPB, f. 7, ed. khr. no. 143, l. 2). Later, the Gospel of Matthew, the Liturgy, the Acts of the Apostles, and others texts were translated. However, the translators encountered difficulties interpreting the biblical texts, which contained many abstract ideas, into a language that lacked many of these ideas. Therefore, the translations were not always satisfactory and sometimes made the Indians laugh during the services (*Doklad Komiteta*, 1863b:Table 5). Kan analyzed the early Tlingit translations of Russian religious texts, and wrote that as a result of an unfortunate translation of the idea of "God" as "Diety of the Distant/High Heavens" (*Haa Shagoon Dikee Kiwaa*), the Tlingit concluded that the Christian God was a god of war inasmuch as, according to the traditional notions of the Indians, the spirits of brave warriors who had died in battle lived in the heavens (see Kan 1999:132–136).

In their addresses to the flock the Russian missionaries appealed to humility and emphasized observing the norms of Christian morals and renouncing human sacrifice. Sometimes they were successful. In 1837, after a sermon to the Stikine people, Veniaminov succeeded in persuading a head chief of the Stikine ḵwáan, Kuatḵu (Kuaḵte), to forego killing two slaves at a potlatch (RGIA, f. 18, op. 5, d. 1306, l. 1; Veniaminov 1840b:34). Missionary activity in 1852 brought even more substantial results for the Russians when a baptized Chilkat chief notified a Novo-Arkhangel'sk archpriest that the Indians would storm Novo-Arkhangel'sk the next night. Only this warning enabled the Russians to prepare their defense, which caused the Indians not to attack the fort (AVPR, f. RAK, op. 888, d. 1020, l. 320).

However, despite the Orthodox missionaries' efforts, very few baptized Indians strictly observed the Church commandments and abandoned pagan ceremonies and potlatches. In most cases the new faith changed the ideology and way of life of the newly Christianized very little. For example, although he had been baptized in 1826, the Sitka chief Nawushkeitl had four wives in 1837, according to A. Erman (1870:2:316). Baptized Tlingit killed Stikine people at the walls of Novo-Arkhangel'sk in 1852. According to Rozenberg, these Christians and their pagan kinsmen decapitated the dead and took their scalps, "which they hung in their boats to carry around while they sang triumphal songs" (AVPR, f. RAK, op. 888, d. 1020, l. 3150b.). What is more, in an 1855 clash with the Russians, the Tlingit occupied the "Kolosh church" and used it as a strategic point from which they first fired on the Novo-Arkhangel'sk garrison, then plundered it and defiled the icons (Golovin 1862:78) (Table 12). In Kan's opinion, the Tlingit were trying to compensate for their losses by taking "church trophies." In 1857 the "Kolosh church" was rededicated by Archbishop Innocent (Veniaminov); however, it was never again the center of Sitkan religious life (Kan 1999:143). The relatively weak influence of the Russian Orthodox Church on the Tlingit's religious awareness was pointed out in the early 1860s by Kostlivtsov and Golovin. The latter wrote: "Many of them were baptized to get gifts and entertainment, so they do not want to go into the church for nothing. If it were announced to them that after each mass they would be given a glass of vodka then the church would be packed, but without this they do not go to pray" (Golovin 1863a:5:178). Kostlivtsov added: "During services not only are they not reverent, but if not stopped, the Koloshi are prepared to go into the church wearing their hat, with a pipe in their mouth, and will laugh and talk during the solemn ceremony" (Kostlivtsov 1863:116).

Christianity was not accepted by most Tlingit for several concrete reasons:

these Natives were independent, Russian-Tlingit connections (especially during the first 20 years of the 19th century) were unstable, the shamans held authority, and the Tlingit clearly realized the threat to their independence that Christianity posed. Veniaminov wrote: "However, I think with complete conviction that though the Koloshi are in need of enlightenment by the Religion of Christianity, they do not quickly agree to accept it; because (in the words of one very sensible Kolosh) they think with the acceptance of Christianity they are placed under the same influence and authority of the Russians as the Aleuts, whom they consider nothing more than slaves or serfs in the service of the Russians" (Veniaminov 1840a:136–137).

The Tlingit's not accepting Orthodoxy can be explained not only by their political independence but also by their fear of the new religion's undermining their traditional system of inheriting property and rank—one of the bases of Tlingit society (Kan 1985:202). In addition, as Kostlivtsov correctly notes, the Natives' traditional way of life and their morals and customs clearly did not conform to the fundamentals of "Christian virtue": gentleness, humility, and charity (Kostlivtsov 1863:116). On the whole, Orthodoxy exerted insignificant influence on Tlingit culture and their way of life in the Russian American period, although it contributed somewhat to mitigating some of their cruel customs.

One reason why the Tlingit thought badly of Orthodoxy was evidently that they were economically completely independent and had an abundance of food that guaranteed the relative stability of their lives during the Russian American period. The American professor A. A. Znamenski (1999) researched the Russians' Christianization of the Tanaina, Chukchi, and northern and southern Altai peoples, convincingly showing that hunters, fishers, and gatherers of the taiga zone—the Tanaina and northern Altai people—were much more receptive to Orthodoxy than were the wandering herders of the Chukchi and southern Altai people. The latter were affected much less by the caprices of nature because they relied not on an appropriating economy but rather on a producing—in this case, herding—one. There were less frequent natural and social crises among them, and therefore there was not a great need among the Chukchi and southern Altai people (analogous to the Tlingit) to borrow a foreign religion as one means to cope with the surrounding world (Znamenski 1999:261–263).

Nevertheless, it would be a mistake to ignore Orthodoxy's influence on the Tlingit in the Russian American period. S. A. Kan, who has studied the spread of Orthodoxy among the Tlingit in depth, points to several factors that might have attracted the Tlingit to Orthodoxy. These factors concerned festive,

Influence of European Contacts on Tlingit Culture

carefully elaborated rituals like baptism. In addition, the Orthodox baptism's ablution by water to purify oneself and remove previous sins was similar to the Tlingit religious practice of purifying one's body and spirit, an indispensable attribute of traditional religious ceremonies. Wearing the crucifix under one's clothing also directly paralleled the Indian religious tradition of using various amulets to maintain good luck (*tlaxetl*) and to protect against bad conduct and misfortune (*ligas*). The Orthodox saint in whose honor the newly baptized received a name could be understood as a personal protective spirit (*ka-kinaa-ek*). Undoubtedly some Indians began to pray to the Christian god and to appeal to him for help in times of danger, and some shamans used crosses and other paraphernalia of Orthodox worship in their own shamanic practice (Kan 1999:83, 172). Russian influence may also have influenced the accessories used in Tlingit funeral rites. For example, the Indians began to enclose their burial houses with wooden fences, which was characteristic of Orthodox cemeteries. Catherine McClellan even considers that the Indians borrowed the construction of such houses from the Russians (McClellan 1975:1:250). Within the sphere of proper religious ideas, some Christian ideas began to be adopted, especially those that conformed with traditional Tlingit myths (for example, the story about the flood). In the 1830s Veniaminov recorded a short version of the Bible story about the flood and the Tower of Babel from the Indians (Veniaminov 1840a:81–82). Having been told about Jesus Christ's origins, Veniaminov's Tlingit informants seemed to have adapted the story to their own culture, reporting that the mythological Raven, who lived on the upper reaches of the Nass River (*Nass-Shaki-Iel*), allegedly has a son who loves people much more than his father (Kan 1999:110). The Dauenhauers note, "It is impossible to say with any determination now whether the custom of commemorating the deceased on the fortieth day after death is properly Tlingit, or whether it was borrowed from Russian Orthodox tradition. At the present time it has become a firm component part of Tlingit commemorative ceremonialism" (Dauenhauer and Dauenhauer 1990b:34).

It is interesting to note that after Alaska was sold to the United States, Orthodoxy among the Tlingit became popular as a distinctive form of protest against American capitalistic colonization. After being ruled by the energetic and pragmatic Americans for two decades, many Tlingit, especially the Sitkans, began to view the Orthodox Church as the sole institution to have survived relatively untouched since Russian America's "golden days" (Kan 1999:170, 173). Until now about eight hundred Tlingit still profess Orthodoxy, which, in the opinion of one Tlingit priest, is the last remains of Russian culture among Southeast Alaska's Indians (Richards 1984:71).

In the 1820s the Americans also endeavored to promote religion among the Tlingit. In 1829 Captain Taylor brought the American missionary Jonathan S. Green from Boston to Southeast Alaska on his ship *Volunteer* to "enlighten" the Natives. However, the American captain so compromised himself in the Indians' eyes by his self-indulgent behavior that not a single person could be found wanting to hear the sermons of his countryman (AVPR, f. RAK, op. 888, d. 351, l. 31–310b.; Duff 1964:92). Green also visited Novo-Arkhangel'sk, where he tried to secure the colonial administration's support in Christianizing the Tlingit. In particular, he asked P. E. Chistiakov's permission to remain in Novo-Arkhangel'sk to study the Native language and religion. The governor politely refused the zealous missionary, citing the fact that without a "permit" from the RAC central board he could not allow him to live in the Russian colonies. In addition, Chistiakov let Green know that the Russians themselves decided religious matters, having noted: "The Koloshi who live around us are already in part prepared for the Christian faith" (AVPR, f. RAK, op. 888, d. 993, l. 3330b.–336). F. P. Wrangell, who replaced Chistiakov, even more decisively rejected American missionaries' proposals to organize missions in Alaska. At the same time, Americans' activities on the "religious front" forced Wrangell to turn special attention to the spread of Orthodoxy among the Tlingit. It was for this reason that the experienced missionary Veniaminov, who proposed to systematically involve the Tlingit in the Christian faith, was moved from Unalaska Island to Novo-Arkhangel'sk in 1834 (AVPR, f. RAK, op. 888, d. 995, l. 1730b.–174, 204–205).

6. Linguistic Borrowings

During the Russian American period the Tlingit were in contact primarily with Russian and English speakers (with regard to Europeans). Dialogue was usually established through an interpreter. But the intensive exchange of goods, as well as other types of contacts, contributed to the Indians' forming new ideas that were naturally bound to require new words. How did the Tlingit respond to the Europeans' languages? Unfortunately, the data is incomplete. Nevertheless, analyzing the information on the Tlingit language that Rezanov, Baranov, and Veniaminov collected in 1805 and 1812, and between 1834 and 1839 (OR GPB, f. 7, ed. khr. no. 139, l. 1–44; ed. khr. no. 143, l. 1–3; Veniaminov 1846), one can confidently assert that the Tlingit vocabulary was only rarely increased with foreign borrowings in relatively pure form, for example, with the word *kottl'* (kettle). Some words that were introduced into the Tlingit language underwent such phonetic regeneration that it is difficult to recognize the source word in them, as, for example, with the Tlingit word *nam*, meaning "rum." Some borrowings entered the Tlingit language because they were associated with similar-sounding words in the Native language. For example, for the concept "Russian" there was a Tlingit word, *kuskekuan*, which means "people of distant clouds" or "people of a celestial horizon" in Tlingit. In the overwhelming majority of cases, the Indians adapted existing Tlingit words to describe new ideas. Russians of that time gave direct indications of this trend: in 1805 Rezanov noted that the Tlingit, unlike other Natives of Russian America, had "their own name for all European things" (OR GPB, f. 7, ed. khr. no. 139, l. 10b.). For example, the Tlingit called a "brick" a *tte*, which in the Tlingit language designates "stone"; "molasses" in Tlingit is *tlinnukuts-ugin*, which literally translates to "sweet water"; "turnip" is *kuskekuankuk-u*, which means "Russian *sarana* {a bulbous root of the lily family}." It is notable that in the Kenai language the borrowing corresponds to the Russian word *repa* {turnip} which was distorted to *lepa* (OP GPB, f. 7, ed. khr. no. 139, 150b.–16, 240b.–25, 320b.–33).

As a result of Tlingit-European contact, the Tlingit vocabulary was enriched in the Russian American period. This enrichment occurred primarily through expanding the meaning of old words and through forming new words.

The American linguist M. Krauss attributes the extremely insignificant number of borrowed Russian words (nine) in the contemporary Tlingit language to the Tlingit's resistance to Russian colonization (Krauss 1981:157). However, it is difficult to make a judgment about a people's borrowings from a language with which it ceased to have contact more than a hundred years ago; in addition, one must consider the constant increase in American cultural-linguistic pressure after 1867. More important, the insignificant number of linguistic borrowings (including borrowings from English) in the Russian American period can be explained by the lack of sufficiently intensive, regular, all-embracing contacts between the bearers of the different languages at that time.

It is well known that bilingualism, resulting from the closest and most constant connections, brings the most changes in an adopted language. Although Tlingit-Russian bilingualism occurred in Tlingit society, it affected an extremely small part of it. Until the 1820s only Tlingit women who lived with the Russians in Novo-Arkhangel'sk and amanaty who were kept at Kodiak were bilingual. For example, Litke mentioned one of the nephews of the head Sitka chief Katlian who, having spent several years at Kodiak (as an amanat), "learned to speak Russian fairly well" (RGA VMF, f. 15, op. 1, d. 8, l. 182). After Tlingit-Russian relations were normalized, the number of Russian-speaking Tlingit began to grow: "Many Koloshi begin to understand and speak Russian," Litke confirmed in 1827 (1834:158). Veniaminov noted that the Tlingit, especially Tlingit women, quickly mastered Russian, speaking it better than, for example, the Kodiak and Aleuts (Veniaminov 1840a:119).

The number of bilingual Indians also grew because some Tlingit worked with Russians in Novo-Arkhangel'sk or served as sailors on RAC ships for a long time, creating grounds for closer linguistic contact; the sale of Alaska ended this progress. How the Tlingit language was influenced by the Russian language could only be confidently judged by vocabularies that recorded the Tlingit language at the end of the 1860s. However, Tlingit-Russian bilingualism and Russian borrowings by the Tlingit language were undoubtedly more widespread in the 19th century than in the 20th century. For example, in 1886 American travelers encountered a group of "*Kolosh*" Natives on Kayak Island who spoke in a mixture of Tlingit, Russian, and Chinook (about the last, see below) (De Laguna 1972:1:103). As late as the early 1890s, there was still one old Indian in Yakutat who knew the Russian language, according to Bishop Nikolai (1893:65).

Finally, regarding Russian borrowings in contemporary Tlingit, researchers encounter particular difficulties in determining the origin of a given word. Because the Tlingit language lacks several sounds inherent in European languages—chiefly consonants—borrowings in Tlingit underwent such phonetic transformation that they were unrecognizably changed. Neither De Laguna nor her Indian informant could determine the origin of the word *savak*, which duplicates the traditional Tlingit word *ketl* (dog) {*sobaka* in Russian}. The word *savak* was also noted at the end of the 19th century in the Kake ḵwáan to mean "large dog" (Swanton 1908:444). However, there is no doubt that this is a case of the borrowing of a Russian word that was adapted because Tlingit lacks the sound "b" and speakers replaced it with "v").

Another example is the word *kaneisdi it*, "house of the cross," by which the Tlingit designate the Orthodox Church. *Kaneist*, in the Dauenhauers' opinion, is a distortion of the Russian word *krest* {cross} (Dauenhauer and Dauenhauer 1990b:350).

Accordingly, the questions of which and how many words the Tlingit borrowed remain open. It would be interesting to trace the number and character of Russian borrowings in the Tlingit of various ḵwáans. Indeed, the depth of Russian contact with members of different Indian societies was uneven.

As trade developed with the Europeans and intensified among the tribes on the Northwest Coast in the 19th century, a special trade jargon, "Chinook" (from the name of an Indian tribe that lived on the lower reaches of the Columbia River), formed among the Indians and Europeans of this region.

The jargon, which was based on the Nutka Indian language on Vancouver Island, borrowed many words from English, French, Spanish, Russian, and several Indian languages. During the second half of the 19th century, Chinook was widely spoken among the Tlingit, primarily the traders and travelers. A Tlingit tradition that Olson recorded says that the Indians of the Tongass ḵwáan learned this jargon on a trip to Fort Simpson and Victoria (Olson 1967:41).

The European colonization of Alaska during the Russian American period only weakly influenced Tlingit personal names. Of course, as European goods entered Indians' daily lives, new names appeared. A chief of the Teiḵweidí clan acquired the name Unashtuku—"Firing Gun," and a slave of the Deisheetaan clan was named Shtin, that is, "Steel" (De Laguna 1960:181; 1972:1:200). But such names were rare.

Another European influence on Tlingit names was the Russian Orthodox Church. The Indians who converted received Christian names, and sometimes the last name of their godfather as well. Russian sources from the early 19th century often mention the Yakutat chief "Fedor"; a chief of the Akoi ḵwáan was known by the name "Pavel Rodionov." Usually the Tlingit who adopted Orthodoxy received only a Christian first name (often a rather exotic one, even for Russian names of the 19th century); the Russians called them by their proper Tlingit last names. Numerous examples are documented: Nartsiss El'k, Neon Kashkinat, Katerina Sakikan, Aleksandr Kunaḵin, and so on (Grinev 1990:139). In 1823 the well-known chief of the Sitka Kiks.ádi, Nawushkeitl, was baptized and received the name "Matvei" after his godfather, Matvei Ivanovich Murav'ev, governor of Russian America (Kan 1999:85). In 1861 the inspector of the RAC, active Councilor of State S. A. Kostlivtsov, became godfather to the influential chief of the Sitka Kaagwaantaan Katliak: upon being baptized Katliak received the name "Sergei" after the name of his godfather, and is often identified in documents as Sergei Sergeev, Sergei Sergeev Kostolivtsov, or simply Toion Sergei (Dean 1995:290; Kan 1999:149; Kostlivtsov 1863:89). The most well-known Tlingit chief with a Christian name was, of course, Mikhail Kukkan. The documents note that his Indian first name was Shchuḵ. After his uncle, the preeminent Sitka chief Kukkan, died in 1841, Mikhail arranged a potlatch, during which he inherited, in addition to his uncle's property, his honorary name (AVPR, f. RAK, op. 888, d. 1008, l. 188–188ob.; Grinev 1990:139). According to the Finnish naturalist Henrik Holmberg, who visited Novo-Arkhangel'sk in early 1850, Mikhail Kukkan had no son, and therefore another of his names was a teknonym formed from the name of his favorite dog (Holmberg 1855:1:38).

Russian Orthodox names given to the Tlingit were evidently rarely used by them in daily intercourse, or at least there is little evidence to suggest they were. Edward Belcher, captain of the English warship *Sulphur*, in 1837 met with the head chief of the Yakutat Tlingit whose name was Anushi, that is, "Russian." This chief, according to Belcher, took the name Ivan Ivatskii (Ivan Ivanovich?), probably in honor of a RAC manager who visited Yakutat for trade. In the 20th century the Yakutat people reported to De Laguna that such male names as Staguan (in honor of the head of the Yakutat fort, Stepan Larionov?) and Shada (Sasha?—the Russian variant of the diminutive, pet form of the name "Alexander") are of Russian origin. The Tlingit suspect that the feminine name Tonkva (Tan'ka? Tanya?) was taken from the same source (De Laguna 1972:1:178; 2:789). In addition, in the list of Tlingit chiefs that J. R. Swanton composed in the early 20th century, Nikana Kukkan, that is, Mikhail Kukkan, is mentioned (Swanton 1908:405). One more example on this theme: an Indian of the Chishkedi clan was named Savak (his mother was known as Savak-tla), which De Laguna translates as "long-eared dog" (De Laguna 1972:2:788). But as a matter of fact, this name, as mentioned above, is a simple loan word of the Russian word *sobaka* {dog}. On the whole, Russian names (or those produced from Russian words) rarely entered Tlingit personal names inasmuch as they were used episodically to designate a particular person and not inherited like clan or honorary names.

Possibly the most substantial influence of European colonization on Tlingit personal names was the Tlingit use of honorary "potlatch" names among the wider circle of the Tlingit (inasmuch as the potlatch was arranged often), as well as the acquisition by one person of several names of this category at a potlatch. The purpose in both cases was the same: to acquire greater prestige. The development of a prestige economy was distinctly reflected in Tlingit personal names in the Russian American period.

§

Thus, Tlingit-European contact during the Russian American period led to definite changes in different areas of the Indians' culture. The greatest change was in material culture, primarily clothing, tools, and weapons. Regarding social relations and spiritual culture, European influence was less significant and amounted to little more than the development of certain tendencies—for example, a decrease in shamans' authority or the erosion of several old customs.

European culture's influence on Tlingit culture was predetermined in character and intensity of contact, which in turn hinged on temporal and spatial factors. This is exemplified by Tlingit-Russian relations. The notable influence of the latter on Tlingit culture did not begin until the 1820s, when contacts became more routine. Contact was most intense around Russian settlements in Tlingit territory: initially at Yakutat, then at Sitka, somewhat at Nuchek, and, for a short period, at the mouth of the Stikine River (Dionisievskii Redoubt). The Sitka people, neighbors of Novo-Arkhangel'sk, were most influenced by the Russians.

The course of the Tlingit tribe's history was partly determined by the fact that, from the late 1700s to 1867, their land fell within the confines of Russian America. Therefore, unlike the overwhelming majority of Northwest Coast Indians, the Tlingit long had contacts not only with the English and Americans but also with the Russians. During the Russian American period five Russian fortifications were established in Tlingit territory (the Yakutat and Mikhailovskii forts, and the Novo-Arkhangel'sk, Ozerskii, and Dionisievskii redoubts) and two settlements founded (at Yakutat and at Hot Springs on Sitka Island).

Research permits one to conclude that it was the Tlingit Indians who played the most important role in Russian America's fate. Their resistance—followed by diplomatic pressure on Russia by the English and the United States—inhibited Russia's southward advance along the Northwest Coast. Tlingit actions from 1802 to 1810 significantly weakened the Russian-American Company's position in Alaska. The notion that the company ever had a monopoly on trade in Southeast Alaska was, in essence, pure fiction. It was not by chance that the Russian Empire, in discussing new regulations for the RAC in 1865, abolished their trade monopoly in the "*Kolosh* archipelago" and adjoining territories (AVPR, f. RAK, op. 888, d. 181, l. 1080b.).

Tlingit in the Russian colonies played the same role as did Iroquois in Canada's French colonies. The Iroquois, bearing Dutch and English firearms, represented the same threat to the French as the Tlingit, armed by the English and Americans, later posed to the Russian settlements in America (these Indians destroyed Fort Mikhailovskii, the settlement at Hot Springs, the "Sitka party," and others). By this author's calculations, a total of about sixty Russians and more than five hundred Native partovshchiki were killed (including members of the Demenenkov party).

Neither the few Russians in the Alaska colonies nor the Russian-American Company itself, which administered these colonies, was in a position to subdue the numerous well-armed and experienced Tlingit fighters. Relying on government help (in the form of a military cruiser sent into the straits of the Alexander Archipelago, diplomatic pressure on Washington, and so on) had little effect, inasmuch as the czarist government itself unwillingly took these steps, and RAC interests and the weak Russian colonies in Alaska did not wish to bear excessive expenditures or strain relations with other powers. Occupied with the notorious "eastern question," problems of European diplomacy, uprisings in the Caucasus, and the exploration of Siberia and Kazakhstan, the czarist government viewed Alaska as an unimportant issue in the game of "big politics." The RAC's ceaseless complaints about foreign smugglers arming the Indians did nothing but irritate the czarist government. Eventually, it came to see Russian America as "useless" since it cost so much to support and protect these colonies, where a significant part of the Native population in no way recognized the Russian Empire's jurisdiction and, even more, represented a potential threat. The Tlingit's active and passive resistance to Russian colonization was thus an indirect reason for selling Alaska to the United States that has not yet been adequately reflected in the scholarly literature (Batueva 1985, Bolkhovitinov 1988, Makarova 1979). Of course, we have succeeded in attracting researchers' attention to this problem, and in recent times some of them have turned their attention to the role of the "Indian factor" in Russia's decision to leave Alaska (Bolkhovitinov 1990:141, 316). Other researchers deny the influence of this factor on the czarist government's decision to sell their transoceanic colonies. These authors cite the fact that documents on the history of Russian America and negotiations to sell Alaska do not mention warlike Tlingit (Polevoi and Okladnikova 1994:79). However, the czarist government, having decided to sell its colonies, would scarcely point out to potential buyers any difficulties that they might expect to have with the Native population since this information could only drive down the price of the territory. But in the published and unpublished documents on the future of Russian America and in discussions of new RAC regulations between 1860 and 1865, the impossibility of thoroughly colonizing Southeast Alaska because of the warlike and independent Native population (whose subjugation the RAC did not deem possible) is repeatedly emphasized. The official *Doklad Komiteta ob ustroistve russkikh amerikanskikh kolonii* for 1863 states that "these tribes, in the present state at least, have more significance as enemies than as Russian subjects, though they occupy land recognized as a possession of Russia" (*Doklad Komiteta*, 1863a:249; see also 370–371). And further:

> The usual occupants who inhabit Russian land never expect complete subjugation of the Kaloshi in proper regard to us; for this it would be necessary for them {the Kaloshi} to acknowledge the authority and advantage of common improvement cooperation; or finally, it would be necessary to risk the cessation of peaceful relations with them {the Kaloshi} and to step forth in never-ending, useless war with the purpose of permanently expelling them from the land the

Russians occupied, or of their final enslavement. Is this possible? The Kaloshi are a purely American tribe, though not one nook of America can boast of such results subduing the Kaloshi—traces of extermination are seen, but subjugation nowhere. . . . From this it should be concluded that since their subjugation is impossible, rather than extermination, as others do this, which would be inhuman, we should never go beyond precautionary measures. This is one of the chief reasons why on the mainland it is impossible to undertake anything with the hope of success in regard to colonization (*Doklad Komiteta*, 1863b:489–490).

Tlingit resistance also deterred English efforts to colonize Canada. The Indians' animosity compelled the English to postpone penetrating the region of the upper reaches of the Stikine and Yukon, as well as fortifying the strip of coast leased from the RAC (as evidenced by the "Stikine incident," the evacuation of the British of Fort Taku, the destruction of Fort Selkirk by the Chilkat, and so on).

It would be incorrect to consider Tlingit-European contact to have been exclusively negative and limited only to conflicts and clashes. On the contrary, the primary relationship between the Tlingit and the Europeans was a mutually beneficial trading relationship that supplied one side with furs and foodstuffs and the other with European manufactured items. Nevertheless, only Tlingit resistance permitted them to preserve their political and economic independence in the Russian American period, which was reflected in Russian legislation. As inhabitants of the empire's territory and nominally its subjects, the Tlingit retained complete independence. They found themselves outside the Russian colonies' social structure, although the Russian-American Company made several attempts to integrate some Tlingit chiefs into the colonial administration. Contrary to the statement of the eminent Soviet Americanist A. V. Efimov, it is not true that the RAC exploited the Tlingit and the Aleuts, "forcing them to work for the needs of the company, conducting inequitable trade with them, and carrying out the dreadful colonial politics of the czarist government" (Efimov 1969:473). The Aleuts and Tlingit belonged to entirely different categories of Russian America's Native population. Whereas the Aleuts were in fact subjected to quasi-feudal exploitation, the RAC used the Tlingit exclusively as civilian workers, and, what is more, on a very limited scale. There was not great inequity in trade between the Russians and the Tlingit, but the value and assortment of wares that the Indians wanted for their furs sometimes caused the RAC managers to temporarily stop trade with them.

The American ethnohistorian Dean finds numerous parallels between the colonial politics of the British in India in the 19th century and those of the Russians in Alaska (Dean 1995:266–267, 294). In essence, both attempted to use "indirect management" of the Natives, relying on the Natives' leaders and traditional institutions. In our view, this practice was much more universal and was especially effective where the number of the Native population was many times greater than that of the colonizers. Dean, comparing the situations in India and Russian America, observes that the colonial powers supported the Native leaders and traditional institutions in an attempt to synthesize "feudalism" and "modernism" (of which capitalism is evidently a part); however, one cannot agree with his view. India was not a feudal country in the full sense of the word. Here, as across Asia, reigned an order that Marx designated the "Asiatic manner of production" (Marx 1957b:222; 1959:7). To designate this order (formation) we use the more precise term *politarism* (from the Greek *politea*, meaning "government"). Politarism is in essence based on the supreme property of the government (which is embodied in the highest ruler with unlimited authority). That supreme property is the basic means of production (largely land) and the individual who is the direct producer. Russian colonization of Alaska did not bear either a capitalistic or a feudal character but rather was politaristic inasmuch as the mother country—the Russian Empire—was itself also politaristic (Grinev 1996b, 1999, 2000; Grinev and Iroshnikov 1998). Therefore, implanting "feudalism" among the Tlingit, as Dean (1995:285) suggests happened, was neither the RAC's wish nor even a possibility for the czarist government.

On the whole, the politics of St. Petersburg regarding the Tlingit were limited to a paternalistic declaration to protect "independent non-Russians" without actively interfering in their internal affairs. It was up to the Russian colonies' governor to establish direct relations with the Indians. But no consistent political course was sustained by the governors, inasmuch as each governor occupied the post for a single five-year period, during which he implemented his own policies. The next governor often began his relations with the Tlingit as though he had a "clean slate." The colonial administrations' inconsistency vis-à-vis "Tlingit politics" was especially apparent in the 1850s and early 1860s when N. Ya. Rozenberg, S. V. Voevodskii, and I. V. Furuhjelm were charged with conducting relations with the independent Indians.

Having found themselves "one-on-one" with the Tlingit, the Russian colonial authorities were forced to carefully implement colonial policies, counting on Russian culture's peacefully spreading among the "independent Natives" and drawing them into the bosom of Orthodoxy in a gradual unforced cultural assimilation.

The Tlingit's economic and political independence in the Russian American period, as distinct from the Aleuts' and Kodiak's situation, enabled them to preserve their traditional culture as an integral system. Their culture not only was not degraded by the clash with European culture but continued to develop throughout the entire Russian period of Alaskan history. The substantial firmness of the old cultural patterns and forms and the flowering of ceremonialism (potlatch) and art attest to this stability. In not one sphere of Indian culture were its traditional elements completely eliminated. In the opinion of F. de Laguna, the period from 1840 to 1867 was an enormously prosperous epoch for the Tlingit (De Laguna 1990b:223).

The Tlingit's political independence in the Russian American period was not the only factor ensuring the stability of their traditional culture. European colonization did not change the economic base or social structure of Tlingit society, and this in turn guaranteed preservation of the traditional culture. The highly developed culture and Indians' self-awareness prefigured the well-known conservatism regarding innovations. The Tlingit took an active and discriminating role in their contacts with Europeans, borrowing only those things that had definite advantages when compared to their own cultural forms (steel blades, firearms, metal kettles, and so on). In addition, Tlingit-European connections in the Russian American period were, on the whole, not overly intense, all-embracing, or continuous. In addition, there were far fewer bearers of European culture than there were Indians. All these factors suppressed Euro-American cultural pressure while permitting traditional Indian culture to adapt. This process stimulated both more frequent contacts between the Tlingit and other Northwest Coast Indians and the formation (already under way) of a single tribal culture in this region, although this formation was interrupted by European capitalistic colonization in the last quarter of the 19th century.

Contacts with Europeans in the Russian American period turned out to have influenced the southern Tlingit's culture more than the northern Tlingit's culture. The latter, with the exception of the Sitka people, largely preserved their traditional culture because English and American fur traders visited less often. These traders' ships visited the southern Tlingit more often, and, with the Hudson's Bay Company's founding forts on the Northwest Coast, the southern Tlingit obtained greater power than the northern Tlingit through trading in the posts and even making trips as far south as Oregon.

As research has shown, Tlingit culture in the Russian American period was a combination of tradition and innovation, where the elements of traditional culture were preserved almost intact though sometimes were intertwined with new elements introduced by European colonization. The Tlingit culture can never be called purely "Indian"—contact with Europeans left its imprint. Some Tlingit in the sphere of European influence were more affected; others remained almost unchanged. Contact with Europeans was especially apparent in Tlingit material culture.

As American historians and ethnographers themselves note, the position of Alaska's Native population, including the Tlingit, largely deteriorated after Alaska was transferred to the United States. Some Tlingit chiefs publicly and outspokenly emphasized that the Americans treated the Indians worse than the Russians had. Others displayed the Russian medals for loyalty that their ancestors had been awarded (Dauenhauer and Dauenhauer 1990b:135). The first decades of American rule were characterized by clashes between the Tlingit and the citizens and army of the United States; widespread alcoholism, prostitution, and illness among the Natives; and the degradation (especially in the 1880s and 1890s) of traditional Indian culture. The effect of all these factors can be seen in the steady drop in the Tlingit population, which declined until the 1920s. Only in the 1930s did this trend abate and the number of Tlingit begin to grow more and more quickly, strengthening their economic position. It was not until the 1950s that a distinctive "renaissance" of certain aspects of their traditional culture and ethnic self-awareness began to emerge.

Since the beginning of the 1960s this process has received support from the Alaskan Native Brotherhood, established in 1912 by educated Tlingit in the struggle for their rights in American society. At present, Indians regularly conduct various ceremonies (in particular, the potlatch) and develop traditional occupations and art. They strive not to forget their past, including the history of their contact with the Russians when Alaska was considered part of the Russian Empire. Modern Tlingit acknowledge the large role of the Russians in their history but suppose that the latter did not have the right to sell Alaska to the Americans (Shnirel'man 2002:480–486). However that may be, it was the Russian American period that became the brightest chapter in Tlingit history, which was accompanied by the flowering of their rich and original culture.

Unpublished Archival Materials

{1} AVPR, f. Gl. arkhiv 1–7, 1802 g., d. 1, papka no. 35, l. 150ob.–151 /copy/

l. 150ob.

Approximate estimate of the Koliuzh people living near the Port of Novo-Arkhangel'sk from Yakutat along the straits, with the names of their villages, known to the Russians

Villages

1. Yakutat village from Bering Yakutat Bay and the former Russian fort lying 10 versts toward Akoi[1] at the river emptying through many arms and called Sakova[2]; 10 large barabaras in it. Male inhabitants in it along with minors, up to 200.
2. Village of the Kilkva on the bank of the river of this same name, 40 versts distance from the first. Male inhabitants with minors, up to 100.
3. The first and chief Akoi village situated on the river at the isthmus between the sea and the river, standing 8 versts from the Kilkva village; how many native occupants in it is not known, but annually in spring, for the preparation of fish oil, people arrive to it from Icy Strait and from Yakobi Island and remain all summer. The population then, less minors, is from 500 to 700.
4. The second Akoi village is close to Marklovskaia Mountain[3] on the Altsek River,[4] the number of native inhabitants unknown for the reason that many people gather from Icy Strait for the preparation of fish oil.
5. On the south side of Yakobi Island is a village named Apolosovo or Vorovskoe by the Russians;[5] in it the male inhabitants reach 100.
6. In Icy Strait near the mouth of Chilkat Inlet, the village of Kaknau, are 25 large barabaras. Male inhabitants, up at least to 600.
7. Opposite the above-mentioned, on the other side of the strait, the village of Kaukatan,[6] male inhabitants, up to 400. Within Chilkat Inlet on a large river on the mainland are three populous villages.[7] In the words of those taken captive after the devastation of Sitka and with the
8. destruction near Kekovskoe village of the party of seized and re-

l. 151

9. sold Kodiak people, according to the number of their large barabaras, probably by all observations the
10. males can be supposed to reach 2000.
11. At the mouth of Aiku Strait in Chilkat Inlet, which flows into Takku Inlet

12. 25 versts distant are four

13. populous villages. Approximately, according to obser-

14. vations, there can be supposed as many males as 1000.

15. At the mouth of Takku Inlet is a not so populous village, but in it live a multitude of people who are occupied with hunting land animals, such as foxes, marmots, and others. They produce very little, but receiving wares, broadcloth, and so on from the Boston Men they carry out trade with the mountain peoples on the mainland, receiving from them elk hides, deer hides, and so on.

16. On the mainland coast from Takku Inlet to Stakin Strait

17. at a distance from Takku of about 25 versts in Icy Bay, called Tsultan[8] by the Koliuzhi, in two villages, which G. Kuskov visited, estimating by the number of structures that there should be in average a ratio of up to 600.

18. In Stakin Bay and Strait, in three

19. villages, there are so many inhabitants that they are high

20. above all other people in population.

21. In the Port of Buldakov is Kekovskoe village; in it, according to the number of barabaras, the males are at least up to 200.

22. In the Port of Delarov is Kuiuvskoe village; in it the male inhabitants are up to 150.

23. On Khutsnovskii Island, named by the Russian Admiralty, is the populous village of Khutsnovo. According to the assurance of the Boston Men, and Kodiak people who have returned from captivity, in addition to the aged and minors, in it the warriors armed with guns are at least 1,700.

24. The Sitka village is at the end of the strait from Novo-Arkhangel'sk, in it, in addition to the old and young, are warriors to 700.

NB. Both of the last villages are close to the Port of Novo-Arkhangel'sk. To the south, the straits are also all filled with inhabitants; all the shores to California itself are an anthill of people.

Notes

This list was compiled by N. P. Rezanov at the end of 1805 with the help of information gathered by A. A. Baranov and other RAC employees.

1. That is, to the southeast.

2. The name of the river comes from the Tlingit word *ssak*, by which the Indians meant candle-fish (eulachon).

3. Mount Fairweather (4,663 meters).

4. The modern Alsek River.

5. Possibly the Tlingit village in Freshwater Bay, or Asanki.

6. Evidently, the village of Gaotakan Hoonah.

7. The villages of Klukwan, Katkwaaltu, and Gantegastaki/Yendestake.

8. Evidently, Sumdum Holkham Bay.

{2} AVPRI, f. Snosheniia Rossii s Angliei, op. 356, d. 507, l. 15–16ob. /Copy/

The Most Humble Report of Governor Baranov of the American Company of Messrs. Golikov and Mrs. Shelikhova [to the Irkutsk Governor Larion Timofeevich Nagel']

l. 15

By force of the many instructions of the Okhotsk administration on the placement in remote locations in America of secret copper plates[1] and emblems, delivered [to the colonies], the execution [of this task] was stopped because of the absence of Russian-born seafarers in the service of the company. But in the past summer, 1797, one such plate (Plate no. 3), because of the presence of Ensign Ivan Rodionov with the hunting party, was put in a place sought out by me, beyond Lituya Bay near Chilkat (or Remeden, according to the English name) Inlet, [on] the large, with inhabitants, Takhanas Island, named Yakobi by me [in] 1795, when [I was] on this [island], in Lodyzhenskii Harbor; while the emblem with proper certificate was entrusted to the chief toion of the villages of Chilkat Inlet who lived close to this island [Yakobi].[2] With the report on this by Mr. Rodionov, an inferior of mine, and the certificate [entrusted to the chief], copies are also enclosed with this; and that place [where the metal plate was hidden] is signified on the map (through the [company] Office), forwarded with this, by the sign of a cross, thus:
†

l. 15ob.

At present, to Second Lieutenant Gavril Terent'evich Talin, sent specially on the company ship *Orel* for thoroughly describing the coasts of America to the northeast[3] and east to 55 degrees at the north latitude here, and if possible also toward Nootka to the Queen Charlotte Islands, named by the English, to set the recommended course and to place [there] two plates: one at the most distant place which is going to be attained in this summer, and the other on the Island of Sitka not far from the mentioned Yakobi [Island], where the English come each year in many ships to trade, and [where] there are capable [that is, favorable] harbors there [on Sitka Island], on which is also Mount Edgecumbe[4] named by them [the English] (which formerly emitted fire). To this end he is provided with two such plates and five state emblems to distribute to reliable inhabitants of the villages there. Regarding this I sent this one [Talin] a report [instructions] by me— I enclose a copy for examination by Your Highness. In addition I have the honor to report that of the plates sent here, five are without any numbers and should such be placed, I beg for a resolution; of the emblems I distributed inside and along the north side of Aliaksa to Ugashenskoe, Kanigomiudskoe, and Katskoe [village] three; and along the mainland coast beyond Aliaksa to Agolomiutskoe village 1, which [settlements] were all arbitrated and hostages taken by me, except from Agolomiutskii, from which time did not permit taking

l. 16

amanaty, and the total [emblems] in this, with the one given by Mister Rodionov, are 5 [emblems].

New arrivals from the English nation try to assert themselves in the neighborhood of our occupation, [maintain] their powers (force) and right by different methods and signs, distributing everywhere they land medals and buttons for the clothing and caps with the English emblem resembling Grenadiers': this is all distributed in great number near Sitka; and in addition, they trade for gunpowder, lead, and guns to our detriment openly and liberally. One such forehead part, from a copper cap with the English emblem, is sent with this [report] and, will it be inappropriate to solicit from the above administration {permission} for us to distribute to the people [natives] something of such [decorations] with the Russian emblem to wear on clothing or on the head, which can be small medals and similar buttons and the like. And though here [in a northern direction] the English no longer come from Nootka beyond Sitka and Yakobi Island, but by all appearances try to acquire for [their] nation the shores and islands to Nootka despite the fact that Captain Chirikov was here first, as [I] heard through Mr. Shields,[5] who met in 1796 in Sitka with the sea-captain Barbarus,[6] who at the same time left one Englishman there with the residents, while Mr. Shields (I do not know why) sent back on his [Barber's] ship our devoted, formerly with him, young lad of Koliuzh people [that is, Tlingit]; and in addition apparently this one [Barber] assured him [Shields] that Nootka was already really occupied by them [the English]

l. 16ob.

and reinforced by many people through resettlement—that it should be expected that they also will not linger to occupy those places where M[r.] Chirikov arrived, if it is not prevented by us [by the occupation of the territories]. But we of the company are now weakened by {having} many people distributed everywhere in the great expanse, [the expanse] occupying from the Shumagin [Islands] to Lituya and in all not 200 men of us, and in addition, in the distance there [on the Northwest Coast] where Chirikov was, several artilleries and people with skills are needed for construction of a regular fort, because the people there have in great number every kind of firearms and equipment [and therefore] it is not possible to be engaged without suitable precaution of these native inhabitants, and even more so if the Europeans try to hinder and force us out. Lieutenant Shields, by virtue of the instructions of Your special high excellency to the managing gentlemen [that is, the owners of the company], with the present transport with my report, is sent to the Okhotsk administration.

About which with obedience I will have the honor of awaiting the permitted kindness.

Governor of the American Company
Aleksandr Baranov
June 7th, 1798
From Pavlov Harbor of the American Island Kodiak.

Notes

1. Meaning metal plates with the inscription "Land of Russian Possession."
2. Evidently, the chief of Klukwan village.
3. Correctly: southeast.
4. The extinct volcano Edgecumbe located not on Sitka (Baranov) Island but on Kruzof Island.
5. James Shields (Yakov Egorovich Shil'ts)—Englishman in the service of the Shelikhov-Golikov Company, former lieutenant of the Ekaterinburg Regiment, shipwright, and seafarer.
6. Henry Barber: captain of the English brig *Arthur*.

{3} AVPR, f. Gl. arkhiv 1–7, 1802 g., d. 1, papka no. 35, l. 97ob.–98ob.

A letter by [N. P.] Rezanov to the Directors of the RAC, 26 June 1806 N.-Arkhangel'sk [fragment]

l. 97ob.–98

This day {there} arrived in our Port [1] the three-masted ship *Vancouver* of the American States, its captain is Brown. . . . He told us frankly that trade becomes more difficult from year to year and that the local Americans and Indians here will not give up beavers for less than 7½ *arshin* of broadcloth and similarly the cost of all wares had increased, saying that in Sitka the Russians give more. He asked what we pay? M[r.] Baranov answered that it was too much and did not say the price. They showed us canvas, caps, and other things obtained from you, Brown said. They take everything they see, answered Baranov. But in fact they do not carry out any barter at all, and imagine how the savages [2] know how to cheat for their own benefit, showing those items, which M[r.] Baranov presented them. Brown said that all these peoples become haughtier day by day and at the same time braver. He went to Kaigani, [3] he was not permitted to get water and he had to go to Khoda, to another place lying nearby, though when he wanted to untie the rope by which {the boat} was fastened, he was not permitted. He threatened to shoot from the cannons—they poured out in swarms shouting that he could not shoot everyone and, at night, one of them untied him for two *arshin* of broadcloth. He said that all the Boston ships

l. 98ob.

are extremely offended and each of them paying for their treacherous and vile acts, {and} upon the leaving of the shores does not spare them and burns villages, and they become all the more fierce."

Notes

1. Novo-Arkhangel'sk.
2. Indians.
3. Evidently, Kaigani village at the south end of Dall Island, settled by Haida-Kaigani Indians.

{4} RGA VMF, f. 1375, op. 1, d. 26. /Copy/

Proposal [of L. A. Hagemeister] to the Novo-Arkangel'sk office [RAC] [of] 6 March [1818], N 68

l. 39

The interpreter of the Kolosh language, Domna, requests as usual that she be provided with various clothing and so on. Since formerly support [from the RAC] was not provided to her, the office has placed, on the 1st of January 1818, 60 rubles a year for clothing that should be given to her in this sum of money. Regarding supplying her with provisions by reason of ill health, the previously established order in this is followed, providing the 20 pounds of cereals per month for [her] not on account [not on credit].

Notes

Leontii Andreevich Hagemeister: first governor of the naval officers who succeeded A. A. Baranov on the 11th of January 1818. He was in charge of the Russian colonies until the 24th of October of the same year when he surrendered his duties to S. I. Yanovskii.

{5} RGA VMF, f. 1375, op. 1, d. 26. /Copy/

Proposal [of S. I. Yanovskii] to the Novo-Arkhangel'sk office [RAC] [of] 9 December [1818], N 295

l. 141ob.

Three Kokoantanskii [Kaagwaantaan] toions, who arrived here, brought us two amanaty, with the proposal of forgetting everything past and with the promise of exchange, asking from us two [hostages], whom they promise to maintain well; being in favor of this proposal, I agreed to it and selected two boys from the Creoles: Nikolai Gychev and Antipatr Beliaev. Then the Novo-Arkhangel'sk office had the kindness to order clothing sewn for them and give them provisions for the road. The amanaty obtained from them [the Kaagwaantaan]: Tunek and Kystyn, being ordered equipped, transferred to an artel, and supplied with provisions equally with the Russians.

Notes

Semion Ivanovich Yanovskii: governor of Russian America from 1818 to 1819

{6} RGA VMF, f. 1375, op. 1, d. 26. /Copy/

Report to the Board of Directors [Lieutenant S. I. Yanovskii][of] 16 April [1819], N 319

l. 152ob.

From that time, since the Koloshi killed two of our people,[1] we were always, as it were, blockaded, always exposed to danger, so that no one would be a victim of their barbarity. They always spied on us around the fort. Everywhere that our people were sent to work, it was always necessary for them to go armed; even in summer they did not dare leave the fort without guns. Almost every person who went for water or to the garden [outside the fortification wall] exposed his life to danger. In order to avert this, it seems to me no other means were left than to go to their fort,[2] ravage it, in a word, it was needed to put them in fear, and this was not possible to do without bloodshed on both sides. Another means was to become reconciled with them; the losses could not be brought back, and therefore vengeance having been put off, gentleness and philanthropy was necessary to show them the difference by which we are distinguished from them and the fact that barbarity does not create happiness in people. During the stay of Captain-Lieutenant Leontii Andreianovich Hagemeister here, he told the Koloshi repeatedly that if they want to be reconciled [with the Russians], it was necessary to bring two amanaty from the Kokoantan clan; then their crime will be pardoned, but they should vow never to cause the smallest insult to anyone of ours in the future. After some time they [the Indians] agreed to this, but only

l. 153

if we give them two amanaty and I found it necessary to risk this for the following reasons. If they give two boys of nearest relation to the chief toion, it can consequently be expected that ours will not be in danger among them; we have a big need of Kolosh interpreters, all the negotiations having to be conducted now through Kolosh women who live with Russians, who are devoted to theirs [their kinsmen], {and so} translate not that which they should, but relate everything to the Koloshi that we are doing, of which we have been convinced more than once. This can be averted when our amanaty learn the Kolosh language. The Koloshi, who have given their amanaty for security, will give up their barbaric intentions and will more often go and trade with the Russians, will bring more goods. Thus, for these chief reasons I decided to give them two of our Creole boys. The 17th of December [1818] Koloshi from the Kokoantan clan arrived in three boats with up to 50 men; in many negotiations with great ceremony we exchanged amanaty with their chief toion Tsoutok; he gave his nephews, who [Tsoutok] swore with his crew to live until his death in friendship with the Russians and to help each other in everything. Since then the Koloshi began to come to us more, to bring wares, sometimes to bring here [to Novo-Arkhangel'sk] with them our amanaty. So far they have been treated well, {and} should be in the future, but nevertheless there is never a guarantee, because they do not have occasion to harm us.

l. 153ob.

The Koloshi took the amanaty with them to show them in Kutenov [Kootzna-hoo]; finally they came to us again to ask to exchange amanaty, and they will give us two girls. I did not want to consent to this, but our boys [amanaty] very much requested that we redeem them and one fell ill from *vered* [illness of the capillaries]. Thus, on the 11th of April [1819], also with a great ceremony, they were exchanged and two girls of the nearest relation to the toion were accepted from them; they are now retained by us. Since among the local people dancing is a great passion, they taught our boys to dance in their way better than they dance themselves; now they [the boy amanaty] understand their conversation, but only a little. I want to give one [for learning the language] to the Kolosh elder who lives among us.

Notes

1. It is the matter of two Russian promyshlenniki who were killed by Tlingit of the Kaagwaantaan clan in the spring of 1818.
2. The Kaagwaantaan fort was on the shore of the Pogibshii {Peril} Strait (between Chichagof and Baranof Islands) not far from Novo-Arkhangel'sk.

{7} RGA VMF, f. 1375, op. 1, d. 2. /Copy/

Under the Highest patronage of His Imperial Majesty
of the Russian-American Company from the Board of Directors
of the Russian-American Colonies
to the Governor, Fleet Captain-Lieutenant and Cavalier
Matvei Ivanovich Murav'ev

l. 16

From the report of the manager of the colonies M[r.] Yanovskii of the 16th of April 1819, under N 319, the Board of Directors of the Company noted that he, with the inclination of the friendship of the Chief Sitka Toion toward the Russians, obtained from him, as assurance of this, two amanaty, and in return gave as amanaty two Creole boys with the intention that they learn to converse in the Kolosh [language]. The last step—that of the Company to give amanaty under whatever pretext—the Board of Directors considers inappropriate; since this lets the savages [Indians] note that the Russians fear them and seem equal to them; which should be shown under no circumstances, rather one should endeavor in all cases to attain the upper hand, and though to deal mercifully

l. 16ob.

with those, who hence-forth show cruelty; but, with proper firmness, peculiar to educated people, to punish their insurgents according to local circumstances, their treacherous customs and those views, which must always secure our colonies and practices [hunting/trade]. In communicating such an idea to you the Board of Directors of the Company will expect that you manage the Koloshi to that degree of humility, as the Kad'iak people [Koniag Eskimos] are managed, though in as humanely a manner as possible so it might act upon the barbarians, and in this way the integrity of the establishment and people to be rendered to your unremitting care.

N 87 [Directors:] Venedikt Kramer
January 23 Andrei Severin
1820 Director of the Office: Zelenin

{8} AVPR, f. RAK, op. 888, d. 992, l. 15–17 /Copy/

[1826] No. 27, February 3. Report to the Board of Directors
[by P. E. Chistiakov]

l. 15

December 6 at 6 o'clock in the evening I was alarmed by news through our interpreter who received the information from arriving Koloshi who had been fishing near Ozerskii Redoubt, that allegedly on the night of the 5th to 6th Koloshi in several boats approached our fortification with the intention of fishing for herring, were hailed several times by our watchmen, but as no answer was given by them, gun shots followed from our fortification, which forced them to move away, and by one of these {gunshots} a Kolosh was killed; from the account of the interpreter I saw clearly that the manager of the redoubt was in need of resorting to such measure, since he

l. 15ob.

could suppose that the Koloshi had the intention of attacking the fortification during the night.—Though I did not receive confirmation of this news from the redoubt and heartily wished that it was false, but if it was true, in such case I could not get news since, because of the early herring run, the Koloshi were temporarily settled close to our redoubt, a distance of one verst from it, numbering up to 300 people, and by the state of the narrowness of the bay they occupied both shores, and, as a result, after such an incident the redoubt would find itself under siege, which in fact happened.—On the next day I sent an armed six-oar launch to the redoubt,

l. 16

with an interpreter, under the command of Midshipman Teben'kov, in order to learn about this incident in detail at the redoubt and from the Koloshi; my order to him and his report to me I forward in copy.—To my dissatisfaction the news was true, but thank God, by this time it had no consequences.—I summoned the relatives of the dead man and the toions, who then were {there}, {and} it seemed, succeeded through an interpreter to persuade them of the necessity to resort to measures hostile to them, they agreed that they knew the prohibition against approaching the fortification at night and that they were guilty, since they heard that they were hailed (according to evidence in the redoubt), but they did not suppose that shooting might begin.—For the killed man I gave his relatives goods

l. 16ob.

on the company account for 250 rubles and, it seems, they were satisfied with this. My opinion of this incident is that though the Koloshi may not have had any evil intent, their approach to the fortification showed impudence, for which they received a good lesson; they probably wanted to test the repair and see if our guns were in order, since the place where the redoubt is located lies at their heart,[1] the run of fish into the lake is so abundant that it supplies all those who live here the whole winter and is known by them. I find for my part that the Manager

l. 17

of the redoubt was entirely right, he has 38 people in his garrison, while their nomadic village is composed of 300 people; at night he in fact was not able to see how many boats there were nor what they intended, since such an event as occurred was the first here since the occupation of Sitka, I add also that thank God that he {the manager} did not resort to his battery.
Slobodchikov,[2] manager of the redoubt, was appointed by Matvei Ivanovich[3] in the place of Shmakov,[4] a man of good conduct and what is called here an old voyager.

Documentary Appendix

Notes

Petr Egorovich Chistiakov: governor of Russian America from 1825 to 1830.

1. That is, the Russians occupied their richest clan grounds.
2. Sysoi Slobodchikov, a Russian promyshlennik (of the "old voyagers").
3. This is M. I. Murav'ev, governor of Russian America from 1820 to 1825.
4. Aleksei Shmakov, Russian promyshlennik from the Tarsk petty bourgeois ("old voyager").

{9} AVPR, f. RAK, op. 888, d. 995, l. 137–139 /Copy/

[1831] No. 190, April 30. Report to the Board of Directors [by F. P. Wrangell]

l. 137

Because of the discord between the Northern and Sitka Koloshi and the Stakin,[1] there was a large conference in Novo-Arkhangel'sk of the former [Northern and Sitka Koloshi], whose number now reaches 2,000. Among them are Chilkat, who came with rather good procurement from the rivers, announced to me their complaint, and which was supported by all the other toions, concerning the refusal [by the Russians] to sell {them}

l. 137ob.

gunpowder, guns, and lead. They said that {the Stakhin}, {and} the Koloshi who lived in their the Stikine neighborhood, received at a low price and in large quantity all military equipment from American ships, they brag in front of the Sitka Koloshi and had become so strong that the latter can not withstand them at the present time: such is their humiliation that they charge the Russians with allowing other nations to sell gunpowder, lead, and guns in the straits, {and} not supplying those Koloshi who consider themselves Soiuznye Rossii [Russian Allies] and whose toions wear the medals with this inscription. "Why, they say, do you call us your allies and invite us to trade with you and not with foreigners, when you do not

l. 138

protect us and our enemies kill, humiliate, and mock us for our loyalty to you, so it is better for us to go to the ships of foreigners, sell them our goods and not know you at all." Such are the consequences of shameless violation of the conventions by the Citizens of the United States!—I for my part told them that in places occupied by us, that no one would offend them and we will be their protectors; but we could not sell them military equipment. It goes without saying that no reasons will convince them since they always insist on the fact that their enemies are supplied with gunpowder by foreigners, consequently it is necessary for us to provide them for warding off attack.

Such logical reasoning of the Sitka Koloshi put

l. 138ob.

me in a difficult situation and in the first instance I deviated as far as possible from the explanation, consoling the toions with small gifts.

Through new colonization by the Hudson Company in Observatory Inlet,[2] perhaps, acting in the same way with the Russian-American Company, the sale of firearms will be somewhat limited, and I consider quite useful to enter into friendly connections with This Company [Hudson's Bay Company], as was proposed by it.

Here I have to note that if the Company does not find great profits from the purchase of sea and river products from the Koloshi for blankets, the delivery of which is difficult for the Board of Directors, we are on the other hand committed solely to these good quality blankets {so} that the Koloshi value our friendship through

l. 139

them, since if there are no profits provided to them from us, then all these allies will enjoy, with the warlike spirit peculiar to them, treating us as enemies, and taking revenge on us during our trips into the woods, while out fishing, and in such cases whenever it is possible.

I have the honor of submitting these thoughts so that the Board of Directors may take them into consideration.

Notes

Ferdinand Petrovich Wrangell: governor of Russian America from 1830 to 1835.

1. It concerned a large clash of the Kaagwaantaan clan of the Chilkat and Sitka ḵwáans with the Naanya.aayí clan of the Stikine ḵwáan.
2. Fort Simpson.

{10} AVPR, f. RAK, op. 888, d. 998, l. 280ob.–281 /Copy/

No. 307. May 12. Under HIS IMPERIAL MAJESTY'S HIGHEST patronage of the Russian-American Company of the Chief Director of the Russian Colonies in America Fleet Captain 1st rank and Baron [F. P.] Wrangell 1st

l. 280ob.

CERTIFICATE

Documentary Appendix

l. 281

This (*Soiuznye Rossii*) is given to the Stakhin Toion Kek-khal'-tsech[1] as a badge of distinction[2] rendered to him in commemoration of zeal shown by him toward the Russians and concessions to the Russian-American Company of a parcel of land for the construction of a Redoubt[3] in that place where his own residence was, for which place he was paid by the Company, that it would remain in Its eternal and irretrievable possession. In the certification of which and given to him, to Toion Kek-khal'-tsech, is this certificate signed by me and with seal affixed. In the Port of Novo-Arkhangel'sk, on the Northwest Coast of America. 12 May 1834.

OF HIS IMPERIAL MAJESTY

MY MOST ALL-MERCIFUL SOVEREIGN,

Fleet Captain 1st rank, holding

various Orders, of the Russian Colonies

in America the Chief Director /genu. sign./

B[aron] Wrangell

Notes

1. Kektl'tsech: one of the wealthiest chiefs of the Stikine people, brother of the head chief of the Naanya.aayí clan, Sheiks {Shakes}, mentioned in Tlingit legends (Olson 1967:49).
2. A silver medal with an inscription on one side "Soiuznye Rossii" {Allies of Russia} and the double-headed eagle on the other.
3. Meaning Dionisievskii Redoubt, the construction of which was begun at the mouth of the Stakhin (Stikine) River in 1833.

{11} AVPR, f. RAK, op. 888, d. 1003, l. 121ob.–122 /Copy/

[1838] No. 391, June 18. To the Commander of the Brig
Chichagov, Fleet Lieutenant [D. F.] Zarembo
[by I. A. Kupreianov]

l. 121ob.

It is known to me that during the present year especially many Kaigani Koloshi were in Khutsnovo, in Icy Strait, and in Chilkat for trade of furs, {and} for resale of these to the English or Americans. There were at that time about 15 boats of Kaigani Koloshi there, while in the past year Kaigani Koloshi who also visited Novo-Arkhangel'sk endeavored as well to coax furs out of the Sitka Koloshi for exchange with

l. 122

Foreigners: Therefore I ask You to convince as much as possible the Koloshi of the Northern Straits [Alexander Archipelago], where you are at present located, that they not enter into such trade with the Kaigani, rather better they traded their catch to us, and what would be more profitable for them is if they {take} wares obtained from us (such as *tyny*)[1] for their catch, {or if} they buy from the Kaigani Koloshi, rather than exchange such directly in trade. I ask this same be explained also to the Stakhin Koloshi. In the present case, having with you the Stakhin Kolosh Nikolai,[2] I suggest that this will facilitate for you the explanation of this circumstance to them in Chilkat.

Notes

Ivan Antonovich Kupreianov: governor of Russian America from 1835 to 1840.

1. More correctly: *tinne*—copper plate.
2. This was the second son of the head chief of the Stikine, Sheiks {Shakes}; he was baptized in Novo-Arkhangel'sk and received a silver medal from the hands of I. A. Kupreianov.f

{12} RGIA, f. 18, op. 5, d. 1306, l. 6 /Copy/

[Letter of the former governor of Russian America F. P. Wrangell to the head of the Department of Manufacture and Internal Trade of the Ministry of Finance Ya. A. Druzhinin]

Sir Yakov Aleksandrovich!

l.6

In the most respected regard[1] of Your Excellency of 15 December No. 5295, I have the honor of reporting that I would propose the following respectable dress for the Stikine Toion Kuakhte Kuatke: a brocade kaftan completely of gold and a hat like a knight's helmet, or those being used by the mountaineers of the Caucasus Region.—The more the dress has a military appearance, the better, in my opinion.

With complete respect and devotion I have the honor of being
Your Excellency's
humble servant
16 December 1838 F. Wrangell

Notes

1. In the official inquiry to F. P. Wrangell of 15 December 1838, Ya. A. Druzhinin asked advice about what form the hat should be and how best to use the brocade for sewing the kaftan for the Stikine toion Kuatke (RGIA, f. 18, op. 5, d. 1306, l. 4–5).

{13} TsGIA, f. 18, op. 5, d. 1306, l. 1–1ob. /Copy/

Report of the Board of Directors of the Russ.-Am. C.
of 2 December 1838. No. 1509.

To His Excellency
General of the Infantry,
Member of the State Council, Senator,
Minister of Finances and Count
Egor Frantsevich Kankrin

l. 1

The governor of the Russian-American Company, Captain of the Guards 1st rank Kupreianov, by dispatch No. 228 of 1 May of the present year, informs the Board of Directors of the Company, that with his, M[r.] Kupreianov's, permission a Kolosh boy of 4 years was brought to Sitka from the Stakhin, whom the Koloshi there assigned to be killed in commemoration of the deaths of their relatives; but the Stakhin toion Kuakhte Kuatke, as a consequence of the admonitions of the priest Veniaminov[1] about the cessation of this ungodly terrible custom, first gave an example and freed those doomed to death, including as well the mentioned boy, having replaced the killing of slaves with donations of another kind, as it were in public certification of his attachment and respect for the Russians. For such praiseworthy behavior, the Governor could not distinguish toion Kuakhte, aside from issuing a certificate with an expression of gratitude, since he had

l. 1ob.

previously already been rewarded for devotion and zeal toward the Russians by a silver *Soiuznye Rossii* medal, and therefore [the governor] asks the Board of Directors about applying to obtain some different reward for Toion Kuakhte.

The young Kolosh, released by toion Kuakhte, was baptized in Sitka in the Greco-Russian faith and received the name Mikhail. He was placed among the number of students of the technical school there, with instruction to have special supervision for him. It may be that later this boy will serve as an intermediary between us and the Koloshi, for the introduction of gentle Christian customs to the barbarous people.

Having the most esteemed honor to report about this to Your Excellency, the Board of Directors of the Company takes the boldness to most humbly ask about petitioning and obtaining for Toion Kuakhte, a reward for such laudable behavior, and as an example to other savages, a golden kaftan or other such perceived sign of distinction.[2]

> Director Ivan Prokof'ev
> Director Nikolai Kusov
> Director Andrei Severin

Notes

1. This case was described by I. E. Veniaminov: in the commemoration potlatch one of the chiefs of the Stikine people did not kill, as usual, two of his slaves, rather set them free: one went to the

Russians, the other to an old Tlingit as a servant on the assumption that after his {the old Tlingit's} death he became an entirely free man (Veniaminov 1840a:134–135).

2. The delivery of the gift to the Stikine chief Kuakhte was sanctioned by the Emperor Nikolai I on the 9th of December 1838. The gift consisted of a brocade kaftan, belt, and hat.

{14} TsGIA, f. 18, op. 5, d. 1312, l. 1ob.–2ob.

November 3

Russian-American His Excellency
Company General of the Infantry
Board of Directors Member of the State Council

Senator, Minister of Finances,
1842 Count Egor Frantsievich
No. 1375 Kankrin

l. 1ob.

The suit MOST HUMBLY awarded to Toion Kuatkhe [1] was delivered to the Board of Directors at the Department of Manufacture and Trade on the 28th of March 1839 for No. 1567 and sent to the colonies to be issued to a proper person.
Meanwhile, in the winter of 1840, before putting in order the execution of the aforesaid HIGHEST will, Toion Kuatkhe was unworthy of the MOST ALL-MERCI-FUL reward, having killed his slave, without any specific reason in Koloshi custom. Such cruelty surprised the Koloshi themselves.—For this reason the colonial administration is resolved not to give Kuatkhe the MOST ALL-MERCIFUL reward.
Bringing this to the attention of the Board of Directors, the present Governor, Captain 1st rank

l. 2

Etolin, offers that for subduing the brutal customs of the Koloshi and for their gradual conversion to the Christian faith, it would be quite useful that as an intermediary between the Russians and Koloshi one of the Sitka Toions served who would for this purpose be raised to title of Head Toion of the Koloshi living in the Russian possessions. For this, in the opinion of the Governor of the colonies, the Sitka Kolosh Shchukh is found to be the most worthy, having entered the Orthodox faith six years ago and named Mikhail at Holy Epiphany, who in the present year received an important inheritance after the death of his close relative, one of the most principal Sitka Toions, and he [Shchukh] will adopt his name, Kukhkan, much respected by the Koloshi. Kolosh Mikhail, of quite good behavior, gentle peaceful disposition, is attached to the Russians and always accepts with gratitude the helpful counsel of the colonial administration, and therefore also deserves encouragement so that his useful example might work in this with great force on his fellow tribesmen.

At the same time Captain of the 1st Rank Etolin offers that for the greatest significance and influence on the head Sitka Kolosh, not only among the Koloshi, but also among

l. 2ob.

the Russians, it would be useful that this honorary title be given with the HIGHEST authorization, for declaring this among all the Koloshi living in the Russian possessions, and be accompanied by the same signs of encouragement as were awarded to the Stakhin Toion, Kuatkhe.

Finding the measure suggested by Captain of the 1st Rank Etolin quite good and, because of the nearness of the English, necessary not only for the benefit of the Company, but in general for increasing our influence on the Koloshi living in the Russian possessions, the Board of Directors of the Russian-American Company is so bold as to most humbly ask Your Excellency about obtaining for the Kolosh Mikhail [Kukhkan] the title of Most Principal Sitka Toion and deigning to give him the honorable clothing intended for the Stakhin Toion Kuatkhe, but for the above-described reasons not given to him.

> [signatures:]
> Wrangell
> Severin
> Directors Prokof'ev
> Kusov

Notes

1. This is another, perhaps more correct, variation of the name of the Stikine chief who has already been mentioned in the documents as Kuakhte.

{15} AVPR, f. RAK, op. 888, d. 1006, l. 102ob.–103 /Copy/

[1840] No. 76, July 23. Under the patronage of
HIS HIGHEST IMPERIAL MAJESTY,
from the Russian-American Company
Governor of the Russian Colonies in America,
Fleet Captain 2nd rank and Cavalier Etolin.

l. 102ob.

CERTIFICATE

This is given to the Icy Strait Kolosh Toion, Gkemkiut, [1] for the fact that he was awarded the Silver badge by me: *Soiuznye Rossii* for the zeal shown by him toward

l. 103

the Russians in delivering procurements to the Russian-American Company, [2] and in the expectation that he, Toion Gkemkiut, will in the future also show such devotion to us making himself worthy of his distinction.—In certification of which this is given to him with My signature and a seal affixed.

Northwest Coast of America, Port of Novo-Arkhangel'sk,
23rd of July 1840
of his imperial majesty my most all-merciful sovereign,
by Fleet Captain 2nd rank and Cavalier,
Governor of the Russian Colonies in America
/signature/
A. Etolin

Notes

1. One of the Tlingit chiefs of the Hoonah k̲wáan.
2. Toion Gkemkiut arrived in Novo-Arkhangel'sk especially to invite the Russians to his village for trade, since the Indians had at this time accumulated about 60 sea otter skins. For this he received the silver medal from A. K. Etolin, which had been awarded sometime before to the other chief of the Hoonah, Koadchini, and after his death was returned by the Indians to the Russians.

{16} AVPR, f. RAK, op. 888, d. 1008, l. 2–2ob. /Copy/

1842, No. 2, January 8. To the Novo-Arkhangel'sk Office
[Instructions of A. K. Etolin]

l. 2

The employee of the company, Arkhangel'sk peasant Pavel Chubarov, by the petition submitted to me of the 5th of January asks permission to enter into legal matrimony with the bride he named, baptized Kolosh woman, Nastasia. If there is no lawful hindrance to this marital union, I propose

l. 2ob

that the Novo-Arkhangel'sk office make a report to the priest here, Andrei Sizykh, about marrying these people by official church regulations.

{17} Ibid., l. 15ob.

1842, No. 14, January 27. To the Novo-Arkhangel'sk Office
[Instructions of A. K. Etolin]

l. 15ob.

I forward with this three silver badges to be kept in the Novo-Arkhangel'sk office: *Soiuznye Rossii*, which remain after the deaths here of the Sitka Kolosh Toions: Liushtykh Ashteinat[1] (having received the name Ion at Holy Epiphany), Kukhkan,[2] and Khudtse;—two badges with certifications issued by My predecessor of the 16th of June and the 22nd of September 1837, for Nos. 348 and 399, and the third without certificate, probably lost by the Koloshi after the death of Toion Khudtse.

Notes

1. This was one of the first Sitka people who accepted Orthodoxy in the time of Baranov. According to I. G. Voznesenskii, "Tayon Ionka" was also a shaman (LO AAN, f. 46, op. 1, ed. khr. No. 3, l. 19).
2. This was the uncle of "the chief Sitka toion" Mikhail Kukhkan.

{18} AVPR, f. RAK, op. 888, d. 1009, l. 421ob.–422ob. /Copy/

[1843] No. 447, May 17. Report to the Board of Directors of the Company [by A. K. Etolin]

l. 421ob.

In consequence of my preliminary notification to the Board of Directors in the dispatch of the 24th of May of the past year under No. 417, about the baptizing of the Sitka Koloshi begun on the 20th of May by the Mission here, and about

l. 422

the instructions I made for the gradual rapprochement of these newly baptized Koloshi with the Russians, at the present time I have the honor to report to the Board of Directors that such baptism is successfully continued, as well as the use of them {the Koloshi}, at their own request, in temporary and daily work for the Company. Some of these Koloshi have even been on voyages on our ships, and three wished to enter permanently into the service of the Company, of whom one is located in Novo-Arkhangel'sk and another sent to Kodiak, while the third is at Mikhailovskii redoubt. With pleasure I repeat that which I indicated in the dispatch under No. 417, that those Koloshi with a present-day significant number of decrepit and incapable people here serve us as great reinforcement for the cutting of firewood for the Steamships, carrying loads, and various other gross work at the Port, which in the future will always be kept in mind here, for the

l. 422ob.

advantageous replacement by them of workers necessary in other occupations. About which I have the honor of reporting to the Board of Directors.

[1843] No. 553, October 10. Under the PATRONAGE
OF HIS IMPERIAL MAJESTY,
the Russian-American Company,
Governor of the Russian Colonies in America Fleet
Captain 1st rank and Cavalier Etolin
CERTIFICATE

l. 539ob.–540

This is given to the Honorable Baptized Sitka Kolosh Mikhail Kukhkan for the fact that the Board of Directors of the Russian-American Company, as a consequence of my idea of starting the institution of the Title of Chief Sitka Kolosh Toion and of the petition for this Title for Mikhail Kukhkan and of his reward of honorable clothing with respect to his personal merits proven by continual devotion to the Russians and zeal in the fulfillment of the will of the Colonial administration, submitted this idea to the Minister of Finances, as a consequence of which His Excellency [1] made it known by written instruction to the Board of Directors of the Company that HIS IMPERIAL MAJESTY, through representation of the Committee of Ministers, on the 8th day of December 1842, by order deigned to allow the institution of the title of Chief Toion in the Russian-American Colonies with the fact that the confirmation of the above-mentioned depended on the Ministry of Finances and on this basis to confirm with the title of Chief Toion the Kolosh Mikhail

l. 540ob.

Kukhkan and with respect to his personal merits to issue him the MOST ALL-MERCIFULLY the awarded honorable clothing. In fulfillment of such will OF HIS MOST HIGH IMPERIAL MAJESTY, proclaimed by me about this to everyone's knowledge, in order that each and all, both the Russians and the native people henceforth recognize Mikhail Kukhkan as the Chief Sitka Kolosh Toion and render to him the proper respect according to his title. The clothing MOST HIGHLY awarded him was entrusted to him by me on the 10th of October 1843, after which in the Cathedral here he was led in the proper oath under the title of Chief Toion. In the certification of which he, Mikhail Kukhkan, was also given this Certificate after being signed by Me and with a seal affixed and in firm assurance that he by all powers will endeavor to completely render himself worthy of such great

l. 541

MONARCHIAL mercy, by customary steadfast devotion to the Russians; by modest behavior to serve as an example for his fellow countrymen and as far as possible to contribute to subduing the brutality of their customs, and in general to honestly zealously and with willingness carry out all the instructions of the Colonial Administration. The Port of Novo-Arkhangel'sk, on the Northwest Coast of America. 10 October 1843.

of his imperial majesty
My MOST ALL-MERCIFUL SOVEREIGN,
Fleet Captain 1st rank,
of the Russian Colonies in America
Governor /origin. signed/
A. Etolin

Notes

1. Count E. F. Kankrin, minister of finances.

{20} AVPR, f. RAK, op. 888, d. 1011, l. 312ob. /Copy/

[1845] No. 267, May 14. To the Novo-Arkhangel'sk Office [Instruction of A. K. Etolin]

l. 312ob.

In respect of the fact that the Employee [RAC] Karl Dal'strem[1] supported a young baptized Kolosh girl, Praskovia Larionova,[2] whose mother ran off to the Koloshi, I suggest the Novo-Arkhangel'sk Office give Dal'strem 100 rubles annually toward the livelihood and dress of this girl until she is of such age, that is, 7 years old, that she can be taken into the girls school here; she is now going on 5 years old.

Notes

1. *Iz findliandskikh urozhentsev* [of Finnish born], that is, a Finnish Swede. He served in the Russian colonies from 1822 as a sail master. He was married to the Russian-Tlingit Mestizo (Creole) Natalia Kabachakova and had four children by her.
2. This was the illegitimate daughter of the RAC "employee" Prokofii Larionov.

{21} Ibid., l. 151ob.

[1845] No. 5, May 30. To the Novo-Arkhangel'sk Office
[Instruction of the governor's aide, D. F. Zarembo]

l. 151ob.

According to the verbal order of the former Governor of the Colonies, Adolph Karlovich Etolin, I suggest in his absence that the Novo-Arkhangel'sk office issue to the Kolosh Toion Nak-akan wares amounting to 150 rubles, for the young Kolosh Fedor, illegitimate son of the Company employee Mikhail Ivanov and write off the amount toward debit [accounts].

{22} AVPR, f. RAK, op. 888, d. 1013, l. 206ob.–207 /Copy/

[1846] No. 270, May 5. To the Board of Directors of the Company [Report of M. D. Teben'kov] Regarding the Kolosh igrushka.

l. 206ob.

Following as far as possible my Predecessor in all actions,[1] upon arrival in Sitka I stated to the Koloshi that in March I intended to organize an *igrushka* for them as evidence of our good will and favor toward them. At the announced time up to 1500 of them gathered, excluding slaves. The *igrushka* lasted, as before, two days, the 12th and 16th of April, and cost 1389 rubles 91 3/4 kopecks.

Regarding the *igrushka* for the Koloshi, I agreed with the opinion of my Predecessor, that it is quite sufficient to have one *igrushka* for each Governor, once in 5 years,—strictly as I mentioned, in order to show the Koloshi good will on our part,—no other motives can be seen for this.

l. 207

I advised [gave notice to] the Koloshi in September that there would be an *igrushka* in March or April, advised {them} not to come with empty hands, but the *igrushka* did not bring any profit in this case, excluding as I mentioned in my Report under No. 256 that during this meeting of the Koloshi, the market was heaped with food supplies: halibut, *yamanina* [wild sheep?], wild fowl, and so on.—This is one benefit which the *igrushka* could provide us.[2]

About which I have the honor to report to the Board of Directors.

Notes

Mikhail Dmitrievich Teben'kov: governor of Russian America from 1845 to 1850.

1. Meaning A. K. Etolin, governor of Russian America from 1840 to 1845.

2. It would be strange to consider reciprocal gifts on the part of the Tlingit: this would be contrary to the order of the traditional potlatch.

{23} AVPRI, f. RAK, op. 888, d. 1014, l. 195 /copy/

[1847] No. 29 April 4. Kodiak Office [M. D. Teben'kov's orders]
About the dispatch on the Schooner Tungus *of a Kolosh family.*

l. 195.

On the schooner *Tungus* now is sent to Kodiak to live a Kolosh family which escaped the persecution of their fellow tribesmen.[1] I suggest the Office place them in a favorable location not far from the [Pavlovskii] harbor where they might sell their industry [the furs and products procured by them]. A barabara and all management, as is necessary, to provide them at Company expense and to try to bring them close to the Russians in order to teach them to speak Russian. We need Kolosh interpreters.—The time smooths hate [the Kolosh toward the exiles] and from this family the children can be later good as interpreters for us.[2]

Notes

1. This is obviously a matter of a Tlingit family that was accused of sorcery and escapes through the protection of the Russians.
2. Little is known about the fate of this Tlingit family. A dispute is mentioned in RAC documents for 1848 that occurred in the family after it was on Kodiak—the mother of the family drove her daughter out of the house in freezing weather and she nearly died of the cold (AVPRI, f. RAK, op. 888, d. 1016, l. 134–134ob.).

{24} AVPR, f. RAK, op. 888, d. 1015, l. 57ob.–61 /Copy/

[1847] No. 370, May 12. To the Board of Directors of the Company
[Report of M. D. Teben'kov] About the ransom of kalgi (slaves)

l. 57ob.

To the Board of Directors of the Company the barbaric inhuman disposition and customs of the Koloshi are of course not obscure. With all the effort on our side, about fifty years in the mollification of this barbarian people, our influence in this case is still only barely noticeable. It

l. 58

is known that the Koloshi are divided into clans, regarding their origin or birth, some from the Raven, others from the Wolf, Eagle, and so on. Each clan knows the place of its birth in its traditions, and that village is considered to be the place where the clan began. After a known period of time (8 years) the whole clan gathers in its ancestral village and organizes the so-called *igrushka* [potlatch]. There they recall past deeds, deliberate on future enterprises, invite guests from other clans, drink, eat, dance, and give to all comers whatever and however. In this last, the vanity sometimes reaches such a frenzy that a Kolosh will carry all his fortune to a sandbank: cut to pieces his best furs or fabrics, scatter beads, tobacco—everything he has—and finally in a rage of liberality comes

l. 58ob.

even to subject (with the help of his family) to death his slaves (*kalgi*), taking in this case the slaves as household items. This inhumane custom, the root of which is vanity, {and} cannot be said to be necessary for this festival, sometimes passes without human blood; but the quite violent desire of vanity arrives in an instant on this occasion in those who love glory, and the unfortunate victims fall under the blows of the dagger or a long stick placed on the neck.[1] Participation in the festival is required by the whole clan, and if any Kolosh of a clan can not be present during this time at the festival in the ancestral village, then he has to act the same in the village where he lives. Thus, the Koloshi of the Raven clan, whose ancestral village is in Icy Strait, had to celebrate this period or its clan festival while living under our walls at Sitka.[2]

l. 59

The frenzy of the festive came, as I mentioned, precisely to the fact that many carried all their fortune to the sand banks and scattered it in shreds, while some who had slaves with them began to stab and choke them.—This was at the beginning of March, and so secret was the accomplishment of the crime that 8 souls had already been killed (all females) when we learned of this. I immediately sent an interpreter[3] to announce that such an evil deed was not to be under our walls, {and if} in this way vanity is {to be} satisfied—not to spare anything— then better to have them sell the *kalgi* to us, to take goods and scatter them as they want.—This acted on the Koloshi, and we thus acquired a one-year-old boy (taken to be brought up by the former bookkeeper Kondakov according to

l. 59ob.

his own desire) and 2 adult girls.[4] This is one of the most important killings among the Koloshi occurring during peace and even for amusement.

Another kind of killing among the Koloshi is from superstition. Among them the honorable [that is, noble] or Toion: he himself or his wife, or children can by no means die a natural death. They look for reasons and the shaman finally finds that the deceased was defiled by so and so (for the most part, women from poor families are guilty). Here the idea exists among the Koloshi of such kind {in which a noble dies}: {and} relatives of the deceased seize the falsely accused and all torture her until she confesses. The measures of the torture are such that there was no example of the presumed guilty not admitting their guilt, that they in fact killed the deceased by corruption.

l. 60

Then the unfortunate takes her final position. If compassion could be found in the torturers, and they wanted to give her life—to pardon her, then at the same time the dagger of a relative of her family strikes her: a brother, uncle, and sometimes even a son—from the shame of having such a relative.

Thus, with the death of some of the honorable Koloshi, two victims are at the present time being tortured: one a young woman, the other a woman who has a husband and four children. The voice of persuasion, and more ransom for the girl of 5 blankets made the Koloshi hesitate, they released her to us in the fort, and I paid for her not on the account of the Company, rather by taking up a collection from the honorable [inhabitants of Novo-Arkhangel'sk], so that they [the Tlingit] saw our [Christian] teaching at work, and along with this saw with their own eyes those individuals who were prepared in such a case to donate in order to save their neighbor.—The woman was released without payment,

l. 60ob.

but she had to be healed: her stomach had been cut with a knife. Through the art of our medics she was healed, and does not for the world want to return to her village. For fear that the Koloshi at sometime would again resume their claim to her, she and all her family: husband, two sons, and two daughters I sent off (at their request) to Kodiak (Protocol No. 29). I sent the girls for the same reason to the Kurile Islands[5] (Protocol 109).

There is a third kind of killing among the Koloshi, and also only slaves (*kalgi*)—this is to send servants to the other world to the deceased: male slaves for men, female slaves for women.[6]

Through my persuasion one such slave has been saved at the present time—and even without payment. I took him and sent him to live in Mikhailovskii Redoubt,

l. 61

in the service.

Representing to the Board of Directors, {regarding} the barbaric customs of the Koloshi and the measures I took in this case toward averting and saving unfortunate victims, I am at present entirely obliged to our interpreter the Koloshi, Niktopolion Gedeonov, for saving 10 of the above-mentioned souls, who Gedeonov announced to the Koloshi my opinion and instruction and who himself took no less part in saving these unfortunates. For which deed, as well as for his continual devotion and zeal toward the Company (since 1822), I most humbly request that the Board of Directors of the Company petition for Gedeonov a respectable Monarchial reward, which can make a great useful influence on the Koloshi.

About which I have the honor to report to the Board of Directors of the Company.

Notes

1. That is, slaves were strangled by pressing a stick on the neck of the victim.
2. Evidently, in this case it was a matter of the L'uknax̱.ádi clan, whose representatives moved to Sitka from the Hoonah ḵwáan.
3. Niktopolion Gedeonov.
4. One of them they called Kattakhel', the other was baptized in Novo-Arkhangel'sk and received the name Irina (Irina Khaske).

5. The Indian women ransomed from slavery were sent off on the brig *Promysel* to Urup Island, where there was a RAC hunting artel at that time.
6. That is, it concerns the funeral potlatch.

{25} Ibid., l. 114ob.

[1847] No. 424, May 21. To Petr Epifanov who is managing Mikhailovskii Redoubt [Instructions of M. D. Teben'kov]
On the account of the
Kolosh Pavel Litinakhkuti

l. 114ob.

The Kolosh Pavel Litinakhkuti, removed in the last year on the brig *Okhotsk* from Mikhailovskii Redoubt, who worked there in the service, launched the complaint that he was not completely satisfied with the salary that has been assigned to him for his service.—Therefore I direct you, Epifanov, for clarification of this affair to present to the Novo-Arkhangel'sk Office a detailed and clear Account of this Kolosh at the time of his presence in your redoubt.

{26} AVPR, f. RAK, op. 888, d. 1018, l. 373ob.–374 /Copy/

[1850] No. 113, December 28. To the Novo-Arkhangel'sk Clerical Administration [Inquiry of N. Ya. Rozenberg]

l. 373ob.

The peasant Pavel Semenov, of the Yaroslav Province, employed in the service of the Russian-American Company, came to me with a request in which he writes that he "in 1843, with the permission of the Colonial Administration, was contracted in legal marriage to the girl Avdot'ia

l. 374

Ignat'eva, daughter of the deceased Company employee Polikarp Ignat'ev, who {the daughter} lived with him Semenov until 1845, {and} for reasons unknown to him, left him for the Koloshi, where she is at this time—and that all the efforts undertaken by him in the course of five years to return her from there remained entirely unsuccessful, therefore he, Semenov, at the present time asks me to use the measures available to me to return his legal wife Avdot'ia from the Koloshi.
For the settlement of this request of the employee of the Company, Pavel Semenov, I need information about this concerning whether the deceased Company employee Polikarp Ignat'ev had been married to the Kolosh woman Makrida, with whom he had had the daughter Avdot'ia—presently Pavel Semenov's wife—or if

he lived with her and had children from her, including the daughter Avdot'ia, outside of marriage?

As a consequence of which I most humbly ask the Novo-Arkhangel'sk Clerical Administration to order the one who should provide information to write a certificate from the original books of metrics {statistics} of the Cathedral here, and to honor me with a following notification.

Notes

Nikolai Yakovlevich Rozenberg: governor of Russian America from 1850 to 1853.

{27} AVPR, f. RAK, op. 888, d. 1020, l. 411ob.–412ob. /Copy/

No. 598, 14 July 1852. To the Board of Directors of the Company [Report of N. Ya. Rozenberg]
About the Kolosh attack on the Goriachie Kliuchi [Hot Springs]

l. 411ob.

In the supplement to my dispatch of the 7th of this past June under No. 501 I hasten to report to the Board of Directors of the Company that about ten days later, after the departure of the ship "Kodiak" to Ayan, on the 14th of this same month of June, not far from Ozerskii Redoubt, the Koloshi (according to suspicion, Stakhin) robbed of completely everything ten people of our redoubt, employees who were seining fish in one of the bays nearest the redoubt, and was done by them or others on this same day, but (through suspicion) also by the Stakhin Koloshi an open attack on our Hot Springs, which ended in complete robbery of all those who lived at the Springs, for use by our people, killing one of them, and burning to the ground all the Company structures existing there.

During this attack on the Springs, those there to use them were: Lieutenant Matskevich; the American Chait, who lived in Sitka; Nikolai, son of Druzhinin who arrived this spring in the

l. 412

Colonies for service; and the employees: Nikolai Matveev, Aleksei Panov, Gustav Lundstrem, and Nikolai Nabokov; in addition to these persons, at the Springs were: the manager of the Springs, doctor's student Platon Benzeman, and M[r.] Matskevich's orderly, Yan Raevskii. Of them: M[essrs.] Matskevich and Chait, and the employees Panov and Lundstrem, as well as Raevskii and Benzeman were saved by flight from the Springs through the forest and mountains to Ozerskii Redoubt, from where on the next day they were brought to Novo-Arkhangel'sk on the Steamer *Nikolai I*. Nikolai [Druzhinin] was saved by Kaigani Koloshi who were in Kliuchevskaia Bay at that time and was also brought on the next day on the

Steamer to the Port. The employee Matveev, being stunned by a blow to the head, lay almost a whole day under a tree stump, not being noticed by the robbers, and was saved only by this. 4 days after the incident that occurred this employee was taken by a Kaigani Kolosh woman to Ozerskii Redoubt, from where he was then brought to the Port on the Steamer. Employee Nabokov was killed. The beheaded body of whom was delivered to the Port by Sitka Koloshi several days later, and by certification

l. 412ob.

of the Medics, that this body was in fact the body of Nabokov, was given burial according to Christian ceremony.

Notes

Hot Springs: Such was called the place south of Novo-Arkhangel'sk where there were hot sulphur springs that were used by the Tlingit and employees of the RAC for the treatment of various ills. The company constructed three small cabins for the ill at the springs.

{28} Ibid., d. 1024, l. 124ob. /Copy/

No. 318, 11 June 1858. To the Novo-Arkhangel'sk Office
About the Kolosh boy Sakhlia [Instruction of S. V. Voevodskii]

l. 124ob.

On the bark *Nakhimov* the Kolosh boy Sakhlia, whom the Novo-Arkhangel'sk Office has decently provided with footwear and clothing as far as the Port of Ayan, will set off to the Port of Ayan for two years for the study of the Russian language.
Up to 300 rubles in bills per year are designated toward his expenses in the Port of Ayan, which expenditure, according to assignments of the Ayan office, as well as the expenditure of the present outfitting of Sakhlia, the Novo-Arkhangel'sk Office writes off toward trade expenditures for Colonial production.

Notes

Stepan Vasil'evich Voevodskii: governor of Russian America from 1854 to 1859.

{29} AVPR, f. RAK, op. 888, d. 1022, l. 78ob.–79 /Copy/

List of wounded and dead during the battle with the Koloshi, 11 March 1855

Documentary Appendix

l. 78ob.

Table 12. Wounded and Dead during the Battle with the Koloshi, 11 March 1855

Name	Year in company service	Wages/ salary	Means of death
1. Ivanov, Aleksandr, 4th Fleet Crew boatswain	1840	700	Killed in service
2. Panfilov, Apolinarii, Tiumen peasant	1850	350	Killed in service
3. Kliuev, Aleksei, 25th Fleet Crew boatswain	1850	500	Died of wounds
4. Kuznetsov, Fedor, Rubinsk townsman, helper	1852	450	Died of wounds
5. Samoilov, Nikolai, S. Petersburg townsman, Keeper of the Company's Store	1849	2,500	Died of wounds
Sailors of the Fleet Crew			
6. Spiridonov, Afonasii, 16th Crew	1854	350	
7. Nemchinov, Ignatii, 16th Crew	1854	350	Died of wounds
l. 79			
8. Ivanov, Ivan, 17th Crew	1854	350	
9. Larionov, Grigorii, 18th Crew	1854	350	
10. Nikolaev, Lavr, 11th Crew	1854	350	
11. Maksimov, Nikolai, 16th Crew	1854	350	
12. Vasil'ev, Mikhailo 26th Crew	1850	350	
13. Patenga, Grzhegoush 22nd Crew	1850	350	[was wounded by Koloshi on the 10th of March when he guarded the woodshed]
14th Siberian Line Battalion			
14. Baranov, Aleksei, ensign	1854	2,338	
15. Baluev, Samoilo, private	1854	350	
16. Karpov, Karp, private	1854	350	
17. Chebukin, Roman, private	1854	350	
Finnish Employees			
18. Il'man, Karl	1851	400	

Table 12. Continued

19. Niulund, Aleksandr	1848	450	
20. Shvedberg, Iogan	1851	350	
21. Anderson, Karl	1851	350	
	Creole		
22. Rysev, Ivan	1821	450	Died of wounds

{30} Ibid., l. 136ob.–137

No. 215, 30 September 1855. To the Board of Directors
About the Stakhin Koloshi [Report of S. V. Voevodskii]

l. 136ob.

Those who were under the authority of the Novo-Arkhangel'sk Clerical Administration seminary, the seminarians Iona Storozhevskii and Ivan Nadezhdin and the
wife of the Artillery Non-Commissioned Officer Lipatov[1] with a 4-year-old foster
child,[2] having engaged two paddlers from the Koloshi, set off in a boat to Ozerskii
Redoubt, but on the way they were met by seven boats of Stakhin Koloshi who,
having fallen upon them, {and} killed the Seminarian Storozhevskii, the Koloshi,
and Lipatov's wife with the first shots, severely wounded Nadezhdin, took him to
the Hot Springs, and, having learned from him that he was a Russian, left him
there.

From the springs Nadezhdin returned through the mountains to Ozerskii Redoubt, and from there was brought up here [to

l. 137

Novo-Arkhangel'sk] and at present is recovering. He gave all the details of this
incident, from which it is evident that the Stakhin people made this attack to get
vengeance against our Koloshi [that is, the Sitka people] for the Stakhin people
they killed in 1850.[3]

At the present time information has reached me through the Koloshi that the
4-year-old foster child that was with Lipatova remained alive and is among the
Stakhin people. Therefore I wrote to Mr. Douglas,[4] Chief manager of the Hudson's
Bay possessions, about ransoming this boy and bringing him to us on the first
occasion.[5]

In general, our relations with the Stakhin people are a hindrance during the
course of the lease of Fort Stakhin, since even with the means to punish the
Stakhin people, the Hudson's Bay Company could lodge complaints for possible
interference in their affairs.

Notes

1. Non-Commissioned Officer Gavrila Lipatov was married to the Creole Ekaterina Eremina.

2. Adopted son, Creole boy Plotnitsyn.
3. The date indicated is inaccurate. It should be: 1852.
4. See the letter from S. V. Voevodskii to J. Douglas of 13 (25) September 1855, in which this episode is described and contains the request for assistance in ransoming the Creole Plotnitsyn (AVPR, f. RAK, op. 888, d. 1022, l. 127–1270b.).
5. Later, the Stakhin people told the Russians that the Creole boy perished during their attack (AVPR, f. RAK, op. 888, d. 1025, l. 164–1640b.).

{31} AVPR, f. RAK, op. 888, d. 1024, l. 106–106ob. /Copy/

No. 293, 20 June 1859. Certificate [from S. V. Voevodskii]

l. 106

This certificate is given to the Kolosh clan Toion Aleksei for the fact that he from April 1855 conducted

l. 106ob.

himself impeccably and humbly and rendered a good disposition toward the Russians—for which he is given by me a copper *tyn* (shield).[1] In the attestation of which this certificate is given to him with my signature and a seal affixed.

Notes

1. That is, a copper plate (in Tlingit: "*tinne*").

{32} Ibid., d. 1025, l. 217 / Copy/

No. 646, 30 December 1860. To the Novo-Arkhangel'sk Office.
About the assignment of salary to Toion Kaliakh [Instructions from I. V. Furuhjelm]

l. 217

I suggested to the office to provide from 1 January of the coming year a payment of 240 rub. *ass.* {rubles in banknotes} per year without rations to the Kolosh toion Aleksei Kaliakh.

Notes

Ivan Vasil'evich Furuhjelm: governor of Russian America from 1859 to 1863.

{33} Ibid., l. 102ob. /Copy/

No. 346, 10 July 1861. Certificate [from I. V. Furuhjelm]

l. 102ob.

Given to the Sitka Kolosh Mikhail Kinukve, because he is well behaved and has always carried out the wishes of the Colonial Administration with zeal.— In certification of which he Kinukve is given this certificate with my signature and a seal affixed.—Port of Novo-Arkhangel'sk. July 10, 1861.

{34} AVPR, f. RAK, op. 888, d. 1025, 120ob. /Copy/

No. 424, 9 October 1861. To the Board of Directors
About the release by the Sitka Koloshi of kalgi
[Report of I. V. Furuhjelm]

l. 120ob.

I have the honor of reporting to the Board of Directors that the Sitka Koloshi, on account of the renewal of barabaras[1] and commemoration of the dead, following my persuasion, gave all the Koloshi they intended to kill to the Company or released them, totaling 3 men and 16 women who now live at the Port.

Notes

Kalgi: by this Kamchadal word the Russians meant slaves taken from the Native inhabitants of Russian America.

1. That is, on account of reconstruction of houses, which usually terminated in a potlatch with human sacrifice.

{35} Ibid., l. 125–125ob. /Copy/

No. 448, 9 October 1861. Certificate [from I. V. Furuhjelm]

l. 125

This is given to the native of the Russian American colonies from the Kolosh tribe, the girl Aleksandra, being this day 14 years of age, to attest that she in 1852,

l. 125ob.

with permission of the Colonial Administration, was taken to be raised by the son of the Akhtyrsk merchant, Aleksandr Ivanov Dziubin, and at present follows him in departing from the Colonies to Russia. In attestation of which this certificate with signature and seal affixed by the Governor of the Colonies is given to her.—

Port of Novo-Arkhangel'sk on the Northwest Coast of America.—October 9th, 1861.

{36} AVPRI, f. RAK, op. 888, d. 1026, l. 110ob. /Copy/

No. 418, 2 November 1862
Certificate [from I. V. Furuhjelm]

1. 110ob.

This is given with a suitable inscription and affixing of the stamp to the Kolosh Kaiur Woman Tsamka, of seven and a half years of age, to attest to the fact that she was ransomed from servitude from the Kolosh Toion Naskhyaan on the 20th of September 1859 by being in the service of the Rus. Amer. company by M[r.] Bergmeister [1] Yalmar Vasil'evich Furuhjelm [2] for six hundred fifty rubles currency. In the presence of the Kolosh Toion Mikhail Kukhkan.—Port of Novo-Arkhangel'sk on the Northwest Coast of America.—November 2, 1862.

Notes

1. An officer's rank in the Corps of Mining Engineers that corresponds to the rank of army captain or captain in the cavalry.
2. Brother of Russian America governor I. V. Furuhjelm.

{37} AVPRI, f. RAK, op. 888, d. 1026, l. 33–33ob. /Copy/

No. 153, 1 May 1863
To the Board of Directors [report of I. V. Furuhjelm]
On the true affair of the Aleut Anisim Bashurov

l. 33

In the addition to my report No. 16, of January 15th of this year, I have the honor of presenting with this a true investigated affair of the Aleut Bashurov, found killed, and to report that for finding the guilty on February 20th of this year, two Kolosh were taken into custody: Kekat and Kutyng, who after several days testified that the killing was carried out by the Kolosh Foma, who was then in Icy Strait.

On the basis of this evidence, in order to find the Kolosh Foma, the steam ship *V[elikii] K[niaz'] Konstantin* was sent off to Icy Strait, which, returning on March 13th to Novo-Arkhangel'sk, delivered the mentioned Kolosh, taken by the commander [of the steamer] Lindfors by force.

The testimony of the Kolosh Foma and the other Koloshi, who caught him in the crime, though there is no clear proof for charging him, there is nevertheless some suspicion by reason of his hasty departure to Icy Strait, this is why I recognized the necessity to remove Kolosh Foma

l. 33ob.

from Sitka, having sent him to reside in Kodiak until the discovery of all the details of the affair about Bashurov.
About which I have the honor to report to the Board of Directors.

{38} AVPRI, f. RAK, op. 888, d. 1027, l. 28ob.–29 /Copy/

No. 86, 6 April 1866
Certificate [from D. P. Maksutov]

l. 28ob.

This is given to the Kolosh Kaagwaantaan Gana<u>k</u>nau in the fact that he is of good conduct and always carried out the wish

l. 29

of the Colonial Authority with zeal. In certification of which he, Gana<u>k</u>nau, is also given this certificate signed by me and affixed with a seal.
Port of Novo-Arkhangel'sk. May 6, 1866.

Notes

Prince Maksutov, Dmitrii Petrovich: Last governor of Russian America 1863–1867.

Introduction

1. Here and henceforth, the collective term "Europeans" refers broadly to the bearers of Euro-American culture: Russian, English, Spanish, American, etc. Correspondingly, in this work the term "European culture" is used to contrast the foreigners' culture with "Indian" or "traditional Tlingit" culture.

2. Most Alaska place names are spelled according to the *Dictionary of Alaska Place Names* by Donald J. Orth (Washington, DC: USGPO, 1967).—Trans.

3. The Russians were still using the Julian calendar, which differs from the Gregorian (whose date appears in parentheses) by 12 days. Present-day Baranof Island was then Sitka Island.—Trans.

4. Here and throughout the manuscript, information in square brackets, except where otherwise noted, is that of A. V. Grinev, the author.

1. Tlingit Indians before Contact with Europeans

1. The descendants of the "early Alaskans" were, according to Swanton, members of the Tlingit clan *Sit'kwedí* (Swanton 1908:412).

2. De Laguna pointed out these differences in the language of the southern and northern Tlingit (De Laguna 1972:1:16).

3. Kan indicated that among the Tlingit there existed a funerary potlatch, which was organized after the funeral, and a potlatch proper—a wake—a year or so after the death of a kinsman (Kan 1983:47).

4. The Tlingit themselves probably did not differentiate the abstract ideas of "clan," "lineage," and "community"). According to De Laguna's (1972:1:212) information, they designated all these social unities by the general word *naa*—clan. However, analysis of the functioning of Tlingit society convinces one of the legitimacy of the division of the named unities. The clan (or part of it—the lineage) was a unit of the social structure, while the clan community (or simply community) was a socioeconomic organism that consisted of representatives of several clans for matrimonial and work purposes.

5. Avunculocality is an anthropological term that applies, in this case, to the fact that a boy's uncle (mother's brother) is his father (though not biological) and that he lives with him, inherits from him, etc.

6. The emergence of the Kaagwaantaan from a sublineage of a separate household is corroborated by the name of the clan: *kaukan'ittan*—designating literally "occupants of the house that was burned by the fire" (Veniaminov 1840a:33). According to the legend, the Kaagwaantaan obtained their nickname after the Wolf House in the settlement of Kaknau of the Hoonah k̲wáan, which belonged to them, burned down (Swanton 1909:326–334, 338). The Kaagwaantaan considered Kaknau (Ka̲knuwu—"the fort of

the ptarmigan") to be the "capital" of their clan (De Laguna 1960:142). However, they were forced to leave this settlement after they were defeated by the Naanya.aayí clan of the Stikine kwáan. This defeat occurred despite the fact that the Kaagwaantaan were known for their warlike character and fearlessness, which both Lisianskii and Litke pointed out (Lisianskii 1812:151; Litke 1834:141). Veniaminov wrote that "the Kukontani were famous not for any heroic deeds but only for their large number of people: their number was so great that they also had their subdivisions." (Veniaminov 1840a:33). One such lineage—the Sitka Kaagwaantaan—settled under the walls of the capital of Russian America, Novo-Arkhangel'sk, where its members formed the most high-strung part of the Native population (see chapter 2 of this monograph).

7. The matri-clan societies are geographically widespread and often form among peoples standing on the threshold of class formation. For example, the Minangkabau of Sumatra Island, the Garo of northeastern India, and the Ashanti of western Africa had a structure of social organization similar to that of the Tlingit (Maretin 1975:60–132; Maretina 1980:119–124; Popov 1982:39–82).

8. The suffixes -idí, -adi, -edi, -iadi, and -iati literally translate to "children," but in the English-language sources it is usually translated as "people" or "people of"; therefore, the name of the Tekweidí clan is interpreted as "people of Teko Island" (Oberg 1973:137).

9. Perhaps the only clan whose name completely corresponds to the "totemic" version was the Tliuknakhadi, whose name literally means "children (people) of the Salmon (Coho) clan." It is true that an Indian informant of De Laguna reported that this name was taken by the clan from a river Tl'iugunakh (or Tl'akunukh or Tl'iuknakh) near present-day Sitka (formerly Novo-Arkhangel'sk) (De Laguna 1972:1:226). It is possible that the name for the Kiksadi (Khikhchadi) clan, "children of the frog," had a similar origin.

10. The Indians came to know the starry heaven rather well and distinguished many constellations (the constellation of the Great Bear [Dipper]—the Yachte—was even a totem of the L'eeneidí clan). The Tlingit called the Milky Way Tlkaiak kosiite ("the tracks of Tlkaiak"), which refers to a mythological hero who undertook a trip through the heavens. Particular omens were connected with the passage of the planet Venus (Kekashagutli) through the heavens: the Indians believed that if the Morning Star rose over the mountains from the southeast, this signified bad weather, but if from the east, then good weather (Swanton 1908:418, 427, 451–452). Veniaminov reported that the Tlingit considered the sun a poor man, but the moon by contrast was thought to be rich. The spots on it, according to legend, were two boys (in J. P. Swanton's version— girls) who were "pulled" up by the moon because they mocked it (Swanton 1908:453; Veniaminov 1840a:85–86).

11. Spirits, which aided shamans in their activities, were chiefly those of different animals, especially the {river} otter. It can be supposed that the Otter was the totem of shamans because the Tlingit attributed to this animal the supernatural power to charm people (Krause 1956:185–186; Swanton 1908:456, 464; Veniaminov 1840a:62–63).

12. Thus, for example, the Raven was especially respected in the G̲aanax̲teidí and L'uknax̲.ádi clans, and the Killer Whale in the Dak̲l'aweidí, Kaagwaantaan, Woosh-keetaan, and Tsagweidi clans (Swanton 1908:416). Delocalized parts of a clan (a lineage)could keep the original totems and acquire new totems, which were often connected with separate sublineages. So, in the G̲aanax̲teidí clan there were such totems as the Raven, Frog, and Whale. At the level of the lineage, clan totems were added as follows: among the Tanta G̲aanax̲teidí were the totems of the Sea Star, Chum Salmon, and Hawk (Kijook in Tlingit), and among the Chilkat G̲aanax̲teidí the Wood Worm, Goose, {River} Otter, Owl, and Tsak̲k̲ini Creek. In the Chilkat Kaagwaantaan lineage only one sublineage had the "right" to the Shark totem, since, according to legend, the men of this lineage once caught shark instead of halibut, which the chief transformed into the totem (Olson 1967:42–44). In connection with the above account, one cannot agree with Dzeniskevich's conclusion that the "small clan associations, which were detached from the primary clan, had their own emblems, though frequently their emblem became the symbol of part of the previous totem. Among the clans that were separated from the Bear clan there were, for example, the Teeth clan or Bear Claws clan, the clan of its Paws" (Dzeniskevich 1985:61–62). In no historical sources have I encountered clans of Teeth, Claws, or Bear Paws. However, there do appear to be some: for example, the Killer Whale Tooth House in Angoon (Kan, personal communication). In addition, the name of a sublineage by no means always reflected the totem held sacred in it.

13. Among the Athapaskans of the interior mainland the Crow, rather than the Raven, is revered. There are also stories about the Raven among the tribes of the Bella Bella and Bella Coola, who live on the coast south of the Tsimshian, though the place of the Raven in their mythology is relatively insignificant, and the subjects are different from those of myths that are spread among the northern tribes (Boas 1928:11–35; McIlwraith 1948:2:386–419). The epic about the Raven was widely scattered among the indigenous population of Kamchatka and Chukotka as well, and also in part among the Eskimos and Aleuts of Alaska, and the Evenks and Yukagir of Siberia (Dzeniskevich 1976; Meletinskii 1981).

14. Teknonymy is the custom of naming a person after his or her child. In many societies people assume a new or additional name from time to time, that is, names are not lifelong, as ours are.

2. History of Tlingit Relations in Russian America

1. The Tlingit called white people "gus'k'ikwáan" (literally, "clouds-base face people") or simply "dleit k̲áa" (literally, "white man") (Emmons 1991:8; Kan 1999:25).

2. See Bolkhovitinov's three-volume *Istoriia Russkoi Ameriki* [The History of Russian America], published in Russia between 1997 and 1999.

3. England's military-diplomatic pressure, the competition posed by English merchants, and the internal decadence of the Spanish colonial empire had, by the mid-

1790s, led Spain to withdraw almost entirely from the political struggle for the North-west Coast. In May of 1789 the so-called Nootka incident occurred: the crews of the Spanish corvette *La Princessa* and the brig *San Carlos* in Nootka Sound (on Vancouver Island) seized the English trading ships *Argonaut, Princess Royal,* and *Northwest America.* The seized ships were dispatched to San Blas, the Spanish naval base on Mexico's west coast. A most acute crisis in Anglo-Spanish relations (1790) nearly ended in war. England readied its naval fleet for military action, and the Madrid envoy in London was presented an ultimatum. Spain, its sea power having significantly declined by this time, was forced to concede, and evacuated its fort in Nootka Sound; in addition, it withdrew all its claims on the Northwest Coast (Gough 1975:71–77). Only their forts and Catholic missions in Upper California (in Monterey, San Francisco, and elsewhere) remained Spanish property.

4. A number of Russian and foreign ethnographers mistakenly indicate that Captain James Cook visited Tlingit territory, made contact with the tribe, and even acquired a collection of Tlingit artifacts (Averkieva 1974:141–142; Corser 1940:12; Oberg 1973:5; Okladnikova 1995:32).

5. Communications were translated from Russian into Koniag (Eskimo), then from Koniag into Tlingit.

6. P. A. Tikhmenev and A. Krause erroneously indicated that the Tlingit attack on Baranov's camp occurred in 1793 (Krause 1956:29; Tikhmenev 1861:1:38), having evidently been misled by the date of Baranov's letter (July 24, 1793) describing this event—although Baranov himself points out in the letter that the attack on his camp had occurred the previous summer, that is, in 1792.

7. Alaskans here refers to people from the Alaska Peninsula.—Trans.

8. These Indians, as Kan suggests, could have been baptized by the Russians on Kodiak. In such a case, they would have been the first Tlingit to accept Orthodoxy (Kan 1999:51).

9. The Russian colony founded in 1796 near Yakutat Bay consisted of a fort and set-tlement. The fort was called "Yakutatskaia" (or simply "Yakutat"), while the settlement, as Shelikhov had instructed, was named "Slavorossiia" ("Novorossiisk"). According to the 19th-century American researchers Dall and Baker, the Russian colony in Yakutat consisted of seven structures surrounded by a palisade (probably the fort proper) and five structures outside the walls, which comprised the settlement (De Laguna 1972:1:74).

10. In the legend it says that the Kodiak and Chugach, who were returning from the hunt (most likely they were going *to* the hunt), were attacked by Eyak and southern Chugach. A Tlingit named Yakegua from Yakutat led the Eyak; the Chugach were led by Irkuk. Soon after the attack Irkuk died and Yakegua was seized, as Birket-Smith (1953:140–141) supposes, by the Russians and was tortured to death. However, judging by the description of the torture to which Yakegua was subjected, it was the Chugach who tortured him then executed him, possibly under orders from the Russian leader.

11. Historical sources and literature indicate that a large number of party members

perished in 1799 from poisoning; numbers vary from 150 to 180 and even to 200 (Hulley 1953:124; Litke 1834:1:129; *Russkaia Amerika: Po lichnym . . .* , 1994:85).

12. Several authors incorrectly identify the year of the founding of the Russian colony on Baranof Island as 1792 (Alekseev 1982:109–111), 1796 (Alekseev 1975:125), 1800 (Lazarev 1832:155; Niblack 1890:234; Oberg 1973:5), 1802 (Olson 1967:3), and 1804 (Kotzebue 1987:205).

13. The Russian-American Company did not especially strive to strengthen its colonies with people. As Svetlana G. Fedorova notes, on the one hand, the company was interested in the influx of contingents of workers and employees from Russia, and on the other, the company limited and regulated hiring and moving Russians to Alaska, since it was costly. According to Fedorova's calculations, the number of Russians in Alaska's large territories was insignificant and fluctuated from 225 to 823 men between 1799 and 1867 (peaking in 1839). From 1799 to 1821 the census reported not more than 400 people from Russia in the territory; between 1822 and 1845 the annual number averaged 670. Then, from 1846 to 1867 the number of Russians in Alaska fluctuated between 517 and 812 men (Fedorova 1971:136–146).

14. Judging by available sources, there were 29 Russians, 5 (or perhaps 7) "English" (American sailors taken into the service of the RAC), about 200 members of the "Sitka" party, and several dozen women and children, generally Natives of Kodiak at Fort Mikhailovskii in spring 1802. In June 1802, before the Tlingit attack, these small forces were distributed in the following way: a party of five Russians, three Americans, and several Kodiak led by V. Kochesov had set out on June 10 to hunt sea lions, and shortly before this I. Urbanov had left with two Russians and an American—the "Sitka" party—to go hunting. In the fort itself there remained 21 Russians, 1 (or perhaps 3) Americans, 2 or 3 dozen Kodiak, and up to 50 women and children. On the day of the attack, there were seven Russians absent from the colony on domestic affairs. Almost everyone else was killed by the Indians (*K istorii Rossiisko-Amerikanskoi . . .* , 1957:106–123; Khlebnikov 1861:45; Tikhmenev 1863:2:Append. 174–180).

15. According to K. T. Khlebnikov, there were only 15 (Khlebnikov 1861:50–51). The so-called Kodiak were Koniag Eskimos who lived on Kodiak Island.

16. According to Davydov and Litke, the fusillade on the Tlingit canoes was indeed the fault of the Indians themselves, because they had hoped to free their chief by force (Davydov 1812:2:112; RGA VMF, f. 15, op. 1, d. 8, l. 183).

17. She was probably a creole (mestizo) or Eskimo from Kodiak since there were no Russian women in Fort Mikhailovskii.

18. If Barber's information is reliable, a quite substantial number of Indians must have been killed: the average canoe held 15 to 20 men, and, of the five canoes seized by the Americans and English sailors, only 7 men survived.

19. Nevertheless, unexamined data continue to appear in scholarly literature. For example, in a book dedicated to the history of the Russian trading fleet, it says: "Thus, still in 1802 the tribe of Tlingit, led by sailors with the English ship of Captain Barber, attacked the Russian colony at Sitka and destroyed the whole garrison" (Mikhailov

et al. 1995:184). (Generalizing to include all the Tlingit and suggesting that the entire garrison was destroyed is implausible at best.) And there is another example from a large, recently published, scholarly monograph: "In 1802 the Tlingit took by storm Fort Arkhangel'skii [Mikhailovskii] at Sitka, set it afire [in fact, they first set it afire, then seized it], along with a merchant ship located in the harbor [actually, in the stocks]. English sailors from the ship of the fur-trading captain Barber actively took part in the attack" (Postnikov 2000:222).

20. Describing the events of 1802 Tikhmenev wrote that the Indians, having learned of the destruction of Fort Mikhailovskii, attacked Kuskov's party (Tikhmenev 1861:1:90). In reality, as De Laguna correctly notes, the attack on Kuskov's party occurred more than a month before the attack on the fort (De Laguna 1972:1:172). Besides, Tikhmenev incorrectly indicated the location of the attack on Kuskov's party—saying it occurred in Yakutat—and made several other mistakes in describing this event, which one will notice when comparing his report with Kuskov's (*K istorii Rossiisko-Amerikanskoi* . . . , 1957:106–123).

21. Based on data from modern Tlingit, the powerful Sitka Kaagwaantaan were not involved in the attack on the Russian fort (Jacobs 1990:3; Kan 1999:58). On this question, S. A. Kan occupies an intermediate position: in his opinion, each Tlingit clan viewed its participation in the attack as a "personal" war with the Russians, and some of the clans/lineages generally distanced themselves from participation in this affair (Kan 1999:59). In my view, the situation could have been still more complex: even within a clan/lineage not all its warriors could take part in the action against the Russians and their allied Native party members. This is confirmed by the facts. Thus, directly before the seizure of Fort Mikhailovskii a Sitkan went to the small party of Vasilii Kochesov and warned the Russians about the impending attack (*K istorii Rossiisko-Amerikanskoi* . . . , 1957:121). Also, as early as 1805, Georg H. von Langsdorff met with the Sitka chief Schinchetaes, who was subjected to ostracism by his kinsmen for refusing to take part in the war with the Russians (Langsdorff 1812:2:106).

22. In Russian documents, *Akoitsy* was the name used to identify the Tlingit of the Akoi kwáan (of the Dry Bay region), who lived to the south of Yakutat.

23. The name "Chesnyga" was mentioned by Kuskov in 1802—one of the Akoi chiefs bore it (*K istorii Rossiisko-Amerikanskoi* . . . , 1957:119). De Laguna identifies this name with the Tlingit name "Jisniya," which was the name of one of the chiefs of the L'uknax̱.ádi Akoi, builder of the Frog House in Kutsek̲ village (De Laguna 1972:1:171). During Baranov's campaign in 1804 he appeared as a truce envoy of the Russians, for which he evidently received a silver medal from Rezanov in 1805 (OR GBL, f. 204, k. 32, ed. khr. no. 4, l. 33).

24. According to Tlingit legends, the failure of Russian-Tlingit negotiations and the subsequent flight of the Tlingit were caused by a mutual misunderstanding. Two Indian women who served as intermediaries and interpreters in the negotiations (I note that this fact does not appear in Russian sources) explained to their fellow tribesmen that the white flag, displayed by the Russians as a sign of peace, in fact meant that the

Russians intended to "wipe them out as snow." This compelled the Indians to secretly leave their fortification and run into the mountains in the territory of their relatives the Kootznahoo ḵwáan in the eastern part of the island (Jacobs 1990:5; Kan 1999:63–64).

25. According to Russian sources the murdered children (all boys) were between the ages of four and nine, that is, at an age when children can take care of themselves, and therefore the Indians knew that the children were not crying from fear, as A. V. Zorin correctly notes. In his opinion, it could have been a matter either of ritual sacrifice or the murder of captive children (creoles and Kodiak) from the destroyed Fort Mikhailovskii (Zorin 2001b:24).

26. For example, Okun' wrote: "After the occupation of Fort Mikhailovskii it was decided to dig it out and move it to a place inaccessible to attack—on the high hill where formerly the village of the Tlingit had been" (Okun' 1939:53). As is well known, it was impossible to dig out and move Fort Mikhailovskii to another place in 1804 since it had been destroyed by the Indians in 1802. The Russians did not tear down but rather burned the fort abandoned by the Tlingits.

In the monograph of the eminent Russian historian Bolkhovitinov on the events of 1804, he reports: "The wooden fort, 'equipped with cannons and other small arms purchased from the Boston men,' was taken by assault only owing to the support of the crew of the newly arrived 'round-the-world' ship *Neva* under the command of Yu. F. Lisianskii" (Bolkhovitinov 1966:313). However, according to all the sources at our disposal, the Tlingit fort was not taken by assault but rather was left by the Indians after the Russians unsuccessfully stormed it. In addition, it seems to us that Bolkhovitinov somewhat exaggerated the role of *Neva*'s crew in this clash, since without Baranov's promyshlenniki and partovshchiki there was no way that 16 sailors could frighten several hundred Indian warriors.

"In the fall of 1804 the *Neva* arrived in Russian America. On 1 (13) October 1804 the landing party, comprised of sailors of the expedition, as well as a detachment led by Baranov, began the storming of the fort on Sitka Island, earlier seized by the Indians. The attack was repelled, with three people among the Russians being killed and 14 wounded, including Baranov," we read in the notes to a document inserted in the collection *Rossiia i SShA: Stanovlenie otnoshenii. 1765–1815* [Russia and the USA: The Formation of Relations: 1756–1815] (1980:116). From the cited passage it follows that the compilers of the collection (Soviet and American historians) do not see the difference between Fort Mikhailovksii, seized and burned in 1802, and the fortification constructed later by the Indians. In addition, the number of Russian losses cited by the collection's authors are clearly underestimated.

In one of A. I. Alekseev's works on the events of 1804 it says the following: "The arrival of the *Neva* in Russian America, besides serving a symbolic, 'watch-dog' function, also had practical significance, since by its armed intervention Yu. F. Lisianskii created a decisive superiority in the forces of the Russians in warding off the latest attack of one of the Indian tribes, provoked by American and English pirates" (Alekseev 1982:116). In this example it is seen that the author confuses the events: in 1802 the Tlingit, being provoked by foreign skippers (but not pirates!), attacked the Russians and destroyed their fort on Sitka Island. While in 1804, when the *Neva* was in Russian America, the Indians did not attack the Russians; instead, the latter, with the support of the *Neva*'s crew, expelled the Indians from their fort.

27. The events of 1804 were fantastically reflected in the folklore of the Skidegate Haida who live in the southern part of the archipelago of the Queen Charlotte Islands (Swanton 1905:378–379).

28. Langsdorff thought that in this party there were about 140 baidarkas (Langsdorff 1812:2:191), while Khlebnikov believed there were 200 (Khlebnikov 1985:45). There is also no precise information on the number of partovshchiki (280–400 men).

29. In the source material there are no precise data on the number in the Demenenkov party who perished. According to Khlebnikov, 250 men in this party were lost (and in another work—"more than 200") (Khlebnikov 1979:25, 1835:99); Tikhmenev says 300 men were lost (Tikhmenev 1861:1:151). However, Khlebnikov's, and even moreso Tikhmenev's, data are probably inaccurate, since Baranov reported in one of his letters that 39 of the baidarkas (about 78 men) of the Demenenkov party escaped, while Khlebnikov cites 30 to 31 (Khlebnikov 1835:101, 1985:45; OR GBL, f. 204, k. 32, ed. khr. no. 6, l. 30b.).

30. The English historian Ernst Sipes cites completely unrealistic numbers of Russian colonists in Yakutat. In his opinion, there were from 80 to 100 "serfs" (Sipes 1998:43–44). In fact, in 1794 only 30 colonists (men), 11 women, and 4 children were sent to America. The lists of Russian settlers for 1794 and 1798 have been published (Grinev 2001:62–63).

31. The Tlaḵaik Teiḵweidí, judging by everything, represented the remains of the autochthonous Eyak-language population, which formed a small clan (De Laguna 1972:1:169, 260–268). It is possible that the Russians ranked them among the Ugalaḵmiut (Eyak), who, according to Dmitrii Tarkhanov, in 1796 still inhabited the "inside of Yakutat Bay," that is, the most sheltered part of Yakutat Bay (Grinev 1987:93, 1988b:114; OR GPB, Sb. Q. IV. 311, l. 23). According to De Laguna, the Tlaḵaik Teiḵweidí governed the settlement of Tlaku-an ("Old Settlement") on Knight Island in the back of the bay (De Laguna 1972:1:76, 221–222).

32. Chesnyga never returned these captives to the Russians, at least until 1808, though his son (or possibly nephew) was with Baranov among the *amanaty*. Details of the captives' fate is not known with certainty. From Baranov's letters we know only that they were kept by the Indians in the settlement of Kaknau (Hoonah ḵwáan); the settler Luka Filipov died there in captivity (no later than 1808). Baranov tried to rescue the captive Russians and Kodiak, for which in September 1806 he sent into the region of Cross Sound (to the settlement of Kaknau) the American captain O. Kimball in the ship *Peacock* (for this the latter was promised a party of Aleuts with baidarkas for hunting sea otters one season) and in 1807 sent N. I. Bulygin on the ship *Kad'iak* into Yakutat Bay. But these actions had limited success. Only a Kodiak man and woman were rescued, as well as a few belongings from the destroyed fort. In addition, Larionov's

wife and child remained in captivity among the Tlingit (OR GBL, f. 204, k. 32, ed. khr. no. 6, l. 10b.–30b., 50b., 10–100b., 12, 14, 20). The latter, according to Heinrich I. Holmberg and A. Krause, was the daughter of a chief (Tlingit? Tlak̲aik Teik̲weidí?) (Holmberg 1855:59; Krause 1956:265). Much later, in 1821, Governor Murav'ev wrote that during the time of his predecessor S. I. Yanovskii in Novo-Arkhangel'sk, one of Larionov's sons, whom the Indians wanted to sacrifice at a potlatch, had been rescued. His older brother had earlier come to Novo-Arkhangel'sk and gone into the service of the RAC (AVPR, f. RAK, op. 888, d. 989, l. 179ob.–180). It is possible that the fate of one of Larionov's sons is reflected in the Tlingit tradition about Jivak (Olson 1967:54–55). In the documents of the RAC for 1830 the creole Larionov brothers are mentioned in connection with their lawsuit against the company concerning the inheritance from their father. All three brothers, by the way, were employed by the RAC. The oldest son, Andrei, worked in the Kodiak office; the middle son, Ivan, served in California at Fort Ross; and the youngest son, Dmitrii, was a "junior interpreter" (translator) with the Tlingit in the redoubt of St. Dionisii and in Novo-Arkhangel'sk. Along with the Larionov brothers there was a sister, Pelageia, "who lived among the *Koloshi*," according to the documents. She was probably born during her mother's captivity among the Tlingit. However, according to the Finnish naturalist H. J. Holmberg, she was the daughter of S. F. Larionov, while her mother was the daughter of a chief of the Yakutat Indians. They were taken captive together. Larionov's daughter grew up among the Indians and was returned to the Russians only as an adult, and settled in Sitka. Though she had been baptized (having received the name "Pelageia" at baptism), and though she had learned to read Russian, by her worldview she remained a true Indian. It was not by chance that she married the "head Sitka toion," Mikhail Kuk̲kan—in January 1845 (Pierce 1990:275, 295–296). Not until 1839 did Larionov's children finally receive his inheritance—1,394 rubles, 7 kopecks (AVPR, f. RAK, op. 888, d. 1001, l. 242–243; d. 1003, l. 124; d. 1004, l. 8–80b.). According to legends De Laguna collected from the Yakutat people, in 1805 only the supervisor of the Russian lighthouse, the watchman of the fish dam, and the daughter of the commandant of the Russian fort (more probably, however, Larionov's wife) were successfully saved (De Laguna 1972:1:236, 259–261).

33. De Laguna (1972:1:175) tried to connect Khlebnikov's version with a Chugach legend telling of the destruction of Yakutat people who came to them allegedly for trade (Birket-Smith 1953:141–142).

34. The Ugalak̲miut-Eyak who lived from the mouth of the Copper River to Yakutat Bay were considered distant relatives of the Yakutat people and would hardly have annihilated them, as Khlebnikov described. There are inaccuracies as well in Khlebnikov's description of the following events: according to him, the American captain Kimball, carrying out Baranov's request, set out to rescue the captives seized by the Indians in Yakutat. Maneuvering at Yakutat, he allegedly seized the main Chilkat chief, Asik (who destroyed Yakutat), took from him as *amanaty* two nephews, and rescued from captivity one of the Aleuts and his wife (Khlebnikov 1835:119). However, from Baranov's letter, which described this episode, it follows that Kimball did not sail to the region

of Yakutat but rather to the settlement of Kaknau (in the vicinity of Cross Sound). He did not manage to capture the Chilkat chief Asik but rather the Akoi chief "Toion Osip" and took from him as a hostage only one nephew. The Aleut (in reality a Kodiak) rescued from captivity was not the husband of the woman released with him (OR GBL, f. 204, k. 32, ed. khr. no. 6, l. 10b.–20b., 50b.). Khlebnikov's erroneous data are then cited by Tikhmenev (1861:1:171–172) and F. De Laguna (1972:1:176); R. A. Pierce (1990:236, 295) also relied on these data.

35. In the scholarly literature it is often erroneously indicated that this incident took place in the Queen Charlotte Islands and that in the Indian attack the party lost eight Aleuts (Okun' 1939:116; Pierce 1990:283; Tikhmenev 1861:1:208).

36. As A. V. Zorin succeeded in establishing from the archival materials, the patronymic of the former Kursk merchant was not Timofei "Osipovich," as is customarily reported in scholarly literature (see, for example, Pierce 1990:497), but rather Timofei Nikitich Tarakanov (Zorin 1997:23).

37. The term *Koloshi* is used here in the broad sense (see chapter 1, section 1.3).

38. It is difficult to judge the authenticity of Tikhmenev's information since in other sources there are no data on this episode.

39. Promyshlenniki who hired on for a four-year period under a "half-share" system received at the end of the period half the take in furs, with the merchant receiving the other half. The promyshlenniki then divided up their half among themselves.

40. In Soviet/Russian historiography the point of view that, in Russian America, capitalistic production relations entailed the supremacy of merchant capital in the person of the Russian-American Company, became widespread (Agranat 1971:182; 1997:55, 58; Makarova 1968:163; 1974:7, 25; Okun' 1939:14–18; Pasetskii 1974:22).

41. It should be noted that this is only partially true since the Tlingit, in spite of the presence in 1823 of the frigate *Kreiser* (commanded by M. P. Lazarev) in Novo-Arkhangel'sk harbor, briefly laid siege to the city. The incident occurred because Indians had robbed a garden farmed by sailors of the frigate on one of the islets in Sitka Bay. M. I. Murav'ev demanded the guilty be handed over for punishment, and the Tlingit in answer laid siege to the fort. Only owing to a successful maneuver by the frigate *Kreiser*, which placed the Indians directly under the guns of the ship, were the latter forced to agree with the demand of the colonial governor and hand over the guilty (Zavalishin 1877, t. 3, no. 11, c. 218).

42. In fact, the connections of the Russians with the Stikine people were complicated by past enmity between the latter and the Kaagwaantaan, who lived in Sitka and in the Chilkat ḵwáan. Therefore Stikine people visiting Novo-Arkhangel'sk were placed under the protection of the Russians.

43. According to the contract, the HBC renounced its suit against the RAC concerning the "Stikine incident" and promised to supply the Russian colonies with provisions ("at moderate prices"), as well as deliver the necessary cargo there. For the territory being leased, the HBC was obliged to pay the RAC 2,000 river otter skins annually (about 118,000 rubles by 1840 prices). It was especially stipulated in the contract that the

RAC would not trade with the Indians of the leased zone of the coast, while the HBC in turn would pledge to give up the purchase of furs from Natives of the Russian possessions. If furs were obtained in violation of the agreement, then they had to be given to the opposite side. The fixed interest is brought forth in the seventh article of the agreement where it speaks about the fact that, in case of war between Russia and Great Britain before the end of the period of the lease, both companies would continue their agreement as if there were no war at all (AVPR, f. RAK, op. 888, d. 351, l. 211–221). This article later served as the basis for the neutrality of the Russian colonies in America during the Crimean War (1853–56). A combined Anglo-French squadron approached Sitka Island in June 1855 but did not undertake any hostile activities against Novo-Arkhangel'sk or other Russian colonies in Alaska (AVPR, f. RAK, op. 888, d. 1022, l. 1090b., 119–120). As the American historian J. S. Galbraith pointed out, not only the Russians but the English had an interest in mutual neutrality. One of the directors of the HBC, George Simpson, feared that well-armed RAC ships under the command of officers of the naval fleet could easily destroy HBC steamships and trading posts on the Northwest Coast, because they were not equipped to defend against European military might. Besides, the Indian tribes might become involved in the conflict, which would also create a real threat to the HBC's interests (Galbraith 1957:165).

44. The Tlingit, at least in Sitka, suspected that the Russian colony was the source of the illness (Kan 1999:95, 97).

45. The date of this event is inaccurately indicated in the work of A. A. Istomin as 1844 (Istomin 1985:151; Pierce 1990:275).

46. Incorrect data concerning this are cited by A. Markov (1856:87). He wrote that Kukkan obtained 10,000 rubles gratis from the RAC. A. A. Istomin (1985:151) later cites this information.

47. The only serious incident that darkened Russian-Tlingit relations in the 1840s was, as far as we know, the wounding of a Russian woman by a Tlingit in Novo-Arkhangel'sk.

48. In the Russian version of this monograph it is mistakenly indicated that the successors of A. K. Etolin and M. D. Teben'kov did not put on igrushka for the Tlingit (Grinev 1991:162).

49. Rozenberg noted that also taking part in the slaughter were other Christian Tlingit, who then took scalps from the murdered Stikine people.

50. The Hudson's Bay Company assigned three tariffs on furs: (1) the lowest—for interior Indians not having contacts with American traders; (2) higher—for the coastal Indians, in order to interest them in trade with the English; and (3) the highest—when it was necessary to grab the furs from under the noses of American fur dealers who had come to the Northwest Coast to trade with the Indians (Galbraith 1957:139–140).

51. The opinion about the unprofitability of Dionisievskii Redoubt for the RAC is confirmed in the literature by P. N. Golovin (Galbraith 1957:157; Gibson 1990:45; Golovin 1862:140; Roppel 1992:313). His assertion is not entirely correct, however. Though maintenance of the redoubt and garrison cost the company an average of

12,000 silver rubles a year, and the local Tlingit charged a high price for their furs, the managers of the RAC nevertheless annually obtained furs there amounting to 70,000 rubles (in banknotes). Especially valuable were the skins of the "Stikine otter," which, according to the RAC's Kiakhta office, were of "excellent quality compared to the usual" and traded for 75 rubles instead of 45 rubles (the price usual for a river otter skin) (AVPRI, f. RAK, op. 888, d. 351, l. 1340b.; d. 1000, l. 35). But the chief articles of trade with the Stikine people at Dionisievskii Redoubt were beavers, which they got in trade from the Athapaskans in the British possessions, from which the RAC, as is mentioned in its official report, "extracted no little profit" (ORAK 1842:62). In addition, Dionisievskii Redoubt began to manufacture bricks, which were then delivered to Novo-Arkhangel'sk.

52. During a drunken dispute among the employees of Fort Stikine, its commandant, J. MacLaughlin Jr. was killed (Andrews 1947:107–108; Klein 1987:104–106). The killers were seized and sent to the Russians by orders of G. Simpson and, with the consent of the colonial governor, placed under guard at Ozerskii Redoubt.

53. These voyages are reflected in legends. For example, a mourning song about an Indian of the Naanya.aayí clan who died en route to Victoria (according to the Tlingit, it was Vaktani) was recorded by Swanton (1909:406).

54. The year of this incident is incorrectly indicated in the work of I. I. Petroff as 1864 (Petroff 1884:120).

3. Influence of European Contacts on Tlingit Culture

1. The Russians also called them "*Kolosh* capes." Sometimes this name was used as well for the traditional Chilkat capes. The latter, at the end of the 1840s, cost six ordinary European blankets or 120 rubles (LO AAN f. 46, op. 1, ed. khr. no. 2, l. 36).

2. Maritime service was dangerous: in 1842 the RAC ship *Naslednik Aleksandr*, on its return from San Francisco, was overtaken by a severe storm, during which its commander, Captain-Lieutenant Kadnikov, and several crew members, including the christened "Kolosh Pavel," were killed. The latter, together with the captain, was buried on the open sea, according to maritime custom (AVPR, f. RAK, op. 888, d. 1009, l. 216–217).

3. The Tlingit believed that river otters had the power to transform themselves into humans, then back again. For an account of this, see F. Boas, "Sagen der Tlingit," *Verhandlungen der Berliner Gesellschaft für Anthropologie, Ethnologie und Urgeschichte,* 1895, S. 222–234. Berlin.—Trans.

4. This was the "chief Sitka toion," Mikhail Kukkan's uncle.

5. A. A. Istomin's indication that the Russians sold the Tlingit rum only from 1832 is incorrect (Istomin 1985:151). According to G. H. von Langsdorff, by 1805 the Russians had offered the Tlingit vodka, but the latter feared drinking it since they were afraid that they would thereby fall under the newcomers' power (Langsdorff 1812:2:96, 112). However, fear of alcoholism's consequences gradually disappeared, and in 1830, for example, the Tlingit received from the Russians almost three *vedro* {about 8 gallons} of rum, in addition to other goods, for a sea otter (Khlebnikov 1985:140).

6. By 1788 Russian sailors on the galliot *Tri Sviatitelia* noted that some Yakutat people they encountered were dressed in European clothing (Shelikhov 1971:99).

7. In the opinion of the head of the Kodiak office of the RAC, Ivan Banner, who observed the Yakutat Tlingit in 1803, these Indians borrowed Russian footwear, "torbasy," that is, leather boots, sewn from tanned hide from the throat of a sea lion, as well as socks made from the fur of sheep and otter (*K istorii Rossiisko-Amerikanskoi . . .*, 1957:128). The latter element of dress was evidently of Athapaskan or Eyak origin.

8. H. J. Holmberg reported that the Tlingit valued "white" metal (such as iron, tin, and silver) the most, not "yellow" (copper, brass, gold) (Holmberg 1855:21).

9. The first medals in Russian America were brought at the beginning of the 1790s by the Billings-Sarychev Expedition to award to Aleut and Kodiak elders, as well as to give to distinguished partovshchiki (in all, the expedition brought about 80 gold, 300 silver, and more than 600 copper medals) (RGA VMF, f. 214, op. 1, d. 29, l. 1170b.). These medals were worn on chains or, more rarely, on a blue ribbon of the order of St. Andrew of the Primordial. On the front of the medal was a bust image in profile of the Empress Catherine II wearing her crown and robe, and the edge was inscribed "B[OZH'EI] M[ILOST'YU] EKATERINA II. IMPERATR [ITSA] I SAMODERZH[ITSA] VSEROSS [IISKAYA]" [Divine Gracious Catherine II. Empress and Absolute Ruler of All Russia]. Under the portrait of the czarina was the year of minting: 1785, and on the back of the medal was an image of the flagship of the Billings expedition with its name: "SLAVA ROSSII" [Glory of Russia] (Chepurnov 1993a:47–48).

10. As N. I. Chepurnov, a specialist in Russian medals, notes, copper and tin medals were awarded that were inscribed "Soyuznye Rossii" (the United Russias). These medals are of a later time, and were evidently minted unofficially, under the RAC's terms (Chepurnov 1993b:99). In our view, these were probably innovations (replicas or copies) made specially for collectors, since in the RAC sources known to us there is nothing about the minting of such medals from nonprecious metals.

11. However, this table does not reflect the difference between the 1803 medals and the 1806 silver badges. In addition, Dean's table does not mention Governor I. V. Furuhjelm's decision to pay the Sitka chief Aleksei Kalyak an annual RAC salary in the amount of 240 rubles in bills starting in 1861 (see documentary appendix entry {32}). A similar sum was given this same year to the chief of the Sitka Kaagwaantaan Sergei Sergeev (Sergei Katliak), whose baptized father, the active councilor of state S. A. Kostlivtsov, was a RAC inspector (Dean 1995:290; Kan 1999:149; Kostlivtsov 1863:89).

12. In J. R. Dean's opinion, the Tlingit's accepting the "Soyuznye Rossii" medals signified their recognition of Russian sovereignty and was similar to *yasak*—a tax that the Natives of Siberia usually paid in furs to the czarist treasury, though, as the American researcher notes, distribution of the medals did not involve paying a tax and was a sign of friendship (Dean 1995:276). In our view, *yasak* and silver medals were entirely different phenomena of Russian colonial practice. *Yasak* was a poll tax (similar to tribute in Spanish America), which fixed the personal dependence of a Native on the Russian government in the person of the czar, whose subject he was. Distribution of the

medals with the very symbolic inscription "Soyuznye Rossii" (not "subjects of Russia," but "united Russias") demonstrated only the outward loyalty to the Russians of the person awarded the medal and did not involve any economic or political obligation.

13. In 1844 the RAC board of directors handed the governmental Department of Mining and Mineral Affairs 3 gold, 131 silver, and 6 bronze medals (a total of 140) from the number of those given out by Rezanov and evidently even by I. I. Billings (RGIA, f. 18, op. 5, d. 1317, l. 2).

14. In 1804, during the siege of the Tlingit fort on Sitka Island, the partovshchiki discovered the Sitka people's hiding place, in which was so much cloth and *yukola* {dried fish} that it filled 150 baidarkas (Lisianskii 1812:20–21).

15. Possibly one important reason for the fact that, for example, the Koniagmiut Eskimo were relatively easily subdued and managed by a small number of Russian promyshlenniki was that the Eskimos lacked a clan structure that "concentrated" the society into a unified organism. "Disagreement of the islanders in general," wrote G. I. Davydov about the Kodiak people in the 1800s, "served as a greater lifesaver for the Russians than being cautious" (Davydov 1810:1:107).

16. The last slave among the Tlingit received freedom at a potlatch in 1910 (De Laguna 1972:1:216).

17. According to J. R. Swanton, the name "Kude'naha" Kudena designated "Narrow Opening of a Bear's Den" and was popular among the Kaagwaantaan—the other clan of the Wolf-Eagle moiety (Swanton 1908:421).

18. According to R. L. Olson, in the Tanta (Tongass) ḵwáan the Ḵas'ittan lineage was considered an independent clan as were the Tekuedi, Daktlauedi, and Ḡaanaxteidí lineages, although they were related to the last (Olson 1967:10). According to other information, the Ḵas'ittan were a lineage of the Koskedi clan, whose representatives also settled in the Sitka, Hoonah, and Akoi ḵwáans (De Laguna 1990b:227; Emmons 1991:436).

19. In Kan's opinion, in 1820 the number of Tlingit women who accepted Orthodoxy clearly exceeded the number of baptized Indian men. Evidently, most women accepted Orthodoxy under the influence of their Russian husbands or lovers (Kan 1999:85).

20. In the original Russian text of the monograph the author mistakenly ascribed the drop in the number of newly baptized Tlingit to the departure from the colonies of Governor A. K. Etolin, who did much to improve Russian-Tlingit relations (Grinev 1991:228).

21. At the same time, as Bishop Petr noted in the official report to the Holy Synod for 1864, the Tlingit themselves followed the bad examples of the Russian and Finnish workers in Novo-Arkhangel'sk. Only rewards attracted the Tlingit to the bosom of Orthodoxy: if they were given a gift they would all become Christians immediately. In the end, the Indians did not adhere to the Church ceremonies and never donated to the Church, the Sitkans being especially selfish and immoral, spoiled by gifts from the colonial leadership (Kan 1999:154).

GLOSSARY

In Russian, plural nouns typically end in *i* or *y*; for example, *amanat, amanaty*.—Trans.

Aank̲áawu. A wealthy person (see Table 3).

Aanyádi. A member of the elite (see Table 3).

Amanat. A voluntarily offered hostage, held to guarantee peace.

Arshin. Old Russian measurement of length, equal to 71.12 centimeters [28 inches].

Ass. (assignatsiia). Banknote.

Baidar. A large skin-covered boat.

Baidarka. A skin-covered boat that held from one to three persons.

Barabara. Semi-subterranean dwelling.

Beaver. In Russian America sea otters were most often identified by the term *bobr* (beaver). The Russian word for sea otter is *kalan'*.

Carronade. A short light iron cannon.

Daby. A kind of Chinese cotton fabric.

Dolia. Russian unit of weight equal to 0.044 grams.

Exploitation (French *exploitation*—utilization, extraction of profits). In Marxism this is the process of appropriating the results of someone else's work or taking their spouse without paying equivalent compensation; according to Marx, exploitation usually arises when the worker is alienated from (i.e., does not own) the means of production.

Falcon. A light piece of ordnance; a swivel gun.

Falconet. A small falcon. *See* **Falcon.**

Galliot. A long, narrow light-draft ship, sometimes having both sails and oars (related to the word *galley*).

Gregorian calendar. Introduced by Pope Gregory XIII in 1582. A revision of the Julian calendar, its dates fall twelve days after those in the Julian calendar.

Gorno. Deer hide.

Hooker. A two-masted trading or cargo ship with a broad bow and rounded stern. From the Dutch *hoeker*.

Igrushka. A celebration, from the Russian word for "toy," derived from the word *igra*, meaning "play" or "game": a domestic *igrushka* involves close neighbors and takes place several times a year; a public *igrushka* involves acquaintances and prominent persons from distant places.

Italian mile. Unit of measure equivalent to 1 nautical mile, 1.75 versts, $\frac{1}{60}$ of a degree, or 1.8669 kilometers.

Julian calendar. A calendar, named for Julius Caesar, introduced in 46 BC. Its dates precede those of the Gregorian calendar by 12 days.

Kalan'. *See* **Beaver.**

Kalgi. The Russians used this Kamchadal word to designate slaves of the Native inhabitants of Russian America.

Kaluzhka. Labret that women wore in the lip.

Kamlanie. A shamanic ceremony.

Kaiur. A Native who was forced to work for the Russian-American Company.

Kaiurka. A female *kaiur*.

Kaiurstvo. The form of servitude endured by a *kaiur*.

Kitaika. Cheap Chinese cotton fabric.

Koliuzh. Tlingit.

Kolosh. Tlingit.

Koshlok. A young sea otter.

Laida. A Finnish word meaning the shore of a sandbank that is bared during low tide.

Method of production. The historically determined method of procuring material goods that is determined by the totality of the production force (workers, means of production, objects produced) and production (economic) relations. Economic relations arise between the people in the process of producing, distributing, exchanging, and using the product. The character of production relations depends on to whom the products and means of production (sometimes including the worker himself or herself, as with politarism or slave owning) belong.

Partovshchik. Members of a sea otter–hunting party, generally applied to the Native members.

Politarism. Social structure (formation) in which the government (embodied in the highest ruler with unlimited authority) owns the land, the basic means of production, and the individual who is the producer; politarism was the first social structure to rely on exploitation (see definition above) and social inequality; it was widely represented in the early civilizations of Asia, Africa, and America, and in the USSR and other "socialistic" countries of the 20th century (industrial politarism).

Potestarnye (from Latin *potestas*, meaning power) or potestarno. Traditional relations, institutions, and systems of authority in pre-classic and pre-state societies.

Prikazchik. A steward or manager of a business or enterprise.

Promyshlennik. Russian hunter/trapper/trader.

Pud. Old Russian measure of weight equal to 16.38 kilograms, or about 36 pounds.

Redoubt. Fort.

Rovduga. A deer hide used as currency.

Sarana. The chocolate, or Kamchatka, lily (*Fritillaria camschatcensis*).

Shebek. A small ship.

Toion. A Siberian word for chief or leader.

Tsukli (*siukluk* in Aleut). Name that the Russians in America borrowed to designate the tubular *Dentalium* shell, which was eight to nine centimeters long.

Ugalentsi. Eyak.

Ukaz. An edict.

Vedro. 21 pints, or about 2.5 gallons.

Versts. 3,500 feet, or about 1 kilometer.

Yasak. Taxes in the form of furs.

Yukola. Dried fish.

Zolotnik. Russian unit of weight equal to 4.266 grams.

BIBLIOGRAPHY

Abbreviations

AN	Akademiia nauk (Academy of Sciences)
ARGO	Arkhiv Russkogo geograficheskogo obshchestva (Archive of the Russian Geographical Society)
AVPR	Arkhiv vneshnei politiki Rossii (Moskva) (Archives of Foreign Politics of Russia in Moscow) (formerly AVPRI)
AVPRI	Arkhiv vneshnei politiki Rossiiskoi imperii (Moskva) (Archive of the Foreign Politics of the Russian Empire in Moscow) (now AVPR)
BAE	Bureau of American Ethnology
HBC	Hudson's Bay Company
LO AAN	Leningradskoe otdelenie Arkhiva Akademii nauk SSSR (Leningrad Division of the Archives of the Academy of Sciences of the USSR) (now SPbOA RAN)
MAE	Muzei antropologii i etnografii im. Petra I AN SSSR (Soiuz Sovietskikh Sotsialisticheskikh Respublik) = USSR (Union of Soviet Socialist Republics) (Peter I Museum of Anthropology and Ethnography)
OR GBL	Otdel rukopisei gosudarstvennoi biblioteki im. V. I. Lenina (Moskva) (Manuscripts Division of the Lenin State Library in Moscow) (now OR RGB)
OR GPB	Otdel rukopisei gosudarstvennoi publichnoi biblioteki im. M. E. Saltykova-Shchedrina (Leningrad) (Manuscripts Division of the Saltykov-Shchedrin State Library [Leningrad]) (now OR RNB)
OR RGB	Otdel rukopisei Rossiiskoi gosudarstvennoi biblioteki (Moskva) (Division of Manuscripts of the Russian State Library in Moscow) (formerly OR GBL)
OR RNB	Otdel rukopisei Rossiiskoi natsional'noi biblioteki im. M. E. Saltykova-Shchedrina (S.-Peterburg) (Division of Manuscripts of the Russian National Saltykov-Shchedrin Public Library) (St. Petersburg) (formerly OR GPB)
RAC	Russian-American Company
RGADA	Russkii gosudarstvennyi arkhiv drevnikh aktov (Moskva); now Rossiiskii gosudarstvennyi arkhiv drevnikh aktov (Moskva) (Russian State Archive of Early Documents) (Moscow)
RGA VMF	Rossiiskii gosudarstvennyi arkhiv Voenno-Morskogo Flota SSSR (S.-Peterburg) (Central [Russian] State Archive of the Naval Fleet of the USSR, St. Petersburg) (formerly TsGA VMF)

RGIA	Ruskii gosudarstvennyi istoricheskii arkhiv SSSR (Leningrad); now Rossiiski gosudarstvennyi istoricheskii arkhiv SSSR (S.-Peterburg) (Russian State Historical Archive of the USSR)
RGA VMF	*Russkii gosudarstvennyi arkhiv voenno-morskogo flota* (Russian State Archive of Naval Fleet of the USSR)
SE	Sovetskaia etnografiia (Soviet Ethnography)
SPbOA RAN	Sankt-Peterburgskoe otdelenie Arkhiva Rossiiskoi Akademii nauk (S.-Peterburg) (St. Petersburg Division of Archives, Russian Academy of Sciences) (formerly LO AAN)
TIE	Sbornik trudy Instituta etnografii (Collection of Works of the Institute of Ethnography)
TSGA VMF	Tsentral'nyi gosudarstvennyi arkhiv Voenno-Morskogo Flota SSSR (Leningrad) (now RGA VMF)

Archival Material

AVPRI (now AVPR)

-f. RAK, op. 888, d. 5, 36, 68, 105, 108, 121, 126, 130, 170, 172–174, 181, 207, 215, 222, 284, 318, 320, 351, 357, 382, 385, 393, 396, 491, 747, 855, 856, 945/25, 947/27, 949/29, 951/31, 961/41, 988, 989, 992, 993, 995, 998, 1000–1016, 1018, 1020–1027;

- f. Gl. arkhiv I–7, 1802 g., d. 1, papki 1, 12, 35, 45;

- f. Gl. arkhiv I–7, 1802 g., op. 6, d. 1, papka 1, l. 2–9

- f. Gl. arkhiv I–7, 1802 g., d. 1, papka No. 33, l. 146ob.

- f. Gl. arkhiv I–9, 1852 g., d. 15; 1859–1867 gg., op. 8, d. 3;

- f. Gl. arkhiv I–13, 1805–1808 gg., d. 12;

- f. Gl. arkhiv II-3, 1805–1811 gg., op. 34, d. 7, 8;

- f. Gl. arkhiv II-3, 1805–1824 gg., op. 34, d. 7

- f. Gl. arkhiv II-5, 1844–1860 gg., op. 38, d. 3.

- f. Snosheniya Rossii s Angliei, op. 35/6, d. 507, l. 16

Ser. I, vol. III–VII, Ser. II, vol. I–VI

LO AAN (now SPbOA RAN)

- f. 46, op. 1, ed. khr. no. 2, 3;

- f. 53, op. 1, ed. khr. no. 2/1–2.

OR GBL (now OR RGB)

- f. 204, k. 32, ed. khr. no. 2–6, 12.

OR GPB (now OR RNB)

- f. 7, ed. khr. no. 139, 143;

- Sb. Q. IV. 311.

RGADA

- f. 1605, op. 1, d. 161, 187, 190, 352, 353, 355, 356, 360–362, 364.

RGIA

- f. 13, op. 1, d. 287, l. 65
- f. 37, op. 19, d. 71, 1. 1–30b.

TSGA VMF (now RGA VMF)

- f. 7, op. 1, d. 8, 14–16;
- f. 15, op. 1, d. 8, 9;
- f. 213, op. 1, d. 104, 110;
- f. 214, op. 1, d. 25, 29.
- f. 1152, op. 1, d. 2, l. 40–41ob.
- f. 1375, op. 1, d. 26, l. 89ob.–90ob.

RGIA

- f. 18, op. 5, d. 1244, 1262, 1270, 1271, 1282, 1291, 1306, 1312, 1316, 1317, 1321, 1329;
- f. 523, op. 1, d. 366;
- f. 796, op. 90, d. 273; op. 174, d. 2949;
- f. 994, op. 2, d. 829, 830, 833, 838, 848, 851, 857, 859, 864, 872.

Reference List

Adam, L.

1913   "Stammesorganisation und Häuptlingstum der Tlinkitindianer Nordwest-
        amerikas" [Tribal Organization and Chiefdom of the Tlingit Indians of
        Northwest America]. *Zeitschrift für vergleichende Rechtwissenschaft* [Journal
        for Comparative Jurisprudence]. Bd. 29. S. 86–120.

Agranat, G. A.

1971   "Ob osvoenii russkimi Aliaski" [On the Opening Up of Alaska by the Rus-
        sians]. *Letopis' Severa* [Chronicle of the North]. 5:190.

1997   "Sud'ba Russkoi Ameriki" [The Destiny of Russian America]. *SShA: ekono-
        mika, politika, ideologiia* [USA: Economics, Politics, Ideology] 11:52–63.

Alekseev, A. I.

1975   *Sud'ba Russkoi Ameriki* [The Destiny of Russian America]. Magadan, Russia:
        Magadanskoe knizhnoe izdatel'stvo.

1977   *Il'ia Gavrilovich Voznesenskii* [Il'ia Gavrilovich Voznesenskii]. Moscow:
        Nauka.

1982   *Osvoenie russkimi liud'mi Dal'nego Vostoka i Russkoi Ameriki* [The Opening
        Up by the Russian People of the Far East and Russian America]. Moscow:
        Nauka.

1987   *Beregovaia cherta* [Coastal Frontier]. Magadan: Magadanskoe knizhnoe izdatel'stvo.

Alekseeva, E. V.

1998   *Russkaya Amerika. Amerikanskaya Rossiaya?* [Russian America. Americanized Russia?]. Yekaterinburg, Russia: UrO RAN.

Al'perovich, M. S.

1993   *Rossiia i Novyi Svet (posledniaia tret' XVIII veka)* [Russia and the New World (the Last Third of the 18th Century)]. Moscow: Nauka.

Anatolii, Archimandrite

1906   *Indiane Aliaski: Byt i religiia ikh* [The Indians of Alaska: Their Way of Life and Religion]. Odessa, Ukraine: Tipografiia E. I. Fesenko.

Andreev, A. I., ed.

1944   *Russkie otkrytiia v Tikhom okeane i Severnoi Amerike v XVIII–XIX vv.: Sb. materialov* [Russian Discoveries in the Pacific Ocean and North America in the 18th and 19th Centuries: Collection of Materials]. Moscow: Izdatel'stvo AN SSSR.

1948   *Russkie otkrytiia v Tikhom okeane i Severnoi Amerike v XVIII veke* [Russian Discoveries in the Pacific Ocean and North America in the 18th Century]. Moscow: Gosudarstvennoe izdatel'stvo geograficheskoi literatury.

Andrews, C. L.

1947   *The Story of Alaska.* Caldwell ID: Caxton Printers.

1967   "The Settlement of Sitka." In *Alaska and Its History.* M. B. Sherwood, ed. Pp. 47–55. Seattle: University of Washington Press.

Antonson, J. M.

1990   "Sitka." In *Russian America: The Forgotten Frontier.* R. Barnett and B. Smith, eds. Pp. 165–173. Tacoma: Washington State Historical Society.

Arkhiv grafov Mordvinovykh

1902   *Arkhiv grafov Mordvinovykh* [Archive of the Mordvinov Counts], vol. 6. St. Petersburg: Tipografiia I. N. Skorokhodova.

Arndt, Katherine L.

1988   "Russian Relations with the Stinkine Tlingit, 1833–1867." *Alaska History* 3(1):27–43.

Atlas geograficheskikh otkrytii . . .

1964   *Atlas geograficheskikh otkrytii v Sibiri i v Severo-Zapadnoi Amerike XVII–XVIII vv.* [Atlas of Geographic Discoveries in Siberia and Northwestern America in the 17th and 18th Centuries]. A. V. Efimov, ed. Moscow: Nauka.

Averkieva, Yu. P.

1941   *Rabstvo u indeitsev Severnoi Ameriki* [Slavery among the Indians of North America]. Moscow: Izdatel'stvo AN SSSR.

1959a   "K istorii metallurgii u indeitsev Severnoi Ameriki" [Toward the History of Metallurgy among the Indians of North America]. *Sovetskaia etnografiia [Soviet Ethnography]*. 2:71–77.

1959b   "K voprosu o totemizme u indeitsev severo-zapadnogo poberezh'ia Severnoi Ameriki" [On the Question of Totemism among the Indians of the North-west Coast of North America]. *TIE Issledovaniia i materialy po voprosam pervobytnykh religioznykh verovanii* [Investigations and Materials on the Question of Primitive Religious Beliefs]. 51:250–265. Moscow: Izdatel'stvo AN SSSR.

1960   "K istorii obshchestvennogo stroia u indeitsev severo-zapadnogo poberezh'ia Severnoi Ameriki (rod i potlach u tlinkitov, khaida i tsimshian)" [On the History of Social Structure among the Indians of the Northwest Coast of North America (Clan and Potlatch among the Tlingit, Haida, and Tsimshian)]. *TIE* (n.s.) 58, Amerikanskii etnograficheskii sbornik [American Ethnographic Collection], 5–126. Moscow: Izdatel'stvo AN SSSR.

1961   "Razlozhenie rodovoi obshchiny i formirovanie ranneklassovykh otnoshenii v obshchestve indeitsev severo-zapadnogo poberezh'ia Severnoi Ameriki" [The Degeneration of Clan Society and Formation of Early Class Relations in the Society of the Indians of the Northwest Coast of North America]. *TIE* 70:1–275. Moscow: Izdatel'stvo AN SSSR.

1967   "Estestvennoe i obshchestvennoe razdelenie truda i problema periodizatsii pervobytnogo obshchestva" [Natural and Social Division of Labor and the Problem of Chronology in Primitive Society]. In *Ot Aliaski do Ognennoi Zemli* [From Alaska to Tierra del Fuego], 72–84. Moscow: Nauka.

1974   *Indeitsy Severnoi Ameriki* [The Indians of North America]. Moscow: Nauka.

1978   "Indeitsy severo-zapadnogo poberezh'ia Severnoi Ameriki (tlinkity)" [Indians of the Northwest Coast of North America (the Tlingit)]. In *Severoamerikanskie indeitsy* [North American Indians], 318–360. Moscow: Izdatel'stvo Progress.

1981   "O kul'te medvedia u indeitsev Severnoi Ameriki" [On the Bear Cult among the Indians of North America]. In *Traditsionnye kul'tury Severnoi Sibiri i Severnoi Ameriki* [Traditional Cultures of Northern Siberia and North America], 142–148. Moscow: Nauka.

Bancroft, H. H.
1970   *History of Alaska, 1730–1885.* Darien CT: Hafner.

Barbeau, C. M.

1954 " 'Totemic Atmosphere' on the North Pacific Coast." *Journal of American Folklore* 67(67):103–122.

1958 *Pathfinders in the North Pacific.* Caldwell ID: Caxton.

1961 "Tsimshian Myths." *National Museum of Canada* 174:1–97.

1987 *Tsimshian Narratives* 1–2. Ottawa: Canadian Museum of Civilization.

Barratt, G.

1981 *Russia in Pacific Waters, 1715–1825.* Vancouver: University of British Columbia Press.

1983 *Russian Shadows of the British Northwest Coast of North America, 1810–1890.* Vancouver: University of British Columbia Press.

1992 "The Afterlife of the Chirikov's Lost Men." In *Bering and Chirikov: The American Voyages and Their Impact.* O. W. Frost, ed. Pp. 265–275. Anchorage: Alaska Historical Society.

Batueva, T. M.

1985 "Ekspansiia sshA na severe Tikhogo okeana i pokupka Aliaski v 1867 godu" [Expansion of the USA in the North Pacific Ocean and the Purchase of Alaska in 1867]. In *Amerikanskii ekspansionizm* [American Expansionism], 66–89. Moscow: Nauka.

Belenkin, I. F.

1988 "Krestiteli" [The Ones Who Baptize]. *Ateisticheskie chteniia* [Atheistic Readings] 17:20–35.

Berg, L. S.

1926 "Otkrytiia russkikh v Tikhom okeane" [Russian Discoveries in the Pacific Ocean]. In *Tikhii okean: Russkie nauchnye issledovaniia* [Pacific Ocean: Russian Scientific Investigations], 1–24. Leningrad: Izdatel'stvo AN SSSR.

Berkh V. N.

1808 "Predislovie" [Introduction]. *Makenzi A. Puteshestvie po Severnoi Amerike k Ledovitomu moriu i Tikhomu okeanu* . . . . [Mackenzie, A. Travels through North America to the Arctic Ocean and the Pacific Ocean. . . .] Pp. 1–13. St. Petersburg: Morskaia tipografiia. English original: *Voyages from Montreal, on the River St. Lawrence, Through the Continent of North America, to the Frozen and Pacific Oceans; in the Years 1789 and 1793.*

1823 *Izvestie o mekhovoi torgovle, proizvodimoi rossiianami pri ostrovakh Kuril'skikh, Aleutskikh i severo-zapadnom beregu Ameriki* [Information on the Fur Trade Conducted by the Russians in the Kurile and Aleutian Islands and Northwest Coast of America]. St. Petersburg: Tipografiia N. Grecha.

Birket-Smith, K.
1953   *The Chugach Eskimo*. Copenhagen: Nationalmuseets publikationsfond.

Birket-Smith, K., and F. de Laguna.
1938   *The Eyak Indians of the Copper River Delta, Alaska*. Copenhagen: Levin and Munksgaard.

Bishop, C. A.
1987   "Coast-Interior Exchange: The Origins of Stratifications in Northwestern North America." *Arctic Anthropology* 24(1):72–83.

Blomkvist, E. E.
1951   "Risunki I. G. Voznesenskogo (ekspeditsiia 1839–1849 gg.)" [The Illustrations of I. G. Voznesenskii (The Expedition of 1839–1849)]. *Sbornik* MAE [Collection of the Museum of Anthropology and Ethnology] 13:230–303.

1975   "Istoriia izucheniia v Rossii severoamerikanskikh yazykov" [The History of Research in Russia of North American Languages]. *Sbornik MAE: Iz kul'turnogo naslediia narodov Ameriki i Afriki* [Collection of the Museum of Anthropology and Ethnology: From the Cultural Legacy of the Peoples of America and Africa] 31:94–117.

Boas, F.
1924   "Ts'ets'aut, an Athapascan Language from Portland Canal, British Columbia." *International Journal of American Linguistics* 3(1):1–35.

1928   *Bella Bella Texts*. New York: Columbia University Press.

1955   *Primitive Art*. New York: Crowell.

Bolkhovitinov, N. N.
1966   *Stanovlenie rossiisko-amerikanskikh otnoshenii: 1775–1815* [The Formation of Russian-American Relationships: 1775–1815]. Moscow: Nauka.

1975   *Russko-amerikanskie otnosheniia: 1815–1832* [Russian-American Relations: 1815–1832]. Moscow: Nauka.

1981   "Izuchenie russko-amerikanskikh otnoshenii: Nekotorye itogi i perspektivy" [The Study of Russian-American Relations: Some Results and Perspectives]. *Novaia i noveishaia istoriia* [Recent and Most Recent History] 6:54–64.

1985a   "Doktrina Monro: proiskhozhdenie, kharakter i evoliutsiia" [The Monroe Doctrine: Origin, Character, and Evolution]. In *Amerikanskii ekspansionizm* [American Expansionism], 49–65. Moscow: Nauka.

1985b   "Zarubezhnye issledovaniia o Russkoi Amerike" [Foreign Research on Russian America]. *SShA: ekonomika, politika, ideologiia* [USA: Economics, Politics, Ideology] 4:81–95.

1988   "Kak prodali Aliasku" [How Alaska Was Sold]. *Mezhdunarodnaia zhizn'* [International Life] 7:120–131.

1990   *Russko-amerikanskie otnosheniia i prodazha Aliaski, 1834–1867 gg.* [Russian-American Relations and the Sale of Alaska, 1834–1867]. Moscow: Nauka.

1991   *Rossiia otkryvaet Ameriku. 1732–1799* [Russia Discovers America. 1732–1799]. Moscow: Mezhdunarodnye otnosheniia.

Bolkhovitinov, N. N., ed.

1997–   *Istoriia Russkoi Ameriki (1732–1867).* [The History of Russian America (1732–
1999   1867)], vol. 3. (1999): *Russkaia Amerika: ot zenita k zakatu, 1825–1867* [Russian America: From Zenith to Decline, 1825–1867]. Moscow: Mezhdunarodnye otnosheniia [International Relations].

Bol'shaia sovetskaia entsiklopediia

1949   *Bol'shaia sovetskaia entsiklopediia* [The Great Soviet Encyclopedia]. Moscow: Izd-vo Bol'shaia sovetskaia entsiklopediia.

Bromlei, Yu. V.

1983   *Ocherki teorii etnosa* [An Essay on the Theory of Ethnos]. Moscow: Nauka.

Bruggeman, M., and P. R. Gerber

1987   *Indianer der Nordwestküste* [Indians of the Northwest Coast]. Zurich: U. Bär.

Bullard, J. B., ed.

1974   *The World of the American Indian.* Washington DC: National Geographic Society.

Chamisso, A. von

1986   *Puteshestvie vokrug sveta* [Voyage around the World]. Moscow: Nauka.

Chekurov, M. V.

1984   *Zagadochnye ekspeditsii* [Mysterious Expeditions]. Moscow: Mysl'.

Chepurnov, N. I.

1993a   *Rossiiskie nagradnye medali* [Russian Award Medals]. Pt. 1. *Medali XVIII veka.* [Medals of the 18th Century] Cheboksary, Russia: Izd-vo Chuvashiia [Chavash Publishers].

1993b   *Rossiiskie nagradnye medali* [Russian Award Medals]. Pt. 2. *Medali XIX veka. Medali epokhi Aleksandra I (1801 po 1824 gg.).* [Medals of the 19th Century. Medals of the Alexander I Era (1801 to 1824)] Cheboksary, Russia: Izd-vo Chuvashiia [Chavash Publishers].

Chevigny, H.

1942   *Lord of Alaska: Baranov and Russian Adventure.* New York: Viking.

1965   *Russian America: The Great Adventure, 1741–1867.* London: Cresset.

Chlenov, M. A.

1985   "Ob eiakakh" [About the Eyaks]. *Sovetskaia etnografiia* [Soviet Ethnography]
        1:166–167.

Clark, H. W.

1930   *Alaska: The Last Frontier.* New York: Grosset and Dunlap.

Colby, M. E.

1945   *Guide to Alaska: Last American Frontier.* New York: Macmillan.

Cook, J.

1971   *Tret'e plavanie kapitana Dzheimsa Kuka: Plavanie v Tikhom okeane v 1776–
        1780 gg.* [The Third Voyage of Captain James Cook: Voyage in the Pacific
        Ocean in 1776–1780]. Moscow: Mysl'.

Cook, W. L.

1973   *Flood Tide of Empire: Spain and Pacific Northwest, 1543–1819.* New Haven:
        Yale University Press.

Corser, H. P.

1940   *Totem Lore of the Alaska Indian and Land of the Totem.* Wrangell, Alaska: W.
        C. Waters.

Crass B. A.

1992   "Vitus Bering, a Russian Columbus?" In *Bering and Chirikov: The American
        Voyages and Their Impact.* O. W. Frost, ed. Pp.394–411. Anchorage: The
        Alaska Historical Society.

Curtis, E. S.

1970   *The North American Indian*, vol. 10. *The Kwakiutl.* New York: Johnson Re-
        print.

Cutter, D. C.

1975   "Spain and the Oregon Coast." In *The Western Shore: Oregon Country Essays.*
        T. Vaughan, ed. Pp. 29–46. Portland: Oregon Historical Society.

Dauenhauer, N. M., and R. L. Dauenhauer

1987a   " 'Who Painted the Face of the Little Old Man?'—The Battle of Sitka, 1802
        and 1804, from the Tlingit, Russian, and British Points of View." *A Report on
        Work in Progress.* August 1987:1–32.

1987b   "Haa Shuká, Our Ancestors: Tlingit Oral Narratives." In *Classics of Tlingit
        Oral Literature*, vol. 1. *Haa Shuk, Our Ancestors: Tlingit Oral Narratives.*
        Seattle: University of Washington Press.

1990a   "The Battle of Sitka, 1802 and 1804, from Tlingit, Russian, and Other Points
        of View." In *Russia in North America.* R. A. Pierce, ed. Pp. 6–23. Fairbanks:
        Limestone.

1990b   "Haa Tuwunáagu Yís, For Healing Our Spirit: Tlingit Oratory." In *Classics of Tlingit Oral Literature*, vol. 2. *Haa Tuwunáagu Yís, For Healing Our Spirit: Tlingit Oratory*. Seattle: University of Washington Press.

1994   "Haa kusteeyí, Our Culture: Tlingit Life Stories." In *Classics of Tlingit Oral Literature*, vol. 3. *Haa _kusteeyí, Our Culture: Tlingit Life Stories*. Seattle: University of Washington Press.

Davidson, D. S.
1941   "Relations of the Hudson's Bay Company with the Russian Company on the Northwest Coast, 1829–1867." *British Columbia Historical Quarterly* 5(1):33–51.

Davydov, G. I.
1810   *Dvukratnoe puteshestvie v Ameriku morskikh ofitserov Khvostova i Davydova, pisannoe sim poslednim* [Twofold Trip to America by the Naval Officers Khvostov and Davydov, Written by the Latter]. Pt. 1. St. Petersburg: Morskaia tipografiia.

1812   *Dvukratnoe puteshestvie v Ameriku morskikh ofitserov Khvostova i Davydova, pisannoe sim poslednim* [Twofold Trip to America by the Naval Officers Khvostov and Davydov, Written by the Latter]. Pt. 2. St. Petersburg: Morskaia tipografiia.

Dean, J. R.
1994   " 'Their Nature and Qualities Remain Unchanged': Russian Occupation and Tlingit Resistance, 1802–1867." *Alaska History* 9(1):1–17.

1995   " 'Uses of the Past' on the Northwest Coast: The Russian-American Company and Tlingit Nobility, 1825–1867." *Ethnohistory* 42(2):265–302.

De Laguna, F.
1947   "The Prehistory of Northern North America as Seen from the Yukon." *Current to American Antiquity* 12(3):3–360.

1960   "The Story of a Tlingit Community: A Problem in the Relationship between Archeological, Ethnological, and Historical Methods." *Bulletin of the* BAE 172:1–254.

1963   "Yakutat Canoes." *Folk* 5:219–229.

1972   *Under Mount Saint Elias: The History and Culture of Yakutat Tlingit*. Pt. 1–3. Washington DC: Smithsonian Institution Press.

1975   "Matrilineal Kin Groups in Northwestern North America." *Proceedings: Northern Athapaskan Conference* 1:17–147. 1971 Paper No. 27. Canadian Ethnohistory Service, National Museum of Canada, Ottawa. A. McFadyen

Clark, ed. 2 vols. National Museum of Man. Mercury Series. Ethnology Service Papers 27. Ottawa.

1983   "Aboriginal Tlingit Sociopolitical Organization." In *The Development of Political Organization in Native North America: 1979 Proceedings of the American Ethnological Society*. E. Tooker, ed. Pp. 71–85. Philadelphia: American Ethnological Society.

1987   "Atna and Tlingit Shamanism: Witchcraft on the Northwest Coast." *Arctic Anthropology* 24(1):84–100.

1990a   "Eyak." *Handbook of North American Indians*, vol. 7. *Northwest Coast*, 189–196. Washington DC: Smithsonian Institution.

1990b   "Tlingit." *Handbook of North American Indians*, vol. 7. *Northwest Coast*, 203–228. Washington DC: Smithsonian Institution.

De Laguna, F., and C. McClellan
1981   "Ahtna." In *Handbook of North American Indians*, vol. 6. *Subarctic*, 641–663. Washington DC: Smithsonian Institution.

De Laguna, F., F. A. Riddell, D. F. McGeein, K. S. Lane, J. A. Freed, and C. Osborne
1964   "Archaeology of the Yakutat Bay Area, Alaska." *Bulletin of the* BAE 192:1–245.

Divin, V. A.
1967   "Russkie moreplavaniia k beregam Ameriki posle Beringa i Chirikova" [Russian Voyages to the Shores of America after Bering and Chirikov]. *Ot Aliaski do Ognennoi Zemli* [From Alaska to Tierra del Fuego], 85–94. Moscow: Nauka.

1971   *Russkie moreplavaniia na Tikhom okeane v XVIII v.* [Russian Voyages on the Pacific Ocean in the 18th Century]. Moscow: Mysl'.

Dmitrishin, B.
1994   "Administrativnyi apparat Rossiisko-Amerikanskoi kompanii, 1798–1867" [The Administrative Apparatus of the Russian-American Company, 1798–1867]. In *Amerikanskii ezhegodnik* [American Annual]. Pp. 96–115. Moscow: Nauka.

Doklad komiteta
1863a   *Doklad komiteta ob ustroistve russkikh amerikanskikh kolonii* [Report of the Committee on the Establishment of the Russian American Colonies]. St. Petersburg: Tipografiia departamenta vneshnei torgovli.

1863b   *Doklad komiteta ob ustroistve russkikh amerikanskikh kolonii: Prilozheniia* [Report of the Committee on the Establishment of the Russian American Colonies: Preface]. St. Petersburg: Tipografiia departamenta vneshnei torgovli.

Donskoi, V.

1893   "Sitkha i koloshi" [Sitka and the Tlingit]. In *Pribavlenie k tserkovnym vedomostiam* [Addendum to Church Bulletin] 22:823–828; 23:856–862.

Doroshin, P. P.

1866   "Iz zapisok, vedennykh v Russkoi Amerike" [From Notes Made in Russian America]. *Gornyi zhurnal* [Mountain Journal] 1(3):365–400.

Drucker, P.

1955   *Indians of the Northwest Coast.* New York: American Museum of Natural History.

1958   "The Native Brotherhoods: Modern Intertribal Organizations of the Northwest Coast." *Bulletin of the Bureau of American Ethnology* 168:1–194.

1965   *Cultures of the North Pacific Coast.* San Francisco: Chandler.

1967   "Rank, Wealth, and Kinship in Northwest Coast Society." In *Indians of the North Pacific Coast.* T. McFeat, ed. Pp. 55–65. Seattle: University of Washington Press.

Duff, W.

1964   "The Indian History of British Columbia," vol. 1. *The Impact of the White Man. Anthropology in British Columbia*, Memoir No. 5. *Victoria: Royal British Columbia Museum.*

Dzeniskevich, G. I.

1976   "Skazanie o Vorone u atapaskov Aliaski" [Legends about Raven among the Athapaskans of Alaska]. *SE* 1:73–83.

1979   "Tovaroobmen u atapaskov Aliaski v pervoi polovine XIX v." [Barter among the Athapaskans of Alaska during the First Half of the 19th Century]. In *Problemy istorii i etnografii Ameriki* [Problems of History and Ethnography in America]. Pp. 254–264. Moscow: Nauka.

1984   "Medved' v fol'klore indeitsev Aliaski" [The Bear in the Folklore of the Indians of Alaska]. In *Fol'klor i etnografiia* [Folklore and Ethnography]. Pp. 16–23. Leningrad: Nauka.

1985   "Medved' v iskusstve indeitsev severo-zapadnogo poberezh'ia Severnoi Ameriki" [The Bear in the Art of the Indians of the Northwest Coast of North America]. *Sbornik* MAE: *Kul'tura narodov Ameriki* [Collection of the Museum of Anthropology and Ethnology: Culture and Way of Life of the Peoples of America] 10:59–73.

1987a   *Atapaski Aliaski: Ocherki material'noi i dukhovnoi kul'tury, konets XVIII–nachalo XIX v.* [The Athapaskans of Alaska: An Outline of the Material and Spiritual Culture, End of the 18th–Beginning of the 19th Century]. Leningrad: Nauka.

1987b   "Rol' totemnoi simvoliki v potlache u tlinkitov" [The Role of the Totemic Symbol in the Potlatch among the Tlingit]. *SE* 3:106–114.

1990   "Legenda khaida 'Proiskhozhdenie gryzushchego Bobra' (k probleme rekonstruktsii obshchestva khaida XIX v)." [The Haida Legend "Origin of the Gnawing Beaver" (Toward the Problem of Reconstruction of Haida Society of the 19th Century)]. In *Fol'klor i etnografiia: Problemy rekonstruktsii faktov traditsionnoi kul'tury* [Folklore and Ethnography: Problems of the Reconstruction of Facts of Traditional Culture]. Pp. 126–137. Leningrad: Nauka.

1992   "K rannei istorii russko-tlinkitskikh otnoshenii" [Toward the Early History of Russian-Tlingit Interrelations]. In *Amerika posle Kolumba: Vzaimodeistvie dvukh mirov* [America after Columbus: The Interaction of Two Worlds]. Pp. 64–73. Moscow: Nauka.

1994   "Religioznye traditsii indeitsev Aliaski i khristianstva" [Religious Traditions of the Indians of Alaska and Christianity]. In *Otkrytie Ameriki prodolzhaetsia* [The Discovery of America Continues], vol. 2. Pp. 88–105. St. Petersburg: Muzei antropologii i etnografii [Museum of Anthropology and Ethnography].

1996   "Simvoly statusa tlinkitskogo vozhdia" [Symbols of Status of the Tlingit Leader]. In *Simvoly i atributy vlasti* [Symbols and Attributes of Authority]. Pp. 285–300. St. Petersburg: Muzei antropologii i etnografii [Museum of Anthropology and Ethnography].

Efimov, A. V.
1948   *Iz istorii russkikh ekspeditsii na Tikhom okeane: Pervaia polovina XVIII veka* [From the History of Russian Expeditions to the Pacific Ocean: First Half of the 18th Century]. Moscow: Voennoe izdatel'stvo Ministerstva Vooruzhennykh sil SSSR [Military Publishers of the Ministry of Armed Forces of the USSR].

1969   *SShA. Puti razvitiia kapitalizma* [The USA. Courses of Development of Capitalism]. Moscow: Nauka.

1971   *Iz istorii velikikh russkikh geograficheskikh otkrytii* [From the History of the Great Russian Geographic Discoveries]. Moscow: Nauka.

Efimov, A. V., and S. A. Tokarev, eds.
1959   *Narody Ameriki* [Peoples of America], vol. 1. Moscow: Izdatel'stvo AN SSSR.

Emmons, G. T.
1903   "The Basketry of the Tlingit." *Memoirs of the American Museum of Natural History* 3:229–277.

1911   *The Tahltan Indians*. Philadelphia: The University of Pennsylvania Museum.

1982   "The Whale House of Chilkat." In *Raven's Bones*. Pp. 68–90. Sitka AK: Sitka Community Association.

1991   *The Tlingit Indians*. F. de Laguna, ed. Seattle: University of Washington Press.

Erman, A.

1870   "Ethnographische Wahrnehmungen und Erfahrungen an den Küsten des Bering-Meers" [Ethnographic Observations and Experiences on the Coasts of the Bering Sea]. *Zeitschrift für Ethnologie* [Periodical for Ethnology] 2:295–327, 369–393.

Fainberg, L. A.

1964   *Obshchestvennyi stroi eskimosov i aleutov ot materinskogo roda k sosedskoi obshchine* [Social Structure of the Eskimos and Aleuts from the Maternal Clan to the Neighborly Community]. Moscow: Nauka.

1971   *Ocherki etnicheskoi istorii zarubezhnogo Severa* [An Outline of the Ethnic History of the Non-Russian North]. Moscow: Nauka.

Feder, N.

1973   *American Indian Art*. New York: Harry N. Abrams.

Fedorova, S. G.

1971   *Russkoe naselenie Aliaski i Kalifornii: Konets XVIII veka–1867 g.* [The Russian Population of Alaska and California: End of the Eighteenth Century–1867]. Moscow: Nauka.

1972   "Pervoe postoiannoe poselenie russkikh v Amerike i Dzh. Kuk" [The First Permanent Colony of Russians in America and J. Cook]. In *Novoe v izuchenii Avstralii i Okeanii* [What Is New in the Study of Australia and Oceania]. Pp. 228–236. Moscow: Nauka.

1973   "Etnicheskie protsessy v Russkoi Amerike" [Ethnic Processes in Russian America]. In *Natsional'nye protsessy v SShA* [National Processes in the USA]. Pp. 158–180. Moscow: Nauka.

1979   "Russkaia Amerika i Tot'ma v sud'be Ivana Kuskova" [Russian America and Tot'ma in the Fate of Ivan Kuskov]. In *Problemy istorii i etnografii Ameriki* [Problems of History and Ethnography in America]. Pp. 229–253. Moscow: Nauka.

1981   "Russkoe nasledie v sud'bakh korennogo naseleniia Aliaski" [The Russian Legacy in the Fate of the Native Population of Alaska]. In *Traditsionnye kul'tury Severnoi Sibiri i Severnoi Ameriki* [Traditional Cultures of Northern Siberia and North America]. Pp. 244–264. Moscow: Nauka.

Feest, K.

1985   *Iskusstvo korennykh narodov Severnoi Ameriki* [The Art of the Native Peoples of North America]. Moscow: Raduga.

Firsov, I. I.

1988   *Polveka pod parusami* [A Half Century under Sail]. Moscow: Mysl'.

Fisher, R.

1977   *Contact and Conflict: Indian-European Relations in British Columbia, 1774–1890*. Vancouver: University of British Columbia Press.

Fradkin, E. K.

1985   "Polieikoniia v iskusstve tlinkitov" [Poly-Iconism in the Art of the Tlingit]. *Sbornik* MAE *Kul'tura i byt narodov Ameriki* [Collection of the Museum of Anthropology and Ethnography: Culture and Way of Life of the Peoples of America] 40: 91–110.

Frost, O. W., ed.

1992   *Bering and Chirikov: The American Voyages and Their Impact*. Anchorage: Alaska Historical Society.

Fuller, G. W.

1931   *A History of the Pacific Northwest*. New York: A. A. Knopf.

Galbraith, J. S.

1957   *The Hudson's Bay Company as an Imperial Factor, 1821–1869*. Berkeley: University of California Press.

Garfield, V. E.

1939   "Tsimshian Clan and Society." *University of Washington Publications in Anthropology* 7(3):167–349.

1947   "Historical Aspects of Tlingit Clans in Angoon." *American Anthropologist* 49:438–452.

Garfield, V. E., and L. A. Forrest

1961   *The Wolf and the Raven*. Seattle: University of Washington Press.

Gibson, J. R.

1975   "Bostonians and Muscovites on the Northwest Coast, 1788–1841." In *The Western Shore: Oregon Country Essays*. T. Vaughan, ed. Pp. 81–120. Portland: Oregon Historical Society.

1976   *Imperial Russia in Frontier America*. New York: Oxford University Press.

1987a   "Russian Expansion in Siberia and America." In *Russia's American Colony*. S. Frederick Starr, ed. Pp. 32–40. Durham: Duke University Press.

1987b   "Russian Dependence upon the Natives of Alaska." In *Russia's American Colony*. S. Frederick Starr, ed. Pp. 77–104. Durham: Duke University Press.

1988   "The Maritime Trade of the North Pacific Coast." In *Handbook of North American Indians*, vol. 4. *History of Indian-White Relations*. Pp. 375–390. Washington DC: Smithsonian Institution.

1990   "Furs and Food: Russian America and the Hudson's Bay Company." In *Russian America: The Forgotten Frontier*. B. S. Smith and R. J. Barnet, eds. Pp. 68–77. Tacoma: Washington State Historical Society.

1992   *Otter Skins, Boston Ships, and China Goods. The Maritime Fur Trade of the Northwest Coast, 1785–1841.* Seattle: University of Washington Press.

Goddard, P. E.
1924   *Indians of the Northwest Coast.* New York: American Museum Press.

Golovin, P. N.
1862   "Obzor russkikh kolonii v Severnoi Amerike" [Survey of the Russian Colonies in North America]. *Morskoi sbornik* [Sea Collection] 57(3):19–192.

1863a   "Iz putevykh zametok P. N. Golovina s predisloviem V. Rimskogo-Korsakova" [From the Traveling Notes of P. N. Golovin with the Preface of V. Rimsky-Korsakov]. *Morskoi sbornik* [Sea Collection] 5:101–182; 6:275–340.

1863b   "Obzor russkikh kolonii v Severnoi Amerike kapitana 2-go ranga Golovina" [Survey of the Russian Colonies in North America by Captain of the 2nd Rank Golovin]. In *Prolozheniia k dokladu Komiteta ob ustroistve Russkikh Amerikanskikh kolonii* [Developing an Address to the Committee about Organization of the Russian-American Colonies]. Pp. 268–462. St. Petersburg: Tipografiia departamenta vneshnei torgovli.

Golovnin, V. M.
1864   *Sochineniia i perevody Vasiliia Mikhailovicha Golovnina* [The Works and Translations of Vasilii Mikhailovich Golovnin], vol. 4, 5. St. Petersburg: Tipografiia Morskogo ministerstva.

1961   *Puteshestvie na shliupe "Diana" iz Kronshtadta v Kamchatku, sovershennoe pod nachal'stvom flota leitenanta Golovnina v 1807–1811 godakh* [Voyage on the Sloop *Diana* from Kronshtadt to Kamchatka, Conducted under the Leadership of Fleet Lieutenant Golovnin in 1807–1811]. Moscow: Geografgiz.

1965   *Puteshestvie vokrug sveta, sovershennoe na voennom shliupe "Kamchatka" v 1817, 1818 i 1819 godakh flota kapitanom Golovninym* [Voyage around the World, Conducted on the Sloop *Kamchatka* in 1817, 1818, and 1819 by Fleet Captain Golovnin]. Moscow: Mysl'.

Gough, B. M.

1975   *The Northwest Coast in Late 18th-Century British Expansion.* In *The Western
Shore: Oregon Country Essays.* T. Vaughan, ed. Pp. 47–80. Portland: Oregon
Historical Society.

Grinev, A. V.

1983   *Kolonizatsiia Russkoi Ameriki i frantsuzskaia kolonizatsiia Kanady: Obshchee i
osobennoe* [The Colonization of Russian America and French Colonization
of Canada: General and Particular]. In *Nauchno-tekhnicheskomu progressu—
tvorcheskii poisk vuzov* [Toward Scientific-Technical Progress—Creative
Quests of Institutions of Higher Education]. P. 66 (Tez. dokl. 1-i Kraevoi
mezhvuz. nauch.-prakt. konf. 27–28 aprelia 1983 g.) [Thesis of a Lecture at
the 1st Regional Interinstitutional Scientific-Practical Conference of April
27–28, 1983]. Barnaul, Russia: Poligrafist.

1986a   "Ob etnonime 'koloshi'" [On the Ethnonym "Koloshi"]. *SE* 1:104–108.

1986b   "Tovaroobmen mezhdu indeitsami tlinkitami i atapaskami Skalistykh gor v
XIX veke" [Barter between the Tlingit Indians and the Athapaskan Indians
of the Rocky Mountains in the 19th Century]. *SE* 5:113–122.

1987   "Zabytaia ekspeditsiia Dmitriia Tarkhanova na Mednuiu reku" [The Forgotten Expedition of Dimitrii Tarkhanov on the Copper River]. *SE* 4:88–100.

1988a   "Godovoi khoziaistvennyi tsikl tlinkitov" [The Annual Economic Cycle of
the Tlingit]. In *Ekologiia amerikanskikh indeitsev i eskimosov* [Ecology of the
American Indians and Eskimos]. Moscow: Nauka.

1988b   "Indeitsy eiaki i sud'ba russkogo poseleniia v Yakutate" [The Eyak Indians
and the Fate of the Russian Colony in Yakutat]. *SE* 5:110–120.

1989a   "Totem v traditsionnom tlinkitskom obshchestve" [The Totem in Traditional
Tlingit Society]. In *Lingvisticheskaia rekonstruktsiia i drevneishaia istoriia Vostoka* [Linguistic Reconstruction and Earliest History of the East]. Pp. 38–40
(Tez. dokl. Mezhdunar. konf. 29 maia–2 iiunia 1989 g.) [Thesis of a Lecture
at the International Conference of May 29–June 2, 1989]. Moscow: Nauka.

1989b   "The Eyak Indians and the Fate of a Russian Settlement in Yakutat." *European Review of Native American Studies* 3(2):1–6.

1990   "Lichnye imena indeitsev tlinkitov" [Personal Names of the Tlingit Indians].
SE 5:132–141.

1991   *Indeitsy tlinkity v period Russkoi Ameriki (1741–1867 g.)* [Tlingit Indians of the
Russian America Period (1741–1867)]. Novosibirsk, Russia: Nauka.

1994a   "Nekotorye tendentsii otechestvennoi istoriografii rossiiskoi kolonizatsii
Aliaski" [Some Tendencies of the Russian Historiography of the Russian
Colonization of Alaska]. *Voprosy istorii* [Questions of History] 11:163–167.

1994b   "Frederika de Laguna i ee vklad v izuchenie korennogo naseleniia Aliaski" [Frederica de Laguna and Her Contribution to the Study of the Native Population of Alaska]. *Etnograficheskoe obozrenie* [Ethnographic Review] 4:120–125.

1995   "Totemizm u indeitsev khaida, tlinkitov i tsimshian" [Totemism among the Haida, Tlingit, and Tsimshian Indians]. *Etnograficheskoe obozrenie* [Ethnographic Review] 4:115–125.

1996a   "Vzaimootnosheniia Rossiisko-Amerikanskoi kompanii i Kompanii Gudzonova zaliva: Problema anglo-russkikh kontaktov v Severnoi Amerike (1821–1867 gg.)" [Interrelations of the Russian-American Company and the Hudson's Bay Company: The Problem of Anglo-Russian Contacts in North America (1821–1867)]. In *Aktual'nye voprosy istorii, istoriografii i mezhdunarodnykh otnoshenii.* [Crucial Questions on History, Historiography, and International Relations] Pp. 61–92. Barnaul, Russia: Izdatel'stvo Altaiskogo gosudarstvennogo universiteta [Publisher of Altai State University].

1996b   " 'Kolonial'nyi politarizm' v Novom Svete" ['Colonial Politarism' in the New World]. *Etnograficheskoe obozrenie* [Ethnographic Review] 4:52–64.

1999   "Russkaia Amerika i SSSR: Udivitel'nye paralleli" [Russian America and the USSR: Strange Parallels]. *Klio* 1:119–127.

2001   "Russko-tlinkitskii konflikt 1818 g. i ego rezreshenie" [The Russian-Tlingit Conflict of 1818 and Its Resolution]. In *Russkaia Amerika i Dal'nii Vostok (konets XVIII v.–1867 g.)* [Russian America and the Far East (End of the 18th Century to 1867)]. For the 200-Year Establishment of the Russian-American Company. Materials of the International Scientific Conference (Vladivostok, October 11–13, 1999).

Grinev, A. V., and M. P. Iroshnikov

1998   "Rossiia i politarizm" [Russia and Politarism]. *Voprosy istorii* [Questions of History] 7:40.

Grinnell, G. B.

1902   "Natives of the Alaska Coast Region." In *Alaska 1899: Essays from the Harriman Expedition, vol. 1: Narrative, Glaciers, Natives.* J. Burroughs, J. Muir, and G. B. Grinnell, eds. Pp. 137–183. New York: Doubleday, Page.

Gul'sen, K.

1849   "Puteshestvie na shliupe *Blagonamerennyi* dlia issledovaniia beregov Azii i Ameriki za Beringovym prolivom s 1819 po 1822 god" [Journey on the Sloop *Blagonamerennyi* for the Investigation of the Coasts of Asia and America beyond Bering Strait from 1819 to 1822]. *Otechestvennye zapiski* [Homeland Notes] 67(10):213–281; 67(11/12):275–340.

Gunther, E.
1972   *Indian Life of the Northwest Coast.* Chicago: University of Chicago Press.

Hallock, C.
1886   *Our New Alaska.* New York: Forest and Steam.

Holm, B.
1965   *Northwest Coast Indian Art.* Seattle: University of Washington Press.

1984   *The Box of Daylight: Northwest Coast Indian Art.* Seattle: University of Washington Press.

Holm, B., and W. A. Reid
1972   *Dialogue on Form and Northwest Coast Freedom Indian Art.* Houston: Institute for the Arts, Rice University.

Holmberg, H. J.
1855   *Ethnographische Skizzen über die Völker des Russischen Amerika* [Ethnographic Sketches of the Peoples of Russian America], vol. 1. Helsingfors, Finland: Gedruckt bei H. C. Friss.

Howay, F. W.
1973   "A List of Trading Vessels in the Maritime Fur Trade, 1785–1825." *Materials for the Study of Alaskan History* 2:1–209.

Howay, F. W., ed.
1941   *Voyages of the* Columbia *to the Northwest Coast 1787–1790 and 1790–1793.* Boston. Reprinted New York: Da Capo, 1969).

Hulley, C. C.
1953   *Alaska, 1741–1953.* Portland: Binford and Mort.

Hunt, W. R.
1976   *Alaska: A Bicentennial History.* New York: Norton.

Indeitsy Ameriki
1955   "Indeitsy Ameriki" [Indians of America]. *Sbornik* TIE 25. Moscow.

Istomin, A. A.
1980   "Selenie Ross i kaliforniiskie indeitsy" [The Ross Settlement and the California Indians]. *SE* 4:57–69.

1985   "Russko-tlinkitskie kontakty (XVIII–XIX vv.)" [Russian-Tlingit Contacts (18th–19th Centuries)]. In *Istoricheskie sud'by amerikanskikh indeitsev* [Historical Fate of the American Indians]. Pp. 146–154. Moscow: Nauka.

Istoriia pervobytnogo obshchestva . . .
1986   *Istoriia pervobytnogo obshchestva: Epokha pervobytnoi rodovoi obshchiny* [The History of Primitive Society: The Epoch of Primitive Clan Community]. Moscow: Nauka.

Istoriia pervobytnogo obshchestva . . .

1988   *Istoriia pervobytnogo obshchestva: Epokha klassoobrazovaniia* [The History of Primitive Society: The Epoch of Class Formation]. Moscow: Nauka.

Ivashintsov, N.

1872   *Russkie krugosvetnye puteshestviia s 1803 po 1849 god* [Russian Round-the-World Voyages from 1803 to 1849]. St. Petersburg: Tipografiia Morskogo ministerstva.

Jacobs, M., Jr.

1990   "Early Encounters between the Tlingit and the Russians." In *Russia in North America*. R. A. Pierce, ed. Pp. 1–6. Proceedings of the 2nd International Conference on Russian America (Sitka AK, August 19–22, 1987). Fairbanks: Limestone.

Jacobs, M., Jr., and M. Jacobs, Sr.

1982   "Southeast Alaska Native Foods." In *Raven's Bones*. Pp. 112–130. Sitka AK: Sitka Community Association.

Johansen, U. von

1963   "Versuch einer Analyse dokumentarischen Materials über die Identitätsfrage und kulturelle Position der Eyak-Indianer Alaskas" [An Attempt to Analyze Documentary Materials on the Question of Identity and Cultural Position of the Eyak Indians of Alaska]. *Anthropos* 58:868–896.

Jonaitis, A.

1986   *Art of the Northern Tlingit.* Seattle: University of Washington Press.

Jopling, C. F.

1989   *The Coppers of the Northwest Coast Indians: Their Origin, Development, and Possible Antecedents.* Philadelphia: American Philosophical Society.

K istorii Rossiisko-Amerikanskoi Kompanii

1957   *K istorii Rossiisko-Amerikanskoi kompanii: Sb. dokumental'nykh materialov* [Toward the History of the Russian-American Company: A Collection of Documentary Materials]. Krasnoyarsk, Russia: Krasnoiarskii gosudarstvennyi arkhiv, Krasnoiarskii gosudarstvennyi pedagogicheskii institut [Krasnoyarsk State Archive, Krasnoyarsk State Pedagogical Institute].

Kabo, V. R.

1986   *Pervobytnaia dozemledel'cheskaia obshchina* [The Primitive Pre-Agricultural Society]. Moscow: Nauka.

Kan, S. A.

1983   "Words that Heal the Soul: Analysis of the Tlingit Potlatch Oratory." *Arctic Anthropology* 20(2):47–59.

1985   "Russian Orthodox Brotherhoods among the Tlingit: Missionary Goals and Native Response." *Ethnohistory* 32(3):196–223.

1987   "Memory Eternal: Orthodox Christianity and the Tlingit Mortuary Complex." *Arctic Anthropology* 24(1):32–55.

1988   "The Russian Orthodox Church in Alaska." In *Handbook of North American Indians*, vol. 4. *History of Indian-White Relations*. Pp. 506–521. Washington DC: Smithsonian Institution Press.

1989   *Symbolic Immortality: The Tlingit Potlatch of the Nineteenth Century.* Washington DC: Smithsonian Institution Press.

1991   "Shamanism and Christianity: Modern-Day Tlingit Elders Look at the Past." *Ethnohistory* 38(4):363–387.

1999   *Memory Eternal: Tlingit Culture and Russian Orthodox Christianity through Two Centuries.* Seattle: University of Washington.

Khazanov, A. M.

1979   "Klassoobrazovanie: faktory i mekhanizmy" [Class Formation: Factors and Mechanisms]. In *Issledovaniia po obshchei etnografii* [Studies in General Ethnography]. Pp. 125–177. Moscow: Nauka.

Khlebnikov, K. T.

1835   *Zhizneopisanie Aleksandra Andreevicha Baranova, Glavnogo pravitelia Rossiiskikh kolonii v Amerike* [Biography of Alexander Andreevich Baranov, Chief Director of the Russian Colonies in America]. St. Petersburg: Morskaia tipografiia.

1861   "Pervonachal'noe poselenie russkikh v Amerike" [The Initial Settlement of the Russians in America]. In *Materialy dlia istorii russkikh zaselenii po beregam Vostochnogo okeana* [Materials on the History of Russian Settlement along the Shores of the Eastern Ocean] 4:40–56. St. Petersburg: Tipografiia Morskogo ministerstva.

1979   *Russkaia Amerika v neopublikovannykh zapiskakh K. T. Khlebnikova* [Russian America in the Unpublished Notes of K. T. Khlebnikov]. R. G. Liapunova and S. G. Fedorova, eds. Leningrad: Nauka.

1985   *Russkaia Amerika v "zapiskakh" Kirila Khlebnikova: Novo-Arkhangel'sk* [Russian America in the "Notes" of Kiril Khlebnikov: New Archangel]. S. G. Fedorova, ed. Moscow: Nauka.

Khrushchov, S. P.

1926   "Plavanie shliupa 'Apollona' v 1821–1824 godakh" [Voyage of the Sloop "Apollon" in 1821–1824]. In *Zapiski, izdavaemye Gosudarstvennym Admiralteiskim departamentom* [Notes Published by the State Admiralty Department] 10:200–272.

Kittlitz, F. H. von

1858   *Denkwürdigkeiten einer Reise nach dem Russischen Amerika, nach Mikronesien und durch Kamtschatka von F. H. von Kittlitz* [Memorabilia of a Trip to Russian America, Micronesia, and through Kamchatka by F. H. von Kittlitz], vols. 1 and 2. Gotha, Germany: Verlag von Justus Perthes.

Klein, L. F.

1987   "Demystifying the Opposition: The Hudson's Bay Company and the Tlingit." *Arctic Anthropology* 24(1):101–114.

Koloshi i ikh . . .

1866   "Koloshi i ikh orudiia" [The Koloshi and Their Tools]. Voskresnyi dosug [Sunday Leisure] 7(159):141–142.

Kostlivtsov, S. A.

1863   "Otchet po obozreniiu Rossiisko-Amerikanskikh kolonii deistvitel'nogo statskogo sovetnika Kostlivtsova" [Report on a Survey of the Russian-American Company by the Active Councillor of State Kostlivtsov]. In *Prilozheniia k dokladu Komiteta ob ustroistve Russkikh Amerikanskikh kolonii* [Developing an Address to the Committee about Organization of the Russian-American Colonies]. Pp. 1–267. St. Petersburg: Tipografiia departamenta vneshnei torgovli.

Kotzebue, O. E.

1821–1823 *Puteshestvie v Yuzhnyi okean i v Beringov proliv dlia otyskaniia Severo-Vostochnogo morskogo prokhoda, predpriniatoe v 1815, 16, 17 i 1818 godakh* . . . [Voyage in the Southern Seas and in Bering Strait for Locating the Northeast Sea Passage, Undertaken in 1815, 1816, 1817, and 1818 . . .]. 1821, pt. 1; 1822, pt. 2; 1823, pt. 3. St. Petersburg: Tipografiia N. Grecha.

1987   *Novoe puteshestvie vokrug sveta v 1823–1826 gg.* [New Voyage around the World 1823–1826]. Moscow: Nauka.

Krause, A.

1956   *The Tlingit Indians.* Seattle: University of Washington Press.

Krauss, M. E.

1975   *Native People and Languages of Alaska* (map). Fairbanks: Alaska Native Language Center.

1981   "Yazyki korennogo naseleniia Aliaski: Proshloe, nastoiashchee i budushchee" [Languages of the Native Population of Alaska: Past, Present, and Future]. In *Traditsionnye kul'tury Severnoi Sibiri i Severnoi Ameriki* [Traditional Cultures of Northern Siberia and North America]. Pp. 149–182. Moscow: Nauka.

Krauss, M. E., ed.

1982   *In Honor of the Eyak: The Art of Anna Nelson Harry*. Michael E. Krauss, ed. Fairbanks: Alaska Native Language Center.

Krauss, M. E., and V. K. Golla

1981   "Northern Athapaskan Languages." In *Handbook of North American Indians*, vol. 6. *Subarctic*. Pp. 67–85. Washington DC: Smithsonian Institution Press.

Kriukov, M. V.

1967   *Formy sotsial'noi organizatsii drevnikh kitaitsev* [Forms of Social Organization of the Early Chinese]. Moscow: Nauka.

Krupnik, I. I.

1992   "Kul'turnye kontakty i ikh demograficheskie posledstviia v raione Beringova proliva" [Cultural Contacts and Their Demographic Consequences in the Region of Bering Strait]. In *Amerika posle Kolumba: vzaimodeistvie dvukh mirov* [America after Columbus: Interaction of Two Worlds]. Pp. 30–47. Moscow: Nauka.

Kubbel', L. E.

1988   *Ocherki potestarno-politicheskoi etnografii* [Outline of Power-Politics Ethnography]. Moscow: Nauka.

Kushner, H. I.

1975   *Conflict on the Northwest Coast: American-Russian Rivalry in the Pacific Northwest, 1790–1867*. Westport CT: Greenwood.

Langsdorff, Georg H. von

1812   *Bemerkungen auf einer Reise um die Welt in den Jahren 1803 bis 1807 von G. H. von Langsdorff* [Observations on a Voyage around the World in the Years 1803 to 1807 by G. H. von Langsdorff], vols. 1 and 2. Frankfurt: F. Wilmans.

La Pérouse, J. F. G. de

1968   *A Voyage 'round the World, Performed in the Years 1785, 1786, 1787 and 1788 by the* Boussole *and* Astrolabe. New York: Da Capo.

Larionova, N.

1988   "Sosedi cherez proliv" [Neighbors across the Strait]. *Pravda* (November 12).

Lazarev, Aleksei P.

1950   *Zapiski o plavanii voennogo shliupa "Blagonamerennogo" v Beringov proliv i vokrug sveta dlia otkrytii v 1819, 1820, 1821 i 1822 godakh, vedennye gvardeiskogo ekipazha leitenantom A. P. Lazarevym* [Notes on the Voyage of the Naval Sloop *Blagonamerennyi* in Bering Strait and around the World for Discoveries in 1819, 1820, 1821, and 1822. Introduced by Lieutenant of Guard Crew, A. P. Lazarev]. Moscow: Gosudarstvennoe izdatel'stvo geograficheskoi literatury [State Publisher of Geographic Literature].

Lazarev, Andrei P.

1832   *Plavanie vokrug sveta na shliupe "Ladoga:" v 1822, 1823 i 1824 godakh shliup-
om nachal'stvoval kapitan-leitenant Andrei Lazarev* . . . [Voyage around the
World on the Sloop *Ladoga*: in 1822, 1823, and 1824 the Sloop was Commanded by Captain-Lieutenant Andrei Lazarev . . .]. St. Petersburg: Morskaia tipografiia.

Lazarev, M. P.

1952   *Dokumenty* [Documents], vol. 1. Moscow: Voeno-morskoe izdatel'stvo
[Naval Publisher].

Lebedev, D. M.

1951   *Plavanie A. I. Chirikova na paketbote "Sv. Pavel" k poberezh'iam Ameriki: S
prilozheniem sudovogo zhurnala 1741 g.* [The Voyage of A. I. Chirikov on the
Packet Boat *St. Pavel* to the Coasts of America: With a Supplement of the
Ship's Journal 1741]. Moscow: Izdatel'stvo AN SSSR.

Lévi-Strauss, C.

1982   *The Way of the Masks.* Seattle: University of Washington Press.

1985   *Strukturnaia antropologiia* [Structural Anthropology]. Moscow: Nauka.

1994   *Pervobytnoe myshlenie* [Primitive Thought]. Moscow: Respublika.

Liapunova, R. G.

1967   "Ekspeditsiia I. G. Voznesenskogo i ee znachenie dlia etnografii Russkoi
Ameriki" [The Expedition of I. G. Voznesenskii and Its Significance for
Ethnography of Russian America]. *Sbornik MAE: Kul'tura i byt narodov
Ameriki* [Collection of the Museum of Anthropology and Ethnology: Cul-
ture and Way of Life of the Peoples of America] 34:5–33.

1975   *Ocherki etnografii aleutov (konets XVIII–pervaia polovina XIX v.)* [A Survey
of the Ethnography of the Aleuts (End of the 18th–First Half of the 19th
Century)]. Leningrad: Nauka.

1979   "Zapiski ieromonakha Gedeona (1803–1807)—odin iz istochnikov po istorii
i etnografii Russkoi Ameriki" [The Notes of Hieromonk Gedeon (1803–
1807)—One of the Sources of History and Ethnography of Russian Amer-
ica]. In *Problemy istorii i etnografii Ameriki* [Problems of History and Ethnography in America]. Pp. 215–229. Moscow: Nauka.

1985   "K probleme etnokul'turnogo razvitiia amerikanskikh aleutov (so vtoroi po-
loviny XVIII v. do nashikh dnei)" [Toward the Problem of the Ethno-
Cultural Development of the American Aleuts (From the Second Half of
the 18th Century to Our Day)]. In *Istoricheskie sud'by amerikanskikh indeitsev*
[Historical Fate of American Indians]. Pp. 293–305. Moscow: Nauka.

1987 *Aleuty: Ocherki etnicheskoi istorii* [The Aleuts: An Outline of the Ethnic History]. Leningrad: Nauka.

Lisianskii, Yu. F.

1812 *Puteshestvie vokrug sveta v 1803, 4, 5 i 1806 godakh . . .* [Voyage around the World in 1803, 1804, 1805, and 1806 . . .]. Pt. II. St. Petersburg: Tipografiia F. Drekhslera.

Litke, F. P.

1834 *Puteshestvie vokrug sveta, sovershennoe . . . na voennom shliupe "Seniavin" v 1826, 1827, 1828 i 1829 godakh . . .* [Voyage around the World, Conducted . . . in the Naval Sloop *Siniavin* in 1826, 1827, 1828, and 1829 . . .]. Pt. I. St. Petersburg: Tipografiia III Otdeleniia sobstvennoi e.i.v. Kantseliarii [Printing House of the 3rd Division of His Imperial Majesty's Own Chancellory].

Liutyi, A.

1989 "Russkaia Amerika" [Russian America]. *Pravda* (16 February).

Lopukhin, A.

1989 "Tam russkii dukh . . ." [There is the Russian Spirit . . .]. *Pravda.* (January 16).

MacLachlan, B. B.

1981 "Tahltan." In *Handbook of North American Indians,* vol. 6. *Subarctic.* Pp. 458–468. Washington DC: Smithsonian Institution Press.

Magidovich, I. P.

1962 *Istoriia otkrytiia i issledovaniia Severnoi Ameriki* [The History of the Discovery and Investigation of North America]. Moscow: Geografgiz.

Magidovich, I. P., and V. I. Magidovich

1984 *Ocherki po istorii geograficheskikh otkrytii: Geograficheskie otkrytiia i issledovaniia novogo vremeni (seredina XVII–XVIII v.)* [An Essay on the History of Geographic Discoveries: Geographic Discoveries and Investigations of Recent Times (Middle of the 17th–18th Century)], vol. 3. Moscow: Prosveshenie.

1985 *Ocherki po istorii geograficheskikh otkrytii: Geograficheskie otkrytiia i issledovaniia novogo vremeni (XIX–nachalo XX v.)* [An Essay on the History of Geographic Discoveries: Geographic Discoveries and Investigations of Recent Times (19th–Beginning of the 20th Century)], vol. 4. Moscow: Prosveshenie.

Makarova, R. V.

1968 *Russkie na Tikhom okeane vo vtoroi polovine XVIII v.* [Russians on the Pacific Ocean during the Second Half of the 18th Century]. Moscow: Nauka.

1974   *Vneshniaia politika Rossii na Dal'nem Vostoke: Vtoraia polovina XVIII v.* [The External Politics of Russia in the Far East: Second Half of the 18th Century]. Moscow: Ministerstvo vysshego i srednego spetsial'nogo obrazovaniia RSFSR, Moskovskii gosudarstvennyi istoriko-arkhivnyi institut [Ministry of Higher and Middle Special Education of the Russian Soviet Federative Socialist Republic, Moscow State Historical-Archival Institute].

1979   "K istorii likvidatsii Rossiisko-Amerikanskoi kompanii" [Toward the History of the Liquidation of the Russian-American Company]. In *Problemy istorii i etnografii Ameriki* [Problems of History and Ethnography in America]. Pp. 264–274. Moscow: Nauka.

Malakhovskii, K. V.
1985   *Istoriia Novoi Zelandii* [The History of New Zealand]. Moscow: Nauka.

Malaspina, A. A.
1824–1827 "Puteshestvie v Yuzhnom more, k zapadnym beregam Amerikii ostrovam Marianskim i Filippinskim, sovershennoe v 1789, 90, 91, 92, 93 i 94 godakh . . ." [Voyage in the South Seas, to the Western Shores of America, and to the Mariana and Philippine Islands, Conducted in the 1789, 1790, 1791, 1792, 1793, and 1794 . . .]. In *Zapiski, izdavaemye Gosudarstvennym Admiralteiskim departamentom* [Notes Published by the State Admiralty Department]. 1824, pts. 6, 7; 1825, pts. 8, 9; 1827, pts. 12, 13.

Mamyshev, V. N.
1855   "Amerikanskie vladeniia Rossii" [The American Possessions of Russia]. *Biblioteka dlia chteniia* [Library for Reading] 130(2):204–292.

Manning, C. A.
1953   *Russian Influence on Early America.* New York: Library Publishers.

Maretin, Yu. V.
1975   Obshchina sosedsko-bol'shesemeinogo tipa u minangkabau (Zapadnaia Sumatra) [Community of the Neighbor–Large Family type among the Minangkabau (Western Sumatra)]. In *Sotsial'naia organizatsiia narodov Azii i Afriki* [Social Organization of the Peoples of Asia and Africa]. Pp. 60–132. Moscow: Nauka.

Maretina, S. A.
1948   *Evoliutsiia obshchestvennogo stroia u gornykh narodov Severo-Vostochnoi Indii* [The Evolution of Social Structure among Mountain Peoples of Southeast India]. Moscow: Nauka.

1980   *Evoliutsiia obshchestvennogo stroia u gornykh narodov Severo-Vostochnoi Indii* [The Evolution of Social Structure among Mountain Peoples of Northeastern India]. Moscow: Nauka.

Markov, A.
1856   *Russkie na Vostochnom Okeane* [Russians on the Pacific Ocean]. St. Peters-
        burg: Tipografiia A. Dmitrieva.

Markov, S. N.
1948   *Letopis' Aliaski* [A Chronicle of Alaska]. Moscow: Izdatel'stvo Glavsevmor-
        puti.

Marx, K.
1957   "Britanskoe vladychestvo v Indii" [British Rule in India]. In *Sochineniia*. 2-e
        izdanie [Works (2nd edition)]. K. Marx and F. Engels. 9:130–136.

1957   "Voennyi vopros—Parlamentskie dela—Indiia" [Military Question—Parlia-
        mentary Affair—India]. In *Sochineniia*. 2-e izdanie [Works (2nd edition)]. K.
        Marx and F. Engels. 9:216–223.

1959   "K kritike politicheskoi ekonomii. Predislovie" [Toward a Critique of Politi-
        cal Economy. Preface]. In *Sochineniia*. 2-e izdanie [Works (2nd edition)]. K.
        Marx and F. Engels. 13:5–9.

Materialy dlia istorii . . .
1861   *Materialy dlia istorii russkikh zaselenii po beregam Vostochnogo okeana* [Materi-
        als for the History of Russian Settlement on the Shores of the Pacific Ocean].
        Issues 1–4. St. Petersburg: Tipografiia Morskogo ministerstva.

Maurelle, F. A.
1781   *Journal of a Voyage in 1775 to Explore the Coast of America, Northward of
        California* . . . London: J. Nichols.

Maurer, E. M.
1977   *The Native American Heritage: A Survey of North American Indian Art*. Chi-
        cago: Congress Printing.

Mauss, M.
1996   *Obshestva. Obmen. Lichnost'* [Society. Exchange. Identity]. Moscow: Nauka.

McClellan, C.
1954   "The Interrelations of Social Structure with Northern Tlingit Ceremonial-
        ism." *Southwestern Journal of Anthropology* 17:103–123.

1963   "Wealth Woman and Frogs among the Tagish Indians." *Anthropos* 58(1–
        2):121–128.

1970a   "Indian Stories about the First Whites in Northwestern America." In *Ethno-
        history in Southwestern Alaska and the Southern Yukon*. R. E. Ackerman, ed.
        Pp. 103–133. Lexington: University Press of Kentucky.

1970b   "The Girl Who Married the Bear." *Canada. National Museum of Man. Pub-
        lications in Ethnology*. 2:1–58. Ottawa.

1975   *My Old People Say: An Ethnographic Survey of Southern Yukon Territory.* Pts. 1–2. Ottawa: National Museums of Canada.

1981a   "Inland Tlingit." In *Handbook of North American Indians*, vol. 6. *Subarctic.* Pp. 469–480. Washington DC: Smithsonian Institution Press.

1981b   "Tutchone." In *Handbook of North American Indians*, vol. 6. *Subarctic.* Pp. 493–505. Washington DC: Smithsonian Institution Press.

1989   "Frederica de Laguna and the Pleasures of Anthropology." *American Ethnologist* 16(4):766–785.

McIlwraith, T. F.

1948   *The Bella Coola Indians.* Pts. 1–2. Toronto: University of Toronto Press.

Meletinskii, E. M.

1979   *Paleoaziatskii mifologicheskii epos: Tsikl Vorona* [Paleo-Asiatic Mythological Epic: The Raven Cycle]. Moscow: Nauka.

1981   "Paleoaziatskii epos o Vorone i problema otnosheniia Severo-Vostochnoi Azii i Severo-Zapadnoi Ameriki v oblasti fol'klora" [The Paleo-Asiatic Epic of Raven and the Problem of the Relationship of Northeast Asia and Northwestern America in the Realm of Folklore]. In *Traditsionnye kul'tury Severnoi Sibiri i Severnoi Ameriki* [Traditional Cultures of Northern Siberia and North America]. Pp. 182–200. Moscow: Nauka.

Mikhailov, Yu. A., A. L. Kolodkin, and V. A. Kontalev, eds.

1995   *Pod flagom Rossii: istoriia zarozhdeniia i razvitiia morskogo torgovogo flota / avtorskii kollektiv V. P. Puzyrev (rukovoditel')* . . . [Under the Flag of Russia: The History of Rise and Development of the Maritime Fleet / Author's Collective V. P. Puzyrev (leader) . . .]. Moscow: "Soglasie."

Miller, P.

1967   *Lost Heritage of Alaska.* New York: Bonanza.

Morgan, L. G.

1934   *Drevnee obshchestvo* [Ancient Society]. Leningrad: Izdatel'stvo Instituta narodov Severa [Publisher of the Institute of Peoples of the North].

1983   *Liga khodenosauni, ili irokezov* [League of the Ho-De-No-Sau-Nee, or Iroquois]. Moscow: Nauka.

Morison, S. E.

1922   *The Maritime History of Massachusetts, 1783–1860.* Boston: Houghton Mifflin.

Morskoi entsiklopedicheskii spravochnik

1986   *Morskoi entsiklopedicheskii spravochnik* [Naval Encyclopedic Reference], vol. 2. Leningrad: Sudosrtoenie.

Moss, M.

1996   *Obshchestva. Obmen. Lichnost'* [Societies. Exchange. Personality]. Moscow: Nauka.

Murdock, G. P.

1965   *Culture and Society*. Pittsburgh: University of Pittsburgh Press.

Narochnitskii, A. L.

1956   *Kolonial'naia politika kapitalisticheskikh derzhav na Dal'nem Vostoke: 1860–1895* [Colonial Politics of Capitalist Powers in the Far East: 1860–1895]. Moscow: Izdatel'stvo AN SSSR.

Narochnitskii, A. L., ed.

1963–1985 *Vneshniaia politika Rossii XIX i nachala XX veka: Dokumenty rossiiskogo Ministerstva inostrannykh del* [Foreign Politics of Russia of the 19th and Beginning of the 20th Centuries: Documents of the Russian Ministry of Foreign Affairs], series 1, vol. 3–7; ser. 2, vol. 1–6. Moscow: Gospolitizdat.

Narody mira . . .

1988   *Narody mira: Istoriko-etnograficheskii spravochnik* [Peoples of the World: Historical-Ethnographic Reference Book]. Moscow: Sovetskaia entsiklopediia.

Nevskii, V. V.

1951   *Pervoe puteshestvie rossiian vokrug sveta* [The First Voyage of Russians around the World]. Moscow: Geografgiz.

Niblack, A. P.

1890   "The Coast Indians of Southern Alaska and Northern British Columbia." In *Annual Report of the United States National Museum, 1888*. Washington DC: Government Printing Office.

Nikolai, Bishop of the Aleuts and Alaskans

1893   *Iz moego dnevnika: Putevye zametki i vpechatleniia vo vremia puteshestviia po Aliaske i Aleutskim ostrovam* [From My Diary: Travel Notes and Impressions during a Voyage to Alaska and the Aleutian Islands]. Pt. 1. St. Petersburg: Sinodal'naia tipografiia.

Novoarkhangel'sk i Koloshi . . .

1862   "Novoarkhangel'sk i Koloshi" [Novo-Archangel'sk and the Tlingit]. *Vokrug sveta* [Around the World] 2:30–36.

Oberg, K.

1967   "Crime and Punishment in Tlingit Society." In *Indians of the North Pacific Coast*. T. McFeat, ed. Pp. 209–222. Seattle: University of Washington Press.

1973   *The Social Economy of the Tlingit Indians*. Seattle: University of Washington Press.

Obozrenie sostoianiia deistvii . . .

1835   "Obozrenie sostoianiia deistvii Rossiisko-Amerikanskoi kompanii s 1797 po 1819 god" [Survey of the State of Activities of the Russian-American Company from 1797 to 1819]. *Zhurnal manufaktur i torgovli* [Journal of Textiles and Trade] (1–3).

Ogden, A.

1941   *The California Sea Otter Trade, 1784–1848.* Berkeley: University of California Press.

Okladnikov, A. P.

1983   "Innokentii Veniaminov." In *Pervoprokhodtsy* [Early Explorers]. Pp. 130–181. Moscow: Molodaia gvardiia.

Okladnikova, E. A.

1995   "Kunstkamera i ee rannie severoamerikanskie kollektsii" [The Kunstkamera Museum and Its Early North American Collections]. *Kur'er Petrovskoi Kunstkamery* [Courier of the Petrovski Art Chamber] 1:29–60.

1996   "Simvoly vlasti v traditsionnoi kul'ture indeitsev Tikhookeanskogo poberezh'ia Severnoi Ameriki" [Symbols of Authority in the Traditional Culture of the Indians of the Pacific Coast of North America]. In *Simvoly i atributy vlasti.* Pp. 250–284. St. Petersburg: Muzei antropologii i etnografii [Museum of Anthropology and Ethnography].

Okonchatel'noe obozrenie severnykh . . .

1839   "Okonchatel'noe obozrenie severnykh beregov Ameriki P. V. Dizom i T. Simpsonom letom i osen'iu 1837 g." [Final Survey of the Northern Shores of America by P. W. Dease and T. Simpson in Summer and Fall of 1837]. *Syn Otechestva* [Son of the Fatherland] 7:83–114.

Okun', S. B.

1938   "K istorii prodazhi russkikh kolonii v Amerike" [On the History of the Sale of the Russian Colonies in America]. *Istoricheskie zapiski* 2:209–239.

1939   *Russiisko-Amerikanskaia kompaniia* [The Russian-American Company]. Moscow: Gosudarstvennoe sotsial'no-ekonomicheskoe izdatel'stvo [State Socio-Economic Publisher].

Olson, R. L.

1936   "Some Trading Customs of the Chilkat Tlingit." In *Essays in Anthropology.* Pp. 211–214. Berkeley: University of California.

1967   "Social Structure and Social Life of the Tlingit in Alaska." *Anthropological Records* 26:1–123.

ORAK

1842–1869 *Otchety Russiisko-Amerikanskoi kompanii za 1840–1863 gg.* (ORAK) [Reports of the Russia-American Company 1840–1863 (ORAK)]. St. Petersburg: for 1842–49 in Tipografiia E. Fishera, for 1850–61 in Tipografiia Shtaba inspektora po inzhenernoi chasti, for 1862 in Tipografiia R. Golike, for 1863–64 in Tipografiia E. Treimana, for 1867–69 in Tipografiia V. Nusval'ta.

Ormsby, M. A.
1958   *British Columbia: A History.* Toronto: Macmillans.

Oswalt, W. H.
1966   *This Land Was Theirs: The Study of the North American Indian.* New York: Wiley.

Paseniuk, A. M.
1985   *Idu po Komandoram* [I Am Going through the Commanders]. Moscow: Sovetskaia Rossiia.

Paseniuk, L. M.
1988   *Belye nochi na reke Mamontovoi* [White Nights on Mammoth River]. Krasnodar, Russia: Krasnodarskoe knizhnoe izdatel'stvo.

1995   "Morekhod Gerasim Izmailov" [Mariner Gerasim Izmailov]. In *Amerikanskii Ezhegodnik* [American Annual]. Pp. 96–115.

Pasetskii, V. M.
1967   *V pogone za tainoi veka* [In Pursuit of the Secret of the Century]. Leningrad: Gidrometeoizdat.

1969   *Vperedi—neizvestnost' puti* [Ahead—Uncertainty of Course]. Moscow: Sovetskaia Rossiia.

1970   *Ocharovannyi nadezhdoi* [Fascinated by Hope]. Leningrad: Gidrometeoizdat.

1974   *Arkticheskie puteshestviia rossiian* [The Arctic Travels of Russians]. Moscow: Mysl'.

Petroff, I. I.
1884   *Report on the Population, Industries, and Resources of Alaska (10th U.S. Census, 1880).* Washington DC: U.S. Government Printing Office.

Petrov, V.
1991   *Russkie v istorii Ameriki* [The Russians in the History of America]. Moscow: Nauka.

Pierce, R. A.
1988   "Russian and Soviet Eskimo and Indian Policies." In *Handbook of North American Indians*, vol. 4. *History of Indian-White Relations*. Pp. 119–127. Washington DC: Smithsonian Institution Press.

1990   *Russian America: A Biographical Dictionary.* Kingston, Ontario: Limestone.

Polevoi, B. P.

1960   *Grigorii Shelikhov—Kolumb rossiiskii: Biograficheskii ocherk* [Grigorii Sheli-
         kov—The Russian Columbus: A Biographical Sketch]. Magadan, Russia:
         Magadanskoe knizhnoe izdatel'stvo.

Polevoi, B. P., and E. A. Okladnikova

1994   "Osobennosti otnoshenii mezhdu russkimi i aborigenami v Russkoi
         Amerike: Ot otkrytiia Ameriki so storony Azii do prodazhi Aliaski" [Pecu-
         liarities of the Relations between the Russians and the Natives in Russian
         America: From the Discovery of America from the Asian Side to the Sale of
         Alaska]. *Otkrytie Ameriki prodolzhaetsia* [Discovery of America Continues]
         2:65–87.

Popov, V. A.

1982   *Ashantiitsy v XIX v.: Opyt etnosotsiologicheskogo issledovaniia* [The Ashanti
         People in the 19th Century: Experiment in Ethno-Sociological Research].
         Moscow: Nauka.

Postnikov, A.V.

2000   Russkaya Amerika v geograficheskikh opisaniyakh i na kartakh. 1741–1867
         gg. [Russian America in Geographic Descriptions and on Maps. 1741–1867].
         St. Petersburg: Izd-vo Dmitrii Bulanin [Dmitrii Bulanin Publisher].

Ratner-Shternberg, S. A.

1927   "Muzeinye materialy po tlingitskomu shamanstvu" [Museum Materials on
         Tlingit Shamanism]. *Sbornik* MAE [Collection of the Museum of Anthropol-
         ogy and Ethnology] 6:79–114; tables 1–4.

1929   "Muzeinye materialy po tlingitam: Ocherk II" [Museum Materials on Tlin-
         git: Essay 2]. *Sbornik* MAE [Collection of the Museum of Anthropology and
         Ethnology] 8:270–301; tables 1–4.

1930   "Muzeinye materialy po tlingitam: Ocherk III" [Museum Materials on Tlin-
         git: Essay 3]. *Sbornik* MAE [Collection of the Museum of Anthropology and
         Ethnology] 9:167–186; tables 1–4.

Razumovskaia, R. S.

1967   "Pletenye izdeliia severo-zapadnykh indeitsev" [Plaited Artifacts of the
         Northwestern Indians]. *Sbornik* MAE: *Kul'tura i byt narodov Ameriki* [Col-
         lection of the Museum of Anthropology and Ethnology: Culture and Way
         of Life of the Peoples of America] 24:93–123.

1985   "Simvolicheskii ornament severo-zapadnykh indeitsev" [The Symbolic Dec-
         oration of the Northwest Indians]. *Sbornik* MAE: *Kul'tura i byt narodov*

Ameriki [Collection of the Museum of Anthropology and Ethnology: Culture and Way of Life of the Peoples of America] 40:74–90.

Rich, E. E.
1960   *Hudson's Bay Company 1670–1870*, vol. 3. Toronto: McClelland and Stewart.

Richards, B.
1984   "A Place Apart." *National Geographic* 164(1):50–87.

Romanov, D. M.
1986   *Buriam navstrechu* [Toward the Storms]. Tula, Russia: Priokskoe knizhnoe izdatel'stvo.

Romanov, V. P.
1825   O Koliuzhakh ili Koloshakh voobshche [About the Tlinkit or Tlingit in General]. *Severnyi Arkhiv* 17(17):1–28.

Roppel, P.
1992   "Russian Expansion to Southeast Alaska." In *Bering and Chirikov: The American Voyages and Their Impact*. O. W. Frost, ed. Pp. 301–313. Anchorage: Alaska Historical Society.

Rosman, A., and P. G. Rubel
1971   *Feasting with Mine Enemy: Rank and Exchange among Northwest Coast Societies*. New York: Columbia University Press.

Rossiia i ssha . . .
1980   *Rossiia i ssha: Stanovlenie otnoshenii: 1765–1815* [Russia and the USA: The Formation of Relations: 1756–1815]. Moscow: Ministerstvo inostrannykh del SSSR, Gosudarstvennyi departament ssha [Ministry of Foreign Affairs of the USSR, State Department of the USA].

Rossiisko-Amerikanskaia kompaniia . . .
1994   *Rossiisko-Amerikanskaia kompaniia i izuchenie Tikhookeanskogo Severa, 1799–1815: Sbornik dokumentov* [Russian-American Company and a Study of the Pacific North, 1799–1815: Collection of Documents]. Moscow: Nauka.

Russkaia Amerika . . .
1994   *Russkaia Amerika: Po lichnym vpechatleniiam missionerov, zemleprokhodtsev, moriakov i drugikh ochevidtsev* [Russian America: According to the Personal Impressions of Missionaries, Explorers, Sailors, and Other Eyewitnesses]. Moscow: Mysl'.

Russkaia Tikhookeanskaia epopeia
1979   *Russkaia Tikhookeanskaia epopeia* [The Russian Pacific Ocean Epic]. Khabarovsk, Russia: Khabarovskoe knizhnoe izdatel'stvo.

Russkie ekspeditsii . . .

1984   *Russkie ekspeditsii po izucheniiu severnoi chasti Tikhogo okeana v pervoi polovine XVIII v.: Sb. dokumentov* [Russian Expeditions for Investigation of the Northern Part of the Pacific Ocean in the First Half of the 18th Century: Collection of Documents]. Moscow: Nauka.

Salisbury, O. M.

1962   *The Customs and Legends of the Tlingit Indians of Alaska.* New York: Bonanza.

Sarychev, G. A.

1952   *Puteshestvie po severo-vostochnoi chasti Sibiri, Ledovitomu moriu i Vostochnomu okeanu* [Voyage along the Northeastern Part of Siberia, the Arctic Ocean, and the Pacific Ocean]. Moscow: Geografgiz.

Schumacher, W. W.

1979   "Aftermath of the Sitka Massacre of 1802. Contemporary Documents with an Introduction and Afterword." *Alaska Journal* 9:58–61.

Segal, D. M.

1972   "Mifologicheskie izobrazheniia u indeitsev severo-zapadnogo poberezh'ia Kanady" [Mythological Representation among the Indians of the Northwest Coast of Canada]. In *Rannie formy iskusstva* [Early Forms of Art]. Pp. 321–369. Moscow: Nauka.

Semenov, Yu. I.

1968   "O nekotorykh teoreticheskikh problemakh istorii pervobytnosti" [On Some Theoretical Problems of the History of Antiquity]. *SE* 4:75–86.

1976   "Pervobytnaia kommuna i sosedskaia krest'ianskaia obshchina" [The Primitive Commune and Neighboring Peasant Society]. In *Stanovlenie klassov i gosudarstva* [Formation of Classes and State]. Pp. 7–86. Moscow: Nauka.

1979   "Evoliutsiia ekonomiki rannego pervobytnogo obshchestva" [The Evolution of the Economics of Early Primitive Society]. In *Issledovaniia po obshchei etnografii* [Studies in General Ethnography]. Pp. 61–124. Moscow: Nauka.

1993   "Ekonomicheskaia etnologiia" [Economic Ethnology]. In *Materialy k serii "Narody i kul'tury"* [Materials for the Series "Peoples and Cultures"]. Bk. 1, Pts. 1–3. Moscow: Nauka.

Shashkov, S. S.

1898   "Rossiisko-Amerikanskaia kompaniia" [The Russian-American Company]. *Sobranie sochinenii* [Collected Works] 2:632–652.

Shelikhov, G. I.

1971   *Rossiiskogo kuptsa Grigoriia Shelikhova stranstvovaniia iz Okhotska po vos-tochnomu okeanu k Amerikanskim beregam* [The Russian Merchant Grigo-rii Shelikov's Travels from Okhotsk on the Pacific Ocean to the American Shores]. Khabarovsk, Russia: Khabarovskoe knizhnoe izdatel'stvo.

Shemelin, F. I.

1816   *Zhurnal pervogo puteshestviia rossiian vokrug zemnogo shara . . .* [Journal of the First Voyage of Russians around the Earthly Globe . . .]. Pt. 1. St. Peters-burg: Meditsinskaia tipografiia [Medicine Publishing House].

1818   *Zhurnal pervogo puteshestviia rossiian vokrug zemnogo shara . . .* [Journal of the First Voyage of Russians around the Earthly Globe . . .]. Pt. 2. St. Pe-tersburg: Meditsinskaia tipografiia [Medicine Publishing House].

Shirokii, V. F.

1942   "Iz istorii khoziaistvennoi deiatel'nosti Rossiisko-Amerikanskoi kompanii" [From the History of the Economic Activity of the Russian-American Com-pany]. *Istoricheskie zapiski* [Historical Notes] 13:207–221.

Shortridge, L.

1919   "War Helmets and Clan Hats of the Tlingit Indians." *Museum Journal* 11:43–48.

1928   "The Emblems of the Tlingit Culture." *Museum Journal* 19:350–377.

Shumilov, A.

1989   " 'Most' cherez Beringov proliv" ["Bridge" across Bering Strait]. *Pravda* (February 28).

Siebert, E., and W. Forman

1967   *Indianerkunst der amerikansichen Nordwestküste* [Indian Art of the American Northwest Coast]. Praha, Czechoslovakia: Artia.

Simpson, G.

1847   *Narrative of a Journey round the World during the Years 1841 and 1842*, vols. 1 and 2. London: Henry Colburn.

Sipes, E.

1998   "Traders and Soldiers in Russian America." *History Today* 48(8):38–44.

Sitnikov, L. A.

1986   "Materialy dlia istorii Russkoi Ameriki: ('Otvety' Filippa Kashevarova)" [Ma-terials for the History of Russian America: (The "Answers" of Filipp Kashe-varov)]. In *Novye materialy po istorii Sibiri dosovetskogo perioda* [New Mate-

rials on the History of Siberia of the Pre-Soviet Period]. Pp. 82–103. Novosibirsk, Russia: Nauka.

Skarbek, I. Yu.
1988   *Za trideviat' zemel'* [At the Other End of the World]. Moscow: Molodaia
        gvardiia.

Soldatkin, E.
1989   "Master iz plemeni tlinkitov" [Craftsman of the Tlingit Tribe]. In *Les i
        chelovek* [Forest and Man]. Pp. 172–173. Moscow: Lesnaia promyshlennost'.

Solovjova, K. G.
1992   "Fortified Structures of the Russian-American Company." In *Bering and
        Chirikov: The American Voyages and Their Impact.* O. W. Frost, ed. Pp. 341–
        354. Anchorage: Alaska Historical Society.

Solovjova, K. G., and A. A. Vovnianko
1994   "Propavshie i zabytye karty kompanii Golikovykh-Shelikhova, 1783–1798
        gg." [Missing and Forgotten Maps of the Golikov-Shelikov Company, 1783–
        1798]. In *Amerikanskii Ezhegodnik* [American Annual]. Pp. 116–136. Moscow:
        Nauka.

Spencer, R. F., and J. Jennings, eds.
1977   *The Native Americans.* New York: Harper and Row.

Staniukovich, A. K., ed.
1995   *Dnevnik plavaniia s Beringom k beregam Ameriki 1741–1742* [G. W. Steller's
        Journal of the Voyage with Bering to the Shores of America, 1741–1742].
        Moscow: PAN.

Sturgis, William
1978   *The Journal of William Sturgis, 1782–1863.* S. W. Jackman, ed. Victoria, Can-
        ada: Sono Nis.

Svet, Ya. M., and S. G. Fedorova
1971   "Istoriia piatnadtsati" [The History of the Fifteen]. In *Brigantina.* Pp. 48–64.
        Moscow: Molodaia gvardiia.

Swanton, J. R.
1905   "Haida Texts and Myths, Skidegate Dialect." *Bulletin of the* BAE 29:1–448.

1908   "Social Conditions, Beliefs, and Linguistic Relationship of the Tlingit Indi-
        ans." *Annual Report of the* BAE 26:391–512.

1909   "Tlingit Myths and Texts." *Bulletin of the* BAE 39:1–451.

Teben'kov, M. D.

1852   *Gidrograficheskie zamechaniia k Atlasu severo-zapadnykh beregov Ameriki* . . .
[Hydrographic Notes for the Atlas of the Northwest Shores of America . . .].
St. Petersburg: Tipografiia Morskogo kadetskogo korpusa.

Teit, J. A.

1906   "Notes on the Tahltan Indians of British Columbia." In *Anthropological Papers Written in Honor of Franz Boas*. B. Laufer, ed. Pp. 337–349. New York: G. E. Stechert.

Tikhmenev, P. A.

1861–   *Istoricheskoe obozrenie obrazovaniia Rossiisko-Amerikanskoi kompanii i deistvii ee do nastoiashchego vremeni* [Historical Survey of the Formation of the Russian-American Company and Its Activities up to the Present Time]. Pt. 1. St. Petersburg: Tipografiia Eduarda Veimara.

1863   *Istoricheskoe obozrenie obrazovaniia Rossiisko-Amerikanskoi kompanii i deistvii ee do nastoiashchego vremeni* [Historical Survey of the Formation of the Russian-American Company and Its Activities up to the Present Time]. Pt. 2. St. Petersburg: Tipografiia Eduarda Veimara.

Tishkov, V. A.

1977   *Strana klenovogo lista: nachalo istorii* [Land of the Maple Leaf: The Beginning of History]. Moscow: Nauka.

Tishkov, V. A., and A. V. Koshelev

1986   *Istoriia Kanady* [The History of Canada]. Moscow: Mysl'.

Tokarev, S. A.

1986   *Religiia v istorii narodov mira* [Religion in the History of the Peoples of the World]. Moscow: Izdatel'stvo politicheskoi literatury [Publisher of Political Literature].

1990   *Rannie formy religii* [Early Forms of Religion]. Moscow: Izdatel'stvo politicheskoi literatury.

Tompkins, S. R.

1945   *Alaska, Promyshlennik and Sourdough*. Norman: University of Oklahoma Press.

Trufanov, I. T.

1967   "Kenaiskie tomagavki iz etnograficheskoi kollektsii I. G. Voznesenskogo" [The Kenai Tomahawks of I. G. Voznesenskii's Ethnographic Collection]. In *Sbornik* MAE : *Kul'tura i byt narodov Ameriki* [Collection of the Museum of Anthropology and Ethnology: Culture and Way of Life of the Peoples of America] 24:85–92.

Tumarkin, D. D.

1964   *Vtorzhenie kolonizatorov v "krai vechnoi vesny": gavaiskii narod v bor'be protiv chuzhezemnykh zakhvatchikov v kontse XVIII–nachale XIX v.* [The Incursion of Colonizers into the "Land of Eternal Spring": The Hawaiian People in the Struggle against Foreign Invaders at the End of the 18th–Beginning of the 19th Centuries]. Moscow: Nauka.

1983   "Materialy ekspeditsii M. N. Vasil'eva—tsenneishii istochnik po istorii i etnografii Gavaiskikh ostrovov" [Materials from the Expedition of M. N. Vasil'ev—the Most Valuable Source on the History and Ethnography of the Hawaiian Islands]. *SE* 6:48–62.

Turner, G.

1979   *Indians of North America.* Poole, England: Blandford.

Unkovskii, S. Ya.

1952   "Iz 'istinnykh zapisok moei zhizni' leitenanta S. Ya. Unkovskogo" [From the "Actual Notes of My Life" of Lieutenant S. Ya. Unkovskii]. *Lazarev M. P. Dokumenty* 1:11–60.

Vancouver, G.

1830   *Puteshestvie v severnuiu chast' Tikhogo okeana i vokrugsveta . . .* [Travel in the Northern Part of the Pacific Ocean and around the World . . .]. Bk. 4. St. Petersburg: Morskaia tipografiia.

1833   *Puteshestvie v severnuiu chast' Tikhogo okeana i vokrugsveta . . .* [Travel in the Northern Part of the Pacific Ocean and around the World . . .]. Bk. 5. St. Petersburg: Morskaia tipografiia.

VanStone, J. W.

1981   "Etnoistoricheskie issledovaniia na Aliaske: obzor" [Ethnohistorical Research in Alaska: A Survey]. In *Traditsionnye kul'tury Severnoi Sibiri i Severnoi Ameriki* [*Traditional Cultures of Northern Siberia and North America*]. Pp. 212–228. Moscow: Nauka.

Varshavskii, S. R.

1982   *Uvekovechennaia slava Rossii* [Immortal Glory of Russia]. Magadan, Russia: Magadanskoe knizhnoe izdatel'stvo.

Vasil'evskii, R. S., and D. Ya. Rezun

1987   *Vospitanie istoriei* [The Upbringing by History]. Novosibirsk, Russia: Novosibirskoe knizhnoe izdatel'stvo.

Vasilov, M. I.

1886   "Poslednie dni v Russkoi Amerike: 1867–1868 gg." [The Last Days of Russian America: 1867–1868]. *Russkaia starina* [The Old Days of Russia] 49:549–560; 50:593–598; 51:605–614.

Veniaminov, I. E.

1840a   *Zapiski ob ostrovakh Unalashkinskogo otdela* [Notes on the Islands of the Unalaska District]. Pt. 3. St. Petersburg: Russian-American Company. See translation: *Notes on the Islands of the Unalaska District*. L. T. Black and R. H. Geoghegan, trans. Kingston, Ontario: Limestone, 1984.

1840b   "Sostoianie pravoslavnoi tserkvi v Rossiiskoi Amerike" [The Condition of the Orthodox Churches in Russian America]. *Zhurnal Ministerstva narodnogo prosveshcheniia* [Journal of the Ministry of Public Education] 26(5):3–58.

1846   *Zamechaniia o koloshenskom i kad'iakskom yazykakh* [Notes on the Tlingit and Koniag Languages]. St. Petersburg: Tipografiia Imperatorskoi Akademii nauk.

Vneshniaia politika Rossii
1995   *Vneshnyaya politika Rossii (VPR) (1828–1830)* [Foreign Politics of Russia], vol. 8 (16). *Mezhdunarodnye otnosheniya* Series 2. [International Relations]. Moscow: Foreign Ministry of Russia (USSR).

Voitov, V.
1984   "Okeanskie dorogi chelovechestva" [Oceanic Roads of Mankind]. *Nauka i zhizn'* 8:143–149.

Wherry, J. H.
1964   *The Totem Pole Indians*. New York: W. Funk.

Whymper, F.
1966   *Travel and Adventure in the Territory of Alaska*. Ann Arbor: University Microfilms.

Wrangell, F. P.
1835   "Kratkie statisticheskie zamechaniia o rossiiskikh koloniiakh v Amerike" [Short Statistical Observations on the Russian Colonies in America]. *Teleskop* 28(13):104–133.

1839a   "Obitateli severo-zapadnykh beregov Ameriki" [The Inhabitants of the Northwest Coasts of America]. *Syn Otechestva* 7:51–82.

1839b   *Statistische und ethnographische Nachrichten über die Russischen Besitzungen an der Nordwestküste von Amerika* [Statistical and Ethnographic Reports of the Russian Possessions on the Northwest Coast of America]. St. Petersburg: Buchdruckerei der Kaiserlichen Akademie der Wissenschaften [Printer of the Royal Academy of Sciences].

Woldt, A.
1884   *Capitain Jacobsen's Reise an der Nordwestküste Amerikas 1881–1883* . . . [Captain Jacobsen's Travels on the Northwest Coast of America 1881–1883 . . .].

Leipzig: M. Spohr. See translation: *Alaskan Voyage, 1881–1883*. Erna Gunther, trans. Chicago: University of Chicago Press, 1977.

Yakimov, O. D.

2001   Nikolai Militov—igumen Kenaiskoi pravoslavnoi missii [Nikolai Militov—the Abbot of the Kenai Orthodox Mission]. *Russkaya Amerika i Dal'nii Vostok (konets XVIII v.–1867 g.)* [Russian America and Far East (the End of the 18th Century–1867]. K 200-letiyu obrazovaniya Rossiisko-Americanskoi kompanii [To 200-years jubilee of Russian-American Company]. Materialy mezhdunaridnoi anuchnoi konferentsii (Vladivistok, 11–13 oktyabrya 1999 g.) [The Materials of International Scientific Conference (Vladivostok, October 11–13, 1999)]. Pp.208–229.

Zagoskin, L. A.

1956   *Puteshestviia i issledovaniia leitenanta Lavrentiia Zagoskina v Russkoi Amerike v 1842–1844 gg.* [The Travels and Investigations of Lieutanant Lavrentii Zagoskin in Russian America in 1842–1844]. Moscow: State Publishing House of Geographic Literature. See translation: *Lieutenant Zagoskin's Travels in Russian America, 1842–1844*. Henry N. Michael, ed. Toronto: Arctic Institute of North America: University of Toronto Press, 1967.

Zavalishin, D. I.

1865   *Rossiisko-Amerikanskaia kompaniia* [The Russian-American Company]. Moscow: Universitetskaia tipografiia (Katkov).

1866   "Delo o kolonii Ross" [Affairs of a Russian Colony]. *Russkii vestnik* [Russian Bulletin] 62(3):36–65.

1877   Krugosvetnoe plavanie na fregate "Kreiser" [Round-the-World Voyage on the Frigate *Kreiser*]. In *Drevniaia i novaia Rossiia* [Early and Recent Russia] 2, nos. 2–7; 3, nos. 9–11.

Zavoiko, V. S.

1840   *Vpechatlenie moriaka vo vremia dvukh puteshestvii krugom sveta* [The Impressions of a Sailor during Two Voyages around the World] Pts. 1 and 2. St. Petersburg: Tipografiia E. Fishera.

Zelenoi, K. S.

1865   "Iz zapisok o krugosvetnom plavanii (1861–1864 gg.)" [From the Notes on a Round-the-World Voyage (1861–1864)]. *Morskoi sbornik* [Sea Collection] 78(5); 79(7, 8); 80(9).

Znamenski, Andrei A.

1999   *Shamanism and Christianity: Native Encounters with Russian Orthodox Missions in Siberia and Alaska, 1820–1917*. Westport CT: Greenwood.

Zorin, A. V.

1994   "Rossiisko-Amerikanskaya kompaniya I tlinkity v nachale XIX veka" [The
        Russian-American Company and the Tlingit at the Beginning of the 19th
        Century]. *Voprosy istorii* [Questions of History] 6:170–173.

1997   "Iz Kurska na Gavaii: Sud'ba pervoprokhodtsa Timofeia Tarakanova" [From
        Kursk to Hawaii: The Fate of Pioneer Timofei Tarakanov]. In *Kurskie tetradi:
        Kursk i kuriane glazami uchenykh* [Kursk Notebook: Kursk and Kuriane
        through the Eyes of Learning]. Tetrad' pervaia [First Notebook]. Kursk,
        Russia: Izd-vo KGPU.

1998a   "Sopernichestvo torgovo-promyslovykh kompanii v Russkoi Amerike (1787–
        1797)" [Competition of the Fur-Trading Companies in Russian America].
        Voprosy istoii 11–12:151–156.

1998b   "Voina mezhdu severnymi kagvantanami I nanyaaii Stikina" [The War be-
        tween the Northern Kagwantan Clan and the Naanya.aayí Clan of the Sti-
        kine]. *Pervye amerikantsy* [First Americans]. *Indeitsy Ameriki: proshloe I nas-
        toyashee* [The American Indians: The Past and Present] 3: 52–57.

2001a   "Beshenye lebedevskie (Sopernichestvo torgovo-promyslovykh kompanii v
        Russkoi Amerike)" [Lebedev's Wild Men (Competition of the Fur-Trading
        Companies in Russian America)]. *Klio* 1:73–84.

2001b   "Bitva za Sitku (1804)" [Battle for Sitka (1804)]. *Pervye amerikantsy* [First
        Americans]. *Indeitsy Ameriki: proshloe I nastoyashee* [The American Indians:
        The Past and Present] 9:10–27.

2001c   "Russkie plenniki Ameriki" [Russian Captives in America]. *Pervye ameri-
        kantsy* [First Americans]. *Indeitsy Ameriki: proshloe i nastoyashee* [The Amer-
        ican Indians: The Past and Present] 8:10–20.

2002   *Indeiskaya voina v Russkoi Amerike* [Indian War in Russian America]. Kursk:
        Izd-vo KGPU.

Aankáawu, 56, 74

Aanyádi, 56, 58, 60, 79, 81, 220, 233

Active. See ships

adzes. *See* tools

Agishanuku, 69, 83

Ahtna, 20, 21, 32, 123, 145, 148, 216, 250, 257

Akoi kwáan. *See* Kwáans

albatross. *See* birds

alder. *See* plants

Aleksandr II, 193

Alert. See ships

Aleut, 22, 94, 106, 119, 123, 125, 130, 135, 175, 193, 236, 241, 242, 245, 247, 248, 258, 313, 317n13, 322n32, 323n34, 324nn35–36, 327n9

Aleutian Islands, 22, 91–94, 124, 260

Alexander Archipelago, 15, 94, 99, 106–109, 113, 115, 118, 131, 133, 139, 141, 145, 148–151, 153, 154, 160–162, 164, 166, 168, 171–174, 178, 195, 200, 203–205, 221, 228, 248, 262, 275

Alexander I, 141, 159

Alsek, 15, 34, 117, 123, 216, 282n4, 329n6

Amanat, 68, 133, 222, 260, 269

Ametist. See ships

amulets. *See* decoration

Anakadzho, 170

Angoon, 7, 211, 262, 317n12

animalism, 70, 73, 74

animals: bears, 16, 30, 75; beaver, 37, 53, 59, 69, 84, 87, 126, 155, 163, 167, 195, 215, 216, 219; caribou, 32, 37; deer, 16, 30, 37, 39, 49, 219, 228, 230, 282n15; dogs, 30, 75, 78, 79, 270–272; elk, 32, 61, 65, 101, 217, 227, 250, 253, 282n15; ermine, 38, 59, 78, 140, 217, 236; frogs, 54, 73, 74, 88, 316n9, 317n12, 320n23; hides, 32, 68, 158, 215, 217, 219, 227, 230, 282n15; horns, 32, 38; killer whales, 54, 70, 71, 74, 84, 88, 183, 238, 317n12; marmots, 37, 216, 217; marten, 37, 59, 216; mountain sheep, 16, 30, 39, 166, 210; mice, 74; porcupines, 32; porpoises, 30, 35, 39; river otters, 16, 73–76, 155, 324n43, 326n3; sea lions, 38, 74, 217, 236, 319n14, 327n7; sea otters, 16, 30, 37, 39, 61, 93, 94,

97, 98, 104, 109, 111, 113, 114, 117, 123, 125, 129, 139, 148–150, 154, 156, 158, 161–163, 210, 237, 298n2, 322n32, 326n5; seals, 16, 30, 35, 39; sheep, 16, 30, 39, 166, 210, 302, 327n7; whales, 16, 39, 83, 84; wolves, 16, 37, 43, 46, 47, 50, 54, 66, 70, 71, 73, 88, 303, 315n5, 328n17

animism, 70, 77

Ankta (Annta, Anta), 172

Annakuts, 167

Apollon. See ships

apparel: blankets, 37, 46, 159, 160, 163, 174, 195, 217–220, 231, 232, 292, 305, 326n1; cloaks, 30, 32, 37, 70, 87, 101, 112, 211, 212, 217, 231, 232; clothing, 30, 32, 37, 96–98, 101, 109, 114, 151, 157, 159, 166, 217, 223, 231–233, 236, 241, 254, 267, 272, 284, 286, 287, 297, 300, 308, 327n6; dress, 37, 59, 140, 214, 221, 230–232, 236, 244, 294, 301, 327n6; hats, 30, 37, 38, 87, 211, 212, 214, 222, 228, 232; helmets, 30, 101, 252; labrets, 22, 38; loincloths, 37; moccasins, 37, 216, 232; shirts, 37, 171, 231, 232; snowshoes, 35

Archimandrite Anatolii (Kamenskii), 6, 17, 39, 59, 62, 64, 65, 77, 82, 91

Argonaut. See ships

Aristocrats, 37, 58, 60, 83, 116, 264

armor. *See* weapons

arrows. *See* weapons

art, 9, 11, 30, 34, 46, 59, 60, 84, 86–88, 256, 279, 326n54

Arthur. See ships

Atahualpa. See ships

Athapaskans, 8, 18, 20, 21, 23, 24, 32, 35, 37, 50, 84, 157, 168, 170, 171, 195, 196, 199, 211, 212, 215–217, 227, 230, 232, 236, 238, 242, 250, 253, 257, 317n13, 326n52, 327n7

Atlin, 217

Atrevida. See ships

Auk kwáan. *See* Kwáans

Avdot'ia, 306–307

Avunculate, 62, 64

Ayan, 187, 190, 191, 222, 259, 307–308

badges. *See* decoration
baidarka. *See* transportation
Balkans, 186
Banner, Ivan, 84, 244, 327n7
Baranof Island, 1–3, 15, 29, 94, 95, 110, 154, 319n12
Baranov, Aleksandrs. *See* governors
Barber, Henry, 108, 120–122, 130–131, 228, 284, 285n6, 319nn18–19
bark, 30, 33, 35–37, 39, 85, 166, 177, 230
baskets. *See* containers
battle, 16, 30, 50, 64, 66, 67, 71, 75, 85, 87, 88, 101, 103, 104, 117, 119, 128, 137, 146, 155, 165, 183, 188, 189, 203, 239, 255, 264, 309
Bear House, 64
bears. *See* animals
beauty, 61, 246
beaver. *See* animals
Beaver. See ships
Behm Canal, 20
beliefs, 5, 65, 67, 69, 74, 75, 124
Bella Coola, 22, 317n15
Bering, Vitus, 5, 92, 93, 105, 205, 206, 281
berries. *See* plants
Billings, Joseph, 327n9, 328n13
birds: albatross, 39; ducks, 16, 210; eagles, 16, 38; gulls, 16; hummingbirds, 16; ravens, 23, 38, 46, 47, 50, 53, 54, 61, 69, 70, 74, 79, 80, 83, 84, 95, 101, 119, 146, 175, 220, 235, 262, 267, 303, 304, 317nn12–13
blankets. *See* apparel
blood feud, 64, 76, 82
blood money, 48
Boas, Franz, 20, 87
boats. *See* transportation
bodyguards, 59
Bolivar Liberator. See ships
bone, 22, 35, 37, 38, 211, 217, 226, 236
Boston men, 99, 114, 282n23, 321n26
bowls. *See* containers
boxes. *See* containers
bracelets. *See* decoration
braids. *See* decoration
buckets. *See* containers

cabins. *See* structures
Cadboro. See ships
calendar, 32, 121, 315n3

California, 5, 10, 12, 91, 95, 139, 147, 150, 212, 213, 224, 249, 318n3, 323n32
candle fish. *See* fish
canoes. *See* transportation
Canton, 114, 226, 243
Cape Spencer, 172
Cape Suckling, 110
capitalistic production, 40, 324n40
caribou. *See* animals
Caroline. See ships
carvers, 30
cedar. *See* plants
ceiling. *See* structures
ceremony, 8, 9, 11, 21, 23, 30, 33, 34, 37, 38, 45, 47, 48, 52, 56, 59, 68, 70, 72, 75, 79, 80, 82, 84, 85, 87, 95, 139, 140, 152, 206, 220, 221, 226, 228, 231, 232, 254, 257, 262, 265, 267, 279, 288, 308, 328n21
Chait, 307–308
Chak-nu, 146
Chatham Strait, 23, 115, 149, 192, 225
Chatlk-nu, 139
Cheerful. See ships
Chesnyga, 133, 144, 146, 234, 258, 320n23, 322n32
chests. *See* containers
Chichagof Island, 95, 122
Chichagov. See ships
chief, 7, 33, 37–38, 43–44, 48–49, 52, 56–59, 66, 70, 73–75, 78–80, 82, 84, 88, 98, 100, 106, 107, 108, 111, 116, 118, 120, 121, 122–124, 126, 133, 141, 142, 147, 148, 151, 152, 155, 161, 163, 164, 166, 167, 168, 170, 172, 175, 176, 181, 184, 185, 187, 189, 193, 196, 198, 199, 204, 206, 213, 219, 220, 228, 231–239, 241–244, 252, 254, 258–260, 263, 265, 271, 272, 277, 280, 283, 285n2, 287, 288, 289, 293n1, 294n2, 296nn1–2, 297n1, 298nn1–2, 299n2, 300, 317n12, 319n16, 320n21, 320n23, 323n3, 323n4, 326n4, 327n11
Chilkat. See ships
Chilkat Inlet, 281–283
Chilkat ḵwáan. *See* Ḵwáans
Chinese, 17, 91, 109, 114, 221, 226, 231, 233, 242
Chinook, 270, 271
Chirikov, Aleksei, 4, 92, 93, 105, 107, 206, 284
chisels. *See* tools

Chishkedi, 272
Chistiakov, Petr. *See* governors
Chuchkan, 127
Chugach, 1, 20, 22, 35, 93, 98, 99, 101, 103–105, 110, 117, 123, 125, 140, 141, 144–146, 148, 157, 162, 178, 214, 215, 228, 244, 245, 257, 318n10, 323n33
Chugach Bay, 98, 99, 101, 104, 125, 141, 178
clan, 8, 21, 24, 36, 38, 43, 46–55, 58–66, 68–74, 76–84, 88, 97, 100, 108, 124, 133, 134, 143, 146, 152, 153, 160, 168, 183, 184, 197, 214, 228, 234, 237–239, 241, 242, 248, 250–255, 262, 271, 272, 287, 288, 288n1, 291n1, 292n1, 293n1, 303, 304, 306n2, 311, 315n1, 315n4, 315n6, 316nn7–10, 317n12, 320n21, 322n31, 326n53, 328n15, 328nn17–18
cloaks. *See* apparel
clothing. *See* apparel
clubs. *See* weapons
cod. *See* fish
collecting, 6, 34, 43, 52, 77, 92, 209, 210
colors, 38, 87, 231
Columbia River, 115, 157, 270
commoners, 55, 56, 58, 60, 241
conflict, 10, 47, 64–66, 108, 110, 145, 162, 170, 174, 183, 184, 194, 198, 199, 238, 253, 325n43
containers: baskets, 30, 33, 37, 39, 88, 211, 214, 215; bowls, 37, 226; boxes, 37, 84, 88, 211, 256; buckets, 32, 37, 226; chests, 37, 256; cups, 37, 87, 226; dishes, 37, 39; ladles, 37; oil lamps, 37; scoops, 37; spoons, 22, 30, 32, 37, 214, 226
Controller Bay, 20
Cook, James, 91, 95–97, 318
copper, 17, 20, 21, 30–32, 35, 37, 38, 49, 61, 81, 93, 100, 105, 112, 124, 140, 141, 143, 163, 211–214, 220, 226, 233, 234, 236, 250, 255, 257, 283, 284, 294n1, 311, 311n1, 323n34, 327nn8–10
Copper River, 20, 21, 31, 32, 214, 250, 257, 323
corner posts. *See* structures
crabs. *See* shellfish
craftsmanship, 30
cremation, 74
Crimean War, 186, 187, 190, 233, 325n43
Crocker, John, 128–130
Cross Sound, 15, 106, 160, 322n32, 324n33

Cunningham, William, 120, 122, 125, 129–130
cups. *See* containers

daggers. *See* weapons
Dal'strem, Karl, 249, 301
dances, 21, 46, 48, 50, 56, 66, 71, 83–85, 112, 218, 228, 257
darts. *See* weapons
Davydov, Gavriil, 109, 112, 114, 119, 121, 123, 124, 127–129, 319n16, 328n15
Dease Lake, 196
death, 16, 61, 63, 64, 67, 74, 76, 82, 84, 105, 110, 136, 146, 155, 175, 206, 222, 229, 236, 240, 250, 256, 267, 271, 288, 295, 296, 296n1, 298n2, 299, 304, 305, 315n3, 318n10
decoration, 37, 68, 230, 233; amulets, 74, 75, 101, 267; badges, 231, 232, 293, 298, 299, 237n11; bracelets, 38, 211–213, 233; braids, 38, 175; hairpins, 38; headdress, 37, 38; masks, 66, 77, 86, 88, 211, 212, 257; medals, 140, 152, 163, 168, 172, 190, 213, 233–236, 241, 255, 280, 284, 291, 293n2, 294n2, 295, 298n2, 320n23, 327nn9–12, 328n13; necklaces, 38, 97; pendants, 38, 233, 236; rings, 38, 233, 252
deer. *See* animals
Deisheetaan, 50, 53, 79, 80, 84, 262, 271
Delarov, Evstratii, 282
Del'fin. See ships
Demenenkov, T. S., 141, 144, 145, 239, 275, 322n29
dentalium, 32, 38, 218
Descubierta. See ships
Destruction Island, 23
Diane. See ships
Dionisievskii Redoubt, 168, 170–172, 174–177, 191, 195, 196, 238, 246, 248, 273, 293n3, 325n51
dip nets. *See* hunting equipment
dishes. *See* containers
Dispatch. See ships
Dixon, George, 97, 98, 200, 226
Dixon Entrance, 200
Dlketin, 245
dogs. *See* animals
Domna, 286
Doroshin, Petr, 38, 224
Dragon. See ships

dress. *See* apparel

Dry Bay, 20, 21, 23, 320n22

ducks. *See* birds

dugout boats. *See* transportation

Duktut, 67

Dundas Island, 149, 194

Eagle moiety, 52, 62, 328n17

eagles. *See* birds

earthquakes, 69

Ebbets, John, 120, 122, 251

Eclipse. See ships

economy, 29, 34, 40, 42, 43, 45, 63, 73, 79, 81, 82, 88, 157, 209, 210, 213, 219, 266, 272

education, 67, 249, 258, 259

eggs, 30, 39

elite, 55, 56, 58, 69

Eliza. See ships

elk. *See* animals

Ermak, 92

Ermak. See ships

ermine. *See* animals

Eskimo, 1, 5, 21, 22, 28, 35, 93, 123, 157, 162, 211, 214, 227, 228, 245, 242, 247, 257, 317n13, 318n5, 319n17, 328n15

ethnonym, 21–23, 126, 127

Etolin, Adolf. *See* governors

excess, 40–42, 45, 56, 63, 64, 76, 166, 223

exchange, 30, 32, 40, 42, 45, 49, 62, 63, 68, 84, 96, 105, 109, 112, 118, 153, 154, 156, 161, 171, 214–219, 240, 268, 287, 288, 293, 294

exogamy, 22, 50, 55, 61

exploitation, 30, 40–45, 49, 54, 57, 58, 60, 63, 123, 124, 139, 157, 176, 260, 277

Eyak, 18, 20, 23, 24, 35, 93, 103–105, 144, 145, 214, 215, 238, 250, 275, 318n10, 322n31, 323n34, 327n7

fabric, 98, 109, 212, 230–232

family, 9, 24, 28, 36, 42, 52, 58, 61–64, 78, 80, 95, 124, 239, 247, 302, 303, 303nn1–2

fetishism, 70, 75

fighting, 28, 59, 64, 65, 67–69, 125, 126, 142, 186, 206, 210, 237, 240, 251, 252, 275

Filipov, Luka, 144, 322n32

firearms, 65, 99, 103, 104, 106, 109, 114, 133, 136, 142, 149, 155, 156, 170, 171, 181, 187, 192,

194, 204, 205, 210, 213–216, 218, 227, 250, 251, 282n23, 284, 287, 290, 291

fish: candle fish, 16, 29, 30, 32, 33, 35, 118, 282n2; cod, 29; halibut, 29, 35, 166, 302, 317; herring, 16, 29, 33, 35, 39, 147, 148, 254, 289, 290; salmon, 16, 17, 29, 33, 39, 43, 52, 73, 74, 79, 216, 316n9, 317n12; shark, 35, 218, 317n12

fish camps, 33, 36

fishing, 17, 29, 30, 32, 34–36, 40, 41, 43, 52, 56, 59, 61, 77, 88, 142, 143, 146, 193, 209, 210, 251, 254, 289, 292

fish oil, 30, 33, 39, 118, 215, 281n4

floor. *See* structures

food, 33, 34, 37, 39, 44, 46, 47, 112, 123, 146, 148, 157, 166, 205, 217, 226, 228, 266, 302

Fort Durham, 196

Fort Highfield, 196

Fort House, 53

Fort Kasatki, 251

Fort Langley, 194

Fort McLoughlin, 194

Fort Mikhailovskii, 112–114, 118–120, 122, 123, 125–131, 133, 139, 209, 239, 245, 275, 319n14, 319n17, 320nn19–21, 321nn25–26

Fort Nass, 194

Fort Ross, 150, 213, 249, 323n32

Fort Selkirk, 199, 277

Fort Simpson, 170, 184, 194, 195, 198–200, 219, 242, 271, 292n2

Fort Stikine, 176, 196, 198–200, 232, 256, 326n52

Fort Taku, 155, 196, 277

Fort Victoria, 196

Frederick. See ships

Frederick Sound, 23, 113, 119

French, 5, 18, 97, 98, 105, 156, 242, 271, 275, 325n43

frogs. *See* animals

furs, 32, 35, 37, 45, 59, 62, 64, 92, 93, 96–98, 100, 105, 106, 109, 111, 113–116, 120–122, 123, 125, 130, 131, 149, 150, 154–158, 159, 161, 162, 163, 167, 168, 171, 173, 176, 181–183, 194–196, 198, 200, 202, 204–206, 210, 214–219, 226, 228, 230–233, 236, 239, 240, 241, 242, 277, 279, 293, 303, 325n43, 325n50, 326n51, 327n7, 327n12

Gaanaxteidí, 21
Gabrillo, Juan, 96
games, 83, 85, 256
Gedeonov, Kalistrat, 222
geese, 16
Giyak kwáan. *See* Kwáans
Glacier Bay, 72
Globe (Globus). *See* ships
goat, 32, 38, 39, 214
Golovin, Pavel, 85, 94, 114, 181, 182, 187–189,
    191–193, 205, 215, 219, 224, 229, 232, 236,
    246, 248, 252, 253, 255, 256, 258, 259, 261,
    262, 265, 325
Golovnin, Vasilii, 4, 114, 149, 185, 221
governors: Baranov, Aleksandr, 101, 104, 106–
    114, 121–125, 128, 133–137, 139–141, 143–
    151, 156–158; Chistiakov, Petr, 161–163, 183,
    194, 244, 248, 268, 289, 291, 329; Etolin,
    Adolf, 167, 175–177, 191, 205, 221, 235, 237,
    240, 257, 296–298, 300–302, 325, 328, 330;
    Furuhjelm, Johan, 191–193, 200–201, 219,
    223, 232, 237, 243, 262, 278, 311–313, 327n11,
    331n69; Hagemeister, Ludwig, 152, 153, 156,
    235, 286, 287, 329; Kupreianov, Ivan, 71,
    173–175, 195, 220, 237, 244, 246, 293–295,
    330; Maksutov, Dmitrii, 193, 202, 203,
    238, 259, 314; Murav'ev, Matvei, 126, 159–
    163, 204, 231, 243, 247, 271, 288, 291, 323,
    324, 329; Rozenberg, Nikolai, 162, 182–
    187, 238, 249, 265, 278, 306, 307, 325, 331;
    Rudakov, Aleksandr, 182, 186; Teben'kov,
    Mikhail, 176, 178, 181, 198, 199, 220, 223,
    224, 249, 290, 302, 325, 330; Voevodskii,
    Stepan, 182, 187, 189–191, 278, 308, 311,
    331; Wrangell, Ferdinand, 294, 295, 330;
    Yanovskii, Semion, 153, 154, 159, 286, 287,
    289, 323, 329
grog, 164, 228
gulls. *See* birds
guns. *See* firearms

Hagemeister, Ludwig. *See* governors
Haida, 18, 20–24, 28, 30, 32, 34, 36, 50, 61, 84,
    88, 115, 125–127, 139, 151, 157, 176, 186, 200,
    205, 214, 217, 227, 230, 235, 253, 286n3,
    322n27
hair, 17, 38, 68, 75, 140, 151, 248, 257
hairpins. *See* decoration

Haisla, 36, 50
halibut, 29, 35, 166, 302, 317n12
Hamilton. See ships
hammers. *See* tools
Han, 216
Hancock. See ships
Hanna, James, 97
harpoons. *See* hunting equipment
hats. *See* apparel
headdress. *See* decoration
hearth, 36
helmets. *See* apparel
hemlock. *See* plants
Henya kwáan. *See* Kwáans
Henya Joy, 243
herring. *See* fish
hides, 32, 37, 65, 68, 101, 158, 215, 217, 219,
    227, 230, 253, 255, 282n15, 327n7
hooks. *See* hunting equipment
Hoonah kwáan. *See* Kwáans
horns, 32, 38
hostages, 68, 79, 103, 105, 106, 108, 136, 153,
    178, 184, 186, 188, 258, 284, 287, 324n34
Hot Springs, 185, 275, 307, 308n, 310
household groups, 55
Hudson's Bay Company, 5, 114, 161, 168, 170,
    172, 173, 175, 194–196, 198, 200, 205, 213,
    226, 230, 236, 242, 244, 247, 248, 279, 310,
    325n50
hummingbirds. *See* birds
hunting, 17, 30, 33–35, 40, 41, 43, 52, 59, 61,
    62, 75, 77, 83, 94, 104–107, 109, 111, 113,
    114, 118, 119, 122, 123, 125–127, 129–131, 139,
    141, 148–150, 161, 162, 164, 209, 210, 227,
    228, 237, 282n15, 322n32
hunting equipment: dip nets, 35; harpoons, 30,
    35, 212; hooks, 30, 35, 209; leisters, 35; nets,
    35, 151, 178; slings, 35; snares, 35; traps, 35,
    210, 216
huts. *See* structures

Icy Bay, 15, 282n17
Icy Strait, 239, 281n6, 293, 298, 304, 313
igrushka, 46, 175, 178, 198, 302, 303, 325n48
Ilkak, 100, 101, 105
Imperator Nikolai I. See ships
intratribal conflict, 253

instruments: rattle, 84, 221, 257; tambourine, 84; whistle, 84, 181

jackets, 231, 253
Japanese, 17, 31, 91
Jenny. See ships
Jivak, 245, 323n32
Juan de Fuca, 96, 115

Kaagwaantaan, 8, 46, 50, 52–54, 62, 71, 73, 117, 136, 137, 151–153, 160, 183, 184, 199, 206, 220, 235, 238, 242, 248, 251, 252, 262, 264, 271, 286, 287, 288nn1–2, 292n1, 314, 315n6, 317n12, 320n21, 324n42, 327n11, 328n17
Kabachakov, Matvei, 222, 249, 254
Kachaty, 259
Kad'iak. See ships
Kaigani, 18, 23, 28, 94, 126, 127, 139, 148, 157, 167, 172, 173, 176, 195, 200, 202, 205, 235, 239, 253, 285, 286n3, 293, 294, 308
Kake k̲wáan. *See* K̲wáans
Kakklen, 250
Kaknau, 97, 160, 281n6, 315n6, 322n32, 324n34
Kaknu River, 224
Kak-tlen, 250
Kamchadal, 67, 312n
Kamchatka, 33, 91–93, 98, 99, 221, 222, 227, 228, 261, 317n13
Kamchatka Expedition, 91–93, 99
Kamchatka lily. *See* plants
kamlanie, 59
K̲as'ittan, 250, 328n18
Kategan, Gavrila, 222, 259
Katlian, 75, 119, 120, 136, 140, 152, 221, 235, 269
Kats, 83
kayak. *See* transportation
Kayak Island, 20, 93, 270
Kekovskoe village, 281, 282n21
Kenai Bay, 97, 101
K̲etl, 83, 254, 270
Khlebnikov, Kirill, 16, 63, 68, 95, 103, 106, 110, 112, 119, 120, 123, 124, 125, 127, 128, 130, 131, 135, 137, 141, 143, 144, 145, 148, 149, 165, 213, 214, 223, 230, 237, 239, 243, 319n15, 322nn28–29, 323nn33–34
Kiks.ádi, 46, 50, 51, 75, 112, 119, 124, 128, 134, 136, 137, 141, 152, 153, 184, 220, 235, 271

Kilk̲va, 281
killer whales. *See* animals
Kitkatla, 250, 253
Kittlitz, Frederich, 162, 236, 244
Kluk̲wáan, 216
knives. *See* tools
Kochesov, Vasilii, 119, 127, 129–131, 319n14, 320n21
Kodiak Island, 1, 93, 94, 99, 100, 104, 142
Kolosh, 22
Konakadet, 77
Kondakov, 106, 304
Koniag, 1, 111, 120, 121, 124, 140, 157, 158, 162, 223, 235, 236
Konstantin. See ships
Kootznahoo k̲wáan. *See* K̲wáans
Koskedi-Kuskedi, 255
Kotzebue, 4, 5, 85, 127, 137, 217, 228, 252, 253, 319n12
Kreiser. See ships
Kruzof Island, 15, 93, 285n4
K̲uaketli, 172
Kuashk̲wáan. *See* K̲wáans
Kuatkau, 197
Kuatk̲e, 172
Kudena, 250, 251
Kuiu k̲wáan. *See* K̲wáans
Kuk̲ka, 174, 175
Kulikalov, D., 104
Kupreianov, Ivan. *See* governors
Kuskov, Ivan, 113, 117, 118, 122–128, 141, 148–150, 320n20
Kurile Islands, 305
Kuznetsov, Fedor, 167, 187, 309
Kwakiutl, 21, 22, 38, 50, 217, 253
K̲wáans, 24, 27; Akoi, 28, 104, 105, 123, 133, 146, 147, 160, 184, 228, 234, 238, 255, 258, 260, 271, 320n22, 328n18; Auk, 28, 105, 216; Chilkat, 28, 30, 61, 64, 66, 99, 147, 148, 160, 183, 184, 257, 263, 292n1, 324n42; Giyak, 119; Henya, 27, 66, 94, 126, 127, 128, 243; Hoonah, 27, 30, 95, 133, 228, 238, 245, 255, 259, 262, 298n1, 306n2, 315n6, 322n32, 328n18; Kake, 51, 128, 202, 206, 262, 270; Kootznahoo, 50, 105, 117, 139, 147, 148, 173, 183, 192, 211, 262, 321n24; Kuashk̲wáan, 53, 79, 107, 143; Kuiu, 117, 124, 127, 128; Sanya,

50, 253; Sitka, 28, 61, 86, 95, 98, 108, 115, 134, 147, 162, 183, 184, 220, 229, 235, 255, 256, 261, 292n1, 328n18; Stikine, 28, 99, 127, 128, 148, 183, 185, 195, 196, 251, 265, 292n1, 316n6; Taku, 196, 202, 216, 253, 262; Tanta, 59, 172, 251, 253, 254, 328n18; Tongass, 172, 195, 225, 271, 328n18; Yakutat, 100, 104, 105, 184, 263

Kwudaktik, 80

Kystyn, 287

labrets. *See* apparel
ladles. *See* containers
Ladoga. See ships
La Favorita. See ships
Lama. See ships
Langsdorff, Georg, 39, 114, 115, 137, 146, 210, 225, 228, 229, 231, 239, 245, 320, 322, 326
language, 6, 16–18, 20–24, 30, 45, 75, 84, 100, 127, 169, 170, 183, 214, 216, 222, 244, 248, 249, 258, 259, 262–264, 268–271, 286, 288, 308, 315n2, 316n8, 322n31
Lankushu, 80
La Pérouse, 5, 18, 95, 97–98
La Princessa. See ships
larch. *See* plants
Larionov, Prokopii, 249, 301n2
Larionov, Stepan, 109, 110, 141, 142, 144, 272, 322n32
La Solide. See ships
laws, 63, 136
Le Bordelais. See ships
legends, 7–9, 18, 47, 50, 53, 59, 60, 64, 66, 69–72, 76, 79, 82–84, 91, 98, 99, 104, 117, 119, 124, 141–143, 146, 183, 225, 228, 229, 245, 251, 257, 293n1, 320n24, 323nn32–33
leisters. *See* hunting equipment
Lescar. See ships
levirate, 63
lineage, 48–55
Lisianskii, Yurii, 4, 28, 31, 54, 68, 84, 86, 128, 134–137, 139, 140, 212, 225, 226, 253, 256, 316n6, 321n26
Litke, Fedor, 4, 30, 39, 45, 58, 60, 64, 67, 83, 151, 152, 154, 162–164, 212, 219, 221, 228, 229, 231, 245, 246, 254, 269, 316n6
Lituya Bay, 15, 23, 97, 98, 100, 107, 283
loincloths. *See* apparel

L'uknax̲.ádi, 50, 77, 79, 97, 98, 146, 184, 220, 234, 238, 306n2, 317n12, 320n23
Lynn Canal, 17, 29, 106, 167

magic, 38, 70, 74, 75, 84
Maksutov, Dmitrii. *See* governors
Malaspina, Alesandro, 5, 22, 96, 226
marmots. *See* animals
marriage, 44, 49–52, 61–63, 82, 245, 247, 249, 250
marten. *See* animals
masks. *See* decoration
Massachusetts, 205
matchmaking, 62
mats, 30, 37, 211, 227
Meares, John, 97, 98
medals. *See* decoration
menstruation, 61
metal, 31, 96, 98, 100, 209, 211–213, 215, 217, 256, 279, 283, 285n1, 327n8
Metlakatla, 251
mice. *See* animals
Mikhail. *See* Skautlelt
Mikhailovskii Redoubt, 224, 299, 305, 306
moccasins. *See* apparel
moiety, 24, 43, 45–48, 52, 59–62, 66, 70, 73, 78, 80, 88, 146, 219, 220, 235, 328n17
Molchanov, Emel'ian, 248, 249
mollusks. *See* shellfish
months, 32, 33, 91, 107, 108, 173, 196
moon, 46, 53, 69, 75, 83
Moon House, 53
mosquitoes, 38, 83
mother-of-pearl, 37, 212, 228, 231, 233
mountain sheep. *See* animals
Mount Edgecumbe, 283
Mt. Edgecumbe, 15
Mt. Fairweather, 15
Mt. St. Elias 2, 15
Murav'ev, Matvei. *See* governors
murder, 48, 49, 58, 63, 65, 82, 85, 117, 124, 126, 136, 137, 152, 174, 183, 193, 229, 250, 321n25, 325n49
mythology, 6–8, 23, 69–71, 83, 84, 87, 88, 267, 316

Naanya.aayí, 47, 54, 66, 77, 160, 168, 183, 184, 197, 198, 238, 239, 256, 292n1, 293n1, 316n6, 326n53

Na-Dene, 18
Nadezhda. See ships
Nakhimov. See ships
Nal'tushkan, 192
names, 18, 26–28, 32, 35, 36, 46–50, 54, 56, 66,
    69, 71, 72, 74, 76, 78–80, 84, 100, 238, 252,
    267, 271–272
Nashukaii, 80
Nass River, 30, 194, 267
Near East, 186
necklaces. *See* decoration
Nekadi, 50
nets. *See* hunting equipment
Neva. See ships
Nikolai I, 236, 271, 296n2, 330n40
Nikolai I. See ships
Niktopolion Gedeonov, 222, 223, 258, 305,
    306n3
Nootka, 45, 96–98, 283, 284, 318n3. *See* Nutka
Northern Lights, 16
Northwest America. See ships
Novo-Arkhangel'sk, 2, 134, 139, 146–157, 160–
    166, 168, 173–178, 181–183, 185–187
Nuchek, 101, 141, 178, 273
Nuestra Señora del Rozario. See ships
Nukva'ik, 216
Nushagak River, 248, 249
Nutka, 217, 227, 271. *See* Nootka

O'Cain. See ships
octopus, 74, 85
Ogden, Peter, 168, 170, 225
oil lamps. *See* containers
Okhotsk, 156, 175, 283, 285
Okhotsk. See ships
Ol'ga. See ships
oral creations, 83
orators, 58, 84
Oregon, 205, 206, 217, 279
Orel. See ships
orphans, 44, 60
Otkrytie. See ships
Otter. See ships
otters. *See* animals: river otters; animals: sea
    otters
Owhyhee. See ships
Ozerskii Redoubt, 153, 161, 163, 185, 190, 289,
    307, 308, 310, 326n52

Peacock. See ships
Pedler. See ships
pendants. *See* decoration
Peril Strait, 111
pine. *See* plants
plants: alder, 16; berries, 30, 39, 151, 166; cedar,
    16, 32, 36, 37, 61, 84, 85, 227; hemlock, 16,
    33; Kamchatka lily, 33; larch, 16; pine, 16;
    roots, 30, 35, 39, 74, 77; seaweed, 30, 32, 33,
    39; spruce, 16, 30, 212
plates. *See* copper; utensils
Plotnikov, Abrosim, 120, 127, 128
politarism, 44, 158, 278
polyandry, 64
polygamy, 63, 64
population, 12, 23, 28, 36, 53, 60, 61, 92, 95,
    131, 154, 173, 214, 225, 238, 239, 241, 242,
    245, 247, 248, 253, 261, 275–278, 280, 281n3,
    316n6, 317n13, 322n31
porcupines. *See* animals
porpoises. *See* animals
Port Gamble, 205
Portland Canal, 15, 20, 23, 172
Portlock, Nathaniel, 95, 97, 98
potlatch, 9, 38, 45–49, 56, 58, 62, 63, 70–73,
    76, 78, 79, 80, 85, 120, 124, 172, 175, 178,
    198, 219–221, 233, 240, 265, 272, 328n16
prestige, 40–42, 45, 48, 49, 53, 63, 70–73, 79,
    81–83, 141, 153, 255, 264, 272
Prince of Wales Island, 18, 20, 93, 94, 126, 156,
    166, 202
Princess Royal. See ships
Prince William Henry. See ships
Prince William Sound, 95, 99, 100, 162
production force, 61
production relations, 40, 41, 324n40
property, 40–45, 47, 50–52, 54, 56, 57, 62, 63,
    65, 70, 72–74, 79, 82, 84, 85, 120, 141, 143,
    199, 219, 220, 236, 266, 271, 278
Puget Sound, 205, 217, 242, 253
Purtov, E., 104–106

Queen Charlotte Islands, 18, 86, 115, 127, 139,
    151, 176, 283, 322n27, 324n35

rakes. *See* tools
rank, 30, 47, 48, 52, 53, 56, 58–62, 64, 67, 77,
    81, 82, 84, 100, 151, 219, 220, 241, 255, 266

rattle. *See* instruments
Raven Bones House, 53
ravens. *See* birds
Rebecca. See ships
redistributive, 44, 56
regalia, 47, 48, 59, 70
reincarnation, 76
Remeden, 283
Rezanov, Nikolai, 28, 31, 130, 141–148, 225, 228,
    233–235, 245, 254, 268, 269, 285, 320n23,
    328n13
rings. *See* decoration
river otters. *See* animals
Rob Roy. See ships
roe, 29, 39
Romanov, V. P., 34, 63, 215, 254
roof. *See* structures
Rostislav. See ships
Royal Charlie. See ships
Rozenberg, Nikolai. *See* governors
Rudakov, Aleksandr. *See* governors
rum, 163, 165, 167, 171, 198, 201, 203–205, 217,
    229, 230, 241, 244, 326n5

Salish, 22
salmon. *See* fish
San Carlos. See ships
Sanya ǩwáan. *See* Ǩwáans
Sarychev, Gavriil, 327n9
scalping, 68
scoops. *See* containers
scrapers. *See* tools
sculptors, 58
sea lions. *See* animals
seal oil, 39
seals. *See* animals
sea otters. *See* animals
seaweed. *See* plants
Senaǩet, 172
Seniavin. See ships
Sergeev, Sergei, 271
Shagóon, 71
Shakes, 47, 155, 168, 170, 171, 196–198, 239,
    254, 256, 259, 264
shamanism, 7, 59, 70, 77, 111, 256
shamans, 38, 59, 65, 68, 70, 74, 75, 77, 88, 251,
    254, 256, 261, 266, 267, 316n11
Shangukeidí, 62

sheds, 36
Shekesti, 172
Shelikhov, Grigorii, 2, 93, 94, 100, 101, 106,
    142, 217, 223, 285, 318, 327, 329
Shelikhov. See ships
shell, 35, 37, 225, 230
shellfish, 33; crabs, 30, 39; mollusks, 30, 32, 39,
    110, 124, 215; octopus, 74, 85
Shields, James, 107–108, 284, 285n5
Shiksi Noow, 134
ships: *Active,* 204; *Alert,* 120–122; *Ametist,*
    165; *Apollon,* 159; *Argonaut,* 318n3; *Arthur,*
    285n6, 329n16; *Atahualpa,* 155; *Atrevida,*
    96; *Beaver,* 205; *Bolivar Liberator,* 225;
    Cadboro, 194; *Caroline,* 114, 115; *Cheerful,*
    114; *Chichagov,* 166–168, 172, 175, 205, 237,
    293; *Chilkat,* 167; *Del'fin,* 107; *Descubierta,*
    96; *Diane,* 254; *Dispatch,* 113; *Dragon,* 115;
    Eclipse, 150; *Eliza,* 114; *Ermak,* 133; *Frederick,*
    204; *Globe* (Globus), 120, 121, 125, 126;
    Hamilton, 204, 205, 243; *Hancock,* 113, 128,
    130; *Imperator Nikolai I,* 243; *Jenny,* 115, 121,
    129, 130; *Kad'iak,* 149, 322n32; *Konstantin,*
    153, 199, 223, 262, 313; *Kreiser,* 159, 324n41;
    Ladoga, 159; *La Favorita,* 95; *Lama,* 171;
    La Princessa, 95, 318n3; *La Solide,* 98; *Le
    Bordelais,* 156, 157; *Lescar,* 204; *Nadezhda,*
    125, 234; *Nakhimov,* 308; *Neva,* 134–136, 150,
    151, 258, 321n26; *Nikolai I,* 175, 178, 192,
    243, 308; *Northwest America,* 318n3; *Nuestra
    Señora del Rozario,* 95; *O'Cain,* 147, 149;
    Okhotsk, 306; *Ol'ga,* 106, 107, 110; *Orel,* 108,
    110, 111, 283; *Otkrytie,* 151; *Otter,* 149, 155;
    Owhyhee, 204; *Peacock,* 149, 322n32; *Pedler,*
    156; *Princess Royal,* 318n3; *Prince William
    Henry,* 115; *Rebecca,* 205; *Rob Roy,* 155, 204;
    Rostislav, 133; *Royal Charlie,* 202; *San Carlos,*
    318n3; *Seniavin,* 231; *Shelikhov,* 223; *Sonora,*
    94, 95; *St. Ekaterina,* 110; *St. Nikolai,* 23,
    149; *St. Simeon,* 101; *Sulphur,* 272; *Tri Ier-
    arkha,* 107; *Trincomalee,* 186; *Tri Sviatitelia,*
    100, 327n6; *Tungus,* 224, 302, 303; *Ulysses,*
    114; *Unicorn,* 120, 121; *Vancouver,* 285; *Velikii
    Kniaz' Konstantin,* 223, 262, 313; *Virgin de
    los Remedios,* 95; *Volunteer,* 268
shirts. *See* apparel
Shmakov, Aleksei, 291n4

Simpson, Emilius, 194, 247

Simpson, George, 5, 173, 186, 197, 239, 243, 248, 259, 325n43, 326n52

Sitka. *See* Novo-Arkhangel'sk

Sitka Island, 4, 106, 109, 110, 113, 125, 127, 133, 139, 141, 150, 161, 245, 321n26, 325n43, 328n14

Sitka k̲wáan. *See* K̲wáans

S̲kagataelch', 240

Skautlelt, 112, 118–120

skin boats. *See* transportation

Skin-Ya, 193

slaves, 20–22, 32, 36, 38, 42, 45, 47–49, 52, 55, 56, 58–62, 64, 66, 75, 79, 81, 95, 100, 115, 124, 136, 137, 139, 157, 164, 172, 174, 176, 182, 183, 212, 214, 215, 217, 219–221, 239–241, 246, 250, 253, 264–266, 295, 296, 296n1, 302, 303–305, 306n1, 306n5, 312n, 328n16

slings. *See* hunting equipment

Slobodchikov, Sysoi, 149, 291n4

smallpox, 28, 95, 173, 174, 192, 193, 216, 256, 261

smokehouses. *See* structures

snares. *See* hunting equipment

snowshoes. *See* apparel

social organization, 5, 9, 50, 55, 70, 237, 238, 316n7

social status, 38, 48, 49, 58, 60, 61, 64, 78, 233, 239

socioeconomic structure, 55

songs, 6, 9, 21, 45–48, 56, 66, 68, 69, 71, 75, 77, 84, 140, 218, 221, 257

Sonora. See ships

sorcery, 58, 60, 75, 80, 124, 256, 303n1

sororate, 63

Spanish, 5, 22, 91, 94–97, 105, 226, 242, 271, 317n3, 327n12

spears. *See* weapons

spirits, 16, 49, 50, 59, 65, 69–72, 74–77, 88, 254, 256, 264, 316n11

spirits (alcohol), 160, 170, 171, 194, 202, 204, 220, 229, 230

spoons. *See* containers

spruce. *See* plants

status, 38, 42, 48, 49, 52, 53, 56, 58, 60–62, 64, 67, 71, 78, 79, 81, 86, 158, 223, 233, 239, 256, 262, 270

steam baths, 36

St. Ekaterina. See ships

Stikine k̲wáan. *See* K̲wáans

St. Michael's Cathedral, 248

St. Nikolai. See ships

stone, 22, 30, 35, 37, 38, 65, 119, 164, 216, 226

St. Petersburg, 3, 12, 122, 155, 161, 171, 176, 178, 186, 189, 193, 194, 234, 236, 243, 249, 252, 258, 261, 278

structures: cabins, 36, 185, 308n; ceilings, 36; corner posts, 36; floors, 36; huts, 34, 36, 88; roofs, 36, 119; smokehouses, 36; wind screens, 36

St. Simeon. See ships

Stunuku, 117

Sulphur. See ships

surplus goods, 40, 41, 44, 45, 56, 63, 89

Suvorov, 243

taboos, 39, 67, 71, 210

Tagish, 20, 215, 233

Tahltan, 20, 215, 216, 238

Takestina, 64

Takhanas Island, 283

Takku Inlet, 282

Taku k̲wáan. *See* K̲wáans

Taku Bay, 167, 196

Taltan, 20, 171, 196, 256

tambourine. *See* instruments

Tanaiaka, 183, 184

Tanaina, 123, 145, 266

Tanak̲ku, 171

Tanta k̲wáan. *See* K̲wáans

tattooing, 38

Tawal Creek, 142

Teben'kov, Mikhail. *See* governors

teeth, 35, 37, 38, 87, 218, 236, 256, 257, 317n12

Teik̲weidí, 20, 50, 54, 64, 71, 83, 108, 143, 146, 172, 214, 228, 245, 250, 271, 322n21, 323n32

Teik̲weidí Valley House, 64

Teko, 54, 316n8

Ten̲kentin, 243–244

Teslin, 217

Thunderbird, 83, 254

Tikhmenev, Petr, 3, 5, 27, 109, 122, 130–131, 141, 150, 188, 189, 210, 255, 318n6, 320n20, 322n29, 324n34, 324n38

Tlakaik, 20, 108, 143, 146, 214, 245, 322n31, 323n32

Tlaktoowu, 250

Tlzhiditin, 77

tobacco, 30, 110, 163, 166, 210, 217, 218, 230, 242, 303

toboggans. *See* transportation

toion, 46, 58, 59, 108, 109, 111, 127, 140, 144–146, 151, 171, 175, 198, 213, 214, 226, 232, 240, 251, 260, 262–264, 271, 283, 287–289, 293, 295, 296, 299, 299n2, 300, 323n32, 326n4

Tongass kwáan. *See* Kwáans

tongs. *See* tools

tools, 30, 33, 35, 40, 41, 65, 98, 210, 214, 226, 227, 252, 272; adzes, 35, 97, 212; chisels, 35; hammers, 30, 35; knives, 30, 35, 114, 122, 209, 212, 215, 227, 305; rakes, 35; scrapers, 35; tongs, 37

torture, 68, 74, 256, 304–305, 318n10

totem, 7, 30, 33, 36, 38, 47, 49, 50, 54, 70–73, 76, 80, 84, 87, 88, 100, 101, 119, 183, 238, 254, 255, 316n11, 317n12

totemism, 70–74, 254

totem poles, 7, 30, 33, 36, 88

transportation, 35, 61, 195, 226, 227; baidarka, 94, 109, 110, 136, 144, 149, 157, 228; boats, 30, 35, 65, 83, 92, 93, 99, 120, 122, 140, 156, 218, 252, 258, 265, 288–290, 293, 310; canoes, 18, 30, 32, 35, 52, 61, 65, 66, 69, 74, 88, 93, 97, 103–105, 115, 118, 120–122, 128, 136, 142, 176, 190, 200, 204–206, 219, 227, 250–252, 258, 319n16; dugout boats, 35; kayaks, 20, 93, 270; skin boats, 35; toboggans, 35

traps. *See* hunting equipment

Tri Ierarkha. See ships

Tri Sviatitelia. See ships

Trincomalee. See ships

trousers, 37, 231, 242

Tsetsaut, 20, 253

Tsimshian, 18, 20–22, 24, 30, 32, 34, 36, 50, 66, 77, 84, 88, 100, 115, 126, 127, 149, 170, 186, 198, 200, 214, 217, 240, 244, 250, 251, 253, 257, 317n13

Tsukane, 259

Tsultan, 282

tubers, 30, 33, 39

Tunek, 287

Tungus. See ships

Tutchone, 20, 199, 215, 216, 233

Tuxekan, 43

Ugalakmiut, 144, 145, 322n31, 323n34

Ugalentsi, 23, 214

Ulysses. See ships

Unashtuku, 271

Unga Island, 227

Unicorn. See ships

utensils, 30, 37, 114

Vancouver, George, 5, 30, 99, 104, 105, 228, 233, 242, 252

Vancouver. See ships

Vancouver Island, 2, 97, 104, 157, 196, 199, 242, 271, 318n3

Velikii Kniaz' Konstantin. See ships

Veniaminov, Ivan, 5, 6, 18, 26–28, 39, 47, 67, 69, 75–77, 82, 172–174, 183, 214, 220, 221, 226, 241, 247–249, 251, 253, 256, 258, 261, 265–268, 270, 295, 296n1, 316n6

Virgin de los Remedios. See ships

Visheksh, 250, 251

vodka, 229, 265, 326n5

Voevodskii, Vasilii. *See* governors

Volunteer. See ships

war leaders, 59, 67, 69

warriors, 51, 65, 67, 71

Washinedi, 50

Washington, 12, 155, 275

wealth, 8, 30, 41, 42, 48, 49, 56, 58, 64, 68, 75–77, 80, 93, 98, 146, 219, 220, 231, 239, 244, 266

weapons, 30, 88, 98, 101, 130, 151, 153, 159, 178, 216, 244, 258, 272; armor, 65, 101, 104, 252, 253; arrows, 30, 35, 65, 85, 101, 114, 210, 212, 216, 254; clubs, 35, 65, 226; daggers, 35, 65, 68, 84, 112, 119, 211, 212; darts, 35; spears, 30, 35, 65, 68, 84, 101, 210, 212

wergeld, 58, 64, 65

whales. *See* animals

whistle. *See* instruments

wind screens. *See* structures

witch, 77

wolves. *See* animals

Wooshkeetaan, 50, 317n12

Wrangel, Ferdinand. *See* governors

Yakobi, I. V., 100

Yakobi Island, 281n5, 283, 284

Yakutat, 15, 20, 22–24, 28, 30, 31, 35, 37, 50, 53, 61, 91, 96–100, 103–112, 116–118, 120, 122, 123, 126, 131, 133, 139, 141–146, 162, 173, 184, 192, 200, 214, 222, 226–228, 233, 239, 244, 245, 255–258, 260, 263, 270–273, 275, 281n1, 318nn9–10, 320n22, 322nn30–31, 323nn32–34, 327nn6–7

Yakutat ḵwáan. *See* Ḵwáans

Yakvan, 184

Yanovskii, Semion. *See* governors

Yel, 69, 79, 83, 97, 101

Yelnawu, 262

Yendestake, 66, 282n7

York, John, 195, 218

Zhukov, Ivan, 248–249